ESSENTIALS OF MARKETING RESEARCH

ESSENTIALS OF MARKETING RESEARCH

FIFTH EDITION

William G. Zikmund

Barry J. Babin
Louisiana Tech University

CENGAGE
Learning®

Australia • Brazil • Japan • Korea • Mexico • Singapore • Spain • United Kingdom • United States

Essentials of Marketing Research, Fifth Edition
William G. Zikmund and Barry J. Babin

Vice President of Editorial, Business:
Jack W. Calhoun

Publisher: Erin Joyner

Executive Editor: Mike Roche

Developmental Editor: Elizabeth Lowry

Editorial Assistant: Megan Fischer

Marketing Manager: Gretchen Swann

Senior Marketing Communications Manager:
Jim Overly

Marketing Coordinator: Leigh Smith

Media Editor: John Rich

Rights Acquisitions Director: Audrey Pettengill

Senior Rights Acquisitions Specialist, Text and
Image: Deanna Ettinger

Manufacturing Planner: Ron Montgomery

Production House/Compositor:
PreMediaGlobal

Senior Art Director: Stacy Shirley

Internal Designer, Production Management,
and Composition: PreMediaGlobal

Cover Designer: Chris Miller

Cover Image: © Dimitri Vervitsiotis/
Getty Images

For product information and technology assistance, contact us at
Cengage Learning Customer & Sales Support, 1-800-354-9706

For permission to use material from this text or product,
submit all requests online at **www.cengage.com/permissions**
Further permissions questions can be emailed to
permissionrequest@cengage.com

Exam*View*® is a registered trademark of eInstruction Corp. Windows is a registered trademark of the Microsoft Corporation used herein under license. Macintosh and Power Macintosh are registered trademarks of Apple Computer, Inc. used herein under license.

© 2013 Cengage Learning. All Rights Reserved.

Cengage Learning WebTutor™ is a trademark of Cengage Learning.

Library of Congress Control Number: 2013935245

ISBN-13: 978-1-285-75203-7

ISBN-10: 1-285-75203-1

Student Edition:

ISBN-13: 978-1-285-75202-0

ISBN-10: 1-285-75202-3

Cengage Learning
200 First Stamford Place, 4th Floor
Stamford, CT 06902
USA

Cengage Learning is a leading provider of customized learning solutions with office locations around the globe, including Singapore, the United Kingdom, Australia, Mexico, Brazil, and Japan. Locate your local office at:
www.cengage.com/global

Cengage Learning products are represented in Canada
by Nelson Education, Ltd.

To learn more about Cengage Learning Solutions, visit **www.cengage.com**

Purchase any of our products at your local college store or at our preferred online store **www.cengagebrain.com**

Printed in the United States of America
1 2 3 4 5 6 7 17 16 15 14 13

To my family.

BRIEF CONTENTS

Preface, xvii

PART ONE **Introduction, 1**
1 The Role of Marketing Research, 2
2 Data Mining Procedures and Knowledge Systems, 26
3 The Marketing Research Process, 46
4 The Human Side of Marketing Research: Organizational and Ethical Issues, 69

PART TWO **Designing Research Studies, 90**
5 Qualitative Research, 96
6 Secondary Data Research in a Digital Age, 127
7 Survey Research, 151
8 Observation, 189
9 Conducting Marketing Experiments, 213

PART THREE **Measurement, 236**
10 Measurement and Attitude Scaling, 245
11 Questionnaire Design, 279

PART FOUR **Sampling and Statistical Theory, 299**
12 Sampling Designs and Sampling Procedures, 311
13 Reviewing statistical theory and Determining Sample Size, 335

PART FIVE **Analysis and Reporting, 351**
14 Basic Data Analysis, 362
15 Testing for Differences Between Groups and for Relationships Among Variables, 383
16 Communicating Research Results, 412

PART SIX **Comprehensive Cases with Computerized Databases, 418**
Case 1 Say It Ain't So! Is This the Real Thing?, 432
Case 2 TABH, INC., Automotive Consulting, 434
Case 3 Knowing the Way, 435

Endnotes, 437
Index, 445

CONTENTS

Preface, xvii

PART ONE
Introduction

CHAPTER 1
The Role of Marketing Research, 2

Introduction, 3

Survey This!, 5

What Is Marketing Research?, 5
Business and Marketing Research, 5
Marketing Research Defined, 6

Research Snapshot Good Fat and Bad Fat, 7

Applied and Basic Marketing Research, 7
Applied Marketing Research, 7
Basic Marketing Research, 8
The Scientific Method, 8

Marketing Research and Strategic Management Orientation, 9
Customer Orientation, 9
Long-Run Profitability, 10
A Cross-Functional Effort, 11
Keeping Customers and Building Relationships, 12

Research Snapshot Harley-Davidson Means Family, 13
Marketing Research: A Means for Implementing the Marketing Concept, 13
Marketing Research and Strategic Marketing Management, 14

Planning and Implementing a Marketing Mix, 16
Product Research, 16
Pricing Research, 17
Distribution Research, 17
Promotion Research, 18
The Integrated Marketing Mix, 18
Analyzing Marketing Performance, 19

When is Marketing Research Needed?, 19
Time Constraints, 20
Availability of Data, 20
Nature of the Decision, 20
Benefits versus Costs, 20

Marketing Research in the Twenty-First Century, 21
Communication Technologies, 21
Global Marketing Research, 21

Research Snapshot "Jacques" Daniels, 22

Tips of the Trade, 23

Summary, 23
Key Terms and Concepts, 24
Questions for Review and Critical Thinking, 24
Research Activities, 25

CHAPTER 2
Data Mining Procedures and Knowledge Systems, 26

Introduction, 27

Data, Information, and Intelligence Equal Value, 27

Survey This!, 28

The Characteristics of Valuable Information, 28
Relevance, 29
Completeness, 29
Quality, 29
Timeliness, 30
Global Marketplace, 30
Near Field Communication (NFC) Devices, 30

Decision Support Systems, 31

Research Snapshot What a Nice Surprise?, 32
Databases and Data Warehousing, 33
Input Management, 33
Data Archives, 36

Research Snapshot MySpace Means My Data, 37
Networks and Electronic Data Interchange, 37
The Internet and Research, 38

Research Snapshot How Did They Know That?, 39
Information Technology, 40

Predictive Analytics, 41

Data Technology and Ethics, 41

Tips of the Trade, 42

Summary, 43
Key Terms and Concepts, 43
Questions for Review and Critical Thinking, 44
Research Activities, 44

CHAPTER 3
The Marketing Research Process, 46

Introduction, 47

Types of Marketing Research, 47
Exploratory Research, 48

Research Snapshot Tupperware Isn't Alone in *Sealing* the Deal, 49
Descriptive Research, 49

Research Snapshot The Squeaky Wheel Gets..., 51
Causal Research, 51
Uncertainty Influences the Type of Research, 54

Stages in the Research Process, 55
Alternatives in the Research Process, 55
Defining the Research Objectives, 56
Planning the Research Design, 61

Research Snapshot Theory Drives Research?, 62
Planning a Sample, 63
Collecting Data, 64
Analyzing Data, 64
Drawing Conclusions, 64
The Research Program Strategy, 65

Tips of the Trade, 65

Summary, 66
Key Terms and Concepts, 66
Questions for Review and Critical Thinking, 67
Research Activities, 67

CHAPTER 4
The Human Side of Marketing Research: Organizational and Ethical Issues, 69

Introduction, 70

Who Should Do the Research?, 70
Do It Yourself or Let Your Fingers Do the Walking?, 70

Survey This!, 71

Working in the Marketing Research Field, 72

Research Snapshot The True Power of Research, 73
Research Suppliers and Contractors, 73
Limited Research Service Companies and Custom Research, 74

Size of the Marketing Research Firm, 74
The Director of Marketing Research as a Manager, 76

Research Snapshot Marketing Research Pays, 77
Cross-Functional Teams, 77

Ethical Issues in Marketing Research, 78
Ethical Questions Are Philosophical Questions, 78
General Rights and Obligations of Concerned Parties, 79
Rights and Obligations of the Research Participant, 80
Rights and Obligations of the Client Sponsor (User), 84

Research Snapshot When Nobody Is Looking?, 85
Privacy, 86
Rights and Obligations of the Researcher, 86
The Role of Society at Large, 90

The Researcher and Conflicts of Interest, 90
A Final Note on Ethics, 91

Tips of the Trade, 91

Summary, 92
Key Terms and Concepts, 92
Questions for Review and Critical Thinking, 93
Research Activities, 93

PART TWO
Designing Research Studies

CHAPTER 5
Qualitative Research, 96

Introduction: What Is Qualitative Research?, 97
Describing Qualitative Research, 97

Survey This!, 98
Qualitative "versus" Quantitative Research, 98

Contrasting Qualitative with Quantitative Methods, 99

Research Snapshot The Other Side of the Coin, 100
Qualitative Research and Exploratory Research Designs, 100
Idea Generation, 101
Probing, 101
Concept Testing, 102

Qualitative Research Orientations, 103
Phenomenology, 103

Research Snapshot "When Will I Ever Learn?", 104
Ethnography, 104
Grounded Theory, 105
Case Studies, 106

Common Techniques Used in Qualitative Research, 107
Focus Group Interview, 108
Depth Interviews, 112
Conversations, 113
Free-Association and Sentence Completion Methods, 114

Preparing a Focus Group Outline, 116
Disadvantages of Focus Groups, 117

Modern Technology and Qualitative Research, 118
Facilitating Interviewing, 118

Research Snapshot Research Knows Almost No Boundaries!, 120

Exploratory Research in Science and in Practice, 121
Misuses of Exploratory Qualitative Research, 122

Tips of the Trade, 124

Summary, 124
Key Terms and Concepts, 125
Questions for Review and Critical Thinking, 125
Research Activities, 126

CHAPTER 6
Secondary Data Research in a Digital Age, 127

Introduction, 128

Using Secondary Data in Marketing Research, 128
Advantages, 128

Survey This!, 129
Disadvantages, 129

Typical Objectives for Secondary-Data Research Designs, 132
Fact-Finding, 132

Research Snapshot Does It Matter?, 133
Model Building, 134
Data Mining, 137
Database Marketing and Customer Relationship Management, 138

Sources of Internal Secondary Data, 138

Research Snapshot What's That Buzzing Sound?, 139
Internal and Proprietary Data, 139

Research Snapshot Uncle Sam Finds You!, 140

External Secondary Data Sources, 140
Information as a Product and Its Distribution Channels, 140

Single-Source and Global Research Data, 145
Single-Source Data-Integrated Information, 145
Government Agencies, 146

Tips of the Trade, 147

Summary, 148
Key Terms and Concepts, 148
Questions for Review and Critical Thinking, 149
Research Activities, 149

CHAPTER 7
Survey Research, 151

Introduction, 152

The Types of Information Gathered Using Surveys, 152

Survey This!, 153

Error in Survey Research, 153
Advantages and Disadvantages of Survey Research, 153

Research Snapshot Like a Good Neighbor?, 154

Sources of Error in Surveys, 154
Random versus Systematic Sampling Error, 154
What Can Be Done to Reduce Survey Error?, 159

Different Ways That Marketing Researchers Conduct Surveys, 159
Interactive Survey Approaches, 160
Noninteractive Media, 160

Conducting Personal Interviews, 160
Advantages of Personal Interviews, 160

Research Snapshot iPod, uPod, FMPod?, 161
Disadvantages of Personal Interviews, 162

Research Snapshot Matters of Taste, 163
Door-to-Door Interviews and Shopping Mall Intercepts, 164

Global Considerations, 164
Telephone Interviews, 165
Phone Interview Characteristics, 167
Central Location Interviewing, 170
Computerized Voice-Activated Telephone Interview, 170
Global Considerations, 170

Surveys Using Self-Administered Questionnaires, 170
Mail Questionnaires, 171
Response Rates, 173
Increasing Response Rates for Mail Surveys, 174
Self-Administered Questionnaires Using Other Forms of Distribution, 176
E-Mail Surveys, 177
Internet Surveys, 178
Text-Message Surveys, 181

Choosing an Appropriate Survey Approach, 181

Pretesting Survey Instruments, 183

Ethical Issues in Survey Research, 183

Tips of the Trade, 184

Summary, 185
Key Terms and Concepts, 186
Questions for Review and Critical Thinking, 186
Research Activity, 187

CHAPTER 8
Observation, 189

Introduction, 190

Observation in Marketing Research, 190
What Can Be Observed?, 190

Survey This!, 191
The Nature of Observation Studies, 191

Research Snapshot Feel Like You Are Alone? Think Again, 192
Observation of Human Behavior, 192
Complementary Evidence, 194

Direct and Contrived Observation, 194
Direct Observation, 194

Research Snapshot Clean as We Say, or
Clean as We Do?, 196
  Contrived Observation, 196

Ethical Issues in the Observation of Humans, 197

Observation of Physical Objects, 198
  Artifacts, 199
  Inventories, 199
  Content Analysis, 200

Mechanical Observation, 201
  Television and Radio Monitoring, 201
  Monitoring Website Traffic, 202
  Scanner-Based Research, 204
  Camera Surveillance, 205
  Smartphones, 205

Measuring Physiological Reactions, 206
  Eye-Tracking, 206
  Pupilometer, 207
  Psychogalvanometer, 207
  Voice-pitch Analysis, 207
  Neurological Devices, 207

Tips of the Trade, 208

Summary, 209
Key Terms and Concepts, 209
Questions for Review and Critical Thinking, 210
Research Activities, 210

CHAPTER 9
Conducting Marketing Experiments, 213

Introduction, 214

The Characteristics of Experiments, 214

Survey This!, 215
  Subjects, 215
  Experimental Conditions, 215
  Effects, 216
  Summary of Experimental Characteristics, 218

Basic Issues in Experimental Design, 218
  Manipulation of the Independent Variable, 218
  Selection and Measurement of the Dependent
    Variable, 220

Research Snapshot Goldfishing or Bluefishing?, 221
  Selection and Assignment of Test Units, 221
  Extraneous Variables, 223

Demand Characteristics and Experimental Validity, 224
  Experimenter Bias and Demand Effects, 224
  Reducing Demand Characteristics, 224
  Establishing Control, 226
  Basic versus Factorial Experimental Designs, 227
  Laboratory Experiments, 227
  Field Experiments, 227
  Advantages of Between-Subjects Designs, 228
  Internal Versus External Validity, 229
  Internal Validity, 229
  External Validity, 231

Research Snapshot Mechanical Students, 232
  Trade-Offs Between Internal and External Validity, 232
  Using Test-Marketing, 233
  Forecasting New Product Success, 233
  Testing the Marketing Mix, 233
  Identifying Product Weaknesses, 234
  Projecting Test-Market Results, 235
  Estimating Sales Volume: Some Problems, 235
  Advantages of Test-Marketing, 236
  Disadvantages of Test-Marketing, 236

Research Snapshot The Hidden in Hidden Valley Ranch, 237

Ethical Issues in Experimentation, 239

Tips of the Trade, 240

Summary, 240
Key Terms and Concepts, 241
Questions for Review and Critical Thinking, 241
Research Activities, 242

PART THREE
Measurement

CHAPTER 10
Measurement and Attitude Scaling, 245

Introduction, 246

What to Measure, 246

Survey This!, 247
  Concepts, 248
  Operational Definitions, 248

Levels of Scale Measurement, 249
  Nominal Scale, 249
  Ordinal Scale, 251
  Interval Scale, 252
  Ratio Scale, 253
  Mathematical and Statistical Analysis of Scales, 253
  Reliable and Valid Index Measures, 255

Indexes and Composites, 255
  Computing Scale Values, 255

Research Snapshot Recoding Made Easy, 256
  Reliability, 257

Validity, 258
  Establishing Validity, 258
  Reliability vs. Validity, 260

What Is an Attitude?, 260

Attitudinal Rating Scales, 261
  Physiological Measures, 262
  Rating Scales, 262
  Assessing Item and Scale Quality, 266
  Semantic Differential, 266
  Constant-Sum Scale, 267
  Graphic Rating Scales, 268

Research Snapshot Click, Click, Click, 269
    Ranking, 269
    Paired Comparisons, 270
    Direct Assessment of Consumer Attitudes, 270
    How Many Scale Categories or Response Positions?, 270
    Balanced or Unbalanced Rating Scale?, 271
    Forced-Choice Scales?, 272
    Single or Multiple Items?, 272

Attitudes and Intentions, 273
    Multi-Attribute Attitude Score, 273
    Behavioral Intention, 275

Tips of the Trade, 275

Summary, 275
Key Terms and Concepts, 276
Questions for Review and Critical Thinking, 277
Research Activities, 278

CHAPTER 11
Questionnaire Design, 279

Survey This!, 280

Introduction, 280

Basic Considerations in Questionnaire Design, 280
    What Should Be Asked?, 281
    Questionnaire Relevancy, 281
    Questionnaire Accuracy, 281

Question Phrasing: Open- or Close-Ended Statements?, 282
    Open-Ended Response versus Fixed-Alternative Questions, 282
    Types of Fixed-Alternative Questions, 285
    Phrasing Questions for Self-Administered, Telephone, and Personal Interview Surveys, 286

Avoiding Mistakes, 287
    Simpler Is Better, 287
    Avoid Leading and Loaded Questions, 288
    Avoid Ambiguity: Be as Specific as Possible, 290
    Avoid Double-Barreled Items, 291
    Avoid Making Assumptions, 292
    Avoid Taxing Respondents Memory, 292

Research Snapshot Who Really Does Housework?, 293

Order Bias, 294
    Question Sequence, 294
    Randomized Presentations, 295
    Randomized Response Techniques, 296

Survey Flow, 296
    Traditional Questionnaires, 297

Survey Technology, 298
    Response Quality, 299
    Timing, 300
    Physical Features, 300

Pretesting and Revising Questionnaires, 302

Research Snapshot I Give Up!, 303
    Designing Questionnaires for Global Markets, 304

Tips of the Trade, 305

Summary, 305
Key Terms and Concepts, 306
Questions for Review and Critical Thinking, 307
Research Activities, 308

PART FOUR
Sampling and Statistical Theory

CHAPTER 12
Sampling Designs and Sampling Procedures, 311

Introduction, 312

Why Sample?, 312
    Pragmatic Reasons, 312

Survey This!, 313
    Accurate and Reliable Results, 313
    Destruction of Test Units, 314

Identifying a Relevant Population and Sampling Frame, 314
    Defining the Target Population, 315

Research Snapshot George Gallup's Nation of Numbers, 317
    The Sampling Frame, 317
    Sampling Units, 318

Random Sampling and Nonsampling Errors, 319
    Random Sampling Error, 319
    Systematic Sampling Error, 319
    Less Than Perfectly Representative Samples, 322

Probability versus Nonprobability Sampling, 322
    Convenience Sampling, 323
    Judgment Sampling, 323
    Quota Sampling, 323
    Probability Sampling, 325
    Simple Random Sampling, 325
    Stratified Sampling, 326
    Proportional versus Disproportional Sampling, 328
    Cluster Sampling, 329

Research Snapshot Had Too Much?, 330
    Multistage Area Sampling, 330

What Is the Appropriate Sample Design?, 330
    Degree of Accuracy, 331
    Resources, 331
    Time, 331
    Advance Knowledge of the Population, 331
    National versus Local Project, 331

Tips of the Trade, 332

Summary, 332
Key Terms and Concepts, 333
Questions for Review and Critical Thinking, 333
Research Activity, 334

CHAPTER 13
Reviewing Statistical Theory and Determining Sample Size, 335

Introduction, 336

Basic Descriptive and Inferential Statistics, 336
What Are Sample Statistics and Population Parameters?, 336

Survey This!, 337
Measures of Central Tendency, 339
Measures of Dispersion, 340

Distinguish Between Sample and Sample Distribution, 343
The Normal Distribution, 344
Population Distribution and Sample Distribution, 347
Sampling Distribution, 347

Central-Limit Theorem, 348

Estimation of Parameters and Confidence Intervals, 350
Point Estimates, 350

Research Snapshot Are You Facebook Normal?, 351
Confidence Intervals, 351

Sample Size, 353
Random Error and Sample Size, 353
Factors in Determining Sample Size for Questions Involving Means, 353

Research Snapshot Target and Walmart Shoppers Really Are Different, 354
Estimating Sample Size for Questions Involving Means, 354
Population Size and Sample Size, 355
Determining Sample Size for Proportions, 356
Determining Sample Size on the Basis of Judgment, 357

Tips of the Trade, 358

Summary, 358
Key Terms and Concepts, 359
Questions for Review and Critical Thinking, 359
Research Activities, 360

PART FIVE
Analysis and Reporting

CHAPTER 14
Basic Data Analysis, 362

Introduction, 363

Coding Qualitative Responses, 363
Structured Qualitative Responses and Dummy Variables, 363

Survey This!, 364

The Nature of Descriptive Analysis, 364

Creating and Interpreting Tabulation, 365
Cross-Tabulation, 366

Data Transformation, 369
Simple Transformations, 369
Problems with Data Transformations, 370

Research Snapshot Wine Index Can Help Retailers, 371
Index Numbers, 372
Tabular and Graphic Methods of Displaying Data, 372

Hypothesis Testing Using Basic Statistics, 372
Hypothesis Testing Procedure, 372

Significance Levels and p-values, 373
Type I and Type II Errors, 373

Research Snapshot The Law and Type I and Type II Errors, 375

Univariate Tests of Means, 375

Tips of the Trade, 378

Summary, 378
Key Terms and Concepts, 379
Questions for Review and Critical Thinking, 379
Research Activities, 381

CHAPTER 15
Testing for Differences Between Groups and for Relationships Among Variables, 383

Introduction, 384

What is the Appropriate Test Statistic?, 384

Survey This!, 386

Cross-Tabulation Tables: The χ^2 Test for Goodness-of-Fit, 387

The t-Test for Comparing Two Means, 390
Independent Samples t-Test, 390
Independent Samples t-test Calculation, 390
Practically Speaking, 392

Research Snapshot Marketing Expert "T-eeze", 393
Paired-Samples t-Test, 394
The Z-Test for Comparing Two Proportions, 395

One-Way Analysis of Variance (ANOVA), 396
Simple Illustration of ANOVA, 396
Partitioning Variance in ANOVA, 397
The F-Test, 399

Research Snapshot Is the Price Right?, 401
Practically Speaking, 402

Statistical Software, 402

General Linear Model, 402
GLM Equation, 402
Regression Analysis, 403

Tips of the Trade, 405

Summary, 406
Key Terms and Concepts, 406
Questions for Review and Critical Thinking, 407
Research Activities, 410

CHAPTER 16
Communicating Research Results, 412

Introduction, 413

What Is a Marketing Research Report?, 413
Report Format, 413

Survey This!, 414
Tailoring the Format to the Project, 415
The Parts of the Report, 415

Research Snapshot Statistics Show 20 Percent of Report Statistics Are Misleading. Oh Yeah??!!, 416
Basic Marketing Research Report, 418

Using Tables Effectively, 419
Creating Tables, 419

Using Charts Effectively, 420
Pie Charts, 422
Line Graphs, 422
Bar Charts, 422

The Oral Presentation, 423

Research Snapshot Presentation Today?, 425

Reports on the Internet, 426

The Research Follow-Up, 426

Tips of the Trade, 426

Summary, 427
Key Terms and Concepts, 427
Questions for Review and Critical Thinking, 427
Research Activities, 428

PART SIX
Comprehensive Cases with Computerized Databases

CASE 1: *Say It Ain't So! Is This the Real Thing?*, 432
CASE 2: *TABH, INC., Automotive Consulting*, 434
CASE 3: *Knowing the Way*, 435

Endnotes, 437

Index, 445

PREFACE

Marketing research has been an exciting field for decades. However, today's dynamic information society places greater importance on marketing research and thereby places a greater value on careers related to marketing research. The explosion in information technology provides decision makers with greater access to timely data about customers and potential customers. Unfortunately for management, very few pieces of data speak for themselves and some order must be brought to the huge volumes of data available. Marketing research can leverage data gathered through new tools such as Qualtrics Survey software or harvested from consumers' comments left behind on Facebook pages into more effective decision making. Researchers employ a wide range of skills and tools in trying to uncover and decipher valuable pieces of information that can be turned into action through effective decision making.

And that's where this text comes in: *Essentials of Marketing Research* acquaints students with basic knowledge and skills involved in the research process that ultimately lead to more informed and therefore enhanced market decisions. Like searching for a needle in a haystack, imagine trying to find a single piece of meaningful market information in a social network. Meaningful information may well be hidden beneath piles and piles of irrelevant stuff! Or how about trying to find a key piece of market information that may be hidden in the mind of a consumer or an employee who isn't consciously aware of all his or her reasons for some preference or behavior and, consequently, can't identify or talk about it? How do you go about finding this information? After finding it, what does this *needle* mean? Researchers employ interpretive and analytical tools in developing meaning. Furthermore, effective marketing means doing things in an ethical manner. This book also focuses on conducting research according to high ethical standards.

Chapter 3 introduces the six-stage research process. Researchers must first work together with decision makers to decide why they are investing resources into a research effort at all. The next two stages apply theory in determining just how to go about acquiring the information needed to provide more informed decisions. Next are two stages that focus on translating raw information obtained from a sample into data and then market intelligence. The process concludes when the market researcher communicates the benefits of finding "pointed" information that can help mend problems or create something really new and special to the decision maker. Success in this process usually merits the researcher a reward that is a bit more valuable than that needle!

New to *Essentials of Marketing Research*

To ensure that students are able to conduct market research with an understanding of all the latest theories and techniques available to them, the fifth edition is newly revised and updated. Certainly, the field of marketing research is dynamic both in terms of the demands placed on it by business and in terms of the technological advances that provide more tools for the researcher's toolbox. This edition integrates the latest technological advances into the methodology of marketing research.

The Internet has revolutionized information gathering and dissemination. As a result, the ways researchers gather secondary data, conduct survey processes, develop sampling plans, design questionnaires, gather qualitative data, apply interpretive and statistical tools, and communicate results are in a state of nearly constant change. The Research Snapshot features continue to get students and instructors directly involved in marketing research by highlighting current events, describing technological innovations, and emphasizing ethical elements of marketing research, among other things. Compared to previous decades, the Internet provides the most common source of information as opposed to face-to-face or home telephone interviews. As a result, the Survey This! feature gives students keen insight into gathering data with online software provided by Qualtrics, a state-of-the-art survey software company. Data provided with the book give students a chance to analyze data gathered using the same questionnaire they take as part of the introduction to the course. Thus, the new edition provides currency and presents marketing research in interesting and engaging style that provides students with real hands-on experience.

In addition to greater currency and attention given to the Internet, key features added to the fifth edition include:

- Survey This!—Students respond to an online questionnaire using Qualtrics software. The questionnaire involves students' opinions, activities, and interests regarding numerous everyday behaviors ranging from study habits to involvement with social networking. The resulting data are provided to instructors and students through the supplemental materials provided with the text. In the early chapters, this feature is useful for critiquing the way questionnaires are constructed and how research hypotheses are addressed in a questionnaire. In later chapters, students can use the data to respond to real research questions about other students. Students also get access to Qualtrics to design their own questionnaires. Several end-of-chapter exercises take advantage of the Qualtrics software and give students the opportunity to apply concepts learned in the text in designing and implementing effective surveys and interpreting the data they provide.

- Tips of the Trade—Each chapter contains a useful list of important tips that correspond to the particular stage of the research process discussed in the chapter. The tips provide information addressing practical questions such as interview length, question wording, interviewer involvement, sample size requirements, and guides for data reliability and validity, as well as useful tips for testing hypotheses using inferential statistics.

- Chapter Vignettes—Each chapter opens with a story relevant to the material featured in that particular chapter. Some of these vignettes involve famous brands and companies, so the reader may well be familiar with some of the topics. Other vignettes involve "slice of life" stories describing a businessperson's struggle to make smart decisions and demonstrate how research is intertwined with this struggle. About half of the vignettes are new to this edition or significantly updated.

- A Simplified Approach and Style—The boxed material, chapter objectives, and end-of-chapter materials are now presented in a simplified form that allows greater focus on the truly important information. Boxed materials highlight Research Snapshots that cover ethical angles of research, provide illustrations of research in practice, and offer relevant tips or detailed examples. The chapter learning objectives ensure an important coherence and structure to the chapters that culminate with the end-of-chapter materials. Learning objectives are keyed to the major headings in each chapter. This facilitates organization around objectives that can be used to develop measurable assessment outcomes.

- Increased Attention to the Impact of Social Networking—Consumers leave more and more data behind on social network sites and Internet blogs all the time. In addition, Facebook sites provide opportunities to invite respondents to take part in marketing research. The fifth edition integrates illustrations of and techniques for leveraging these tools into more effective research throughout the text. This material can be found in both the Research Snapshot features and in the body of the text.

- Greater Attention to Qualitative Research—Chapter 5 continues to focus more exclusively on qualitative research. Qualitative research is dramatically being changed by the Internet as consumers leave more and more artifactual data behind on social networking websites, company chat rooms, blogs, micro-blogs (such as tweets left on Twitter), and more.

■ More on analytics—Analytic tools are discussed throughout, but in particular, the closing chapters present an introduction to more analytic techniques than in the previous edition.

Organization of the Book

The organization of the fifth edition of *Essentials of Marketing Research* follows the logic of the marketing research process. The book is organized into six parts. Each part presents the basic research concepts for one of the stages in the research process and discusses how these concepts relate to decisions about conducting specific projects.

Part 1: Introduction begins the book by discussing the scope of marketing research. An overview of the problem definition and the entire marketing research process is provided. The interplay between research and business is emphasized throughout this discussion. Research is not equally important among all firms. The way that the importance and scope of research varies with the type of business orientation that characterizes some company is illustrated. An overview of computerized data management and information systems and an explanation of how all of this is changing due to the Internet follows. Without high ethical standards, no business is good. Thus, the introductory materials also include an emphasis on business ethics and the special ethical problems associated with marketing research.

Part 2: Designing Research Studies covers essentials that provide a starting place to studying business problems. In this context, Part 2 discusses the need for exploratory research and secondary data collection. Research proposals are covered in some detail, and the reader is encouraged to see these as the written agreement that helps put the decision maker and the researcher on the same page.

Chapter 5 emphasizes qualitative research applications. One role played by qualitative research is helping to separate business problem symptoms from true issues that can be attacked with marketing research. However, qualitative research is a topic extending far beyond problem definition by allowing greater potential for discovery and greater potential for deeper and potentially more meaningful explanations.

Part 2 includes a detailed discussion of secondary data and emphasizes its increasing importance in an increasingly data rich world. This part also examines some topics most closely associated with marketing research. For example, the chapters describe issues related to planning, conducting, and administering surveys. Surveys remain a mainstay for collecting consumer and employee opinion. Part 2 concludes with material dealing specifically with market experiments. As such, this part emphasizes test marketing, which to many is synonymous with marketing research.

Part 3: Measurement is critical to research. This part of the text discusses the basics of measurement theory. Two chapters offer practical explanations of measurement and questionnaire design. Key topics include descriptions of the different levels of scale measurement and how this affects the interpretation of results.

Part 4: Sampling and Statistical Theory examines sampling designs and sample size. These chapters explain the difference between a population and a sample. The reasons why sampling is needed and why it can be used to confidently allow predictions about larger numbers of people are covered. The fieldwork process also is discussed, including the importance of supervision of the work that goes on in the field.

Part 5: Analysis and Reporting covers important processes necessary in translating raw data into market intelligence. Included among these topics, the data must be edited and coded. The coded data are then ready for analysis. Some of the most commonly used methods for analyzing data also are presented. For instance, basic descriptive statistics are discussed as ways of portraying key results like central tendency. Inferential statistics also are discussed, including often-used univariate and bivariate approaches such as *t*-tests.

Part 6: Comprehensive Cases with Computerized Databases make up the last section of the book. These cases provide materials to challenge students to apply and integrate concepts learned. Instructors will find that these cases provide some flexibility either to expand or simplify the assignment to suit the demands of varying course assignments. The three cases provide more variety and involve analysis of internal marketing problems as well as an opportunity to use qualitative research. When quantitative data are included, they can be easily analyzed with basic statistical tools like SPSS. Excel files are also included with the same data. These files can be read directly by statistical programs like SAS or other programs. One case is new to the fifth edition.

For this edition of *Essentials*, the Appendix and Glossaries have been moved to the website.

Superior Pedagogy

More than other marketing research textbooks, the fifth edition of *Essentials of Marketing Research* addresses students' need to comprehend all aspects of the marketing research process. The following features facilitate learning throughout the book:

■ **Learning Objectives.** Each chapter begins with a concise list of learning objectives that emphasize the major areas of competency the student should achieve before proceeding to the next chapter. The key is to avoid labeling everything a major learning objective and to provide the instructors with flexibility for emphasizing additional material from each chapter as they see fit.

■ **Major Headings Keyed to Learning Objectives.** All first-level headings, with the exception of those labeled "Introduction," are keyed to learning objectives. This should be an aid in developing assessment rubrics and makes the book more user friendly in terms of identifying key material. Example assessment rubrics are available in the instructional resources.

■ **Research Snapshots.** All of the box materials share a common title, Research Snapshots. Each chapter contains three Research Snapshots. The boxes explore marketing research processes in a variety of modern businesses situations, ranging from international considerations to research ethics. Some boxes also illustrate research techniques and applications in a step-by-step fashion. Every attempt is made to make the box material lively and relevant to the subject matter of the chapters.

■ **Writing Style.** An accessible, interesting writing style continues as a hallmark of this book. With a careful balance between theory and practice and a sprinkling of interesting examples and anecdotes, the writing style clarifies and simplifies the market research process. In addition, the text offers a comprehensive treatment of important and current topics.

■ **Statistical Approach.** A short review of statistical theory in Chapter 13 provides students with an overview of the basic aspects of statistics. Because this text stresses managerial applications more than statistical theory, students are given some basic tools to perform common data analysis. More sophisticated data analysis approaches are left for further reference. Thus, the readers can learn how to test simple hypotheses involving differences between means or relationships among variables. Cross-tabulation, *t*-tests, ANOVA, and regression are covered in sufficient depth to allow a student to use these techniques. The text includes screenshots to get students started running statistics using EXCEL, SAS, or SPSS, which is available with this text.

In addition, easy-to-follow, click-through sequences can walk a student through a few of the most basic approaches to producing statistical results.

■ **Key Terms.** Learning the vocabulary of marketing research is essential to understanding the topic, and *Essentials of Marketing Research* facilitates this with key terms. First, key concepts are boldfaced and completely defined when they first appear in the textbook. Second, all key terms and concepts are listed at the end of each chapter, and many terms are highlighted in a marginal glossary. Third, a glossary summarizing all key terms and definitions appears online. A glossary of frequently used symbols is also included.

■ **Ethics Questions.** Identified by a special icon, ETHICS, ethics questions are included in most chapters. Among the compelling issues students are asked to explore is redefining the right to privacy in light of new technology. The ethical issues also provide a great opportunity for building critical thinking skills.

■ **Internet Questions.** Internet questions also are identified by a special icon, 'NET. Nearly all chapters include multiple questions and research activities that illustrate advances in Internet applications common to marketing research.

- **Research Activities.** The end-of-chapter materials include a few real-world research activities intended to provide actual research experience for the student. Most provide an opportunity for the student to gain experience with multiple content areas. Some involve ethical aspects of research, and some involve Internet usage.
- **Cases.** Extensive cases taken from real-life situations illustrate marketing research concepts and build knowledge and research skills. These cases offer students the opportunity to participate actively in the decision-making process, one of the most effective forms of learning. The fifth edition includes multiple new end-of-chapter cases and a new comprehensive end-of-book case. Video cases are also available via the instructor section of the book's website (**www.cengage.com/marketing/zikmund**).

Resources for Students

To promote learning and competency, it is also important to provide students with well-crafted resources. In addition to covering the latest information technology (described above), the fifth edition includes the following student resources:

- The dedicated website **www.cengage.com/marketing/zikmund**, developed especially for the new edition, includes chapter quizzes that allow you to test and retest student knowledge of chapter concepts. Each chapter has a quiz to encourage retesting. In addition, the website features downloadable flashcards of key terms, the very best online marketing research resources available, and much more.
- The Qualtrics Research Suite was built for researchers by researchers. Enclosed with each new copy of *Essentials of Marketing Research* is an access code that gives you access to a tool that makes survey creation easy enough for a beginner while at the same time sophisticated enough for the most demanding academic or corporate researcher. Qualtrics allows you to create and deploy surveys, and provides data for analysis. A survey included in the book in the Survey This! box on page 5 has you fill out an initial survey. Then the survey data collected from students using *Essentials of Marketing Research* around the globe are used throughout the rest of the book in a variety of ways, from critiquing questionnaire construction to using the data to respond to real research questions about other students. Access to Qualtrics requires an access code that is provided with each new copy of the book.

Acknowledgments

Certainly, no list of acknowledgments will be complete. So many people have assisted in this project. Chief among these would be to the late Bill Zikmund for carrying the weight of this project for the first editions. I am privileged to be able to carry the project along into hopefully many more editions as the premier marketing research text. Also, thanks go to some of my team. My graduate assistants Kevin James, David Shows, Melanie Gardner, and Christina Chung have helped with research for this text and helped share some of the workload on other endeavors, freeing up time for me to spend on this project. David was particularly helpful in getting the Survey This! feature underway. Thanks also to Julia Callaway for helping to manage my crazy schedule. I would be remiss not to also mention the support and patience of my family. All have contributed to the project, and my kids were particularly helpful in judging the relevance of vignettes and examples. Also, thanks go to all the great faculty who mentored me during my days in the Ph.D. program at LSU. Most notable among these are Joseph F. Hair, Jr., and the late William R. Darden.

Special thanks go to all the good people at Cengage Learning who helped make this project possible. Thanks to my publisher, Mike Roche, for motivating the whole team to stay on schedule. Thanks to Gretchen Swann for creative inspirations and marketing support. Also, a special thanks to Elizabeth Lowry and Jerusha Govindakrishan. They provided tremendous support through the writing and production process, including assistance with proofing, permissions, photos, and exhibits.

Many colleagues contributed ideas for this book. They made many suggestions that greatly enhanced this book. For their insightful reviews of the manuscript for the fifth or previous editions of *Essentials of Marketing Research*, I would like to thank the following:

Karen Goncalves
Nichols College

David R. Dunaetz
Azusa Pacific University

Carol Bienstock
Radford University

Curt Dommeyer
California State University at Northridge

Steven V. Cates
Averett University

John Durham
University of San Francisco

Stephanie Noble
The University of Tennessee

Ron Eggers
Barton College

Bob Lauman
Webster University

Trish Fisher
Vanguard University

Natalie Wood
St. Joseph's University

H. Harry Friedman
City University of New York–Brooklyn

Robert Jaross
Florida International University

Rama Ganesan
University of Arizona

Terry Paul
The Ohio State University

Susan D. Geringer
California State University, Fresno

Mike Parent
Utah State University

Ron Goldsmith
Florida State University

Stephen Batory
Bloomsburg University

Larry Goldstein
Iona College

Michael R. Hyman
New Mexico State University

David Gourley
Arizona State University

Rick Saucier
St. John's University

Jim Grimm
Illinois State University

Xin Zhao
University of Utah

Christopher Groening
University of Missouri

Gerald Albaum
University of Oregon

Al Gross
Robert Morris College

William Bearden
University of South Carolina

Don Heinz
University of Wisconsin

Joseph A. Bellizzi
Arizona State University–West

Fu Nin Ho
San Francisco State University

Pamela Braden
West Virginia University at Parkersburg

Craig Hollingshead
Texas A&M University–Kingsville

James A. Brunner
University of Toledo

Victor Howe
University of Kentucky

F. Anthony Bushman
San Francisco State University

Roy Howell
Texas Tech University

Thomas Buzas
Eastern Michigan University

Lexi Hulto
Metro State College of Denver

Roy F. Cabaniss
Huston-Tillotson College

Rhea Ingram
Columbus State University–Georgia

Faith Chakirian
California Lutheran University

P. K. Kannan
University of Maryland

Michael d'Amico
University of Akron

Iksuk Kim
California State University, Los Angeles

Susan Kleine
Arizona State University

David B. Klenosky
Purdue University

C. S. Kohli
California State University–Fullerton

Russ Laqczniak
Iowa State University

Jerome L. Langer
Assumption College

JungKook Lee
Indiana University

James H. Leigh
Texas A&M University

Larry Lowe
Bryant College

Karl Mann
Tennessee Technological University

Charles R. Martin
Wichita State University

Marlys Mason
Oklahoma State University

Tom K. Massey
University of Missouri–Kansas City

Sanjay Mishra
University of Kansas

G. M. Naidu
University of Wisconsin–Whitewater

Gail O'Connor
Massachusetts College of Liberal Arts

Talai Osmonbekov
Northern Arizona University

Rodney Oudan
Worcester State University

Charles Prohaska
Central Connecticut State University

Alan Sawyer
University of Florida

Robert Schaffer
California State University–Pomona

Leon G. Schiffman
City University of New York–Baruch

Jeff Seyfert
Southern Nazarene University

David Shows
Louisiana Tech University

K. Sivakumar
Lehigh University

David F. Smith
Bemidji State University

Mark Speece
Central Washington University

Harlan Spotts
Western New England College

Wilbur W. Stanton
Old Dominion University

Jon Steele
Mid-State Technical College

Bruce L. Stern
Portland State University

James L. Taylor
University of Alabama

Dr. Robert J. Tielman
Bradman University

James L. Thomas, Ph.D.
Jacksonville State University

Gail Tom
California State University–Sacramento

Deborah Utter
Boston College

David Wheeler
Suffolk University

Richard Wilcox
Carthage College

Margaret Wright
University of Colorado

Clifford E. Young
University of Colorado–Denver

William Lee Ziegler
Bethune-Cookman College

Thanks also to all of the students who have inspired me and reinforced the fact that I made a great career decision about two decades ago. Thanks also to my close colleagues Mitch Griffin and Jon Carr for their continued support and insight.

Barry J. Babin
Louisiana Tech University
November, 2011

BARRY J. BABIN

Barry Babin has authored over seventy research publications in some of the most prestigious research periodicals including the ***Journal of Marketing, Journal of Consumer Research, Journal of Business Research, Journal of Retailing, Psychological Reports, Psychology and Marketing,*** and ***Journal of the Academy of Marketing Science***, among others.

Barry is currently Max P. Watson, Jr., professor of business and department chair of the Department of Marketing & Analysis at Louisiana Tech University. He has won numerous honors for his research including the USM Louis K. Brandt Faculty Research Award (which he won on three occasions while a member of that faculty), the 1996 Society for Marketing Advances (SMA) Steven J. Shaw Award, and the 1997 Omerre Deserres Award for Outstanding Contributions to Retail and Service Environment Research. He is also an affiliate member of the Scientific Research Committee at Reims Management School in France.

Barry is past-president of the Academy of Marketing Sciences and former president of the Society of Marketing Advances. He is also the marketing editor for the ***Journal of Business Research***.

Barry's research focuses on the effect of the service environment in creating value for both employees and customers. His expertise is in building and understanding value that leads to long-lasting, mutually beneficial relationships with employees and customers. He also has expertise in creative problem solving and in wine marketing. His primary teaching specialties involve consumers and service quality, marketing research, and creative problem solving. He is well respected internationally and has lectured in many countries outside of the United States including Australia, South Korea, France, Germany, Canada, Sweden, and the United Kingdom, among others.

:::::::: **PART ONE**

Introduction

CHAPTER 1
The Role of Marketing Research

CHAPTER 2
Data Mining Procedures and Knowledge Systems

CHAPTER 3
The Marketing Research Process

CHAPTER 4
The Human Side of Marketing Research: Organizational and Ethical Issues

The Role of Marketing Research

LEARNING OUTCOMES

After studying this chapter, you should be able to

1. Know what marketing research is and what it does for business
2. Understand the difference between basic and applied marketing research
3. Understand how the role of marketing research changes when a firm is truly marketing oriented
4. Be able to integrate marketing research results into the strategic planning process
5. Know when marketing research should and should not be conducted
6. Appreciate the way that technology and internationalization are changing marketing research

Chapter Vignette:

"Crunch Time for Research"

New technologies are better than old ones, right? Not always, and the managers at PepsiCo are learning this the hard way. What could be better than a "compostable" chip bag? Early in 2010, Sun Chips, a PepsiCo brand, introduced new packaging for all of its Sun Chips products. The new packaging was positioned as more environmentally friendly than traditional chips packages based on the fact that the packaging decomposes more quickly. The new bag included a bold header claiming the each bag represented a "100% Compostable Chip Package." Within weeks of the launch, Sun Chips realized the decision to switch packaging was a huge mistake. A few consumers e-mailed complaints to the company, but what really spoke *volumes* was an almost overnight 11 percent drop in sales! Customers clearly had cooled to Sun Chips and by summer, Sun Chips returned to their traditional packaging.

Sun Chips management believed they would have a green advantage over competitors by touting the compostableness of their new packaging. But, in hindsight, the decision makers only got wind of packaging's

©AriWasaabi /Shutterstock

problems after the product launch, which is far more damaging than hearing something before a launch. In their rush to capture an advantage due to the new green positioning, they overlooked some of the basic functions of product packaging, some of which only became obvious with actual product use. In particular, the new packaging's crunch overwhelmed the crunch of the chips. In fact, the packaging registered a whopping 95 decibels on a sound meter, which comes in as louder than a lawnmower, coffee grinder, most barking dogs, and, according to European Union employee safety regulations, requires ear protection. The packaging became the butt of jokes and customers rushed to post YouTube videos about the bag. "Sorry, I can't hear you over my Sun Chip bag." Additionally, the new packaging's cruch outlasted that of the chips as the new packaging did not maintain crispiness as well as the old packaging.

Will consumers buy environmentally friendly packaging? Yes, but only when it still accomplishes its primary function in a satisfying way. Was the packaging properly researched? Could the obnoxiousness of the noise been determined prior to the expense and embarrassment of an actual product launch? Is "compostable" a good label for chips? These are basic questions that market research can address. Maybe then PepsiCo could've avoided a green product that became a major source of noise pollution.

Lessons are sometimes hard to learn. Later the same year, PepsiCo had to pull back new Tropicana Orange Juice packaging because consumers were turned off by its new appearance.[1]

Introduction

When one considers all the complexities involved in getting a product to the market successfully, the packaging may easily seem like a minor detail. However, when managers make decisions without adequate information, they can quickly realize that some details are not so minor after all. Snack company decisions, like companies marketing any product, require information as input to effective decision making. Research can provide that information. Without the input that research provides, key business decisions including those shaping product and pakage design, pricing, distribution, and promotion become guesswork.

We open with two examples illustrating how business decisions require intelligence and how research can provide that intelligence. The following illustrations focus specifically on how marketing research encourages innovation in the form of new products or improvements in existing goods and services. Imagine yourself in the role of brand manager as you read these examples and think about the information needs you may have in trying to build a successful brand.

Splenda is a leading name in the artificial sweetener industry. Splenda realizes the value of consumer input in discovering and testing new product ideas. Over the years, Splenda's customers have recognized how important the benefit of convenience is to the overall value of its products. Many of its product ideas focus on ways to make Splenda more convenient for consumers to use anywhere.

Toward that end, Splenda introduced prototype of a new pocket-sized, spray mist sweetener. The prototype was intended to be tested by actual consumers. Given the expense of introducing a new product on a full scale, Splenda looked to get accurate information about real consumers' reactions. In contrast to traditional means of collecting data, Splenda's research team turned to Facebook as a way of quickly gathering information from customers. Splenda released a description of the product to its Facebook fans and then offered a free sample to interested consumers. In just two days, Splenda sent 16,000 samples to consumers through a request app and eventually recorded 3,100 *Likes*. More importantly, 1,500 consumers responded to a questionnaire detailing their reaction to the new sweetener format. The information they gathered was truly sweet and helped them make informed decisions about their product line.[2] This testing eventually led to the introduction of Splenda Minis.

The coffee industry, after years of the "daily grind," has proved quite dynamic over the past few years. After a steady decline, research on consumers' beverage purchases shows that coffee sales began rebounding around 1995. Telephone interviews with American consumers estimated that there were 80 million occasional coffee drinkers and 7 million daily upscale coffee drinkers in 1995. By 2001, estimates suggested there were 161 million daily or occasional U. S. coffee drinkers

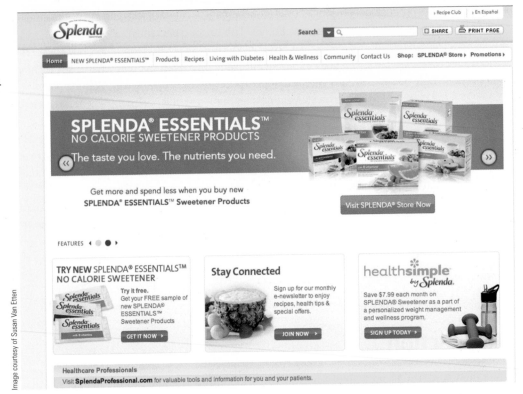

Image courtesy of Susan Van Etten

and 27 million daily upscale coffee drinkers.[3] By 2007, research indicates that although practically all coffee drinkers visit gourmet coffee shops, younger coffee consumers, particularly those under the age of 30, drink most of their coffee the *gourmet* way.[4]

Coffee drinking habits have also changed. In 1991 there were fewer than 450 coffeehouses in the United States. Today, places such as Starbucks, Second Cup, The Coffee Bean, and Gloria Jean's are virtually everywhere. Starbucks has more than 15,000 Starbucks stores today.[5] Research can play a big role in Starbucks or its competitors' success. Just imagine how useful information gathered from research is in deciding where to locate a coffee shop. Currently, over two of three Starbucks locations are in the United States, but Starbucks' management believes that eventually China will be its biggest market. Although Chinese consumers do not drink a lot of coffee, at nearly two billion potential customers, just a little coffee consumption from each adds up to success.[6] Traditionally, countries from cold climates have led the world in per capita coffee consumption, with Denmark leading the world at about a liter and a half per day (the United States comes in sixteenth at about 1/3 liter per day), but an interesting trend suggests that as a country's standard of living increases, so does its coffee consumption. Brazilians are turning to coffee in large numbers now, so perhaps China will follow. Starbucks may be able to use this information in its location strategy. However, also consider the information needs when designing stores for different venues. Should the same products be offered everywhere? Is WiFi availability equally important? How important is parking? All of these are important questions that can be addressed better using research.

These examples illustrate the need for information in making informed business decisions. Splenda provides consumers with free samples of new offerings in return for feedback. The statistics about coffee demonstrate how research can track trends that may lead to new business opportunities. Also, one can easily see how research can be used to examine new concepts and product changes in progressively more complex stages, setting the stage for a more successful product introductions. These are only the tip of the iceberg when it comes to the types of marketing research that are conducted every day. This chapter introduces basic concepts of marketing research and describes how research can play a crucial role in successful marketing and business success in general.

This book introduces the reader to the world of mareking research. Marketing research represents the eyes and the ears of the competitive business firm. The researcher's job is to determine what information is needed so that data can be analyzed and become intelligence. Consumers play a crucial role in this process. They often are research participants and, with or without their knowledge, they provide the information. One way that consumers (and sometimes employees or managers) take part is by participating in surveys. Most readers have probably participated in surveys previously. Here is another chance to do so, only this time, you will first play the role of a research participant. Later, you will fill the role of a research analyst and even a key marketing decision maker as you try to make sense of data provided by the many users of this textbook.

Your first interaction with the "Survey This!" feature is simply to play the role of respondent and respond to the entire survey as honestly and completely as possible. Go to the URL provided in the preface and by your instructor, and simply participate. Your answers will be anonymously stored in the database along with all the other students using this book around the country and, in some cases, the world. Once you've completed the survey, you can visit the course website and get a copy of the questions contained in the questionnaire.

Courtesy of Qualtrics.com

What Is Marketing Research?

Part of business involves studying the different things that come together to create a business environment. Marketing research would not exist if business didn't exist. Thus, understanding marketing research requires at least a cursory understanding of business.

Business and Marketing Research

In its essence, business is very simple. Successful companies offer things to consumers that they are willing to buy. That means that consumers view offers as providing valuable bundles of benefits. Many factorsaffect value and successful companies are those that understand the value equation. With this in mind, several key questions help provide answers to help you understand.

1. *What do we sell?* This includes not only the benefits that are easily seen, but also the more emotional benefits such as the comfort and relaxation of enjoying a cup of gourmet coffee in a pleasant atmosphere or the esteem that comes from having the latest electronic gadget. Companies offer value propositions that provide the potential for value from more than tangible product features.
2. *How do consumers view our company?* Companies likewise often define themselves too narrowly based only on the physical *product* they sell. They should think about just whom their customers would choose if they chose another alternative? For instance, how is Starbucks viewed relative to its competitors? Who are the competitors? Does Starbucks compete more directly with Maxwell House, Tassimo, McDonald's, or something completely unassociated with coffee like a local lounge? If Starbucks provides value through relaxation and social interaction, a lounge may sometimes be an alternative. Ultimately, companies ask themselves "Are we viewed more or less favorably relative to alternatives?"

3. *What does our company/product mean?* What knowledge do people have of the company and its products? Do they know how to use them? Do they know all the different needs the company can address? What does our packaging and promotion communicate to consumers? Does our total value proposition signal the quality that we offer?

4. *What do consumers desire?* How can the company make the lives of its customers better, and how can it do this in a way that is not easily duplicated by another firm? Part of this lies in uncovering the things that customers truly desire, but which they can often not put into words.

Answering these questions requires information. Marketing research's function is to supply information that helps provide these answers, thereby leading to more informed and more successful decision making. Managers that use this information reduce the risk associated with decision making.

All business problems require information for effective decision making. Can the right information be delivered and can it be delivered in a useful form? Research seeks to deliver accurate and precise information that can make marketing strategy and management more effective.[7] Marketing research attempts to supply accurate information that reduces the uncertainty in decision making. Very often, decisions are made with little information for various reasons, including insufficient time to conduct research or management's belief that enough is already known. Relying on seat-of-the-pants decision making—decision making without research—is like betting on a long shot at the racetrack because the horse's name is appealing. Once in a while the long shot pays off. More often, long-run uninformed decision making is unwise. Marketing research helps decision makers shift from intuitive guesswork to a more systematic, objective, and effective approach.

Marketing Research Defined

Marketing research

The application of the scientific method in searching for the truth about marketing phenomena. These activities include defining marketing opportunities and problems, generating and evaluating marketing ideas, monitoring performance, and understanding the marketing process.

Marketing research is the application of the scientific method in searching for the truth about marketing phenomena. Research applications include defining marketing opportunities and problems, generating and evaluating marketing ideas, monitoring performance, and generally understanding the marketing process. Marketing research is more than conducting surveys.[8] This process includes idea and theory development, problem definition, gathering information, analyzing data, and communicating the findings including potential implications.

This definition suggests that the marketing research process is neither intuitive or haphazard. Literally, research (*re*-search) means "to search again." The term connotes patient study and scientific investigation wherein the researcher takes another, more careful look to try and successively know more. Ultimately, all findings are tied back to some theory.

The definition also emphasizes, through reference to the scientific method, that any information generated should be accurate and objective. The researcher should be personally detached and free of bias attempting to find truth. Research isn't performed to support preconceived ideas but to test them. If bias enters into the research process, the value of the research is considerably reduced. We will discuss this further in a subsequent chapter.

Clearly, marketing research is relevant to all aspects of the marketing mix. Research can facilitate managerial decision making about each of the four Ps: product, pricing, promotion, and place (distribution). By providing valuable input marketing mix decisions, marketing research decreases the risk of making bad decisions in each area.

Finally, this definition of marketing research is limited by one's definition of *marketing*. Although one could hardly argue that research aimed at designing better products for a for-profit corporation like Pepsico is clearly marketing research, marketing research also includes efforts that assist nonprofit organizations such as the American Heart Association, the university alumni association, or a parochial elementary school. Every organization exists to satisfy social needs, and each requires marketing skills to produce and distribute their products and services. Governments also can use research in much the same way as managers at Starbucks or Pepsico. For instance, the FDA is an important user of marketing research, employing it to address the way people view and use various food and drugs. One such study commissioned and funded research to address

Good Fat and Bad Fat

American consumers can be seen every day scouring nutrition labels. Most likely, the item they show the most interest in recently is the amount of fat. The Food and Drug Administration (FDA) is concerned that consumers get information that is not only accurate, but that also conveys the proper message to achieve a healthy diet. But all fat is not created equal. In particular, dieticians warn of the dangers associated with excess amounts of trans fats; diet nutrition labels break fats into saturated and unsaturated fats. Among numerous factors that complicate the interpretation of the nutrition label, trans fat (hydrogenated) is technically a nonsaturated fat, but it acts more like a saturated fat when consumed. So, where should it be placed? The FDA cannot address this problem intelligently without marketing research addressing questions such as the following.

1. If trans fats are listed as a saturated fat, would consumers' beliefs about their consumption become more negative?
2. If the saturated fat amount includes a specific line indicating the amount of "saturated fat" that is really trans fat, would consumers become more confused about their diet?
3. If all amounts of fat are given equal prominence on the label, will consumer attitudes toward the different types of fats be the same?
4. Will consumers interpret foods free of trans fats as healthy?
5. Do consumers interpret fat information on the front of a label in a way that interferes with an understanding from a nutrition label?

Nutrition Facts
Serving Size 1 oz. (28g)
Servings Per Container: 4

Amount Per Serving
Calories 130   Calories from Fat 50

	% Daily Value*
Total Fat 5g	8%
Saturated Fat 0.5g	3%
Trans Fat 0g	0%
Cholesterol 0mg	0%
Sodium 90mg	4%
Total Carbohydrate 7g	6%
Dietary Fiber 1g	4%
Sugars 1g	
Protein 2g	

Vitamin A 15%   •   Vitamin C 10%
Calcium 2%   •   Iron 2%

*Percent Daily Values are based on a 2,000 calorie diet. Your daily values may be higher or lower depending on your calorie needs:

©Susan Van Etten

Making this even more complicated is the fact that some consumer segments, such as teenagers in this case, may actually use the nutrition labels to select the brands that are least nutritious rather than most nutritious. So, they may actually seek out the one with the worst proportion of trans fats! The FDA specifically addressed trans fats in labeling regulations that took effect in 2006. Under these labels, the FDA allows labels to claim zero trans fat as long as less than half a gram of hydrogenated oil per serving is contained. Simple? Interest now focuses on whether the company can make a low-fat claim on package fronts.

Sources: "Health Labels are in the Eye of the Beholder," *Food Management*, 40 (January 2005), 80; Weise, E., "Food Labels Now Required to Mention Trans Fat, Allergens," *USA Today*, (January 2, 2006), H1. Nestle, M., and D. S. Ludwig (2010), "Front-of-Package Food Labels," *Journal of the American Medical Association*, 303 (August), 771–72.

the question of how consumers used the risk summaries that are included with all drugs sold in the United States.[9] The Research Snapshot describes a typical FDA market research project. This book explores marketing research as it applies to all organizations and institutions engaging in marketing activities.

Applied and Basic Marketing Research

One useful way to describe research is based on the specificity of its purpose. Is the research intended to address a very specific problem or is it meant to describe some overall marketing phenomenon?

Applied Marketing Research

Applied marketing research is conducted to address a specific marketing decision for a specific firm or organization. The opening vignette describes a situation in which companies like Pepsico could use applied marketing research. The research could have proved useful in designing or deciding

Applied marketing research

Research conducted to address a specific marketing decision for a specific firm or organization.

whether to launch new product packaging. In other instances, research may suggest how to modify a value proposition for a particular market segments. Applied research is relatively specific.

Basic Marketing Research

Basic marketing research

Research conducted without a specific decision in mind that usually does not address the needs of a specific organization. It attempts to expand the limits of marketing knowledge in general and is not aimed at solving a particular pragmatic problem.

Basic marketing research does not address the needs of a specific organization and does not typically address a specific business decision. Instead, basic research expands marketing knowledge in general and as such is not aimed at solving a particular business's problem. Basic research can test the validity of a general marketing theory (one that applies to all of marketing) or to learn more about some market phenomenon like social networking. A great deal of basic marketing research addresses the ways in which retail atmosphere influences consumers' emotions and behavior.[10] From such research, we can learn how much the physical place creates value for consumers above and beyond any items purchased. This basic research does not examine the problem from any single retail or service provider's perspective. However, Starbucks' management may become aware of such research and apply the results in deciding how to design its stores. Thus, the two types of research are not completely independent.

Researchers sometimes use different terms to represent the same distinction. Some reserve the term *marketing research* to refer to basic research. Then, the term *market research* is used to capture applied research addressing the needs of a firm within a particular market. Although the distinction is very useful in describing research, very few aspects of research apply only to basic or only to applied research. Here, we will use the term *marketing research* more generally to refer to either type of research.

The Scientific Method

Scientific method

The way researchers go about using knowledge and evidence to reach objective conclusions about the real world

All marketing research, whether basic or applied, involves the scientific method. The **scientific method** is the way researchers go about using knowledge and evidence to reach objective conclusions about the real world. The scientific method is the same in social sciences such as marketing as in physical sciences such as physics. Marketing researchers apply the scientific method as their way to understand marketing phenomena.

Exhibit 1.1 briefly illustrates the scientific method. Researchers usually begin with some understanding of theory in the problem area. Consumer researchers usually are familiar with consumer behavior theory and by elaborating on this theory and/or combining theoretical knowledge

EXHIBIT 1.1

A Summary of the Scientific Method

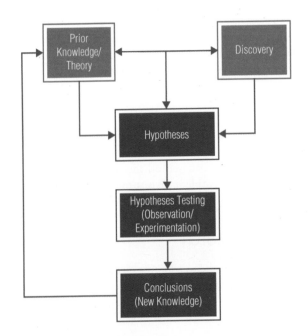

Source: © Cengage Learning 2013.

with pure discovery, research questions emerge. Discovery can involve any means of developing new thoughts, including exploratory techniques that we will discover later or even eureka types of experiences like the apple falling on Newton's head! The research then develops formal research hypotheses that play a key role through the remainder of the process. The next step involves testing hypotheses against empirical evidence (facts from observation or experimentation). Results either support a particular hypothesis or do not support thathypothesis. From these results, new knowledge is acquired which may lead to a new thory or modification of an existing theory.

Use of the scientific method in applied research ensures objectivity in gathering facts and testing creative ideas for alternative marketing strategies. In basic research, scientific research contributes to conclusions that over time contribute to the development of general laws about phenomena like price and value. The scientific method is the philosophy and way of doing *scientific* research, the results of which are the basis for knowledge growth and better decision making. Much of this book deals with scientific methodology.

Marketing Research and Strategic Management Orientation

In all of business strategy, there are only a few business orientations. A firm can be **product oriented**. A product-oriented firm prioritizes decision making in a way that emphasizes technical superiority in the product. Thus, input from technicians and experts in the field are very important in making critical decisions. A firm can be **production oriented**. Production orientation means that the firm prioritizes efficiency and effectiveness of the production processes in making decisions. Here, input from engineers and accounting becomes important as the firm seeks to drive costs down. Production-oriented firms are usually very large firms manufacturing products in very large quantities resulting in good economies of scale. Marketing research may take a backseat with these orientations.

In contrast, marketing research is a primary tool enabling implementation of a marketing orientation.[11] The **marketing concept** is a central idea in modern marketing thinking that focuses more on how the firm provides value to customers than on the physical product or production process. It has evolved over time as product- and production-oriented firms respond to changes in the competitive and economic environments. When a firm adapts the marketing concept, it develops a **marketing orientation**. A marketing-oriented firm must:

1. Be **customer oriented**—meaning that all firm decisions are made with a conscious awareness of their effect on the consumer
2. Emphasize long-run profitability rather than short-term profits or sales volume
3. Adopt a cross-functional perspective, meaning that marketing is integrated across other business functions

Going further, a **stakeholder orientation** recognizes that multiple parties are affected by firm decisions. When a company makes a decision to change a product line based on marketing research, that decision affects customers, employees, and their families; the owners of the company (shareholders in a public company); and even society in general. Good decision making considers how all are affected when making decisions.

Customer Orientation

According to the marketing concept, the consumer should be the primary focus of attention, the pivot point about which the business moves to achieve the balanced best interests of all other stakeholders in the long run. According to this philosophy, the firm creates offers with consumers' needs in mind. The creation of value for consumers, after all, is the reason that a firm exists. Therefore, unlike the other two orientations, marketing research addressing consumer desires, beliefs, and attitudes becomes essential.

To the Point

"If you have knowledge, let others light their candle with it."

—WINSTON CHURCHILL

Product oriented

Describes a firm that prioritizes decision making in a way that emphasizes technical superiority in the product.

Production oriented

Describes a firm that prioritizes efficiency and effectiveness of the production processes in making decisions.

Marketing concept

A central idea in modern marketing thinking that focuses on how the firm provides value to customers more than on the physical product or production process.

Marketing orientation

The corporate culture existing for firms adopting the marketing concept. It emphasizes customer orientation, long-term profitability over short-term profits, and a cross-functional perspective.

Customer oriented

Describes a firm in which all decisions are made with a conscious awareness of their effect on the consumer.

Stakeholder orientation

A way of doing business that recognizes that multiple parties are affected by firm decisions.

To the Point

"Knowledge has to be increased, challenged, improved constantly, or it vanishes"

—PETER DRUCKER

● ● ● ● ● ● ●
Marketing research allows the right combination of fashion and style by describing the way people use their bags.

Image courtesy of Susan Van Etten

How could a good piece of luggage be designed without consumer research? Those who travel frequently, particularly by air, are very picky about the bag they carry. When all is considered, research shows that price is hardly the most important criteria for the frequent travelor. These consumers are willing to plunk down hundreds and sometimes even over $1,000 for the right bag. Well-known companies like Samsonite and lesser well-known companies, at least to the general public, like Mandarina Duck, use consumer input to design *perfect* bags. What factors do consumers consider more important than price and essential in a good bag? First, rollers. Not just any rollers, smooth and sturdy rollers and increasingly, four instead of two wheels. That enables the bag to stand up and provide an easy place to rest a computer or purse. Second, size. It has to hold at least a few days' attire but has to fit in the overhead bin of an airplance. Third, separate storage for items like shoes and toiletries and preferably, a garment compartmet for more dressy attire. Fourth, sturdiness. The bag should stand abuse and last years, not months! Fifth, unique and fun appearance. When you travel a lot, the bag should have personaity that says something about the consumer. Thus, a bag that is a special khaki orange color with grey accents not only is fun, but unique engough to stand out in a crowd and much easier to pick out on a carousel should you have to check it. Mandarina Duck is a leader in style but does not take a back seat in function.[12] Consumer research plays a big role in this research.

Long-Run Profitability

Customer orientation does not mean slavery to consumers' every fleeting whim. Implicit in the marketing concept is the assumption of the continuity of the firm. Thus, the firm must eventually experience profitability to survive (see Exhibit 1.2). High fuel prices have stifled the market for large SUVs and trucks. This has contributed to troubles at automotive companies including GM. GM also dropped several brands from its portfolio. Surprisingly, one of the brands that GM dropped was Saturn. Saturn produced fuel-efficient, economy cars generally recognized as innovative by

Goods	Services	EXHIBIT **1.2**
Gas	Day Care	Long-Run Profitability
Corn	Spas	
Tools	Internet Service Provider	

Provide Benefits by Meeting Customers
Needs and Desires

Value

When the Firm Provides Benefits,
It Creates Value for Customers and Itself

Source: © Cengage Learning 2013.

automotive experts. Saturn customers displayed among the highest average customer satisfaction among GM brands. Originally intended to change American's minds about GM products, Saturn struggled to become profitable.[13] Pricing the cars higher was not a good option because consumers show too much price sensitivity and would likely have switched to other brands.

The second aspect of the marketing concept argues against profit less volume or sales volume for the sake of volume alone. Sometimes, the best decision for a customer and the best decision in the long run for the firm is the sale that is not made. For instance, a parts supplier might be able to mislead a customer about the relative quality of the parts he or she sells and make an immediate sale. However, when the parts begin to fail sooner than expected, the customer will almost certainly not do business with this firm again. If instead the salesperson had been honest and suggested another supplier, he or she may be able to find another opportunity to do business with that firm.

A Cross-Functional Effort

The marketing concept requires marketing information to be provided to and used by all the functional areas of a business. Information must be integrated into decisions for all areas. Production needs accurate forecasts to know how much should be produced, the design team needs input on consumer tastes, strategic management personnel need to understand the meaning of the brand, and so on. Problems are almost certain to arise from lack of an integrated, company-wide effort. The marketing concept stresses a cross-functional perspective to achieve consumer orientation and long-term profitability. The first panel of Exhibit 1.3 illustrates a firm in which every department works independently; the walls between the areas of the firm illustrate a lack of cross-functionality and, consequently, a lack of market orientation. The second panel illustrates a firm without barriers between the functions where marketing personnel work cross-functionally with other areas to achieve long-term profitability.

When a firm lacks organizational procedures for communicating marketing information and coordinating marketing efforts, the effectiveness of its marketing programs will suffer. Marketing research findings produce some of the most crucial marketing information; thus, such research is management's key tool for finding out what customers want and how best to satisfy their needs. In a competitive marketplace, managers recognize the critical need for conducting marketing research. When conducted competently, the firm's decisions are based on valid and reliable facts that are communicated effectively to decision makers.

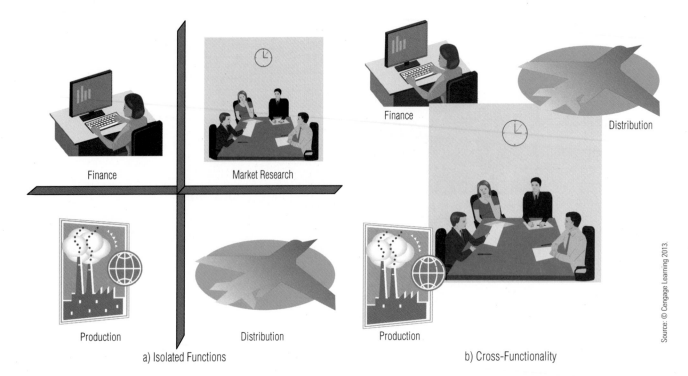

a) Isolated Functions

b) Cross-Functionality

Source: © Cengage Learning 2013.

EXHIBIT 1.3
Isolation versus
Crossfunctionality of
Marketing in a Firm

In a marketing-oriented firm, marketing researchers serve more than the external customers who buy the firm's offerings. Marketing research also serves internal customers with information. The internal customers include employees all along the value production chain from frontline service and sales employees, to production managers to the CEO. In fact, in a market-oriented organization, all employees are marketers in that they serve internal and external customers. An accountant who prepares a report for a sales manager should view the manager as a customer who uses the information to make decisions benefiting external customers. All employees share the common focus of providing value to customers.[14]

Keeping Customers and Building Relationships

Relationship marketing

Communicates the idea that a major goal of marketing is to build long-term relationships with the customers contributing to their success.

Marketers often talk about getting customers, but keeping customers is equally important. Effective marketers work to build long-term relationships with their customers. The term **relationship marketing** communicates the idea that a major goal of marketing is to build long-term relationships with the customers contributing to their success. Once an exchange is made, effective marketing stresses managing the relationships that will bring about additional exchanges. Effective marketers view making a sale not as the end of a process but as the start of the organization's relationship with a customer. Satisfied customers will return to a company that has treated them well if they need to purchase the same product in the future. If they need a related item, satisfied customers know the first place to look. Harley Davidson is a company that over time has developed a familial-type bond with its loyal customers. The research snapshot describes some of the ways Harley seeks for and uses information to better serve its markets at home and abroad.

In a company that practices total quality management, manufacturing's orientation toward lowest-cost productivity should harmonize with marketing's commitment to quality products at acceptable prices. For example, when Ford Motor Company advertises that "Quality Is Job One," the production department must make sure that every automobile that comes off the assembly line meets consumers' quality specifications. The notion that quality improvement is every employee's job must be integrated throughout the organization so that marketing and production will be in harmony. If this notion conflicts with manufacturing's desire to allow for variations from quality standards, the firm must implement statistical quality controls and other improvements in the manufacturing operation to improve its systems and increase productivity.

Chapter 8 discusses the measurement of quality, customer satisfaction, and value in detail. Throughout this book, however, we will explain how marketing research can help a company achieve the goal of creating valuable experiences for customers.

Harley-Davidson Means Family

A good family doesn't keep secrets. Harley-Davidson treats customers like family and believes that in a good relationship, one doesn't keep secrets from the other. Harley practices a wide variety of research and one recent tool involves mining social media sites. For instance, Harley-Davidson discovered a link between Kirchart skateboards and the Hog. Searching for the brand's name on social network sites like Facebook, they discovered a link to a YouTube video in which professional skateboarders for Heath Krichart rode Harley-Davidson motorcycles across the country on their summer tour. As a result of this information, Harley leveraged this information by becoming an official sponsor of Kirchart's tours.

Harley, an iconic Amerian brand, is an international company. Before Harley-Davidson goes overseas, Harley needs considerable research on each international market. In late 2009, Harley opened its first dealerships in India. Indian consumers were more accustomed to scooters than Hogs but the rising middle class and a new demand for luxury products creates opportunity. Survey research among Indian consumers showed a favorable opinion since the early 2000s. However, high duties imposed by the Indian government and difficult emission regulations proved too much of a barrier for Harley for several years.

©AP Photo/Krishnendu Kes

Successful lobbying of the Indian government eased some of the restrictions and Harley now offers twelve models ranging from a smallish 883 cc model to the 1800 cc model more fitting of the title Hog. In this way, Harley can address the needs of the luxury market and those desiring a more practical bike that still makes a statement.

Sources: Fournier, S., and J. Avery (2011), "The Uninvited Brand," *Business Horizons* (in press). NDTV (2010), "Harley-Davidson Opens First Outlet in India," *Press Trust of India* (July 9), www. ndtv.com/article/india/harley-davidson-opens-first-outlet-in-india-36610, accesed January 30, 2011. "Harley Davidson Rules Out India Foray for Near Future," *Asia-Africa Intelligence Wire* (September 2, 2005).

Marketing Research: A Means for Implementing the Marketing Concept

Home building used to be a business completely dominated by local construction contractors. If a customer wanted a home that would provide maximum satisfaction, a custom home at a custom price was the only option. Several home builders have grown into national companies. In doing so, they have implemented market-driven design processes that integrate research into the home designs. The research tracks consumers' actual living patterns to build homes with maximum livability. Thus, rather than "wasting space" on things like hallways that add little or even distract from a home's livability, that space is cannibalized, allowing more space allocated to the places where families really "live." In addition, research shows that consumers will make use of outdoor living areas if they are properly designed. Thus, the homes often include covered porches or lanais in place of less used indoor space like a formal living room.[15] In addition, younger homeowners are more and more eschewing large lawns because they view them as a hassle. They'd prefer a common green-space shared by multiple home owners than the responsibility of caring for their own. Research on preferred domicile space helps shape not only home design, but community living spaces as well.

By improving efficiency, research also facilitates profitability. For instance, during the introduction of a new product, accurate forecasting of the product's potential sales volume is an essential basis for estimating its profitability. A firm considering the introduction of a cat snack that contains hairball medicine might rely on a test market experiment to determine the optimal price for this new concept. Extensive testing should be done to ensure that the marketing program is fine-tuned to maximize the firm's profitability while satisfying consumers.

Analysis of data may also be a form of marketing research that can increase efficiency. Marketing representatives from Exxon Chemical Company used laptop computers to present a complex set of calculations to sales prospects to show them the advantage of Exxon products over competitors' products. Such analysis of research data improves the salesperson's batting average and the firm's efficiency. A good marketing researcher needs some knowledge of the ways information might be used to best provide the most useful information.

Marketing Research and Strategic Marketing Management

Effective marketing management requires research. Think about the role that celebrity endorsers plays to many companies. In 2010, Accenture quickly dissacociated itself with Tiger Woods but Nike golf stuck with him. Given their importance, numerous firms monitor the favorability of different celebrities and firms seek this research information in making endorsement decisions. The Davie-Brown Index is maintained as an independent research source providing such data. Among football quarterbacks, Tim Tebow is seen as more appealing and trendsetting than others like Tom Brady, Tony Romo, or Drew Breeze.[16] The prime managerial value of marketing research comes from the reduced uncertainty that results from information and facilitates decision making about marketing strategies and tactics to achieve an organization's strategic goals.

Developing and implementing a marketing strategy involves four stages:

1. Identifying and evaluating market opportunities
2. Analyzing market segments and selecting target markets
3. Planning and implementing a marketing mix that will provide value to customers and meet organizational objectives
4. Analyzing firm performance

Exhibit 1.4 illustrates the integration of research and marketing strategy and the way they come together to create value in the marketplace.

EXHIBIT **1.4**

Marketing Research Cuts Decision Risk with Input that Leads to Value

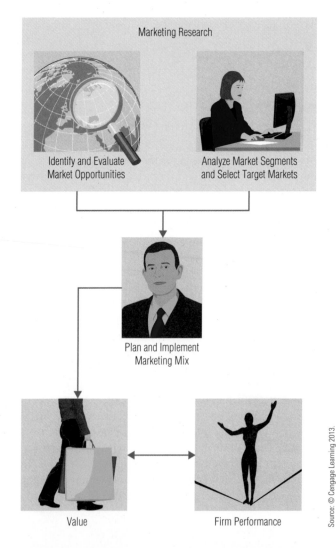

Source: © Cengage Learning 2013.

Identifying and Evaluating Market Opportunities

One job that marketing research performs is monitoring the environment for signals indicating a business opportunity. A mere description of a social or economic activity, such as trends in consumer purchasing behavior, may help managers recognize problems and identify opportunities for enriching marketing efforts. In some cases, this research can motivate a firm to take action to address consumer desires in a way that is beneficial to both the customers and to the firm.

At times, evaluating opportunities may involve something as mundane as tracking weather trends. Consumers have a physical need to maintain some degree of physical comfort. Thus, changes in temperature patterns may create business opportunities for utility companies, appliance companies, and even beverage companies as more consumers will select a hot beverage like hot chocolate when the weather is cold and dreary. Companies can also adjust their logistic distribution patterns based on the weather. When Hurricane Katrina hit the Gulf Coast of the United States, several chainsaw companies (such as Poulan) and companies that manufacture generators (such as Honda) began directing inventory toward those areas even before the hurricane actually struck. As a result, many home supply stores like Home Depot and Lowe's were able to maintain inventories of these vital products despite an increase in demand of over 1,000 percent! Thus, the misfortune of a hurricane created a business opportunity that also provided real value to consumers. In this case, the businesses and the consumers all benefited from the fact that firms scan the opportunity for trends.

Malls sometimes have research firms housed within them because the firm can interact with a steady stream of consumers. Some shopping centers in Texas near the U. S.–Mexican borders spotted an opportunity when they realized that a significant number of the shoppers in their mall indicated their residency in Mexico. A survey project was launched to profile these consumers. The results revealed that these consumers were typically from somewhere near Monterey, Mexico, typically households with children and typically relatively high in household income.[17] The results to that study can be used to market to other consumers living near Monterey who match this profile and encourage them to take a day trip across the border to do some shopping.

Market opportunities may be evaluated using many performance criteria. Estimates of market sales potential allow managers to evaluate the profitability of various opportunities. Accurate sales forecasts are among the most useful pieces of planning information a marketing manager can have. Complete accuracy in forecasting the future is not possible because change is one of the few constants in marketing. Nevertheless, objective forecasts of demand or of changes in the environment can provide a strong foundation for a sound marketing strategy.

Geo-demographics

Refers to information describing the demographic profile of consumers in a particular geographic region.

● ● ● ● ● ● ●

Fun in the snow depends on weather trends, equipment, and clothing—all subjects for a market researcher.

Analyzing and Selecting Target Markets

The second stage in developing a marketing strategy involves analyzing market segments and selecting target markets. Marketing research is a major source of information for determining which characteristics of market segments distinguish them from the overall market. Such research can help "locate" or describe a market segment in terms of demographic and characteristics. Geo-demographics can be important to study and track in this effort. **Geo-demographics** refers to information describing the demographic profile of consumers in a particular geographic region.

© agefotostock/SuperStock

The company may learn that consumers in a particular postal code within a region tend to be middle-aged, have multiple children over the age of twelve, and have college degrees and white-collar jobs. Once the company knows the geo-demographics of a market segment, the consumers within that segment can be reached by choosing media appealing to that particular profile. For example, *Architectural Digest* is a magazine that is read predominantly by consumers with very high social status in the most exclusive ZIP codes in the United States.

Planning and Implementing a Marketing Mix

Using the information obtained in the two previous stages, marketing managers plan and execute a marketing-mix strategy. Marketing research may be needed to support specific decisions about any aspect of the marketing mix. For instance, the research can evaluate an alternative course of action. For example, advertising research might investigate whether an actress like Julia Roberts or a singer like Katy Perry would make a better spokesperson for a specific brand of hair coloring. Research might be conducted involving test ads with each celebrity examining questions such as whether or not attitudes toward the brand are higher for Julia or for Katy. Perhaps not as obviously, research also would address how much credibility is associated with each celebrity based on how much a consumer would believe that the celbrity would actually use that particular product.

An overall research plan involves all marketing strategy elements. Once research identifies a target market and media that can be used in promotion, the benefits required to create value for the customers must be known and communicated, the appropriate price to capture that value must be determined and not overlooked, the best channel of distribution to reach the targeted consumers must be determined. The integration of all of this research leads to effective brand management.[18] The following examples describe marketing research for each element of the marketing mix.

● ● ● ● ● ● ●

Product testing research provides valuable input to companies, customers and policy makers.

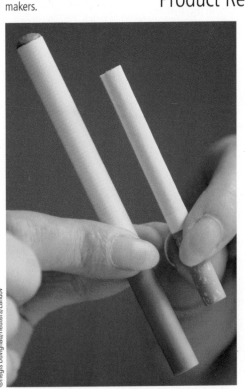

©Regis Duvignau/Reuters/Landov

Product Research

Product research takes many forms and includes studies designed to evaluate and develop new products and to learn how to adapt existing product lines. Concept testing exposes potential customers to a new product idea to judge the acceptance and feasibility of the concept. Product testing reveals a product prototype's strengths and weaknesses or determines whether a finished product performs better than competing brands or according to expectations. Brand-name evaluation studies investigate whether a name is appropriate for a product. Package testing assesses size, color, shape, ease of use, and other attributes of a package. Product research encompasses all applications of marketing research that seek to develop product attributes that will add value for consumers.

The idea of a smokeless cigarette has been around for decades. Products like Reynold's Premier, perhaps the most famous (or infamous) smokeless cigarette typically failed because the experience was too different than traditional smoking. After all, one can hardly smoke if there is no smoke! The latest concept is an E-cigarette. E-cigarettes contain a battery-powered tube that heats a liquid containing varying degrees of nicotine. When a user puffs on the device, it produces smoke, or more precisely, a steamlike (but smokeless) vapor. Research suggested the importance of something that looks like smoke in simulating an authentic smoking experience. Proponents, such as the National Vapors Club, argue that the product is a safer alternative to regular cigarettes. However, further product testing is under way to provide input to policy makers like the U. S. FDA to determine both the actual safety and the perceptions that the various brands of E-cigarettes send to consumers.[19]

Pricing Research

In many ways, pricing research represents typical marketing research. Many test markets address the question of how consumers will respond to a product offering two different prices. **Pricing** strategy involves finding the amount of monetary sacrifice that best represents the value customers perceive in a product after considering various market constraints. Most organizations conduct pricing research. Starbucks may seem expensive now, but if the price doubled, would Starbucks lose half of its customers? How much extra are Toyota customers willing to pay for each extra mpg? How much is one willing to pay to place a bid in an online auction? Pricing research also investigates the way people respond to pricing tactics. How do consumers respond to price reductions? How much are people willing to pay for some critical product attribute? Do consumers view prices and/or quantity discounts as fair in a given category?[20] Do price gaps among national brands, regional brands, and private labels exist? Most importantly, research also addresses the way consumers determine perceived value.

Pricing research addresses consumer quality perceptions by its very nature. A great deal of research addresses consumer reactions to low prices and documents the fact that, in quite a few instances, prices can actually be too low. In other words, sales can actually decrease with lower prices instead of increasing.[21]

Recently, Walmart test-marketed a Starbucks-type coffee shop called Medina's Kicks.[22] A Kicks coffee shop was set up in a Texas Walmart store. They are testing prices relative to the nearby Starbucks. At prices 25 percent below Starbucks, sales remain relatively low, while Starbucks remains popular. By lowering the price, they may also have lowered the perceived product quality. By raising the price, might quality perceptions improve and get consumers to think the coffee may be more similar to Starbucks? These are typical pricing questions.

Distribution Research

Distribution involves the marketing channels that will physically "distribute" products from a producer to a consumer. A **marketing channel** is a network of interdependent institutions that perform the logistics necessary for consumption to occur. Some channels are very short and involve only a producer and a consumer, and some are very long involving much transportation, wholesale, and retail firms. It may be somewhat obvious why the term **supply chain** is sometimes used to refer to a channel of distribution. Distribution is necessary to remove the separations between buyers and sellers.

Distribution research is typified by studies aimed at selecting retail sites or warehouse locations. A survey of retailers or wholesalers may be conducted because the actions of one channel member can greatly affect the performance of other channel members. Distribution research often is needed to gain knowledge about retailers' and wholesalers' operations and to learn their reactions to a manufacturer's marketing policies. It may also be used to examine the effect of just-in-time ordering systems or exclusive distribution on product quality. Research focused on developing and improving the efficiency of marketing channels is extremely important.

Netflix revolutionized the home movie business by bypassing retail outlets altogether and distributing movie rentals directly to the home consumer. More recently, Netflix allows consumers to access movies directly online. The customer can download the movie and then watch at their own convenience. Blockbuster responded by entering the online market despite

Pricing

Involves finding the amount of monetary sacrifice that best represents the value customers perceive in a product after considering various market constraints.

Marketing channel

A network of interdependent institutions that performs the logistics necessary for consumption to occur.

Supply chain

Another term for a channel of distribution, meaning the link between suppliers and customers.

● ● ● ● ● ● ●

What types of marketing research would be useful to Redbox.

research suggesting that such a move would cannibalize some of their in-store business.[23] Marketing research forecasts that the percentage of online video delivery will continue to grow to at least 12 percent by 2012.[24] A key determinant in the growth is the speed with which technology will allow videos to be downloaded. Consumers lack the patience for downloads counted in hours and not minutes or seconds. Thus, the research suggests that as download speeds increase, online distribution will grow even more. As an example that advanced technology is not always the answer, Redbox has found success with an old technology—delivering movies via vending machines, many located at Walgreens drugstore locations. Location is critical for Redbox. Location studies are indeed important for retailers and other members of the distribution channel.

Promotion Research

Promotion

The communication function of the firm responsible for informing and persuading buyers.

Promotion research

Investigates the effectiveness of advertising, premiums, coupons, sampling, discounts, public relations, and other sales promotions.

Promotion is the communication function of the firm responsible for informing and persuading buyers. **Promotion research** investigates the effectiveness of advertising, premiums, coupons, sampling, discounts, public relations, and other sales promotions. However, among all of these, firms spend more time, money, and effort on advertising research.

The marketing research findings of Zales, a large jewelry retailer, helped in the creation of advertising with large, one-word headlines that simply asked, "Confused?" "Nervous?" or "Lost?" The advertisements overtly acknowledged the considerable emotional and financial risks that consumers face in jewelry purchases. Research had shown that typical consumers felt unable to determine the relative quality of various jewelry items, believed jewelry purchases were expensive, and needed reassurance about their purchases, especially because they often purchased jewelry for someone else. This promotion helped communicate an effective message of empathy with the consumer.

Similarly, a business in transition must effectively communicate its meaning. As AT&T's business shifts from that of a pure long-distance provider into that of a distanceless cable, Internet, and wireless communication specialist, it is trying to make sure its image changes, too. But research showed its brand name still conjured up the image of an old-fashioned telephone company.[25] Marketing research also indicates great familiarity with the blue-and-white striped globe that served as AT&T's logo. A survey found 75 percent unaided recognition among the broad consumer market, 77 percent recognition among 18- to 24-year-olds, and 80 percent recognition among "high-value, active networkers"—consumers spending seventy-five dollars or more per month on long-distance and wireless services. Because of this high level of recognition, AT&T produced numerous TV commercials featuring an animation of the logo bouncing around, giving fun, high-intensity demonstrations of the various ways the company is transforming itself in the broadband-enabled world, accompanied by voice-over explanations of these new services.

Future research may even consider placing the logo as a product placement in video games as a way of further transforming AT&T's image from "Ma Bell" into a modern technology service provider.[26] AT&T's association with Apple may also have fostered the transformation, but beginning in 2011, other mobile providers such as Verizon can also sell and service iPhones and iPads. Will this hurt AT&T's image?

The Integrated Marketing Mix

Integrated marketing communication

Means that all promotional efforts (advertising, public relations, personal selling, event marketing, and so forth) should be coordinated to communicate a consistent image.

Integrated marketing mix

The effects of various combinations of marketing-mix elements on important outcomes.

Marketing today focuses increasingly on the fact that different promotional decisions should not be made in isolation. Instead, the concept of **integrated marketing communication** is adopted, meaning that all promotional efforts (advertising, public relations, personal selling, event marketing, and so forth) should be coordinated to communicate a consistent image. Likewise, more generally marketing firms realize that the elements of the marketing mix itself must work together. For instance, a change in price can affect the quality of the product, which may also influence decisions about distribution. From a research standpoint, the **integrated marketing mix** means that research studies often investigate effects of various combinations of marketing mix elements on important outcomes like sales and image. Research suggests that consumer-oriented firms are particularly oriented toward integrating all aspects of their marketing into a single message.[27]

Best Buy, a U. S.-based electronic and appliance retailer, recently showed the success of integrating sales and service with promotion. You'll find a Geek in every Best Buy. The Geeks are technology experts (i. e., "computer geeks") that provide knowledgeable sales advice and technical service. To be a Geek, you have to look like a Geek! Their attire is carefully co-ordinated: white socks with black shoes, black pants that are just a little too short, a white sport shirt, and a narrow black tie. Today, the Geeks have become prominent in Best Buy television ads, and they even provide in-home setup and technical service. The Geeks are transforming Best Buy in the minds of consumers.[28] Companies that integrate the use of consistent spokespeople, such as the Geeks, across marketing elements enjoy more favorable brand images among consumers and are better able to communicate relevant information.[29]

● ● ● ● ● ● ●

Best Buy has reinvented the traditional Geek image and made it work for them.

Analyzing Marketing Performance

After a marketing strategy has been implemented, marketing research may serve to inform managers whether planned activities were properly executed and are accomplishing what they were expected to achieve. In other words, marketing research may be conducted to obtain feedback for evaluation and control of marketing programs. This aspect of marketing research is especially important for successful **total value management**, which attempts to manage the entire process by which a consumer receives benefits from a company.

Performance-monitoring research refers to research that regularly, sometimes routinely, provides feedback for evaluation and control of marketing activity. For example, most firms continuously monitor wholesale and retail activity to ensure early detection of sales declines and other anomalies. In the grocery and drug industries, sales research may use Universal Product Codes (UPCs) on packages read by electronic cash registers and computerized checkout counts to provide valuable market-share information to store and brand managers interested in the retail sales volumes of their products. Market-share analysis and sales analysis are the most common forms of performance-monitoring research. Almost every organization compares its current sales with previous sales and with competitors' sales. However, analyzing marketing performance is not limited to the investigation of sales figures.

Marketing metrics refer to quantitative ways of monitoring and measuring marketing performance. Research is needed to determine marketing metrics that allow a firm to know whether the resources invested in marketing activities have met their quantitative business goals. Marketing metrics allow the firm to assess the return on investment (ROI) associated with marketing activities. Recent research suggests that the more firms emphasize value creation in their marketing, the higher are these key performance metrics.[30] Thus, value appears to pay.

Total value management

Trying to manage and monitor the entire process by which consumers receive benefits from a company.

Performance-monitoring research

Refers to research that regularly, sometimes routinely, provides feedback for evaluation and control of marketing activity.

Marketing metrics

Quantitative ways of monitoring and measuring marketing performance.

When Is Marketing Research Needed?

The need to make intelligent, informed decisions ultimately motivates marketing research. Not every decision requires marketing research. Thus, when confronting a key decision, a marketing manager must initially decide whether or not to conduct marketing research. The determination of the need for marketing research centers on (1) time constraints, (2) the availability of data, (3) the nature of the decision to be made, and (4) the value of the research information in relation to costs.

Time Constraints

Systematic research takes time. In many instances management believes that a decision must be made immediately, allowing no time for research. Decisions sometimes are made without adequate information or thorough understanding of market situations. Although making decisions without researching a situation is not ideal, sometimes the urgency of a situation precludes the use of research. The urgency with which managers often want to make decisions often conflicts with the marketing researchers' desire for rigor in following the scientific method.

Availability of Data

Often times, managers already possess enough information to make sound decisions without additional marketing research. When they lack adequate information, however, research must be considered. This means that data need to be collected from an appropriate source. If a potential source of data exists, managers will want to know how much it will cost to get the data.

If the data cannot be obtained or obtained in a timely fashion, this particular research project should not be conducted. For example, many African nations have never conducted a population census. Organizations engaged in international business often find that data about business activity or population characteristics that are readily available in the United States are nonexistent or sparse in developing countries. Imagine the problems facing marketing researchers who wish to investigate market potential in places like Uzbekistan, Yugoslavian Macedonia, and Rwanda.

Nature of the Decision

The value of marketing research depends on the nature of the managerial decision to be made. A routine tactical decision that does not require a substantial investment may not seem to warrant a substantial expenditure for marketing research. For example, a computer company must update its operator's instruction manual when it makes minor product modifications. The research cost of determining the proper wording to use in the updated manual is likely too high for such a minor decision. The nature of the decision is not totally independent of the next issue to be considered: the benefits versus the costs of the research. In general, however, the more strategically or tactically important the decision, the more likely it is that research will be conducted.

Benefits versus Costs

Marketing research can be costly but it can also be of great benefit. Earlier we discussed some of the managerial benefits of marketing research. In any decision-making situation, managers must identify alternative courses of action and then weigh the value of each alternative against its cost. Marketing research can be thought of as an investment alternative. When deciding whether to make a decision without research or to postpone the decision in order to conduct research, managers should ask three questions:

1. Will the payoff be worth the investment?
2. Will the information gained by marketing research improve the quality of the marketing decision enough to warrant the expenditure?
3. Is the proposed research expenditure the best use of the available funds?

In the opening vignette, PepsiCo failed to do enough market testing to identify critical problems with the new Sun Chip bags. Conducting extensive research was judged to be an unwise investment. The value of the research information was not positive because its cost exceeded its benefits. Perhaps the change in packaging was seen as so inconsequential that extensive testing beyond concept testing was seen as unnecessary to make a quality decision. In hindsight, perhaps more research was merited although a comparison of the loss in sales revenue with the costs of conducting further market tests would be needed to better address this question. Exhibit 1.5 outlines the criteria for determining when to conduct marketing research.

EXHIBIT **1.5**
Should We Conduct
Marketing Research?

Factor	Conduct Market Research	Do Not Conduct Market Research
Time	Sufficient time is available before decision will be made.	Time pressure requires a decision before adequate research can be completed.
Data Availability	Firm does not have access to data but data can be obtained.	Firm already has relevant data or data cannot be obtained.
Nature of Decision	Decision of considerable strategic or tactical importance.	Decision is not critical and involves relatively little risk.
Benefits versus Costs	Potential value of research exceeds costs of conducting research.	Costs of research exceed potential value of project.
	GO!	STOP!

Source: © Cengage Learning 2013.

Marketing Research in the Twenty-First Century

Marketing research, like all business activity, continues to change. Changes in communication technologies and the trend toward an ever more global marketplace have played a large role in many of these changes.

Communication Technologies

Virtually everyone is "connected" today. Increasingly, many people are "connected" nearly all the time. The typical college student spends hours a day on Facebook or other social networking sites that connect him or her to the Internet. Each move provides access to information but also leaves a record of data that tells a great deal about that particular consumer. Today, the amount of information formally contained in an entire library can rest easily in a single personal computer.

The speed with which information can be exchanged continues to increase. During the 1970s, exchanging information overnight from anywhere in the continental United States was heralded as a near miracle of modern technology. Today, we can exchange information from nearly anywhere in the world to nearly anywhere else in the world almost instantly. A researcher can get on Skype and interview decision makers anywhere in the world as long as both are connected to the Internet. Our mobile phones and handheld data devices can be used not only to converse, but also as a means of communication that can even involve marketing research data. Marketing researchers arm trained interviewers with iPads and similar devices which can display graphic images to respondents and provide a structured guide to the interview. Thus, the expressions "time is collapsing" and "distance is disappearing" capture the tremendous revolution in the speed and reach of our communication technologies.

As recently as the 1970s, most computer applications required expensive mainframe computers found only in very large corporations, major universities, and large governmental/military institutions. Researchers could expect to wait hours or even longer to get results from a statistical program involving 200 respondents. Today, even the most basic laptop computers can solve complicated statistical problems involving thousands of data points in practically a nanosecond. Soon, small, inexpensive appliances like an iPad will access software and data existing on the cloud (large servers that supply information and software to large numbers of Internet users), illiminating the need for specialized software and a conventional laptop computer.

Global Marketing Research

Marketing research has become increasingly global as more and more firms take advantage of markets that have few, if any, geographic boundaries. Some companies have extensive international marketing research operations. Upjohn conducts marketing research in 160 different countries.

"Jacques" Daniels

Sales of U. S. distilled spirits have declined over the last ten to fifteen years as more Americans turn to wine or beer as their beverage of choice. As a result, companies like Bacardi and Brown-Forman, producers of Jack Daniels, have pursued market development strategies involving increased efforts to expand into international markets. The Brown-Forman marketing budget for international ventures includes a significant allocation for marketing research. By doing research before launching the product, Brown-Forman can learn product usage patterns within a particular culture. Some of the findings from this research are indicated as follows.

1. Japanese consumers use Jack Daniels (JD) as a dinner beverage. A party of four or five consumers in a restaurant will order and drink a bottle of "JD" with their meal.
2. Australian consumers mostly consume distilled spirits in their homes. Also in contrast to Japanese consumers, Australians prefer to mix JD with soft drinks or other mixers. As a result of this research, JD launched a mixture called "Jack and Cola" sold in 12-ounce bottles all around Australia. The product has been very successful.
3. British distilled spirit consumers also like mixed drinks, but they usually partake in bars and restaurants.

"Jacques" Daniels

4. In China and India, consumers more often choose counterfeit or "knock-offs" to save money. Thus, innovative research approaches have addressed questions related to the way the black market works and how they can better educate consumers about the differences between the real thing and the knock-offs.
5. Chinese consumers enjoy their Jack mixed with green tea.

The result is that more than half of all Jack Daniels made is now consumed outside of the United States. The global sales growth has contributed to impressive sales growth of over 40 percent since 2002.

Sources: Swibel, Mathew, "How Distiller Brown-Forman Gets Rich by Exploiting the Greenback's Fall—and Pushing its Brands Abroad," *Forbes*, 175, no. 8 (2005), 152–55; Kiley, D., "Jack Daniel's International Appeal," *Businessweek*, October 10, 2007, accessed at http://www.businessweek.com/innovate/content/oct2007/id20071010_651037.htm, September 14, 2008.

ACNielsen International, known for its television ratings, is the world's largest marketing research company. Two-thirds of its business comes from outside the United States. Nielsen researchs all manner of topics internationally. For instance, the candy market is changing globablly.[31] North American consumers are buying more confectionary product, in particular non-chocolate bars with some utilitarian benefit beyond good taste. However, North America lags behind Asian consumers who are purchasing and consuming candies loaded with things like amino acids and tea extracts. Asian consumers are nuts about health candy it seems. International candy companies like Hershey's, Nestlé, and Mars are keen to learn such trends for obvious reasons.

Companies that conduct business in foreign countries must understand the nature of those particular markets and judge whether they require customized marketing strategies. For example, although the fifteen nations of the European Union share a single formal market, marketing research shows that Europeans do not share identical tastes for many consumer products. Marketing researchers have found no such thing as a typical European consumer; language, religion, climate, and centuries of tradition divide the nations of the European Union. Scantel Research, a British firm that advises companies on color preferences, found inexplicable differences in Europeans' preferences in medicines. The French prefer to pop purple pills, but the English and Dutch favor white ones. Consumers in all three countries dislike bright red capsules, which are big sellers in the United States. This example illustrates that companies that do business in Europe must research throughout Europe to adapt to local customs and buying habits.[32]

Even companies that produce brands that are icons in their own country are now doing research internationally. The Research Snapshot discusses how Brown-Forman, the parent company of Jack Daniels (the classic American "Sour Mash" or Bourbon Whiskey), are now interviewing consumers in the far corners of the world. The internationalization of research places greater demands on marketing researchers and heightens the need for research tools that allow us to

culturally cross-validate research results, meaning that the empirical findings from one culture also exist and behave similarly in another culture. The development and application of these international research tools are an important topic in basic marketing research.

Cultural cross-validation

To verify that the empircal findings from one culture also exist and behave similarly in another culture.

TIPS OF THE TRADE

1. Throughout this text, a Tools & Tips section is provided to provide helpful hints for using and doing marketing research. The first tip is to pay attention to these sections as helpful references.
2. Customers and employees are valuable sources for input that leads to innovation in the marketplace and in the workplace.
3. Business problems ultimately boil down to information problems because with the right information, the business can take effective action.
4. Research plays a role before, during, and after key marketing decisions.

- Research helps design marketing strategies and tactics before action is taken.
- Once a plan is implemented, research monitors performance with key metrics providing valuable feedback.
- After a plan is implemented, research assesses performance against benchmarks and seeks explanations for the failure of success of the action.

5. Research that costs more than the right decision could return should not be conducted.

Source: © Cengage Learning 2013.

∷ SUMMARY

This chapter had six learning objectives. After reading the chapter, the student should be competent in each area described by a learning objective.

1. Know what marketing ia and does for business. Marketing research is is the application of the scientific method in searching for the truth about marketing phenomena. Thus, it is the intelligence-gathering function in business. The intelligence includes information about customers, competitors, economic trends, employees, and other factors that affect marketing success. This intelligence assists in decisions ranging from long-range planning to near-term tactical decisions. Although many business decisions are made "by the seat of the pants" or based on a manager's intuition, this type of decision making carries with it a large amount of risk. By first researching an issue and gathering intelligence on customers, competitors, and the market, a company can make a more informed decision. The result is less risky decision making.

2. Understand the differences between basic and applied marketing research. Applied marketing research seeks to facilitate managerial decision making. Basic or pure research seeks to increase knowledge of theories and concepts. Both are important. Applied research examples are emphasized in this text although practically all of the tools and techniques that are discussed are appropriate to either type of research. Some use the term market research to refer to applied research and marketing research to refer to basic research.

3. Understand how the role of marketing research changes when a firm is truly marketing oriented. Every company has a particular operating orientation. Production-oriented companies emphasize producing outpus as efficiently as possible. Generally, this leads to an emphasis on low-cost production and low-cost positioning in the marketplace. Product-oriented companies emphasize producing a sophisticated product that is also technologically advanced. Firms that are oriented around the marketing concept become very consumer oriented. Market-oriented firms view all employees as customers who need marketing intelligence to make good decisions. Marketing-oriented companies tend to do more marketing research and emphasize marketing research more than do other firms.

4. Be able to integrate marketing research results into the strategic planning process. Marketing research is a means of implementing the marketing concept, the most central idea in marketing. The marketing concept says that a firm must be oriented both toward consumer satisfaction and toward long-run profitability (rather than toward short-run sales volume). Marketing research can help implement the marketing concept by identifying consumers' problems and needs, improving efficiency, and evaluating the effectiveness of marketing strategies and tactics. The development and implementation of a marketing strategy consist of four stages: (1) identifying and evaluating opportunities, (2) analyzing market segments and selecting target markets, (3) planning and implementing a marketing mix that will provide value to customers and meet the objectives of the organization, and (4) analyzing firm performance. Marketing research helps in each stage by providing information for strategic decision making. In particular, marketing research aimed at the marketing mix seeks information useful in marking better decisions about product design, promotion, distribution, and pricing.

5. Know when research should and should not be done. Marketing managers determine whether marketing research should be conducted based on (1) time constraints, (2) availability of data, (3) the nature of the decision to be made, and (4) the benefit of the research information versus its cost. Research should only be conducted when time is available, relevant data can be found and does not already exist, the decision can be shaped by information, and the benefits outweigh the cost of doing the research.

6. Appreciate how technology and internationalization are affecting the way research is conducted and used. Technology has changed almost every aspect of marketing research. Modern computing and communications technologies including social networking make data collection, study design, data analysis, data reporting, and practically all other aspects of research easier and better. Furthermore, as more companies do business outside their own borders, companies are doing research in an international marketplace. This places a greater emphasis on research that can assess the degree to which research tools can be applied and interpreted the same way in difference cultures. Thus, research techniques often must cross-validate results.

⠶ KEY TERMS AND CONCEPTS

applied marketing research, 7	marketing concept, 9	promotion, 18
basic marketing research, 8	marketing metrics, 19	promotion research, 18
cultural cross-validation, 23	marketing orientation, 9	relationship marketing, 12
customer oriented, 9	marketing research, 6	scientific method, 8
geo-demographics, 15	performance-monitoring research, 19	stakeholder orientation, 9
integrated marketing communication, 18	pricing, 17	supply chain, 17
integrated marketing mix, 18	product oriented, 9	total value management, 19
marketing channel, 17	production oriented, 9	

⠶ QUESTIONS FOR REVIEW AND CRITICAL THINKING

1. What advantages does research offer to the decision maker over seat-of-the-pants decision making?

2. Define a marketing orientation and a product orientation. Under which strategic orientation is there a greater need for marketing research?

3. Who might represent an internal customer for marketing research to a market-oriented company?

4. Name some products that logically might have been developed with the help of marketing research.

5. Define *marketing research* and describe its task. How is it different from research in the physical sciences?

6. Which of the following organizations are likely to use marketing research? Why? How?
    a. Manufacturer of breakfast cereals
    b. An online auction Internet site
    c. Manufacturer of nuts, bolts, and other fasteners
    c. The Federal Trade Commission
    d. A hospital
    e. A company that publishes marketing textbooks

7. An automobile manufacturer is conducting research in an attempt to predict the type of car design consumers will desire in the year 2022. Is this basic or applied research? Explain.

8.   What is the definition of an *integrated marketing mix*? How might this affect the research a firm conducts?

9.   Comment on the following statements:
   a.   Marketing managers are paid to take chances with decisions. Marketing researchers are paid to reduce the risk of making those decisions.
   b.   A marketing strategy can be no better than the information on which it is formulated.
   c.   The purpose of research is to solve marketing problems.

10. List the conditions that help a researcher decide when marketing research should or should not be conducted.

11. How have technology and internationalization affected marketing research?

12. What types of tools does the marketing researcher use more given the ever-increasing internationalization of marketing?

13. Apple, Facebook, Coca-Cola, Microsoft, Walmart, Pfizer. Given the introduction to marketing research presented here, rank the companies based on how important you believe marketing research is to each's success.

:: RESEARCH ACTIVITIES

1.   Suppose you owned a jewelry store in Denton, Texas. You are considering opening a second store just like your current store. You are undecided on whether to locate the new store in another location in Denton, Texas, or in Birmingham, Alabama. Why would you decide to have some marketing research done before making the decision? Should the research be conducted? Go to **http://www. census. gov.** Do you think any of this information would be useful in the research?

2.   Find recent examples of news articles from the most recent week involving the use of marketing research in making decisions about each element of the marketing mix. The *Wall Street Journal* is a good source for such stories.

3.   Find a list of the ten most popular mobile phone apps at the current time. Is there anything in common among the apps? Do they indicate any trends about consumers in general or a particular segment of consumers? What is that trend? Which companies may benefit from such a trend?

Data Mining Procedures and Knowledge Systems

CHAPTER
2

LEARNING OUTCOMES

After studying this chapter, you should be able to:

1. Know why concepts like data, information, and intelligence represent value
2. Understand the four characteristics that describe data
3. Know what a decision support system is and does
4. Describe marketing research's role in predictive analytics
5. Recognize the major categories of databases
6. Be sensitive to the potential ethical abuse of tracking consumers electronically

Chapter Vignette:

Data Can Give You a Lift!

Online technologies have dramatically changed the way we shop for travel services, especially airline tickets. Consumers most often buy tickets without any person-to-person contact. Airline consumers spend a lot of time online trying to get the best deals. At any given time, a major airline is serving approximately 1,000

© Paul Prescott/Shutterstock

customers through its website. In a typical day, that means over one million customers have *touched* the company. Each touch leaves behind a record that researchers can mine to guide managerial decision making.

Even occasional flyers probably know that airline prices can be difficult to predict. A consumer may find a higher price for a roundtrip flight from Tampa to Atlanta than for a roundtrip flight from Tampa to San Francisco! A direct flight from New York to Paris may cost less than an indirect flight from New York to Paris with a two-hour layover in Houston! Airline pricing does not always make sense to consumers, but does make sense to managers. Dynamic pricing approaches like this rely greatly on research using data describing who is flying to where and when they are flying. At times, the airline's attempt to maximize yield can lead to very attractive price offers to consumers. In fact, airline travel can sometimes compete with or even beat the price of driving, particularly when airlines target consumers with specific profiles with a special fare between specific locations.

Airlines use sophisticated yield management systems, aiming to maximize the revenue realized on any given flight, and thereby on every flight. An empty seat is the worst thing for a positive yield. However, how can an airline predict how many consumers will be on each flight? When someone books a flight online, the system records a lot of information beyond the fact that one more seat is unavailable. Information can be taken from the consumer's Web cookies so that the company knows what cities the consumer searched for, if different dates were considered, how long it took to make a decision, how the ticket was paid for, and much more. The yield management system uses all of this data to predict the probability that a seat will be occupied and then determine the price that a particular customer will be offered. From a profitability standpoint, allowing someone to fly for a ridiculously low price is better than having an empty seat on the airplane. Although it may seem strange to consumers, the results of yield management systems like these show that airlines actually increase profits when the disparity between the lowest prices and highest prices that passengers pay is greatest.

Airlines use a host of sophisticated data systems. The pricing systems also now get involved in offering customers upgrades based on the portion of first-class customers on a flight. Baggage pricing also is a new reality. Airlines know that baggage is a priority because data show that poor baggage handling results in customers booking with other airlines. Delta Airlines, fresh off a bankruptcy in 2007, invested $100 million for a new baggage handling system. Take a look at the baggage ticket they put on your bag and you will see a barcode that contains all the routing information for the bag and information about the customer as well. Fixed and handheld scanners track this baggage throughout its time at the airport and the result of using this data is fewer upset customers. In fact, airlines with good performance misdirect fewer than four in every 1,000 bags handled. Airlines give us a lift and sophisticated data systems give their bottom lines a lift, too.[1]

Introduction

Dynamic pricing refers to a systematic adjustment of prices with each transaction in an effort to optimally achieve the firm's margin objectives.[2] Check an airline site on Monday and you may very well find different prices than you would have on Sunday. In fact, the adjustments that these pricing systems make based on Internet traffic mean that customers can usually find lower prices on Tuesday or Wednesday than on Friday or Saturday.[3] Pricing, shipping, and promotion decisions today are often automated or at least supplemented with intelligence generated from data collected in routine transactions and warehoused electronically.

Airlines aren't alone in this effort. Imagine all the market-relevant information that consumers pass daily through Facebook communications. Did Home Depot or Lowe's get more *Likes* today? Did any of their customers share a complaint with their friends? Maybe they even tweeted about the event. All of this data, and a great deal of less obvious data left as traces on each computer, can prove very valuable to companies. So valuable that Facebook's ability to use personal data about its more than 500 million users to specifically and automatically target advertisements to receptive users proves a major source of their revenue.[4] The Research Snapshot below describes how this works in more detail.

This chapter discusses data systems and the role decision support systems and predictive analytics play in helping firms make informed marketing decisions. The decision support systems can be complicated and extensive, extending beyond the internal organizational walls. Marketing research plays an important role in making sense out of the glut of data now available. Today, data technology allows businesses to more easily integrate research findings into marketing strategy and operations.

dynamic pricing

A systematic adjustment of prices with each transaction in an effort to optimally achieve the firm's margin objectives.

Data, Information, and Intelligence Equal Value

In everyday language, terms like *information* and *data* are often used interchangeably. Researchers use these terms in specific ways that emphasize how useful each can be. Marketing managers may not be as intimately involved in finding and analyzing data; however, the decisions that they make based on the input received from research will make or break the firm. In this way, data, information, and intelligence all have the potential to create value to the firm through better decision making. One way in which these terms are not interchangeable lies in how closely linked they are to creating value for consumers and businesses.

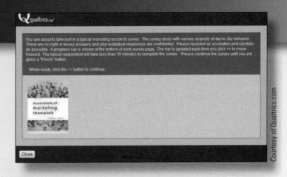

Review the questionnaire that you responded to last chapter. Later, you'll be asked to analyze data with the hope of predicting and explaining some important outcomes with marketing implications. Now, which sections do you think would provide the most value to a firm that provides online access to Blu-ray videos of late release movies and television specials? How could the information be used by a DSS that included a predictive analytics component? How would the question change if instead of an online provider of video files, the client was a private university seeking to increase admissions from students with strong prospects for success?

Source: © Cengage Learning 2013.

data

Facts or recorded measures of certain phenomena (things).

information

Data formatted (structured) to support decision making or define the relationship between two facts.

market intelligence

The subset of data and information that actually has some explanatory power enabling effective decisions to be made.

Data are simply facts or recorded measures of certain phenomena (things or events). **Information** is data formatted (structured) to support decision making or define the relationship between two facts. **Market intelligence** is the subset of data and information that actually has some explanatory power enabling effective decisions to be made. So, there is more data than information, and more information than intelligence. Most data are irrelevant to any specific decision-making situation and therefore not always valuable. When data become information, there relevance is examined more closely through some analytical procedure. Conclusions are drawn from the structured data (i.e., information) to actually shape marketing decisions. The result is market intelligence and this should enable better decision making, better value provided to customers in that their desires are more closely met and, thereby, more value for the firm in the form of improved performance.[5]

Think again about the thousands upon thousands of facts recorded by eBay each day. Each time a product is sold, that facts about that transaction are recorded and become data. The data include the final selling price, the amount of time the item was available for sale, the number of consumers making an offer, and the seller feedback scores. Similarly, major retailers like Lowe's record information about each customer transaction. Their inventory system structures the data in a way that allows automatic generation of stocking reports and product orders. In this way, the automated inventory system turns data into information. Further, analysts track sales trends by harvesting the information from each store's sales and inventory records. Selected suppliers like Black and Decker also integrate the POS (point-of-sale) data to adjust their manufacturing and distribution processes.[6] All of this helps Lowe's get the right products into each store. The system even suggests places for new Lowe's locations. In this way, data become transformed into intelligence.

Recent technologies produce tremendous quantities of data. In this chapter, we discuss how various **sensing systems** automatically collect data and make it available for conversion into intelligence. Sensing systems involve more than just sales data and include information collected by medical scanners, digital cameras, audio recording devices, environmental sensors, and more. While in previous eras, problem solvers felt constrained by a lack of information, researchers worry now that we are deluged with data so much so that it outstrips our ability to effectively convert it into intelligence. In fact, in 2010 the world generated 1,250 billion gigabytes of data, which means more data than there are stars in the universe.[7] The deluge challenges marketing researchers with harnessing market data. The deluge of data suggests greater demand for marketing analysts.

sensing systems

General term for combined hardware and software that automatically records phenomena.

The Characteristics of Valuable Information

Four important characteristics do much to determine the value of information. Exhibit 2.1 provides an overview of the characteristics discussed below.

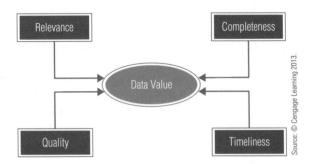

Source: © Cengage Learning 2013.

EXHIBIT 2.1
Characteristics of
Valuable Data

Relevance

Relevance is the characteristics of data reflecting how pertinent these particular facts are to the situation at hand. Put another way, the facts are logically connected to the situation. Unfortunately, irrelevant data and information often creep into decision making. One particularly useful way to distinguish relevance from irrelevance is to think about how things change. Relevant data are facts about things that will materially alter the situation if they change. So, this simple question becomes important:

Will a change in the data coincide with a change in some important outcome?

American consumers' dietary trends are relevant to the restaurant industry. For instance, if American diets become more health-conscious, sales of doughnuts are likely to change. This may lead a restaurant like Dunkin' Donuts to rethink its product offering. However, information on the height of Mount Washington is irrelevant because it isn't going to change any time soon and even if it did, it would not affect U.S. doughnut preferences.

relevance
The characteristics of data reflecting how pertinent these particular facts are to the situation at hand. When data are relevant, a change in that fact is associated with a change in an important outcome.

Completeness

Information completeness refers to having the right amount of information. Marketing managers must have sufficient relevant information to develop explanations and predictions useful in decision making. For example, managers trying to make a key decision about launching a technological innovation to their current software commission a quick research study in which consumers are asked to rate the perceived usefulness of the technological improvement. Based on the high usefulness scores, the managers launch the innovation only to find decreased sales and increased customer complaints. The complaints send a loud signal that the innovation made the product too complex. In their haste to act, the managers acted without input on this critical variable.

A follow-up study demonstrated that perceived complexity was equally as important in predicting adoption of new technologies and that as consumers see innovations as more complex, they find less value in the product. Theory can play a big role in helping to make information more complete and in this case a theory known as the *technology acceptance model* describes some key pieces of information in predicting the success of technological innovations.[8]

information completeness
Having the right amount of information.

Quality

Data quality reflects how accurately the gathered actually match reality. High quality data are valid and reliable—both concepts we'll turn to in detail later. In this chapter, we emphasize the vast quantity of data now available, not in small part due to Web 2.0 technologies. In fact, the chief scientist at Amazon.com estimated that in 2009, consumers left behind more data than they had in all of history through 2008.[9]

Not all data are equal in quality. Professional sales managers equip their salespeople with a plethora of technology to record information about sales calls. The data have numerous uses, not the least of which is allowing data systems to compute an expected value of the customer. In this way, the salesperson can know how much effort to put into winning each particular prospect. However, salespeople often are pinched for time and wait until the end of the day or even the end

data quality
How accurately the data actually match reality.

of the week to enter the required information. A pharmaceutical salesperson may wonder, "Did I spend 5 minutes or 12 minutes answering questions?" "Did the doctor make me wait 10 minutes or more?" "Did the doctor ask for samples or did I just leave them?" Each inaccurate answer lowers data quality and means the decision system's statistical models are less reliable. Managers can take advantage of technology by placing a GPS tracking device on the sales manager's smartphone or tablet. The tracking devices record the time spent in each location automatically. However, sales managers might weigh the increased accuracy against management spying on salespeople. Researchers offer this advice as a guide to enhanced data quality:[10]

1. Automate data collection and entry when feasible.
2. Inspect the data and cleanse for obvious errors.
3. Be mindful of the costs and benefits of efforts at improving data quality.

Timeliness

timeliness

Means the data are not so old that they are irrelevant.

Timeliness means the data are not so old that they are irrelevant. Generally, timeliness requires highly current data. Imagine car companies trying to predict the types of cars consumers would be most interested in recently. Think of all the changes in the operating environment that have taken place since 2007. The economy went from boom to bust and consumer confidence dropped consequently. Fuel prices have fluctuated wildly ranging anywhere from a U.S. average for regular gas of $1.60 per gallon in late 2008 to nearly $4.10 per gallon in July of that same year. Car preference will change with these environmental factors so data collected in one time period may not be entirely accurate. Similarly, imagine how the dramatic pace of technology change in the electronics industry hinders predicting consumer acceptance of mobile phones. The term **market dynamism** represents the rate of change in environmental and competitive factors.[11] Highly dynamic markets mean greater risk in relying on data, particularly on untimely data.

market dynamism

Represents the rate of change in environmental and competitive factors.

Global Marketplace

"Facts are stubborn things."

—RONALD REAGAN

By now, marketers around the world realize the potential marketplace is the entire world. A start-up company in Topeka, Kansas, only needs a website and the company's business isn't just in Kansas anymore. Large companies use a plethora of technology ranging from handheld tablets to satellites to gather and exchange data in an effort to keep track of business details globally.

Consider a simple example. At any moment, United Parcel Service (UPS) can track the status of any shipment around the world. UPS drivers use handheld electronic clipboards called *delivery information acquisition devices* (DIADs) to record appropriate data about each pickup or delivery. The data are then entered into the company's main computer for record-keeping and analysis. A satellite telecommunications system allows UPS to track any shipment for a customer. Consumers also can get near real-time information on the status of a delivery as information from the DIADs is available through **www.ups.com**.

Near Field Communication (NFC) Devices

RFID tag

Abbreviation for radio frequency identification tags that use a small microchip to communicate with data systems.

RFID stands for radio frequency identification. A tiny chip, which can be woven onto a fabric, placed in packaging, attached to a card, or otherwise affixed to virtually any product, sends a radio signal that identifies that particular entity uniquely. When the tag comes into proximity of a reader, the reader records the programmed information allowing products and/or consumers to be tracked virtually anywhere. The U.S. military pioneered RFID technology as a logistical tool and Walmart is one of the leading proponents of the technology as it can greatly assist in its global information system.[12] Pharmaceutical companies also use RFID tags to track the whereabouts of medicines.

Retailers use RFID technology both to offer customers uniquely tailored promotions and to keep track of customers' shopping behavior. La Croissanterie, a fresh but fast-food chain based in Paris, replaced its traditional cardboard loyalty card with a plastic wallet-sized card that

Loyalty cards like this bring rewards to good customers and a wealth of data to the retailer.

includes an RFID chip.[13] Once a customer enters the store, they can activate tap a smart poster that contains NFC (near field communication) technology. **NFC** works like a WiFi system communicating with specific devices within a defined space like inside of a retail unit. The NFC essentially talks to the RFID chip. The smart poster identifies the customer's loyalty status, offers them a promotion based on this status, records all purchases, and updates the customer's status automatically (no hole punchers or stamps used here), but most importantly from a research standpoint, records all the customer data no matter which of about 200 La Croissanterie units the customer visits.

NFC

Abbreviation for near field communication or WiFi-like systems communicating with specific devices within a defined space like inside of a retail unit or near a poster billboard.

NFC doesn't require RFID tags to communicate with consumers. Smartphone technologies allow consumers to download applications that allow their phones to act as their loyalty card. More than half of the smartphones in France can use an app to replace the card system described above. Interactive billboards are popping up in major metropolitan areas like London, which both encourage passersby to download such an app on the spot or, if they already have the app, to use it to get special deals on the spot. Nokia invested $1 million to test interactive posters in the United States, United Kingdom, Australia, and South Africa and realized good returns.[14] Once the consumer accepts an app, data systems go to work recording information aimed at finding out just what makes customers like him/her receptive to offers.

Decision Support Systems

Marketing research serves four possible business functions. These functions align with purposes of marketing research:

1. Foundational—answers basic questions such as "What consumers or consumer segments should the company serve and with what types of products?"
2. Testing—addresses things like new product concepts, product innovations, pricing, or promotional ideas. "How effective will they be?"
3. Issues—examine how specific, broad issues impact the firm. "How will a new competitor, a change in organizational structure, or increased investments in advertising influence the company?"

©Omni Terra Images

What a *Nice* Surprise?

Darlene lets her Facebook friends know that she may feel a cold coming on. Almost instantly, a friend chats back recommending Zicam (a brand of cold remedies). Much to Darlene's surprise, she receives an offer to download a $2 off coupon for any Zicam product. "What a coincidence," she thinks. However, such an event isn't a coincidence at all. Data miners create algorithms that search social network sites for uses of their brand name or other key phrases strongly related to their brand. The use of the brand name triggered a device that tracked the location of the recommender and recipient via the computers' IP addresses. Data tracking companies and research personnel have other ways of tracking consumer preferences. For instance, the cookies on Darlene's computers leave behind a virtual map of her web activities; what sites she visits and how long she spends on the page. She tries to close a United Airlines web page and receives an offer from Travelocity. Today's Web 2.0 technologies leave little room for coincidence and demonstrate how quickly companies can act on accurate and timely data.

Sources: Mullan, E. (2009). "Mom 3.0: Marketing to High-Tech Moms," *Econtent*, 32 (March), 14–15. Steel, E. (2010). "Some Data Miners Ready to Reveal What They Know," *Wall Street Journal* (December 3), B1–B2. Courtesy. Division of Public Affairs, United States Marine Corps, Department of Defense, USA.

4. Performance—this type of research monitors specific metrics including financial statistics like profitability and delivery times with questions such as "How is variation in product lead time affecting performance metrics?"

The performance category is most relevant in decision support systems. Monitored metrics feed into automated decision-making systems and/or trigger reports for specific managers. These form the basis of a decision support system and best typify the way marketing research assists managers with day-to-day operational decisions.

decision support system (DSS)

A computer-based system that helps decision makers confront problems through direct interaction with databases and systems.

customer relationship management (CRM)

Part of the DSS that characterizes interactions between firm and customer.

A marketing **decision support system (DSS)** is a system that helps decision makers confront problems through direct interaction with computerized databases and systems. A decision support system stores and transforms data into organized information that is easily accessible to marketing managers and other specific internal customers of information. DSSs save managers countless hours by making decisions that might take days or even weeks otherwise in minutes or even seconds.

Modern decision support systems greatly facilitate **customer relationship management (CRM)**. A CRM system is the part of the DSS that characterizes the interactions between firm and customer. It brings together information about customers including sales data, market trends, marketing promotions, and the way consumers respond to them based on customer preferences. A CRM system describes customer relationships in sufficient detail so that managers, salespeople, customer service representatives, and perhaps the customers themselves can access information directly, match customer needs with satisfying product offerings, remind customers of service requirements, and know what other products a customer has purchased. CRM systems compute the overall lifetime value of each customer, which becomes a key metric for triggering decisions.

The CRM systems are specifically responsible for promotions customized to individual customers. Casinos use loyalty or "player's" cards that the customer swipes with each activity. All this information gets stored and eventually the casino knows how to manage the customer by directing offers that the customer's previous behavior suggests a liking-for. An auto repair shop uses information about a car to schedule routine maintenance and help diagnose problems before they occur.

Exhibit 2.2 illustrates how data systems like NFC work with a decision support system. Raw, unsummarized data are input to the DSS. Data collected in marketing research projects are a major source of this input, but the data may be purchased or collected by accountants, sales managers, production managers, or company employees other than marketing researchers. Effective marketers spend a great deal of time and effort collecting information for input into the decision support system. Useful information is the output of a DSS. A decision support system requires both databases and software. For firms operating across national borders, the DSS becomes part of its global information system.

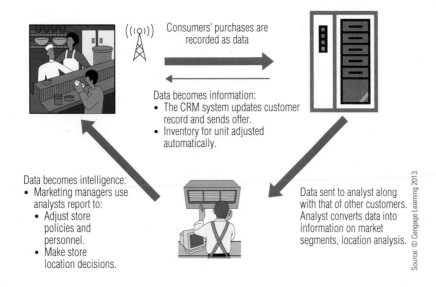

Source: © Cengage Learning 2013.

EXHIBIT **2.2**
Decision Support Systems Use Data to Create intelligence

Databases and Data Warehousing

A **database** is a collection of raw data arranged logically and organized in a form that can be stored and processed by a computer. A customer mailing list is one type of database. Population characteristics may be recorded by state, county, and city in another database.

Data warehousing is the process allowing important day-to-day operational data to be stored and organized for simplified access. More specifically, a **data warehouse** is the multi-tiered computer storehouse of current and historical data. Data warehouse management requires that the detailed data from operational systems be extracted, transformed, placed into logical partitions (for example, daily data, weekly data, etc.), and stored in a consistent and secure manner. Organizations with data warehouses may integrate databases from both inside and outside the company. Data warehousing allows for sophisticated analysis, such as data mining, discussed later in the book.

Input Management

How does data end up in a data warehouse? In other words, how is the input managed? Input includes all the numerical, text, voice, behavioral, and image data that enter the DSS. Systematic accumulation of pertinent, timely, and accurate data is essential to the success of a decision support system.

DSS managers, systems analysts, and programmers are responsible for the decision support system as a whole, but many functions within an organization provide input data. Marketing researchers, accountants, corporate librarians, sales personnel, production managers, and many others within the organization help to collect data and provide input for the DSS. Input data can also come from external sources.

Exhibit 2.3 shows six major sources of data input: internal records, proprietary marketing research, salesperson input, behavioral tracking, Web tracking, and outside vendors and external distributors of data. Each source can provide valuable input.

Internal Records

Internal records, such as accounting reports of sales and inventory figures, provide considerable data that may become useful information for marketing managers. An effective data collection system establishes orderly procedures to ensure that data about costs, shipments, inventory, sales, and other aspects of regular operations are routinely collected and entered into the computer.

database

A collection of raw data arranged logically and organized in a form that can be stored and processed by a computer.

data warehousing

The process allowing important day-to-day operational data to be stored and organized for simplified access.

data warehouse

The multitiered computer storehouse of current and historical data.

EXHIBIT 2.3

Six Major Sources of
Marketing Input for Decision
Support Systems

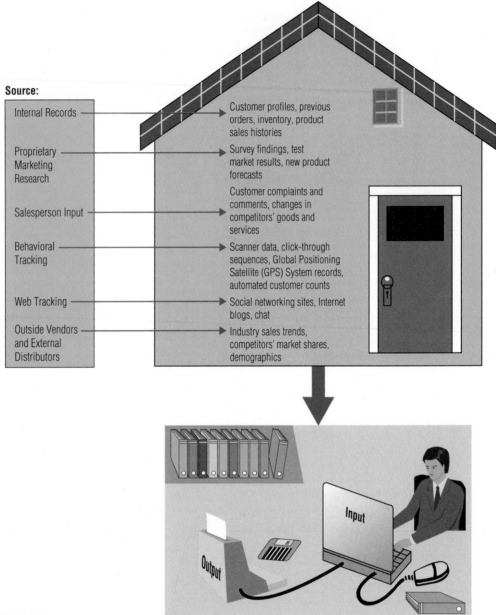

Proprietary Marketing Research

proprietary marketing research

The gathering of new data to investigate specific problems.

Research projects conducted to study specific company problems generate data; this is **proprietary marketing research**. Providing managers with nonroutine data that otherwise would not be available is a major function of proprietary marketing research. Earlier, we discussed four categories of research. Proprietary marketing research may involve either or both of the "testing" and "issues" types of research.

Salesperson Input

Salespeople work in firms' external environments, so they commonly provide essential marketing data. Sales representatives' reports frequently alert managers to changes in competitors' prices and new product offerings. Salespeople also hear customer complaints. As complaint trends become evident, this data may become marketing intelligence that leads to a change in service delivery.

Behavioral Tracking

Modern technology provides new ways of tracking human behavior. Global positioning satellite (GPS) systems allow management to track the whereabouts of delivery personnel at all times. This is the same system that provides directions through an automobile's navigation system. For example, if your delivery person takes a quick break for nine holes of golf or decides to stop at Neil's Bar for a couple of beers mid-afternoon, management can spot these as deviations from the appropriate delivery route. Smartphones generally have GPS capabilities that potentially allow systems to track customer whereabouts and maybe even driving patterns.

Retailers also track purchase behavior at the point of sale. **Scanner data** refers to the accumulated records resulting from point-of-sale data recordings. The **Universal Product Code**, or **UPC**, is the bar code on a product containing information on the category of goods, the manufacturer, and product identification based on size, flavor, color, and so on. This is what the optical scanner actually reads. Each time a reader scans a bar code, the information can be stored. Bar code readers are used in many places where data needs to be recorded and used including in package delivery and on the bag check tickets at the airport.

scanner data

The accumulated records resulting from point-of-sale data recordings.

Universal Product Code (UPC)

UPC is the bar-coded information that contains product information that can be read by optical scanners.

Web Tracking

The Internet greatly facilitates customer behavior tracking. For instance, Google tracks the "click-through" sequence of customers. Therefore, if a customer is searching for information on refrigerators, and then goes to BestBuy.com, Google tracks this behavior and uses the information to calculate the value of a click-through provides an advertising offer to Best Buy. The tracking data also allows Google and other search engines to know how much to charge advertisers for premium listings in search results. Search for "used cars" and the first results, usually indicated by background shading, are listings that Google sells, like advertising. Companies listed on top of a list of search results pay more than companies listed at the bottom.

Marketing researchers monitor postings and create vehicles, such as contests which invite consumers to leave ideas and feedback about the brand. The Research Snapshot on the next page demonstrates how publishing and production companies use input from social networking sites. Other sources for information include Internet blogs and chat rooms where consumers share

● ● ● ● ● ●

GPS devices like this or even your smartphone facilitate behavioral tracking of the user.

©kaczor58/Shutterstock

information about their own experiences, including complaints that serve as a type of warning to other consumers. BlueKai and eXelate are companies that specialize in Web tracking.[15] BlueKai trades data on over 200 million U.S. consumers.

Some companies also supply real-time data on web traffic. Do more consumers visit Amazon. com or Ebay.com? Alexa (alexa.com) provides access to this data. A visit to this website reveals the answer to that question and also provides a demographic breakdown of the visitors to each website. Are women more frequent visitors to Amazon relative to men? This information may be useful when choosing a possible Internet retail channel for goods.

Outside Vendors and External Distributors

Companies called *data specialists* record and store certain marketing information. Computer technology has changed the way many of these organizations supply data, favoring the development of computerized databases. Many organizations specialize in the collection and publication of high-quality information. One outside vendor, the ACNielsen Company, provides television program ratings, audience counts, and information about the demographic composition of television viewer groups. Other vendors specialize in the distribution of information.

Media sources like *Advertising Age, Wall Street Journal, Sales and Marketing Management,* and other trade- and business-oriented publications are important sources of information. These publications keep managers up to date about the economy, competitors' activities, and other aspects of the marketing environment. In addition, they provide demographic and lifestyle statistics about their particular readers which can be very useful in advertisers' media planning.

Data Archives

The *Statistical Abstract of the United States* is a typical example of a data archive. The *Abstract* provides a comprehensive statistical summary of U.S. social, political, and economic organization. Users can access the *Abstract* as well as data from the 2010 census with projections through the current year via the Internet at **http://www.census.gov**.

Numerous computerized search and retrieval systems and electronic databases are available as subscription services or in libraries. Today, businesspeople access online information search and retrieval services, such as Dow Jones News Retrieval and Bloomberg Financial Markets, without leaving their offices. In fact, some information services can be accessed from remote locations via digital wireless devices.

data wholesalers

Companies that put together consortia of data sources into packages that are offered to municipal, corporate, and university libraries for a fee.

Data wholesalers put together consortia of data sources into packages offered to municipal, corporate, and university libraries for a fee. Information consumers then access the data through these libraries. Some of the better known databases include Wilson Business Center, Hoovers, PROQUEST, INFOTRAC, LEXIS-NEXIS, and Dow Jones News Retrieval Services. These databases provide all types of information, including recent news stories and data tables charting statistical trends.

The DIALOG catalog, for example, maintains more than 600 databases in areas including business, law, and humanities. A typical database may have a million or more records, each consisting of a one- or two-paragraph abstract that summarizes the major points of a published article along with bibliographic information. The DIALOG catalog can be searched through PROQUEST, which is available through most university libraries.

Several types of databases from outside vendors and external distributors are so fundamental to decision support systems that they deserve further explanation. The following sections discuss statistical databases, financial databases, and video databases in slightly more detail.

Statistical Databases

Statistical databases contain numerical data for market analysis and forecasting. Often demographic, sales, and other relevant marketing variables are recorded by geographical area. Geographic information systems use these *geographical databases* and powerful software to prepare computer maps of relevant variables. Companies such as Claritas, Urban Decision Systems, and CACI all offer geographic or demographic databases used widely in the industry.

Image courtesy of Susan Van Etten

MySpace Means My Data

Social networking sites have become perhaps the most important marketing tool for companies wanting to reach youth markets. Facebook and Twitter receive the most attention but social media has changed communication. For young consumers, it's hard to imagine a world without these sites. Social media even played a prominent role in the overturning of governments, as was seen in Egypt in 2011.

Information gathered from these websites has become input into product designs including music, movies, and books aimed at teen markets. The publishers of the Clique series of teen books such as the Twilight Saga create MySpace and Facebook pages and encourage fans to visit the sites and leave input. Fans even give input that will shape the content of the novels. The publishers set up polls asking questions such as who Bella should choose. The polls record thousands of votes and the publishers use the information to help keep authors in tune with the teen markets.

Another benefit of Web tracking is international access. As of late 2010, nearly 12 million Indian consumers have a Facebook account and India accounts for the second most Facebook hits behind the United States. The popularity of Facebook over more regional networking sites like Hi5 or Orkut is thought to lie in a simple fact—Indian consumers find Facebook fun! By creating entertaining activities and experiences, consumers become practically addicted. The more time consumers spend, the more information they leave behind.

Source: © Cengage Learning 2013.

Financial Databases

Competitors' and customers' financial data, such as income statements and balance sheets, may interest managers. These are easy to access in financial databases. CompuStat publishes an extensive financial database on thousands of companies, broken down by industry and other criteria. To illustrate the depth of this pool of information, CompuStat's Global Advantage offers extensive data on approximately 7,000 companies in more than thirty countries in Europe, the Pacific Rim, and North America.

Video Databases

Video databases and streaming media are having a major impact on the marketing of many goods and services. For example, movie studios provide clips of upcoming films and advertising agencies put television commercials on the Internet (see AdCritic at **http://www.creativity-online.com**, for example). McDonald's maintains a digital archive of television commercials and other video footage to share with its franchisers around the world. YouTube.com is the world's largest video database and companies routinely produce video commercials for release on YouTube. In 2011, Volkswagen, Old Spice, and Go Daddy SuperBowl ads were available on YouTube prior to the game. Just imagine the potential value of digital video databases to advertising agencies' support systems as firms monitor the number of hits on different videos, monitor how long most people view a video, and track online buzz on Facebook and Twitter.

Networks and Electronic Data Interchange

Electronic data interchange (EDI) systems integrate one company's computer system directly with another company's system. Much of the input to a company's decision support system may come through networks from other companies' computers. Companies such as Computer Technology Corporation and Microelectronics market data services that allow corporations to exchange business information with suppliers or customers. For example, every evening Walmart transmits

electronic data interchange (EDI)

Type of exchange that occurs when one company's computer system is integrated with another company's system.

● ● ● ● ● ● ●

YouTube provides a digital archive that can be mined for data or used as a vehicle to test ideas and concepts.

©AP Photo/Matt Sayles

millions of characters of data about the day's sales to its apparel suppliers. Wrangler, a supplier of blue jeans, receives the data and applies a model that sends orders to replenish Walmart stock. This DSS lets Wrangler's managers know when to send specific quantities of specific sizes and colors of jeans to specific stores from specific warehouses.

open source innovation

shared structured data between companies to facilitate the development of innovations

Many firms share information in an effort to encourage more innovation. **Open source innovation** is a term that captures structured data openly shared between companies. Boeing builds innovative aircraft including the Dreamliner 787 passenger jet and the Phantom Ray unmanned airborne system with sophisticated stealth technology designed for military applications. Hundreds of suppliers manufacture components for these aircraft. Boeing came to a realization around the turn of the century that their core competency is more in systems integration than in manufacturing.[16] As a result, Boeing designs the electronic systems for nearly all of these components but to do so, the suppliers need open access to Boeing data. Without this access, Boeing's pace of innovation would be slower.

"The Net is 10.5 on the Richter scale of economic change."

—NICHOLAS NEGROPONTE

The Internet and Research

The Internet is useful to researchers in many ways. In fact, more and more applications become known as the technology. Over 2,000,000,000 (2 billion) people use the Internet.[17] Web tracking means that billions, if not trillions, of traces of data are left behind. Thus, the Internet is a repository for data and a good tool for gathering data on these billions of consumers.

Navigating the Internet

content providers

Parties that furnish information on the World Wide Web.

Parties that furnish information on the World Wide Web are called **content providers**. Content providers maintain websites that contain information about the entity as well as links to other sites. Increasingly, users are able to add content to websites as well. In these cases, such as Wikipedia, the users manage the content. Most Web browsers also allow the user to enter a **Uniform Resource Locator (URL)** into the program. The URL is really just a website address that Web browsers recognize.

Uniform Resource Locator (URL)

A website address that Web browsers recognize.

keyword search

Takes place as the search engine searches through millions of Web pages for documents containing the keywords.

Google revolutionized search engines by changing the way the search was actually conducted. It searches based on a mathematical theory known as *graph theory*.[18] Google greatly improved the accuracy and usefulness of the search results obtained from a keyword search. A **keyword search** searches through the Internet almost instantly looking for content containing the keywords (usually entered as a phrase). Other search engines now use similar approaches

How Did They Know That?

Major state universities have thousands and thousands of alumni, but, typically, the university has limited resources to personally call on alumni to financially support the university. Historically, only one out of every hundred or so alumni would provide gifts sufficient to balance the average unit costs of marketing to all alums. What if the university could improve the hit ratio and better target relatively expensive marketing approaches like personal meetings to those who are 50 percent likely to give a major gift instead of 5 percent likely. This is exactly what modern predictive analytic tools can do. Using all the information on alumni, much of it gathered through various touchpoints with the university, a statistical model can be built which predicts responsiveness to appeals and places a potential donor value on each alumnus. So, perhaps an alum with football season tickets who also attends at least three orchestra performances and who majored in marketing becomes registered as a donor with high value. More marketing efforts can be directed their way and in this way, marketing is made much more efficient.

Similarly, pharmaceutical firms use data mining approaches based on volumes of input on physicians in their directories to better predict the types of drugs each doctor is likely to prescribe. When a doctor switches prescriptions for a patient, the program identifies a probable reason such as side effects,

©aceshot1/Shutterstock

insurance coverage, cost, and so on; and this feedback allows them to adjust production and marketing accordingly. In this manner, they can design products that doctors are more likely to prescribe. Predictive outcomes of programmed research of this type truly represent win-win propositions. The physicians (customers) get products that more closely match their desires and the company performs better through increased sales. Modern technology enhances firms' ability to be opportunistic in their relationships in a good way.

Sources: Crosno, J. L., and R. Dahlstrom, "A Meta-Analystic Review of Opportunism in Exchange Relationships," *Journal of the Academy of Marketing Science*, 36 (June 2008), 191–201; Goldman, L., "Web 2.0 Brings Web Analytics 2.0," *DM Review*, 17 (March 2007), 28; "SAS Helps ImpactRX Provide Real Time Marketing Intelligence to Pharma Companies," *Business Wire*, (March 17, 2008), retrieved July 14, 2008, from ABI/INFORM Dateline database (document ID: 1447327611); "SPSS Text Mining Reveals Greater Customer Insights as Organizations Worldwide Tap into Unstructured Data," *Business Wire* (June 16, 2008), retrieved July 15, 2008, from ABI/INFORM Dateline database (document ID: 1495884601).

so that different search engines return nearly identical results when the same keywords are input. Paid listings at each search engine are an exception. The search results are so similar that Google accused Bing in 2011 of copying their results.[19] Bing's response included an admission that they use Web tracking, including clickstream data showing how consumers interact with Google, but that this is only one of thousands of pieces of information that are used to build their search algorithms.

Most keyword searches are formed by simply entering a name or phrase. A student doing a term paper on Winston Churchill might simply put Churchill in the search window. A Boolean search is a search that combines relevant keywords in very specific ways. The operators include words like *and*, *or*, and *not*. So, a search of Churchill will bring up thousands of hits including Churchill Downs, the home of the Kentucky Derby, as well as a cigar store or two. However, enter "war" and "Churchill" and the search becomes quickly limited to sites that contain both words and enter "war and Churchill" and the search looks for content with that exact expression. Modern data mining approaches can actually automate Web searches using Boolean operators. Researchers can monitor the Web for negative information about a brand by taking advantage of these search mechanisms.

Environmental Scanning

Environmental scanning entails all information gathering designed to detect changes in the external operating environment of the firm. Even things beyond the control of the firm can have a significant impact on firm performance.

environmental scanning

Entails all information gathering designed to detect changes in the external operating environment of the firm.

Information Technology

pull technology

Consumers request information from a Web page and the browser then determines a response; the consumer is essentially asking for the data.

Data and information are delivered to consumers or other end users via either **pull technology** or **push technology**. Conventionally, consumers request information from a Web page and the browser then determines a response. Thus, the consumer is essentially asking for the data. In this case, it is said to be pulled through the channel. The opposite of pull is push. Push technology sends data to a user's computer without a request being made. In other words, software is used to guess what information might be interesting to consumers based on the pattern of previous responses. Push technology delivers personalized information to consumers without any intentional effort on the consumers' part. When airline customers go to a website to search for flights from Columbus to Riverside, they are pulling information. When those same customers get "Dinged" with a special on flights from Columbus to Riverside, they have had the information pushed to them based on their previous behavior. Technology could feasibly even use webcams such as those on the Microsoft Xbox Kinect to observe gamers and the way they interact with the devices in an effort to provide more relevant advertising.[20] Microsoft and other firms are weighing the benefits of such an approach against privacy concerns.

push technology

Sends data to a user's computer without a request being made; software is used to guess what information might be interesting to consumers based on the pattern of previous responses.

Today's information technology uses "smart agents" or "intelligent agents" to deliver customized content to a viewer's desktop. **Smart agent software** is capable of learning an Internet user's preferences and automatically searching out information and distributing the information to a user's computer. My Yahoo! and MyExcite are portal services that personalize Web pages. Users can get stock quotes relevant to their portfolios, news about favorite sports teams, local weather, and other personalized information. Users can customize the sections of the service they want delivered. With push technology, pertinent content is delivered to the viewer's desktop without the user having to do the searching.

smart agent software

Software capable of learning an Internet user's preferences and automatically searching out information in selected Web sites and then distributing it.

Cookies

cookies

Small data files that a content provider can save onto the computer of someone who visits its website.

Cookies, in computer terminology, are small data files that record a user's Web usage history. If a person looks up a weather report by keying a ZIP code into a Web page, the fact that the user visited the website and the ZIP code both become information stored in a cookie. This is a clue that tells where the person lives (or maybe where he or she may be planning to visit). Websites can then direct information to that consumer based on information in the cookie. So, someone in College Station, Texas, may receive pop-up ads for restaurants in College Station. If that person visits graduate program sites, he or she may receive an advertisement from University of Phoenix. Information technology is having a major impact on the nature of marketing research.

Intranets

Intranet

A company's private data network that uses Internet standards and technology.

An **Intranet** is a company's private data network that uses Internet standards and technology.[13] The information on an Intranet—data, graphics, video, and voice—is available only inside the organization or to those individuals whom the organization deems as appropriate participants. Thus, a key difference between the Internet and an Intranet is that security software programs, or "firewalls," are installed to limit access to only those employees authorized to enter the system. Intranets then serve as secure knowledge portals that contain substantial amounts of organizational memory and can integrate it with information from outside sources. The challenge in designing an Intranet is making sure that it is capable of delivering relevant data to decision makers. Research suggests that relevance is a key in getting knowledge workers to actually make use of company Intranets.[14]

The Intranet can be extended to include key consumers as a source of valuable research. Their participation in the Intranet can lead to new product developments. Texas Instruments, like other companies, uses an Intranet that integrates communications between customers and researchers as a way of providing input into the modification of its calculators. An Intranet lets authorized users, possibly including key customers, look at product drawings, employee newsletters, sales figures, and other kinds of company information.

Predictive Analytics

The term *predictive analytics* did not exist prior to the widespread usage of the Internet. In fact, no other facet of business better illustrates how the Internet can be leveraged for business success than predictive analytics. Broadly speaking, **predictive analytics** refers to linking computerized data sources to statistical tools that can search for predictive relationships and trends. Predictive analytics also eliminates manual scanning of data. Software companies like SPSS and SAS offer products that both look for data and then use statistical tools to reveal key predictive relationships. We'll learn more about SPSS and specific statistical tools later in the book. Marketing researchers use predictive analytics to provide explanations and forecasts of consumer opinions and actions.

The airline systems described in the opening vignette represent a type of predictive analytics. Information taken from consumers' actual archived behavior along with preference data provided by direct input from the consumer is used to model sales levels that can be achieved with various amounts of discounts. Financial companies like Merrill Lynch use predictive analytics to find service innovations needed to enhance specific customers' satisfaction. In addition, financial firms also apply predictive analytics in fraud detection.[21] Previously, fraud detection was like finding a needle in a haystack. In the big picture, predictive analytics allows companies to better allocate resources (see the Research Snapshot on the next page for an illustration). Beats finding a needle in a haystack!

predictive analytics

A system linking computerized data sources to statistical tools allowing more accurate forecasts of consumers' opinions and actions.

Data Technology and Ethics

By this point in the chapter, one may feel a little like *big brother* could be watching. Well, maybe not big brother, but the advances in data technology make privacy seem like a thing of the past. The rapid advancement has outpaced society's ability to understand the ethical and moral implications of the high volumes of electronic communication, so much of which leaves an enduring and at least semipublic record. After all, text messages, device cameras, Web browsing, social media posts, not to mention e-mail and mobile phone calls, all leave behind some type of record. Background checks now routinely involve mining records from social media sites. Some of these records can be used in market research and consumers experience some benefits from the intelligence produced.

Technology is continuing to evolve. Blackberry even has technology that allows a message to be transposed from someone's mobile device onto their skin! **Geolocation technologies**, typified by Foursquare (**www.foursquare.com**), check consumers into bars, restaurants, or theaters through their mobile phone. A consumer takes an account at Foursquare or a competitor like Jiepang, places the app on his/her smartphone, and now the consumer's friends know his/her whereabouts whenever he/she is out and about.[22] The behavioral tracking possible with this technology could be used by marketing research firms to feed data systems to push promotional offers to "friends," but the data could be used more strategically to understand the paths consumers take when they are out and about. Data like this could aid in location strategies for service providers. However, what are the ethical implications when the data become available to people who are not exactly friends?

One way consumers can enhance security when using the Internet is to enhance security settings including placing limits or prohibiting the storage of cookies once the browser is closed. The consumer may a price in convenience for doing this as the browser will no longer be able to fill in URLs, names and passwords, etc. automatically. Once again however, technology creates workarounds to these security precautions. **History sniffing** is a term for activities that covertly discover and record the websites that a consumer visits. Perhaps not totally surprisingly, the Internet

geolocation technologies

Technologies that work through smartphone apps to broadcast a person's location through an electronic network.

history sniffing

Activities that covertly discover and record the websites that a consumer visits.

● ● ● ● ● ● ●

Geolocation technologies are typified by Foursquare. Among other things, they enable marketing messages to be pushed to consumers.

Image courtesy of Susan Van Etten

porn industry advanced the use of this technology—realizing that some of its customers would try to prevent their cookies from being traced. One history sniffing technique relies on the fact that hyperlinks change color from blue to purple when a user clicks through.[23] A browser code uses this technology to build profiles of users based on the sites they visit.

Legal battles are under way in an effort to understand where limits should be legally placed on these types of activities. Technology may eventually provide an answer. A company called Tiger-text, claiming the product has nothing to do with Tiger Woods, offers an app for Blackberry users that enables text messages to self-erase after a user-specified period of time.[24] Regulation in the area must consider the same question that consumers face. That question involves trading off the convenience and benefits that come from having our electronic communications and browsing be snooped with a concern for privacy.

Later, we discuss research ethics in more detail. Here though, four factors are relevant for considering the ethics of data gathered through means like those discussed here.

1. Has the consumer implicitly or explicitly consented to being traced? When a consumer places information on Twitter for instance, that consumer is making the information publicly available and therefore consenting to others seeing and using the information. However, phone conversations are generally considered private communications between two individuals. Thus, researchers tracking Facebook or Foursquare information are acting fairly by essentially only joining in on information users have agreed to make public to some extent. Conversely, researchers who might think about eavesdropping on conversations between two individuals are violating their privacy and acting in an unjust manner.

2. Does the tracking behavior violate any explicit or implicit contracts or agreements? As the legal issues involving electronic privacy development, agreements for use of various technologies will increasingly include statements regarding the limits to which behavior can be traced. Researchers should be mindful of staying within these limits.

3. Can researchers enable users to know what information is available to data miners? Behavioral tracking companies like BlueKai Inc. participate in an **open data partnership**, which gives consumers access to the information collected from their Web behavior and even provides them an opportunity to edit the information.[25] The open data partnership represents a fair way of handling data mining activities as at least consumers come to know what information researchers gather and can act to be more secretive if some of that information represents things they would rather keep private.

4. Do the benefits to consumers from tracking their behavior balance out any potential invasion of their privacy? Ethically, any imposition of consumers should be smaller than the benefit consumers obtain from the research activity. Greater convenience to the consumer and being able to better communicate to them about desirable products are benefits enhanced from electronic data mining activities.

open data partnership

Researchers agree to make the information they collect from activities like Web tracking available to the consumers from whom they gather the information.

TIPS OF THE TRADE

- Researchers should focus on relevance as the key characteristic of useful data.
  - Do so by asking, "Will knowledge of some fact change some important outcome?"
- Automate data collection when possible to enhance data quality.

- Weigh the costs of technology investments against the benefits they will bring.
- Be mindful of ethical concerns when using today's sophisticated data mining techniques.

Source: © Cengage Learning 2013.

:: SUMMARY

1. Know why concepts like data, information, and intelligence represent value. Increased global competition and technological advances in interactive media have spurred development of global information systems. From a research perspective, there is a difference between data, information, and intelligence. Data are simply facts or recorded measures of certain phenomena (things); information is data formatted (structured) to support decision making or define the relationship between two facts. Market intelligence is the subset of data and information that actually has some explanatory power enabling effective decisions to be made. The proper use of data, information, and intelligence means better decision making and better decision making means greater value for the firm.

2. Understand the four characteristics that describe data. The usefulness of data to management can be described based on four characteristics: relevance, completeness, quality, and timeliness. Relevant data have the characteristic of pertinence to the situation at hand and when relevant facts change, the decision is affected. Completeness means having the right amount of information for decision making. Missing information can lead to erroneous conclusions. The quality of information is the degree to which data represent the true situation. High-quality data represent reality faithfully and present a good picture of reality. Timely means the data are not so old that they are irrelevant. Generally, timeliness requires highly current data.

3. Know what a decision support system is and does. A marketing decision support system (DSS) is a system that helps decision makers confront problems through direct interaction with computerized databases and systems. Decision systems systematically integrate marketing data. Marketing data come from four major sources: internal records, proprietary marketing research, marketing intelligence, and outside vendors and external distributors. Data warehousing is the process allowing important day-to-day operational data to be stored and organized for simplified access. Data warehouse management requires that detailed data from operational systems be extracted, transformed, and stored (warehoused) so that the various database tables from both inside and outside the company are consistent. All of this feeds into the decision support system that automates or assists business decision making.

4. Describe marketing research's role in predictive analytics. Predictive analytics refers to linking computerized data sources to statistical tools that can search for relationships and trends which allow more accurate prediction of consumers' opinions and actions. Thus, it combines automated data mining with multivariate statistical tools to enhance prediction. The marketing researcher's job in predictive analytics is twofold. First, identify the key sources of information that may create predictive intelligence and second, use analytic tools to build predictive models.

5. Recognize the major categories of databases. The Internet is a worldwide network of computers that allows users access to information and documents from distant sources. It is a combination of a worldwide communication system and the world's largest public library. The World Wide Web is a system of thousands of interconnected pages, or documents, that can be easily accessed with Web browsers and search engines.

6. Ethics of electronically tracking consumers. Privacy is becoming a rare commodity as consumers enter a myriad of information into websites and pass information through their smartphones. The tracking of consumers can be made more ethical when a) consumers have implicitly or explicitly consented to being tracked, b) tracking activities do not violate any agreements with the consumer, c) systems exist that allow consumers to know what information is gathered, and d) the benefits to consumers in general outweigh any imposition from the data gathering process.

:: KEY TERMS AND CONCEPTS

content providers, *38*

cookies, *40*

customer relationship
    management (CRM), *32*

data, *28*

database, *33*

data quality, *29*

data warehouse, *33*

data warehousing, *33*

data wholesalers, *36*

decision support system (DSS), *32*

dynamic pricing, *27*

electronic data interchange (EDI), *37*

environmental scanning, *39*

geolocation technologies, *41*

history sniffing, *41*

information, *28*

information completeness, *29*

Intranet, *40*

keyword search, *39*

market dynamism, *30*

market intelligence, *28*

NFC, *31*

open data partnership, *42*

open source information, *38*

predictive analytics, *41*

proprietary marketing research, *34*

pull technology, *40*

push technology, *40*

relevance, *29*

RFID tag, *30*

scanner data, *35*

sensing systems, *28*

smart agent software, *40*

timeliness, *30*

uniform resource locator (URL), *38*

universal product code (UPC), *35*

∷ QUESTIONS FOR REVIEW AND CRITICAL THINKING

1. What is the difference between data, information, and intelligence?
2. What are the characteristics of useful information?
3. What is the key question distinguishing relevant data from irrelevant data?
4. Define the technologies of NFC and RFID. How can each provide input to a DSS?
5. What types of databases might one find in the following organizations?
   a. Holiday Inn
   b. Major university athletic department
   c. AB-InBev
   d. Quibids (online auction website)
   e. iTunes
6. What type of operational questions could a delivery firm like UPS expect to automate with the company's decision support system?
7. What makes a decision support system successful?
8. What is data warehousing?
9. How does data warehousing assist decision making? Visit **http://www.kbb.com**. While there, choose two cars that you might consider buying and compare them. Which do you like the best? What would you do now? What are at least three pieces of data that should be stored in a data warehouse somewhere based on your interaction with *Kelly Blue Book*?
10. Give three examples of computerized databases that are available at your college or university library.
11. What is predictive analytics? Think about the three websites that you interact with most. List at least ten pieces of information that you exchange with these websites that you believe have potential to become useful data that can be made into intelligence through predictive analytics.
12. Suppose a retail firm is interested in studying the effect of lighting on customer purchase behavior. Which of the following pieces of information is the least relevant and why?
    a. Amount of natural light in the store
    b. Compensation system for store salespeople
    c. Color of the walls in the store
    d. Type of lighting: fluorescent or incandescent
13. Imagine the data collected by eBay each day. List at least five types of data that are collected through the daily operations. Describe how each type illustrates in it data, information, or intelligence. Make sure you list at least one example of each.
14. How could New Balance, a maker of athletic shoes, use RFID technology to collect data?
15. What are four questions researchers can ask in deciding whether their electronic data gathering systems violate good ethical principles?

∷ RESEARCH ACTIVITIES

1. To learn more about data warehousing, go to **http://www.dwinfocenter.org**. How could a company that provides music and video files via the Internet (such as Netflix) use a data warehouse?
2. Use the Internet to see if you can find information to answer the following questions:
   a. What is the exchange rate between the $US and €Euro?
   b. What are four restaurants in the French Quarter in New Orleans?
   c. What is the most popular novel among teenage girls age 14–16?
   d. Do more people visit the foxnews.com or cnn.com websites?

Harvard Cooperative Society

Case 2.1

From his office window overlooking the main floor of the Harvard Cooperative Society, CEO Jerry Murphy can glance down and see customers shopping. They make their way through the narrow aisles of the crowded department store, picking up a sweatshirt here, trying on a baseball cap there, checking out the endless array of merchandise that bears the Harvard University insignia.

Watching Murphy, you can well imagine the Coop's founders, who started the store in 1882, peering through the tiny windowpanes to keep an eye on the shop floor. Was the Harvard Square store attracting steady traffic? Were the college students buying enough books and supplies for the Cooperative to make a profit? Back then, it was tough to answer those questions precisely. The owners had to watch and wait, relying only on their gut feelings to know how things were going from minute to minute.

Now, more than a hundred years later, Murphy can tell you, down to the last stock-keeping unit, how he's doing at any given moment. His window on the business is the PC that sits on his desk. All day long it delivers up-to-the-minute, easy-to-read electronic reports on what's selling and what's not, which items are running low in inventory and which have fallen short of forecast. In a matter of seconds, the computer can report gross margins for any product or supplier, and Murphy can decide whether the margins are fat enough to justify keeping the supplier or product on board. "We were in the 1800s, and we had to move ahead," he says of the $55 million business.

Questions

1. What is a decision support system? What advantages does a decision support system have for a business like the Harvard Cooperative Society?
2. How would the decision support system of a business like the Harvard Cooperative Society differ from that of a major corporation?
3. Briefly outline the components of the Harvard Cooperative Society's decision support system.

Source: © Cengage Learning 2013.

The Marketing Research Process

LEARNING OUTCOMES

After studying this chapter, you should be able to:

1. Classify marketing research as either exploratory research, descriptive research, or causal research
2. List the major stages of the marketing research process and the steps within each
3. Understand the concepts of theory and hypothesis and the critical role they play in research
4. Know the difference between a research project and a research program

Chapter Vignette:

Changing for Wired Students

Some might say that college students always have been at least a little wired. In this high-tech world though, students don't even need a wire.[1] Changing educational technologies mean today's students enjoy many more choices than did their parents or even their older siblings. Universities offer new degree programs in varied and specific fields including areas like sports marketing and gaming management, and degrees can be obtained without ever physically stepping foot on an actual university campus.

Options for nontraditional students who have difficulty attending day classes or devoting years of study to obtaining a degree have grown exponentially. The University of Phoenix, Strayer University, and Nova Southeast typify institutions that specifically cater to those seeking a nontraditional degree program. The University of Phoenix alone boasts an enrollment of over 400,000 students. Competitive pressures and budgetary concerns have led even traditional universities to rethink the traditional "sage on the stage" approach and conventional academic calendars offering a multitude of weekend and e-learning opportunities.[2]

Over a quarter of a million U.S. students alone attend MBA classes of one form or another at any given time. In urban areas, such as the Dallas-Fort Worth, Texas, area, a dozen or more institutions offer an MBA. Clearly, the market for the MBA degree is particularly competitive and the fact is that those universities that offer a market-oriented program are most attractive to students. Marketing research can help accomplish this by addressing questions such as the following:

- How do consumers trade off added convenience against quality perceptions or price?
- Will offering courses online expand the pool of MBA program applicants?

- When is the best time to offer classes? Should schools offer a weekend program?
- Where is the best place to hold classes? Should classes be offered in multiple locations? Should a program be offered overseas?
- How are nontraditional vis-à-vis traditional MBA programs viewed in terms of value, quality, and prestige?
- What is the demand? Are there enough potential students to make a particular program financially feasible?
- How can a particular MBA program be differentiated from competing schools?

- Can a business school better accomplish the mission of the university with an online MBA program?

The competitive MBA market typifies the landscape of many marketing firms. Clearly, universities could benefit from marketing research addressing some of these key questions. Each university maintains its own academic standard while still trying to attract enough students to make its MBA program feasible. Potential opportunities and potential problems fill this competitive landscape. Decisions made by university faculty and administrators will determine how successfully each school deals with the changing marketplace.

Introduction

This chapter focuses on the marketing research process. This process informs business decisions aiding in solving problems and seizing on opportunities. Quality decision making drives business success. Marketing researchers contribute to decision making in several key ways. These include

1. Helping to better define the current situation and identifying useful decision statements
2. Defining the firm—determining how consumers, competitors, and employees view the firm
3. Providing ideas for product improvements or possible new product development
4. Testing ideas that will assist in implementing marketing strategy
5. Examining how well a marketing theory describes marketing reality

The chapter introduces the types of research that allow researchers to provide input to key marketing decisions. The chapter first discusses stages in the marketing research process and concludes by demonstrating the role that theory plays in better decision making.

Types of Marketing Research

Effective marketing research reduces uncertainty and helps focus marketing decision making. Sometimes marketing researchers know exactly what their marketing problems are and can design careful studies to test specific hypotheses. Universities, even not-for-profit universities, face marketing problems. For instance, input from employers, students, and alumni might suggest that a school's curriculum is outdated. The problem could even be contributing to low enrollment motivating university administration to address the problem. Thus, marketing researchers working for the university may devise a careful test exploring which of three new, alternative curricula would most improve the public's perception that the curriculum is high quality. This type of research is problem oriented and seems relatively unambiguous. The marketing research may culminate with researchers preparing a report suggesting the relative effect of each alternative curriculum on enrollment. The decision should follow relatively directly from the research.

In more ambiguous circumstances, marketing managers may be totally unaware of a marketing problem. Alternatively, the company may be scanning the environment for opportunities. For example, a small, private undergraduate university in a mid-sized Colorado town may consider adding an online MBA program. University administrators may have little idea as to how this would affect the image of their school among current students, employers, alumni, or faculty. They also may not know exactly what programs would be most desired by its current or potential customer bases. Some preliminary research may be necessary to gain insights into the nature of such

"There is no great trick to doing research…the trick is getting people to use it…[most people use research] as a drunkard uses a lamppost—for support, not for illumination."

—DAVID OGILVY[3]

a situation. Without it, the situation may remain too ambiguous to make more than a seat-of-the-pants decision. The decision makers almost certainly need input from marketing research.

The technique or purpose underlying marketing research provides a basis for classification. Experiments, surveys, and observational studies are just a few common research techniques. Classifying research by its purpose shows how the nature of a decision situation influences the research methodology. The following section introduces the three types of marketing research:

1. Exploratory
2. Descriptive
3. Causal

Matching the particular decision situation with the right type of research is important in obtaining useful research results.

Exploratory Research

exploratory research

Conducted to clarify ambiguous situations or discover ideas that may be potential business opportunities.

Exploratory research aims to clarify ambiguous situations or discover ideas that may amount to true business opportunities. Exploratory research does not provide conclusive evidence from which to determine a particular course of action. In this sense, exploratory research is not an end unto itself. Researchers usually undertake exploratory research with the full expectation that managers will need more research to supply more conclusive evidence. Using exploratory research can sometimes also make the difference in determining the relevance of follow-up research. Rushing into detailed surveys before knowing exactly what the key decisions should be will likely produce irrelevant data and therefore waste time, money, and effort.

Innovation and Exploratory Research

Exploratory research is particularly useful in new product development.[4] Sony and Honda have each been instrumental in developing robot technology.[5] Making a functional robot that can move around, perform basic functions, carry out instructions, and even carry on a conversation isn't really a problem. What Sony and Honda have to research is what market opportunities may exist based on robot technology. One research approach allows consumers to interact with robots freely as a form of exploratory research. The observational research suggests that consumers interact much more when the robot has human qualities, including the ability to walk on two legs. Researchers noticed that people will actually talk to the robot (which can understand basic oral commands) more when it has human qualities. In addition, consumers do seem entertained by a walking, talking, dancing robot. Thus, this has allowed each company to form more specific research questions focusing on the relative value of a robot as an entertainment device or as a security guard.

Exploratory Research and Problem Solving

In our university example, exploratory research is perhaps called for to help identify constituency concerns about nontraditional course delivery for business classes. This exploratory research should include open-ended interviews with faculty, students, and alumni. These open-ended responses may help build specific hypotheses concerning the relative attractiveness of alternative curricula to students and the effect of online instruction on job satisfaction and on alumni quality perceptions.[6] The resulting hypotheses may motivate researchers to test the propositions using one of the two remaining types of research. The Research Snapshot describes how exploratory research helps identify sources of indirect competition identified through research.

symptoms

Observable cues that serve as a signal of a problem because they are caused by that problem.

Exploratory research can be useful in helping to better define a marketing problem or identify a market opportunity. Problems are usually not as obvious as they may seem. In fact, they usually are not easily observable. Instead, researchers infer problems from **symptoms**, which are observable cues that send a signal of some problem because the problem itself causes the symptom. A drop in market share, for instance, is generally only a symptom of a market problem and not a problem itself. Exploratory research may help identify what is causing this symptom so that decision makers

© Jean-Philippe Ksiazek/Getty Images

Tupperware Isn't Alone in *Seal*ing the Deal

Many U.S. college students may not know about Tupperware and even those that do may not associate Tupperware with hedonic value (i.e., fun)! Tupperware's early success centered on selling products at house parties primarily aimed at gathering women together in a festive atmosphere. One woman would agree to host a party where her friends and family gathered to share some food and drink and then sit through a dazzling display of Tupperware plastic bowls—which of course party goers could order for a price. The combination of a light atmosphere and social pressure proved successful in closing a lot of deals for Tupperware. Tupperware's first fifty years of success came to a halt in the late 1900s in part because of higher-quality products from competitors and the dual-career families putting a premium on family time at home. In the early 2000s, Tupperware turned toward the Internet to revive its brand with less than enthusiastic results.

Meanwhile, Tupperware commissioned market research, examining the way that women around the world purchase different types of products. Exploratory research suggests that women prefer to buy some products only after a thorough demonstration of the way one should use the product. As a result, Tupperware researchers concluded that women do not care to buy "beauty online," as CEO Rick Goeings claims. Furthermore, descriptive research showed that a large number of young working women in European countries like France and

in developing countries like Brazil enjoy spending time away from work with their female coworkers. As a result, Tupperware house parties are back in and are extremely successful internationally. So much so that Tupperware's U.S. sales account for less than 15 percent of their total business. The combination of a little wine and relaxation does indeed *seal the deal* for plastic bowls. However, House Party Inc., a company that helps others arrange parties like these, has taken the concept into other industries. Little Black Dress, the wine label, hosts parties where women swap items from their wardrobes while sipping and buying wines and for women who celebrate the potty dance while promoting Pull-Ups training pants. Thus, research led the way to an effective selling appeal.

Sources: Barrett, J. (2006), "Can a 50s Icon Do It Again?" *Newsweek*, 147 (3/20), E20; Shah, A. (2010), "Enthusiastic Brands Welcome the Return of the House Party," *PRWeek*, (April 1), 23–24. *Wall Street Journal* (2011), "Tupperware CEO Rick Goings: Our Hip New Customers," Video Interview 1/28/2011, http://online.wsj.com/video/tupperware-ceo-rick-goings-our-hip-new-customers/EC05AA5F-AD48-4A59-A7B5-37B8479BEC2F.html?mod=WSJ_WSJ_US_VideoModule_2.

can actually attack the problem, not just the symptom. Patients don't usually go to the doctor and point out their problem (like an ulcer). Instead, they point out symptoms (upset stomach). Similarly, decision makers usually hear about symptoms and often need help from research to identify and attack problems. Whether facing an opportunity or a problem, businesses need quality information to deal effectively with these situations. The amount of certainty or ambiguity also characterizes all decision situations.

Descriptive Research

Descriptive research, as the name implies, describes characteristics of objects, people, groups, organizations, or environments. Put more simply, descriptive research tries to "paint a picture" of a given situation. Marketing managers frequently need to determine who purchases a product, portray the size of the market, identify competitors' actions, and so on. Descriptive research addresses who, what, when, where, why, and how questions.

Descriptive research often helps describe market segments. What does the organic food market look like? Marketing researchers used simple descriptive surveys to describe consumers who are heavy consumers (buy a lot) of organic food products. One report shows that the 2010 global organic food market was just over $60 billion and expects the market to grow to nearly $100

descriptive research

Describes characteristics of objects, people, groups, organizations, or environments; tries to "paint a picture" of a given situation.

billion by 2014.[7] Fruits and vegetables (i.e., fresh produce) account for more than 30 percent of those sales with prepared foods accounting for just over 20 percent. The global organic food market segment is predominantly North American (49 percent) and European (48 percent). Growth is taking place in these markets but at a decreasing rate. Analysts, as a result, are looking to Asia where organic food companies see great potential.

Competition for this segment is considerable. Over half of Whole Foods' food products are organic and as a result, they appeal to the organic food segment in the United States. Whole Foods' sales have increased since 2005, reaching over $8 billion in 2009. However, profit margins dipped from nearly 4 percent to just over 1 percent during the most recent depressed economy. One reason for this is that organic food segment became more price sensitive and deprioritzed quality organic foods and turned increasingly to lower priced alternatives with correspondingly lower price margins. Whole Foods temporarily responded by dropping many higher-priced, higher-margin items from their store shelves in favor of low-price alternatives.[8] The resulting lower margins reversed after a refocus on quality over price in 2010.

Research on the segment during this time also suggests that the organic market lacks brand loyalty—but its store loyalty remains a question. Walmart, at approximately the same time, increased its organic and higher-quality offerings in an effort to capitalize on the organic consumer market. However, this move also proved unproductive and they stepped back to more lower-priced alternatives after realizing the high-priced products confused their segment. Thus, each store made decisions aimed at better serving the organic food segment, but did so without considering how the changes in policies would affect their customers' perceptions. Thus, some survey research to support the descriptive research showing sales and sales growth in the organic segment overall may have led to better decision making.

Similarly, the university considering the addition of an online MBA program might benefit from descriptive research profiling the market and the potential customers. Online customers are not identical to the traditional MBA student. They tend to be older, averaging about 30 years of age. Another key statistic is that the dropout rate for online students is significantly higher than for traditional MBA students. Nearly 14 percent of online students drop before completing a course, compared to 7.2 percent for traditional in-class students. For this and other reasons, online students are much more costly to serve.[9] The Research Snapshot describes descriptive research results focusing on what makes a worker irritating.

Food retailers are interested in descriptive research describing what specific types of consumers are buying.

©Corbis/Jupiter Images

The Squeaky Wheel Gets...

Marketing problems are often people problems. Disgruntled marketing employees can lack creativity and lose the motivation that drives a strong work ethic. What appears to be a marketing problem can really be an internal people problem. With this in mind, what kind of things do coworkers do that irritate other coworkers? Several descriptive research studies address this by surveying employees and having them rate potentially problematic behaviors based on how annoying they actually are. Perhaps the resulting list isn't surprising, but some of the most problematic coworker habits and practices include the following.

- Slacking—the perception that a coworker is simply not pulling his or her share of the work is one of the most frequently mentioned annoying behaviors.
- Abusing the printer or copier—printing things unnecessarily, wasting paper, occupying the printer or copier or both with personal documents and slowing down the work.
- Leaving used tea bags in the office sink.
- Currying favor with the boss.
- Constantly eating and leaving behind crumbs and warming things in the microwave that leave behind strong odors (i.e., pickled cabbage, fish, popcorn, etc.).
- Over air-conditioning the office making it cold as a meat locker.
- Being fortunate enough to have a window and then keeping the shade closed all day.
- Coming in late but leaving on time.
- Noisiness—squeaky chairs, loud laughter, loud phone calls, aggravating smartphone noises, and annoying body noises.

The question becomes, how should management deal with these annoying habits? Should employees confront each other or should management create policies that restrict all possible annoying behavior? Is that possible? Maybe this calls for more research. Do you know an annoying coworker?

Sources: "What Your Workers Find Most Annoying," *Legal Alert for Supervisors*, 3, no. 64 (2008) 3; Piccolo, C. "Irritating Coworkers," Medhunters.com (2008), http://www.medhunters.com/articles/irritatingCoworkers.html, accessed July 20, 2008; "Xerox Survey Reveals Environmental Pet Peeves Among Office Workers," *Graphic Arts Online* (April 17, 2008), www.graphicartsonline.com, accessed June 18, 2008; Nudd, T., "Pet Peeves," *Adweek*, 46 (September 26, 2005), 33.

Accuracy is critically important in descriptive research. If a descriptive study misestimates a university's demand for its MBA offering by even a few students, it can mean the difference between the program sustaining itself or being a drain on already scarce resources. For instance, if a research predicts that twenty students will enroll in a cohort, but only fifteen students actually sign up, the program will likely not generate enough revenue to sustain itself. Therefore, descriptive research forecasting sales revenue and costs or describing consumer attitudes, satisfaction, and commitment must be accurate or decision-making quality will suffer.

Unlike exploratory research, researchers usually conduct descriptive studies with a considerable understanding of the marketing situation. This understanding, perhaps developed in part from exploratory research, directs the study toward specific issues. Later, we will discuss the role of research questions and hypotheses. These statements help greatly in designing and implementing a descriptive study.

Survey research typifies a descriptive study. Many surveys try to answer questions such as "Why are store A's sales lower than store B's sales?" In other words, a **diagnostic analysis** seeks to detect reasons for market outcomes and focuses specifically on the beliefs, feelings, and reactions consumers have about and toward competing products. A research study trying to diagnose slumping French wine sales might ask consumers their beliefs about the taste of French, Australian, and American wines. The results might indicate a deficiency in taste, suggesting that consumers do not believe French wines taste as fruity as do the others. Descriptive research can sometimes provide an explanation by diagnosing differences among competitors, but descriptive research does not provide direct evidence of causality.

diagnostic analysis

Seeks to detect reasons for market outcomes and focuses specifically on the beliefs, feelings, and reactions consumers have about and toward competing products.

Causal Research

If a decision maker knows what *causes* important outcomes like sales and employee satisfaction, then he or she can shape firm decisions in a positive way. Causal inferences are very powerful because they lead to greater control. **Causal research** allows decision makers to make causal

causal research

Allows causal inferences to be made—they identify cause-and-effect (x brought about y) relationships.

inferences. What brought some event about? That is, causal research seeks to identify cause-and-effect relationships to show that one event actually makes another happen. Heat causes ice to melt. Heat is the cause and melted ice (water) is the effect.

Exploratory and/or descriptive research usually precedes causal research. In causal studies, researchers typically have a substantial understanding of the decision-making situation. As a result, the researcher can make an educated prediction about cause-and-effect relationships that the research will test. The tests are usually quite focused, which is a good thing, but the trade-offs must be considered. Causal research designs can take a long time to implement. Also, they often involve intricate designs that can be very expensive. Thus, even though managers may often want the assurance that causal inferences can bring, they are not always willing to spend that much time and money.

Causality

Ideally, managers want to know how a change in one event (say, using a new product logo) will change another event of interest, like sales. Causal research attempts to establish that when we do one thing, another thing will follow. A **causal inference** is just such a conclusion. Although we use the term *cause* all the time in everyday language, scientifically establishing something as a cause is not so easy and even researchers sometimes confuse causality with correlation. A researcher requires very specific evidence to draw a causal inference. Three critical pieces of causal evidence are

causal inference

A conclusion that when one thing happens, another specific thing will follow.

1. Temporal Sequence
2. Concomitant Variance
3. Nonspurious Association

Temporal Sequence

temporal sequence

One of three criteria for causality; deals with the time order of events—the cause must occur before the effect.

Temporal sequence deals with the time order of events. In other words, having an appropriate causal order, or temporal sequence, is a necessary criterion for causality. The cause must occur before the effect. How could a restaurant manager blame a decrease in sales on a new chef if the drop in sales occurred before the new chef arrived? If advertising causes sales, the advertising must appear before the change in sales.

Concomitant Variation

concomitant variation

One of three criteria for causality; occurs when two events "covary," meaning they vary systematically.

Concomitant variation occurs when two events "covary," meaning they vary systematically. In causal terms, concomitant variation means that when a change in the cause occurs, a change in the outcome also is observed. We often use the term correlation, discussed in a later chapter, to represent what concomitant variation means. Causality cannot possibly exist when there is no systematic variation between the variables. For example, if a retail store's competition has not changed, then the competitors cannot possibly be responsible for changes in store sales. There is no correlation between the two events. On the other hand, if two events vary together, one event may be causing the other. If a university increases its number of online MBA course offerings and experiences a decrease in enrollment in its traditional in-class MBA offerings, the online course offerings may be causing the decrease. But, the systematic variation alone doesn't guarantee it.

Nonspurious Association

nonspurious association

One of three criteria for causality; means any covariation between a cause and an effect is true and not simply due to some other variable.

Nonspurious association means any covariation between a cause and an effect is indeed due to the cause and not simply due to some other variable. A spurious association is one that is not true. Often, a causal inference cannot be made even though the other two conditions exist because both the cause and effect have some common cause; that is, both may be influenced by a third variable. For instance, a city worker notices an alarming trend. On days when a large number of ice cream cones are sold at Virginia Beach, more people drown. So, when ice cream sales go up, so does drowning. Should the city decide to ban ice cream? This would be silly because the concomitant variation observed between ice cream consumption and drowning is spurious. On days when the beach is particularly crowded, more ice cream is sold and more people drown. So, the number of people at the beach, being associated with both, may cause both. Exhibit 3.1 illustrates the concept of spurious association.

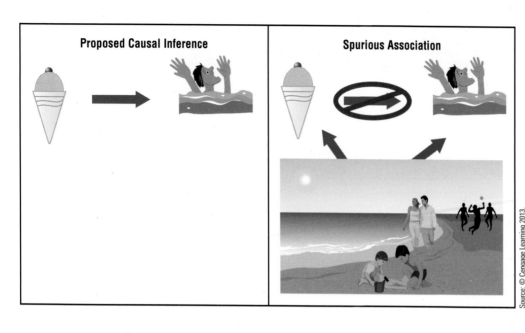

Source: © Cengage Learning 2013.

EXHIBIT 3.1

Ice Cream is a Spurious Cause of Drowning

Establishing evidence of nonspuriousness can be difficult. If a researcher finds a third variable that covaries with both the cause and effect, causing a significant drop in the correlation between the cause and effect, then a causal inference becomes difficult to support. Although the researcher would like to rule out the possibility of any alternative causes, it is impossible to observe the effect of all variables on the correlation between the cause and effect. Therefore, the researcher must use theory to identify the most likely "third" variables that would relate significantly to both the cause and effect. The research must control for these variables in some way, as we will see in Chapter 9. In addition, the researcher should use theory to make sure that the cause-and-effect relationship truly makes sense.

In summary, causal research should do all of the following:

1. Establish the appropriate causal order or sequence of events
2. Measure the concomitant variation (relationship) between the presumed cause and the presumed effect
3. Examine the possibility of spuriousness by considering the presence of alternative plausible causal factors

Experiments

Marketing experiments hold the greatest potential for establishing cause-and-effect relationships. An **experiment** is a carefully controlled study in which the researcher manipulates a proposed cause and observes any corresponding change in the proposed effect. An **experimental variable** represents the proposed cause and the researcher controls this variable by manipulating its value. **Manipulation** means that the researcher alters the level of the variable in specific increments. So, managers often want to make decisions about the price and distribution of a new product. Both price and the type of retail outlet in which a product is placed are considered potential causes of sales. A causal research design would manipulate both the price and distribution and assess the consequences on key outcome variables.

Suppose a company produces a new video game console called the Wee Station. They may manipulate price by offering it for $100 among some consumers and $300 among others. Likewise, they manipulate retail distribution by selling the Wee Station at discount stores in some consumer markets and at specialty electronic stores in others. The retailer can examine whether price and distribution cause sales by comparing the sales results in each of the four conditions created. Exhibit 3.2 illustrates this study.

A marketing research experiment examined the effect of adding a higher priced alternative to the set of products sold by a retailer. The researchers manipulated price by creating a scenario that

experiment

A carefully controlled study in which the researcher manipulates a proposed cause and observes any corresponding change in the proposed effect.

experimental variable

Represents the proposed cause which the researcher controls by manipulating its value.

manipulation

Means that the researcher alters the level of the variable in specific increments.

Source: © Cengage Learning 2013.

EXHIBIT **3.2**
Testing for Causes with an
Experiment

	Wee Station Sales by Condition	
	High Price	**Low Price**
Specialty Distribution	Peoria, Illinois: Retail Price: $300 Retail Store: Best Buy	Des Moines, Iowa: Retail Price: $100 Retail Store: Best Buy
General Distribution	St. Louis, Missouri: Retail Price: $300 Retail Store: Big Cheap-Mart	Kansas City, Missouri: Retail Price: $100 Retail Store: Big Cheap-Mart

Assuming that Wee Station consumers are the same in each of these cities, the extent to which price and distribution cause sales can be examined by comparing the sales results in each of these 4 conditions.

either added a higher or lower priced alternative to a set of products reviewed by a consumer. The results show that for frequently purchased products, adding a higher–priced alternative causes consumers to believe that prices in general were lower.[10] We will say much more about manipulations and experimental designs in Chapter 9.

Uncertainty Influences the Type of Research

The amount of uncertainty surrounding a marketing situation does much to determine the most appropriate type and amount of research needed. Exhibit 3.3 contrasts the types of research, illustrates this idea, and shows researchers conduct exploratory research during the early stages of decision making. At this point, the decision situation is usually highly ambiguous and management is very uncertain about what actions to take. When management is aware of the problem but lacks some key knowledge, researchers conduct descriptive research. Causal research requires tightly defined problems.

Each type of research produces a different type of result. In many ways, exploratory research is the most productive because it produces many ideas. Exploratory research is discovery oriented and relatively unstructured. Too much structure in this type of research may lead to more narrowly focused types of responses that could stifle creativity. At times, managers do take managerial action

EXHIBIT **3.3** Characteristics of Different Types of Marketing Research

	Exploratory Research	**Descriptive Research**	**Causal Research**
Amount of Uncertainty Characterizing Decision Situation	Highly ambiguous	Partially defined	Clearly defined
Key Research Statement	Research question	Research question	Research hypothesis
When Conducted?	Early stage of decision making	Later stages of decision making	Later stages of decision making
Usual Research Approach	Unstructured	Structured	Highly structured
Examples	"Our sales are declining for no apparent reason" "What kinds of new products are fast-food customers interested in?"	"What kind of people patronize our stores compared to our primary competitor?" "What product features are most important to our customers?"	"Will consumers buy more products in a blue package?" "Which of two advertising campaigns will be more effective?"
Nature of Results	Discovery oriented, productive, but still speculative. Often in need of further research.	Can be confirmatory although more research is sometimes still needed. Results can be managerially actionable.	Confirmatory oriented. Fairly conclusive with managerially actionable results often obtained.

Source: © Cengage Learning 2013.

based only on exploratory research results because management may not be able to or may not care to invest the time and resources needed to conduct further research. Decisions made based only on exploratory research can be more risky because exploratory research does not test ideas.[11] For instance, a business school professor may ask a class of current MBA students for ideas about an online program. Although the students may provide many ideas that sound very good, that particular research design does not test any idea scientifically. An exploratory design is adequate for discovering ideas, but not for testing ideas.

The discovery process often culminates with research questions. These research questions can guide descriptive research designs. Research questions focus the research on specific variables, allowing for a more structured approach capable of producing managerially actionable results. For example, descriptive research might profile a market segment both demographically and psychographically. Results like this can greatly assist firms in taking action by deciding when and where to offer their service for sale.

Researchers who employ causal designs focus very specifically on a small number of research hypotheses. Experimental methods require tight control of research procedures. Thus, causal research is highly structured to produce specific results. Causal research results are often managerially actionable because they suggest that if management changes the value of a "cause," some desirable effect will come about. So, by changing a package's color (i.e., the cause, from orange to blue), higher sales occur. The increased control associated with experiments reduces uncertainty in testing hypotheses.

Stages in the Research Process

Marketing research, like other forms of scientific inquiry, involves a sequence of highly interrelated activities. The stages of the research process overlap and not every research project follows exactly through each stage. Nevertheless, marketing research generally follows a pattern represented by these stages:

1. Defining research objectives
2. Planning a research design
3. Planning a sample
4. Collecting data
5. Analyzing data
6. Formulating conclusions and preparing a report

Exhibit 3.4 portrays these six stages as a cyclical or circular-flow process. The circular-flow concept illustrates how one research project can generate new ideas and knowledge that lead to further investigation. Thus, the conclusions and reporting stage connects with the defining the research objectives stage with a dotted line. Notice also, that management is in the center of the process. The researcher cannot properly define research objectives without managerial input. After all, management must ultimately make a decision. Management also may ask for additional research once a report is given. This same general research process applies in basic marketing research and applied market research, whether for profit or non-profit organizations.[12]

Alternatives in the Research Process

The researcher must choose among a number of alternatives during each stage of the research process. Like choosing a route on a map, no single path fits all journeys. The map analogy is useful because the marketing researcher faces multiple alternatives at each stage. When there are severe time constraints, these constraints override validity, resulting in choosing the fastest alternative. When money and human resources are more plentiful, the appropriate path differs and likely emphasizes validity over speed. Exhibit 3.5 shows the decisions that researchers must make in each stage.

Libraries contain a wealth of information – whether it is a physical or virtual library

©AP Photo/Eric Audras RF

EXHIBIT **3.4**
Stages of the Research Process

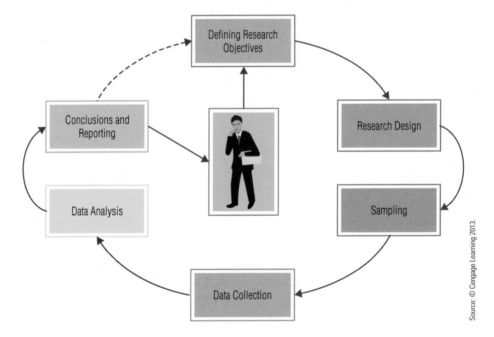

Source: © Cengage Learning 2013.

Defining the Research Objectives

research objectives
The goals to be achieved by conducting research.

deliverables
The term used often in consulting to describe research objectives to a research client.

Exhibit 3.5 shows how the research process begins with defining research objectives. **Research objectives** are the goals that researchers intend to achieve through this particular effort. In consulting, researchers use the term **deliverables** to describe the objectives to a research client. The genesis of the research objectives lies in the type of decision situation faced. The objectives may involve exploring a new market's reaction to some a new product offering. Alternatively, they may involve testing the effect of a policy change like self-service checkout on perceived service quality. A deliverable may be to quantify any change in service quality in the latter instance. Different types of objectives lead to different types of research designs.

EXHIBIT **3.5** Flowchart of the Marketing Research Process

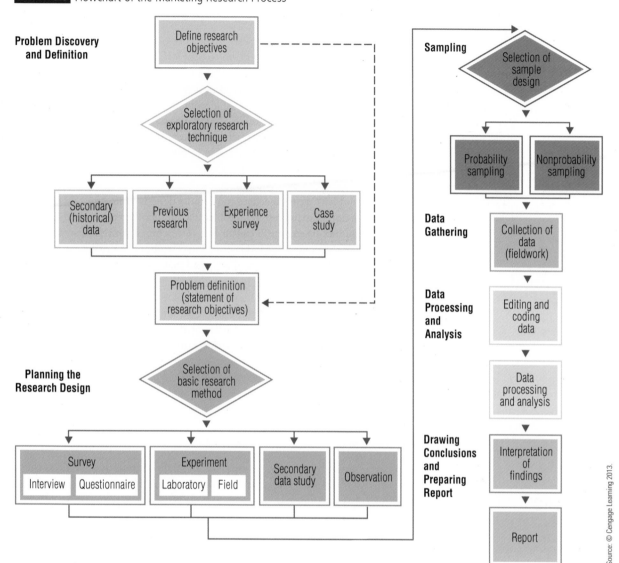

Note: Diamond-shaped boxes indicate stages in the research process in which a choice of one or more techniques must be made. The dotted line indicates an alternative path that skips exploratory research.

In applied or market research, the researcher cannot list objectives until there is an understanding of the decision situation. The lead researcher and the chief decision maker must share this understanding for effective research. We often describe this understanding as a *problem statement*. In general usage, the word *problem* suggests that something has gone wrong. This isn't always the case. Actually, the research objective may be to simply clarify a situation, define an opportunity, or monitor and evaluate current operations. The research objectives cannot be developed until managers and researchers have agreed on the actual business "problem" that will be addressed by the research. Thus, they set out to "discover" this problem through a series of interviews and through a document called a *research proposal*.

Managers and researchers alike may not have a clear-cut understanding of the situation at the outset of the research process. Managers may only be able to list symptoms that could indicate a problem. Sales may be declining, but management may not know the exact nature of the problem. Thus, the researcher in this case may only be able to state a research objective in general terms:

"Identify factors contributing to reduced sales."

The researcher needs this preliminary research to discover things that he/she should research more specifically.

Defining the Managerial Decision Situation

In marketing research, the adage "a problem well defined is a problem half solved" is worth remembering. This adage emphasizes that an orderly definition of the research problem lends a sense of direction to the investigation. Careful attention to problem definition allows the researcher to set the proper research objectives. If the purpose of the research is clear, the chances of collecting necessary and relevant information and not collecting surplus information will be much greater.

Albert Einstein noted that "the formulation of a problem is often more essential than its solution."[13] This is good advice for marketing managers. Managers naturally concentrate on finding the right answer rather than asking the right question. They also want one solution quickly rather than having to spend time considering many possible solutions. Properly defining a problem can be more difficult than solving it. If a researcher collects data before carefully thinking out the nature of the marketing problem, the data will probably not allow useful results.

Marketing research must have clear objectives and definite designs. Unfortunately, little or no planning goes into the formulation of many research problems. Consider the case of the Ha-Pah-Shu-Tse brand of Indian fried bread mix (the name "Ha-Pah-Shu-Tse" comes from the Pawnee Indian word for red corn). The owner of the company, Mr. Ha-Pah-Shu-Tse, thought that his product, one of the few Native American food products available in the United States, was not selling because it was not widely advertised. He wanted a management consulting group to conduct some research concerning advertising themes. However, the management consultants pointed out to the Ha-Pah-Shu-Tse family that using the family name on the bread mix might be a foremost source of concern. They suggested that consumer behavior research investigating the brand image might be a better initial starting point rather than advertising copy research. Family management agreed.

The summary of the managerial decision making, the research objectives and/or deliverables, and a basic description of the research process are described in a research proposal. Put simply, a **research proposal** is a written statement of the research design emphasizing what the research will accomplish.

research proposal

A written statement of the research design emphasizing what the research will accomplish.

Exploratory Research

Researchers can use exploratory research to help discover and define the decisions themselves. The preliminary activities undertaken can yield results that place the situation into a more easily researched context. Exploratory research can progressively narrow the scope of the research topic and help transform ambiguous problems into well-defined ones that yield specific research objectives. By investigating any existing studies on the subject, talking with knowledgeable individuals, and informally investigating the situation, the researcher can progressively sharpen the concepts. After such exploration, the researcher should know exactly what data to collect and how to obtain the data. Exhibit 3.5 indicates that researchers must decide whether to use one or more exploratory research techniques or bypass this stage altogether.

The marketing researcher can employ techniques from four basic categories to obtain insights and gain a clearer idea of the problem: previous research, pilot studies, case studies, and experience surveys. This section will briefly discuss previous research and pilot studies interviews, the most popular type of pilot study.

Previous Research

As a rule, researchers should first investigate previous research to see whether others may have addressed the same research problems previously. Researchers should search previous research reports within the company's archives. In addition, some firms specialize in providing various types of research reports, such as economic forecasts. The Census of Population and the Survey of Current Business are each examples of previous research conducted by an outside source.

literature review

A directed search of published works, including periodicals and books, that discusses theory and presents empirical results that are relevant to the topic at hand.

Literature Review

Previous research may also exist in the public domain. A **literature review** is a directed search of published works, including periodicals, books, as well as government, industry, or company reports. The reports may discuss theory and/or present empirical results relevant to the research objectives. A literature survey is common in applied market research studies but it is a fundamental requirement of a basic (i.e., marketing) research report. Researchers conduct literature reviews using

Courtesy, www.perkinsrowe.com

A business endeavor this big is best done with a lot of research. Luckily, there is a lot of previous research in the form of previous literature and reports to provide a start.

traditional library search tools and Internet search tools. Modern electronic search engines make finding literature simple and fast. Given the vast amount of hits a search of key terms may generate, the researcher faces the challenge of separating relevant literature from irrelevant literature.

Suppose a real estate developer is interested in developing a piece of commercial property. In particular, she has identified this property as a location for a lifestyle center containing places for people to shop, be entertained, dine, work and live—all in one location. Success will depend on attracting people to this place and creating the right feel. The decision to move forward with the project involves many dimensions including the location, tenant mix, the physical design or atmosphere of the place, which is affected by things like color, scents, and architecture. Obviously, prudence calls for more than a cursory study of the feasibility of this project and the implications for different types of designs. Before launching an exhaustive study, the researcher can first look through research journals and find hundreds of studies that address the different decision dimensions.[14] The review may give some idea on what type of architecture will work best to create the right atmosphere and enable the research to focus on a smaller set of possibilities.

Pilot Studies

Almost all consumers take a test drive before buying a car. A **pilot study** serves a similar purpose for the researcher. A pilot study is a small-scale research project that collects data from respondents like they are planned in the full study as sort of a dry run. Pilot studies are critical in refining measures and reducing the risk that the full study design contains a fatal flaw that will render its results useless. This is particularly true for experimental research, which depends critically on valid manipulations of experimental variables.[15] Pilot studies also often are useful in fine-tuning research objectives. Researchers sometimes refer to a pilot study as a **pretest**. A *pretest* is a very descriptive term indicating a small-scale study in which the results are only preliminary and intended only to assist in design of a subsequent study.

A pilot study sometimes includes a focus group interview. A **focus group** interview brings together six to twelve people in a loosely structured format. The technique assumes that individuals are more willing to talk about things when they are able to do so within a group discussion format. Focus group respondents sometimes feed on each other's comments to develop ideas that would be difficult to express in a different interview format. We discuss focus groups in much more detail in Chapter 5.

Suppose a consultant is hired by Carrefour to research the way consumers react to sales promotions. Carrefour is second in size only to Walmart, operating nearly 11,000 stores in twenty-nine

pilot study

A small-scale research project that collects data from respondents similar to those to be used in the full study.

pretest

A small-scale study in which the results are only preliminary and intended only to assist in design of a subsequent study.

focus group

A small group discussion about some research topic led by a moderator who guides discussion among the participants.

countries (**www.carrefour.fr**). Carrefour began in France over forty-five years ago and pioneered the discount hypermarket format. More specifically, the researcher may be asked to help management decide whether the size of promotions should vary with national culture. In other words, the basic research question is whether culture influences consumer perceptions of sales promotions.[16] A pretest examines whether or not differences in currency might interfere with these perceptions, or whether or not the different terms that refer to promotions and discounts vary in meaning when translated into another language. For example, is a discount expressed in Korean won interpreted the same way as a discount expressed in euros? If each euro equals about $1.60, and a single dollar is worth about 1,020 won, a €1 (1 Euro) discount means a savings of over 1,600 won!

Exploratory research need not always follow a structured design. Because the purpose of exploratory research is to gain insights and discover new ideas, researchers may use considerable creativity and flexibility. Some companies perform exploratory research routinely as part of environmental scanning. If the conclusions made during this stage suggest marketing opportunities, the researcher is in a position to begin planning a formal, quantitative research project.

Stating Research Objectives

After identifying and clarifying the problem, with or without exploratory research, the researcher must formally state the research objectives. This statement delineates the type of research needed and what intelligence may result that would allow the decision maker to make choices that are more informed. The statement of research objectives culminates the process of clarifying the managerial decision into something actionable.

A written decision statement expresses the business situation to the researcher. The research objectives try to address directly the decision statement or statements. As such, the research objectives represent a contract of sorts that commits the researcher to producing the needed research. This is why market researchers express these as deliverables in applied market research. Research objectives drive the rest of the research process. Indeed, before proceeding, the researcher and managers must agree that the objectives are appropriate and will produce relevant information.

What Is a Theory?

theory

A formal, logical explanation of some events that includes predictions of how things relate to one another.

Ultimately, theory plays a role in determining the appropriate research objectives. A **theory** is a formal, logical explanation of some events that includes descriptions of how things relate to one another. Researchers build theory through a process of reviewing previous findings of similar studies, simple logical deduction, and knowledge of applicable theoretical areas. For example, if a Web designer is trying to decide what color the background of the page should be, the researcher may first consult previous studies examining the effects of color on things like package design and retail store design. He or she may also find theories that deal with the wavelength of different colors or theories that explain retail atmospherics. This may lead to specific predictions that predict blue as a good background color.[17]

Although some may see theory as only relevant to academic or basic marketing research, theory plays a role in understanding practical market research as well. Before setting research objectives, the researcher must be able to describe the business situation in some coherent way. Without this type of explanation, the researcher would have little idea of where to start. Ultimately, the logical explanation helps the researcher know what variables need to be included in the study and how they may relate to one another. The Research Snapshot illustrates how theory and practice come together in marketing research.

What Is a Hypothesis?

hypothesis

A formal statement explaining some outcome.

A **hypothesis** is a formal statement explaining some outcome. Hypotheses (pl.) must be testable. In other words, when one states a hypothesis, one makes a proposition. In its simplest form, a hypothesis is a guess. Using our opening vignette as an example, the researcher may use theoretical reasoning to develop the following hypothesis:

H1: The more hours per week a prospective MBA student works, the more favorable his/her attitude toward online MBA class offerings.

EXHIBIT **3.6** Examples of Decision Statements, Research Objectives, and Research Hypotheses

Decision Statement	Relevant Theory	Research Objective	Hypothesis
Should we allocate more resources toward social networking or television advertising?	Source Credibility	Identify attitude change associated with message communicated through each media.	A target market consumer's attitude will become more positive when exposed through a Facebook posting than through a television advertisement.
In what ways can we improve our service quality?	Atmospherics (Stimulus – Organism – Response)	Determine how much the physical environment influences consumer perceptions of service quality.	Consumers' emotional responses to the service environment (colors, odors, lighting, etc.) are related positively to perceived service quality.
How much price promotion should be used in marketing brand X?	Brand equity	Determine the effects of price reduction on sales and brand image.	The more a product is promoted with price reductions, the more its brand image is reduced.

Source: © Cengage Learning 2013.

We often apply statistics to data to test hypotheses empirically. **Empirical testing** is done by comparing a hypothetical prediction, such as a hypothesis, against reality using data. When the data are consistent with a hypothesis, we say, "The hypothesis is supported." When the data are inconsistent with a hypothesis, we say, "The hypothesis is not supported." We are often tempted to say that we prove a hypothesis when the data conform to the prediction; this isn't really true. Statistical results cannot prove anything because there is always the possibility that our conclusion is wrong. Perhaps the sample drawn does not match the population. Now, at times we can be very, very confident in our conclusion, but from an absolute perspective, statistics cannot prove a hypothesis is true.

Exhibit 3.6 illustrates how decision statements are linked to research objectives, which are linked to research hypotheses. Although the first two objectives each have one hypothesis, notice that the third has two. In reality, most research projects will involve more than one research objective, and each of these may often involve more than one hypothesis. Think about how you might go about trying to test the hypotheses listed in Exhibit 3.6.

empirical testing

Means that some prediction has been examined against reality using data.

Planning the Research Design

After the researcher has formulated the research problem, he or she must develop the research design as part of the research design stage. A **research design** is a master plan that specifies the methods and procedures for collecting and analyzing the needed information. A research design provides a framework or plan of action for the research. Objectives of the study determined during the early stages of research are included in the design to ensure that the information collected is appropriate for solving the problem. The researcher also must determine the sources of information, the design technique (survey or experiment, for example), the sampling methodology, and the schedule and cost of the research.

research design

A master plan that specifies the methods and procedures for collecting and analyzing the needed information.

Selection of the Basic Research Method

Here again, the researcher must make a decision. Exhibit 3.5 shows four basic approaches for descriptive and causal research: surveys, experiments, secondary data, and observation. The objectives of the study, the available data sources, the urgency of the decision, and the cost of obtaining the data influence technique selection.

The most common method of generating primary data is the survey. Most people have seen the results of political surveys by Gallup or Harris Online, and some have been respondents (members of a sample who supply answers) to marketing research questionnaires. A **survey** is a

survey

A research technique in which a sample is interviewed in some form or the behavior of respondents is observed and described in some way.

Theory Drives Research?

This chapter makes clear the fact that theory drives research. Well, theories also might explain driving. Public policy makers rightly are concerned with making the roads safer. To do so, they observe and commission research explaining what makes consumers drive more recklessly. This research may address the goal of determining what type of PSA (public service announcement) might alter a person's driving in a way that makes them a safer driver.

In Great Britain, British Monitoring Schools play on fear by employing a two-factor theory of driving. The two factors are freedom and independence. If safety messages emphasize to consumers that they will lose a great deal of freedom and independence if driving privileges are lost, the consumers will drive more safely. In other words, perceptions of freedom and independence are related to plans to drive more safely.

Others worry that children who play video games involving simulated car chases, car races, or other risky driving behaviors will drive differently than others. One theory suggests that this

causes consumers to become better drivers. Another suggests that these games desensitize consumers to dangers associated with risky driving so that they become relatively dangerous drivers. Researchers' empirical tests support this latter hypothesis so be careful with the Xbox race games!

Sources: Costa, M. (2010), "BSM Puts Dual Theory to Test," *Marketing Week*, 33 (36), 20–21; Beullins, K., K. Roe, and J. Van Den Buick (2011), "Excellent Gamers, Excellent Drivers? The Impact of Adolescent Video Game Playing on Driving Behavior: A Two-Wave Panel Study," *Accident Analysis and Prevention*, 43 (January), 58–65.

research technique involving interviews of sample units in some form or recorded observations of some behavior. The term *surveyor* is most often reserved for civil engineers who describe a piece of property using a transit. Similarly, marketing researchers describe some market segment using a questionnaire. The task of writing a list of questions and designing the format of the printed or written questionnaire is an essential aspect of the development of a survey research design.

Research investigators may choose to contact respondents by telephone, mail (snail or e), via a website, a social network page, a smartphone, or even in person. An advertiser spending nearly $3 million for thirty seconds of commercial time during the Super Bowl may telephone people to gather quickly information concerning their reactions to the advertising. A forklift truck manufacturer trying to determine a cause for low sales in the wholesale grocery industry might choose a mail questionnaire because the appropriate executives are hard to reach by telephone. A researcher trying to determine the decision approaches consumers use when making important purchases may seek descriptions via Facebook or other network sites.[18] Although personal interviews are expensive, they are valuable because investigators can use visual aids and supplement the interviews with observations. Each of these survey methods has advantages and disadvantages. A researcher's task is to find the most appropriate way to collect the needed information.

The objective of many research projects is merely to record what can be observed—for example, the number of automobiles that pass by a proposed site for a gas station. An automatic device is best to *observe* this data. Research personnel known as *mystery shoppers* act like customers while observing and recording data. Companies pay mystery shoppers to gather data about the way employees treat consumers, the cleanliness of the environment, price points, and other important marketing information. This data addresses questions like: How often are store policies followed? How often are customers treated courteously?

The main advantage of the observation technique is that it records behavior without relying on reports from respondents. Researchers collect observations unobtrusively and passively, meaning without a respondent's direct participation. For instance, the ACNielsen Company created a "people meter," which they attached to television sets to record the programs watched by each household member. Today, Nielsen automatically collects TiVo and other digital recording activity to help know what people are watching. Automatic recording eliminates the possible bias of respondents stating that they watched the president's State of the Union address rather than the *Family Guy* or *The Simpsons*.

Observation is more complex than mere "nose counting," and the task is more difficult than the inexperienced researcher would imagine. Observation cannot capture all kinds of data. Researchers are often interested in things such as attitudes, opinions, motivations, and other intangible states of mind that they cannot directly observe.

The "Best" Research Design

No single best research design fits all situations. Researchers often have several alternatives that can achieve a stated research objective. Consider a researcher who must forecast product sales for the upcoming year. Some commonly used forecasting methods are surveying executive opinion, collecting sales force composite opinions, surveying user expectations, projecting trends, and analyzing market factors. Any one of these may yield a reliable forecast.

The ability to select the most appropriate research design develops with experience. Inexperienced researchers often jump to the conclusion that a survey methodology is usually the best design because they are most comfortable with this method. Chicago's Museum of Science and Industry wanted to determine the relative popularity of each exhibit. Museum personnel considered a survey approach. Instead, a creative researcher suggested a far less expensive alternative: an unobtrusive observation technique. The researcher suggested that the museum merely keep track of the frequency with which the floor tiles in front of the various exhibits needed replacing, indicating where the heaviest traffic occurred. The tile observation method showed that the chick-hatching exhibit was the most popular. This method provided the same results as a survey but at a much lower cost.

Planning a Sample

The research design outlines a sampling plan but the sampling stage is a distinct phase of the research process. For convenience, however, we will treat the sample planning and the actual sample generation processes together in this section.

If you take your first bite of a steak and conclude that the entire steak needs salt to taste good, you have just conducted a sample. **Sampling** involves any procedure that draws conclusions based on measurements of a portion of the entire population. In other words, a sample is a subset from a larger population. In the steak analogy, the first bite is the sample and the entire steak is the population. If certain statistical procedures are followed, a researcher need not select every item in a population because the results of a good sample should have the same characteristics as the population as a whole. Of course, when errors are made, samples do not give reliable estimates of the population. So, should the first bite come from the edge or the center of a steak?

A famous example of error due to sampling is the 1936 Literary Digest fiasco. The magazine conducted a survey and predicted that Republican Alf Landon would win over Democrat Franklin D. Roosevelt by a landslide in that year's presidential election. This prediction was wrong—and the error was due to sample selection. The postmortems showed that *Literary Digest* had sampled its readers as well as telephone subscribers. In 1936, these people were not a representative cross-section of voters, because a disproportionate number of them were Republicans.

The first sampling question to ask is "Who is to be sampled?" The answer to this primary question requires the identification of a target population. Defining this population and determining the sampling units may not be so easy. If, for example, a savings and loan association surveys people who already have accounts for answers to image questions, the selected sampling units will not represent potential customers. Specifying the target population is a crucial aspect of the sampling plan.

The next sampling issue concerns sample size. How big should the sample be? Although management may wish to examine every potential buyer of a product or service, doing so may be unnecessary as well as unrealistic. Typically, larger samples are more precise than smaller ones, but proper probability sampling can allow a small proportion of the total population to give a reliable measure of the whole. A later discussion will explain how large a sample must be in order to be truly representative of the universe or population.

The final sampling decision is how to select the sampling units. Simple random sampling may be the best known type, in which every unit in the population has an equal and known chance of

> *"You cannot put the same shoe on every foot."*
> —PUBLIUS SYRUS

sampling
Involves any procedure that draws conclusions based on measurements of a portion of the population.

being selected. However, this is only one type of sampling. For example, a cluster-sampling procedure may reduce costs and make data-gathering procedures more efficient. If members of the population are found in close geographical clusters, a sampling procedure that selects area clusters rather than individual units in the population will reduce costs. Rather than selecting 1,000 individuals throughout the United States, it may be more economical to first select twenty-five counties and then sample within those counties. This will substantially reduce travel, hiring, and training costs. In determining the appropriate sampling plan, the researcher will have to select the most appropriate sampling procedure for meeting the established study objectives. Chapter 12 provides a full discussion of sampling.

Collecting Data

The data-collection stage begins once the researcher has formalized the sampling plan. Data gathering is the process of gathering or collecting information. Human observers or interviewers may gather data, or machines like scanners or online stat counters may record data automatically.

Obviously, the many research techniques involve many methods of gathering data. Surveys require direct participation by research respondents. This may involve filling out a questionnaire or interacting with an interviewer. In this sense, they are obtrusive. **Unobtrusive methods** of data gathering are those in which the subjects do not have to be disturbed for data to be collected. They may even be unaware that research is going on at all. For instance, a simple count of motorists driving past a proposed franchising location is one kind of data gathering method. However the data are collected, it is important to minimize errors in the process. For example, the data gathering should be consistent in all geographical areas. If an interviewer phrases questions incorrectly or records a respondent's statements inaccurately (not verbatim), major data collection errors will result.

unobtrusive methods

Methods in which research respondents do not have to be disturbed for data to be gathered.

Editing and Coding

After a research team completes the fieldwork, someone must convert the data into a format that will answer the marketing manager's questions. This is part of the data processing and analysis stage. Here, the information content is mined from the raw data. Data processing generally begins with editing and coding the data. Editing involves checking the data collection forms for omissions, legibility, and consistency in classification. The editing process corrects problems such as interviewer errors (an answer recorded on the wrong portion of a questionnaire, for example) before the data are transferred to the computer.

Data have to be coded to become useful. Computer-assisted data collection tools provide data in multiple formats including Excel and SPSS. However, researchers usually need to perform some manual coding. Like mentioned previously, automatic coding offers the advantage of reduced human error.

Analyzing Data

data analysis

The application of computation, summarizing, and reasoning to understand the gathered information.

Data analysis is the application of computation, summarizing, and reasoning to understand the gathered information. In its simplest form, analysis may involve determining consistent patterns and summarizing the relevant details revealed in the investigation. The nature of the data, the research design, and management's requirements help determine what type of data analysis is most appropriate. Statistical analyses may range from portraying a simple frequency distribution to more complex multivariate analyses approaches. Later chapters will discuss three general categories of statistical analysis: univariate analysis, bivariate analysis, and multivariate analysis.

Drawing Conclusions

The research ends by drawing conclusions from the data analysis. These conclusions speak directly to the research questions developed in the early phases of the project and should fulfill the deliverables promised in the research proposal. Conclusions are what managers and other users of the research are interested in. As a result, the researcher highlights the main conclusions in both a written report and in any oral or electronic presentations resulting from the project. We return to this topic in detail at the end of the book because the importance of effective communication cannot be overstated.

Now that we have outlined the research process, note that the order of topics in this book follows the flowchart of the research process presented in Exhibit 3.5. Keep this flowchart in mind while reading later chapters.

The Research Program Strategy

Our discussion of the marketing research process began with the assumption that the researcher wished to collect data to achieve a specific marketing objective. When the researcher has only one or a small number of research objectives that can be addressed in a single study, that study is referred to as a **research project**. We have emphasized the researcher's need to select specific techniques for solving one-dimensional problems, such as identifying market segments, selecting the best packaging design, or test-marketing a new product.

However, if you think about a firm's marketing mix activity in a given period of time (such as a year), you'll realize that marketing research is not a one-shot activity—it is a continuous process. An exploratory research study may be followed by a survey, or a researcher may conduct a specific research project for each aspect of the marketing mix. If a new product is being developed, the different types of research might include market potential studies to identify the size and characteristics of the market; product usage testing to record consumers' reactions to prototype products; brand name and packaging research to determine the product's symbolic connotations; and test-marketing the new product. Thus, when numerous related studies come together to address issues about a single company, we refer to this as a **research program**. Because research is a continuous process, management should view marketing research at a strategic planning level.

research project

A single study that addresses one or a small number of research objectives.

research program

Numerous related studies that come together to address multiple, related research objectives.

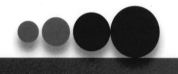

TIPS OF THE TRADE

- Extra effort spent distinguishing symptoms from problems usually pays off. A diagnostic analysis can help with this.
- Use exploratory research tools in the interviews with managers to help establish research objectives.
- Vague questions usually call for exploratory research. Very specific research questions usually call for a causal design. For example:
  - In what ways can Oracle leverage its brand name into new industries? Because this is a broad and relatively vague question, some exploratory research addressing the way consumers view the Oracle brand is a potential starting place for research.
  - The use of an animated character in a pop-up help window will lead consumers to be more satisfied

with the information they receive from the www. edmunds.com website than will the use of a video-taped person. This hypothesis is very specific and suggests a causal research design.
- Don't overlook the first stage of the research process—defining research objectives. The deliverables are in many ways the most important part of a research proposal.
- Good deliverable: Provide a measure of consumer shopping value perceptions for Anthropolgie consumers (both store and online shoppers) and its major competitor, Urban Outfitters.
- Poor deliverable: Increase profitability at Anthropologie by luring customers from Urban Outfitters.

Source: © Cengage Learning 2013.

∷ SUMMARY

1. Classify marketing research as either exploratory research, descriptive research, or causal research. Exploratory, descriptive, and causal research are three major types of marketing research projects. The clarity with which the team defines a decision situation determines whether exploratory, descriptive, or causal research is most appropriate. When the decision is very ambiguous, or the interest is on discovering ideas, exploratory research is most appropriate. Descriptive research attempts to paint a picture of the given situation by describing characteristics of objects, people, or organizations. Causal research identifies cause-and-effect relationships. Or, in other words, what change in "X" will bring about some change in "Y"? Three conditions must be satisfied to establish evidence of causality: 1) temporal sequence—the cause must occur before the effect; 2) concomitant variation—a change in the cause is associated with a change in the effect; and 3) nonspurious association—the cause is true and not eliminated by the introduction of another potential cause.

2. List the major stages of the marketing research process and the steps within each. The six major stages of the research process are 1) defining research objectives, 2) planning the research design, 3) sampling, 4) data gathering, 5) data processing and analysis, and 6) drawing conclusions and report preparation. Each stage involves several activities or steps. For instance, in planning the research design, the researchers must decide on the type of study and, if needed, recruit participants and develop experimental stimuli. Quite often researchers conduct projects as parts of a research program. Such programs can involve successive projects that monitor an established product or a group of projects undertaken for a proposed new product to determine the optimal form of various parts of the marketing mix.

3. Understand the concepts of theory and hypothesis and the critical role they play in research. A hypothesis is a testable, formal statement explaining some outcome. A theory is a formal, logical explanation of some events that includes predictions of how things relate to one another. Researchers build theory through a process of reviewing previous findings of similar studies, simple logical deduction, and knowledge of applicable theoretical areas. The explanations in a theory are often in the form of hypotheses. They are extremely useful in research because they give the research an idea of what to expect prior to testing. As such, they also help to identify the variables that need to be included in the study. Often, certain types of hypotheses point to the need for a specific type of research design.

4. Know the difference between a research project and a research program. A research project addresses one of a small number of research objectives that can be included in a single study. In contrast, a research program represents a series of studies addressing multiple research objectives. Many marketing activities require an ongoing research task of some type.

∷ KEY TERMS AND CONCEPTS

causal inference, *52*
causal research, *51*
concomitant variation, *52*
data analysis, *64*
deliverables, *56*
descriptive research, *49*
diagnostic analysis, *51*
empirical testing, *61*
experiment, *53*
experimental variable, *53*

exploratory research, *48*
focus group, *59*
hypothesis, *60*
literature review, *58*
manipulation, *53*
nonspurious association, *52*
pilot study, *59*
pretest, *59*
research design, *61*
research objectives, *56*

research program, *65*
research project, *65*
research proposal, *58*
sampling, *63*
survey, *61*
symptoms, *48*
temporal sequence, *52*
theory, *60*
unobtrusive methods, *64*

:: QUESTIONS FOR REVIEW AND CRITICAL THINKING

1. List five ways that marketing research can contribute to effective business decision making.
2. Define *market symptoms*. Give an example as it applies to a university business school.
3. Consider the following list, and indicate and explain whether each best fits the definition of a problem, opportunity, or symptom:
   a. A 12.5 percent decrease in store traffic for a children's shoe store in a medium-sized city mall.
   b. FedEx's fuel costs increase 200 percent between 2009 and 2010.
   c. A furniture manufacturer and retailer in North Carolina reads a research report indicating consumer trends toward Australian Jara and Kari wood. The export of these products is very limited and very expensive.
   d. Marlboro reads a research report written by the U.S. FDA. It indicates that the number of cigarette smokers in sub-Saharan Africa is expected to increase dramatically over the next decade.
   e. The Starwood Hotel group faces exchange rates between the United States and Europe, Great Britain, and Canada that have changed dramatically between 2006 and 2011.
4. What are the three types of marketing research? Indicate which type each item in the list below illustrates. Explain your answers.
   a. Establishing the relationship between advertising and sales in the beer industry
   b. Identifying target market demographics for a shopping center located in Omaha, Nebraska
   c. Estimating the 5-year sales potential for Cat-Scan machines in the Ark-La-Tex (Arkansas, Louisiana, and Texas) region of the United States
   d. Testing the effect of the inside temperature of a clothing store on sales of outerwear
   e. Discovering the ways that people who live in apartments actually use vacuum cleaners, and identifying cleaning tasks for which they do not use a vacuum
5. Describe the type of research evidence that allows one to infer causality.
6. What is an experimental manipulation?
7. A marketing researcher is hired by a specialty retail firm. The retailer is trying to decide what level of lighting and what temperature it should maintain in its stores. How can the researcher manipulate these experimental variables within a causal design?
8. Describe how a literature search is useful in marketing research.
9. Do the stages in the research process seem to follow the scientific method?
10. Why is the "define research objectives" of the research process probably the most important stage?
11. Suppose Auchan (http://www.auchan.fr), a hypermarket chain based out of France, was considering opening three hypermarkets in the midwestern United States. What role would theory play in designing a research study to track how the shopping habits of consumers from the United States differ from those in France and from those in Japan? What kind of hypothesis might be examined in a study of this topic?
12. Define research project and research program. Referring to the question immediately above, do you think a research project or a research program is needed to provide useful input to the Auchan decision makers?
13. What type of research design would you recommend in the situations below? For each applied market research project, what might be an example of a "deliverable"? Which do you think would involve actually testing a research hypothesis?
   a. The manufacturer and marketer of flight simulators and other pilot training equipment wish to forecast sales volume for the next five years.
   b. A local chapter of the American Lung Association wishes to identify the demographic characteristics of individuals who donate more than $500 per year.
   c. A major music producer wonders how buzz initiated through Facebook might affect the online revenue for new artists.
   d. A food company researcher wishes to know what types of food are carried in brown-bag lunches to learn if the company can capitalize on this phenomenon.
   e. A researcher wishes to explore the feasibility of a casino in a community where gaming had previously been banned.
   f. A researcher wonders how much consumers retain from Tweats about new products.

:: RESEARCH ACTIVITIES

1. **'NET** Look up information about the online MBA programs at the University of Phoenix (http://business.phoenix.edu/business/graduate.aspx). Compare it to the traditional MBA program at your university. Suppose each was looking to expand the numbers of students in their programs. How might the research design differ for each?
2. **'NET** Use a web Browser to go to the Gallup Organization's home page (http://www.gallup.com). The Gallup home page changes regularly. However, it should provide an opportunity to read the results of a recent poll. For example, a poll might break down Americans' sympathies toward Israel or the Palestinians based on numerous individual characteristics such as political affiliation or religious involvement. After reading the results of a Gallup poll of this type, learn how polls are conducted (hint: see "About Gallup" for "FAQs"). You may need to click on the Frequently Asked Questions List (FAQ) to find this information. List the various stages of the research process and how they were (or were not) followed in Gallup's project.
3. Any significant business decision requires input from a research project. Write a brief essay either defending this statement or refuting it.

A New "Joe" on the Block

Joe Brown is ready to start a new career. After spending thirty years as a market researcher and inspired by the success of Starbucks, he is ready to enter the coffee shop business. However, before opening his first shop, he realizes that a great deal of research is needed. He has some key questions in mind.

- What markets in the United States hold the most promise for a new coffee shop?
- What type of location is best for a coffee shop?
- What is it that makes a coffee shop popular?
- What coffee do Americans prefer?

A quick trip to the Internet reveals more previous research on coffee, markets, and related materials than he expected. Many studies address taste. For example, he finds several studies that in one way or another compare the taste of different coffee shop coffees. Most commonly, they compare the taste of coffee from Starbucks against coffee from McDonald's, Dunkin' Donuts, Burger King, and sometimes a local competitor. However, it becomes difficult to draw a conclusion as the results seem to be inconsistent.

- One study had a headline that poked fun at Starbucks' high-priced coffee. The author of this study personally purchased coffee to go at four places, took them to his office, tasted them, made notes and then drew conclusions. All the coffee was tasted black with no sugar. Just cups of joe. He reached the conclusion that McDonald's Premium Coffee (at about $1.50 a cup), tasted nearly as good as Starbucks House Blend (at about $1.70 a cup), both of which were much better than either Dunkin' Donuts (at about $1.20) or Burger King (less than $1). This study argued that McDonald's was best, all things considered.
- Another study was written up by a good critic who was simply interested in identifying the best-tasting coffee. Again, he tasted them all black with nothing added. Each cup of coffee was consumed in the urban location near the inner city center in which he lived. He reached the conclusion that Starbucks' coffee had the best flavor although it showed room for improvement. McDonald's premium coffee was not as good, but better than the other two. Dunkin' Donuts coffee had reasonably unobjectionable taste but was very weak and watery. The Burger King coffee was simply not very good.
- Yet another study talked about Starbucks becoming a huge company and how it has lost touch with the common coffee shop coffee customer. The researchers stood outside a small organic specialty shop and interviewed 100 consumers as they exited the shop. They asked, "Which coffee do you prefer?" The results showed a preference for a local coffee, tea, and incense shop, and otherwise put Starbucks last behind McDonald's, Burger King, and Dunkin' Donuts.
- Still another study compared the coffee-drinking experience. A sample of 50 consumers in St. Louis, Missouri, were interviewed and asked to list the coffee shop they frequented most. Starbucks was listed by more consumers than any other place. A small percentage listed Dunkin' Donuts but none listed McDonald's, despite their efforts at creating a premium coffee experience. The study did not ask consumers to compare the tastes of the coffee across the different places.
- Joe also wants to find data showing coffee consumption patterns and the number of coffee shops around the United States, so he spends time looking for data on the Internet. His searches don't reveal anything satisfying.

As Joe ponders how to go about starting "A Cup of Joe," he wonders about the relevance of this previous research. Is it useful at all? He even questions whether he is capable of doing any primary research himself and considers hiring someone to do a feasibility study for him. Maybe doing research is easier than using research.

Sources: Shiver, J., "Taste Test: The Little Joes Take on Starbucks," *USA Today*, (March 26, 2008), http://www.usatoday.com/money/industries/food/2006-03-26-coffee_x.htm, accessed July 20, 2008; Associated Press, "McDonald's Coffee Beats Starbucks, Says Consumer Reports," *The Seattle Times*, (February 2, 2007), http://seattletimes.nwsource.com/html/businesstechnology/2003553322_webcoffeetest02.html, accessed July 20, 2008; "Coffee Wars: Starbucks v McDonald's," *The Economist* 386 (January 10, 2008), 58.

Questions

1. What are the top three key decisions faced by Joe?
2. What are the key deliverables that an outside researcher should produce to help Joe with the key decisions?
3. How relevant are the coffee taste studies cited above? Explain.
4. What flaws in the coffee taste studies should Joe consider in trying to weigh the merits of their results?
5. Briefly relate this situation to each of the major stages of the marketing research process.
6. Try to do a quick search to explore the question: "Are American consumer preferences the same all across the United States?"
7. Would it be better for Joe to do the research himself or have a consultant perform the work?
8. If a consultant comes in to do the job, what are three key deliverables that would likely be important to Joe in making a decision to launch the Cup of Joe coffee shop.

The Human Side of Marketing Research: Organizational and Ethical Issues

LEARNING OUTCOMES

After studying this chapter, you should be able to:

1. Know when research should be conducted externally and when it should be done internally

2. Be familiar with the types of jobs, job responsibilities, and career paths available within the marketing research industry

3. Understand marketing ethics and ways that researchers can face ethical dilemmas

4. Appreciate the rights and obligations of a) research respondents—particularly children, b) research clients or sponsors, c) marketing researchers, and d) society

5. Avoid situations involving a conflict of interest in performing marketing research

Chapter Vignette:

If It Feels Green Then It Is Green?

Consumers today are concerned about environmental sensitivities and as a result, companies are becoming *greener*. Marketing efforts communicate a company's environmental sensitivity through product packaging, labeling, advertising, and public relations. These efforts are complicated by the fact that knowing what truly is best for the environment is itself a complicated exercise. Do electric cars powered by high-powered batteries containing toxic chemicals really do less harm than would high-efficiency diesel-powered cars with matching power? Consider also that consumers may recharge the electric cars with electricity taken from an oil-burning or coal-burning power plant. These questions are difficult enough for scientists to answer much less for the average consumer. Research suggests that even "environmentally aware consumers" cannot discern the most green product alternative even half of the time.

Several policy organizations rank firms based on their environmental impact. Unfortunately, numerous factors make gleaning information from these rankings difficult, including the fact that comparing brands across industries is practically impossible and the fact that rankings provided by different ranking organizations do not correspond to one another. For instance, some rankings place Dell as more environmentally friendly than Apple, whereas others

put Apple in the top spot! Thus, how much can consumers rely on these types of ranking? As a result, consumers easily can become victims of green washing—the false or unjustified belief that a product is more environmentally friendly than alternatives.

Put yourself in the place of a young researcher asked to conduct research for consumer food products firm that grows grapes. The company grows grapes the same way they have for almost 100 years. The practices were organic before anybody knew what that meant. They ship grapes all over North America

©Howard Sayer/Shutterstock

and to South Africa. Management asks the researcher for information useful in developing snack packaging that might help tap into consumers' green sensitivities. Management believes that sales will increase by placing the grapes in a green wrapper and putting the word *sustainable* on the packaging. In fact, management believes this so strongly that they have already invested in equipment and materials to produce the packaging. The researcher plans experiments comparing consumer beliefs about environmental friendliness, attitudes toward the brand, purchase intentions, and perceived tastiness using the green packaging versus using the traditional packaging (no plastic at all with crated grapes selected by the consumer stem by stem). In particular, the researcher examines whether or not consumers perceive this national brand as better than other national brands and the locally grown grapes that it competes with regionally. One thing seems clear, buying green makes consumers feel better and this means the packaging decisions are meaningful to the company.[1]

Introduction

The vignette describes a situation emphasizing marketing research's human side. A company is looking for research to help sell a product, in this case produce. The researcher faces a number of dilemmas. Some of these introduce business ethics into the arena of marketing research. This chapter focuses on marketing research's human side by discussing the people who do, use, and participate in research.

Who Should Do the Research?

The vignette opening this chapter involves a situation in which a company is hiring an outside researcher to conduct a study critical to its marketing strategy. Although this is very typical, many companies have their own employees perform research projects and research programs. Thus, companies sometimes perform in-house research, meaning that employees of the company affected by the research project perform the research. In other cases, companies use an **outside agency** to perform the research, meaning that the company hires an independent, outside firm to perform a research project. Although it would seem that **in-house research** would usually be of higher quality because of the increased knowledge of the researchers conducting the studies, several reasons why employees of the firm may not always be the best people to do the job exist.

outside agency

An independent research firm contracted by the company that actually will benefit from the research.

in-house research

Research performed by employees of the company that will benefit from the research.

Do It Yourself or Let Your Fingers Do the Walking?

When the firm facing a decision encounters one of the following situations, they should consider having the research performed by an outside agency.

- An outside agency often can provide a fresh perspective. Too much knowledge potentially hinders creativity. When a firm desires new ideas, like those that come from discovery-oriented research, an outsider is not constrained by the groupthink that often affects a company employee. In other words, employees who spend so much time together in their day-to-day work activities begin to act and think alike to a large degree. History reveals many stories of products that remained unsuccessful commercially for years until someone from outside the company discovered a useful application. Most people think of the microwave oven as a marvel of the late twentieth century. A company called Raytheon invented the technology for a microwave oven in the 1940s. Raytheon worked on radar systems for the Allied military in World War II. Not until Raytheon acquired an electronics company called Amana in 1965 did anybody realize that the technology could be a huge commercial success as a kitchen appliance. Today, a kitchen would be incomplete without a microwave oven.
- An outside agency often can be more objective. When a firm is facing a particularly sensitive situation that may even affect a large number of jobs within the company, researchers may have

> "*To manage a business is to manage its future; and to manage the future is to manage information.*"
> —MARION HARPER

By now, you are becoming familiar with the student questionnaire that accompanies this book. Examine the items in the questionnaire and the questionnaire overall for the following issues.

1. Were you required to identify yourself by name in completing the survey?

2. Can the results (you can access the results through your instructor) be linked to respondents by name?

3. Do any items need to be tied to a name to be useful to the researcher?

4. Consider the portion of the survey shown below. What if another instructor asked for the results from this particular section of the survey but was only interested in them if the names of the students also can be provided? The instructor believes that he can use the results to encourage particular students to change their study habits. Take the role of the researchers who implemented this research. Should you provide the information this instructor is asking for? Why or why not?

Source: © Cengage Learning 2013.

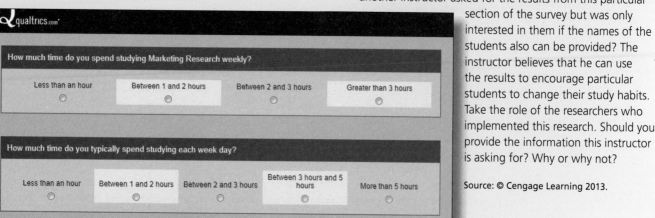

Courtesy of Qualtrics.com

difficultly being objective. Alternatively, if a particular chief executive within the firm is in love with some new idea, researchers may feel a great deal of pressure to present results that are supportive of the concept. In these cases, outside researchers may be a good choice. Outsiders don't have to work for the company and interact with the players involved in the decision on a daily basis. Therefore, they are less concerned about presenting results that may not be truly welcome.

■ An outside agency may have special expertise. When a firm needs research requiring a particular expertise that some outside agency specializes in, it may be a good idea to use that firm to conduct the research. For example, if a company is searching for new ideas about how to use its Facebook site, an online focus group interview may be a good idea. Online focus groups may not be a prevalent skill among company employees. However, multiple research firms specialize in this particular type of research. Thus, an outside agency may have greater competency in this specific area.

■ An outside agency often has local expertise allowing it to specialize in research from its home area. When a company needs consumer research from a particular country or even from a particular part of a country, the outside agency becomes advantageous because of its knowledge of customs and values. The company probably also knows acceptable ways to get information from consumers in that particular area. For example, a research agency based here in the United States would probably not strongly consider a door-to-door survey for consumer research. However, in other parts of the world, particularly with a less developed communication infrastructure, door-to-door interviews may be a viable option.

Likewise, certain conditions make in-house research more attractive, as described below:

■ If a research project needs a quick completion, chances are that in-house researchers can get started more quickly and get quicker access to internal resources that can help get the project done in short order.

■ If the research project requires close collaboration of many other employees from diverse areas of the organization, then in-house research may be preferable. The in-house research firms can usually gain cooperation and can more quickly ascertain just whom they need to interview and where to find those people.

■ A third reason for doing a project in-house has to do with economy. Researchers nearly always save money by doing the research in-house relative to hiring an outside agency.

■ If secrecy is a major concern, the company should conduct the research in-house. Even though an outside firm might be trusted, that same company may take slightly less care in disguising the research efforts. Thus, other companies may pick up signals in the marketplace that suggest the area of research for a firm.

Working in the Marketing Research Field

About three-fourths of all U.S. organizations have a department or individual responsible for marketing research. Consumer products companies, manufacturers, service firms, health-care organizations and retailers are most likely to have an in-house marketing research department. Marketing research clearly has a presence and this is particularly true for larger firms. The amount of companies doing research is likely increasing because as times get tough or as competition increases, firms actually increase the attention paid to marketing research. Further, the increase in data described in the previous chapter creates a proportionate need for more researchers trained in analytical skills.

The insurance industry relies significantly on marketing research as competition increases and the economy remains sluggish. Dozens or even hundreds of people are involved with a major company's marketing research. MetLife has been singled out as a role model for exemplary performance and integration of its marketing research team into strategic decision making. The marketing research team has helped MetLife:[2]

■ Build stronger relationships with customers
■ Integrate customer and competitor information into decision processes
■ Have better working relationships with vendors
■ Become more marketing oriented and entrepreneurial by targeting tailor-made financial advice to generational segments

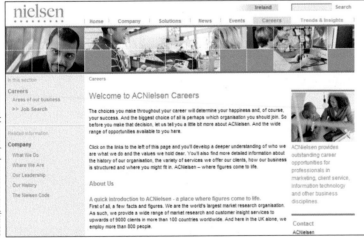

The marketing research field offers many opportunities. Nielsen alone employs over 30,000 employees.

The placement of marketing research within a firm's organizational structure and the structure of the research department itself vary substantially, depending on the firm's degree of marketing orientation and research sophistication. A marketing research department can easily become isolated with poor organizational placement. Researchers may lack a voice in executive committees when they have no continuous relationship with marketing management. Firms that place the research department at an inappropriately low level end up suffering this mishap. Given the critically important nature of the intelligence coming out of a research department, the organizational structure should place research high enough to ensure that senior management is well informed. Research departments also need to interact with a broad spectrum of other units within the organization. Thus, the position they occupy in the organizational hierarchy should allow them to provide credible information both upstream and downstream. MetLife's marketing research informs senior all levels of the organization and seeks input from all levels of the organization.

Research departments that perform a staff function must wait for management to request assistance. Often the term *client* is used by the research department to refer to line management, the entity for whom services are being performed. The research department responds to clients' requests and is responsible for the design and execution of all research.

The True Power of Research

©Clive Rose/Getty Images

The customer's voice is powerful in many ways. How can a company get the power that comes from the customer's voice? Many companies turn to J.D. Power to find powerful research results. J.D. Power rates competing company's products and services in many industries. For instance, want to know what tires make consumers the happiest? This might be an important question for retail dealers considering product lines and for auto manufacturers looking to enhance the value of their new cars by using quality OEM component parts. A sample of 30,000 consumers ranks Michelin highest based on good wear and the smallest number of problems. However, Pirelli tire owners thought their tires looked the best! Value comes in many forms. J.D. Power also breaks results down by region. In the southern United States, consumers rate Bright House Networks as the highest-performing cable company based on customer service, price, and product offerings. However, in the upper Midwest, WideOpenWest (WOW) is the leading provider. Perhaps cable companies or even competitors like DIRECTV will find information like this full of *power*.

Sources: CED (2010), "Ops Fare Well in J.D. Power Phone Study," *Upfront* (October), 14; *The Business* (2010), "Michelin, Pirelli Brands top J.D. Power OE Tire Consumer Satisfaction Study," 28 (May 10), 22–23.

Research Suppliers and Contractors

As mentioned in the beginning of the chapter, sometimes obtaining marketing research from an outside organization makes good sense. In these cases, marketing managers must interact with **research suppliers**, who are commercial providers of marketing research services. Marketing research is carried out by firms that may be variously classified as marketing research consulting companies, such as Burke or the Walker Information Research Company; advertising agencies, such as JWT Worldwide; suppliers of syndicated research services, such as The Nielsen Company; as well as interviewing agencies, universities, and government agencies, among others. The Nielsen Company alone employs over 34,000 people in more than 100 countries.[3] Research suppliers provide varied services which can be classified into several types.

research suppliers

Commercial providers of marketing research services.

Syndicated Service

No matter how large a firm's marketing research department is, some projects are too expensive to perform in-house. A **syndicated service** is a marketing research supplier that provides standardized information for many clients in return for a fee. They are a sort of supermarket for standardized research results. For example, J.D. Power and Associates (see research snapshot above) sells research about customers' experiences with products they purchase and their reasons for satisfaction or dissatisfaction with those products. Consumers are perhaps most familiar with J.D. Power for their automobile ratings. For instance, J.D. Power traditionally lists Lexus, Toyota, and Honda as the most dependable automobiles. In 2011, Buick also found a place among the most dependable autos.[4] Most automobile manufacturers and their advertising agencies subscribe to this syndicated service because the company provides important industry-wide information it gathers from a national sample of thousands of consumers. By specializing in this type of customer satisfaction research, J.D. Power gains certain economies of scale.

syndicated service

A marketing research supplier that provides standardized information for many clients in return for a fee.

Syndicated services provide information economically because the information is not specific to one client but interests many. In a way, the costs for producing the results are spread among all subscribers. Syndicated service companies offer standardized information measuring media audiences, wholesale and retail distribution data, Internet usage, and other forms of data.

Standardized Research Services

Standardized research service providers develop a unique methodology for investigating a business specialty area. Several research firms, such as Retail Forward (**http://www.retailforward.com**), provide location services for retail firms. Standardized research suppliers conduct studies for multiple individual clients using the same methods.

Even when a firm could perform the research task in-house, research suppliers may be able to conduct the project at a lower cost, faster, and relatively more objectively. A company evaluating a new advertising strategy may find an ad agency's research department better able to provide technical expertise on copy development research than could be done within the company itself. Researchers also may wisely seek outside help with research when conducting research in a foreign country in which the necessary human resources and knowledge to collect data effectively are lacking.

Limited Research Service Companies and Custom Research

Limited-service research suppliers specialize in particular research activities, such as field interviewing, data warehousing, or data processing. Full-service research suppliers sometimes contract these companies for ad hoc marketing research projects. The client usually controls these marketing research agencies or management consulting firms, but the research supplier handles most of the operating details of **custom research** projects. These are projects tailored specifically to a client's unique needs.

Exhibit 4.1[5] lists the top twenty suppliers of global research. Most provide multiple services ranging from designing activities to fieldwork. These services are described throughout the book. Clearly, the exhibit reveals that marketing research is a massive, global industry. Just a few decades ago, the list would comprise solely firms based in the United States. Large research firms now base their operations in places around the globe including London, Tokyo, and Germany. The explosion in global data availability will only add to the growth in the industry. Therefore, attractive career opportunities are numerous for those with the right skills and desires.

The top 15 global marketing research firms employ nearly 100,000 full-time employees and generate over $17 billion in annual revenue. Other large firms based that don't make the list of the fifteenth largest include:

Savitz Research of Dallas with revenue of about $15 million
IBOPE Group of San Paulo, Brazil, with revenues of $146 million
Mediametrie of Paris, France, with revenues of $89 million

Size of the Marketing Research Firm

Marketing research organizations themselves consist of layers of employees. Each employee has certain specific functions to perform based on his or her area of expertise and experience. A look at these jobs describes the potential structure of a research organization and gives insight into the types of careers available in marketing research.

Small Firms

The boundary between small firms, mid-sized firms, and large firms, generally speaking, is not precise. Government statistics usually consider firms with fewer than 100 employees to be small. In small firms, the vice president of marketing may be in charge of all significant marketing research. This officer generally has a sales manager collect and analyze sales histories, trade association

©Rhoda Sidney/PhotoEdit

Research in a foreign country is often better done by an outside agency with resources in those places.

standardized research service

Companies that develop a unique methodology for investigating a business specialty area.

custom research

Research projects that are tailored specifically to a client's unique needs.

EXHIBIT 4.1 World's Largest Research Firms (2010)

Rank	Organization	Headquarters	Home Country	Web Site	Employees (Full-Time)	Number of Countries	Approximate Revenue ($ millions)
1	The Nielsen Co.	New York	USA	nielson.com	33,100	100	4,628
2	Kantar	London	UK	kantar.com	19,400	80	2823
3	IMS Health Inc.	Norwalk, CT	USA	imshealth.com	7,300	75	2190
4	GfK	Neuremberg	Germany	gfk.com	10,100	59	1622
5	Ipsos	New York	USA	ipsos.com	8,800	64	1315
6	Westat Inc.	Rockville, MD	USA	wesstat.com	2,100	1	1,000
7	Synovate	London	UK	synovate.com	6,000	62	817
8	Symphony IRI	Chicago, IL	USA	symphonyiri.com	700	8	706
9	Arbitron Inc.	Columbia, MD	USA	arbitron.com	1,029	2	385
10	JD Power	Westlake Village, CA	USA	jdpower.com	800	8	370
11	INTA6E, Inc.	Tokyo	Japan	intage.co.jp	2000	3	369
12	NPD Group Inc.	Port Washington, NY	USA	npd.com	1,000	12	226
13	dunnhumbyUSA	Cincinnati, OH	USA	dunnhumby.com	1,100	18	203
14	Video Research Ltd.	Tokyo	Japan	videor.co.jp	400	3	201
15	Harris Interactive	New York	USA	harrisinteractive.com	800	8	167

Source: © Cengage Learning 2013.

statistics, and other internal data. Small marketing companies usually have few resources and special competencies to conduct large-scale, sophisticated research projects. If a small firm needs a large-scale survey, it often contacts an advertising agency or a firm that specializes in marketing research. Small businesses will generally have fewer than five employees regularly involved in marketing research.

Small marketing research firms are less likely to have major corporate clients; rather, they will probably work for other small firms, especially start-up firms. Typically, small marketing research firms conduct feasibility studies, studies assess consumer attitudes and studies assessing the relationship between customer satisfaction and customer loyalty.[6] A small firm can be a good place to start a career or to start your own business. Researchers working for a small firm will probably have to be involved in many, if not all, of the stages of research.

Mid-Sized Firms

Mid-sized firm are those with between 100 and 500 employees. In a mid-sized firm, someone usually holds the position of **director of marketing research**. This person provides leadership in research efforts and integrates all staff-level research activities.

A **research analyst** is responsible for client contact, project design, preparation of proposals, selection of research suppliers, and supervision of data collection, analysis, and reporting activities. Normally, the research analyst is responsible for several projects simultaneously covering a wide spectrum of the firm's organizational activities. He or she works with product or division management and makes recommendations based on analysis of collected data.

Research assistants (or associates) provide technical assistance with questionnaire design, data analyses, and so forth. Another common name for this position is *junior analyst*. The **manager of decision support systems** supervises the collection and analysis of sales, inventory, and other periodic customer relationship management (CRM) data. Research assistants develop sales forecasts for product lines using analytical and quantitative techniques. They provide sales information to

director of marketing research

This person provides leadership in research efforts and integrates all staff-level research activities into one effort. The director plans, executes, and controls the firm's marketing research function.

research analyst

A person responsible for client contact, project design, preparation of proposals, selection of research suppliers, and supervision of data collection, analysis, and reporting activities.

research assistants

Research employees who provide technical assistance with questionnaire design, data analyses, and similar activities.

manager of decision support systems

Employee who supervises the collection and analysis of sales, inventory, and other periodic customer relationship management (CRM) data.

©Andrew Holt/Alamy

When market research departments grow, they begin to specialize by product or business unit. This happened in the Marriott Corporation, which now has a specific director of marketing research for its lodging facilities.

forecast analyst

Employee who provides technical assistance such as running computer programs and manipulating data to generate a sales forecast.

decision makers to satisfy the planning, analysis, and control needs. A **forecast analyst** who provides technical assistance, such as running computer programs and manipulating data to forecast sales, may assist the manager of decision support systems.

Personnel within a planning department may perform the marketing research function in a mid-sized firm. At times, they may outsource some research functions. The planner may design research studies and then contract with outside firms that supply research services such as interviewing or data processing. They can combine the input from these outside agencies with their own work to write research reports.

Large Firms

As marketing research departments grow, they tend to specialize by product or strategic business unit. Major firms are those with over 500 employees. Marriott Corporation, for instance, has a director of marketing research for lodging (for example, Marriott Hotels and Resorts, Courtyard by Marriott, and Fairfield Inn) and a director of marketing research for contract services (for example, Senior Living Services). Each business unit's research director reports to the vice president of corporate marketing services. Many large organizations have managers of customer quality research who specialize in conducting surveys to measure consumers' satisfaction with product quality.

Exhibit 4.2 illustrates the organization of a major firm's marketing research department. Within this organization, the centralized marketing research department conducts research for all the division's product groups. This is typical of a large research department that conducts much of its own research, including fieldwork. The director of marketing research reports to the vice president of marketing.

The Director of Marketing Research as a Manager

A director of marketing research plans, executes, and controls the firm's marketing research function. This person typically serves on company executive committees that identify competitive opportunities and formulate marketing strategies. The various directors from each functional area generally make up this committee (such as finance, sales, production, and so forth). The director of marketing research provides the research perspective during meetings. For instance, he or she can let the committee know what types of market intelligence can be feasibly obtained given the decision being discussed. Marketing research directors typically face on-the-job issues like these:

EXHIBIT 4.2 Example of a Market Research Firms Organizational Chart

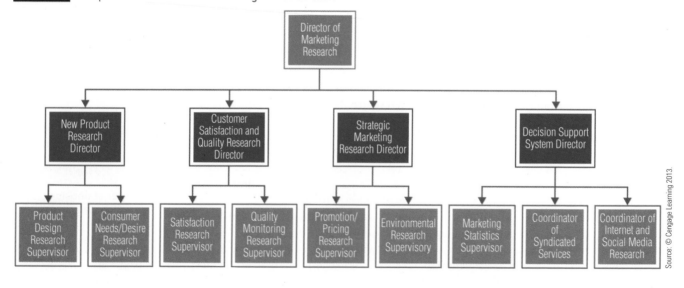

Source: © Cengage Learning 2013.

Marketing Research Pays

Marketing research can pay! Careers in marketing research can be very lucrative. This is particularly true if one has the right attributes. These attributes include being a good people person as well as having good quantitative skills and a good education. The fastest career tracks in marketing research are for those with at least a master's degree.

The prospects of finding a job remain good. Marketing researchers have long been in greater demand than the supply can address. The salaries also can be very lucrative. The 2009 U.S. Department of Labor Salary Survey suggests that marketing research analysts' salaries are generally between $45,000 and $85,000, although some analysts have salaries well over $100,000 per year. These are for actual research analysts and not research directors. Beginning research employees, with little or no experience, generally enter the firm as a survey researcher. Those salaries are considerably less, generally between $22,500 and $55,000. However, they require no significant work experience.

Job opportunities in marketing research exist outside the United States as well. The salaries also are lucrative in other countries. The chart shows typical salary ranges for non-managerial marketing research positions in the United States, Australia, Japan, and the United Kingdom. For comparison purposes, salaries for non-managerial sales employees also are provided. The salaries are expressed in thousands of U.S. dollars and reflect the latest available statistics. As can be seen, research

©Photodisc/Getty Images

Common Currency (US$1,000)	Australia	UK	Japan	United States
Sales Executive				
High	80	72	120	75
Low	55	24	65	45
Marketing Research Analyst				
High	90	90	170	110
Low	50	38	65	55

jobs compare very favorably. In addition, researchers that move into research director positions see a substantial increase in pay. Perhaps you'll give marketing research a try?

Sources: Enright, A., "Carve out a Niche," *Marketing News* (November 15, 2005), 17; "Occupational Employment and Wages," U.S. Department of Labor, (2008), http://www.bls.gov/oes/current/oes193022.htm, accessed March 10, 2011; http://www.bls.gov/oes/current/oes193021.htm, accessed March 11, 2011; Walters, Robert, "Market Research Search Results," (2010), http://www.robertwalters.com, accessed March 10, 2011.

- Skilled research professionals like conducting research better than managing people. They pride themselves on being hands-on researchers. However, a director is a manager and spends more time in meetings and managing than actually conducting research.
- The research management role often is not formally recognized.
- Outstanding research professionals often have trouble delegating responsibility. The pride that comes with being a knowledgeable researcher makes it difficult to give up control. As a result, they delegate only elementary or tedious tasks to subordinates who sometimes become disenchanted and unhappy with their work.
- Finally, other top managers see research as a hodgepodge of techniques available to answer individual, unrelated questions. According to this view, a research operation encompasses an array of equally important and equally involving projects. A project director oversees each project and hence, many firms view a full-time director as unnecessary.[7]

Marketing research jobs range across a large spectrum of activities and salaries. Jobs are available practically all over the world. The Research Snapshot gives a rough idea of what marketing research salaries are like internationally.

Cross-Functional Teams

In a truly marketing-oriented organization, all employees are involved in the intelligence-gathering and dissemination process. Therefore, employees from different areas of the organization are more likely to communicate and act on marketing information in marketing-oriented firms.

cross-functional teams

Employee teams composed of individuals from various functional areas such as engineering, production, finance, and marketing who share a common purpose.

Cross-functional teams are composed of individuals from various functional areas such as engineering, production, finance, and marketing who share a common purpose. Cross-functional teams help organizations focus on a core business process, such as customer service or new-product development. Working in teams reduces the tendency for employees to focus single-mindedly on an isolated functional activity. In marketing-oriented firms, cross-functional teams help employees increase customer value because communication about the customer and their specific desires and opinions spreads throughout the firm more naturally and fully.

At trendsetting organizations, many marketing research directors are members of cross-functional teams. New-product development, for example, may be done by a cross-functional team of engineers, finance executives, production personnel, marketing managers, and marketing researchers who take an integrated approach to solve a problem or exploit opportunities. In the old days, marketing research may not have been involved in developing new products until long after many key decisions about product specifications and manufacturing had been made. Now marketing researchers' input is part of an integrated team effort. Researchers act both as business consultants and as providers of technical services. Researchers working in teams are more likely to understand the broad purpose of their research and less likely to focus exclusively on research methodology.

Ethical Issues in Marketing Research

As in all human interactions, ethical issues exist in marketing research. This book considers various ethical issues concerning fair business dealings, proper research techniques, and appropriate use of research results in other chapters. The remainder of this chapter introduces ethical issues with an emphasis on societal and managerial concerns.

Ethical Questions Are Philosophical Questions

Ethical questions are philosophical questions. Several philosophical theories address how one develops a moral philosophy and how the resulting morals affect behavior. The theories include those about cognitive moral development, the bases for ethical behavioral intentions, and opposing moral values.[8] Although ethics remains a somewhat elusive topic, what is clear is that not everyone involved in business, or in fact involved in any human behavior, comes to the table with the same ethical standards or orientations.[9]

marketing ethics

The application of morals to behavior related to the exchange environment.

moral standards

Principles that reflect beliefs about what is ethical and what is unethical.

ethical dilemma

Refers to a situation in which one chooses from alternative courses of actions, each with different ethical implications.

relativism

A term that reflects the degree to which one rejects moral standards in favor of the acceptability of some action. This way of thinking rejects absolute principles in favor of situation-based evaluations.

Marketing ethics is the application of morals to business behavior related to the exchange environment. Generally, good ethics conforms to the notion of "right," and a lack of ethics conforms to the notion of "wrong." Highly ethical behaviors are those that are fair, just, and do not cause one to feel shame.[10] Ethical values can be highly influenced by one's moral standards. **Moral standards** are principles reflecting one's beliefs about what is ethical and unethical. More simply, moral standards are rules distinguishing right from wrong. The Golden Rule, "Do unto others as you would have them do unto you," is one such ethical principle.

An **ethical dilemma** refers to a situation in which one chooses from alternative courses of actions, each with different ethical implications. Each individual develops a philosophy or way of thinking that guides decisions when facing moral dilemmas. Many people use moral standards to guide their actions when confronted with an ethical dilemma. Other people adapt an ethical orientation that rejects absolute principles. These individuals determine ethics based more on the social or cultural acceptability of behavior. To them, an act conforming to social or cultural norms is an ethical act. The sections below contrast these two ethical orientations.

Relativism

Relativism is a term that reflects the degree to which one rejects moral standards in favor of the acceptability of some action. This way of thinking rejects absolute principles in favor of situation-based evaluations. Thus, an action judged as ethical in one situation is unethical in another.

Idealism

In contrast, **idealism** is a term that reflects the degree to which one bases one's morality on moral standards. Someone who is an ethical idealist will try to apply ethical principles like the Golden Rule in all ethical dilemmas.

For example, a student may face an ethical dilemma when taking a test. Another student may arrange to exchange multiple-choice responses to a test via electronic text messages. This represents an ethical dilemma because there are alternative courses of action each with differing moral implications. An ethical idealist may apply a rule that cheating is always wrong and therefore would not likely participate in the behavior. An ethical relativist may instead argue that the behavior is acceptable because many other students are doing the same thing. In other words, the consensus is that this sort of cheating is acceptable, so this student would be likely to go ahead and participate in the behavior. Marketing researchers, marketing managers, and even consumers face ethical dilemmas practically every day.

idealism

A term that reflects the degree to which one bases one's morality on moral standards.

General Rights and Obligations of Concerned Parties

Everyone involved in marketing research can face an ethical dilemma. For this discussion, we can divide stakeholders involved in research into four parties:[11]

1. The people actually performing the research; the "doers" of research
2. The research client, sponsor, or the management team requesting the research, who can be thought of as "users" of marketing research
3. The research participants, meaning the actual research respondents or subjects who are the source of the data
4. Society at large, which forms governments that oversee all aspects of commerce and benefits from effective research.

Each party has certain rights and obligations toward the other parties. Exhibit 4.3 diagrams these relationships. The research process works correctly and benefits stakeholders when all parties respect their respective rights and obligations. Like the rest of business, research works best when all parties act ethically.

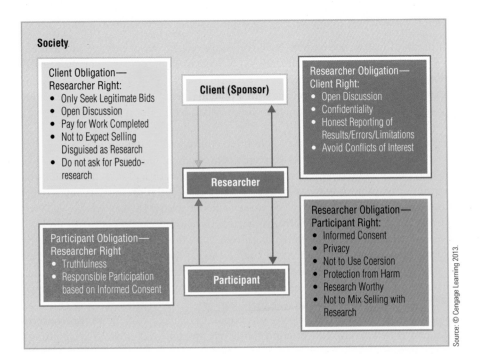

EXHIBIT 4.3

The Rights and Obligations of Marketing Research

Source: © Cengage Learning 2013.

Rights and Obligations of the Research Participant

Most marketing research takes place with the research participant's consent. In other words, the participation is active. Increasingly, marketing researchers rely on participants' passive participation. The researcher's job requires a degree of nosiness that potentially brings some vulnerability to the participant. Thus, marketing researchers need to examine the question, "What ethical duties and obligations are exchanged between the researcher and the research participant?"

Participant's Right to Privacy

informed consent

When an individual understands what the researcher wants him or her to do and agrees to the research study.

Traditional survey research requires that a respondent voluntarily answer questions in one way or another. This may involve answering questions on the phone, responding to an e-mail request, or even sending a completed questionnaire by regular mail. In these cases, **informed consent** means that the individual understands what the researcher wants him or her to do and agrees to be a participant in the research study. Before asking questions, the interviewer provides an opportunity for the participant to decline the invitation. In other cases, research participants may not be aware that someone is monitoring them in some way. The ethical responsibilities vary depending on whether participation is active or passive.

Active Research

Americans traditionally relished their privacy. The right to privacy is an important issue in marketing research. If a research participant believes the researcher is being too nosy, he or she has the right to refuse participation. However, critics argue that the very old, very young, the poorly educated, and other underprivileged individuals are sometimes unaware of their right to provide informed consent or refuse. Although the researcher should provide a clear indication of the nature of the questions, some surveys initially ask questions that are relatively innocuous and then move to questions of a highly personal nature. The respondent should know their right to refuse includes breaking off an interview at any time.

The privacy issue goes further into other ways that a research project could invade a person's privacy. Do any questions below illustrate any privacy concerns?

■ "When is a telephone call that interrupts family dinner an invasion of privacy?"
■ "When is an e-mail requesting response to a 30-minute survey an invasion of privacy?"
■ "When is capturing information from one's Facebook site an invasion of privacy?"
■ "When is a researcher's follow-up to a previous response an invasion of privacy?"

As a practical matter, respondents may feel more relaxed about privacy and feel better informed about the consent decision if they know who is conducting the survey. Thus, field interviewers should state up front that they are legitimate researchers and name the organization they are working for upon initial contact with a potential respondent. In a face-to-face interview, interviewers should wear official nametags and provide identification giving their name and the names of their companies.

do-not-call legislation

Restricts any telemarketing effort from calling consumers who either register with a no-call list or who request not to be called.

Generally, interviewing firms practice common courtesy by trying not to interview late in the evening or at other inconvenient times. Research companies should adhere to the principles of the "do-not-call" policy and should respect consumers' "Internet privacy" even if the company might be technically exempt from the legislation.[12] **Do-not-call legislation** restricts any telemarketing effort from calling consumers either who register with a national or statewide no-call list or who ask the firm directly not to call. U.S. legislators aimed these laws at sales-related calls but legislation in several states, including California, Louisiana, and Rhode Island, extends the laws to apply to "those that seek marketing information." Thus, the legislation effectively protects consumers' privacy from researchers as well as salespeople.[13] Research firms, particularly in these states, should consider subscribing to the do-not-call registry to avoid breeching the law or ethical practice.

Consumers often are confused about the difference between telemarketing efforts and true marketing research. Part of this is because unscrupulous telemarketing firms sometimes disguise their sales efforts by opening conversations with "we are doing research." The resulting confusion contributes to both increased refusal rates and lower trust from the public. A 1980 public opinion poll found that 19 percent of Americans reported refusing to participate in a marketing survey within the previous year. That number approached 50 percent by 2001 when a majority of Americans also expressed doubt that marketers would take actions to protect a consumer's privacy.[14]

Companies using the Internet to do marketing research also face legislative changes. Much of this legislation aims at properly notifying respondents about the collection of data and informing them of to whom the results will be provided. Researchers should make sure to provide consumers a clear and easy way either to consent to participation in active research on the Internet or to opt out easily. Furthermore, companies should ensure that the information consumers send via the Internet is secure.[15]

Passive Research

Passive research involves different types of privacy issues. Generally, researchers do not view unobtrusive observation of public behavior in places such as stores, airports, sidewalks, and museums as an invasion of a person's privacy. Researchers justify this type of observation on the fact that the participants are willfully performing the actions publicly and they are indeed anonymous so long as they are never identified by name nor is any attempt made to identify them. They are "faces in the crowd." As long as the behavior observed is typical of behavior commonly conducted in public, then there is no invasion of privacy; the public behaviors are tantamount to **implicit consent**. In contrast, recording behavior not typically conducted in public would be a violation of privacy. For example, recording people (without consent) taking showers at a health club using hidden cameras is inappropriate, even if the research addresses ways of improving the shower experience.

implicit consent
Behaviors that are openly performed in public implies that one is willing to have others observe them.

Technology improvements also provide new ways of collecting data passively that have privacy implications.[16] Researchers are very interested in consumers' online behavior. As described in Chapter 2, the paths that consumers take while browsing the Internet can be extremely useful in understanding what kinds of information consumers value most. Researchers sometimes have legitimate reasons to use this data such as improving consumers' abilities to make wise decisions. Some type of consent, either implied or informed, provides a means of ensuring that the research is ethical. This is particularly so when the data are shared with companies who may follow up with some sort of sales appeal. A statement such as this can provide consent:

> *From time to time, the opportunity to share your information with other companies arises and this could be very helpful to you in offering you desirable product choices. We respect your privacy, however, and if you do not wish us to share this information, we will not. Would you like us to share your information with other companies?*

- *Yes, you can share the information*
- *No, please keep my information private*

Internet browsing is not as public as walking down the sidewalk. However, consumers should consider their browsing history as public information in most cases. If this makes a consumer uncomfortable, he or she can set the security level of the computer to high and make sure that all the "cookies" are erased when the browser is closed. If the consumer expresses no concern through their actions or instructions, then he or she is providing the equivalent of implicit consent to allow firms to use the browsing histories recorded in these files. Similarly, postings on social networking sites are public and placing it in a forum like this provides implicit consent for firms to extract information from the content. The safest rule for a consumer concerned about privacy is not to put anything on a virtual social network that he or she would not want to broadcast to the public.

Not all of attempts to gain information from one's computer behavior are legitimate. Most readers have probably encountered spyware on their home computer. **Spyware** is software placed on your computer while browsing the Web without consent or knowledge. This software then tracks your usage and sends the information back through the Internet to the source. Then, based on these usage patterns, the user will receive push technology advertising, usually in the form of pop-up ads. Sometimes, the user will receive so many pop-up ads that the computer becomes unusable. The use of spyware is illegitimate when done without consent, thus violating the right to privacy and confidentiality.

spyware
Software placed on a computer without consent or knowledge of the user.

The Obligation to Be Truthful

When someone willingly consents to participate actively, the researcher assumes he or she will provide truthful answers. Honest cooperation is the primary obligation of the research participant. In return for being truthful, the subject has the right to expect confidentiality. **Confidentiality** means that researchers will not share any individual's information with others. Individuals who truly believe that the researcher maintain confidentiality are more likely to respond truthfully, even about potentially sensitive topics. Likewise, the researcher and research sponsor also may expect the respondent to maintain confidentiality. For instance, if the research involves a new food product from Nabisco, then they may not want the respondent to discuss the idea for fear that the idea may fall into the competition's hands. Thus, confidentiality helps ensure truthful responses and protects sensitive information.

confidentiality
The information involved in a research will not be shared with others.

Kids' Stuff Is Complicated

Children are involved in at least half of all spending in the United States. Thus, researchers need input from them to be able to deliver high-value products. However, legislators rightly have special concern for privacy when business interacts with children in some way. Researchers have a special obligation to ensure the safety of children. COPPA, the Children's Online Privacy Protection Act, defines a child as anyone under the age of thirteen. Anyone engaging in contact with a child through the Internet is obligated to obtain parental consent before a child can provide any personal information or identification. Therefore, a researcher collecting a child's name, phone number, or e-mail address without parental consent is violating the law. Although the law and business ethics do not always correspond, in this case, it is probably pretty clear that a child's personal information should not be collected without parental consent.

Policy makers consider children vulnerable because they may not be able to reasonably reach decisions that keep them safe in all cases. Should researchers allow a child to consent to participating in research without parental consent? Even something as innocuous as offering a child a cupcake for participating in research might not meet all parents' approval. Clearly, researchers should interview children under a certain age only in the presence of a parent. However, will the child respond the same way when a parent is present as when alone? Imagine asking a fourteen-year-old if he or she enjoys smoking cigarettes. How might a parent's presence change the response?[17] The age of consent for marketing research isn't clear even when research is within the guidelines of COPPA. To be safe, researchers should conduct most standard research with children under the age of sixteen only with parental consent. When the research involves matters that are for "mature audiences," such as human sexuality or alcohol consumption, then the researchers should seek parental consent for anyone under the age of eighteen.

● ● ● ● ● ●

Researchers have a special duty to protect children involved in research.

Doing research with children can yield extremely useful information. However, it is also more risky than doing research with adults. When in doubt, researchers should consider how they would like to see their own child treated and then go even further to make sure that there are no ethical problems with the use of children in research.

Deception and the Right to Be Informed

Experimental Designs

Experimental manipulations often involve some degree of deception. In fact, without some deception, a researcher would never know if a research subject was responding to the actual manipulation or to their perception of the experimental variable. This is why researchers sometimes use a placebo.

A **placebo** is a false experimental effect used to create the perception of a true effect. Imagine two consumers, each participating in a study of the effect of a new herbal supplement on hypertension. One consumer receives a packet containing the citrus-flavored supplement, which is meant to be mixed in water and drunk with breakfast. The other also receives a packet, but in this case, the packet contains a mixture that will simply color the water and provide a citrus flavor. The second consumer also believes he or she is drinking the actual supplement. In this way, the psychological effect is the same on both consumers, and any actual difference in hypertension must be due to the actual herbs contained in the supplement. Interestingly, experimental subjects often display a placebo effect in which the mere belief that some treatment has been applied causes some effect.

This type of deception can be considered ethical. Primarily, researchers conducting an experiment must generally (1) gain the willful cooperation of the research subject and (2) fully explain the actual experimental variables applied following the experiment's completion. Every experiment should include a **debriefing** session. The debriefing session is the researcher's opportunity to fully inform subjects about the experiment's purpose and provide a chance for them to ask any questions that they may have about the experiment.

Mystery Shopper Research

Researchers sometimes will even withhold the actual research questions from respondents in simple descriptive research. A distinction can thus be made between deception and discreet silence. For instance, sometimes providing the actual research question to respondents is simply providing them more information than they need to give a valid response. A researcher may ask questions about the perceived price of a product when his or her real interest is in how consumers form quality impressions.

Research aimed at marketing employees also sometimes involves deception. For instance, employees are sometimes passive respondents in observational research involving a mystery shopper. **Mystery shoppers** are employees of a research firm paid to "pretend" to be actual shoppers. A mystery shopper would rarely identify him- or herself as anything other than a customer. However, because most employees perform their jobs in public, and perform behaviors that are easily observable, mystery shopper observation does not invade the employee's privacy. Companies in nearly all areas of retailing and other services use mystery shoppers to gather performance information.

Protection from Harm

Researchers should do everything they can to make sure that participation in research does not endanger participants' safety in any respect. Most marketing research does not expose participants to any harm. However, the researcher should consider every possibility. For example, if the research involves tasting food or drink, the possibility exists that a research participant could have a severe allergic reaction. Similarly, researchers studying retail and workplace atmospherics often manipulate odors by injecting certain scents into the air.[18] The researcher is sometimes in a difficult situation. He or she has to somehow find out what things the subject is allergic to, without revealing the actual experimental conditions. One way the researcher can do this is by asking the subjects to provide a list of potential allergies ostensibly as part of a separate research project.

placebo
A false experimental effect used to create the perception that some effect has been administered.

debriefing
Research subjects are fully informed and provided with a chance to ask any questions they may have about the experiment.

mystery shoppers
Employees of a research firm that are paid to pretend to be actual shoppers.

Other times, research may involve some potential psychological harm. This may come in the form of stress or in the form of some experimental treatment, which questions some strongly held conviction. For instance, a researcher studying helping behavior may lead a subject to believe that another person is being harmed in some way. In this way, the researcher can see how much a subject can withstand before doing something to help another person. In reality, the other person is usually a research confederate simply pretending to be in pain. Three key questions that can determine whether the experimental procedures treat a research participant unethically are:

1. Has the research subject provided consent to participate in an experiment?
2. Is the research subject subjected to substantial physical or psychological trauma?
3. Can the research subject be easily returned to his or her initial state?

The issue of consent is tricky in experiments because the researcher cannot reveal exactly what the research is about ahead of time without threatening the validity of the experiment. In addition, the researcher generally provides experimental research subjects with some incentive to participate. We will have more on this later in the book, but ethically speaking, the incentives should always be noncoercive. In other words, a faculty member seeking volunteers should not withhold a student's grade if he or she does not participate in an experiment. Thus, the volunteer should provide consent without fear of harm for saying no and with some idea about any potential risk involved.

If the answer to the second question is yes, then the researcher should not go forward with the research design. If the answer to the second question is no and consent is obtained, then the manipulation does not present an ethical problem, and the researcher can proceed.

The third question is really helpful in understanding how far one can go in applying manipulations to a research subject. If the answer to the third question is no, then the research should not be conducted. Consider the use of hypnosis in marketing research Advertising researchers sometimes use hypnosis to reach deep thoughts of focus group participants.[19] If however, a research design involved inducing hypnosis that caused a consumer to make a large number of purchases, causing debt and trauma, returning the respondent to the original state may be difficult. If so, that application of hypnosis is inappropriate. If the answer to this question is yes, then the manipulation is ethical.

human subjects review committee

Carefully reviews proposed research design to try to make sure that no harm can come to any research participant. Otherwise known as an Institutional Review Board or IRB.

Institutional Review Board

Another name for a human subjects review committee.

Many research companies and practically all universities now maintain a **human subjects review committee**. This committee carefully reviews a proposed research design to try to make sure that no harm can come to any research participant. A side benefit of this committee is that it can also review the procedures to make sure that the research design does not create any legal problems. Sometimes, an organization may use the name **Institutional Review Board** (IRB) to refer to this committee.

Rights and Obligations of the Client Sponsor (User)

Ethical Behavior between Buyer and Seller

The general business ethic expected between a purchasing agent and a sales representative should hold in a marketing research situation. For example, if a purchasing agent has already decided to purchase a product from a friend, the agent would be acting unethically by soliciting bids from others because those bids have no chance of being accepted. Similarly, a client seeking research should only seek bids from firms that have a legitimate chance of actually doing the work. In addition, any section on the ethical obligation of a research client would be remiss not to mention that the user is obligated to pay the provider the agreed-upon wage within the agreed-upon time.

An Open Relationship with Research Suppliers

The client/sponsor has an obligation to encourage the researcher to seek out the truth objectively. Managers and researchers must openly and honestly discuss the key issues and come to a consensus about what decision statement(s), and thus what research question(s), best describes the need for the research. The more a decision maker refuses to answer the researcher's questions, the less likely are the parties to come to a useful consensus about the research. Therefore, the researcher is better off not taking this particular job.

When Nobody Is Looking?

An old adage says that one's character is defined not by doing the right thing when people are looking, but by the actions one takes when nobody is looking. Sometimes the stakeholders involved in research are presented with subtle or perhaps even invisible ways to influence the research process in potentially unethical ways. The client, for example, can simply withhold information. In some instances, the decision to proceed with a project may have already been made behind the scenes but not disclosed to the researcher. Client firms also have "donated" coupons for new products to schools while a test market for that product was under way. The decision makers were motivated to show that their new product ideas would be successful. The results biased the research.

Researchers can also subtly cross the boundary between good and questionable ethical practices. One way that this takes place is in the tactics used to try to get research respondents to agree to participate. Consider these attempts at social persuasion:

- Tell the potential respondent that the interview will take only a few minutes when the average time to complete is more like 15 to 18 minutes.
- Tell the potential respondent that the interview contains only 5 questions and will take only 2 minutes. However, after responding to the fifth question, the respondent is informed that another set of questions has just been added to the survey.
- Telling the potential respondent that "only a few select individuals" qualify to give their opinion when the survey sample is really broad-based.

Field interviewers sometimes practice these techniques even when instructed not to do so. Thus, researchers need to be extremely cautious about the amount of pressure put on research assistants to get participants. Too much pressure may cause the assistants to cross the line and perform actions that question the character of the research firm and the industry overall.

Sources: Bednall, H.B.D., S. Adam, and K. Polcinski (2010), "Using Compliance Techniques to Boost Telephone Response Rates," *International Journal of Market Research*, 52 (2), 155–68; Slsmadi, S. (2010), "Marketing Research and Social Responsibility: Ethical Obligations toward the Society," *Journal of Accounting—Business & Management*, 17 (1), 42–47.

Once agreed upon, the research sponsor should support the research team in their effort to obtain information and perform analyses that will provide answers to the research questions. This means that the client needs to be open to actually using the research results. All too often, decision makers want the research results only if they will support some preconceived answer—in other words the decision is already made and the research is needed for political cover. This is unethical. Time is simply too valuable to ask a researcher to perform a project when the sponsoring agent knows ahead of time that the results will not be used. Unfortunately, as a firm's performance suffers and as top management fails to show ethical leadership, that company tends to practice less ethical research practices as well.[20]

> *"We are what we repeatedly do. Excellence then is not act but a habit."*
>
> —ARISTOTLE

An Open Relationship with Interested Parties

Conclusions should be based on data—not conjecture. Users should not knowingly disseminate conclusions from a research project in a manner that twists them into some desirable interpretation. Twisting the results in a self-serving manner, or to support some political position, poses serious ethical questions. Such actions are morally inappropriate and the client-researcher relationship should be open enough to avoid encouraging anything but honest results.

Advocacy research—research undertaken to support a specific claim in a legal action or to represent some advocacy group—puts a client in a unique situation. Researchers often conduct advocacy research in their role as an expert witness. For instance, a law firm may ask a researcher to present evidence addressing how much a "knock-off" brand diminishes the value of a better-known name brand. In conventional research, the researcher weighs research attributes such as sample size, profiles of people actually interviewed, and number of questions asked, against cost. Trade-offs become appropriate if the research is too costly to conduct relative to the benefit. However, a court's

advocacy research

Research undertaken to support a specific claim in a legal action or represent some advocacy group.

opinion on whether research results are reliable might rely exclusively on any one specific research aspect. Thus, an opposing attorney may magnify the slightest variation from technically correct procedures attempting to demonstrate to the judge or jury that the project is flawed.

Advocacy research presents a number of serious issues that can lead to an ethical dilemma:

- Lawyers' first responsibility is to represent their clients. Therefore, they might not be interested as much in the truth as they are in evidence that supports their client's position. Presenting accurate research results may harm the client.
- A researcher should be objective. However, he or she runs the risk of conducting research that does not support the desired position. In this case, an unethical lawyer may ask the researcher to present the results in a manner that obfuscates the truth.
- Should the lawyer (in this case a user of research) ask the researcher to take the stand and present an inaccurate picture of the results?

Ethically, the attorney should certainly not put the researcher on the stand and encourage an act of perjury. The attorney may hope to ask specific questions that are so limited that taken alone, they may appear to support the client. However, this is risky because the opposing attorney likely also has an expert witness that can suggest questions for cross-examination. Returning to our branding example, if the research does not support an infringement of the known brand's name, then the brand name's attorney should probably not ask the researcher take the stand.

The question of advocacy research is one of objectivity: Can the researcher seek out the truth when the sponsoring client wishes to support its position at a trial? The ethical question stems from a conflict between legal ethic and research ethic. Although the courts have set judicial standards for marketing research methodology, perhaps only the client and individual researcher can resolve this question.

Privacy

The privacy rights of research participants create a privacy obligation on the part of the research client. Suppose a database marketing company is offering a mailing list compiled by screening millions of households to obtain brand usage information. The list would be extremely valuable to your firm, but you suspect the interviewers misled the individuals who filled out the information forms by telling them they were participating in a survey. Would it be ethical to purchase the mailing list? If respondents were deceived into providing their names, the practice is certainly unethical. The client and the research supplier have the obligation to maintain respondents' privacy, so selling it or buying it breaches good ethics.

Consider another example. Sales managers know that a marketing research survey of their business-to-business customers' buying intentions includes a means to attach a customer's name to each questionnaire. This confidential information could be of benefit to a sales representative calling on a specific customer. A client who is ethical would resist the temptation to identify those accounts (that is, those respondents) that are the hottest prospects.

Rights and Obligations of the Researcher

Marketing research firms and marketing research departments should practice good business ethics. Researchers are often the focus of discussions of business ethic because of the necessity that they interact with the public. Several professional organizations offer codes of ethics for marketing researchers, including the American Marketing Association, the European Society for Opinion and Market Research, and the Marketing Research Society.[21] Many of these codes are lengthy and the full contents are available at the associations' Web sites. Key code components generally reflect the content of this chapter and prohibit:

- Representing a sales pitch as marketing research
- Providing the name of respondents who were promised anonymity for some purpose other than the research
- Breaching the confidentiality of the research client or research participant
- Doing research for multiple firms competing in the same market

- Disseminating false or misleading results
- Plagiarizing the work of other researchers
- Violating the integrity of data gathered in the field

In addition, the researchers have rights. In particular, once a research consulting firm is hired to conduct some research, they have the right to cooperation from the sponsoring client. Also, the researchers have the right to be paid for the work they do as long as it is done professionally. Sometimes, the client may not like the results. But not liking the results is no basis for not paying. The client should pay the researcher for competent work in full and in a timely manner.

The Purpose of Research Is Research

Mixing Sales and Research

Consumers sometimes agree to participate in an interview that is supposedly pure research, but it eventually becomes obvious that the interview is really a sales pitch in disguise. This is unprofessional at best and fraudulent at worst. The Federal Trade Commission (FTC) has indicated that it is illegal to use any plan, scheme, or ruse that misrepresents the true status of a person seeking admission to a prospect's home, office, or other establishment. No research firm or basic marketing researcher should engage in any sales attempts. Applied market researchers working for the sponsoring company should also avoid overtly mixing research and sales. However, the line is becoming less clear with increasing technology.

Research That Isn't Research

Consider the following typical exchange between a product manager and a marketing researcher. The manager wants to hire the firm to do a test market for a new product:

Researcher:	*What if the test results are favorable?*
Product manager:	*Why, we'll launch the product nationally, of course.*
Researcher:	*And if the results are unfavorable?*
Product manager:	*They won't be. I'm sure of that.*
Researcher:	*But just suppose they are.*
Product manager:	*I don't think we should throw out a good product just because of one little market test.*
Researcher:	*Then why test?*
Product manager:	*Listen, Smith, this is a major product introduction. It's got to have some research behind it.*

The product manager really wants research that will justify a decision he or she has already made. If the test market's results contradict the decision, the product manager will almost certainly disregard the research. This type of study falls into the category of **pseudo-research** because the purpose is not to gather information for marketing decisions but to bolster a point of view and satisfy other needs.

In this situation, a researcher should walk away from the project if it appears that management strongly desires the research to support a predetermined opinion only. Although it is a fairly easy matter for an outside researcher to walk away from such a job, it is another matter for an in-house researcher to refuse such a job. Thus, avoiding pseudo-research is a right of the researcher but an obligation for the manager.

Occasionally, managers request marketing research simply to pass blame for failure to another area. A product manager may deliberately request a research study with no intention of paying attention to the findings and recommendations. The manager knows that the particular project is in trouble but plays the standard game to cover up for his or her mismanagement. If the project fails, marketing research will become the scapegoat. The ruse may involve a statement something like this: "Well, research should have identified the problem earlier!"

Push Polls

Politicians concocted and specialize in a particular type of pseudo-research A **push poll** is telemarketing under the guise of research intended to "sell" a particular political position of point of view. The purpose of the poll is to push consumers into a predetermined response. For instance, a polling organization calls thousands of potential voters inviting each to participate in a survey. The interviewer then may ask loaded questions that put a certain spin on a candidate. "Do you think that candidate X, who is involved with people linked to scandal and crime, can be trusted with

pseudo-research

Conducted not to gather information for marketing decisions but to bolster a point of view or satisfy other needs.

push poll

Telemarketing under guise of research intended to "sell" a particular political position of point of view.

©AP Photo/Beth Hall

the responsibility of office?" This is a push poll. An honest question may simply ask how much candidate X can be trusted.

Push polling doesn't always involve political candidates. Residents do not always welcome new Walmart locations based on factors, including the increase in traffic and congestion that the store can bring to an area. In 2009, residents of Chicago received a polling call that went something like this:

> *Mayor Daley says that the proposed Walmart would bring over 400 jobs to this area and allow neighborhood residents access to fresh food. Do you support the new Walmart store's construction?*

The results indicated that over 70 percent of residents supported the new store.[22] However, the framing of the question by referencing the mayor and the mention of jobs without mentioning potential problems almost certainly swayed the results.

Service Monitoring

Occasionally, the line between research and customer service is not completely clear. For instance, Toyota may survey all of its new car owners after the first year of ownership. Although the survey appears to be research, it may also provide information that could be used to correct some issue with the customer. For example, if the research shows that a customer is dissatisfied with the way the car handles, Toyota could follow up with the specific customer. The follow-up could result in changing the tires of the car, resulting in a smoother and quieter ride, as well as a more satisfied customer. Should a pattern develop showing other customers with the same opinion, Toyota may need to switch the original equipment tires used on this particular car.

Both research and customer service are involved and because the car is under warranty, no selling attempt exists. Researchers often design satisfaction surveys that include a means of opening a dialog between the company and the customer. Such practice is acceptable as long as the researcher makes the follow-up contact optional. The contact may provide a means of avoiding an experience that diminishes the value of a product.

Misrepresentation of Research

Obviously, one sees that an ethical researcher does not misrepresent study results. This means, for instance, that the researcher states the statistical accuracy of a test precisely and does not overstate or understate the meaning of the findings. Both the researcher and the client share this obligation. Consider a researcher reporting a positive relationship between advertising spending and sales. The researcher may also discover that this relationship disappears when the primary competitors' prices are taken into account. In other words, the competitor's prices account for at least part of the

"He uses statistics as a drunken man uses a lamppost—for support rather than illumination."

—ANDREW LANG

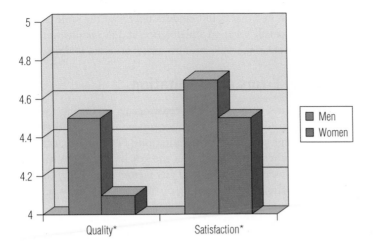

Source: © Cengage Learning 2013.

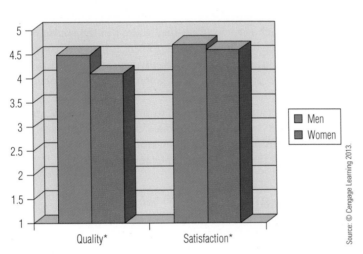

EXHIBIT **4.4**
How Results Can Be
Misrepresented in a Report
or Presentation

observed fluctuation in sales. Thus, it would be questionable, to say the least, to report a finding suggesting that sales could be increased by increasing ad spending without also mentioning the role that competitors' price play in explaining sales.

Honesty in Presenting Results

Misrepresentation can also occur in the way a researcher presents results. For instance, charts can be created that make a very small difference appear very big. Likewise, they can be altered to make a meaningful difference seem small. Exhibit 4.4 illustrates this effect. Each chart presents exactly the same data. The data represent consumer responses to service quality ratings and satisfaction ratings. Both quality and satisfaction are collected on a 5-point (strongly disagree to strongly agree) scale. In frame A, the chart appears to show meaningful differences between men and women, particularly for the service-quality rating. However, notice that the scale range is shown as 4 to 5. In frame B, the researcher presents the same data but shows the full scale range (1 to 5). Now, the differences are reported as trivial.

All charts and figures should reflect fully the relevant range of values reported by respondents. If the scale range is from 1 to 5, then the chart should reflect a 1-to-5 range unless there is some value that is simply not used by respondents. If no or only a very few respondents had reported a 1 for their service quality or satisfaction rating, then it may be appropriate to show the range as 2 to 5. However, if there is any doubt, the researcher should show the full scale range.

The American Marketing Association's Code of Ethic states that, "a user of research shall not knowingly disseminate conclusions from a given research project or service that are inconsistent with or not warranted by the data." A dramatic example of a violation of this principle occurred in an advertisement of a cigarette smoker study. The advertisement compared two brands and stated that "of those expressing a preference, over 65 percent preferred" the advertised brand to a competing brand. The misleading portion of this reported result was that most of the respondents did *not* express a preference; they indicated that both brands tasted about the same. Thus, only a very small percentage of those studied actually revealed a preference, and the results were somewhat misleading. Such shading of results violates the obligation to report accurate findings.

Honesty in Reporting Errors and Limitation

Likewise, researchers should not keep any major error occurring during the course of the study a secret. Hiding errors or variations from the proper procedures can distort or shade the results. Similarly, every research design presents some limitations. For instance, the sample size may be smaller than ideal. The researcher should point out the key limitations in the research report and presentation. In this way, the users can understand any factors that qualify the findings. The decision maker needs this information before deciding on any risky course of action.

Confidentiality

Confidentiality comes into play in several ways. The researcher must abide by any confidentiality agreement with research participants. For instance, a researcher conducting a descriptive research survey may have identified each participant's e-mail address in the course of conducting the research. After seeing the results, the client may ask for the e-mail addresses as a logical prospect list. However, as long as the researcher assured each participant's confidentiality, he or she cannot provide the e-mail addresses to the firm. Indeed, a commitment of confidentiality also helps build trust among survey respondents.[23]

The marketing researcher often is obligated to protect the confidentiality of the research sponsor. In fact, business clients value marketing researchers' confidentiality more than any other attribute of a research firm.[24] Researchers must honor all implied and expressed promises of confidentiality, whether made to a research participant or research client.

The Role of Society at Large

Societies create and condone governments that oversee and regulate business activities. The do-not-call legislation provides an example of a way that governments restrict marketing research behavior. Society has an obligation to be fair and enact restrictions only when the benefits are justified in light of the difficulties those restrictions create. Furthermore, one point summarizes all the ethical obligations of marketing research in general. Marketing research offers benefits for individual members of and for society at large. However, research often involves some inconvenience in the forms of intrusions like surveys. The potential benefits of the research should always outweigh the burdens placed on members of society. When this is true, the research is justified.

The Researcher and Conflicts of Interest

Imagine a researcher conducting a test market for an Apple iPad that allows interactive video among its benefits. Just after conducting the research, the same researcher is contacted by Motorola. Motorola, who has yet to develop video capability, wants research that addresses whether or not an interactive video feature enhances the tablet market. The researcher is now in a difficult position. Certainly, an ethical dilemma exists presenting multiple choices to the researcher, including the following:

■ Agreeing to do the research for Motorola and using some results from the Apple study to prepare a report and recommendation for Motorola
■ Agreeing to sell the new concept to Motorola without doing any additional research. In other words, provide Apple's company secrets to Motorola
■ Conducting an entirely new project for Motorola without revealing any of the results or ideas from the Apple study
■ Turning down the chance to do the study without revealing any information about Apple to Motorola

Which is the best choice? Obviously, both of the first two options violate the principle of maintaining client confidentiality. Thus, both are unethical. The third choice, conducting an entirely new study, may be an option. However, it may prove nearly impossible to do the entire project as if the Apple study had never been done. Even with the best of intentions, the researcher may inadvertently violate confidentiality with Apple. The last choice is the best option from a moral standpoint. It avoids any potential **conflict of interest**. In other words, actions that would best serve one client, Motorola, would be detrimental to another client, Apple. Generally, it is best to avoid working for two direct competitors.

This would be a good time to revisit the opening chapter vignette. Does the situation present the researcher with any potential conflicts of interest? How can they be addressed?

conflict of interest

Occurs when one researcher works for two competing companies.

A Final Note on Ethics

Certainly, there are researchers who would twist results for a client or who would fabricate results for personal gain. However, these are not professionals. When one is professional, one realizes that one's actions not only have personal implications, but also implications for one's field. Indeed, just a few unscrupulous researchers can give the field a bad name. Thus, researchers should maintain the highest integrity in their work to protect our industry. Research participants should also play their role, or else the data they provide will not lead to better products for all consumers. Finally, the research users must also follow good professional ethic in their treatment of researchers and research results. When all three parties participate with integrity, consumers in general, and society overall, gain the most benefit from professional marketing research.

TIPS OF THE TRADE

- A good way to get started in the marketing research industry is to target either a large marketing research firm or a local research firm with offers to serve as an intern. An internship will provide insight and experience that can provide a leg up on others in getting the job.
- When a company faces a very emotional decision, it is usually better to have the research needed to address the related research questions done by an outside firm.
- Those involved in research should consider the position of others involved in the process. When considering conducting or using research in some manner, one way to help ensure fair treatment of others involved

in research is to consider whether you would like to be treated in this manner or whether you would like someone to treat a close member of your family in such a manner.
- Research with particularly vulnerable segments such as children involves special care. When doing research with children under the age of sixteen, parental consent is nearly always needed.
- Even the appearance of a conflict of interest can taint the research and the researcher. So, the wise researchers stay away from such appearances.

Source: © Cengage Learning 2013.

∷ SUMMARY

1. **Know when research should be conducted externally and when it should be done internally.** The company who needs the research is not always the best company to perform the research. Sometimes an outside supplier is more effective. An outside agency is better when the company desires a fresh perspective, when it would be difficult for inside researchers to be objective, and when the outside firm has some special expertise. In contrast, research in-house is better when the company needs it done very quickly, when the project requires close collaboration of many employees within the company, when the budget for the project is limited, and when secrecy is a major concern. The decision to go outside or stay inside for research depends on these particular issues.

2. **Be familiar with the types of jobs, job responsibilities, and career paths available within the marketing research industry.** A marketing research function may be organized in any number of ways depending on a firm's size, business, and stage of research sophistication. Marketing research managers must remember they are managers, not just researchers. Marketing research offers many career opportunities. Entry-level jobs may involve simple tasks such as data entry or performing survey research. A research analyst may be the next step on the career path. Whereas there are several intermediate positions that differ depending on whether one works for a small or large firm, the director of marketing research is the chief information officer in charge of marketing information systems and research projects. The director plans, executes, and controls the marketing research function.

3. **Define ethics and understand how it applies to marketing research.** Marketing ethics is the application of morals to behavior related to the exchange environment. Generally, good ethic conforms to the notion of "right" and a lack of ethic conforms to the notion of "wrong." Those involved in marketing research face numerous ethical dilemmas. Researchers serve clients or, put another way, the doers of research serve the users. A doer may find him/herself tempted to compromise professional standards in an effort to please the user. After all, the user pays the bills. Given the large number of ethical dilemmas involved in research, ethics is highly applicable to marketing research.

4. **Appreciate the rights and obligations of (a) research respondents—particularly children, (b) research clients or sponsors, (c) marketing researchers, and (d) society.** Each party involved in research has certain rights and obligations. These are generally interdependent in the sense that one party's right often leads to an obligation for another party. Although the rights and obligations of all parties are important, the obligation of the researcher to protect research participants is particularly important. Experimental manipulations can sometimes expose subjects to some form of harm or involve them in a ruse. The researcher must offer subjects the chance to be informed fully of the true purpose of the research during a debriefing. The researcher must also avoid subjecting participants to undue physical or psychological trauma. In the end, the total value of research should exceed the cost to society.

5. **Avoid situations involving a conflict of interest in performing marketing research.** A marketing research conflict of interest occurs when a researcher faces doing something to benefit one client at the expense of another client. One situation where this occurs is when a researcher could use results obtained in a study done for Brand A to prepare a report for its primary competitor Brand B. The researcher might consider recollecting the data anew for Brand B, but even this opens up the researcher to the appearance of a conflict of interest. The best way to avoid a conflict of interest is to avoid getting involved with multiple projects involving competing firms within some market.

∷ KEY TERMS AND CONCEPTS

advocacy research, 85
confidentiality, 82
conflict of interest, 91
cross-functional teams, 78
custom research, 74
debriefing, 83
director of marketing research, 75
do-not-call legislation, 80
ethical dilemma, 78
forecast analyst, 76
human subjects review committee, 84

idealism, 79
implicit concent, 81
informed consent, 80
in-house research, 70
Institutional Review Board, 84
manager of decision support
   systems, 76
marketing ethics, 78
moral standards, 78
mystery shoppers, 83
outside agency, 70

placebo, 82
pseudo-research, 87
push poll, 87
relativism, 78
research analyst, 75
research assistants, 76
research suppliers, 73
spyware, 81
standardized research
   service, 74
syndicated service, 73

:: QUESTIONS FOR REVIEW AND CRITICAL THINKING

1. What are the conditions that make in-house research preferable? What are the conditions that make outside research preferable? Would the company in the opening vignette have been better off to do the marketing research desired in-house rather than out-house?

2. Read a recent news article from the *Wall Street Journal* or other key source that deals with a new-product introduction. Would you think it would be better for that firm to do research in-house or to use an outside agency? Explain.

3. What might the organizational structure of the research department be like for the following organizations?
   a. A large advertising agency
   b. A founder-owned company that operates a 20-unit restaurant chain
   c. Your university
   d. An industrial marketer with four product divisions
   e. An Internet search engine firm

4. What problems do marketing research directors face in their roles as managers?

5. Search Internet job sites like **www.monster.com.** Try to gather three to five ads that are for marketing research positions of some type. Comment on the salary ranges and expected qualifications listed in these ads.

6. What is a cross-functional team? How is it relevant to marketing research?

7. What is the difference between research and pseudo-research? Cite several examples of each.

8. **ETHICS** What are marketing ethics? How are marketing ethics relevant to research?

9. **ETHICS** What is the difference between ethical relativism and ethical idealism? How might a person with an idealist ethical philosophy and a person with a relativist ethical philosophy differ with respect to including a sales pitch at the end of a research survey?

10. **ETHICS** What obligations does a researcher have with respect to confidentiality?

11. How should a marketing researcher help top management better understand the functions and limitations of research?

12. **ETHICS** List at least one research obligation for researcher participants (respondents), marketing researchers, and research clients (sponsors).

13. **ETHICS** What is a conflict of interest in a research context? How can such conflicts of interest be avoided?

14. **ETHICS** What key questions help resolve the question of whether or not research participants serving as subjects in an experiment are treated ethically?

15. Identify a research supplier in your area and determine what syndicated services and other functions are available to clients.

16. **'NET** Use the Internet to find at least five marketing research firms that perform survey research. List and describe each firm briefly.

17. What actions might the marketing research industry take to convince the public that marketing research is a legitimate activity and that firms that misrepresent their intentions and distort findings to achieve their aims are not true marketing research companies?

18. **ETHICS** Comment on the ethics of the following situations.
   a. A food warehouse club advertises "savings up to 30 percent" after a survey showed a range of savings from 2 to 30 percent below average prices for selected items.
   b. A radio station broadcasts the following message during a syndicated rating service's rating period: "Please fill out your diary" [which lists what media the consumer has been watching or listening to].
   c. A sewing machine retailer advertises a market test and indicates that the regular price will be cut to one-half for three days only.
   d. A researcher tells a potential respondent that an interview will last ten minutes rather than the thirty minutes he or she actually anticipates.
   e. A respondent tells an interviewer that she wishes to cooperate with the survey, but her time is valuable and, therefore, she expects to be paid for the interview.
   f. When you visit your favorite sports team's home page on the Web, you are asked to fill out a registration questionnaire before you enter the site. The team then sells your information (team allegiance, age, address, and so on) to a company that markets sports memorabilia via catalogs and direct mail.
   g. An academic research performs basic research based on Facebook comments from guys talking about women they know using salacious terms.

19. **ETHICS** Comment on the following interview:

   Interviewer: *Good afternoon, sir. My name is Mrs. Johnson, and I am with Counseling Services. We are conducting a survey concerning Memorial Park. Do you own a funeral plot? Please answer yes or no.*
   Respondent: *(pauses)*
   Interviewer: *You do not own a funeral plot, do you?*
   Respondent: *No.*
   Interviewer: *Would you mind if I sent you a letter concerning Memorial Park? Please answer yes or no.*
   Respondent: *No.*
   Interviewer: *Would you please give me your address?*

20. **ETHICS** Try to participate in a survey at a survey website such as **http://www.mysurvey.com or http://www.themsrgroup.com.** Write a short essay response about your experience with particular attention paid to how the sites have protections in place to prevent children from providing personal information.

:: RESEARCH ACTIVITIES

1. **'NET** Find the mission statement of at least three of the top research firms described earlier in the chapter (see Exhibit 4.1). What career opportunities exist at these firms? Would you consider each firm a small, mid-sized, or large firm? How might a job with one of these firms differ from starting your own research business?

2. **'NET—Ethics** One purpose of the United Kingdom's Market Research Society is to set and enforce the ethical standards to be observed by research practitioners. Go to its website at **http://www.mrs.org.uk.** Click on its code of conduct and evaluate it.

Qualitative Research

LEARNING OUTCOMES

After studying this chapter, you should be able to:

1. Contrast qualitative research with quantitative research
2. Know the role of qualitative research in exploratory research designs
3. Describe the basic orientations of qualitative research
4. Recognize common qualitative research tools and know the advantages and limitations of their use
5. Prepare a focus group interview outline
6. Recognize ways social networking and the blogosphere provide opportunities for qualitative research
7. Appreciate the role of exploratory qualitative research in scientific decision making

Chapter Vignette:

What's in the Van?

The Vans brand, with its standard bearer checkerboard slip on tennis shoes, and skateboarding were nearly synonymous until a corporate acquisition pegged the company with ambitious growth objectives. Success at Vans depended too much on the roller coaster skateboard market. Growth would mean changing the meaning of the brand. The "skateboard footwear" company needed to become a "lifestyle" company. Researchers sought to address the question of "What other segments share cultural meanings and values with the skateboard culture?" Answering this question required a deeper interpretation of the meaning of the "Vans" and the skater lifestyle. Questions like these call for qualitative research methods.[1]

So, what exactly is in the mind and heart of a "boarder"? Some men and women simply find skateboarding a good alternative to more mundane exercise routines and Vans shoes are made for skateboarding. However, Vans growth goals meant tapping into more than the utilitarian value of the brand.[2] Researchers addressed the research questions using an ethnographic approach and discovered that a carefree and detached attitude, a free spirit, and a rejection of conventional society were characteristics defining the Vans brand and the skateboard culture. Vans was more about feelings that extend beyond comfortable feet. Vans transition into a lifestyle brand led to the creation of offthewall.tv—a user-inspired television network that captures the brand's essence. The network praises celebrity skateboarders like Tony Hawk but celebrates irreverent humor in many other ways.[3]

The more qualitative research revealed an understanding of the Vans brand, the more managers realized the overlap between skateboarding and the hip-hop culture, or more generally, with urban culture. As a result, "urban" retailers like Moe's & Co. and Journey's were convinced to stock Vans shoes.[4] Eventually, many of these retailers realized they were onto something and opened up skating sections right inside of their stores. This new retail channel represents a source of growth for the Vans brand. A deep understanding of the brand, its core segment, and the segments who share similar values become essential in making good strategic brand decisions.

Courtesy Vans Classic Slip-on

Image courtesy of Susan Van Etten

Introduction: What Is Qualitative Research?

Chemists sometimes use the term *qualitative analysis* to refer to research that determines the makeup of a compound. In other words, the focus is on the inner meaning of specific chemicals—their *qualities*. As the word implies, *qualitative research* is interested more in *qualities* than quantities. Therefore, qualitative marketing research is unique in not applying specific numbers to measure marketing variables or using statistical procedures to specify a relationship's strength numerically.

Describing Qualitative Research

Qualitative marketing research is research that addresses marketing objectives through techniques allowing the researcher to provide elaborate interpretations of market phenomena without depending on numerical measurement. The focus is on discovering new insights and true inner meanings. Qualitative research is very widely applied in practice and many research firms specialize in qualitative research.

Qualitative research designs employ less structure than most quantitative approaches. Participants in qualitative research do not choose numerical (or multiple choice) responses to a specific question. Instead, qualitative approaches are more **researcher-dependent** in that the researcher must extract meaning from open-ended responses, such as text from a recorded interview or a posting on a social networking website like Facebook, or from a collage representing the meaning of some experience, such as skateboarding. The researcher interprets the data to extract its meaning and converts it to information.

Uses of Qualitative Research

Mechanics can't use a hammer to fix everything that is broken. Instead, a mechanic chooses a tool from which a toolbox that he/she believe matches best to a given problem. Marketing research is the same. The researcher has many tools available and the research design should try to match the best tool to the research objective. Also, just as a mechanic is probably not an expert with every tool, each researcher usually has special expertise with a small number of tools. Not every researcher has expertise with tools that would comprise qualitative research.

Generally, the less specific the research objective, the more likely that qualitative research tools will be appropriate. Also, when the emphasis is on a deeper understanding of motivations or on developing novel concepts, qualitative research is very appropriate. The following list represents common situations that often call for qualitative research.[5]

qualitative marketing research

Research that addresses marketing objectives through techniques that allow the researcher to provide elaborate interpretations of market phenomena without depending on numerical measurement; its focus is on discovering new insights and true inner meanings.

researcher-dependent

Research in which the researcher must extract meaning from unstructured responses such as text from a recorded interview or a collage representing the meaning of some experience.

Although we most often think of surveys as ways of collecting quantitative data, we can also use them to collect qualitative data. Take a look at the question that was part of the in-class survey at the left in the screenshot.

Find at least three responses from students in the data and try to interpret the results. What approach best fits your attempt to interpret this data? What do you think (what theory) can be learned from the responses to this question? Compare your interpretation to those of other students. How much do you agree with other students and what do you think is the source of disagreement, if any?

Sean is highly involved in social networking. She started with facebook but now spends most of her time on habbo and friendster spending several hours a day posting news and communicating with her networks. Studying really is getting in the way. One day, her younger sister asks which are the best social networking sites.

Comment on Sean. What do you think she will tell her sister and what are some of Sean's other characteristics?

Close

Source: ©Cengage Learning 2013.

1. When a researcher faces difficulty developing specific and actionable decision statements or research objectives. For instance, if, after several interviews with a research client, a researcher still cannot determine what things he/she needs to measure, qualitative research approaches may help with problem definition and, as a result, identify research questions indicating what to measure.

2. When the research objective involves developing a very detailed and in-depth understanding of some phenomena. Qualitative research tools help reveal the primary themes indicating human motivations and the documentation of activities is usually very complete.

3. When the research objective is to learn how consumers use a product in its natural setting or to learn how to express some concept in colloquial terms. A survey can probably ask many useful questions, but watching how someone actually experiences a product will usually be more insightful. Qualitative research produces many product improvement ideas.

4. When some behavior the researcher is studying is particularly context-dependent—meaning the reasons something is liked or some behavior is performed depends very much on the particular situation surrounding the event. The skating environment frames the situation in which researchers understand the Vans brand best.

5. When the researcher needs a fresh approach. This is particularly the case when quantitative research results on some issue have been less than satisfying. Qualitative tools can yield unique insights, many of which may lead to new product ideas.

Each situation also describes a situation that may require an exploratory orientation. In Chapter 3, we indicated that researchers sometimes need exploratory research just to reach the appropriate decision statement and research objectives. Although equating qualitative research with exploratory research is an oversimplification, the application of qualitative tools can help clear up ambiguity and provide innovative ideas.

Qualitative "versus" Quantitative Research

In social science, one can find many debates about the superiority of qualitative research over quantitative research or vice versa.[6] We'll begin by saying that this is largely a superfluous argument in either direction. The truth is that qualitative research can accomplish research objectives that quantitative research cannot. Similarly truthful, but no more so, quantitative research can accomplish objectives that qualitative research cannot. The key to successfully using either is to match the right approach to the right research context.

Many good research projects combine both qualitative and quantitative research. For instance, developing valid survey measures requires first a deep understanding of the concept measured and second a description of the way people express these perceptions in everyday language. Both of these are tasks best suited for qualitative research. However, validating the measure formally to make sure it can reliably capture the intended concept will likely require quantitative research.[7] Also, qualitative research may be needed to separate symptoms from problems and then quantitative research may follow to test relationships among relevant variables.

Quantitative marketing research addresses research objectives through empirical assessments that involve numerical measurement and analytical approaches. Qualitative research is more apt to stand on its own in the sense that it entails less interpretation. Quantitative research is quite appropriate when a research objective involves a managerial action standard. For example, a salad dressing company considered changing its recipe.[8] Researchers tested the new recipe using a sample of consumers who rated the product using numeric scales. Management established a rule requiring 90 percent confidence that a majority of consumers would rate the new product higher than the old product, replacing the old formula. A project like this can involve both quantitative measurement in the form of numeric rating scales and quantitative analysis in the form of applied statistical procedures.

quantitative marketing research

Addresses research objectives through empirical assessments that involve numerical measurement and statistical analysis.

Contrasting Qualitative with Quantitative Methods

Exhibit 5.1 illustrates some differences between qualitative and quantitative research. Certainly, these are generalities and exceptions apply but it covers some of the key distinctions.

Quantitative researchers direct a considerable amount of activity toward measuring concepts with scales that directly or indirectly provide numeric values. The user inputs the resulting numeric values into statistical computations and hypothesis testing. As will be described in detail later, this process involves comparing numbers in some way. In contrast, qualitative researchers are more interested in observing, listening, and interpreting. The qualitative researcher intimately involves him/herself in the research process and in constructing study results. For these reasons, qualitative research results are relatively researcher-dependent or **subjective**. Different researchers may reach different interpretations based on the same data input. In contrast, when a survey respondent provides a satisfaction score on a quantitative scale, the score is more objective because the number will be the same no matter what researcher is involved in the analysis.

subjective results

Researcher-dependent results meaning different researchers may reach different interpretations about the same piece of data such as a focus group comment

EXHIBIT 5.1

Comparing Qualitative and Quantitative Research

Qualitative Research	Research Aspect	Quantitative Research
Discover Ideas, Used in Exploratory Research with General Research Objects	Common Purpose	Test Hypotheses or Specific Research Questions
Observe and Interpret	Approach	Measure and Test
Unstructured, Free-Form	Data Collection Approach	Structured Response Categories Provided
Researcher Is Intimately Involved. Results Are Subjective.	Researcher Independence	Researcher Uninvolved Observer. Results Are Objective.
Small Samples—Often in Natural Settings	Samples	Large Samples to Produce Generalizable Results (Results that Apply to Other Situations)
Exploratory Research Designs	Most Often Used	Descriptive and Causal Research Designs

Source: © Cengage Learning 2013.

The Other Side of the Coin

Some brands get all the good publicity and seem to have a virtual halo. Business succeeds when consumers like the firm's products—Right? After all, how many social networking sites are dedicated to accumulating "likes"? Product developers need information on what consumers like about brands' current products, but they also need to reliably guess at what people might like. Obviously, brand managers can learn from what customers like, but perhaps brand managers also can learn from what the consumers who don't like the brand have to say.

A great deal of social network sites are devoted to dislike of brands. One Facebook site seeks to find 1,000,000 consumers who hate Heineken. The site's wall and discussion board are filled with sometimes humorous and sometimes crude stories about consumers' true feelings of Heineken beer. Much of it reflects a disdain for all mass-marketed products. Perhaps fewer brands are more written about than Apple. A qualitative analysis of comments about Apple and anti-Apple social network sites and blogs reveals a striking contrast between those who "like" Apple and others. Apple fans' comments focus more on

©AP Photo/Robert Decelis

design (appearance) and the hedonic gratification that comes from owning the latest electronics. In contrast, the comments left by the anti-Apple folks reflect a more utilitarian concern: How does an electronic device's attributes help electronics accomplish tasks? The actual owning does less for these consumers.

Sources: Cliff, E. (2010), "Tablet Mania: What's Now and What's Next?" *Bloomberg Businessweek*, 4201 (October 29), 46. Dolliver, M. (2009), "Mac/PC Duality Isn't so Strict in Real Life," *Adweek*, 50 (October 19), 19. Gruber, T., J. Szmigin, A.E. Reppel, and R. Voss (2008), "Designing and Conducting Online Interviews to Investigate Interesting Consumer Phenomena," *Qualitative Marketing Research: An International Journal*, 11 (June), 256–74.

Qualitative research seldom involves samples with hundreds of respondents. Instead, a handful of consumers are usually the source of qualitative data. This is perfectly acceptable in discovery-oriented research. All ideas still need testing before the adoption decision. Does a smaller sample mean that qualitative research is cheaper than quantitative? Perhaps not. Although researchers observe fewer respondents, the greater researcher involvement in both the data collection and analysis can drive up the costs of qualitative research.

Small samples, interpretive procedures that require subjective judgments and the unstructured interview format all make traditional hypotheses testing difficult with qualitative research. Thus, these procedures are not best suited for drawing definitive conclusions such as results from causal designs involving experiments. These disadvantages for drawing inferences, however, become advantages when the goal is to draw out potential explanations. The researcher spends more time with each respondent and is therefore able to explore much more ground due to the flexibility of the procedures. Even varying interpretations can be advantageous when in the discovery mode because an expansion of the idea space opens up possibilities for innovation.

Qualitative Research and Exploratory Research Designs

When researchers have limited experience or knowledge about an issue, exploratory research is useful. Exploratory research can be an essential first step to a more rigorous, conclusive, confirmatory study by reducing the chance of beginning with an inadequate, incorrect, or misleading set of research objectives.

Philosophically, we can classify research as either exploratory or confirmatory. Confirmatory research tests hypotheses. The test results help decision making by suggesting a specific course of action. Exploratory research, on the other hand, is different and plays a key role in developing ideas that lead to research hypotheses in the first place.

Most exploratory research designs produce **qualitative data**. These data are not characterized by numbers and instead are textual, visual, or oral. The focus of qualitative research is not on numbers but on stories, visual portrayals, meaningful characterizations, interpretations, and other

qualitative data

Data that are not characterized by numbers, and instead are textual, visual, or oral; focus is on stories, visual portrayals, meaningful characterizations, interpretations, and other expressive descriptions.

expressive descriptions. Exploratory designs do not usually produce **quantitative data**, which represent phenomena by assigning numbers in an ordered and meaningful way.

For example, a quantitative researcher may search for numbers that indicate economic trends. This may lead to hypothesis tests concerning how much the economy influences movie consumption. An exploratory researcher is more likely to adopt a qualitative approach that might involve trying to develop a deeper understanding of how families are impacted by changing economic times and why people suffering economically spend scarce resources on movie consumption. This may lead to the development of a hypothesis, but would not test one.

Researchers can sometimes conduct a qualitative study very quickly. Others take a very long time. For example, Coca-Cola researchers can arrange, conduct, and interpret a single focus group analysis involving the company's sales force in a matter of days. This would provide faster results than most descriptive or causal designs. However, other types of qualitative research, such as a participant-observer study aimed at understanding skateboarding, could take months to complete. A qualitative approach can, but does not necessarily, save time.

Idea Generation

Exploratory research plays a big role in new product development, including developing and screening new product ideas. Exploratory research is particularly useful in idea generation and screening by producing multiple ideas and then narrowing the choices down to a small number of alternatives. In this process, exploratory research may indicate that some new product ideas are unworkable.

Qualitative research can generate ideas for new products, advertising copy, promotional ideas, and product improvements in numerous ways. Researchers using qualitative approaches can ask consumers to describe their product experiences in great detail. This data can reveal the consumer needs that a product can truly address. For example, a consumer may describe their dog food experiences. When asked what he or she wants in a dog food, the reply likely will be "Something that is good for the dog." Once the consumer is encouraged to continue, however, we may learn that the dog food "smells bad in the refrigerator" and "is messy to clean up." Thus, the interview reveals that needs related to dog food are not entirely centered on the dog.

Technology also can assist in this effort. For example, automobile marketers have consumers design their dream cars using computerized design systems similar to those used by automotive designers. This exploratory research might generate ideas that would never have occurred to the firm's own designers.[9]

Probing

Probing is an interview technique that tries to draw deeper and more elaborate explanations from a respondent. Oftentime, researchers may conduct interviews with key decision makers in trying to separate symptoms from the relevant issues that should be the focus of the research. Probing techniques often are applied in such interviews. In addition, researchers apply probing techniques in interviews trying to reveal consumer values and motivations that drive specific consumer behaviors. For instance, why do some consumers avoid personal contact and try to communicate with companies only via web communication? Researchers will find probing useful for any of the following reasons:

1. Clarification – ask respondent to explain exactly what certain phrases or terms mean.
2. Free-form thinking – ask for top of mind associations by saying, "What does _____ make you think of?"
3. Pause – the researcher may simply wait in silence briefly. The silence can encourage the respondent to explain more deeply as a way of coping with the awkwardness that the silence brings.
4. Contrast – ask respondent to contrast events as similar or different from other events.
5. Meaning – ask respondent to "tell me something" or "tell me more" about an interesting point.
6. Change – ask respondent, "what has changed?" This is particularly useful in separating symptoms from issues when interviewing key decision makers.

quantitative data

Represent phenomena by assigning numbers in an ordered and meaningful way.

"Innovation... endows resources with a new capacity to create wealth."
—PETER DRUCKER

probing

Interview technique that tries to draw deeper and more elaborate explanations from respondents.

Concept Testing

concept testing

A frequently performed type of exploratory research representing many similar research procedures all having the same purpose: to screen new, revised, or repositioned ideas.

Research's main role in idea screening is concept testing. **Concept testing** is a frequently performed type of exploratory research representing many similar research procedures all having the same purpose: to screen new, revised, or repositioned ideas. Despite the term *testing*, concept testing approaches are largely qualitative. Typically, respondents read a written statement, view a pictorial representation, or examine a model or sample, and then provide comments. The questions almost always include whether the idea is likable, whether it would be useful, and whether it seems new. Respondents then elaborate on the idea orally, in writing, or through some visual communication. Concept testing allows an initial evaluation prior to the commitment of any additional research and development, manufacturing, or other company resources. Perhaps just as importantly, respondent comments are interpreted qualitatively and provide themes for potentially improving the product.

Concept testing processes work best when they not only identify ideas with the most potential, but they also lead to important refinements. Beiersdorf, the German company that produces Nivea skin care products (http://www.beiersdorf.com, http://www.nivea.com), like all consumer product firms, is constantly developing and screening new product ideas. One idea included a blemish-hiding skin crème that worked by reflecting light from the blemish, causing it to "disappear." During concept testing, most consumers were interested but asked questions about its moisturizing abilities. As a result, Beiersdorf introduced the product by emphasizing both its ability to hide blemishes and to moisturize the skin.[10]

Likewise, if Vans introduces snowboarding and biking products as a way of increasing sales revenues, those products will have to undergo concept screening. Will consumers respond favorably to the ideas of a Vans Cushioned Snowboard or Vans Biking Shoes? Clearly, concept testing including probing interview techniques will be helpful in this effort.

Exhibit 5.2 shows excellent concept statements for two new alternative chain restaurant concepts. A national franchise that operates various chain restaurants that compete with the likes of Hooters and Outback Steakhouse is interested in this concept. The statements portraying the intangibles (brand image, product appearance, name, and price) and a description of the product simulate reality. A researcher conveys the product idea clearly to the research participant who then responds in some way. Their comments become the key information gleaned from the study.

EXHIBIT 5.2

Testing New Product Concepts

Component	Concept	
	Havana's	**Bekkah**
Brand Image	Family oriented, Cuban themed, with generous portions of modestly priced food	Upscale hangout for on–the–go individuals looking for a change of pace
Atmosphere	Bright colors, Cuban music all day and every day with every restaurant built around a bar featuring genuine '57 Chevys	Muted colors and stone walls giving the appearance of an oasis in an arid climate
Product Assortment	Traditional Cuban slow-cooked meats with generous sides like black beans and fried plantains. Cuban sangria and a wide assortment of beer are featured.	Lebanese meats sliced very thin with traditional Middle Eastern seasonings, a variety of pita breads, feta cheese, and yogurt relishes. Lebanese wines are featured and supplement an otherwise domestic collection.
Price Points	Average ticket per customer is projected to be around $14.	Average ticket per customer is projected to be around $26.
Location	Suburban location around the top 10 largest metropolitan areas in the United States and Canada	Major SMSAs (standard metropolitan statistical areas) across the southern United States from San Diego, CA to Jacksonville, FL

Source: © Cengage Learning 2013.

Qualitative Research Orientations

Researchers perform qualitative research in many ways using many techniques. Each researcher's orientation toward qualitative research is influenced by the different fields of study. These orientations are each associated with a category of qualitative research. The major categories of qualitative research include

1. Phenomenology—originating in philosophy and psychology
2. Ethnography—originating in anthropology
3. Grounded theory—originating in sociology
4. Case studies—originating in psychology and in business research

Precise lines between these approaches are difficult to draw and a particular qualitative research study may involve elements of two or more approaches. However, each category does reflect a somewhat unique approach to human inquiry and approaches to discovering knowledge. Each will be described briefly, followed by a description of some of the more common qualitative techniques used to generate qualitative data.

Phenomenology

What Is a Phenomenological Approach to Research?

Phenomenology represents a philosophical approach to studying human experiences based on the idea that human experience itself is inherently subjective and determined by the contexts in which people live.[11] The phenomenological researcher focuses on how relationships between a person and the physical environment, objects, people, or situations shape a person's behavior. Phenomenological inquiry seeks to describe, reflect upon, and interpret experiences.

Researchers with a phenomenological orientation rely largely on conversational interview tools. The phenomenological interviewer is careful to avoid asking direct questions when at all possible. Instead, the interviewer asks respondents to tell a story about some experience. In addition, the researcher must do everything possible to make sure a respondent is comfortable telling his or her story. One way to accomplish this is to become a member of the group (for example, becoming a skateboarder in the scenario described earlier in this chapter). Another way may be to avoid having the person use his or her real name. This might be particularly necessary in studying potentially sensitive topics including smoking, shoplifting, or employee theft.

A phenomenological approach to studying the Vans brand may require considerable time. The researcher may first spend weeks or months fitting in with the person or group of interest to establish a comfort level. The researcher makes careful notes of conversations. If the interview seeks an actual interview, he or she would likely not begin by asking a skateboarder to describe his or her shoes. Rather, asking for favorite skateboard incidents or talking about what makes a skateboarder unique may generate productive conversation. Generally, the approach is very unstructured as a way of avoiding leading questions and to provide every opportunity for new insights.

What Is Hermeneutics?

The term *hermeneutics* is important in phenomenology. **Hermeneutics** is an approach to understanding phenomenology that relies on analysis of texts in which a person tells a story about him- or herself.[12] The interpretive research extracts meaning by connecting text passages to one another or to themes expressed outside the story. The connections provide a way of coding the key meanings expressed in a story. Although a full understanding of hermeneutics is beyond the scope of this text, qualitative tools often employ some of the key terminology. For instance, a **hermeneutic unit** refers to a text passage from a respondent's story that is linked with a key theme from within this story or provided by the researcher.[13] The qualitative researcher uses these passages to interpret the data.

Listening is a necessary skill for phenomenological researchers. A researcher with keen listening skills picks up on the meaningful themes. Furthermore, listening isn't always oral. The Coca-Cola company invites consumers to tell stories about themselves and Coke products on their Facebook

---

phenomenology

A philosophical approach to studying human experiences based on the idea that human experience itself is inherently subjective and determined by the context in which people live.

hermeneutics

An approach to understanding phenomenology that relies on analysis of texts through which a person tells a story about him- or herself.

hermeneutic unit

Refers to a text passage from a respondent's story that is linked with a key theme from within this story or provided by the researcher.

©AP Photo/Lenny Igneizi

"When Will I Ever Learn?"

A hermeneutic approach can be used to provide insight into car shopping experiences. The approach involves a small number of consumers providing relatively lengthy stories about recent car shopping experiences. The goal is trying to discover particular reasons why they eliminate certain car models from consideration. The consumer tells a story of comparing a Ford and a GM (General Motors) minivan. She describes the two vehicles in great detail and ultimately concludes, "We might have gone with the Ford instead because it was real close between the Ford and the GM." The Ford was cheaper, but the way the door opened suggested difficulties in dealing with kids and groceries and the like, and so she purchased the GM model. The researcher in this story goes on to interpret the plotline of the story as having to do with her responsibility for poor consumption outcomes. Consider the following passage.

"It has got GM defects and that is really frustrating. I mean the transmission had to be rebuilt after about 150 miles…and it had this horrible vibration problem. We took a long vacation where you couldn't go over sixty miles an hour because the thing started shaking so bad.… I told everybody, 'Don't buy one of these things.' We should have known because our Buick—the Buick that is in the shop right now—its transmission

lasted about 3,000 miles. My husband's parents are GM people and they had one go bad. I keep thinking, When I am going to learn? I think this one has done it. I don't think I will ever go back to GM after this."

The research concludes that a hermeneutic link exists between the phrase "When I am going to learn?" and the plot of self-responsibility. The resulting behavior including no longer considering GM products and the negative word-of-mouth behavior are ways of restoring esteem given the events.

Sources: Republished with permission of the American Marketing Association from "Interpreting Consumers: A Hermeneutical Framework for Deriving Marketing Insights from the Tests of Consumers' Consumption Stories," by Craig J. Thompson, *Journal of Marketing Research*, 34 (November 1997), 438–455; permission conveyed through Copyright Clearance Center, Inc.

sites. After all, this is where a large portion of consumer conversation takes place in these virtual communities these days.[14] Here, hermeneutic units from conversations taking place in an environment where consumers are comfortable and candid reveal key themes about the ways products are used and can spur ideas for product improvement, advertising, or new products.

Computerized software exists to assist in listening by making coding texts and images easy. ATLAS.ti is one such software package that adopts the term *hermeneutic unit* in referring to groups of phrases that are linked with meaning. One useful component of computerized approaches is a word counter. The word counter will return counts of how many times words appear in a story or recorded interview. Frequently occurring words suggest a key theme and greatly assist the researcher in developing an interpretation.[15] The Research Snapshot demonstrates the use of hermeneutics in interpreting a story about a consumer shopping for a car.

Ethnography

What Is Ethnography?

ethnography

Represents ways of studying cultures through methods that involve becoming highly active within that culture.

participant-observation

Ethnographic research approach where the researcher becomes immersed within the culture that he or she is studying and draws data from his or her observations.

Ethnography represents ways of studying cultures through methods that involve becoming highly active within that culture. **Participant-observation** typifies an ethnographic research approach. Participant-observation means the researcher immerses him/herself within the culture that he or she is studying and draws data from the resulting observations. A *culture* can be either a broad culture, like American culture, or a narrow culture, like urban gangs or skateboarding enthusiasts.[16]

Organizational culture also is relevant for ethnographic study.[17] At times, researchers actually become employees of an organization for an extended period of time. In doing so, they become part of the culture and over time other employees come to act quite naturally around the researcher. The researcher may observe behaviors that the employee would never reveal otherwise. For instance, a researcher investigating the ethical behavior of salespeople may have difficulty

Ethnographic (participant-observation) approaches may be useful to understanding how children obtain value from their experiences with toys.

getting a car salesperson to reveal any potentially deceptive sales tactics in a traditional interview. However, ethnographic techniques may result in the salesperson letting down his or her guard, resulting in more valid discoveries about the car-selling culture.

Observation in Ethnography

Observation plays a key role in ethnography. Researchers today sometimes ask households for permission to place video cameras in their home. In doing so, the ethnographer can study the consumer in a "natural habitat" and use the observations to test new products, develop new product ideas, and develop marketing strategies in general.[18]

Ethnographic study can be particularly useful when a certain culture is comprised of individuals who cannot or will not verbalize their thoughts and feelings. For instance, ethnography has advantages for discovering insights among children because it does not rely largely on their answers to questions. Instead, the researcher can simply become part of the environment, allow the children to do what they do naturally, and record their behavior.[19]

The opening vignette describes a situation in which ethnographic research may be appropriate. A researcher might blend into a skateboard group. The artifacts shared by the group, including photos posted on the group's wall, may provide meaning. Also, researchers who act as customers can perform ethnography by becoming a natural part of the environment. Researchers posing as restaurant customers developed lists of the most critical service failures in restaurants and interpreted meanings for things such as slow service, inappropriate server behavior, and food waste.[20]

"You can tell a lot about a person by the way he eats his jellybeans."

—RONALD REAGAN

Grounded Theory

What Is Grounded Theory?

Grounded theory represents an inductive investigation in which the researcher poses questions about information provided by respondents or taken from historical records. The researcher asks the questions to him- or herself and repeatedly questions the responses to derive deeper explanations. Grounded theory is particularly applicable in highly dynamic situations involving rapid and significant change. Two key questions asked by the grounded theory researcher are "What is happening here?" and "How is it different?"[21] The distinguishing characteristic of grounded theory is that it does not begin with a theory but instead extracts one from whatever emerges from an area of inquiry.

grounded theory

Represents an inductive investigation in which the researcher poses questions about information provided by respondents or taken from historical records; the researcher asks the questions to him- or herself and repeatedly questions the responses to derive deeper explanations.

Focus Group Interview

The focus group interview is so widely used that many advertising and research agencies do nothing but focus group interviews. A **focus group interview** is an unstructured, free-flowing interview with a small group of people, usually between six and ten. Focus groups are led by a trained moderator who follows a flexible format, encouraging dialogue among respondents. Common focus group topics include employee programs, brand meanings, problems with products, advertising themes, or new-product concepts. Unfortunately, the term *focus group* is all too often used loosely referring to any discussion among a small group of people. Without the appropriate structure and trained leader, a group discussion probably lacks the appropriate focus.

Focus group participants may range from consumers talking about hair coloring, petroleum engineers talking about problems in the "oil patch," children talking about toys, or employees talking about their jobs. A moderator begins by providing an opening statement intended to steer discussion in the intended direction. Ideally, discussion topics emerge at the group's initiative more than that of the moderator. Consistent with phenomenological approaches, moderators should avoid direct questioning unless absolutely necessary.

Advantages of Focus Group Interviews

Focus groups allow people to discuss their true feelings, anxieties, and frustrations, as well as the depth of their convictions, in their own words. Although other approaches may also do much the same, focus groups offer several advantages.

1. Relatively fast
2. Easy to execute
3. Allow respondents to piggyback off each other's ideas
4. Provide multiple perspectives
5. Flexibility to allow more detailed descriptions
6. High degree of scrutiny

Speed and Ease

In an emergency situation, a research company can conduct, analyze, and report on three or four group sessions within about a week. The large number of research firms that conduct focus group interviews makes it easy to find someone to conduct the research. Practically every state in the United States contains multiple research firms that have their own focus group facilities. Companies with large research departments likely have at least one qualified focus group moderator so that they need not outsource the focus group.

Piggybacking and Multiple Perspectives

Furthermore, the group approach may produce thoughts that would not be produced otherwise. The interplay between respondents allows them to **piggyback** off of each other's ideas. In other words, one respondent stimulates thought among the others and, as this process continues, increasingly creative insights are possible. A comment by one individual often triggers a chain of responses from the other participants. The social nature of the focus group also helps bring out multiple views as each person shares a particular perspective.

Flexibility

The flexibility of focus group interviews is advantageous, especially when compared with the more structured and rigid survey format. Numerous topics can be discussed and many insights can be gained, particularly with regard to the variations in consumer behavior in different situations. Responses that would be unlikely to emerge in a survey often come out in group interviews: "*If* it is one of the three brands I sometimes use and *if* it is on sale, I buy it; otherwise, I buy my regular brand" or "*If* the day is hot and I have to serve the whole neighborhood, I make Kool-Aid; otherwise, I give them Dr Pepper or Coke."

If a researcher is investigating a target group to determine who consumes a particular beverage or why a consumer purchases a certain brand, situational factors must be included in any

● ● ● ● ● ● ●

Traditional focus group facilities typically include a comfortable room for respondents, recording equipment, and a viewing room via a two-way mirror.

interpretations of respondent comments. For instance, in the previous situation, the focus group moderator would note the preference for a particular beverage. However, it would be inappropriate to say that Kool-Aid is preferred in general. The proper interpretation is situation-specific. On a hot day the whole neighborhood gets Kool-Aid. When the weather isn't hot, the kids may get nothing, or if only a few kids are around, they may get lucky and get Dr Pepper. A possible interpretation may be: Kool-Aid is appropriate for satisfying large numbers of hot kids while Dr Pepper is a treat for a select few.

Scrutiny

A focus group interview allows closer scrutiny in several ways. First, multiple people can observe the interview live because they are usually conducted in a room containing a two-way mirror. The respondents and moderator are on one side, an invited audience that may include both researchers and decision makers is on the other. If the decision makers are located in another city or country, they may watch through an Internet connection (perhaps using Skype or similar technology) or through another video media. No matter how agents from the decision maker observe, the fact that they can look in provides a check on the eventual interpretations offered in the report. Second, the focus group organizers generally videotape the session. If video is not feasible then they will produce an audio recording. Later, detailed examination of the recorded session can offer additional insight and help clear up disagreements about what happened.

Focus Group Illustration

Researchers often use focus group interviews for concept screening and concept refinement. Product development involves a continuous process of examining potential modifications, refinements, and idea generation. This process applies to existing and new products. Although RJR's initial attempts at smokeless cigarettes failed in the United States, Philip Morris developed a smokeless, electronic cigarette for the U.K. market with similar products already available in the United States. Focus groups are being used to help understand how the product will be received and how it might be improved.[24] The voluntary focus group respondents are presented with samples of the product and then they discuss it among themselves. The interview results suggest that consumers like the key product features related to tidiness, such as the fact that it produces no ashes, no side smoke, and very little odor. Focus group respondents show little concern about how the cigarette actually functions but hope that they will be able to use the product around nonsmokers without irritating them. This example illustrates how focus groups are used in developing and refining products and ideas for effectively marketing the product once released.

• • • • • • •

What do you think would be the differences in reactions to legislation further restricting smoking behavior that would be found among a group of smokers compared to a group of nonsmokers.

© Tudor Caralin Gheodhe/Shutterstock

Focus Group Respondents

What is a research supplier's responsibility when recruiting individuals to participate in a focus group? Practically every focus group interview requires that respondents be screened based on some relevant characteristic. For example, if the topic involves improving parochial school education, the group should probably not include non-parents or parents with no plans of having children. The respondents in this case should be parents who are likely to put or are currently putting a child through school.

Even after careful screening, some consumers that fit the desired profile make poor focus group participants. Respondents are inappropriate if they are either unwilling to express their views or they are overbearing. The group dynamics suffer when one or more respondents is too quiet or is a loud mouth. When a researcher finds good focus group participants, he or she may be tempted to use them over and over again. Is this appropriate? This is a dilemma a focus group planner may well face. Consider a research client viewing videotapes of a series of six focus groups conducted about new kitchen appliance designs. The client realizes that four respondents appear in more than one of the six focus group interviews and that ten respondents appear in focus groups videos conducted by the same researcher on another topic six months previously. Whenever diversity of opinion is needed, relying on what essentially become professional focus group respondents is not likely appropriate. The researcher should take the extra effort to find new respondents rather than relying on conveniently available and appropriately talkative respondents.

Group Composition

A traditional focus group's ideal size is six to ten people. A very small group has less potential for good ideas and each person is very susceptible to influence from the others. In a very large group, some participants may have difficulty getting their ideas across.

Homogeneous groups allow researchers to concentrate on consumers with similar lifestyles, experiences, and communication skills. When every participant is more or less similar to the others, the discussion carries forward with less likelihood of becoming overly confrontational. Additionally, marketing campaigns generally communicate with specific market segments consisting of relatively homogenous consumers. Ethnographers like to deal with unique cultures. If an ethnographic researcher is looking to do a focus group about Vans, he or she may recruit participants from a local skate park.

Imagine how the opinions of the electronic cigarette would vary among a group of smokers and nonsmokers. Management would probably be nearsighted not to consider the input from nonsmokers because they ultimately will influence the acceptable places where these devices can be used. Although any one focus group consisting of both smokers and nonsmokers might be lively, it is very likely to be confrontational. If the researcher involves multiple interviews, the researcher may consider doing one with a mixed group, but researchers generally prefer separate interviews for disparate groups. The researcher obtains diversity in the sample by using different groups even though each group is homogeneous. For instance, in discussing smokeless cigarettes, four groups might be used.

1. Single current smokers
2. Married smokers whose spouses do not smoke
3. Former smokers
4. Nonsmokers

Although each group is homogenous, researchers obtain opinions from diverse respondents. Many research firms apply a rule of thumb that four different focus group sessions, each in a different city, can satisfy exploratory research needs dealing with common consumer product issues.

Environmental Conditions

A focus group session may typically take place at the research agency in a room specifically designed for this purpose. These agencies' facilities include the studio-like rooms where the focus groups are conducted, viewed, and recorded. Participants receive refreshments prior to the interview to help create a more relaxed atmosphere conducive to a free exchange of ideas. A relaxed atmosphere helps create a more open and intimate discussion of personal experiences and sentiments.

The Focus Group Moderator

During a focus group interview, a **moderator** ensures that everyone gets a chance to speak as he or she facilitates the discussion.

Several qualities characterize a good focus group moderator.

1. A moderator must develop rapport with the group and make all participants feel comfortable. Good moderators show genuine interest in people, establish rapport, gain participants' confidence, and make them feel eager to talk.
2. A moderator must be a good listener. Careful listening allows the researcher to separate productive discussion directed toward accomplishing the stated research objective from discussions that will take the group in an irrelevant direction. Without good listening skills, the interview may fail to address the issues that motivated the effort.
3. A good does not interject his/her personal opinion. Good moderators usually say less rather than more. They can stimulate productive discussion with generalized follow-ups such as, "Tell us more about that incident," or "How are your experiences similar or different from the one you just heard?" The moderator must be particularly careful not to ask leading questions such as "You do like Red Bull, don't you?"
4. A moderator directs verbal traffic capably without turning off productive participants. The discussion needs to remain focused around the research objective. A moderator does not give the group total control of the discussion because it may well quickly lose focus. He or she normally has prepared questions on topics that aimed to draw out ideas related to the research objective and therefore managerial issues. Normally, he or she starts out by encouraging a general discussion (i.e., "tell me what comes to mind when you think of a skate park") but usually *focuses* in on specific topics as the session progresses. Ideally, the topics get covered with little to no prompting.

moderator
A person who leads a focus group interview and ensures that everyone gets a chance to speak and facilitates the discussion.

Focus Groups as Diagnostic Tools

Focus groups typify exploratory research but they also can be helpful in later stages of a research project. Sometimes, the findings from surveys or other quantitative techniques raise more questions than they answer. Managers who are puzzled about survey research results may use focus groups as a way of better understanding what consumer surveys are actually saying. In such a situation, the focus group supplies diagnostic help as a follow-up to other research.

Focus groups are also excellent diagnostic tools for spotting problems with ideas as an idea screening technique. The moderator presents a marketing concept to the group and then seeks elaborate comments on the idea. This usually leads to lengthy lists of potential product problems and some ideas for overcoming them. People are naturally inclined to offer reasons why things won't work so this approach can be effective. Mature products can also be "focused-grouped" for improvements in this manner.

Depth Interviews

depth interview

A one-on-one interview between a professional researcher and a research respondent conducted about some relevant business or social topic.

An alternative to a focus group is a depth interview. A **depth interview** is a one-on-one interview between a professional researcher and a research respondent. Depth interviews are much the same as a psychological, clinical interview, but with a different purpose. The researcher asks many questions and follows up each answer with probes for additional elaboration. Exhibit 5.4 provides an excerpt from a depth interview. The interviews allow the researchers to develop a theory of the way children react to product advertisements. In each case, the child was elaborating on their reactions to or memories of advertisements.

Like focus group moderators, the interviewer's role is critical in a depth interview. He or she must be a highly skilled individual who can encourage the respondent to talk freely without influencing the direction of the conversation. Probing questions are critical. Interviews often employ the "what has changed approach" in depth interviews with managerial employees. Exhibit 5.5 illustrates the approach.

laddering

A particular approach to probing, asking respondents to compare differences between brands at different levels that produces distinctions at the attribute level, the benefit level, and the value or motivation level. Laddering is based on the classical repertory grid approach.

Laddering is a term used for a particular approach to probing, asking respondents to compare differences between brands at different levels. A repertory grid interview is an approach developed in the mid-twentieth century to conduct interviews that drew out the way people distinguished concepts. Laddering evolved from the repertory grid approach and is very useful in identifying the potential meaning of brand names. What usually results with laddering is that respondents first distinguish things using attribute-level distinctions, second are benefit-level distinctions, and third are distinctions at the value or motivation level. Laddering, for example, can then distinguish two brands of skateboarding shoes based on a) the materials they are made of, b) the comfort they provide, and c) the excitement they create.

EXHIBIT **5.4** Example Results from a Depth Interview

Respondent Comments	Interpreted Meaning
"I like to watch [Barbie ads] because I like to see how pretty the Barbies are and if there is going to be, like, a new kind of Barbie. There is one Barbie . . . that comes with some little lipstick-type thing on a towel. You dip it in water and put the lipstick on the Barbie. The Barbie's lipstick turns darker."	Children look forward to seeing some advertisements and take value from viewing them.
"It's like a fairy tale on the commercial, I mean people can't really be thin. And they can't just pop out of it like that. That's not real."	Children are not detached from reality when viewing the ads.
"The Honey Comb commercial has never left my head because it's got all those details in it. It's got bright colors, and music and kids with interesting things in it. That's what makes it stay in my head. I don't like that kind of cereal or the new kinds. I don't like sweet cereal. I just like the commercials though."	Children appreciate the hedonic value aspects of viewing advertisements.
"I don't like that one (Chip's Ahoy ad) because it made me too hungry. Cookies are my favorite. And we're not allowed to have snacks."	Signifies the role of parents in facilitating the consumption of children.

©Elena Elisseeva/Shutterstock

Source: Adapted from Moore, E. S. and R. J. Lutz, "Children, Advertising, and Product Experiences: A Multimethod Inquiry," *Journal of Consumer Research*, 27 (June 2000), 31–48. ©2000 University of Chicago Press. Reprinted by permission.

Question: What changes have occurred recently?

Probe: Tell me about this change.

Probe: What has brought this about?

Problem: How might this be related to your problem?

Question: What other changes have occurred recently (i.e., competitors, customers, environment, pricing, promotion, suppliers, employees, etc.)?

Continue Probing

EXHIBIT **5.5**
What Has Changed?

Source: ©Cengage Learning 2013.

Depth Interview Procedure

Each depth interview may last more than an hour. Not only does the researcher conduct the interview, with each interview producing about the same amount of text as does a focus group interview, but the resulting data must be analyzed and interpreted. Thus, depth interviews are time consuming. The interviewer also must be keenly aware of what is happening and record both surface reactions and subconscious motivations of the respondent. Analysis and interpretation of such data are highly subjective, and it is difficult to settle on a true interpretation.

Depth interviews provide more insight into a particular individual than do focus groups. In addition, because the setting isn't really social, respondents are more likely to discuss sensitive topics than are those in a focus group. Buick recently took depth interviews into respondents' homes. Here, respondents discussed their ideas about cars and car brands in great detail, sometimes going on for two hours or more.[25] The comfortable surroundings no doubt aided the discussion. Following the interviews, Buick researchers felt as though Buick customers desire premium items and special features but they aren't inclined to pay a premium price for a car. Also, they also picked up on perceptions that consumers viewed Buick as a brand for older people.

Depth interviews are particularly advantageous when the focus is on a unique or unusual behavior. For instance, depth interviews revealed characteristics of adolescent behavior, ranging from the ways they get what they want from their parents to shopping, smoking, and shoplifting.[26] Depth interviews are similar to focus groups in many ways. Focus groups and depth interviews cost about the same as long as only one or two respondents are interviewed in depth. However, if a dozen or more depth interviews are included in a report, the costs are higher than focus group interviews, due to the increased interviewing and analysis time.

Conversations

Holding **conversations** in qualitative research is an informal data-gathering approach in which the researcher engages a respondent in a discussion of the relevant subject matter. This approach is almost completely unstructured and the researcher enters the conversation with few expectations. The goal is to have the respondent produce a dialogue about his or her lived experiences.

A conversational approach to qualitative research is particularly appropriate in phenomenological research and for developing grounded theory. In our Vans experience, the researcher may simply tape-record a conversation about becoming a "skater." The resulting dialogue can then be analyzed for themes and plots. The result may be some interesting and novel insight into the consumption patterns of skaters, for example, if the respondent said,

"I knew I was a real skater when I just had to have Vans, not just for boarding, but for wearing."

This theme may connect to a rite-of-passage plot and show how Vans play a role in this process.

conversations

An informal qualitative data-gathering approach in which the researcher engages a respondent in a discussion of the relevant subject matter.

Technology is also influencing conversational research. Online communications such as online product reviews like those found at www.bestbuy.com and Facebook discussions represent conversational dialog that can be interpreted for meaning. Companies may discover product problems and ideas for overcoming them through computer-based consumer conversations.[27]

A conversational approach is advantageous because conducting a single interview is usually inexpensive. Unlike depth interviews or focus groups, the researcher doesn't have to pay respondents because they are enthusiasts freely discussing their behavior. Often, the conversation takes place spontaneously, with little setup or with little need for any formal setting such as a focus group studio. They are relatively effective at getting at sensitive issues once the researcher establishes a rapport with them. Conversational approaches, however, are prone to produce a small portion of relevant information because they are not steered in the same way as a depth interview or focus group. Additionally, the data analysis is very much researcher-dependent.

Semi-Structured Interviews

Semi-structured interviews usually come in written form and ask respondents for short essay responses to specific open-ended questions. Respondents are free to write as much or as little as they want. The interview design separates questions into sections typically and within each section, probing questions follow the opening question. In face-to-face semi-structured, oral interviews, structured follow-ups are more difficult than with the written approach.

Advantages to semi-structured interviews include an ability to address more specific issues and the fact that responses are usually easier to interpret than with other qualitative approaches. In written form, the researcher prepares all questions ahead of time and thus the presence of an interviewer is not necessary. For this reason, among others, semi-structured interviews are relatively cost-effective.

Some researchers interested in studying car salesperson stereotypes used qualitative semi-structured interviews to map consumers' cognitions (memory). The semi-structured interview began with a free-association task:

List the first five things that come into your mind when you think of a "car salesman."

A probing question followed:

Describe the way a typical "car salesman" looks.

Questions about how the car salesperson acts and how the respondent feels in the presence of a car salesperson followed this probe. The results led to research showing how the information that consumers process differs in the presence of a typical car salesperson as opposed to a less typical car salesperson.[28] One suggestion that followed addressed the way car salespeople dress. Perhaps something other than the prototypical attire would help create a less negative reaction.

Free-Association and Sentence Completion Methods

free-association techniques

Record respondents' first (top-of-mind) cognitive reactions to some stimulus.

Free-association techniques simply record a respondent's first cognitive reactions (top-of-mind) to some stimulus. The Rorschach or inkblot test typifies the free-association method. Respondents view an ambiguous figure and say the first thing that comes to their mind. Free-association techniques allow researchers to map a respondent's thoughts or memory.

The sentence completion method is based on free-association principles. Respondents simply are required to complete a few partial sentences with the first word or phrase that comes to mind. For example:

People who drink beer are _____.
A man who drinks a dark beer is _____.
Light beer is most liked by _____.

Answers to sentence-completion questions tend to be more extensive than responses to word-association tests. Although the responses lack the ability to probe for meaning as in other qualitative techniques, they are very effective in finding out what is on a respondent's mind. They can also do so in a quick and very cost-effective manner. Researchers often employ free-association and sentence-completion tasks in conjunction with other approaches. For instance, they provide effective icebreakers in focus group interviews.

Observation

Throughout this chapter, we describe how observation is an important qualitative tool. The participant-observer approach typifies how researchers use observation to explore various issues. The researcher's field notes play a large role in this process. **Field notes** are the researchers' descriptions of what he/she actually observes in the field. These notes then become the text from which he/she extracts meaning.

field notes

The researcher's descriptions of what he/she actually observes in the field; these notes then become the text from which meaning is extracted.

Observation may also take place in visual form. Researchers may observe consumers in their home, as mentioned above, or try to gain knowledge from photos observed there or posted on an Internet site like Snapfish.com. Observation can either be very inexpensive, such as when a research associate sits at Starbucks and simply observes customer behavior, or it can be very expensive as is the case in most participant-observer studies. Observational research is keenly advantageous for gaining insight into things that respondents cannot or will not verbalize.

Collages

Marketing researchers sometimes have respondents prepare a collage to represent their experience with some good, service, or brand. Harley-Davidson commissioned research comparing collages depicting feelings about Harley-Davidson created by Harley owners with those of collages created by owners of a competing brand. The collages of "Hog" owners revealed themes of artwork and the freedom of the great outdoors. These themes did not emerge in the non-Hog groups. Confirmatory research followed which helped Harley continue its growth by appealing more specifically to sensitivities of its market segments.[29]

Thematic Apperception Test (TAT)

A **thematic apperception test (TAT)** presents subjects with an ambiguous picture(s) in which consumers and products are the center of attention. The investigator asks the subject to tell what is happening in the picture(s) now and what might happen next. Hence, the approach illicits themes (*thematic*) on the basis of the perceptual-interpretive (*apperception*) use of the pictures. The researcher then analyzes the contents of the stories provided by respondents.

thematic apperception test (TAT)

A test that presents subjects with an ambiguous picture(s) in which consumers and products are the center of attention; the investigator asks the subject to tell what is happening in the picture(s) now and what might happen next.

The picture or cartoon stimulus must be sufficiently interesting to encourage discussion but ambiguous enough not to disclose the nature of the research project. Clues should not be given to the character's positive or negative predisposition. Researchers interested in exploring the different thoughts of men and women about receiving gifts might show a simple cartoon of either a man or a woman about to unwrap a gift. Respondents would provide the thoughts in each person's mind as they go about opening the gift. Another TAT might include several ambiguous cartoon frames depicting a skateboarder heading to a store. This might reveal ideas about the brands and products that fit the role of skateboarder.

A **picture frustration** version of the TAT uses a cartoon drawing in which the respondent suggests a dialogue in which the characters might engage. Exhibit 5.6 is a purposely ambiguous illustration of an everyday occurrence. The picture depicts two office workers and the respondent describes what the woman might be saying. This approach could be used for discussions about products, packaging, the display of merchandise, store personnel, and so on.

picture frustration

A version of the TAT using a cartoon drawing in which the respondent suggests a dialogue in which the characters might engage.

Projective Research Techniques

A TAT represents a projective research technique. A **projective technique** is an indirect means of questioning, enabling respondents to project beliefs and feelings onto a third party, an inanimate object, or a task situation. Projective techniques usually encourage respondents to describe a situation in their own words with little prompting by the interviewer. The typical assumption is that respondents interpret the situation within the context of their own experiences, attitudes, and personalities. This allows respondents to express opinions and emotions otherwise hidden from

projective technique

An indirect means of questioning enabling respondents to project beliefs and feelings onto a third party, an inanimate object, or a task situation.

EXHIBIT 5.6
Picture Frustration
Version of TAT

others and possibly even themselves. All projective techniques are particularly useful in studying sensitive issues.

Researchers interested in motivations for buying a hybrid automobile may ask a question like, "What would a person like you do to decide whether or not to trade their current automobile for a hybrid car such as a Prius."[30] This question may illicit far different answers than the obvious one of concern for the environment. They deal more with questions of status or image portrayed by the car. However, despite decades of application, uncertainty remains about whether or not people do project their true feelings onto others based on projective questioning.[31] Nonetheless, the resulting answers can be useful in exploratory research.

Preparing a Focus Group Outline

discussion guide

A focus group outline that includes written introductory comments informing the group about the focus group purpose and rules and then outlines topics or questions to be addressed in the group session.

Focus group researchers use a discussion guide to help control the interview and guide the discussion into product areas. A **discussion guide** includes written introductory comments, informing the group about the focus group purpose and rules and then outlines topics or questions to be asked in the group session. Thus, the discussion guide serves as the focus group outline. Some discussion guides will have only a few phrases in the entire document. Others may be more detailed. The amount of content depends on the nature and experience of the researcher and the complexity of the topic.

A marketing researcher conducting a focus group interview for a cancer center had the following objectives in mind when preparing the guide for the interview and conducting the interview:

■ The first question was very general, asking that respondents describe their feelings about being out in the sun as an icebreaker. This opening question aimed to elicit the full range of views within in the group. Some individuals might view being out in the sun as a healthful practice, whereas others view the sun as deadly. The hope is that by exposing the full range of opinions, respondents would be motivated to fully explain their own position. This was the only question asked specifically of every respondent. Each respondent had to give an answer before free discussion began. In this way, individuals experience a nonthreatening environment encouraging their free and full opinion.

■ The second question asks whether participants could think of any reason they should be warned about sunlight exposure. This question was simply designed to introduce the idea of a warning label.

■ Subsequent questions became increasingly specific. They first asked about possible warning formats that might be effective. The moderator allows focus group participants to react to any formats suggested another respondent. After this discussion, the moderator will introduce some specific formats the cancer center personnel have in mind.

■ Finally, the moderator presents the "bottom-line" question: "What format would be most likely to induce people to take protective measures?" There would be probing follow-ups of each opinion so that a respondent couldn't simply say something like "the second one." All focus groups finish up with a catch-all question asking for any comments, including any thoughts they wanted passed along to the sponsor (which was only then revealed as the Houston-based cancer center).

Researchers who planned the outline established certain objectives for each part of the focus group. The initial effort was to break the ice and establish rapport within the group. The logical flow of the group session then moved from general discussion about sunbathing to more focused discussion of types of warnings about danger from sun exposure.

In general, the following steps allow for an effective focus group discussion guide.

1. Welcome and introductions should take place first. Respondents begin to feel more comfortable after introducing themselves.

2. Begin the interview with a broad icebreaker that does not reveal too many specifics about the interview. Sometimes this may even involve respondents providing some written story or their reaction to some stimulus like a photograph, film, product, or advertisement.

3. Questions become increasingly more specific as the interview proceeds. However, the moderator will notice that a good interview will cover the specific question topics before they are asked. This is preferable as respondents do not feel forced to react to the specific issue; it just emerges naturally.

4. If there is a very specific question to ask, such as explaining why a respondent would either buy or not buy a product, the moderator should save that question for last.

5. A debriefing statement should provide respondents with the actual focus group objectives and answer any questions they may have. This is also a final shot to gain some insight from the group.

Disadvantages of Focus Groups

Focus groups offer many advantages. Like practically every other research technique, the focus group has some limitations and disadvantages, too. Problems with focus groups include those discussed as follows.

First, focus groups require objective, sensitive, and effective moderators. Moderators may often find it difficult to remain completely objective. In large research firms, a lead researcher may provide the focus group moderator only enough information to conduct the interview effectively. The focus group interview's opinion shouldn't influence the interview or its results. Although many people, even some with little or no background to do so, conduct focus groups, good moderators become effective through a combination of objectivity, good people skills (which cannot be taught), training (in qualitative research), and experience. Without them, the exercise could provide misleading results.

Second, researchers do not select focus group participants randomly and thus a focus group is not a representative, random sample. Participants do not represent the entire target market in any statistical sense. Thus, focus group results are not useful in making inferences about a larger population.

Third, although not so much an issue with online formats where respondents can remain anonymous, traditional face-to-face focus groups may not be useful for discussing sensitive topics. A focus group is a social setting and usually involves people with little to no familiarity with each other. Therefore, issues that people normally do not like to discuss in public may also prove difficult to discuss in a focus group.

Fourth, focus groups cost a considerable amount of money, particularly when not conducted by someone employed by the company desiring the focus group. Focus group prices vary regionally, but the following figures provide a rough guideline.

Renting Facilities and Equipment	$1,000
Paying Respondents ($100/person)	$1,000
Researcher Costs	
• Preparation	$ 800
• Moderating	$1,000
• Analysis and Report Preparation	$1,500
Miscellaneous Expenses	$ 400

Thus, a client can expect a professional focus group to cost more than $5,000. However, most marketing topics will call for multiple focus groups. A series of interviews does not increase the costs proportionately however because the only element repeated is the interview itself. Thus, the research firm's price for doing two or three interviews only increases about $2,000 to $3,000 per interview.

Modern Technology and Qualitative Research

Technological advances have greatly improved researchers ability to perform all aspects of marketing research, but perhaps they are changing qualitative marketing research more than any other area. Software is increasingly able to identify text data and group it in some way. This section focuses on how technology enables and facilitates modern qualitative research.

Facilitating Interviewing

Videoconferencing and Streaming Media

The videoconferencing industry has grown dramatically in recent years. Most managers routinely conduct meetings using some Internet-based interface such as Skype, Megameeting, or some similar tool. Researchers can use these tools to conference with managers scattered in offices all around the world. However, researchers also apply the tools to conduct focus group interviews.

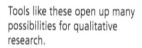

Tools like these open up many possibilities for qualitative research.

Focus Vision Network of New York is a marketing research company that provides specialized videoconferencing equipment and services. The Focus Vision system is modular, allowing for easy movement and an ability to capture each group member close-up. The system operates allows observers in far-off locations to pan the focus group room or zoom in on a particular participant. Managers viewing at remote locations can even send the moderator messages during the interview. For example, while testing new product names in one focus group, an observant manager contacted the moderator with a potential name and the moderator then asked respondents for a reaction to the new name on the spot.[32]

Interactive Media and Online Focus Groups

Internet applications of qualitative exploratory research are growing rapidly and involve both formal and informal applications. Formally, the term **online focus group** refers to a qualitative research effort in which a group of individuals provides unstructured comments by entering their remarks into an electronic Internet display board of some type. Participants use a keyboard and mouse to make their remarks during a chat-room session or in the form of a blog. Because respondents enter their comments into the computer, transcripts of verbatim responses are available immediately after the group session. Online groups can be quick and cost-efficient. However, because there is less interaction between participants, group synergy and snowballing of ideas may be diminished.

Online focus groups allow access to groups that might be hard to tap otherwise. Sermo (sermo.com) is an online community of physicians that provides data to advertising agencies and other institutions. At Sermo, on-demand focus groups comprised of physicians provide fast and efficient feedback on numerous issues related to product effectiveness, usage, and brand messaging.[33] Compared to the price of an in-person physician focus group, the $10,000 to $16,000 price per interview is a bargain.

Several companies have established a form of informal, "continuous" focus group by establishing an Internet blog for that purpose.[34] We might call this technique a **focus blog** when the intention is to mine the site for business research purposes. General Motors, P&G, American Express, Fandango, and Lego all use ideas harvested from their focus blogs. Lego blogs can be found at http://www.thenxtstep.blogspot.com. Although real life, in-person focus group respondents are paid to participate for ninety minutes, bloggers usually participate for absolutely no fee at all! Thus, technology provides some cost advantages over traditional focus group approaches.[35]

Online Versus Face-To-Face Focus Group Techniques

A research company can facilitate a formal online focus group by setting up a private, electronic chat room for that purpose. Participants in formal and informal online focus groups feel that their anonymity is very secure. Often respondents will say things in this environment that they would never say otherwise. For example, a lingerie company was able to get insights into how it could design sexy products for larger women. Online, these women freely discussed what it would take "to feel better about being naked."[36] One can hardly imagine how difficult such a discussion might be face to face. Increased anonymity can be a major advantage for a company investigating sensitive or embarrassing issues.

Because participants do not have to be together in the same room at a research facility, the number of participants in online focus groups can be larger than in traditional focus groups. Twenty-five participants or more is not uncommon for the simultaneous chat-room format. Participants can be at widely separated locations, even in different time zones, because the Internet does not have geographical restrictions. Of course, a major disadvantage is that often the researcher does not exercise as much control in precisely who participates. In other words, a person could very easily not match the desired profile or even answer screening questions in a misleading way simply to participate.

A major drawback with online focus groups is that moderators cannot see body language and facial expressions (bewilderment, excitement, interest, and so forth). Thus, they cannot fully interpret how people are reacting. Also, moderators' ability to probe and ask additional questions on the spot is reduced in online focus groups. Research that requires focus group members to actually touch something (such as a new easy-opening packaging design) or taste something is not generally suitable for an online format.

online focus group

A qualitative research effort in which a group of individuals provides unstructured comments by entering their remarks into an electronic Internet display board of some type.

focus blog

A type of informal, "continuous" focus group established as an Internet blog for the purpose of collecting qualitative data from participant comments.

"Necessity, mother of invention."
—WILLIAM WYCHERLEY

Research Knows Almost No Boundaries!

Qualitative research knows *almost* no boundaries! Well, at least not for Ford. Large companies like Ford are increasingly using qualitative research including phenomenology, ethnography, and grounded theory. Ford now relies on qualitative input to help with ideas for product design, marketing campaign design, concept testing, and even relationships with suppliers. The advances in technologies have helped make automakers more willing to base decisions on consumer input. Some feel that, for perhaps the first time, companies like Ford may now place consumer input above cost cutting in making key decisions.

Ford used information posted online, in-home ethnography, and traditional focus groups to refine a global marketing campaign centered around the Ford Mustang. Marketing researchers interpreted all of this input in a way that placed great emphasis on the feelings associated with driving a Mustang. As a result, Ford developed a slogan and campaign built around "No boundaries!" However, early concept testing showed that this slogan did not create a positive impression in some Asian cultures. Thus, after a few adjustments and further testing, they settled on "Make Every Day Exciting!" Additionally, grounded theory approaches are helping companies better see into the future by building predictive theories about what characteristics might create value for consumers into the future.

Sources: Flint, D. and B. Woodruff, "The Initiators of Changes in Customers' Desired Values: Results from a Theory Building Study," *Industrial Marketing Management*, 30 (2008), 321–30; "Market Research Drives Product Development at Ford," *RP News Wire* (2008), www.reliableplant.com/article. asp?articleid=3802, accessed June 30, 2008; "Changan Ford's Focus Finishes First and Second at China Circuit Championship Beijing Race," *Ford Motor Company Press Release* (2006), http://media.ford.com/newsroom/release_display.cfm?release=24292, accessed August 4, 2008.

Social Networking

Social networking is one of the most impactful trends in recent times. For many consumers, particularly younger generations, social networking sites like Facebook, MySpace, Ning, Bebo, and Twitter are primary tools for communicating with friends both far and near, known and unknown. Social networking takes the place of large volumes of e-mail, phone calls, and even face-to-face communications. Although the impact that social networking will eventually have on society is an interesting question, what is most relevant to marketing research is the large portion of this information that discusses marketing and consumer-related information.

Companies can assign research assistants to search these sites for information related to their particular brands. A Twitter search, for instance, shows quickly who is talking about the product. Companies can get a sense for what these customers are thinking through their tweets.[37] The research analyst codes the information as either positive or negative. When too much negative information appears, the company can take steps to try and protect the brand. In addition, many companies like P&G (Proctor & Gamble) and Ford maintain their own social networking sites for the purpose of gathering research data. In a way, these social networking sites are a way that companies can eavesdrop on consumer conversations and discover key information about their products.

Field Approaches for Interpreting Online Text

Interpretative researchers apply specialized approaches to making sense of consumers' online postings. Some researchers look at the posting as a drama consisting of an act, agency, scene, and purpose.[38] For instance, the wall of a Facebook group, like "I bet I can find 1,000,000 people who hate Heineken," provides a scene in which an act takes place. The act consists of the various posts consumers leave on the site. Classifying the posts into categories found in a dramatic play helps bring sense to the texts consumers openly leave behind.

Other interpretative researchers use the term **netnography** to describe the application of ethnography to comments made in online communities. The researcher blends in as part of a

netnography
The application of ethnography to comments made in online communities.

virtual community and in doing so, he or she gains access to the myriad of comments consumers leave behind about all manner of businesses.[39] Like other uses of social networking in marketing research, the reduced costs relative to traditional ethnography is an important motivator of netnography.

Ethics

Netnography also illustrates ethical dilemmas that qualitative researchers face when dealing with online data. For instance, should the online researcher identify him- or herself to the community as a researcher? If so, the community may not respond the same way. Alternatively, the researcher is extracting data without the informed consent of the participants otherwise. If a researcher takes the latter approach, he/she has a special duty to protect the identity of participants and to protect the brand community itself from harm. If this is the case, the netnography approach is similar to anonymously observing consumers moving about in a public environment.

Software Development

Interpretive Software

Computerized qualitative analysis is now commonly used. Two commonly used programs are ATLAS.ti and NVivo. These can save a lot of time by helping to identify themes and connections within text. In fact, today's programs can even assist in interpreting videotapes and photographs for meaning.

Computerized analysis of depth interviews with service providers and their customers revealed interesting key themes dealing with the friendship or bond that forms between them. Some of the themes that emerged included the feeling that meetings were more like get-togethers with a friend, the feeling that the service provider wants to give something back to a client, and the belief that one can share one's true thoughts and feelings with a client. On the not-so-positive side, a theme that also emerged was that sometimes the friendships are not mutual. Comments like, "I thought she would never leave" or "Won't he give me a break?" would be consistent with that theme.[40]

Some interpretative software are available as freeware. AnSWR is available from the U.S. Centers for Disease Control and Prevention (http://www.cdc.gov/hiv/software/answr.htm) as is EZ-Text (http://www.cdc.gov/hiv/software/ez-text.htm). Transana will read video and audio tape data and is available from the Wisconsin Center for Education Research (http://www.transana.org).

Text Mining

Generally, when managers think of data mining capabilities, they think of statistical analyses of large volumes of quantitative data. However, modern predictive analytic software enables text data to be mined from various sources including social networking sites, recorded conversations from call centers, e-mail contacts, and many more sources. Large companies including Sikorsky Aircraft, one of the largest helicopter companies in the world, and Cablecom, a Swiss telecommunications firm, have used text mining software to help reveal and interpret issues related to customer churn.[38] Leading statistical analysis companies such as SAS and SPSS offer advanced text mining capabilities. Although these programs can be expensive, they offer companies the ability to extract meaning from the tremendous amounts of verbal information generated by their customers, partners, and competitors.

Exploratory Research in Science and in Practice

Any research tool, qualitative or quantitative, can be misapplied. Some people believe that a good statistician can support practically any argument. Well, this may be part urban legend but certainly statistics can be misleading. Qualitative research is no exception and researchers can apply these tools improperly and produce misleading results. Hopefully, the researcher has simply erred when this occurs. Intentionally misleading others with research results is blatantly unprofessional. A researcher needs to know what research tool to apply, how to apply, and when to apply it to practice the craft professionally.

Misuses of Exploratory Qualitative Research

Exploratory research cannot take the place of conclusive, confirmatory research and confirmatory research cannot take the place of discovery-oriented exploratory tools. Qualitative tools generally offer the researcher a great deal of flexibility to cover a wide degree of topics. As such, they are well suited to explore marketing issues. Subjectivity is a drawback of interpretive approaches but that weakness predominantly limits testing, particularly hypothesis testing. The term *interpretive* research sometimes is nearly synonymous with qualitative research. When only one researcher interprets the meaning of what a single person said in a depth interview, one should be very cautious before making major marketing decisions on these results. Is the result **replicable**? Replicable means the same conclusion is intersubjectively certifiable—another researcher's interpretation would match (or they would get the same result by conducting the same research procedures)? The temptation is to act on one interpretation because having other researchers interpret things like depth interviews takes resources that are not always readily available.

replicable

Something is intersubjectively certifiable meaning the same conclusion would be reached based on another researcher's interpretation of the research or by independently duplicating the research procedures.

Indeed, many researchers frowned on qualitative methodologies for years based on a few early and public misapplications during the so-called "motivational research" era. Although many of the ideas produced during this time had some merit, as can sometimes be the case, too few researchers did too much interpretation of too few respondents. Compounding this, marketers were quick to act on the results, believing that the results peaked inside one's subliminal consciousness and therefore held some type of extra power. Thus, often the research was flawed based on poor interpretation, as was the decision process when the deciders acted prematurely. Psychologists applied projective techniques and depth interviews to consumers frequently in the late 1950s and early 1960s, producing some interesting and occasionally bizarre reasons for consumers' purchasing behavior:

- A woman is very serious when she bakes a cake because unconsciously she is going through the symbolic act of giving birth.
- A man buys a convertible as a substitute mistress and a safer (and potentially cheaper) way of committing adultery.
- Men who wear suspenders are reacting to an unresolved castration complex.[41]

Decades later, researchers for McCann-Erickson and other advertising agencies interviewed women about roaches. Among other qualitative techniques, a form of TAT involving story completion about an encounter with an insect was applied in understanding the meanings of insects in consumers' lives. Research like this revealed themes including:

- The joy of victory over roaches (watching them die or seeing them dead).
- Using the roach as a metaphor through which women can take out their hostility toward men (women generally referred to roaches as "he" instead of "she" in their stories).
- A pervasive fear and hatred of roaches. When Orkin tested ads depicting roaches running on the television screen, viewers actually threw things at the screen before even thinking about whether the bugs were real. Although viewers felt real fear during the ads, Orkin decided to run the ads and even started a contest for people who could tell stories about damaging a television during the ad.[42]

Even today, we have the Pillsbury Doughboy as evidence that useful ideas originated from motivational research. In other cases, interpretations were either misleading or too ambitious (taken too far). However, many companies became frustrated when decisions based upon motivational research approaches proved poor. Thus, marketing researchers moved away from qualitative tools during the late 1960s and 1970s. Today, however, qualitative tools have won acceptance once again as researchers realize they have greater power in discovering insights that would be difficult to capture in typical survey research (which is limited as an exploratory tool).

Scientific Decision Processes

Objectivity and replicability are two characteristics of scientific inquiry. Are focus groups objective and replicable? Would three different researchers all interpret focus group data identically? How should a facial expression or nod of the head be interpreted? Have subjects fully grasped the idea or concept behind a nonexistent product? Have respondents overstated their interest because they tend to like all new products? Many of these questions reduce to a matter of opinion that may vary from researcher to researcher and from one respondent group to another. Therefore, a focus group, or a depth interview, or TAT alone does not best represent a complete scientific inquiry.

However, if the thoughts discovered through these techniques survive preliminary evaluations and are developed into research hypotheses, they can be further tested. These tests may involve survey research or an experiment testing an idea very specifically (for example, if Diet Cherry Dr. Pepper is liked better than Diet Pepsi, and so forth). Thus, exploratory research approaches using qualitative research tools are very much a *part* of *scientific* inquiry.

An exploratory research design is the most productive design, meaning the tools used produce more discoveries than do other research designs. A company cannot determine the most important product benefits until all benefits obtained from consuming the product are known.

Before making a *scientific* decision, a research project should include a confirmatory study using objective tools and an adequate sample in terms of both size and how well it represents a population. But, is a *scientific* decision approach always used or needed?

In practice, many marketing managers make decisions based solely on the results of focus group interviews or some other exploratory result. Given that some decisions involve relatively small risk, a scientific decision process is not always justified. However, as risk increases, the confidence that comes along with a rigorous research and decision process becomes well worth the investment. The primary barriers to scientific decisions are (1) time, (2) money, and (3) emotion.

Time

Sometimes, researchers simply lack sufficient time to follow up on exploratory research results. Marketing companies feel an increasingly urgent need to get new products to the market faster. Thus, a seemingly good idea generated in a focus group (like Diet, Vanilla, or Cherry Dr Pepper) is never tested with a more conclusive study. Managers may see the risk of delaying a decision as greater than the risk of proceeding without completing the scientific process. Thus, although the researcher may wish to protest, there may be logical reasons for such action. The decision makers should be aware, though, that the conclusions drawn from exploratory research designs are just that—exploratory. Thus, there is less likelihood of good results from the decision than if the research process had involved further testing.

Money

Similarly, researchers sometimes do not follow up on exploratory research results because the cost is too high. The research team may already have spent thousands of dollars on qualitative research. Managers who are unfamiliar with research will be very tempted to wonder, "Why do I need yet another study?" and "What did I spend all that money for?" Thus, they choose to proceed based only on exploratory results. Again, the researcher has fulfilled the professional obligation as long as he/she makes the tentative nature of any ideas derived from exploratory research clear in the research report.

This approach may seem haphazard but it isn't always bad. If a decision does not involve a great deal of risk or can be reversed easily, the best course of action may be to proceed to implementation without spending more time and money on confirmatory research. Remember, research should never cost more than the benefits that can come from an effective decision.

Emotion

Time, money, and emotion are all related. Decision makers sometimes become so anxious to have something resolved, or they get so excited about some novel discovery resulting from a focus group interview, they may act rashly. Perhaps some of the ideas produced during the motivational research era sounded so enticing that decision makers got caught up in the emotion of the moment and proceeded without the proper amount of testing. Thus, as in life, when we fall in love with something, we are prone to act irrationally. The chances of emotion interfering in this way are lessened, but not eliminated, by making sure multiple decision makers are involved in the decision process.

TIPS OF THE TRADE

- Qualitative research tools are most helpful when
  - The decision makers don't know exactly what issues to take action on
  - A specific behavior needs to be studied in depth
  - When the value of a product changes dramatically from situation to situation or consumer to consumer
  - When exploring a research area with the intent of studying it further
  - Concept testing
- The focus group moderator is key to a successful interview. Not just anyone can moderate a focus group. Generally speaking, a good moderator can get more out of a respondent by saying less.

- Focus group questions should start with more general questions and work to the more specific.
- Don't be afraid to use props such as advertisements, photos, or actual products to get respondents talking.
- Apply qualitative tools to data already existing on the Internet such as social networking sites, corporate feedback listings and blogs.
- Exploratory research approaches are not useful in hypothesis testing.
- The overall value of a research tool is not determined by whether it is quantitative or qualitative but by the value that it produces.

Source: © Cengage Learning 2013.

:: SUMMARY

1. Contrast qualitative research with quantitative research. The chapter emphasized that any argument about the overall superiority of qualitative versus quantitative research is misplaced. Rather, each approach has advantages and disadvantages that make it appropriate in certain situations. The most noticeable difference is the relative absence of numbers in qualitative research. Qualitative research relies more on researchers' subjective interpretations of text or other visual material. In contrast, the numbers produced in quantitative research are objective in the sense that they don't change simply because someone else computed them. Qualitative research involves small samples, whereas quantitative research usually uses large samples. Qualitative procedures are generally more flexible and produce deeper and more elaborate explanations than quantitative research.

2. Know the role of qualitative research in exploratory research designs. The high degree of flexibility that goes along with most qualitative techniques makes it very useful in exploratory research designs. Therefore, exploratory research designs most often involve some qualitative research technique. Many of the things that some criticize qualitative research for, such as lack of structure, actually are advantageous in an exploratory design.

3. Describe the basic orientations of qualitative research. Phenomenology is a philosophical approach to studying human experiences based on the idea that human experience itself is inherently subjective and determined by the context within which a person experiences something. It lends itself well to conversational research. Ethnography represents ways of studying cultures through methods that include high involvement with that culture. Participant-observation is a common ethnographic approach. Grounded theory represents inductive qualitative investigation in which the researcher continually poses questions about a respondent's discourse in an effort to derive a deep explanation of their behavior. Collages are sometimes used to develop grounded theory. Case studies simply are documented histories of a particular person, group, organization, or event.

4. Recognize common qualitative research tools and know the advantages and limitations of their use. Two of the most common qualitative research tools include the focus group interview and the depth interview. The focus group has some cost advantage per respondent because it would take ten times as long to conduct the interview portion(s) of a series of depth interviews compared to one focus group. However, the depth interview is more appropriate for discussing sensitive topics. Researchers today though have a wide variety of tools at their disposal aside from the focus group and depth interview.

5. Prepare a focus group interview outline. A focus group outline should begin with introductory comments followed by a very general opening question that does not lead the respondent. More specific questions should be listed until a blunt question directly pertaining to the study objective is included. It should conclude with debriefing comments and a chance for questions and answers with respondents.

6. Recognize ways social networking and the blogsphere provide opportunities for qualitative research. Facebook postings are replete with postings about brands, products, and consumer experiences. These natural conversations are fertile data for interpretative researchers. Some companies have even established a focus blog that is a source for continuous commentary on a company. Others companies set up their own social networking sites intended to collect information about their brand and products. A key strength of these approaches is cost effectiveness, although virtually no control can be exercised over the respondents. Internet-based communication tools also greatly facilitate focus groups involving participants who need not travel to a focus group facility. This can be particularly useful when groups consist of professionals who would be unlikely to take the time to participate otherwise.

7. Appreciate the role of exploratory qualitative research in scientific decision making. Qualitative research has a rightful place in scientific discovery and the idea that qualitative research is somehow lacking in rigor because it is not quantitative is simply misplaced. Risks do come with using exploratory research procedures in general to make scientific decisions. Not all decisions require a scientific decision process and companies sometimes do make major decisions using only exploratory research. Several explanations for this behavior involve time, money, and emotion. A lack of time, a lack of money and strong emotions to move on all represent barriers to a scientific decision process. Ultimately, the researcher's job is to make sure that decision makers understand the increased risk that comes along with basing a decision only on exploratory research results.

∷ KEY TERMS AND CONCEPTS

case studies, *106*

concept testing, *102*

conversations, *113*

depth interview, *112*

discussion guide, *116*

ethnography, *104*

field notes, *115*

focus blog, *119*

focus group interview, *108*

free-association techniques, *114*

grounded theory, *105*

hermeneutic unit, *103*

hermeneutics, *103*

laddering, *112*

moderator, *111*

netnography, *120*

online focus group, *119*

participant-observation, *104*

Phenomenology, *103*

picture frustration, *115*

piggyback, *108*

projective technique, *115*

qualitative data, *100*

qualitative marketing research, *97*

quantitative data, *101*

quantitative marketing research, *99*

replicable, *122*

researcher-dependent, *97*

subjective results, *99*

thematic apperception test (TAT), *115*

themes, *106*

∷ QUESTIONS FOR REVIEW AND CRITICAL THINKING

1. Define *qualitative* and *quantitative* research. Compare and contrast the two approaches.
2. Describe the term *interpretive research.*
3. Consider the chapter vignette. Illustrate how researchers could apply at least four different qualitative tools to the business situation described in the opening vignette.
4. Define probing. Describe an illustration of the way probing might reveal ideas for a new product or a product improvement in the grocery or fast-food industry.
5. What are the basic categories (orientations) of qualitative research?
6. Of the four basic categories of qualitative research, which do you think is most appropriate for a qualitative approach designed to better define a marketing situation prior to conducting confirmatory research?
7. How might ethnography be used in concept testing?
8. What type of exploratory research would you suggest in the following situations?
   a. A product manager suggests development of a non-tobacco cigarette blended from wheat, cocoa, and citrus.
   b. A research project has the purpose of evaluating potential brand names for a new insecticide.

c. A manager must determine the best site for a drive-in convenience store in an urban area.

d. An advertiser wishes to identify the symbolism associated with cigarette smoking.

e. Searching for ideas for new smartphone or tablet applications.

9. What are the key differences between a focus group interview and a depth interview?

10. 'NET Visit some websites for large companies like Honda, Qantas Airlines, Target, Auchan, and Marriot. Is there any evidence that they are using their Facebook sites in some way to conduct a continuous online focus blog or intermittent online focus groups?

11. What is *laddering*? How might it be used in trying to understand which fast-food restaurant different segments of customers prefer?

12. How is a focus group outline used by a focus group moderator?

13. List at least four ways that recent technological advances have advanced the use of qualitative research. Explain your choices. Do you know any even newer ways that technological advancements could provide data in the form of text or picture

messages? Can you think of a way that SMS text messages or MMS messages might provide qualitative input?

14. Comment on the following remark by a marketing consultant: "Qualitative exploration is a tool of marketing research and a stimulant to thinking. In and by itself, however, it does not constitute market research."

15. ETHICS A researcher tells a manager of a wine company that he has some "cool ethnography results from Facebook postings" suggesting that young consumers like the idea of a plastic individual serving size bottles that could be vended or offered at the cash register. Even before the decision maker sees the report, the manager begins purchasing small plastic bottles and the new bottling equipment. Comment on this situation.

16. ETHICS Under what circumstances might it be unethical to use consumer postings on a brand community Facebook site as data in qualitative research?

17. A bottled water company receives many thousands of customer e-mails every year. Some are complaints; some are compliments. Are these e-mails a possible source for interpretative research? How about for exploratory research? For confirmatory research? Why or why not?

:: RESEARCH ACTIVITIES

1. 'NET How might the following industries use an Internet social networking site for exploratory research? Search several well-known brand names on Facebook. Do you see any evidence that the brands in these industries are using the site to collect data useful in qualitative research?
   a. Energy drinks
   b. Vacation resorts
   c. Video game manufacturers
   d. Insurance companies

2. Go back to the opening vignette. What if Vans approached you to do a focus group interview that explored the idea of offering casual attire (off-board) aimed at their primary segment

(skateboarders) and offering casual attire for male retirees? How would you recommend the focus group(s) proceed? Prepare a focus group outline(s) to accomplish this task.

3. Interview two people about their exercise behavior. In one interview, try to use a semi-structured approach by preparing questions ahead of time and trying to have the respondent complete answers for these questions. With the other, try a conversational approach. What are the main themes that emerge in each? Which approach do you think was more insightful? Do you think there were any "sensitive" topics that a respondent was not completely forthcoming about?

Disaster and Consumer Value

Case 5.1

After September 11, 2001, U.S. consumers showed a desire to tone down their consumer activities. They ordered simpler foods in restaurants and spent more time at home. Therefore, a lot of marketing campaigns began emphasizing down-home themes.

At some point after a disaster, it is time to get back to business. But, major catastrophic events are likely to leave permanent changes on consumers and employees in those areas. Suppose you are approached by the owner of several delicatessens and full-service wine stores in the Gulf Coast area. It is January 2006, and they want to get back to business. But they are uncertain about whether they should simply maintain the same positioning they had previous to Hurricane Katrina and Hurricane Rita. They would like to have a report from you within eighty days.

Questions

1. How could each classification of qualitative research be used here?

2. What qualitative research tool(s) would you recommend be used and why?

3. Where would you conduct any interviews and with whom would you conduct them?

4. ETHICS Are there ethical issues that you should be sensitive to in this process? Explain.

5. What issues would arise in conducting a focus group interview in this situation?

6. Prepare a focus group outline.

Source: © Cengage Learning 2013.

Secondary Data Research in a Digital Age

CHAPTER 6

LEARNING OUTCOMES

After studying this chapter, you should be able to:

1. Discuss the advantages and disadvantages of using secondary data
2. Understand the typical objectives addressed by secondary data
3. Identify various internal and proprietary sources of secondary data
4. Give examples of various external sources of secondary data
5. Describe the impact of single-source data and globalization on secondary data research

Chapter Vignette:

Every (Virtual) Move You Make

So, do you like *Big Brother*? This reality television concept has been copied and altered many times since its advent in Europe. Do people like to eavesdrop on others? Do people like to be eavesdropped upon? Considering the contents conveyed via social networking sites like Facebook, Baidu, Bebo, Twitter, and foursquare.com, perhaps privacy isn't what it used to be! But, nonetheless, a wealth of information is left behind. Many researchers would like to eavesdrop to address the research questions they face. Today, the fact that many of the "moves" that people make are online means that these people are easier to "watch" than ever before.

Researchers with different motives are watching. All of these parties are very interested in the electronic records of behavior left behind when we do things online.

- A marketing research firm hired by a mobile phone service company is trying to find the appropriate target market for different types of products, including pay-as-you-go media devices.
- An online university is looking for target markets expressing dissatisfaction with their life situations. They want to test to see if these segments will be more receptive to marketing appeals to attend the online university than segments identified through more traditional methods.

- Employers hire a research firm to identify employees who have serious issues in their personal lives, as evidenced by messages posted on their social networking sites or who are shirking on the job based on the amount of time they spend logged on to different websites.
- Security officials at the Pentagon and MI6 (British intelligence service) mine material posted on social networking sites, looking for potential security threats.
- T.G.I. Friday's searches for a new location site in Vancouver, B.C.

Image courtesy of Susan Van Etten

■ Political candidates have researchers mine data from blogs and social networks to identify potential targets for significant donations.

These efforts have led to successful marketing appeals, dismissal of employees, and security operations that may have prevented terrorist acts. One company in the United Kingdom identified an employee who spent 35 hours a week logged onto a social networking site when he was supposed to be working. So, 35 out of 40 hours were spent logged on. The employee had no idea that the company could monitor the amount of time spent on the site.

The information that we leave behind in our online behaviors can become stored as secondary data. Advances in technology, particularly something called *Resource Description Framework* or RDF, are enabling better communication across different Web-based interfaces so that once an individual is identified, information taken from different sources about different aspects of the individual's life can all be gathered together in a single record.

Obviously, the sheer volume of secondary data available reveals how important information that is collected and stored as a matter of routine or for some purpose other than a specific research purpose can be. But, perhaps questions about the morality or ethics of using this data are worth debating. Nonetheless, for marketing researchers who specialize in analyzing secondary data, this is a very good time to watch every virtual move consumers make.[1]

Introduction

Market researchers are always working under budget constraints. So, they are wise to ask if the data researchers need to examine the research questions already exists. If so, the analysis can proceed quickly and efficiently. If not, a much more laborious process lies ahead. This chapter focuses on instances where the data may indeed already exist in some usable format.

Using Secondary Data in Marketing Research

secondary data

Data that have been previously collected for some purpose other than the one at hand.

Researchers often look for secondary data at some point in the research process. **Secondary data** are facts and information collected and recorded by someone else prior to and for purposes other than the current project. Secondary data usually are historical and already assembled. They require no additional access to the people who provided the observations that comprise the data.

Advantages

"If I have seen farther than others, it is because I have stood on the shoulders of giants."

—ISAAC NEWTON

The primary advantage of secondary data is availability. Obtaining secondary data is almost always faster and less expensive than acquiring primary data. This is particularly true when researchers use electronic retrieval to access data stored digitally. In many situations, collecting secondary data is instantaneous.

Consider the money and time saved by researchers who obtained updated population estimates for a town during the interim between the 2000 and 2010 censuses. Instead of doing the fieldwork themselves, researchers acquired estimates from sources such as Claritas or the U.S. Census Bureau. The use of secondary data eliminates many of the activities normally associated with primary data collection, such as sampling and data processing. In this case, no workers need to be sent out canvasing neighborhoods to get counts.

Secondary data are essential in instances when data cannot be obtained using primary data collection procedures. For example, a manufacturer of farm implements could not duplicate the information in the Census of Agriculture because much of the information there (for example, amount of taxes paid) might not be accessible to a private firm. In India, researchers use census estimates to track sensitive topics like the child labor rate between the years when an actual census takes place.[2] The results suggest that in the mid-2000s, the rate of child labor, ages as low as five years of age are considered, decreased relative to the 1990s but that the overall number of children in the Indian workplace increased.

Secondary data are collected for a purpose other than the immediate research question at hand. When you participated in the survey as part of taking this course, you contributed to a database that your instructor can use to illustrate concepts with and provide assignments with which you can analyze real-world data. However, collecting fresh data by having your class respond is more like primary data collection. In most primary data collections, the researcher could perhaps find secondary data that may not provide the precise information needed to address a research question, but it might at least be in the same general area as the research question. In our survey, the researcher had some interest in students' communication behaviors. Thus, quite a few questions address text messaging, e-mailing, and so on. Consider the accompanying screenshot from the survey.

Can you find secondary data, aside from the database that goes with this questionnaire, that address similar issues among consumers? If so, what do you find? Do you think the results reveal similar patterns of behavior to that exposed in the class survey? Discuss your results.

Source: © Cengage Learning 2013.

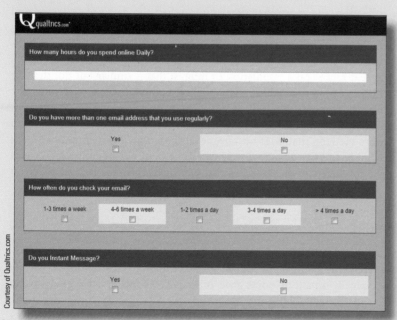

Courtesy of Qualtrics.com

Disadvantages

The researchers using secondary data in nearly every case did not collect the data. Thus, some reason other than the specific research question at hand motivated the data collection. In fact, they could have been collected for an entirely different reason. The data are not tailored to the particular research question but do they fit well enough to be useful? Researchers should ask questions such as these in evaluating this question:

- Do the data apply to the population of interest?
- Do the data apply to the time period of interest or are they too old?
- Do the secondary data appear in the correct units of measurement?
- Do the data offer facts relevant to the research question?
- Do the data include enough variables to describe the phenomena of interest in adequate detail?
- Are the data reliable and valid?

Researchers have to take care not to assume that secondary information is relevant, useful, and reliable simply because it is available. Consider the following typical situations:

- A researcher interested in forklift trucks finds twelve-year-old secondary data on forklift trucks grouped together in a broader category also counting industrial trucks and tractors.
- An investigator who wishes to study consumers earning more than $150,000 per year finds secondary data in which household income is reported in levels with the highest indicating the number of households at $100,000 per year or more.
- A brewery that wishes to compare its per-barrel advertising expenditures with those of competitors finds that some companies' data report the cost of point-of-purchase promotional expenditures with advertising and others do not. Thus, the units of measure differ across companies.
- Data from a previous warranty card study show where consumers like to buy a product but provide no reasons why.

Secondary data often do not adequately satisfy research needs because:

1. the data are too old,
2. of variation in definitions of terms,
3. the use of different units of measurement, and
4. inadequate information to verify the data's validity.

In a primary data collection, the researcher determines when the data are collected and defines the variables included in the research question(s). Contrast this to a researcher asked to investigate market potential for a new product within the African-American market using secondary data reported as "percent white," "percent nonwhite," and "other." Researchers frequently encounter secondary data that report on a population of interest that is similar but not directly comparable to their population of interest. Arbitron and Nielson both report television audience geographical areas based on in-home viewing. In other words, they estimate the percentage of households viewing any particular program such as *American Idol*. A major problem with these estimates is that they ignore viewing that goes on outside of the home. More and more, both Arbitron and Nielsen recognize this fact and now provide estimates of out-of-home viewing as well.[3] Now the researcher also can account for folks that get together at a tavern to cheer on their idols on TV.

Units of Measurement

Units of measurement may cause problems if they do not conform exactly to a researcher's needs. For example, consider a researcher comparing college students' grades across countries. In the United States, grades are typically on a four-point scale. In France, records indicate grades using a twenty-point scale. Places like Turkey, China, and Indonesia use other scales. Can the researcher directly compare students' grades to assist university administrators in making graduate school admission decisions? In contrast, standardized tests like the GMAT or the GRE use the same scale no matter where a student would take the test. Thus, administrators may find it easier to compare students based on standardized test scores. Interestingly though, the GMAT and GRE each use a different scale, making comparisons across the two tests difficult.

data transformation

The process of changing the original form of the data to a format suitable to achieve the research objective; also called *data transformation*.

Sometimes, data using different scales is amenable to rescaling. **Data transformation** is the process of changing the original form of data to a format more suitable for achieving a stated research objective. Researchers may find it easy to compare sales over the years by transforming all sales figures mathematically to a base year by using the inflation rate. For instance, $1 in 1980 = $2.95 in 2010. Government statistics provide GDP estimates in constant (i.e., transformed) dollars. Similarly, one can easily convert dollar values to euros or any other major currency using the exchange rate for that particular day. However, each standardized test covers and assigns points differently so transforming a GRE score to a GMAT score is questionable. Thus, transformations are not always possible.

Reliability and Validity

Another disadvantage of secondary data is that the user has no control over their reliability and validity—topics we will discuss in more detail later but for now, think of these as representing data accuracy or trustworthiness. Although timely and pertinent secondary data may fit the researcher's requirements, the data could be inaccurate. The research methods used to collect the data may have somehow introduced bias to the data. For example, media often publish data from surveys to identify the characteristics of their subscribers or viewers. These data will sometimes exclude derogatory data from their reports. Good researchers avoid data with a high likelihood of bias or for which bias cannot be determined.

Investigators are naturally more prone to accept data from reliable sources such as the census bureaus for major developed nations. Nevertheless, the researcher must assess the reputation of the organization that gathers the data and critically assess the original research design. Unfortunately, such evaluation may be impossible because he/she cannot find or obtain full information explaining the original research's procedures in detail.

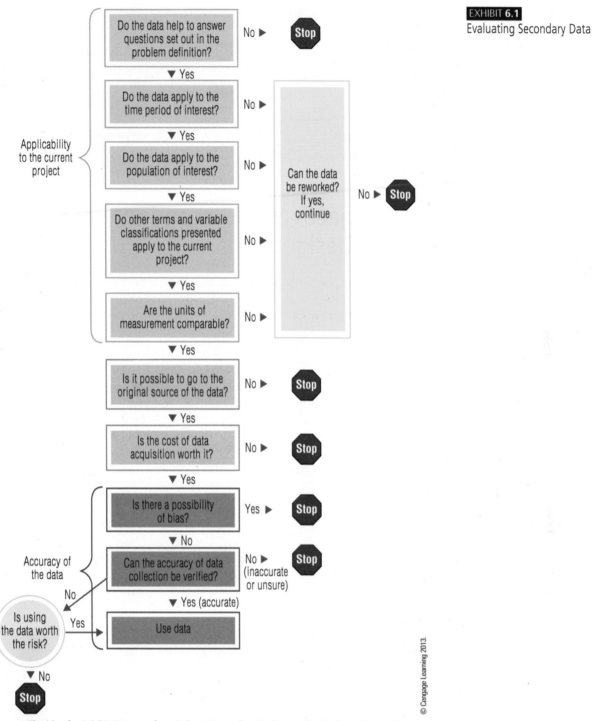

EXHIBIT 6.1
Evaluating Secondary Data

Source: The idea for Exhibit 6.1 came from Robert W. Joselyn, *Designing the Marketing Research Project* (NewYork: Petrocelli/Charter, 1977).

Researchers should verify data whenever possible. **Cross-checks** from multiple sources—that is, comparison of the data from one source with data from another—should be made to determine the similarity of independent projects. When the data are not consistent, researchers should attempt to identify reasons for the differences or to determine which data are most likely correct. When the researcher cannot verify the reliability and validity of the data, he/she must determine whether using the data is worth the risk. Exhibit 6.1 illustrates a detailed series of questions he/she should be asked to evaluate secondary data before they are used.

cross-checks

The comparison of data from one source with data from another source to determine the similarity of independent projects.

EXHIBIT 6.2
Common Research Objectives
for Secondary-Data Studies

Broad Objective	Specific Research Example
Fact-finding	Identifying consumption patterns Tracking trends
Model building	Estimating market potential Forecasting sales Selecting trade areas and sites
Database marketing	Enhancing customer databases Developing prospect lists

Typical Objectives for Secondary-Data Research Designs

We could never list all possible purposes of secondary data in marketing research. However, secondary data plays a role in many commonly occurring marketing research questions. Exhibit 6.2 shows three general categories of research objectives: fact-finding, model building, and database marketing.

Fact-Finding

The simplest form of secondary-data research is fact-finding. A restaurant serving breakfast might be interested in knowing what new products are likely to entice consumers. Secondary data available from National Eating Trends, a service of the NPD Group, show that the most potential may be in menu items customers can eat on the go.[4] According to data from the survey of eating trends, the increased prevalence of nutrition and calorie counts on menus has not significantly affected consumer choices. In addition, although overall restaurant sales dropped during the economic downturn of 2009 and 2010, fast casual restaurants such as Chili's have seen their sales go up. Another research firm, Market Facts, says almost half of consumers say they would pay extra for cheese. These simple facts would interest a researcher who was investigating today's dining market.

• • • • • • •

Fact-finding for restaurant data can begin with secondary data.

©AP Photo/Chris O'Connor

©Beth Hall/Landov

Does It Matter?

Secondary data, by its name, may seem to lack power compared to primary data. However, with secondary data, researchers can test research questions that would be difficult to examine any other way. For example, what matters when it comes to firm performance? Does customer satisfaction ultimately lead to superior firm performance? Given that firm performance is a property of the company and not of its customers or employees, the researcher cannot directly capture this with surveys. Therefore, researchers turn to secondary data to try to isolate controllable variables that drive firm performance.

Basic marketing research addresses this issue by tapping into secondary data sources such as the Nielsen database, Compustat, and the American Consumer Satisfaction Index (the ACSI). What should companies emphasize? Advertising, services, value, or satisfaction? Statistical models using secondary data suggest that advertising, satisfaction, and services all play a role. But, as an industry is more competitive, services

and value come to the top in shaping a firm's stock value. Thus, what matters? It seems like firms should allocate scarce resources toward increasing services and greater value. That's a recipe for success.

Sources: Grewal, P., M. Chandrashkaran, and A. V. Citrin (2010), "Customer Satisfaction Heterogeneity and Shareholder Value," *Journal of Marketing Research*, 47 (August), 612–26; Fang, E., R. W. Palmatier, and J. B. Steencamp (2008), "Effect of Service Transition Strategies on Firm Value," *Journal of Marketing*, 72 (September), 1–14; Luo, X., and C. Homburg (2007), "Neglected Outcomes of Consumer Satisfaction," *Journal of Marketing*, 71 (April), 133–49.

Identification of Consumer Behavior for a Product Category

A typical objective for a secondary research study might be to uncover all available information about consumption patterns for a particular product category or to identify demographic trends that affect an industry. For example, a company called Servigistics offers software that scans a company's own parts inventory data and compares it with marketing objectives and competitors' prices to suggest potential price adjustments. Kia Motors tried using this service in place of the usual method of marking up cost by a set fraction. By considering secondary data, including internal inventory data and external data about competitors' prices, it was able to make service parts a more profitable segment of its business.[5] This example illustrates the wealth of factual information about consumption and behavior patterns available by carefully collecting and analyzing secondary data.

Trend Analysis

Marketers watch for trends in the marketplace and the environment. **Market tracking** is the observation and analysis of trends in industry volume and brand share over time. Scanner research services and other organizations provide facts about sales volume to support this work.

Almost every large consumer goods company routinely investigates brand and product category sales volume using secondary data. This type of analysis typically involves comparisons with competitors' sales or with the company's own sales in comparable time periods. It also involves industry comparisons among different geographic areas.

market tracking

The observation and analysis of trends in industry volume and brand share over time.

Environmental Scanning

In many instances, fact-finding's purpose is simply to study the environment to identify trends. Environmental scanning entails information gathering and fact-finding designed to detect indications of environmental changes in their initial stages of development. As mentioned in Chapter 2, the Internet provides an easy tool for environmental scanning; however, there are other means, such as periodic review of contemporary publications and reports. Environmental scanning continues to show marketers that consumer demand in China is on the rise. Chinese authorities in the early 1990s stopped discouraging the use of makeup, and sales of these products took off—hitting

$524 million in 2005 and reaching $705 million by 2009.[6] Marketers, including Procter & Gamble, L'Oréal, and Shiseido, have captured a sizable share of this market by realizing the potential and developing products to get into the market early.

A number of online information services, such as Factiva and LexisNexis, routinely collect news stories about industries, product lines, and other topics of interest that have been specified by the researcher. Push technology uses "electronic smart agents," custom software that filters, sorts, prioritizes, and stores information for later viewing.[7] The true value of push technology is that the researcher who is scanning the environment can specify the kinds of news and information he or she wants, have it delivered to his or her computer quickly, and view it at leisure. However, early push technologies proved bothersome because they provided too much irrelevant information.[8] Today's technologies work together with search engine histories to direct users toward more relevant information faster.

Model Building

model building

A mathematical representation of the relationship between two or more variables; shows how one thing responds to changes in another.

Model building, the second general objective for secondary research, is more complicated than simple fact-finding. **Model building** involves specifying relationships between two or more variables, perhaps extending to the development of descriptive or predictive equations. The models try to specify how one thing changes in coordination with another. Models need not include complicated mathematics, though. In fact, decision makers often prefer simple models that everyone can readily understand to complex models that are difficult to comprehend. For example, market share is company sales divided by industry sales. This simplistic mathematical representation represents the firm's prowess in the marketplace. Mathematical model builders often use secondary data.

Estimating Market Potential for Geographic Areas

Marketers often estimate market potential using secondary data. In many cases, a trade association or another source publishes exact sales figures. However, when the desired information is unavailable, the researcher may estimate market potential by transforming secondary data from two or more sources. For example, managers may find secondary data about market potential for a country or other large geographic area, but this information may not be broken down into smaller geographical areas, such as by metropolitan area, or in terms unique to the company, such as sales territory. In this type of situation, researchers often need to make projections for the geographic area of interest.

Suppose a Belgian beer company is looking for opportunities to expand sales by exporting or investing in other countries. Managers decide to begin by estimating market potential several potential target markets. Secondary research uncovered data for per capita beer consumption in numerous sources including reports from Data Monitor, a company that catalogs commercial statistics by country. Population estimates are available in several places, including the Census Bureau and through the CIA (see www.cia.gov to access the World Factbook). Exhibit 6.3 illustrates the main findings compiled.

The trade area market potential for the Czech Republic in 2012 is found by multiplying the country's population estimate[9] by the per capita beer consumption:

$$10,190,000 \text{ people} \times 160 \text{ liters/person} = 1,630,400,000 \text{ liters}$$

That's over a bottle a day per person. To get a sense of the expected sales volume, the marketer would have to multiply this amount by the price per liter at which beer typically sells. Although the Czech Republic may be an attractive market, greater overall volume might be offered by other markets with larger overall populations. As Exhibit 6.3 reveals, China offers the largest potential market for beer sales in the world.[10] Brazil and the United States also display relatively high total beer consumption. Although those countries aren't known so much for beer consumption, the sheer size of the markets makes them attractive targets for the brewery.

Of course, the calculated market potential for each country in Exhibit 6.3 is a rough estimate. Also, the marketer will want to consider whether each country is experiencing growth or decline in demand. For example, beer consumption is barely growing in Europe and Japan, but it is

Country	2012 Population Estimate (thousands)	Annual per Capita Beer Consumption (liters)	Market Potential Estimate (k liters)
United States	315,000	85	26,775,000
Germany	81,000	105	8,505,000
Australia	22,000	107	2,354,000
Brazil	205,000	55	11,275,000
China	1,400,000	25	35,000,000
Czech Republic	10,190	160	1,630,400

Source: © Cengage Learning 2013.

EXHIBIT 6.3
Market Potential for Select Geographic Areas by Country

expanding in Latin America (at about 4 percent a year) and even faster in China (by at least 6 percent a year). Additionally, the researcher can probably find information on competitive intensity (how many beer companies are marketing in the country) in each area to adjust the projections for the amount of competition. Perhaps this information will cause the marketer to investigate market potential in additional countries where more growth is expected.

Forecasting Sales

Sales forecasting is the process of predicting sales totals over a specific time period. Accurate sales forecasts, especially for products in mature, stable markets, frequently come from secondary-data research that identifies trends and extrapolates past performance into the future. Marketing researchers often use internal company sales records to project sales. A rudimentary model would multiply past sales volume by an expected growth rate. A researcher might investigate a secondary source and find that industry sales normally grow about 10 percent per year; multiplying company sales volume by 10 percent would give a basic sales forecast.

Exhibit 6.4 provides data for making projections using a moving average projection of growth rates. Average ticket prices for a major-league baseball game are secondary data from Team Marketing Report (http://www.teammarketing.com). The moving average is the sum of growth rates for the past three years divided by 3 (number of years). The resulting number is a forecast of the percentage increase in ticket price for the coming year. Using the three-year average growth rate of 1.9 percent for the 2009, 2010, and 2011 sales periods, we can forecast the average ticket price for 2012 as follows:

$$\$26.92 + (\$26.92 \times .019) = \$27.43$$

A major-league baseball team is probably more interested in financial metrics like revenue. Using the ticket price for any season, one can compute average ticket sales revenue for any upcoming season by multiplying the average major league attendance projection times the number of home games (81) times the average ticket price. For the year 2012, the estimated attendance using the three-year moving average is 30,281. Thus, the estimated revenue for a typical team is:

$$30,281 \ tickets/game \times 81 \ games \times \$27.43 \ per \ ticket = \$67,279,234$$

The moving average forecasting is best suited to a static competitive environment. More dynamic situations make other sales forecasting techniques more appropriate.

Often, more sophisticated forecasting approaches are used. We'll discuss other forecasting methods later in the book, but simple moving averages like the three-year moving average are often applied in practice.

Analysis of Trade Areas and Sites

Marketing managers examine trade areas using **site analysis techniques** that help management select the best locations for retail or wholesale operations. Secondary-data research helps managers make these site selection decisions. Some organizations, especially franchisers, have

site analysis techniques
Techniques that use secondary data to select the best location for retail or wholesale operations.

EXHIBIT 6.4

Secondary Data for Major League Baseball Ticket Prices with Moving Average

Year	Average Ticket Price ($)	Percentage Change from Previous Year	3-Year Moving Average
1996	11.20	5.2%	3.5%
1997	12.36	10.4%	5.8%
1998	13.59	10.0%	8.5%
1999	14.91	9.7%	10.0%
2000	16.67	11.8%	10.5%
2001	18.99	13.9%	11.8%
2002	18.30	–3.6%	7.4%
2003	19.01	3.9%	4.7%
2004	19.82	4.3%	1.5%
2005	21.17	6.8%	5.0%
2006	22.21	4.9%	5.3%
2007	22.70	2.2%	4.6%
2008	25.43	12.0%	6.4%
2009	26.21	3.0%	5.7%
2010	26.60	1.5%	5.5%
2011	26.92	1.2%	1.9%

developed special computer software based on analytical models to select sites for retail outlets. The researcher must obtain the appropriate secondary data for analysis with the computer software.

index of retail saturation

A calculation that describes the relationship between retail demand and supply as a ratio of sales potential per unit area of retail sales space.

The **index of retail saturation** offers one way to investigate retail sites and to describe the relationship between retail demand and supply.[11] The calculation gives an idea of how much revenue a market generates per a specific amount of retail space:

$$\text{Index of retail saturation} = \frac{\text{Local market potential (demand)}}{\text{Local market retailing space}}$$

For example, Exhibit 6.5 shows the relevant secondary data for shoe store sales in a five-mile radius surrounding a Florida shopping center. Data like these are available from numerous vendors of market information such as Mapping Analytics. First, to estimate local market potential (demand), we multiply population by annual per capita shoe sales in the trade area. Then, we sum the selling floor size over all shoe stores in the trade area. These two figures make the numerator and denominator of the calculation, respectively:

$$\text{Index of Retail Saturation} = \frac{\$14,249,000}{94,000 \text{ sq.ft.}} = \$152/\text{sq.ft.}$$

An index value above 200 is considered to indicate exceptional opportunities. Trade area maps represent market potential using colors that indicate varying degrees of market potential. The result is a geographic information system (GIS) that pull secondary data together from multiple sources to provide useful information for better decision making.

1. Population	261,785
2. Annual per capita shoe sales	$54.43
3. Local market potential (line 1 x line 2)	$14,249,000
4. Square feet of retail space used to sell shoes	94,000 sq. ft.
5. Index of retail saturation (line 3/line 4)	152

Source: © Cengage Learning 2013.

Advertising Response

A great deal of modeling in marketing research focuses on how advertising influences consumers and business performance including the way advertising intensity affects the rate at which a service is adopted or disadopted (meaning a consumer ends the service agreement). Particularly in public services such as cable television, historic records on diffusion and firm advertising are readily available. The models include a relationship between the firm's own advertising and the primary competitor's advertising.[12] Additionally, other models show that although banner ad click-through rates are very low, they do contribute to increased sales.

Some models are more focused on classification than response. They may try to show overlap between groups of people or communication. For instance, they may mine social networking data to identify common networks of people whose communication overlaps across Facebook, Twitter, and MySpace.[13] Advertisers can use this knowledge to send a carefully targeted message to a consumer in one social network that will then expand to others by virtue of the overlap.

Data Mining

Large corporations' decision support systems often contain millions or even hundreds of millions of records of data. In Chapter 2, we introduced the term *data mining* in discussing what happens after huge volumes of data become stored electronically and are accessible by a firm's research analysts. Data mining helps clarify the underlying meaning of the data.

The term **data mining** refers specifically to the use of powerful computer analytical routines to dig automatically through huge volumes of data searching for useful patterns of relationships. The analytics can take many forms from simple correlational routines to routines that are more like artificial intelligence. For example, **neural networks** are a form of artificial intelligence in which a computer mimics the way that human brains process information. One computer expert put it this way:

A neural network learns pretty much the way a human being does. Suppose you say "big" and show a child an elephant, and then you say "small" and show her a poodle. You repeat this process with a house and a giraffe as examples of "big" and then a grain of sand and an ant as examples of "small." Pretty soon she will figure it out and tell you that a truck is "big" and a needle is "small." Neural networks can similarly generalize by looking at examples.[14]

Market-basket analysis is a form of data mining that analyzes anonymous point-of-sale transaction databases to identify coinciding purchases or relationships between products purchased and other retail shopping information.[15] Auchan, a large French hypermart firm, identified an interesting pattern among the scanner data gathered as

Reprinted by courtesy of ESRI

customers pay for the things they buy. They noticed that a higher-than-expected number of customers who bought baby diapers also bought beer (they end up in the market basket together). A quick follow-up suggested further that most of the diaper and beer buyers were men. As a result, management decided to move some beer displays closer to the diapers and, as a result, they raised the proportion of beer and customer buyers even higher.

customer discovery

Involves mining data to look for patterns identifying who is likely to be a valuable customer.

Customer discovery is a data-mining application that similarly involves mining data to look for patterns that can increase the value of customers. For example, Macy's commissioned data-mining techniques, looking for patterns of relationships among the huge volumes of previous sales records. In 2011, Macy's sent out millions of catalogs. Not every customer got the same catalog though and, in fact, tens of thousands of versions of the catalog were carefully tailored to specific customers.[16] Female customers 30 years of age will see more handbags, accessories, shoes and women's clothing, than will a middle-aged man. Further, if her individual records show purchases of baby clothing, she'll probably see lots of things for toddlers. The end result is that the customer sees more purchase possibilities that have a high probability of addressing a current need or desire.

Similarly, most catalog merchants have information for each customer, revealing the sets of products that the customer buys in every purchase order. A sequence detection function searches and discovers sets of purchases that frequently precede the purchase of, say, an Internet TV console. The company can then direct-tailor marketing to this customer. As a different type of example, a sequence of insurance claims could lead to the identification of frequently occurring medical procedures performed on patients, which in turn could be used to detect cases of medical fraud.

Researchers are not always trying to find customers in data mining. The research snapshot shows how management can stay in touch with buzz online that may indicate events might impact the brand's image and overall equity.

Database Marketing and Customer Relationship Management

As we have already mentioned, a CRM (customer relationship management) system is a decision support system that manages the interactions between an organization and its customers. A CRM maintains customer databases containing customers' names, addresses, phone numbers, past purchases, responses to past promotional offers, and other relevant data such as demographic and financial data. **Database marketing** is the practice of using CRM databases to develop one-to-one relationships and precisely targeted promotional efforts with individual customers. For example, a gourmet fruit company CRM contains a database of previous customers, including what purchases they made during the Christmas holidays. Each year the company sends last year's gift list to customers to help them send the same gifts to their friends and relatives.

database marketing

The use of customer databases to promote one-to-one relationships with customers and create precisely targeted promotions.

Effective database marketing requires vast amounts of secondary data to be integrated into a CRM system. Transaction records, which often list items purchased by individual customers, its price, the customer name, address, and ZIP code, are the building block for many databases. Analysts supplement these records with data customers provide directly, such as data on a warranty card, short survey, or even other secondary data purchased from third parties. For example, credit services may sell databases about applications for loans, credit card payment history, and other financial data. Several companies, such as Donnelley Marketing (with its BusinessContentFile and ConsumerContentFile services) and Claritas (with PRIZM), collect primary data and then sell demographic data that can be related to small geographic areas, such as those with a certain ZIP code. (Remember that when the vendor collects the data, they are primary data, but when the database marketer incorporates the data into his or her database, they are secondary data.)

Sources of Internal Secondary Data

More and more, the exact distinction between internal and external secondary data becomes blurry with modern information technology. Some accounting documents are indisputably internal records of the organization. Researchers in another organization cannot have access to them. Clearly, a book published by the *Wall Street Journal* and located at a public library is external to the company. However, in today's world of electronic data interchange, data gathered by an industry

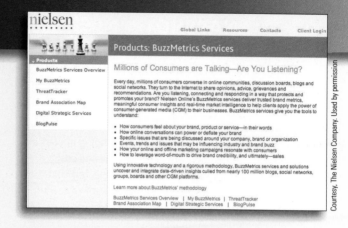

What's That Buzzing Sound?

Bees aren't the only creatures that buzz. Consumers do, too, and more and more they create that buzz online. Just think about it, the Internet is filled with billions of consumer conversations. Obviously, these billions of data points contain a lot of useful information. But, a lot of it is useless, too. How can a firm make sense of this? One solution: data-mining software designed for the blogosphere.

Buzzmetrics, a part of Nielsen online, serves firms by monitoring Internet conversation letting firms know whether conversation about their brand is up or down on any given time period. Want to know if a Super Bowl ad had any impact? The buzz an ad creates from the time it becomes public is good indicator. No buzz, probably not much sizzle in terms of market effectiveness. Is *Dancing with the Stars* still popular? If people aren't talking about it online then that show too may be losing its sizzle. For large brands, companies like Buzzmetrics monitor thousands of websites for brand mentions and whether those mentions are positive or negative. Thus, secondary data can provide a buzz that can come with or without a sting based on whether the conversations spread good or bad news about the brand.

Sources: Hargrave, S. (2008), "Ears to the Ground," *New Media Age* (January 17), 21; Notarantonio, E.M. (2009), "The Effectiveness of a Buzz Marketing Approach Compared to Traditional Advertising: An Exploration," *Journal of Promotion Management*, 15 (October–December), 455–64; Alahnah, M., and D. Khazanchi (2010), "The Importance of Buzz," *Marketing Research*, 22 (Summer), 20–25.

organization may appear in a catalog and may be purchased. For example, international beverage consumption statistics broken down by category are available for purchase from an online information vendor and then made available to company analysts for instantaneous access within the DSS. The formerly external data is now available internally.

Internal data are data that originate in the organization and represent events recorded by or generated by the organization. **Proprietary data** is perhaps a more descriptive term and emphasizes the fact that company owns and controls the data.

Internal and Proprietary Data

Most organizations routinely gather, record, and store internal data to help them solve future problems. An organization's accounting system can usually provide a wealth of information. Routine documents such as sales invoices allow external financial reporting, which in turn can be a source of data for further analysis. If company employees properly code the data into a company database, the researcher may be able to conduct more detailed analysis using the decision support system. Companies organize sales information in several different ways including by account, by product, or by sales territory. The coding allows retrieval of information about orders delivered, back orders, and unfilled orders. Other useful sources of internal data include salespeople's call reports, customer complaints, service records, warranty card returns, product returns, archived focus group recordings, and other records. As you can see, the data provides opportunities to forecast and potentially explain important outcomes to the firm including sales and return rates.

Researchers frequently aggregate or disaggregate internal data. A wine store compared its sales records to names registered on its e-mail mailing list. As a result, the store owner realized that the old 20–80 rule was no exaggeration. In fact, about 15 percent of customers accounted for 80 percent of all sales. As a result, the store concentrated on extra incentives for the best customers to visit the store even more often.

Internet technology is making it easier to research internal and proprietary data. Often companies set up secure, internal networks allowing employees to store and share proprietary data within the organization. An **enterprise search**, which is like an Internet search but focuses on data within the enterprise's internal network, considers not only how many views a particular

internal data

Data that originate in the organization and represent events recorded by or generated by the organization.

proprietary data

Secondary data owned and controlled by the organization.

enterprise search

A search driven by an Internet-type search engine that focuses on data within an organization's internal network.

Uncle Sam Finds You!

In a nation with an all-volunteer military, finding recruits is an ongoing need. The project is especially challenging in wartime, when more service members are necessary but the costs of serving are too daunting for many citizens. One way that the Department of Defense meets this challenge is by reviewing data that exist in a variety of sources. Its Joint Advertising, Market Research & Studies (JAMRS) project operates over a dozen research initiatives that make data available to military recruiters in all branches of the U.S. armed services. Some involve data collection, but many apply already-existing data (secondary data) to the task of recruitment.

JAMRS is partly a data warehouse storing all information gathered as potential recruits visit or contact recruiting stations. JAMRS also pays for data from third-party research firms. For example, it uses the PRIZM market segmentation data gathered and sold by Claritas, a marketing research firm. The PRIZM data describe the purchasing and media behavior of many market segments. Recruiters can use the data to identify the activities of potential recruits that live in their region—for example, to identify the magazines they read. This information can help local recruiters or branches of the military target messages likely to appeal to particular groups of young men and women. Research suggests that recruits are most likely to come from households with lower-middle incomes or below in rural areas and small towns. However, the PRIZM data go much deeper,

Courtesy, U.S. Department of Defense

showing, for example, that U.S. army recruits often come from households that listen to Spanish-language radio and that prospective Marines tend to read *Outdoor Life* and enjoy fishing and hunting.

For the Defense Department, recruiting would no doubt be far more difficult and far less effective without access to secondary data; in this case, data gathered for purposes other than military recruitment. But the data are useful only with careful analysis and interpretation. In this way, Uncle Sam can communicate with receptive audiences in an efficient manner.

Sources: "Market Research and Studies," *Joint Advertising, Market Research & Studies*, JAMRS website, http://www.jamrs.org/mrs.php, accessed April 5, 2011; Arndorfer, James B., "Target Practice," *Advertising Age* (November 28, 2005), 76, 1–41; Margolis, Emanuel, "Building a Database of Potential Soldiers," *Connecticut Law Tribune* (October 24, 2005), http://www.ctlawtribune.com; Arndorfer, James B., "Army Looking for a Direct Hit," *Advertising Age* (July 11, 2005), 76, 4–36.

data page records, but also users' historical search patterns in determining what data might be useful. In addition, other companies have purchased specialized enterprise search software, such as Autonomy, which searches internal sources plus such external sources as news and government websites.[17]

External Secondary Data Sources

external data

Facts observed, recorded, and stored by an entity outside of the researcher's organization.

External data are facts observed, recorded, and stored by an entity outside of the researcher's organization. The government, universities, newspapers and journals, trade associations, and other organizations perform these services either to serve industry or to offer for sale. Today, computerized access is the rule of the day making external data nearly as accessible as internal data. The Research Snapshot illustrates a company that specializes in data archives.

Information as a Product and Its Distribution Channels

Secondary data offers value and thus, companies buy and sell data access regularly. Just as bottles of perfume or plumbers' wrenches go from production to consumers in different ways, secondary data also flow through various channels of distribution. Many users, such as the *Fortune* 500 corporations, purchase documents and computerized lifestyle and population data from companies like Claritas. However, smaller companies lacking the budget necessary to buy data from these companies can get a wealth of data free from sources like the U.S. Census Bureau (**www.census.gov**).

Libraries

Traditionally, libraries' vast storehouses of information have served as a bridge between users and producers of secondary data. The library staff deals directly with the creators of information, such as the federal government, and intermediate distributors of information, such as abstracting and indexing services. The user need only locate the appropriate secondary data on the library shelves (physical or virtual). Libraries provide collections of books, journals, newspapers, and so on for reading and reference. They also stock many bibliographies, abstracts, guides, directories, and indexes, as well as offer access to basic databases. University students don't actually visit the library as much as in the past. Instead, they access many data sources through the school library's website. Large corporations also maintain libraries, as do public institutions like the United Nations and Library of Congress.

The Internet

Today, of course, much secondary data is conveniently available over the Internet. Its creation also means that the data industry is truly global. For example, Library Spot, at **http://www.libraryspot.com**, provides links to online libraries, including law libraries, medical libraries, and music libraries. The virtual reference desk features links to calendars, dictionaries, encyclopedias, maps, and other sources typically found at a traditional library's reference desk. However, today's search engines provide a good start in a search. Remember though, not all sources are equal as some are more credible than others. Exhibit 6.6 lists some popular Internet addresses where one can find potentially useful data.

The opening vignette illustrates how companies find a lot of secondary data via the Internet. Consumers also use information posted online as a form of secondary data to aid in their own purchases. J.D. Power (jdpower.com) provides consumer ratings of many, many products. For instance, a consumer can look there and find the mobile phones and smartphones that are rated most favorably on dimensions such as reliability, ease of use, and battery performance. In 2011, Samsung led in mobile phones and the Apple iPhone topped the smartphone list. Consumers also leave behind comments and ratings and ask questions and get answers from other consumers who they may not even know. Consumers place more value on information provided by consumers who respond quickly to Internet queries for information, whose previous responses are positively evaluated by other consumers and who seem to show knowledge in their responses.[18] Marketing researchers similarly weigh information posted by consumers based on some assessment of credibility.

Vendors

The information age offers many channels besides libraries through which to access data. Many external producers make secondary data available directly from the organizations that produce the data or through intermediaries, which are often called *vendors*. Vendors such as Factiva now allow managers to participate in a community and access thousands of external databases. Hoovers (**http://www.hoovers.com**), for instance, specializes in providing information about thousands of companies' financial situations and operations.

Producers

Classifying external secondary data by the nature of the producer of information yields five basic sources: publishers of books and periodicals, government sources, media sources, trade association sources, and commercial sources. The following section discusses some secondary data sources briefly.

Periodicals

Professional journals, such as the *Journal of the Academy of Marketing Science, Journal of Marketing, Journal of Marketing Research, The Journal of Business Research, Journal of Advertising Research, American Demographics,* and *The Public Opinion Quarterly,* as well as commercial business periodicals such as the *Wall Street Journal, Fortune,* and *BusinessWeek,* contain much useful material. *Sales and Marketing Management's Survey of Buying Power* is a particularly useful source of information about markets.

"The man who does not read good books has no advantage over the man who cannot read them."

—MARK TWAIN

EXHIBIT 6.6

Selected Internet Sources for Secondary Data

Source	Description	URL
U.S. Census Bureau	Demographic information about the United States overall and by state and county. Information about U.S. business and the economy.	www.census.gov
CIA Factbook	Profiles of 286 countries providing descriptive statistics of population, commerce, geography, history, and much more.	www.cia.gov
Federal Statistics	A portal containing links to reports and data compiled by most federal agencies ranging from agriculture to education.	www.fedstats.gov
Data Monitor	Offers a very large collection of current business reports on industries, countries, markets, and consumption statistics as well as tracking data for new product launches. Subscription required.	www.datamonitor.com
Advertising Age	Media source for advertising industry news and access to hundreds of research reports on specific issues within and affecting the industry (for a fee).	www.adage.com
Kantar Media	Source focusing on the integrated global media industry. Excellent source for statistics and reports on viewership, Internet usage, and basic consumer profiles such as the British teen market.	www.kantarmedia.com
European Union Commission	Comprehensive collection of statistics on Europe overall and the individual nations within the European Union. Statistics include detailed economic performance data, immigration, demographic data, and much more.	ec.europa.eu/eurostat
The Wall Street Journal Online	Provides a real-time view of business news and financial statistics including stock values, exchange rates, and more. Some content is free.	www.wsj.com
Harvard Business School	Not a database per se but like at most libraries, links to dozens of sources for data both public and private can be found here.	http://www.library.hbs. edu/all_databases.html
The ACSI	Customer satisfaction ratings for hundreds of large firms doing business in the United States. Data are available by industry and free of charge.	http://theacsi.org/
Chinability	A convenient collection of reports and links to data reports and other sources related to the Chinese economy and business climate.	www.chinability.com

To locate data in periodicals, indexing services such as the *ABI/INFORM and Business Periodicals Index* and the *Wall Street Journal Index* are very useful. Guides to data sources also are helpful. For example, *American Statistical Index and Business Information Sources* is a very valuable source. Most university libraries provide access to at least some of these databases.

Government Sources

Government agencies produce data prolifically. Most of the data published by the federal government can be counted on for accuracy and quality of investigation. Most students are familiar with the U.S. *Census of Population*, which provides a wealth of data.

The *Census of Population* is only one of many resources that the government provides. Banks and savings and loan companies rely heavily on the *Federal Reserve Bulletin* and the *Economic Report of the President*. Builders and contractors use the information in the *Current Housing Report and Annual Housing Survey* for their research. The *Statistical Abstract of the United States* is an extremely valuable source of information about the social, political, and economic organizations of the United States.

The federal government is a leader in making secondary data available on the Internet. Visit FedStats (**http://www.fedstats.gov**) for a central access point and links to many useful statistics. FedStats provides links to the sources mentioned above. Additionally, the following list provides illustrations of the types of facts easily found by exploring this portal:

- Energy production statistics by state and for the country overall. The top three energy-producing states in the United States are Texas, Wyoming, and Louisiana.[19]
- Demographic information for the world overall and for practically every country. Links to reports about international markets also are found here. China, India, the United States, Indonesia, and Brazil are projected to be the five largest countries in the world based on population in the year 2015.
- Economic data series, current and historical, such as gross domestic product, retail sales data, and personal income by state. A map of personal income shows that states in the South tended to experience economic growth, whereas other areas, particularly in the West, showed economic declines during the end of the last decade.
- Over a dozen reports documenting and providing statistics about what people eat across the United States broken down by state, by in home versus out of home, food category, and how much people pay.

State, county, and local government agencies can also be useful sources of information. Many state governments publish state economic models and forecasts, and many cities have metropolitan planning agencies that provide data about the population, economy, and transportation systems in their town. Fortunately, many state and community statistics can be accessed from fedstats.gov, but each state's economic development agency website is a good place to look for more on a particular state.

Media Sources

Information on a broad range of subjects is available from broadcast, Internet, and print media. The *Wall Street Journal* (WSJ.com), *Financial Times* (ft.com), and Bloomberg *BusinessWeek* (businessweek.com) are valuable sources for information on the economy and many markets. The latest stock values for publicly traded companies are available and may prove useful as a measuring stick to assess effectiveness of these companies' major strategic initiatives. WSJ.com is an excellent source for video updates on the latest business trends and news stories.

Some media sources focus on particular aspects of business. *Hispanic Business* (hbinc.com) reports that the number of Hispanic-owned companies in the United States grew at a rate of 55 percent between 2004 and 2010, reaching 3.2 million firms, with 70 percent revenue growth for the period. According to the report, California and Florida are home to half of these businesses. The growth in Hispanic-owned companies is the largest trend in U.S. small business. For researchers willing to pay a modest fee, *Hispanic Business* offers a more detailed report about Hispanic-owned businesses.[20]

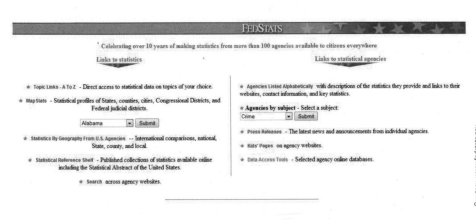

Fedstats.gov is a convenient portal to volumes of secondary data on the economy, demographics, education, crime and much more.

Courtesy. www.fedstats.gov

• • • • • • •

This chart comes from fedstats. gov. The blue states show personal income growth and the beige states have personal income declines for this period.

Personal Income: Percent Change, 2009–2010

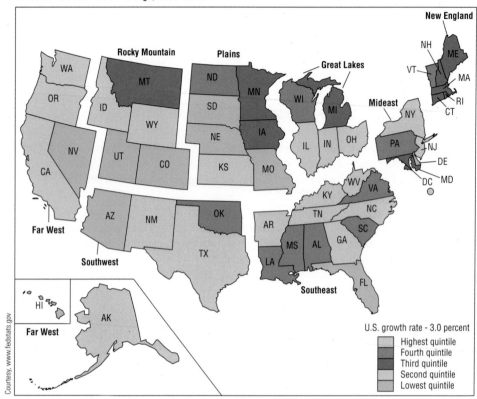

Courtesy, www.fedstats.gov

Trade Association Sources

Trade associations, such as the Food Marketing Institute or the American Petroleum Institute, serve the information needs of a particular industry. The trade association collects data on a number of topics of specific interest to firms, especially data on market size and market trends. Association members have a source of information that is particularly germane to their industry questions. For example, the Recording Industry Association of America (RIAA) provides reports tracking trends in the music industry that are useful to the artists, management companies, and the media in general. As one area of focus, the RIAA compiles a great deal of information related to protecting intellectual and creative property rights.

Commercial Sources

Numerous firms specialize in selling and/or publishing information. For example, the Polk Company specializes in information relevant to automobile marketing, such as the percentage of car buyers relying on the Internet in the search process and the relative health of dealerships by area. Data Monitor offers subscribers an impressive collection of reports, many of which are interactive, and they allow tracking of industry leaders globally, basic descriptions of markets, and statistics on new product introductions. *Fortune* rates the most admired companies annually in addition to providing the *Fortune* 500 list of the largest U.S. companies. Walmart tops that list with revenue approaching $½ trillion.[21] Here are a few sources of specialized data not mentioned above or in Exhibit 6.6.

Market-Share Data. A number of syndicated services supply either wholesale or retail sales volume data based on product movement. Information Resources, Inc., collects market-share data using Universal Product Codes (UPC) and optical scanning at retail store checkouts. Symphonies' INFOSCAN is a syndicated retail tracking service that collects scanner data from more than 32,000 U.S. supermarkets, drug stores, and mass merchandisers. This data allows an estimate of market share for just about any consumer goods brand. INFOSCAN now tracks sales in other countries too including France, Germany, Italy, and the United Kingdom. The *World Market Share Reporter* also is available at the reference desk in many university libraries and available online to subscribers. Gale Research publishes and markets the *Reporter* in a domestic and global version each year.

Walmart operates its own in-store scanner system called RetailLink. Key suppliers can have online access to relevant data free of charge.[22] Given Walmart's dominant role in the U.S. marketplace, share estimates from RetailLink are good proxies for overall market share.

Consumer Attitude and Public Opinion Research. Many research firms offer specialized syndicated services that report findings from attitude research and opinion polls. For example, Yankelovich provides custom research, tailored for specific projects, and several syndicated services. Yankelovich's public opinion research studies, such as the voter and public attitude surveys that appear in *Time* and other news magazines, are a source of secondary data. One of the firm's services is the *Yankelovich MONITOR,* a syndicated annual census of changing social values and an analysis of how they can affect consumer marketing. The *MONITOR* charts the growth and spread of new social values, characterizes the types of customers who support the new values and those who continue to support traditional values, and outlines the ways in which people's values affect purchasing behavior.

Harris/Interactive is another public opinion research firm that provides syndicated and custom research for business. One of its services is the Harris survey. This survey, released three times per week, monitors the pulse of the American public on topics such as inflation, unemployment, energy, consumer products, politics, and so on. A recent poll gauges Americans' opinions about nuclear power in the wake of the Japanese earthquake and tsunami disaster. Only three weeks after the disaster, 41 percent of Americans favored building more nuclear plants in the United States, whereas 39 percent opposed the idea.[23] Despite a great deal of media coverage, that represents a small drop in favorability from 49 percent ten years earlier.

Consumption and Purchase Behavior Data. NPD's National Eating Trends (NET) is the most detailed database available on consumption patterns and trends for more than 4,000 food and beverage products. This is a syndicated source of data about the types of meals people eat and when and how they eat them. The data, called *diary panel data,* are based on records of meals and diaries kept by a group of households that have agreed to record their consumption behavior over an extended period of time.

National Family Opinion (NFO), Marketing Research Corporation of America (MRCA), and many other syndicated sources sell diary panel data about consumption and purchase behavior. Since the advent of scanner data, diary panels are more commonly used to record purchases of apparel, hardware, home furnishings, jewelry, and other durable goods, rather than purchases of non-durable consumer packaged goods. More recently, services have been tracking consumer behavior online and collecting data about sites visited and purchases made over the Internet.

Advertising Research Advertisers can purchase readership and audience data from a number of firms. W. R. Simmons and Associates measures magazine audiences; Arbitron measures radio audiences; ACNielsen Media Measurement estimates television audience ratings. By specializing in collecting and selling audience information on a continuing basis, these commercial sources provide a valuable service to their subscribers.

Assistance in measuring advertising effectiveness is another syndicated service. For example, Roper Starch Worldwide measures the impact of advertising in magazines. Roper provides readership information for the client's or its competitors' ads.

Single-Source and Global Research Data

As business has become more global, so has the secondary data industry. Many private companies exist solely to provide secondary data and many marketing research firms provide this canned data as a big part of their business. Additionally, many government entities provide secondary information based on statistics that they must collect in administering programs in their own country. It's hard to think of a topic for which no secondary data would exist.

Single-Source Data-Integrated Information

ACNielsen Company offers data from both its television meters and scanner operations. The integration of these two types of data helps marketers investigate the impact of television advertising on retail sales. In other ways as well, users of data find that merging two or more diverse types of data into a single database offers many advantages.

PRIZM by Claritas Corporation (a Nielsen entity), CACI, ClusterPlus by SMI, Mediamark Research Inc., and many other syndicated databases report product purchase behavior, media usage, demographic characteristics, lifestyle variables, and business activity by geographic area such as ZIP code. Although such data are often called *geodemographic,* they cover such a broad range of phenomena that no one name is a good description. These data use small geographic areas as the unit of analysis.

The marketing research industry uses the term **single-source data** for diverse types of data offered by a single company. Exhibit 6.7 identifies three major marketers of single-source data.

single-source data

Diverse types of data offered by a single company; usually integrated on the basis of a common variable such as geographic area or store.

Government Agencies

The Japan Management Association provides secondary research data to government and industry. One ongoing survey tracks Japanese executives' opinions on pressing business matters. The Institute's goal is to allow global firms access to its enormous store of data about Japan to develop and plan business in Japan.

Secondary data compiled outside the United States have the same limitations as domestic secondary data. However, international researchers should watch for certain pitfalls that frequently are associated with foreign data and cross-cultural research. First, data may simply be unavailable in certain countries. Second, researchers may question the accuracy of some data. This is especially likely with official statistics that may be adjusted for the political purposes of foreign governments. Finally, although economic terminology may be standardized, various countries use different definitions and accounting and recording practices for many economic concepts. For example, different countries may measure disposable personal income in radically different ways. International researchers should take extra care to investigate the comparability of data among countries. Exhibit 6.8 lists some potential sources for marketing information about various parts of the world.

The U.S. government and other organizations compile databases that may aid international marketers. The U.S. government offers a wealth of data about foreign countries. The CIA's World Factbook and the National Trade Data Bank are especially useful. The National Trade Data Bank (NTDB), the U.S. government's most comprehensive source of world trade data, illustrates what is available. The National Trade Data Bank was established by the Omnibus Trade and Competitiveness Act of 1988.[24] Its purpose was to provide "reasonable public access, including electronic access" to an export promotion data system that was centralized, inexpensive, and easy to use.

EXHIBIT 6.7

Examples of Single-Source Databases

CACI Marketing Systems http://www.caci.com	Provides industry-specific marketing services, such as customer profiling and segmentation, custom target analysis, demographic data reports and maps, and site evaluation and selection. CACI offers demographics and data on businesses, lifestyles, consumer spending, purchase potential, shopping centers, traffic volumes, and other statistics.
PRIZM by Claritas Corporation **http://www.claritas.com/MyBestSegments/ Default.jsp**	PRIZM which stands for Potential Rating Index for Zip Markets, is based on the "birds-of-a-feather" assumption that people live near others who are like themselves. PRIZM combines census data, consumer surveys about shopping and lifestyle, and purchase data to identify market segments. Colorful names such as Young Suburbia, Shot Guns, and Pickups describe 40 segments that can be identified by zip code. Claritas also has a lifestyle census in the United Kingdom (http://www.claritas.co.uk).
MRI Cable Report—Mediamark Research Inc. **http://www.mediamark.com**	Integrates information on cable televisionviewing with demographic and productcom usage information.

Source: © Cengage Learning 2013.

EXHIBIT **6.8**
Some Example Sources of
Global Marketing Information

• United States	• South America
http://www.fedstats.gov	http://www.internetworldstats.com/south.htm
• South Africa	• Norway
http://www.statssa.gov.za	http://www.ssb.no
• Australia	• United Nations
http://www.nla.gov.au/oz/stats.html	http://www.un.org/esa
• Japan	• Global Information from the CIA Factbook
http://www.stat.go.jp/	http://www.cia.gov
• U.K.	
http://www.statistics.gov.uk	
• France	
http://www.insee.fr	

©MICHAEL NEWMAN/PHOTOEDIT

© Cengage Learning 2013.

The U.S. Department of Commerce has the responsibility for operating and maintaining the NTDB and works with federal agencies that collect and distribute trade information to keep the NTDB up to date. Over 1,000 public and university libraries offer access to the NTDB through the Federal Depository Library system. The National Trade Data Bank consists of 133 separate trade- and business-related programs (databases). By using it, small and medium-sized companies get immediate access to information that until now only *Fortune* 500 companies could afford.

Topics in the NTDB include export opportunities by industry, country, and product; foreign companies or importers looking for specific products; how-to market guides; demographic, political, and socioeconomic conditions in hundreds of countries; and much more. NTDB offers one-stop shopping for trade information from more than twenty federal sources. You do not need to know which federal agency produces the information: All you need to do is consult NTDB.

TIPS OF THE TRADE

- Always consider the possibility that secondary data may exist which can address the research question at hand adequately.
- Check on the reliability and validity of secondary data. Most reputable source provide details describing details of the research methods that allow the data quality to be assessed.
- Secondary data are particularly useful for trend analysis, environmental scanning, and estimating market potential for geographic areas.

- Government sites such as the Census Bureau (www.census.gov), the CIA Factbook (www.cia.gov), and FedStats (www.fedstats.gov) are great sources for data about industries, businesses, and consumers, not only in the United States but also around the world.

Source: © Cengage Learning 2013.

Like a Good Neighbor?

Door-to-door surveys represent a special challenge. During the 1950s the approach was synonymous with survey research but even then, like now, they require well- trained, and therefore well-paid, survey administrators helping to make them a costly way of getting data. In addition to the costs, ensuring that you have the correct population of interest complicates the process further.

Door-to-door surveys are occasionally still used as a way of tapping into captive populations in particular those that are not as likely to communicate online or with a mobile phone—like the elderly. Two St. Louis college students undertook a service learning project aimed at identifying special needs of the elderly population in the area. They mapped the neighborhoods and divided the city into zones. Students conducted 680 door-to-door surveys from older St. Louis adults. Their hard work led to the inclusion of elderly adult needs as part of the Good Neighbor Initiative, which included programs for literacy, hunger, homelessness, and health.

Researchers in Brazil investigated the relationship between income and happiness. They too needed data from a broad

cross-section of the population, some of whom may be less inclined to communicate electronically. Door-to-door surveys with 576 Brazilians helped reveal that income does cause happiness, but that relationship depended on income also creating the perception that a household belonged to a higher social class.

Sources: Halsband, D., Welch, G., & Fuller, M. (2008), "Community Survey Leads to Learning from and Caring for Our Elders," (paper presented at the17th annual National Conference, for the Community College National Center for Community Engagement, May 2008); Islam, G., E.W. Herrera, and M. Hamilton (2009), "Objective and Subjective Indicators of Happiness in Brazil: The Mediating Role of Social Class," *Journal of Social Psychology*, 149 (April), 267–72.

One of the key disadvantages is that survey results are no better than the quality of the sample and answers obtained. A survey opens the door to errors in general and those errors contribute to misleading results. In addition to these general disadvantages, each individual survey tool introduces unique disadvantages. By understanding the nature of the errors that can result, researchers can hopefully better match a survey data collection approach and reduce the likelihood of erroneous or useless results.

Sources of Error in Surveys

A manager who is evaluating the quality of a survey must estimate its accuracy. Exhibit 7.1 outlines the various forms of survey error.[4] They have two major sources: random sampling error and systematic error.

Random versus Systematic Sampling Error

sampling error

Error arising because of inadequacies of the actual respondents to represent the population of interest.

systematic error

Error resulting from some imperfect aspect of the research design that causes respondent error or from a mistake in the execution of the research.

population parameter

Refers to some true value of a phenomenon within a population.

Successful surveys portray a representative cross-section of a particular population. Even with technically proper random probability samples, however, statistical errors will occur because of chance variation in the elements selected for the sample. These statistical problems are unavoidable without large samples. **Sampling error** refers to inadequacies of the actual respondents to represent the population of interest. Part of sampling error arises because of random fluctuation but part occurs because of inappropriateness of the sampling frame. We'll learn more about the sources of sampling error in the next chapter.

Conversely, **systematic error** results from some imperfect aspect of the research design or from a mistake in the execution of the research. Systematic errors include all sources of error other than those introduced directly by the sampling procedure. Therefore, systematic errors are nonsampling errors. The term **population parameter** refers to some true value of a phenomenon within

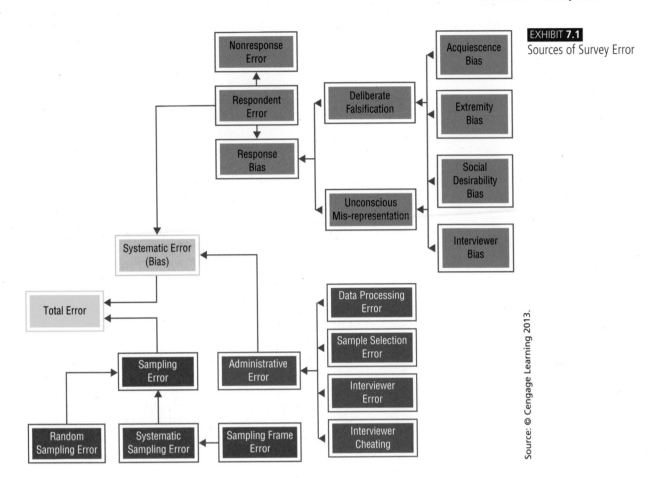

Source: © Cengage Learning 2013.

EXHIBIT 7.1
Sources of Survey Error

a population. For instance, the number of Red Bulls consumed in 2012 by first-year university students in Indiana truly exists and researchers may estimate the number using a sample of these students. A **sample bias** exists when the results of a particular sample deviate in one direction from the true value of the population parameter. For instance, if the researcher selects respondents at final exam time, the Red Bull parameter may be biased upward. Systematic errors arise from two general categories: respondent error and administrative error.

Respondent Error

Surveys ask people for answers and hopefully people give truthful answers. Error exists otherwise and **respondent error** results. Response bias and nonresponse error bias are the two major categories of respondent error.

Nonresponse Error

Surveys rarely obtain 100 percent response rates, but a researcher employing a text message questionnaire about energy drink consumption may face a serious problem. The researcher must believe that sample members who respond to a text message questionnaire are not any different from sample members who did not respond. Sample members who refuse or cannot respond are **nonrespondents**. **Nonresponse error** is the statistical differences between parameter values obtained using only actual survey respondents compared to parameter values obtained from a (hypothetical) survey including input from those who did not respond (i.e., the nonrespondents). Of course, knowing exactly how big this error truly is becomes practically impossible because nonrespondents, by definition, do not provide input.

In a phone survey, nonresponse occurs when a call goes unanswered. The number of **no contacts** in survey research has been increasing for a host of reasons, including restrictions in who can be contacted and changes in technology that allow people to screen out unwanted communications. An e-mail request sent to a potential respondent via an old unused e-mail address likewise is

sample bias

A persistent tendency for the results of a sample to deviate in one direction from the true value of the population parameter.

respondent error

A category of sample bias resulting from some respondent action such as lying or inaction such as not responding.

nonrespondents

Sample members who are not contacted or who refuse to cooperate in the research.

nonresponse error

The statistical differences between a survey that includes only those who responded and a perfect survey that would also include those who failed to respond.

no contacts

Potential respondents in the sense that they are members of the sampling frame but who do not receive the request to participate in the research.

a nonresponse. A consumer who ignores an interviewer's request in a shopping center also creates a nonresponse.

refusals

People who are unwilling to participate in a research project.

Refusals occur when people are unwilling to participate in the research. A research team reviewed fifty mail surveys of pediatricians conducted by the American Academy of Pediatrics (AAP) and found that response rates declined through the first decade of the twenty-first century. In the early years of the study period, an average 70 percent of pediatricians returned completed surveys; the response rate fell to an average 63 percent in the second half of the period.[5] No contacts and refusals can seriously bias survey data. In the case of the pediatricians, the researchers found little difference in the response rates attributable to differences in such easy-to-measure variables as age, sex, and type of membership in the AAP, leaving them to wonder whether the cause of refusals was some unknown but important difference among these doctors.

Because of this problem, researchers investigate the causes of nonresponse. For example, a study analyzed a large database collected by AT&T and found that the effort required to participate in an ongoing study contributes to the problem.[6] People tend not to respond to questions that are difficult to answer. Also, more people respond to the first in a series of surveys and participation can fall off on subsequent follow-up surveys.

How can a researcher assess nonresponse error? Comparing the sample demographics with the demographics of the target population is one means of inspecting for possible response bias. For instance, if we know that 54 percent of freshmen college students in Indiana are female, and our sample asking about Red Bull consumption turns out to be 75 percent male, we know females are underrepresented. Thus, the Red Bull consumption estimate would exhibit bias to the extent that men and women do not drink the same amount.

self-selection bias

A bias that occurs because people who feel strongly about a subject are more likely to respond to survey questions than people who feel indifferent about it.

Researchers know that those who are most enthusiastic about an issue are more likely to respond. **Self-selection bias** is a problem that frequently plagues self-administered questionnaires. Consumers decide where to shop, eat, and get their cars serviced. In each case the consumer chooses the marketers. Thus, a researcher conducting a questionnaire in such environments should expect more favorable responses than normal because the customer made a conscious selection to be at this retailer. Self-selection bias distorts survey results because favorable respondents are overrepresented.

response bias

A bias that occurs when respondents either consciously or unconsciously answer questions with a certain slant that misrepresents the truth.

Response Bias

A **response bias** occurs when respondents answer questions in a way that slants meanings away from true population values. As a result, willfully or not, the respondent contributes to misleading results. If a distortion of measurement occurs because respondents' answers are false or misrepresented, the resulting sample bias will be a response bias. When researchers identify response bias, they should include a corrective measure.

● ● ● ● ● ●

Inactive email addresses contribute to low response rates because they are in effect no contacts.

©Yuri Arcurs/Shutterstock

Deliberate Falsification. Occasionally people deliberately give false answers. A response bias occurs when people misrepresent answers. Rather than appear ignorant or unconcerned about prices, they may provide their best estimate and not tell the truth—namely, that they cannot remember. Sometimes respondents become bored with the interview and provide answers just to finish the survey. Other times, respondents try to look smart by giving answers they think are expected. Similarly, respondents sometimes give answers simply to please the interviewer or to qualify as a respondent to obtain some incentive.

Unconscious Misrepresentation. Even when a respondent is consciously trying to be truthful and cooperative, response bias can arise from the question format, the question content, or some other stimulus. For example, the administration technique can bias results. The results of two in-flight surveys concerning aircraft preference illustrate this point. Passengers flying on Boeing 747s preferred that plane over an Airbus A-380 (74 percent versus 19 percent), whereas passengers flying on an Airbus A-380 preferred it to the 747 (56 percent versus 38 percent). Obviously, presence in one company's aircraft biased the results.[7] Respondents could hardly make a fair comparison of planes when the awareness of one alternative was so much greater.

Respondents may not be able to give precise answers in some cases. Consider the following question:

When was the last time you went 48 hours without checking Facebook? _____days

Respondents may have to guess to answer because they do not know the exact answer. In other cases, consumers cannot adequately express their feelings in words. The cause may be questions that are vague, ambiguous, or not specific enough. Researchers may ask someone to describe his or her frustration when using a computer. If the researcher has a specific interest in software usage, he or she will likely be disappointed with the answers. Language differences also may be a source of misunderstanding. A French researcher used an instrument developed in France to assess lunch habits. However, the French word for lunch, *dejeuner*, means "breakfast" in Quebec.

Many respondents will answer questions even though they have given them little thought. For example, in most investigations of consumers' buying intentions, the predictability of the intention scales depends on how close the subject is to making a purchase. The intentions of subjects who have little knowledge of the brand or the store alternatives or who have not yet made any purchase plans are relatively unlikely to predict purchase behavior accurately. Additionally, the more time passing since a purchase or a shopping event the more people tend to underreport information about that event. Time lapse influences people's ability to communicate specific factors precisely.

Unconscious misrepresentation bias may also occur because consumers unconsciously avoid facing the realities of a future buying situation. Housing surveys record that Americans overwhelmingly continue to aspire to own detached, single-family dwellings (preferably single-level, ranch-type structures that require two to five times the amount of land per unit required for attached homes). However, builders know that *attached* housing purchases by first buyers are more common than respondents expect.

Types of Response Bias

Response bias falls into four specific categories: acquiescence bias, extremity bias, interviewer bias, and social desirability bias. These categories overlap and are not mutually exclusive. A single biased answer may be distorted for many complex reasons, some distortions being deliberate and some being unconscious misrepresentations.

Acquiescence Bias. A tendency to agree with the viewpoints expressed by a survey is known as **acquiescence bias**. This bias is particularly prominent in new-product research. Questions about a new-product idea generally elicit some acquiescence bias because respondents give positive connotations to most new ideas. For example, consumers responded favorably to survey questions about pump baseball gloves (the pump inserts air into the pocket of the glove, providing more cushioning). However, when these expensive gloves hit the market, they sat on the shelves. When conducting new-product research, researchers should recognize the high likelihood of acquiescence bias.

A less common form of acquiescence is evident in respondents tend to disagree with all questions. A survey administered by a group protesting a new Walmart location in a residential area may show abnormally high disagreement about supporting the development. Thus, acquiescence bias is a response bias due to the respondents' tendency to concur with a particular position.

Extremity Bias. Some individuals tend to use extremes when responding to questions. In other words, they will tend to use the furthest left or right ends of a scale. Response styles vary from person to person, and extreme responses may cause an **extremity bias** in the data.[8] Extremity bias is common in consumer satisfaction scales.

Interviewer Bias. Response bias may arise from the interplay between interviewer and respondent. If the interviewer's presence influences respondents to give untrue or modified answers, **interviewer bias** results. Sometimes respondents may give answers they believe will please the interviewer rather than the truthful responses. Respondents may wish to appear intelligent and wealthy—of course they read *Architectural Digest* rather than the *National Enquirer*.

Interviewer characteristics, including age, sex, style of dress, tone of voice, facial expressions, or other nonverbal characteristics, may influence a respondent's answers. In a research

acquiescence bias
A tendency for respondents to agree with the viewpoints expressed by a survey.

extremity bias
A category of response bias that results because some individuals tend to use extremes when responding to questions.

interviewer bias
A response bias that occurs because the presence of the interviewer influences respondents' answers.

study on sexual harassment against saleswomen, male interviewers might not obtain as candid responses from saleswomen as female interviewers would. Thus, interviewer techniques in which the interviewer remains unseen have an advantage of preventing this particular type of interviewer bias.

Many interviewers, contrary to instructions, shorten or rephrase questions to suit their needs. A researcher doing survey research for major U.S. newspapers asked a question about the Nazi holocaust in the following fashion:

"Do you believe it seems possible or does it seem impossible to you that the Nazi Extermination of the Jews never happened?"[9]

–Institute for Historical Review

Obviously, this question is confusing and yielded a result that should be meaningless. Instead, an unscrupulous blogger may use the results to state that 1 in 4 respondents believe the holocaust never occurred when the survey results have no clear meaning.

This potential influence on responses can be avoided to some extent if interviewers receive training and supervision that emphasize the necessity of appearing neutral. Also, researchers with strong opinions may be steered toward other projects or be made aware that misleading results are unethical and likely do not further their cause in the long run.

social desirability bias

Bias in responses caused by respondents' desire, either conscious or unconscious, to gain prestige or appear in a different social role.

Social Desirability Bias. **Social desirability bias** occurs because a respondent wishes to create a favorable impression or somehow save face during an interview. Respondents may inflate income, overstate education, or report heightened sensitivity to environmental issues. In contrast, answers to questions that seek factual information or responses about matters of public knowledge (zip code, home ownership and so on) usually are quite accurate. An interviewer's presence may particularly bias answers to sensitive questions such as "Did you vote in the last election?," "Do you have termites or roaches in your home?," or "Do you color your hair?"

The social desirability bias is especially significant in the case of research that addresses sensitive or personal topics, including respondents' sexual behavior. A researcher surveyed teens, asking the following question:

- Have you ever received any nude pictures of a friend or peer via text message or Facebook?

Fifteen percent of teens reported "yes" to this question. The research also asked the following:

- Have you ever sent nude pictures to your friends or posted them on Facebook?

Only 4 percent indicated "yes" to this question.[10] Do you believe that the large difference in percentage is due to socially desirable responding? Do teens feel pressure to say they receive nude photos? Are teens unwilling to admit to sending messages? An alternative explanation is that a few individuals send large numbers of photos of themselves or others in the nude to large numbers of teens. The social desirability makes it difficult to attribute any definitive meaning to this survey result.

Administrative Error

administrative error

An error caused by the improper administration or execution of the research task.

When a research employee improperly administers or executes his/her task he/she creates **administrative error**. Administrative errors result from carelessness, confusion, neglect, omission, or some other blunder. Four terms describe the different types of administrative error:

data processing error

A category of administrative error that occurs because of incorrect data entry, incorrect computer programming, or other procedural errors during data analysis.

- **Data processing error** results when data are improperly edited, coded, or entered into a computer. The accuracy of data processed by a computer depends on correct data entry and programming. Data processing error is reduced by establishing careful procedures for verifying each step in the data processing stage.

sample selection error

An administrative error caused by improper sample design or sampling procedure execution.

- **Sample selection error** is systematic error that results in an unrepresentative sample because of error in either sample design or execution of the sampling procedure. Executing a sampling plan free of procedural error is difficult. A firm that selects its sample from a telephone directory introduces systematic error, because unlisted and cell phone numbers are not included. Stopping respondents during daytime hours in shopping centers excludes working people who shop by mail, Internet, or telephone. A telephone interviewer may take responses from a female answering the phone when questions are intended for a man.

One problem with many surveys is that there is no way of knowing who exactly responded to the questionnaire.

■ **Interviewer error.** Interviewer error occurs when interviewers record answers incorrectly, such as checking the wrong response or not writing fast enough to record respondents' statements verbatim. Also, selective perception may cause interviewers to misrepresent subtlety contrary opinions.

■ **Interviewer cheating** occurs when an interviewer falsifies entire questionnaires or fills in answers to questions that respondents skipped. Some interviewers cheat to finish an interview as quickly as possible or to avoid questions about sensitive topics. The term *curb-stoning* refers to interviewers filling in responses for respondents that do not really exist. Research firms can reduce interviewer cheating by recontacting a small number of respondents to verify previously recorded responses. In this way, curb-stoners might get revealed and face the consequences associated with this unethical behavior.

interviewer error

Mistakes made by interviewers failing to record survey responses correctly.

interviewer cheating

The practice of filling in fake answers or falsifying questionnaires while working as an interviewer.

What Can Be Done to Reduce Survey Error?

Knowing the many sources of error in surveys, you may have lost some of your optimism about survey research. Don't be discouraged! The discussion above emphasizes negativity because it is important for marketing managers to realize that surveys are not a panacea. Once one knows about the problems, steps can be applied to reduce survey errors. We'll discuss some ways to reduce error through effective questionnaire and sampling design in upcoming chapters. The good news lies ahead!

Different Ways That Marketing Researchers Conduct Surveys

When most people think of interviewing, they envision two people engaged in face-to-face dialogue or in a phone conversation. However, people don't always communicate in a two-way fashion. Sometimes, communication is one-way with little chance for spontaneous interaction. For example, traditional print advertisements employ one-way communication because they are noninteractive. The ad provides no mechanism in which the consumer talks back to the company. Likewise, we can summarize marketing communications with survey respondents into interactive and noninteractive media.

©Michael Newman/PhotoEdit

● ● ● ● ● ● ●

Electronic dating services have become a popular, successful example of electronic interactive media.

interactive survey approaches

Communication that allows spontaneous two-way interaction between the interviewer and the respondent.

noninteractive survey approaches

Two-way communication by which respondents give answers to static questions that do not allow a dynamic dialog.

personal interview

Face-to-face communication in which an interviewer asks a respondent to answer questions.

Interactive Survey Approaches

Interactive survey approaches allow spontaneous two-way interaction between interviewer and respondent. Even when the communication is electronic, interactive approaches try to capture the dynamic exchange made possible through face-to-face interviews. Survey respondents, thus, need not be passive audience members. Today's interactive approaches allow respondents to be involved in two-way communication using electronic media such as smartphones or live Web interfaces. More detail on various electronic survey tools follows later in this chapter.

Noninteractive Media

Noninteractive survey approaches do not facilitate two-way communications and are thus largely a vehicle by which respondents give answers to static questions. The traditional questionnaire received by mail, completed by a respondent, and mailed back to the researcher does not allow a real-time, dynamic exchange of information and is therefore noninteractive. Noninteractive questionnaires do have merit, but this type of survey is less flexible than surveys using interactive communication media. In fact, noninteractive media can be the best approach in some situations. Simple opinion polls, awareness studies, and even surveys assessing consumer attitudes can generally be collected adequately via one-way communication.

The Research Snapshot provides an example of how survey research can provide market intelligence.

Conducting Personal Interviews

A **personal interview** is a form of direct communication in which an interviewer asks respondents questions face-to-face. This versatile and flexible method is a two-way conversation between interviewer and respondent. Personal interviews are truly interactive. Traditionally, researchers have recorded interview results using paper and pencil, by reading questions and recording answers. Today, computers are increasingly supporting survey research by automatically recording responses. In this section, we examine the general characteristics of face-to-face personal interviews, then compare and contrast door-to-door personal interviews with personal interviews conducted in shopping malls and those conducted on the phone.

Gathering information through face-to-face contact with individuals goes back many years. Military inscription and tax rates were set based on periodic censuses in ancient Egypt and Rome. During the Middle Ages, the merchant families of Fugger and Rothschild prospered in part because their far-flung organizations enabled them to get information before their competitors could. [11] Today, survey researchers present themselves in shopping centers and train stations and announce, "Good afternoon, my name is ___. I am with ___ Research Company, and we are conducting a survey on ___."

Advantages of Personal Interviews

Marketing researchers find that personal interviews offer many unique advantages.

iPod, uPod, FMPod?

Apple revolutionized the way consumers listen to music by providing portability for personalized high-fidelity listening. The iPod is a fraction of the size of the now nearly forgotten Sony Walkman and allows the user to store a virtually unlimited number of songs. Of course, the iPod owner can also store movies, games ,and even class lectures. iPods and MP3 players even are standard equipment on smartphones. Nothing is perfect, however, and Apple and other companies that offer MP3 players are constantly searching for potential improvements. So, what's the best method of survey to communicate with this market?

A survey of iPod suggested that more than anything else, users would like the device to include an FM radio tuner; 40 percent of respondents indicated that an FM tuner is desirable. However, when iPod users found the new FM tuners offered as a $50 accessory, the sell-through rate failed to reach 40 percent. Follow-up surveys studying the poor performance revealed several issues that make the 40 percent market penetration forecast inaccurate.

- The survey was implemented through a noninteractive format so respondents couldn't elaborate. Thus, Apple overlooked the fact that customers didn't want to have to add in an FM tuner but rather expected it to be integrated into the design. As a result, Apple may have missed an opportunity to get consumers to upgrade to a newer iPod had the company simply introduced and emphasized new models with built-in FM tuners.

Is it an Iphone?

- The noninteractive survey also took advantage of a mailing list used by a group of FM radio stations that may have not represented the entire iPod population very well.
- The survey failed to ask questions about how customers actually use the iPod.

Eventually, the iPod Nano (5th generation) incorporated an FM tuner and iPod Touch now includes better game interfaces and face-time technologies. Apple's strategy turned based on survey results indicating large numbers of very young users and tweens' attachment to the iPod. The Touch's design is very similar to an iPhone and Apple believes, as a result, iPod Touch users will be easy pickings when they enter the smartphone market.

Sources: http://ipod.about.com/od/misc/tp/fm_tuners.htm, accessed April 22, 2011; Harris Interactive (2010), "First Annual Harris Poll Youth Equitrend Study Uncovers Brand with Highest Equity Among 8-24 Year Olds," www.harrisinteractive.com, accessed April 22, 2011; Elliott, A.M., "iPod Use Sees Increase with under 10-year-olds," *Pocket-Lint* (2008), accessed at http://www.pocket-lint.com/news/12398/kids-growing-ipod-users-report, on April 22, 2011.

Opportunity for Feedback

Personal interviews provide the opportunity for feedback and clarification. For example, if a consumer is reluctant to provide sensitive information, the interviewer may offer reassurance that his or her answers will be strictly confidential. Personal interviews offer the lowest chance that respondents will misinterpret questions, because an interviewer who senses confusion can clarify the instruction or questions. Circumstances may dictate that at the conclusion of the interview, the respondent be given additional information concerning the purpose of the study. This clarification is easily accomplished with a personal interview. If the feedback indicates that some question or set of questions is particularly confusing, the researcher can make changes that make the questionnaire easier to understand.

Probing Complex Answers

Another important characteristic of personal interviews is the opportunity to follow up by probing. If a respondent's answer is too brief or unclear, the researcher may request a more comprehensive or clearer explanation. The interviewer probes for clarification with standardized questions such as "Can you tell me more about what you had in mind?" (See the chapter 5 for an expanded discussion of probing.) Depending on the research purpose, personal interviews vary in the degree to which questions are structured and in the amount of probing required. The personal interview is especially useful for obtaining unstructured information. Skilled interviewers can handle complex questions that cannot easily be asked in telephone or mail surveys.

Length of Interview

If the research objective requires an extremely lengthy questionnaire, personal interviews may be the only option. A general rule of thumb on mail and e-mail surveys is that they should not take more than 12 minutes to complete and telephone interviews typically should take less than 10 minutes. In contrast, a personal interview can be much longer, perhaps an hour or even more. However, the longer the interview, no matter what the form, the more the respondent should be compensated for their time and participation. Researchers should also be clear about how long participation should take in the opening dialogue requesting participation.

Completeness of Questionnaire

The social interaction between a well-trained interviewer and a respondent in a personal interview increases the likelihood that the respondent will answer all the items on the questionnaire. The respondent who grows bored with a telephone interview may terminate the interview at his or her discretion simply by hanging up. Self-administered mail questionnaires require more effort from respondents and as such, they may just skip questions that require lengthy written answers. **Item nonresponse**—failure to provide an answer to a question—occurs less often when an experienced interviewer asks questions directly.

item nonresponse

Failure of a respondent to provide an answer to a survey question.

Props and Visual Aids

Interviewing respondents face-to-face allows the investigator to show them new product samples, sketches of proposed advertising, or other visual aids. When Lego Group wanted to introduce new train model sets for its famous building bricks, the company targeted adults who build complex models with its product. The company invited adults who were swapping ideas at the Lego website to visit the New York office, where they viewed ideas and provided their opinions. The respondents wound up rejecting all the company's ideas, but they suggested something different: the Santa Fe Super Chief set, which sold out within two weeks of introduction due only to enthusiastic word of mouth.[12] Telephone interviews could not have yielded some rich results.

Marketing research that uses visual aids has become increasingly popular with researchers who investigate film concepts, advertising problems, and moviegoers' awareness of performers. Research for movies often begins by showing respondents videotapes of the prospective cast. Respondents see film clips and evaluate a movie's appeal and help researchers know which scenes to use in trailers. The Research Snapshot demonstrates how respondents can even taste new products—a real advantage for examining new products—at least until the virtual tongue takes over.

High Participation Rate

Although some people are reluctant to participate in a survey, the presence of an interviewer generally increases the percentage of people willing to complete the interview. People are often more hesitant to tell a person "no" face-to-face than they are over the phone, in a mail request, or through another impersonal contact. Respondents typically are required to do no reading or writing—all they have to do is talk. A personable interviewer can also do much to improve response rates. Many people enjoy sharing information and insights with friendly and sympathetic interviewers.

Disadvantages of Personal Interviews

Personal interviews also have disadvantages. Respondents are not anonymous and as a result may be reluctant to provide confidential information to another person. Suppose a survey asked top executives, "Do you see any major internal instabilities or threats to the achievement of your marketing objectives?" Many managers may be reluctant to tell the interviewer his/her thoughts about this sensitive question because complete anonymity is impossible.

Matters of Taste

Asking an opinion is easy to do over the phone or online, but not if you want people's reactions to a new food, wine, or perfume. For those opinions, you probably want people to sample the new product first, so a face-to-face interview seems to be the only option. But, researchers have some creative options.

Sometimes researchers simply want to know whether consumers like the product, but in other situations they are trying to meet objectives such as maintaining the same taste after substituting a new ingredient. Sartori Foods uses a chart it calls the Italian Cheese Flavor Wheel to ask consumers to describe various cheeses. The chart matches consumer-friendly terms like *nutty, buttery,* and *creamy* with terms useful in the industry (for example, *aromatic amino acids* and *sulfur compounds*). Researchers can use an alternative to face-to-face interviews by sending both a sample of the product to potential respondents along with a color wheel. A phone interview can then have the respondent use the wheel to describe the taste.

Better yet, scientists have developed a virtual tongue. That's right! A synthetic surface absorbs foods and identifies certain tastes by feeding information into a computer. This may eliminate the need for a respondent altogether. For instance, the virtual tongue has quite a wine palate. It can tell Chardonnay from Malvasia and it can tell a 2009 vintage from a 2007 vintage. Well, this may be reliable, but many consumers are willing to stand in line to verify the wine's characteristics by tasting it for themselves!

Sources: Based on Claudia D. O'Donnell (2005), "Tips for Sensory Tests," *Prepared Foods* (January), http://www.preparedfoods.com/articles/tips-for-sensory-tests, accessed April 19, 2011; Abend, L. (2008), "E-Tongue Passes Wine Taste Test," *Time* (August 12), http://www.time.com/time/business/article/0,8599,1831413,00.html, accessed April 19, 2011.

Interviewer Influence

Imagine telling others about the past weekend. Would you have the same conversation with your mother as with your grandfather? Or, what about a roommate? In the same way, respondents act differently with different interviewers. One study's results suggest that male interviewers produced larger amounts of variance compared to female interviewers when 85 percent of respondents are female. Older interviewers who interviewed older respondents produced more variance than other age combinations, whereas younger interviewers who interviewed younger respondents produced the least variance.

Differential interviewer techniques may be a source of bias. The rephrasing of a question, the interviewer's tone of voice, and the interviewer's appearance may influence respondents' answers. Consider the interviewer who has conducted 100 personal interviews. During the next one, he or she may lose concentration and either selectively perceive or anticipate the respondent's answer. The interpretation of the response may differ somewhat from what the respondent intended. Typically, the public thinks of a person who does marketing research as a dedicated scientist. Unfortunately, some interviewers do not fit that ideal. Considerable interviewer variability exists. Cheating is possible; interviewers cut corners to save time and energy or fake parts of their reports by dummying up part or all of a questionnaire. Control over interviewers is important to ensure that difficult, embarrassing, or time-consuming questions are handled properly.

Lack of Anonymity of Respondent

Because a respondent in a personal interview is not totally anonymous, he or she may be reluctant to provide confidential information to the interviewer. Researchers take care to phrase sensitive questions to avoid social desirability bias. For example, the interviewer may show the respondent a card that lists possible answers and ask the respondent to read a category number rather than be required to verbalize sensitive answers.

Cost

Personal interviews are expensive, generally substantially more costly than mail, e-mail, Internet, or phone surveys. The geographic proximity of respondents, the length and complexity of the questionnaire, and the number of people who are nonrespondents because they could not be contacted (not-at-homes) all influence the cost of personal interviews.

Door-to-Door Interviews and Shopping Mall Intercepts

mall-intercept interview

Personal interviews conducted in a shopping center or similar public area.

Interviewers conduct personal interviews in respondents' homes or offices or in many other places including shopping centers and airports. The phrase **mall-intercept interview** applies to a technique involving random approaches to respondents asking for participation in survey. Interviewers intercept potential respondents in a public area and then complete the interview in a convenient place. Sometimes interviewees are asked to taste new food items or to view advertisements. The locale for the interview generally influences the participation rate, and thus the degree to which the sample represents the general population.

Each shopping center has its own market characteristics, and there is likely to be a larger bias if the research requires a sample representative of the population overall. However, personal interviews in shopping centers are appropriate when the target group is a special market segment such as the parents of children of bike-riding age. The mall-intercept interview allows the researcher to show large, heavy, or immobile visual materials, such as bicycles or television commercials. A mall interviewer can give an individual a product to take home to use and obtain a commitment that the respondent will cooperate when recontacted later. Mall intercepts are great when a type of product demonstration is part of the research design. For example, electronics manufacturers often do not want to test new appliances in consumers' homes because of difficulty in moving and setting up appliances. Thus, bringing respondents to the appliances is a better option.

Door-to-Door Interviews

door-to-door interviews

Personal interviews conducted at respondents' doorsteps in an effort to increase the participation rate in the survey.

The presence of an interviewer at the door generally increases the likelihood that a person will be willing to complete an interview. Because **door-to-door interviews** increase the participation rate and are conducted at a person's residence, they provide a more representative sample of the population than mail questionnaires. For example, response rates to mail surveys are substantially lower among Hispanics whether the questionnaire is printed in English or Spanish.[13] People who do not have telephones, who have unlisted telephone numbers, or who are otherwise difficult to contact may be reached using door-to-door interviews. However, door-to-door interviews may underrepresent some groups and overrepresent others based on the geographic areas covered.

Door-to-door interviews may exclude individuals who live in multiple-dwelling units with security systems, such as high-rise apartment dwellers, or executives who are too busy to grant personal interviews during business hours. Other people, for security reasons, simply will not open the door when a stranger knocks. Telephoning an individual in one of these subgroups to make an appointment may make the total sample more representative. However, obtaining a representative sample of this security-conscious subgroup based on a listing in the telephone directory may be difficult. For these reasons, door-to-door interviews are becoming a thing of the past.

Callbacks

callbacks

Attempts to try and contact those sample members missed in the initial attempt.

CATI

Acronym for computer-assisted telephone interviews.

When an interviewer's first attempt to contact a potential respondent fails, a systematic procedure calling for more attempts should be in place. **Callbacks**, or attempts to try and contact those sample members missed in the initial attempt, can substantially reduce nonresponse error. Calling back a sampling unit is more expensive than interviewing the person the first time around for a host of reasons including the extra labor. Callbacks in door-to-door interviews are important because not-at-home individuals (for example, working parents) may systematically vary from those who *are* at home (nonworking parents, retired people, and the like). In computer-assisted telephone interviews (sometimes referred to by the acronym **CATI**), the computer automatically schedules a call-back when a call to that number is unanswered.

Global Considerations

"People have really odd opinions. They tell me I'm skinny as if that's supposed to make me happy."

—ANGELINE JOLINE

Willingness to participate in a personal interview varies dramatically around the world. For example, in some Arab nations, a male mall-intercept interviewer could never interview a woman. In many countries, the idea of discussing grooming behavior and personal-care products with a stranger would be highly offensive. Personal interviews on such topics would be a bad idea.

● ● ● ● ● ● ●
Phone surveys were less complicated back when phones were phones.

The norms about appropriate business conduct also influence businesspeople's willingness to participate. For example, conducting business-to-business interviews in Japan during business hours is difficult because managers, strongly loyal to their firm, believe that they have an absolute responsibility to stick to the job! Managers also understandably feel uncomfortable answering too many questions about their decision making asked by a company researcher. In these instances, an outside research company might get better responses.

Telephone Interviews

Remember when a telephone was a just telephone? Probably not. Phones come in many forms these days. The interviewer these days typically sits at a computer that lists the questions and provides a survey form upon which the interviewer records the respondent's answers (another example of how CATI takes place). Researchers using phone interviews these days need to ponder this question: Are all types of phones equally prone to error?

Landline Phones

Landline telephone interviews have been a mainstay of commercial survey research since the 1940s. Traditionally, researchers consider data gathered in a phone interview comparable to that collected in a face-to-face interview. Phone interviews even possess advantages over face-to-face interviews as respondents are sometimes more forthcoming with information on a variety of personal topics while tucked away comfortably at home out of the sight of the interviewer.

Pollsters and many market researchers still consider an in-home phone interview survey capable of providing samples relatively representative of the U.S. population. Several recent events including legislation making calls more difficult and decreasing landline phone ownership are challenging this assumption.

No Call Legislation

"No-call" legislation dates back to the mid-2000s. Marketers cannot call phone numbers listed on the do-not-call registry. The legislation exists at the federal and state level and is not unique to the United States. The legislation originally targeted telemarketers and although marketing research efforts do not always fall under the legislation, many commercial marketing research firms honor the do-not-call registry.

Marketers and marketing researchers can obtain the do-not-call lists of phone numbers from the FTC for $55 per area code. A subscriber can purchase the entire registry for $15,058. Although

● ● ● ● ● ● ●

Information about do-not-call lists for each state can be found at the Direct Marketing Association's Web site at http://www.the-dma.org/government/donotcalllists.shtml.

National Do Not Call Registry

REGISTRY HOME

REGISTER A PHONE NUMBER

VERIFY A REGISTRATION

MORE INFORMATION

EN ESPAÑOL

FILE A COMPLAINT

PRIVACY AND SECURITY

REGISTER YOUR HOME OR MOBILE PHONE NUMBER

Follow the registration steps below. Click here for detailed registration instructions.

1. Enter up to three phone numbers and your email address. Click Submit.
2. Check for errors. Click Register.
3. Check your email for a message from Register@donotcall.gov. Open the email and click on the link to complete your registration.

If you share any of these telephone numbers with others, please remember that you are registering for everyone who uses these lines.

STEP ONE

NATIONAL
DO NOT CALL
REGISTRY

Phone Number:

Email Address:

Confirm Email Address:

Your email address MUST be correct to process your registration. Learn why your email address is required. If you do not receive the verification email within a few minutes, please check your spam filter or junk email folder.

Enter phone numbers with or without a dash. Do not use spaces or periods.

Submit

Courtesy, www.donotcall.gov

this may seem expensive, the FTC levies fines on the order of $10,000 per violation (per call), so obtaining the registry is a wise investment for those wishing to contact consumers via the telephone. AT&T faced fines of over three-quarters of a million dollars for making 78 unwanted calls to 29 consumers listed on the do-not-call list. The Feds do take violations very seriously. The FTC's do-not-call website (**http://www.ftc.gov/donotcall**) provides access to detailed information for consumers and organizations.

Likewise, the Canadian government instituted a nearly identical do-not-call program. The Canadian Radio-television and Telecommunications Commission imposes fines up to $11,000 per call for calls made to people on the Canadian do-not-call list. Other countries in Europe and elsewhere are also considering similar or even more aggressive legislation.

Ownership

We used to think that every household had a phone. Think again. Landline phone penetration is about 80 percent in the United States and under 90 percent in Europe.[14] That means that marketing researchers interested in representative samples in either place are starting out with a big piece of population excluded from the list when landline phones are used.

Issues

When calls do get through to someone's house, an all-too-often outcome results:

> *Good evening, I'm with a nationwide marketing research company. Are you watching television tonight?*
> *A: Yes.*
> *Did you see American Idol?*
> *A: "Click."*

Thus, the extent of hang-ups, the do-not-call legislation and the dropping percentage of households with landline phones, are all issues. To the extent that any of these issues are associated systematically with respondent characteristics, systematic error becomes a strong possibility due to the survey's reduced ability to represent the population. Does one's personality relate to hanging up or getting on a don't-call list? Are demographics related to landline phone ownership? Obviously, the chance of administrative error in the form of sample selection bias seems highly plausible. Thus, landline phone interviews are still widely used, but researchers no longer automatically think of them as producing pristine data.

Mobile Phones

Mobile-phone interviews differ from landline phones most obviously because they reach individuals rather than households. However, there are other less obvious distinctions.

- In the United States, telemarketing toward mobile phone numbers is prohibited unless the user opts in. The primary reason for enacting this law was because recipients often have to pay for a call received.
- The recipient of a mobile phone call is more likely to be distracted than are other respondents. The respondent may be driving a car, on the metro, or walking down a noisy street. Factors such as this are not conducive to a high-quality interview.
- The area codes for mobile phones are not necessarily geographic. For instance, a person who moves from Georgia to Arizona can choose to keep the old phone number. As a result, a researcher may be unable to determine whether or not a respondent fits into the desired geographic sampling population.
- The phones have varying abilities for automated responses and differing keypads. Some requests, such as "hit pound sign," may be more difficult to do on some keypads than on others.

Mobile phones are ubiquitous in most developed and even in some not so developed countries. Approximately 90 percent of North American adults own a mobile phone of some type which is comparable to the 83 percent of Europeans who own a phone. Over sixty percent of all Chinese own mobile phones and that's a lot of consumers.[15] In some countries, such as the UAE, Bahrain, and Qatar, mobile phone ownership exceeds two phones for every person![16] Thus, mobile phones allow access to the vast majority of people in developed nations. The consumer movement toward solely mobile phones may have less effect on research in Europe and other nations where mobile phone numbers can be included in samples alongside landline phone numbers. However, each sampling unit's chance of being contacted is multiplied by the number of phones.

Phone Interview Characteristics

Phone interviews have several distinctive characteristics that set them apart from other survey techniques. These characteristics present significant advantages and disadvantages for the researcher.

Random Digit Dialing

People with unlisted phones typically differ demographically and psychologically from other people. Thus, unlisted phone numbers can introduce bias. The problem of unlisted phone numbers can be partially resolved through the use of random digit dialing. **Random digit dialing**, in its simplest form, takes telephone exchanges (area code + the first three numbers) for a geographic area and using computer-generated random numbers, adds the last four digits to obtain a phone number to call. The process excludes mobile phone numbers and if the firm complies, numbers on the do-not-call list. Random digit dialing also helps overcome the problem due to unlisted numbers, new listings, and recent changes in phone numbers. In the vast majority of random digit dialing, the computer actually selects the number from the list of potential respondents and places the call. Unfortunately, the refusal rate in commercial random digit dialing studies is higher than the refusal rate for telephone surveys that use only listed telephone numbers.

random digit dialing

Use of telephone exchanges and random numbers to develop a sample of respondents in a landline phone survey.

Landline versus Mobile Phone Results

Exhibit 7.2 provides a summary of potential differences in surveying by landline or mobile phones. Researchers should not be surprised to observe differences in the characteristics of heavy mobile phone users versus consumers who rely mostly on landline phone communications. For instance, compared to mobile phone users:[17]

- Calls to mobile phone numbers are more likely than landline numbers to result in someone answering the phone—particularly during working hours on weekdays. About one in three calls to mobile phones are answered as opposed to about one in four calls to landline numbers.
- Calls to mobile phone numbers are less likely to result in someone answering the phone on weekends than are landline numbers. Respondents answer less than one in three calls to mobile phones on the weekends as opposed to nearly four in ten calls to landline numbers.
- Refusals are higher for calls to mobile phone numbers than for calls to landline numbers. About half of mobile phone calls result in refusals to participate in the survey, whereas landline refusals average around 30 percent.

Source: © Cengage Learning 2013.

EXHIBIT **7.2**
Comparing and Contrasting
Landline and Mobile Phones

	Landline Phone	Mobile Phones
Sampling Units	Better for sampling households	Better for sampling individuals
Reaching Respondents	Low probability of contact during working hours	Higher probability of getting an answer except on weekends
Cooperation	7 in 10 agree to participate-more willing to talk	5 in 10 agree to participate – usually preoccupied with some other activity
Restrictions	Do not call legislation restrictions may apply	Mobile phone numbers usually cannot be called in USA
Cost to Respondent	Generally none	Depending on service plan, charges may apply and respondent should receive compensation
Geography	Area codes and exchanges indicate location of household	Phone numbers are not good indicators of individuals' locations
Population	Tends to be older than median, married, own fewer durable goods per person	Tend to be younger, single, college-educated, likely to own more durable goods per person
Technology	Relatively static	Changing rapidly w greater likelihood for visual presentation and text input
Ownership	About 80 percent in US and decreasing here and abroad	Over 80 percent in US and increasing – more than 2 phones per capita in some countries

- Mobile phone users should be duly compensated for their responses given the potential costs involved and the calls should be kept to a short duration given that a mobile phone user is more likely in a situation involving attention to some other activity.
- Mobile phone users are different demographically than landline users. Mobile phone consumers tend to be younger, more likely college educated, and more affluent.
- Mobile phone users own different things than landline users. A survey suggests that mobile phone users are more likely to own durable goods like DVD players, computers, and even music players.[18]

These factors all affect the equality of data and samples obtained from landline and mobile-phone sampling. Researchers should consider these factors before making a quick decision that any type of phone interviewing will satisfy the data needs at hand. In the end, a thorough understanding of the population of interest is essential in judging which type of interview is most appropriate.

Speed

One advantage of telephone interviewing is the relative speed of data collection. Data collection with mail or personal interviews can take weeks. In contrast, interviews can conduct hundreds of telephone interviews within a few hours. When an interviewer enters a respondent's answers directly into a computerized system, data processing speeds up even more relative to any other approach involving manual data coding and entry.

Cost

As the cost of personal interviews continues to increase, phone interviews appear relatively inexpensive. Estimates indicate that telephone interviews cost 25 percent of a comparable door-to-door personal interview. However, the typical Internet survey is even less expensive than a phone-based survey.

Absence of Face-to-Face Contact

Telephone interviews are more impersonal than face-to-face interviews. Respondents may answer embarrassing or confidential questions more willingly in a telephone interview than in a personal interview. However, mail and Internet surveys, although not perfect, are better media for gathering extremely sensitive information because they seem more anonymous. Some evidence suggests that people provide information on income and other financial matters only reluctantly, even in telephone interviews. Such questions may be personally threatening for a variety of reasons, and high refusal rates for this type of question occur with each form of survey research.

The inability of the interviewer to see respondents can cause problems. If a respondent pauses to think about an answer, the interviewer may simply interpret the pause as "no response" and go on to the next question. Hence, there is a greater tendency for interviewers to record no answers and incomplete answers in telephone interviews than in personal interviews.

Cooperation

One trend is very clear. In the last few decades, telephone response rates have fallen. Analysis of response rates for the long-running Survey of Consumer Attitudes conducted by the University of Michigan found that response rates fell from a high of 72 percent to 67 percent during the period from 1979 to 1996 and then even faster after 1996, dropping to 60 percent.[19] Lenny Murphy of the data collection firm Dialtek says he has observed a decline in survey response rates from a typical range of 30 to 40 percent in the past down to below 20 percent.[20] Fewer calls are answered because more households use caller ID or answering machines to screen their calls. Famous research companies may choose to identify themselves by name as evidence suggests that respondents may answer if they recognize the firm to be a research firm and not a telemarketer.[21] A lot of phone lines also are dedicated to fax machines or other electronic devices. However the rate of refusal actually grew faster in the more recent period than the rate of not answering researchers' calls. Respondents who answer the call but do not provide data are not particularly helpful in the research process.

Despite the restrictions in the United States, other countries may not adopt laws restricting calls to mobile phones. In addition, consumers in other countries are more open to responding to research delivered by voice or by text messaging. Thus, the mobile phone may be a better interview tool outside of the United States than in the United States.

Refusal to cooperate with interviews is directly related to interview length. Survey research finds that interviews of 5 minutes or less have refusal rates about 20 percent; interviews of between 6 and 12 minutes have 40 percent refusal rates; and about half of people refuse to participate in phone surveys of more than 12 minutes. A good rule of thumb is to keep telephone interviews under 10 minutes long. In general, 30 minutes is the maximum amount of time most respondents will spend unless they are highly interested in the survey subject.

Another way to encourage participation is to send households an invitation to participate in a survey. The invitation can describe the purpose and importance of the survey and the likely duration of the survey. The invitation can also encourage subjects to be available and reassure them that the caller will not try to sell anything. In a recent study comparing response rates, the rates were highest among households that received an advance letter, somewhat lower when the notice came on a postcard, and lowest with no notice.[22]

Incentives to Respond

Respondents should receive some incentive to respond. Research addresses different types of incentives. For telephone interviews, tests of different types of survey introductions suggest that not all introductions are equally effective. A financial incentive or some significant chance to win a desirable prize will produce a higher telephone response rate than a simple assurance that the research is not a sales pitch, a more detailed description of the survey, or an assurance of confidentiality.[23]

Callbacks

An unanswered call, a busy signal, or a respondent who is not at home requires a callback. Telephone callbacks are much easier to make than callbacks in personal interviews. However, as mentioned, the ownership of telephone answering machines and the use of voice-mail is widespread, and their effects on callbacks are not well understood. However, if a respondent decides not to answer a number the first time, one has to wonder why they would decide to answer it on a callback.

Lack of Visual Medium

Visual aids cannot be used in traditional telephone interviews, meaning that they are not ideal for packaging/design research, copy testing of television and print advertising, and concept tests that require visual materials. Likewise, certain attitude scales and measuring instruments require the respondent to see a graphic scale, so they are difficult to use over the phone. Facetime or Skype video calls via a smartphone, tablet, or computer offer the possibility of presenting still or video images to respondents to accompany verbal dialog. Researchers may take greater advantage of this technology in the coming years.

Central Location Interviewing

Research agencies or interviewing services typically conduct all telephone interviews from a central location. Such **central location interviewing** allows firms to hire a staff of professional interviewers and to supervise and control the quality of interviewing more effectively. When telephone interviews are centralized and computerized, an agency or business can benefit from additional cost economies. Research firms gain even better cost economies by outsourcing interviews to offshore call centers where labor costs are very low. However, a respondent will quickly become impatient with an interviewer who is difficult to understand The costs savings that come from using interviewers who have difficulty communicating are soon outweighed by subsequent problems.

Computerized Voice-Activated Telephone Interview

Technological advances have combined computerized telephone dialing and voice-activated computer messages to allow researchers to conduct telephone interviews without human interviewers. However, researchers have found that computerized voice-activated telephone interviewing works best with very short, simple questionnaires. One system includes a voice-synthesized module controlled by a microprocessor. With it the sponsor is able to register a caller's single response such as "true/false," "yes/no," "like/dislike," or "for/against." Media outlets to register callers' responses to certain issues have used this type of system. The system initiates the calls and automatically records responses. If respondents do not answer the first two questions, the computer disconnects and goes to the next call. This process automates the entire data collection process because a recorded voice asks the questions and responses are recorded automatically.

Global Considerations

Different cultures often have different norms about proper telephone behavior. For example, business-to-business researchers have learned that Latin American businesspeople will not open up to strangers on the telephone. So, researchers in Latin America usually find personal interviews more suitable than telephone surveys. In Japan, respondents consider it ill-mannered if telephone interviews last more than 20 minutes. Laws governing researchers' ability to call via landline or mobile phones also vary based on factors such as do-not-call laws and the legality of calling mobile phone numbers. Researchers generally cannot call cell phone numbers in the United States, but that is not the case in other countries including much of Europe.

Surveys Using Self-Administered Questionnaires

Noninteractive surveys do not require an interviewer to ask questions. Marketing researchers distribute questionnaires to consumers in many ways (see Exhibit 7.3). They insert invitations to participate via pop-ups in websites and Facebook posts (or other social networking sites). They insert questionnaires in packages and magazines. They may place questionnaires at points of purchase,

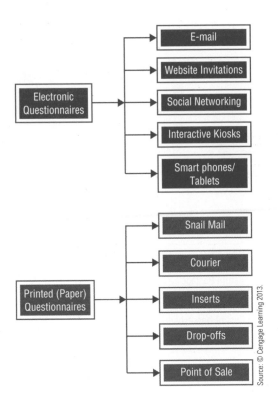

Source: © Cengage Learning 2013.

EXHIBIT 7.3
Options for Self-Administered Questionnaires

in high-traffic locations in stores or malls, or on table tops in restaurants. Traditionally, survey researchers sent printed questionnaires via snail mail. No matter how the **self-administered questionnaires** are distributed, they are different from interviews because the respondent takes responsibility for reading and answering the questions him/herself.

In mall intercepts, a research assistant usually stands by to answer any questions and/or provide basic instructions. But this person does not read the questions to the respondent. More and more, the assistant hands the person an electronic tablet or takes them to a kiosk upon which the respondent receives the survey. Without such assistance, the response quality is totally dependent on the ability to communicate clearly and unambiguously with the respondent in writing. Below, we elaborate on a few of the more widely used survey techniques for self-administered questionnaires.

self-administered questionnaires

Surveys in which the respondent takes the responsibility for reading and answering the questions without having them stated orally by an interviewer.

Mail Questionnaires

A traditional **mail survey** is a self-administered questionnaire sent to respondents through a postal service. Most often, the general postal service, or snail mail, provides delivery. However, when fears of a low response rate, as typically occurs when the sample consists of professional workers like physicians or consultants, an overnight courier service like FedEx is a better but more expensive option.

Mail questionnaires have several advantages and disadvantages.

mail survey

A self-administered questionnaire sent to respondents through the mail.

Geographic Flexibility

Mail questionnaires can reach a geographically dispersed sample simultaneously because interviewers are not required. Researchers can reach respondents who are located in isolated areas or those who are otherwise difficult to reach. For example, a pharmaceutical firm may find that doctors are not available for personal or telephone interviews. However, a mail or courier survey can reach both rural and urban doctors who practice in widely dispersed geographic areas.

Cost

Mail questionnaires are relatively inexpensive compared with personal interviews, though they are not cheap. Most include follow-up mailings, which require additional postage and printing costs. And it usually isn't cost-effective to try to cut costs on printing—questionnaires photocopied on

EXHIBIT **7.4**

Costs of Snail Mail versus
Courier Surveys

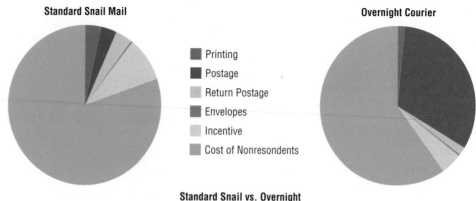

Standard Snail Mail

Overnight Courier

- Printing
- Postage
- Return Postage
- Envelopes
- Incentive
- Cost of Nonresondents

Standard Snail vs. Overnight

Item	Mail	Courier
Printing	0.75	0.75
Postage	0.75	15.00
Return Postage	0.75	0.75
Envelopes	0.10	0.10
Incentive	2.00	2.00
Cost of Nonresondents	17.4	27.9
Cost per Response	**$21.75**	**$46.50**

low-grade paper have a greater likelihood of being thrown in the wastebasket than those prepared with more expensive, high-quality printing.

Low response rates contribute to the high cost as researchers mail multiple questionnaires for every one that respondents send back. Each questionnaire goes out with a return postage paid reply envelope, otherwise researchers should not expect respondents to return completed questionnaires. Very often, a second wave of questionnaires follows the first in an effort to increase responses. So, printing and postage costs add up quickly; not to mention the costs of any incentive provided to increase response rate.

Exhibit 7.4 illustrates the cost of mail questionnaires per response. Typically, researchers mail out 1,000 or more questionnaires. Nonrespondents represent the biggest cost item. This exhibit assumes a two times higher response rate for a courier over snail mail. As that ratio increases, the cost of using a courier approaches that of snail mail.

Respondent Convenience

Respondents complete mail surveys at their convenience so respondents are more likely to take time to think about their replies. Mail questionnaires allow the respondent to check records before responding. A manager replying to a survey about the number of workers hired in the last six months could easily check the records to get a more accurate answer than memory would provide. The added convenience helps minimize the annoyance factor of survey research.

Respondent Anonymity

In the cover letter that accompanies a mail or self-administered questionnaire, marketing researchers almost always state that the respondents' answers will be confidential. With this promise, the researcher cannot share information about any particular respondent by name. Respondents are even more likely to provide sensitive or embarrassing information when the researcher provides anonymity, meaning responses cannot be traced to any individual. Researchers can guarantee confidentiality in practically any research. Anonymity becomes difficult in a personal interview.

A market researcher asked the following question through two approaches, "Have you borrowed money at a regular bank?" Researchers noted a 17 percent response rate for personal interviews and a 32 percent response rate for the mail survey. Although random sampling error may have accounted for part of this difference, the results suggest that for research on personal and sensitive financial issues, mail surveys are more confidential than personal interviews—the likely explanation being anonymity.

Absence of Interviewer

Although the absence of an interviewer can induce respondents to reveal sensitive or socially undesirable information, this lack of personal contact can also be a disadvantage. The respondent does not have the opportunity to question the interviewer. Problems that might be clarified in a personal or telephone interview can remain misunderstandings in a mail survey.

Standardized Questions

Mail questionnaires typically are highly standardized, and the questions are quite structured. Questions and instructions must be complete but straightforward. Any ambiguity likely leads to response error. With a mail survey, once the company mails the questionnaires, it is difficult to change the format or the questions.

Time Is Money

If time is a factor in management's interest in the research results, or if attitudes are rapidly changing, mail surveys may not be a good communication medium. A minimum of two or three weeks is necessary for receiving the majority of the responses. Follow-up mailings require an additional two or three weeks. The time between the first mailing and the cut-off date (when questionnaires will no longer be accepted) normally is six to eight weeks. Even personal interviews are faster in many cases.

Length of Mail Questionnaire

Mail questionnaires vary considerably in length, ranging from extremely short postcard questionnaires to multipage booklets that require respondents to fill in thousands of answers. A general rule of thumb is that a paper questionnaire should not exceed six pages in length. Time wise, any questionnaire taking more than 10 minutes is considered lengthy and response rates will be low. When a questionnaire requires a respondent to expend significant effort, an incentive is generally required to induce the respondent to return the questionnaire. The following sections discuss several ways to pursue higher response rates even when questionnaires are relatively long.

Response Rates

Fewer than 5 percent of respondents return poorly designed mail questionnaires. The basic calculation for obtaining a **response rate** is to the number of completed questionnaires returned divided by the total number of sample members provided a chance to participate. Typically, the number in the denominator is adjusted for faulty addresses and similar problems that reduce the number of eligible participants.

response rate
The number of questionnaires returned or completed divided by the number of sample members provided a chance to participate in the survey.

Response rates represent a major issue of mail questionnaires. When response rates are extremely low, one wonders whether people who responded are unusual, meaning somehow not representative of the population. Nonresponse error might be high if so. If response rates are very high, respondents could be complying due to undue incentives that amount to coercion. The incentive may be more responsible for answers than honest cooperation. In any event, rarely will a mail survey exceed a 50 percent response rate and those types of response rates usually require tremendous effort and expense.

Mail survey respondents are usually better educated and more likely to be a homeowner than nonrespondents. If they return the questionnaire at all, poorly educated respondents who cannot read and write well may skip open-ended questions to which they are required to write out their answers. Thus, systematic differences may correspond to differences between groups.

A researcher also has no assurance that the intended subject is the person who fills out the questionnaire. The wrong person answering the questions may be a problem when surveying corporate executives, physicians, and other professionals, who may pass questionnaires on to subordinates to complete. This probably is not unique to mail surveys because electronic surveying suffers similarly.

Increasing Response Rates for Mail Surveys

Who responds to mail surveys? Individuals who are interested in the general subject of the survey are more likely to respond than those with little interest. Wine enthusiasts are more likely than the average supermarket consumer to answer a survey addressing wine purchases. If the survey aims at measuring the typical supermarket attitudes and behaviors toward wine buying, the heavy responses by enthusiasts could represent error. People who hold extreme positions on an issue are more likely to respond than individuals who are largely indifferent to the topic. To minimize this bias, researchers have developed a number of techniques to increase the response rate to mail surveys. Designing and formatting attractive questionnaires and wording questions so that they are easily understand also help ensure a good response rate. However, special efforts beyond reply postage and follow-ups may be required even with a sound questionnaire.

Cover Letter

cover letter

Letter that accompanies a questionnaire to induce the reader to complete and return the questionnaire.

A **cover letter** that accompanies a questionnaire is an important means of inducing a reader to complete and return the questionnaire. Exhibit 7.5 illustrates a cover letter and some of the points considered by a marketing research professional to be important in gaining respondents' attention and cooperation. The first paragraph of the letter explains why the study is important. The basic appeal alludes to the social usefulness of responding. Two other frequently used appeals are asking for help ("Will you do us a favor?") and the egotistical appeal ("Your opinions are important!"). Most cover letters promise confidentiality, invite the recipient to use an enclosed postage-paid reply envelope, describe any incentive or reward for participation, explain that answering the questionnaire will not be difficult and will take only a short time, and describe how the person was scientifically selected for participation.

A personalized letter addressed to a specific individual shows the respondent that he or she is important. Including an individually typed cover letter on letterhead rather than a printed form is an important element in increasing the response rate in mail surveys.[23]

Incentives Help

Researchers can increase a respondent's motivation for returning a questionnaire by offering monetary incentives or premiums. Although pens, lottery tickets, and a variety of premiums have been used, monetary incentives appear to be the most effective and least biasing incentive. Money attracts attention and creates a sense of obligation. Often, cover letters try to boost response rates with messages such as "We know that the attached dollar cannot compensate you for your time, but please accept it as a token of our appreciation." Response rates increase dramatically when a monetary incentive goes to a charity of the respondent's choice rather than directly to the respondent.

Interesting Questions

The topic of the research—and thus the point of the questions—cannot be manipulated without changing the definition of the marketing problem. However, certain interesting questions can be added the questionnaire, perhaps at the beginning, to stimulate respondents' interest and to induce cooperation. By including questions that are of little concern to the researchers but that the respondents want to answer, the researchers may give respondents who are indifferent to the major questions a reason for responding.

Advance Notification

Advance notification that a questionnaire will be arriving can increase response rates in some situations. ACNielsen has used this technique to ensure a high cooperation rate in filling out diaries

EXHIBIT 7.5
A Cover Letter Requesting
Participation in a Survey

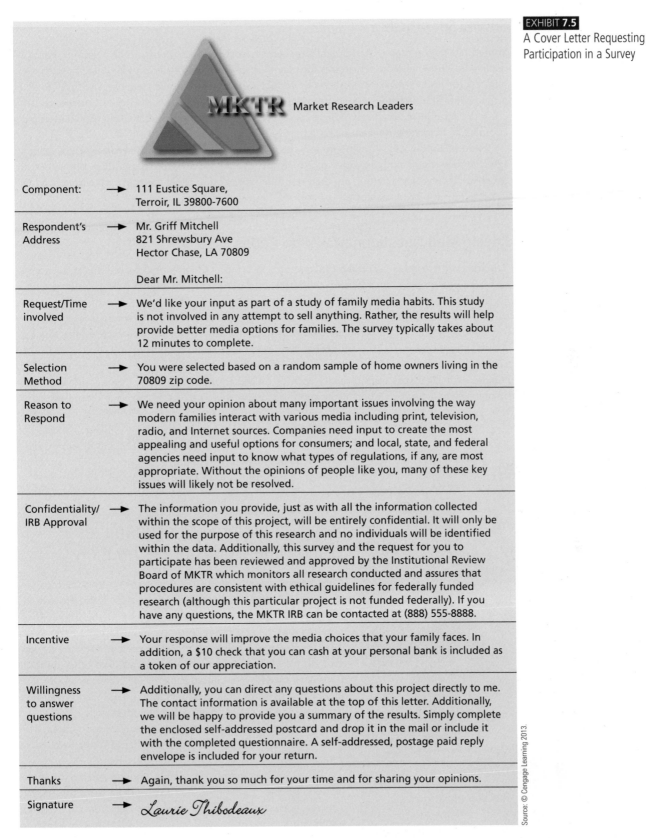

MKTR Market Research Leaders

Component:	→	111 Eustice Square, Terroir, IL 39800-7600
Respondent's Address	→	Mr. Griff Mitchell 821 Shrewsbury Ave Hector Chase, LA 70809 Dear Mr. Mitchell:
Request/Time involved	→	We'd like your input as part of a study of family media habits. This study is not involved in any attempt to sell anything. Rather, the results will help provide better media options for families. The survey typically takes about 12 minutes to complete.
Selection Method	→	You were selected based on a random sample of home owners living in the 70809 zip code.
Reason to Respond	→	We need your opinion about many important issues involving the way modern families interact with various media including print, television, radio, and Internet sources. Companies need input to create the most appealing and useful options for consumers; and local, state, and federal agencies need input to know what types of regulations, if any, are most appropriate. Without the opinions of people like you, many of these key issues will likely not be resolved.
Confidentiality/ IRB Approval	→	The information you provide, just as with all the information collected within the scope of this project, will be entirely confidential. It will only be used for the purpose of this research and no individuals will be identified within the data. Additionally, this survey and the request for you to participate has been reviewed and approved by the Institutional Review Board of MKTR which monitors all research conducted and assures that procedures are consistent with ethical guidelines for federally funded research (although this particular project is not funded federally). If you have any questions, the MKTR IRB can be contacted at (888) 555-8888.
Incentive	→	Your response will improve the media choices that your family faces. In addition, a $10 check that you can cash at your personal bank is included as a token of our appreciation.
Willingness to answer questions	→	Additionally, you can direct any questions about this project directly to me. The contact information is available at the top of this letter. Additionally, we will be happy to provide you a summary of the results. Simply complete the enclosed self-addressed postcard and drop it in the mail or include it with the completed questionnaire. A self-addressed, postage paid reply envelope is included for your return.
Thanks	→	Again, thank you so much for your time and for sharing your opinions.
Signature	→	*Laurie Thibodeaux*

of television watching. Advance notices that go out closer to the questionnaire mailing time produce better results than those sent too far in advance. The optimal lead time for advance notification is three days before the mail survey is to arrive. Advanced notification can come in the form of a postcard, a phone call, or even an e-mail.

Survey Sponsorship

Sometimes response quality is enhanced when the survey sponsor remains anonymous. Respondents who know who the research is for may, perhaps unintentionally, provide biased results. One business-to-business marketer wished to conduct a survey of its wholesalers to learn their stocking policies and their attitudes concerning competing manufacturers. A mail questionnaire sent on corporate letterhead very likely will yield a much lower response rate than a questionnaire using a commercial marketing research firm's letterhead.

Sponsorship by well-known and prestigious organizations such as universities or government agencies may significantly improve response rates. A mail survey sent to members of a consumer panel will receive an exceptionally high response rate because panel members have already agreed to cooperate as part of membership.

Keying Mail Questionnaires with Codes

drop-off method

A survey method that requires the interviewer to travel to the respondent's location to drop off questionnaires that will be picked up later.

● ● ● ● ● ● ●

Snail mail still plays a role in self-administered surveys.

©David De Lossy/Getty Images

A marketing researcher planning a follow-up letter, postcard, or e-mail would prefer not to disturb respondents who already have completed and returned a completed questionnaire. However, if the survey process is completely anonymous, the researcher has no way of knowing who has responded and who has not. Thus, the researcher has no choice but to send any second waves to everyone in the sample. One alternative is to clandestinely code questionnaires in a way that allows the researcher to know who has responded and remove them from the sample list. In this way, individual codes key questionnaires to individual members of the sampling frame. This code can appear on the questionnaire itself or on the envelope. For instance, blind keying might involve using a room number in the reply address as the code. Each envelope would contain a different room number and the sample list would include that number beside each person's name. The code might also appear somewhere on the questionnaire itself and in some cases a statement might indicate the number's purpose in identifying individual responses and not individual people.

Self-Administered Questionnaires Using Other Forms of Distribution

Other forms of self-administered printed questionnaires share many characteristics with mail questionnaires. Airlines occasionally pass out questionnaires to passengers during flights. Restaurants, hotels, and other service establishments print short questionnaires on cards so that customers can evaluate the service. *Tennis Magazine, Advertising Age, Wired,* and other publications have used inserted questionnaires to survey current readers inexpensively. Many manufacturers use postage-paid owner registration cards to collect demographic and lifestyle information economically. Again, problems may arise because people who return these self-administered questionnaires differ from those who do not.

When the research involves a long questionnaire, the drop-off method may be helpful. The **drop-off method** means that a research assistant physically drops the questionnaire off at a respondent's office or home. The assistant may arrange a time to come back and get the completed questionnaire. Clearly, this is an expensive method of distributing questionnaires but the response rate is generally improved. In the United States, researchers employ drop-offs when the sample involves businesspeople who are best reached at their place of work.

E-Mail Surveys

E-mail surveys involve making the questionnaire available to a potential respondent via e-mail. Today, respondents receive requests to participate in surveys more by e-mail than any other distribution method. E-mail surveys can put a respondent together with a questionnaire in one of three ways.

e-mail surveys

Survey requests distributed through electronic mail.

Using E-Mail

Three ways to contact respondents via e-mail include the following.

- A questionnaire can be included in the body of an e-mail. In this case, the questionnaire should be very short (no more than ten questions). These are likely to receive a high response rate.
- Questionnaires can be included as attachments. To complete the questionnaire, a respondent must open the questionnaire, respond via radio boxes and areas to write short answers, save the questionnaire, and then reattach it to a reply e-mail. Researchers can use common software such as Microsoft Word or Adobe Acrobat to create these files. Alternatively, the respondent may have the option of marking the questionnaire with a pen or pencil and returning via fax or mail. As might be expected, response rates are low with this approach given all the effort and inconvenience of dealing with the attachment and, as a result, professional researchers typically avoid this approach.
- A third option is to include a hyperlink within the body of an e-mail that will direct the respondent to a web-based questionnaire. The respondent then completes the response directly on that website. This approach is now the most common way of soliciting responses via e-mail. In essence, the e-mail survey becomes an Internet survey at this point.

Sampling and E-Mail

Like phone surveys, most, but not all, people in developed countries have access to e-mail. In particular, researchers targeting senior citizens may wish to avoid this approach if they desire a true cross-section of their opinion. In contrast, e-mail easily reaches businesspeople, middle-aged, and young adults. Researchers now consider e-mail a viable alternative for contacting research respondents and perhaps as representative as the landline for contacting wide cross-sections of the population.

Please answer the following for the computer you will be using most often to complete our online surveys.

Operating System
Select one from this list

- ○ Windows (any version)
- ◉ Mac OS (any version)
- ○ Linux
- ○ WebTV
- ○ Other
- ○ Don't Know/Not sure

Internet Browser Used Most Often
Select one from this list

- ○ Internet Explorer
- ○ Firefox
- ○ Netscape
- ◉ Safari
- ○ Mozilla
- ○ Opera
- ○ Konqueror
- ○ Lynx
- ○ Web TV
- ○ Other
- ○ Don't Know/Not sure

Online panel members get requests to respond to surveys and get small incentives in return.

Image courtesy of Susan Van Etten

Advantages and Disadvantages of E-Mail

The benefits of incorporating a questionnaire in an e-mail include the speed of distribution, lower distribution and processing costs, faster turnaround time, more flexibility, and less manual processing of paper questionnaires. The speed of e-mail distribution and the quick response time are major advantages when dealing with time-sensitive issues.

Some researchers also believe that respondents are more candid in e-mail than in person or on the telephone. One caveat would exist when dealing with research directed at employers using company e-mail addresses. Employees often believe that their e-mails are not secure and "eavesdropping" by a supervisor could possibly occur. The belief that a response is not secure is particularly strong when the questionnaire is contained in the e-mail itself and a reply e-mail is needed to return a completed questionnaire. When the questionnaire deals with confidential subject matter, the respondent should enter responses via a questionnaire accessed through a hyperlink-accessible Web questionnaire. In this way, the ability to get candid responses remains an advantage.

In general, the guidelines for printed mail surveys apply to e-mail surveys. For example, delivering the material in the cover letter is more difficult because people generally do not like e-mails that are more than two or three lines. Thus, a traditional cover letter may need to be made as brief as possible if it is contained in the e-mail request itself. Another option is to move some of the cover letter material, such as the assurances of confidentiality and IRB approval, to the actual questionnaire introduction.

Also, if the e-mail lists more than one address in the "to" or "CC" field, all recipients will see the entire list of names. This lack of anonymity has the potential to cause response bias and nonresponse error. E-mail requests should be addressed to a single person. Alternatively, the blind carbon copy, or BCC, field can be used if the same message must be sent to an entire sample. A drawback to this approach is that some spam filters will identify any message addressed to a large number of respondents as junk e-mail. Bulk-mailing programs exist that attempt to work around this problem by e-mailing potential respondents a few at a time. As can be seen, the problems associated with successful delivery to respondents remain a disadvantage of e-mail surveys.

Internet Surveys

Internet survey
A self-administered survey administered using a Web-based questionnaire.

click rate
The portion of potential respondents exposed to a hyperlink to a survey who actually click through to view the questionnaire.

An **Internet survey** is a self-administered questionnaire posted on a website. Response rates remain an issue with Internet and e-mail surveys. Typically, respondents know the questionnaire exists either by simply coming across it while browsing, through a pop-up notification, or via an e-mail containing a hyperlink, as described above.

With Internet surveys, we can track both **click rate**, which assesses the portion of potential respondents who actually take a look at the questionnaire, and, if an e-mail request is sent, response rates based on the number of invitations. Generally, except for very long questionnaires, many respondents who click through to view a questionnaire also respond to it. Some researchers argue that the true response rate for an Internet survey initiated by an email invitation should be the ratio of completed questionnaires to the number of click-throughs. This opinion argues that logically, the only respondents with a chance to respond are those that clicked through and many surveys close once a quota of completes is obtained. With this rationale, Internet survey response rates equal or exceed telephone and snail mail surveys.[24] Like every other type of survey, Internet surveys have both advantages and disadvantages.

Speed and Cost-Effectiveness

Internet surveys allow marketers to reach a large audience (possibly a global one), personalize individual messages, and secure confidential answers quickly and cost-effectively. The computer-based survey eliminates the costs of printing, postage, data entry, as well as other administrative costs. Once the researcher develops the questionnaire, the incremental cost of reaching additional respondents is minimal. The low incremental cost means that large samples are possible relative to other interview techniques. Speed isn't greatly affected either as even surveys using large samples can be conducted in a week or less.

Visual Appeal and Interactivity

Internet survey designs allow more interactivity than paper-based surveys. For instance, questions can change based on the specific responses provided. A respondent might initially write in the name of the last retailer in which he or she spent more than $100: Walmart. Subsequent questions asking the respondent to rate the shopping experience can "pipe in," or fill in, the name Walmart into questions. The Internet also is an excellent medium for the presentation of visual materials, such as photographs or drawings of product prototypes, advertisements, videos, or movie trailers.

Respondent Participation and Cooperation

Internet survey respondents who intentionally click through a link they stumble across while browsing display high category involvement. For example, Ticketmaster quickly obtained more than 10,000 responses based on a survey invitation placed on their home page. The responses helped Ticketmaster better understand its customer purchase patterns and evaluate visitor satisfaction with the site. A response like this is possible only when consumers are involved and believe their cooperation will help make the experience better.

Today, many e-mail surveys employ members of consumer panels who have previously indicated a willingness to cooperate by completing questionnaires. Panel members click through a hyperlink to a survey hosted on a server like the one maintained by Qualtrics. Different security settings can provide more confidence that the respondent who received the e-mail request is the one who actually responds. Panel members also need an incentive to respond. A study of German consumers showed that nothing beats financial incentives. In other words, the best way to get responses was to simply pay consumers for participating in surveys.[25] However, as with any incentive, one can question whether paid respondents participate only for the incentive and may even be giving bogus responses simply to earn the reward. Researchers using panel surveys need to be particularly vigilant in screening responses for authenticity.

Accurate Real-Time Data Capture

Internet surveys in effect allow respondents to record their own answers directly into a data file. Survey software also can prohibit improper data entry. For example, on a paper questionnaire a respondent might incorrectly check two responses even though the instructions call for a single answer. Online survey tools can make this type of mistake impossible by barring a second response and/or activating a warning message. Thus, the data capture is more accurate than when humans do the data entry. The researcher can watch the surveys come in and give input into when to stop the survey process.

Callbacks

E-mail survey samples drawn from consumer panels allow for easy callbacks via e-mail. Computer software sends e-mail reminders automatically and like other survey forms, they can marginally increase responses.[26] Computer software can sometimes identify nonrespondents or respondents who started but did not complete a questionnaire and send those people customized messages. Sometimes follow up e-mails offer additional incentives to those individuals who previously quit with only a few additional questions left to answer. When researchers assure respondents of complete anonymity, no individual computer tracking should take place leaving the only callback option a reminder sent to the entire sample qualified by an "excuse me" message for those who may have already responded.

Personalized and Flexible Questioning

Survey software allows questioning to branch off into two or more different lines depending on a respondent's answer to a filtered question. In other words, the computer program asks questions in a sequence determined by the respondent's previous answers. This ability to sequence questions based on previous responses is a major advantage of computer-assisted surveys. The computer can be programmed to skip from question 6 to question 9 if the answer to question 6 is "no." Information can be piped in based on previous responses making questions less ambiguous and more relevant. Fewer, less ambiguous and more relevant questions means a survey that is easier to answer and thus increases response rates and response quality.

A related advantage of using a Web survey is that it can prompt respondents when they skip over a question. In a test comparing telephone and Internet versions of the same survey, the rate of item nonresponse was less for the Internet version, which issued a prompt for each unanswered item.[27] This was likely not a simple matter of motivation, because the rate of respondents who actually took the Web version was less than for the telephone version, even though the researchers offered a larger incentive to those asked to go online. Online survey software can force a respondent to answer questions by blocking them from moving further if they've left a forced response question blank. Research suggests that forced responding does not increase survey nonresponse nor does it present evidence of biased answers.[28] However, researchers may not always be comfortable with this choice as we will see below.

Respondent Anonymity

Respondents are more likely to provide sensitive or embarrassing information when they remain anonymous. The anonymity of the Internet encourages respondents to provide honest answers to sensitive questions.

Improving Response Rates

Methods for improving response rates for an Internet survey are similar to those for other kinds of survey research. A request delivered through Facebook may improve response likelihood. The subject line should refer to a topic likely of interest the audience, and legal as well as ethical standards dictate that it may not be deceptive. Thus, the line might be worded in a way similar to the following: "Please give your opinion on [subject matter of interest]." Researchers should avoid gimmicks like dollar signs and the word *free,* either of which is likely to alert the spam filters installed on most computers.

Unlike mail surveys, Internet surveys do not offer the opportunity to send a physical incentive, such as a dollar bill, to the respondent. Incentives to respond to a survey must be in the form of a coupon or a promise of a future reward. A coupon can be included that contains a discount code which can be applied at a retail website or even in a store. For example, a respondent might receive a $10 coupon good at **www.target.com** or in any Target store as a thanks for participating. Otherwise, a promise can be offered: "As a token of appreciation for completing this survey, the sponsor of the survey will make a sizable contribution to a national charity. You can vote for your preferred charity at the end of the survey." Generally, promises are less effective than an incentive in hand.

Researchers also can use prenotification for Web surveys. The research firm can send e-mail notices, phone messages, postcards, and/or letters informing potential respondents that an e-mail will be arriving containing a survey invitation. Researchers studying why students enroll in the universities that they attend might involve contacting recent college applicants. The applicants might first receive a letter indicating that a survey invitation will arrive via e-mail. With a study like this, one might expect about 20 percent of potential respondents to click through to the questionnaire, and all but a small percentage of these would respond, for an overall response rate of just under 20 percent and a click-through response rate of about 90 percent. Recall that highly engaged respondents are more likely to respond. Alternatively, they may receive only the e-mail invitation.

Mail notification has several potential advantages. Spammers do not send notifications via mail, so the survey may end up having a little more legitimacy. Additionally, the prenotification establishes the potential for a relationship and can even include a request to put the sender on the recipient's safe sender list. However, research provides no evidence of substantial response rate gains by using snail mail prenotification and any gains need to be weighed against the extra costs involved with physically mailing notices.[29] Telephone call prenotifications are slightly more effective but also add costs. Thus, nonautomatic prenotifcations are used only when there are great concerns about responses.

Internet surveys, even those not associated with a panel, are often directed toward a finite population. For example, all members of the Atlanta area Sales and Marketing Executives Association might comprise a population of interest for researchers studying attitudes toward customer relationship management programs. Recent research shows that a combination of pop-up notification on a software user forum's home page plus a single e-mail notification (to all members of the forum) yields an overall response rate of about 14 percent.[30] Thus, respondent characteristics that indicate a stake in the issues studied are most responsible for increasing response rates.

Compared to Snail Mail

Overall, previous data suggest that mail surveys generate higher response rates than e-mail surveys. However, under some conditions, such as with college students or company employees, e-mail surveys get a comparable or higher response rate.[31] Also, more recent evidence suggests changing trends that legitimize electronic communication formats. In part, this is due to the fact that more and more people have grown up with text messages, e-mails, and Facebook postings.[32] Thus, the response rate gap trend suggests better responses to electronic survey requests.

Response Quality

Internet surveys are still in their infancy in many ways. However, the prospects for a bright future are good. Surveys asking potential respondents questions that can be compared with known population demographics can be used to compare the response quality of different survey media. For instance, basic demographic information for each U.S. ZIP code is available through **http://www.census.gov**. Random samples taken from ZIP codes asking respondents to report these basic statistics should produce results that match the census data with allowance for a small amount of error.[33] Thus far, indications are that Web-based survey approaches produce data that is as good as or better in quality than traditional phone surveys.

Text-Message Surveys

This technique is perhaps the newest survey approach. It has all the advantages of mobile-phone surveys in terms of reach and but shares the disadvantages in terms of reaching only respondents who have somehow opted in. However, text-message surveys are catching on in other countries and are ideal for surveys involving only a few very short questions. Additionally, MMS messages can include graphic displays or even short videos. This technology is likely to see more applications in the near future.

Choosing an Appropriate Survey Approach

Each survey administration technique has advantages and disadvantages. A researcher who must ask highly confidential questions may use an anonymous mail survey, thus sacrificing follow-up possibilities to avoid interviewer bias. If a researcher must have considerable control over question phrasing, and the questions involve open-ended responses, centralized location telephone interviewing may provide both control and a user-friendly format.

To determine the appropriate technique, the researcher must ask several questions:

- Is the assistance of an interviewer necessary?
- Are respondents interested in the issues being investigated?
- Will cooperation be easily attained?
- How quickly is the information needed?
- Will the study require a long and complex questionnaire?
- How large is the budget?

The criteria—cost, speed, anonymity, and so forth—may differ for each project.

Exhibit 7.5 summarizes some major advantages and disadvantages of different survey approaches. It emphasizes typical types of surveys. For example, a creative researcher might be able to design highly versatile and flexible mail questionnaires, but most researchers use standardized questions. An elaborate mail survey may be far more expensive than a short personal interview, but generally this is not the case.

EXHIBIT 7.6 Advantages and Disadvantages of Typical Survey Methods

	Door-to-Door Personal Interview	Mall Intercept Personal Interview	Telephone Interview	Mail Survey	Internet Survey
Speed of data collection	Moderate to fast	Fast	Very fast	Slow; researcher has no control over return of questionnaire	Instantaneous; 24/7
Geographic flexibility	Limited to moderate	Confined, possible urban bias	High	High	High (worldwide)
Respondent cooperation	Excellent	Moderate to low	Good	Moderate; poorly designed questionnaire will have low response rate	Varies depending on website; high from consumer panels
Versatility of questioning	Quite versatile	Extremely versatile	Moderate	Not versatile; requires highly standardized format	Extremely versatile
Questionnaire length	Long	Moderate to long	Moderate	Varies depending on incentive	Moderate; length customized based on answers
Item non-response rate	Low	Medium	Medium	High	Software can assure none
Possibility for respondent misunderstanding	Low	Low	Average	High; no interviewer present for clarification	High
Degree of interviewer influence on answers	High	High	Moderate	None; interviewer absent	None
Supervision of interviewers	Moderate	Moderate to high	High, especially with central-location interviewing	Not applicable	Not applicable
Anonymity of respondent	Low	Low	Moderate	High	Respondent can be either anonymous or known
Ease of callback or follow-up	Difficult	Difficult	Easy	Easy, but takes time	Difficult, unless e-mail address is known
Cost	Highest	Moderate to high	Low to moderate	Lowest	Low
Special features	Visual materials may be shown or demonstrated; extended probing possible	Taste tests, viewing of TV commercials possible	Fieldwork and supervision of data collection are simplified; quite adaptable to computer technology	Respondent may answer questions at own convenience; has time to reflect on answers	Streaming media software allows use of graphics and animation

Note: The emphasis is on *typical* surveys. For example, an elaborate mail survey may be far more expensive than a short personal interview, but this generally is not the case.

Pretesting Survey Instruments

A researcher spending $300,000 to survey a few thousand consumers does not want to find out after data collection that most respondents misunderstood some questions, all gave the same answer to a key variable, or misinterpreted the response instructions for an entire set of items. Researchers can minimize these possibilities by employing various screening procedures during *pretesting*. **Pretesting** involves trial runs using the survey instrument with a group of colleagues or actual respondents to iron out fundamental problems in instructions, items, or design of a questionnaire. Researchers benefit by spotting problems in the pretest and rightly inferring that a problem with this very small sample will likely be a problem in the full sample once data collection actually begins.

Broadly speaking, researchers choose from three basic ways of pretesting. The first two involve screening the questionnaire with other research colleagues, and the third—the one most often called pretesting—is a trial or pilot test with an actual group of respondents. First, when screening the questionnaire with other research professionals, the investigator asks them to look for such problems as difficulties with question wording, leading questions, and bias due to question order. An alternative type of screening might involve a client or the research manager who ordered the research. Often, managers ask researchers to collect information, but when they see the questionnaire, they feel that it does not really address their decision statements. The researchers then need either to explain things better to the client and/or make changes. Secondly, other research experts may sometimes be asked to judge the content of survey items as a way of trying to verify that the items are measuring what the researcher intended. Later, we return to this idea under the heading of validity.

The third form is basically a trial run of the entire research project. Once the researcher has decided on the final questionnaire, data are collected with a small number of respondents (perhaps as many as 100 but sometimes as few as three dozen) to determine whether the questionnaire needs refinement. The researcher is keen to spot problem items and analyses these data for suspicious patterns indicating potential problems. For example, a researcher might find that all respondents indicate the same answer to a specific question. Such a result is highly unlikely when more than a handful of respondents are included. Thus, a response like this probably indicates a problem with item wording.

Unfortunately, although the value of a pretest is readily apparent, researchers often press forward without it due to time and budget concerns. The risk of collecting some items that end up not being very helpful increases without a pretest. Needless to say, pretests are highly recommended in almost all types of primary data collection efforts.

pretesting

Screening procedure that involves a trial run with a group of respondents to iron out fundamental problems in the survey design.

"Practice is the best of all instructors."

—PUBLIUS SYRUS, CIRCA 42 BC

Ethical Issues in Survey Research

Chapter 4 mentioned that codes of ethics express researchers' obligation to protect the public from misrepresentation and exploitation under the guise of marketing research. Thou shall not disguise selling as research! Many ethical issues apply to survey research, such as respondents' right to privacy, the use of deception, respondents' right to be informed about the purpose of the research, the need for confidentiality, the need for honesty in collecting data, and the need for objectivity in reporting data.

At this time, a few points are worth emphasizing. Researchers should not ask for information in a misleading way. Also, researchers must be careful to guard the resulting data carefully. For instance, a researcher may end up with data that identifies children's responses to several different new products. The data may also contain demographics and other material. Once that data becomes stored on a laptop or server, it is vulnerable to theft or misplacement. The researcher should follow good security procedures in protecting the data stored on various storage mediums.

Additionally, technology brings new issues to the forefront. Although e-mail is an extremely useful tool, researchers should avoid needlessly contributing to spam volume by sending unsolicited e-mails seeking survey respondents. At times, this may be the only way to reach a population,

Complementary Evidence

The results of observation studies may amplify the results of other forms of research by providing *complementary evidence* concerning individuals' "true" feelings. Focus group interviews often are conducted behind two-way mirrors from which marketing executives observe as well as listen to what is occurring. This additional source allows for interpretation of nonverbal behavior such as facial expressions or head nods to supplement information from interviews.

For example, in one focus group session concerning how women use hand lotion, researchers observed that all the women's hands were above the table while they were casually waiting for the session to begin. Seconds after the women were told that the topic was to be hand lotion, all their hands were placed out of sight. This observation, along with the group discussion, revealed the women's anger, guilt, and shame about the condition of their hands. Although they felt that people expected them to have soft, pretty hands, their household tasks include washing dishes, cleaning floors, and doing other chores that are hard on the hands.

Other research studies combine visible observation with personal interviews. During or after in-depth observations, researchers ask individuals to explain their actions.[3] Direct observation of women applying hand and body lotion identified two kinds of users. Some women slapped on the lotion, rubbing it briskly into their skin. Others caressed their skin as they applied the lotion. When interviewed asked about their behavior, the researchers were able to interpret this finding. Women who slapped the lotion on were using the lotion as a remedy for dry skin. Those who caressed their skin were more interested in making their skin smell nice and feel soft.

When researchers examine focus group videos, observation of the nonverbal communication symbols can add even more to marketers' knowledge of the situation. Researchers also may follow up observations of customers in a shopping center with survey research. For example, if customers are observed looking into the window of a store for more than 30 seconds but then moving on without going in, researchers may intercept them with a few questions potentially revealing reasons for this behavior.

Recording the decision time necessary to make a choice is a relatively simple, unobtrusive task easily accomplished through direct observation; it is also an example of complementary evidence. Survey responses combined with information on how long the respondent took to make a choice reveal more than either type of data alone. Recorded choice time is a measure of **response latency.** This measure is based on the hypothesis that the longer a decision maker takes, the more difficult that decision was and the more thought the respondent put into the choice. A quick decision presumably indicates an easy or obvious choice. Computer-administered surveys can incorporate an automatic measure of response latency and thereby offer a big advantage over paper-and-pencil approaches. Imagine how cumbersome a survey would become if respondents had to manually time themselves and enter the number of seconds it took to make responses.

response latency

The amount of time it takes to make a choice between two alternatives; used as a measure of the strength of preference.

Direct and Contrived Observation

Researchers need to always take care of how much they interject themselves into the data collection situation. In a phenomenological approach, the researcher is often very much within the research situation. Consider the case where researchers ask restaurant employees to talk about working in a restaurant and how much emphasis restaurant management places on hygiene and customer safety. The researcher has to ask questions and may even provide some prop or stimulus to help get the respondent started. On the other hand, hidden cameras placed within the restaurants could record behavior and provide data without the need for a researcher's presence. Alternatively, an ethnographer may actually take a job in the restaurant and perform certain acts to see how other employees react. This brings us to the difference between direct and contrived observation.

Direct Observation

direct observation

A straightforward attempt to observe and record what naturally occurs; the investigator does not create an artificial situation.

Direct observation can produce detailed records of what people actually do during an event. The observer plays a passive role, making no attempt to control or manipulate a situation, instead merely recording what occurs. He or she must make every effort not to interject him- or herself into the situation. For example, recording traffic counts and traffic flows within a supermarket can help managers design store layouts that maximize a typical customer's exposure to the merchandise offered while also facilitating search efforts. This data gathered through observation often are more accurate than what one would get by asking consumers about their movement through a store. A manufacturer can then better determine shelf locations, sales displays, the arrangement of departments and merchandise within those departments, the location of checkout facilities, and other characteristics that improve the shopping value consumers obtain from visiting a store.

For instance, if directly questioned in a survey, most shoppers would inaccurately portray the time they spent in each department. Observation such as described in the Research Snapshot dealing with way-finding eliminates that error. In the museum study described in the Research Snapshot, the observer carefully recorded the amount of time spent in each exhibit room. The results allowed the research team to assess the popularity of the various exhibits based on time spent in each area.

With the direct observation method, the data consist of records of events made as they occur. An observation form often helps keep researchers' observations consistent and ensures that they record all relevant information. A respondent is not required to recall—perhaps inaccurately— an event after it has occurred; instead, the observation is instantaneous. For instance, a response latency measure embedded in an online survey will "observe" how long a respondent took to answer a question without the respondent ever knowing the measure was taken. Will this provide more accurate information than if a research assistant asked respondents to report how many seconds it took to respond? Almost certainly the answer is yes!

Why Use Direct Observation?

In many cases, direct observation is the most straightforward form of data collection—or the only form possible. A produce manager for Auchan (a France-based hypermart firm) may periodically gather competitive price information from Carrefour (also a France-based hypermart firm) stores within competing areas. Both Carrefour and Auchan can monitor each other's promotions by observing advertisements posted on the competitor's website (see **http://www.auchan.fr** and **http://www.carrefour.fr**), for example. In other situations, observation is the most economical technique. In a common type of observation study, a shopping center manager may observe the license plate (tag) numbers on cars in its parking lot. These data, along with automobile registration information, provide an inexpensive means of determining where customers live.

Researchers sometimes can obtain certain data more quickly or easily using direct observation than by other methods. If a research question involves what demographic characteristics are associated with spending time in a food court, a researcher can simply observe the gender, race, and other visible respondent characteristics rather than employing a survey. Researchers investigating a diet product may use observation when selecting respondents in a shopping mall. Overweight people may be prescreened by observing pedestrians, thus eliminating a number of screening interviews. Direct observation's advantages often make it the simplest, quickest, and most accurate way to gather data. On the other hand, direct observation has limited flexibility because not all phenomena are observable.

Errors Associated with Direct Observation

Although direct observation involves no interaction with the subject, the method is not error-free; the observer may record events subjectively. The same visual cues that may influence the interplay between interviewer and respondent (e.g., the subject's age or sex) may come into play in some direct observation settings, such as when the observer subjectively attributes a particular economic status or educational background to a subject. We refer to a distortion of measurement resulting from the cognitive behavior or actions of the witnessing observer as **observer bias**. For example, in a research project using observers to evaluate whether salesclerks are rude or courteous, fieldworkers may be required to rely on their own interpretations of people or situations during the observation process.

observer bias

A distortion of measurement resulting from the cognitive behavior or actions of a witnessing observer.

©M. Thomsen/zefa/CORBIS

Clean as We Say, or Clean as We Do?

Most people know that hand washing is a fundamental way to stay healthy, not to mention simple good manners. So, when you ask them, most people say they faithfully wash their hands. But according to observational research, what people say about this behavior is not what they necessarily do.

The American Society for Microbiology and the Soap and Detergent Association together arranged for a nationwide study of hand washing by U.S. adults. In an online survey by Harris Interactive, 91 percent of adults said they always wash their hands after using a public restroom. Men were somewhat less likely to make this claim—88 percent, versus 94 percent of women. The researchers followed up on the survey results by observing adults in public restrooms in Atlanta, Chicago, New York City, and San Francisco. A 2007 tally of the percentage who washed their hands found that only 77 percent did so. About 66 percent of men were observed washing their hands after going to the restroom, whereas women washed their hands 88 percent of the time. The difference between reporting of hand washing and actual hand washing was greater for the men (about a 22 percent difference) than for the women (6 percent). Additionally, hand washing is down 6 percent since 2005.

In many industries, hand washing is critical to patron health, in particular in the health care and food preparation industries. Companies in these industries often provide formal training programs designed specifically to increase hand washing among employees. However, even after training, employees in these industries still often do not wash their hands when and as they should. In fact, a recent observational study showed that even the best performing companies reached only 85 percent success in having employees wash when they should.

Research teams often conduct observational hand-washing studies by having observers discreetly watch and record the frequency of the number of people using a public toilet facility and the number of people who washed their hands properly. Observers pretend to be grooming themselves while watching the visitors. In the Harris study cited above, researchers observed over 6,000 people in four U.S. cities. Do you think a hidden camera would reveal different results? What might they be if so?

Sources: Based on "Hygiene Habits Stall: Public Handwashing Down," *Cleaning 101*, www.sciencedaily.com/releases/2007/09/070917112526.htm, accessed September 2, 2011; Harris Interactive, "Many Adults Report Not Washing Their Hands When They Should, and More People Claim to Wash Their Hands than Who Actually Do," news release (December 14, 2005); Constable, K. (2011), "Clean Hands—Old Dirt, New Dirt," *Foodmagazine* (February 11), 16.

"What we see depends mainly on what we look for."

—SIR JOHN LUBBOCK

Also, accuracy may suffer if the observer does not record every detail that describes the persons, objects, and events in a given situation. Generally, the observer should record as much detail as possible. However, the pace of events, the observer's memory, the observer's writing speed, and other factors will limit the amount of detail that can be recorded.

Interpretation of observation data is another potential source of error. Facial expressions and other nonverbal communication may have several meanings. Does a smile always mean happiness? Does the fact that someone is standing or seated next to the president of a company necessarily indicate the person's status? Error creeps in the more pure observation moves into subjective judgment.

Contrived Observation

contrived observation

Observation in which the investigator creates an artificial environment in order to test a hypothesis.

Most observation takes place in a natural setting, but sometimes the investigator intervenes to create an artificial environment to test a hypothesis. This approach is called **contrived observation**. Contrived observation can increase the frequency of occurrence of certain behavior patterns, such as employee responses to complaints. An airline passenger complaining about a meal or service from the flight attendant may actually be a researcher recording that person's reactions. If situations were not contrived, the research time spent waiting and observing would expand considerably. A number of retailers use observers called *mystery shoppers* to visit a store and pretend to be interested in a particular product or service. After leaving the store, the "shopper" evaluates the salesperson's performance.

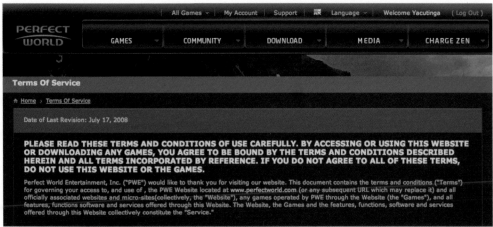

● ● ● ● ● ● ●

Included in the Terms of Service of some sites is an agreement to let the site collect observational data about you.

The Research Snapshot discusses direct observation of hand washing in public restrooms. Similarly, a study compared results from self-reported questionnaire data, focus group data, and observational data concerning hygiene among restaurant employees. The questionnaire responses suggested that 95 percent of employees washed their hands thoroughly after handling raw chicken, but that number averaged about 82 percent in the face-to-face interview condition, and when observation provides the data, 75 percent of the restaurant employees did not wash their hands adequately after handling raw chicken.[4] This direct observation could be turned into a contrived situation if a participant observer, pretending to be a new employee, asked another employee to assist by in some way handling raw chicken, and then observed the other employee's behavior. In the latter case, the researcher has interjected him- or herself into a situation, but perhaps for a very good reason. This may allow a hypothesis stating that interruptions will be associated with less hand washing compared to a no interruption condition.

Ethical Issues in the Observation of Humans

Observational researchers' tools are sometimes akin to snooping or spying.[5] Observation methods introduce a number of ethical issues, many raising the issue of the respondent's right to privacy. Suppose a research firm approaches a company interested in acquiring information about how women put on their bras by observing behavior in a spa dressing area. The researcher considers approaching spas in several key cities about placing small cameras inconspicuously to observe women getting dressed. Obviously, such a situation raises an ethical question. Even if the dressing room is an area where women often do dress where others can observe them, women do not expect to have their dressing behavior recorded and viewed. Therefore, unless the researcher can find a way to have women consent to such observation, this observational approach is unethical.

If the researcher obtains permission to observe someone, the subject may not act naturally. So, at times there is a strong temptation to observe without obtaining consent or gaining input from an IRB (Institutional Review Board). Many times, such as monitoring people walking through and waiting in an airport, obtaining consent from individual respondents is impractical if not impossible. Further, asking for consent just before the actual observation will likely change the behavior.

New technologies afford new opportunities to observe behaviors of interest to marketing managers. Deep-packet inspection refers to the ability of an Internet service provider to read data transmitted by users. The observation of this data might clue researchers in on how consumers search for marketing information. Cloud computing similarly involves the transfer of data from a private computer onto some server making information susceptible to be observed by others. Smartphones also record an individual's movements using GPS technologies. Observers may also

EXHIBIT 8.3
Is the Observation Ethical?

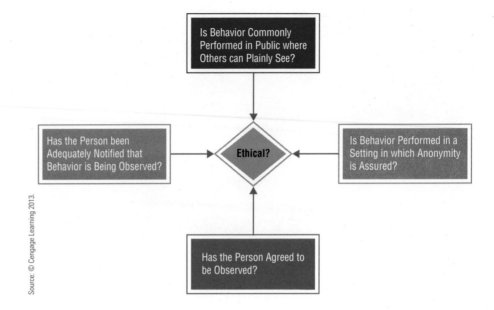

Source: © Cengage Learning 2013.

snoop on Facebook and other social networking sites and both observe and provoke online comments all motivated by the need to discover information about consumers.

So, when should researchers feel comfortable collecting observational data? Although exceptions exist to every rule, here are four questions that can help address this question:

1. Is the behavior being observed commonly performed in public where it is expected that others can observe the behavior?
2. Is the behavior performed in a setting in which the anonymity of the person being observed is assured (meaning there is no way to identify individuals)?
3. Has the person agreed to be observed?
4. Has the person been adequately notified that their behavior (including data transfers) is being observed?

If the answer to the first two questions is "yes," then there is not likely a violation of privacy in collecting observational research data. If the answer to the third and/or fourth question is "yes," then gathering the data also is likely ethical. Otherwise, the researcher should carefully consider input from an IRB or other authority before proceeding with the research.

Also, some might see contrived observation as unethical based on the notion of entrapment. To *entrap* means to deceive or trick into difficulty, which clearly is an abusive action. For instance, in the hand-washing example above, when the experimenter interrupts the real employee, he/she may entrap the employee into a lower probability of washing hands thoroughly. In this instance, if the employee was caused or caused harm to others (by getting in trouble with a superior or making someone ill) then clearly the intrusion is unethical. However, if no possibility of harm exists, then the researcher can likely proceed although this particular instance should be done under the auspices of an IRB.

Observation of Physical Objects

"What would you rather believe? What I say, or what you saw with your own eyes?"

—GROUCHO MARX

Physical phenomena may be the subject of observation study. Physical-trace evidence is a visible mark of some past event or occurrence. For example, the wear on library books indirectly indicates how many people actually handle and/or check out books and, therefore, wear represents a proxy for popularity based on the assumption that more wear means more readers. A classic example of physical-trace evidence in a nonprofit setting was erosion on the floor tiles around the hatching-chick exhibit at Chicago's Museum of Science and Industry. These tiles were replaced every six weeks; tiles in other parts of the museum did not need to be replaced for years. The selective erosion of tiles, indexed by the replacement rate, was a measure of the relative popularity of exhibits.

Artifacts

Clearly, a creative marketing researcher has many options for determining the solution to a problem. The story about Charles Coolidge Parlin, generally recognized as one of the founders of commercial marketing research, examining garbage cans at the turn of the twentieth century illustrates another study of physical traces. Physical traces often involve artifacts. **Artifacts** are things that people made and consumed within a culture that signal something meaningful about the behavior taking place at the time of consumption. Ethnographers are particularly interested in examining artifacts and Parlin's garbage can escapades illustrate how a marketing researcher can apply an ethnographic approach involving observation of artifacts.

Parlin designed an observation study to persuade Campbell's Soup Company to advertise in the *Saturday Evening Post*. Campbell's was reluctant to advertise because it believed that the *Post* was read primarily by working people who would prefer to make soup from scratch, peeling the potatoes and scraping the carrots, rather than paying ten cents for a can of soup. To demonstrate that rich people weren't the target market, Parlin selected a sample of Philadelphia garbage routes. Garbage from each specific area of the city that was selected was dumped on the floor of a local National Guard Armory. Parlin had the number of Campbell's soup cans in each pile counted. The results indicated that the garbage from the rich people's homes didn't contain many cans of Campbell's soup. Although they may not have made soup from scratch themselves, their housekeepers may have. The garbage piles from the blue-collar area showed a larger number of Campbell's soup cans. This observation study was enough evidence for Campbell's. They advertised in the *Saturday Evening Post*.[6]

A scientific project conducted at the University of Arizona adopted this research approach in which aspiring archaeologists sifted through garbage for over thirty years. They examine soggy cigarette butts, empty milk cartons, and half-eaten Big Macs in an effort to understand modern life. Like other research involving observation, we can compare the observed garbage data with the results of surveys about food consumption. Garbage does not lie. This type of observation can correct for potential overreporting of healthful item consumption and underreporting of, say, cigarettes or fast food.

Even if fashion companies could learn a lot about the types of problems consumers typically have when purchasing and wearing clothes, would observation through two-way mirrors be appropriate?

artifacts

The things that people made and consumed within a culture that signal something meaningful about the behavior taking place at the time of consumption.

Inventories

Another application of observing physical objects is to count and record physical inventories through retail or wholesale audits. This method allows researchers to investigate brand sales on regional and national levels, market shares, seasonal purchasing patterns, and so on. Marketing research suppliers offer audit data at both the retail and the wholesale levels.

An observer can record physical-trace data to discover information a respondent could not recall accurately. For example, measuring the number of ounces of liquid bleach used during a

● ● ● ● ● ● ●

Picking through the garbage
on the side of the road can
reveal behaviors of fast-food
customers.

©Kuzma/Shutterstock

test provides precise physical-trace evidence without relying on the respondent's memory. The accuracy of respondents' memories is not a problem for the firm that conducts a pantry audit. The pantry audit requires an inventory of the brands, quantities, and package sizes in a consumer's home rather than responses from individuals. The problem of untruthfulness or some other form of response bias is avoided. For example, the pantry audit prevents the possible problem of respondents erroneously claiming to have purchased prestige brands. However, gaining permission to physically check consumers' pantries is not easy, and the fieldwork is expensive. In addition, the brand in the pantry may not reflect the brand purchased most often if consumers substituted it because they had a coupon, the usual brand was out of stock, or another reason.

Researchers studying hand washing employed an interesting observational approach involving inventories. They decided to measure hand washing by electronically monitoring the portion of people using public restrooms who used soap.[7] In other words, the soap use unobtrusively assessed whether a user washed his or hands or not. In addition, the researchers posted either knowledge based or disgusting messages about the implications of not washing hands. In this way, they implemented an experiment within the observational research approach. The results showed that just over 30 percent of men and 65 percent of women washed their hands, and that men were more likely to wash after exposure to a disgusting message but women were more likely to wash after receiving knowledge. Thus, the soap inventory served as an observational measurement tool (compare to results in the research snapshot).

Content Analysis

content analysis

The systematic observation and quantitative description of the manifest content of communication.

Besides observing people and physical objects, researchers may use **content analysis**, which obtains data by observing and analyzing the contents or messages of advertisements, newspaper articles, television programs, letters, and the like. This method involves systematic analysis as well as observation to identify the specific information content and other characteristics of the messages. Content analysis studies the message itself and involves the design of a systematic observation and recording procedure for quantitative description of the manifest content of communication. This technique measures the extent of emphasis or omission of a given analytical category. For example, content analysis of advertisements might evaluate their use of words, themes, characters, or space and time relationships. Content analysis often counts the frequency of themes or occurrences within a given hermeneutic unit. For instance, the frequency with which women, African Americans, Hispanics, or Asians appear in advertising displayed on a cable network represents a topic amenable to content analysis.

Content analysis might be used to investigate questions such as whether some advertisers use certain themes, appeals, claims, or deceptive practices more than others or whether recent consumer-oriented actions by the Federal Trade Commission have influenced the contents of advertising. A cable television programmer might do a content analysis of network programming to evaluate its competition. Every year researchers analyze the Super Bowl telecast to see how much of the visual material is live-action play and how much is replay, or how many shots focus on the cheerleaders and how many on spectators. Content analysis also can explore the information content of television commercials directed at children, the company images portrayed in ads, and numerous other aspects of advertising.

Study of the content of communications is more sophisticated than simply counting the items; it requires a system of analysis to secure relevant data. After one employee role-playing session involving leaders and subordinates, researchers analyzed videotapes to identify categories of verbal behaviors (e.g., positive reward statements, positive comparison statements, and self-evaluation requests). Trained coders, using a set of specific instructions, then recorded and coded the leaders' behavior into specific verbal categories. Ideally, two or three coders perform the task, allowing for an assessment of rater reliability or how replicable are the results.

Mechanical Observation

In many situations, the primary—and sometimes the only—means of observation is mechanical rather than human. Video cameras, traffic counters, and other machines help observe and record behavior. Some unusual observation studies have used motion-picture cameras and time-lapse photography. An early application of this observation technique photographed train passengers and determined their levels of comfort by observing how they sat and moved in their seats. Another time-lapse study filmed traffic flows in an urban square and resulted in a redesign of the streets. Similar techniques may help managers design store layouts and resolve problems in moving people or objects through spaces over time.

Television and Radio Monitoring

Perhaps the best-known marketing research project involving mechanical observation and computerized data collection is ACNielsen's **television monitoring** system for estimating national television audiences. Nielsen Media Research uses a consumer panel and a monitoring device called a People Meter to obtain ratings for television programs nationwide.[8] The Nielsen People Meter gathers data on what program is on a television and who is watching it at the time. The electronic devices capture information on program choices and the length of viewing time. This observational data is supplemented with consumer diaries which together provide valuable input on ratings which helps price advertising time by program and lets advertisers know what programs will reach the targeted audience. Over 5,000 consumers comprise Nielsen's television panel.

television monitoring
Computerized mechanical observation used to obtain television ratings.

Critics of the People Meter argue that subjects in Nielsen's panel grow bored over time and don't always record when they begin or stop watching television. Arbitron, best known for measuring radio audiences, has attempted to answer this objection with its own measuring system, which it calls the Portable People Meter.[9] Each participant receives points for the time he or she uses the meter. The participant's pay is based on the total points displayed in the base station. Arbitron's meter simplifies the participants' role and collects data on exposure to radio and television programming outside the home. However, the device records only signals that the radio or television system embeds using Arbitron's equipment.

Other devices gather data about the viewing of advertisements. The TiVo digital television recorder collects detailed viewing data, such as what commercials people skip by using fast-forward. The PreTesting Company sets up contrived observational studies in which viewers equipped with a remote control watch any of three prerecorded channels playing different programs and advertisements, including the client's ads to be tested.[10] The system records the precise points at which the viewer changes the channel. By combining the results from many participants, the company arrives at a Cumulative Zapping Score, that is, the percentage of viewers who had exited the

● ● ● ● ● ● ●

Traffic cameras that monitor speeding on major highways are becoming commonplace in Europe, Australia, and even in some parts of the United States. Would car companies learn anything from the observed behavior?

client's advertisement by each point in the ad. So that viewing behavior will be more natural, Pre-Testing tells respondents they are evaluating the programming, not the ads.

Mobiltrak, a Virginia-based research technology firm, produces a device that can passively observe what is playing on cars' stereos. The company installs their shoebox-sized equipment on towers located at heavily traveled intersections. Sensors on the equipment measure the level of electronic radiation emitted by the radio of each car as it passes by. The data describe the volume of traffic listening to each station, not the stations on individual vehicle's radios or any demographic data about the vehicles' drivers or passengers.[11] By paying a subscription fee to Mobiltrak, radio stations in the company's service areas can obtain data about their listeners. They can use the data to sell advertising time to businesses located where the most listeners are driving. In addition, advertisers can pay for data collected at particular locations. For example, Home Depot, which has used Mobiltrak, can find out which stations people are listening to as they travel on roads leading past one of the company's stores.

Monitoring Website Traffic

Computer technology makes gathering detailed data about online behavior easy and inexpensive. The greater challenges are to identify which measures are meaningful and to interpret the data correctly. For instance, most organizations record the level of activity at their websites. They may count the number of *hits*—mouse clicks on a single page of a website. If the visitor clicks on many links, that page receives multiple hits. Similarly, they can track *page views,* or single, discrete clicks to load individual pages of a website. Page views more conservatively indicate how many users visit each individual page on the website and may also be used to track the path or sequence of pages that each visitor follows. Additionally, companies can track comments about their brands left on blogs and social networking sites.

Web Traffic and Buzz

click-through rate (CTR)

Proportion of people who are exposed to an Internet ad who actually click on its hyperlink to enter the website.

A **click-through rate (CTR)**, in the same way as for assessing survey responses, is the percentage of people who exposed to an advertisement who actually click on the corresponding hyperlink which takes them to the company's website. Counting hits or page views can suggest the amount of interest or attention a website is receiving, but these measures are flawed. First, hits do not differentiate between a lot of activity by a few visitors and a little activity by many visitors. In addition, the researcher lacks information about the meaning behind the numbers. If a user clicks on a site many times, is the person finding a lot of useful or enjoyable material, or is the user trying unsuccessfully to find something by looking in several places? Additionally, some hits are likely made by mistake. The consumers may have had no intention of clicking through the ad or may not have known what they were doing when they clicked on the ad.

A more specific count is the number of *unique visitors* to a website. This measurement counts the initial access to the site but not multiple hits on the site by the same visitor during the same day or week. Operators of websites can collect the data by attaching small files, called *cookies*, to the computers of visitors to their sites and then tracking those cookies to see whether the same visitors return. Some marketing research companies, notably Forrester Research and Nielsen, monitor Internet activity related to brands, industries, and consumers. These companies maintain panels of hundreds of thousands of consumers who agree to provide their Internet activities by making their cookies available as data. The information that remains stored in cookies and other system files can also help researchers know about the habits of Internet usage for consumers. Researchers supplement panel data with information tracked on Internet users who are not members of the panel.

The research companies provide their clients with assessments of more than website effectiveness as the resulting data includes assessments of advertising effectiveness and social media buzz. Imagine how a company like Paramount might be interested in whether or not news about new products stirs up any activity online. **Conversation volume** represents a measure of the amount of Internet postings that involve a specific name or term. Paramount relies heavily on Web traffic and buzz data to help predict how successful a movie might be.[12] A company can even help gauge interest in a new product before releasing it. The movie studio leaked news about both *Paranormal Activity II* and *Waiting for Superman* and then sat back to see whether consumers visited Paramount's websites more, searched for the movie titles more, or made comments or Tweets about the movies on social network sites.

Extrapolating product success purely based on Web traffic or even online conversation volume can produce inaccurate projections. Mere counts of brand-name usage do not reveal whether the usages are in a positive or negative light. In addition, many brand names can be confounded by other meanings.[13] Just imagine all the reasons why someone may search or use the word "kiss." Further, outside the panel users, consumers employ differing levels of computer security systems limiting researchers' access to information. Difficulties such as these strongly point toward the need for observational data from the Internet to be professionally analyzed before relying on it for important decisions.

Numerous websites provide basic Web traffic statistics. Some sites provide services for free and others for a fee. Alexa.com allows free access where users can compare traffic among competing websites and get basic demographic information about the consumers who frequent those sites. Exhibit 8.4 illustrates how one can use these sites to better understand Web traffic. Other providers include statcounter.com and Google Analytics, among others.

conversation volume

A measure of the amount of Internet postings that involve a specific name or term.

Alexa.com makes information about the most popular web sites and product interest available based on actual web traffic.

Top Sites
The top sites on the web, ordered by Alexa Traffic Rank.

1. Google	4. Yahoo	7. Wikipedia	10. Tencent
2. Facebook	5. Live	8. Blogger	11. Twitter
3. Youtube	6. Baidu	9. MSN	More ▶

Hot Products
Products that people are coveting right now...

1. The Life Plan: How Any Man Can Achieve Lasting Health
2. Disney Epic Mickey
3. Winning
4. Hawke & Co Men's Cobre Jacket
5. Kindle
More ▶

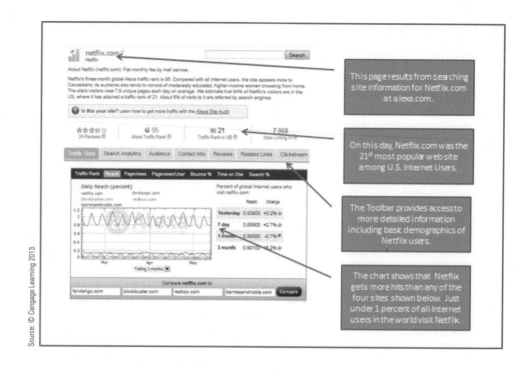

Source: © Cengage Learning 2013.

CTR and Online Advertising

As online advertising has become more widespread, marketing research has refined methods for measuring the effectiveness of the advertisements. Applying the CTR to the amount spent on the advertisement gives the advertiser a *cost per click.* This presents a practical way to evaluate advertising effectiveness. However, marketers rarely see getting consumers to click on an ad as its primary objective. Companies more often expect advertising to help them meet sales goals.

Google has benefited from CTR research indicating that the highest click-through rates tend to occur on pages displaying search results. Not surprisingly, someone who searches for the term *kayaks* is more likely to be interested in an advertisement offering a good deal on kayaks. The company showed Vanguard, for example, that banner ads cost the financial firm less than fifty cents per click and generated a 14 percent click-through rate. That CTR is far above typical response rates for direct-mail advertising, but it does not indicate whether online clicks are as valuable in terms of sales.[14] If the company makes more than fifty cents per customer clicking through, the ads are an effective sales tool.

Scanner-Based Research

Lasers performing optical character recognition and bar code technology like the universal product code (UPC) and RFID tags have accelerated the use of mechanical observation in marketing research. Chapter 6 noted that a number of syndicated services offer secondary data about product category movement generated from retail stores using scanner technology.

This technology allows researchers to investigate questions that are demographically or promotionally specific. Scanner research has investigated the different ways consumers respond to price promotions and the effects of those differences on a promotion's profitability. One of the primary means of implementing this type of research is through the establishment of a **scanner-based consumer panel** to replace consumer purchase diaries. In a typical scanner panel, each household carries a shopper card, which members present at checkout. A scan of the card allows recording of a household's purchase information as data.

Aggregate data, such as actual store sales as measured by scanners, are available to clients and industry groups. For instance, data from Information Resources Inc. (IRI) have indicated a downward trend in sales of hair-coloring products. Demographic data suggest that an important reason is the aging of the population; many consumers who dye their hair reach an age at which they no

scanner-based consumer panel

A type of consumer panel in which participants' purchasing habits are recorded with a laser scanner rather than a purchase diary.

longer wish to cover their gray hair. A smaller segment of the population is at an age where consumers typically begin using hair coloring.[15]

Data from scanner research parallel data provided by a standard mail diary panel, with some important improvements:

1. The data measure observed (actual) purchase behavior rather than reported behavior (recorded later in a diary).
2. Substituting mechanical for human record-keeping improves accuracy.
3. Measures are unobtrusive, eliminating interviewing and the possibility of social desirability or other bias on the part of respondents.
4. More extensive purchase data can be collected, because all UPC categories are measured. In a mail diary, respondents could not possibly reliably record all items they purchased.
5. The data collected from computerized checkout scanners can be combined with data about advertising, price changes, displays, and special sales promotions. Researchers can scrutinize them with powerful analytical software provided by the scanner data providers.

Camera Surveillance

Modern society increasingly relies on cameras to keep tabs on all sorts of behaviors. In 2005, terrorist attacks on the famous Tube (subway) System rocked London. Within just a few hours of the attacks, analysis of London's video surveillance recordings revealed potential suspects who were quickly identified using database technology. On a typical day, cameras record a Londoner's behavior automatically hundreds of times. Likewise, cameras planted inconspicuously in places can be useful in marketing research. Shopping center security video can help identify problems with merchandising and the types of things that attract consumers to come into and remain in an environment. However, cameras have many more applications.

Researchers sometimes ask and get permission to place cameras inconspicuously in consumers' homes, offices, or even cars.[16] Microsoft commissioned research involving the observation of fifty homes via inconspicuous, in-home cameras. The research addressed problems encountered by consumers encountered when using Windows products in their homes, Microsoft was able to study the consumer behavior involved and try to find a way to reduce the problems identified. Other companies including Kimberly-Clark, Sony, and Old Spice have also successfully applied observational research using cameras. The Old Spice research involved videos of guys taking showers in their homes (with permission and swimsuits) and the Kimberly-Clark research involved young parents wearing small hat cams while changing a baby's diaper. This type of observation allows close inspection of activities in places and at times when having an actual observer present would not work.

Marketing researchers are also using something dubbed a Mindcam to understand various aspects of consumer activity, such as shopping.[17] A small camera and microphone combination records all the sights and sounds experienced by the shopper. Typically, an interview follows up where the consumer tries to explain his or her behavior and any purchases made. Small cameras and other recording devices make these types of developments possible.

Smartphones

Modern people are increasingly dependent upon their smartphones and other devices such as tablet computers. Most people don't realize how much information is recorded through their everyday use of the phone. All text messages and phone calls leave behind some kind of record. In this way, phones serve as a type of mechanical behavior recorder. Smartphones also contain GPS devices capable of recording the phone's, and thus most likely the user's, whereabouts anytime the phone is connected. Observations from smartphones might reveal:[18]

- When people are happy based on their message content.
- Their political opinions.
- When the customer may be unhappy with their smartphone service provider.
- Where a person likes to party on the weekend based on GPS information.

● ● ● ● ● ● ●

Physiological responses to advertising can be recorded with a device like this one.

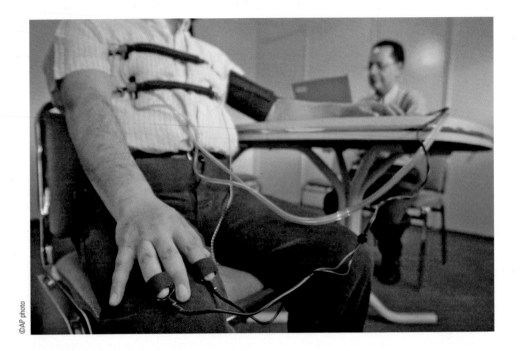

©AP photo

Like other areas, technology may outpace the ethics of using this type of data. The benefits of allowing researchers access to the data are being weighed against privacy concerns as policy makers ponder legal limits on what can be recorded and shared.

Measuring Physiological Reactions

Marketing researchers have used a number of other mechanical devices to evaluate consumers' physical and physiological reactions to advertising copy, packaging, and other stimuli. Four major categories of mechanical devices are used to measure physiological reactions: (1) eye-tracking monitors, (2) pupilometers, (3) psychogalvanometers, (4) voice-pitch analyzers, and (5) neurological activity.

Eye-Tracking

eye-tracking monitor

A mechanical device used to observe eye movements; some eye monitors use infrared light beams to measure unconscious eye movements.

A magazine or newspaper advertiser may wish to grab readers' attention with a visual scene and then direct it to a package or coupon. Or a television advertiser may wish to identify which selling points to emphasize. Eye-tracking equipment records how the subject reads a print ad or views a television commercial and how much time a respondent spends looking at various parts of a stimulus. In physiological terms, the gaze movement of a viewer's eye is measured with an **eye-tracking monitor**, which measures unconscious eye movements. Originally developed to measure astronauts' eye fatigue, modern eye-tracking systems need not keep a viewer's head in a stationary position. The devices track eye movements with invisible infrared light beams that lock onto a subject's eyes. The light reflects off the eye, and eye-movement data are recorded while another tiny video camera monitors which magazine page is being perused. The data are analyzed by computer to determine which components in an ad (or other stimuli) were seen and which were overlooked. Eye-tracking monitors have recently been used to measure the way subjects view e-mail and Web marketing messages. OgilvyOne has used this technology to learn that people often skip over more than half of the words in e-mail advertising, especially words on the right side of the message. Interestingly, consumers generally ignore the word *free*.[19]

Other physiological observation techniques are based on a common principle: that adrenaline is released when the body is aroused. This hormone causes the heart to enlarge and to beat harder and faster. These changes increase the flow of blood to the fingers and toes. The blood vessels dilate, and perspiration increases, affecting the skin's electrical conductivity. Other physical changes following the release of adrenaline include dilation of the pupils, more frequent brain wave activity, higher skin temperature, and faster breathing. Methods that measure these and other changes associated with arousal can apply to a variety of marketing questions, such as subjects' reactions to advertising messages or product concepts.

Pupilometer

A **pupilometer** observes and records changes in the diameter of a subject's pupils. A subject is instructed to look at a screen on which an advertisement or other stimulus is projected. When the brightness and distance of the stimulus from the subject's eyes are held constant, changes in pupil size may be interpreted as changes in cognitive activity that result from the stimulus, rather than from eye dilation and constriction in response to light intensity, distance from the object, or other physiological reactions to the conditions of observation. This method of research is based on the assumption that increased pupil size reflects positive attitudes toward and interest in advertisements.

pupilometer

A mechanical device used to observe and record changes in the diameter of a subject's pupils.

Psychogalvanometer

A **psychogalvanometer** measures galvanic skin response (GSR), a measure of involuntary changes in the electrical resistance of the skin. This device is based on the assumption that physiological changes, such as increased perspiration, accompany emotional reactions to advertisements, packages, and slogans. Excitement increases the body's perspiration rate, which increases the electrical resistance of the skin. The test is an indicator of emotional arousal or tension and can be used to help detect dishonest responses as a lie detector.

psychogalvanometer

A device that measures galvanic skin response, a measure of involuntary changes in the electrical resistance of the skin.

Voice-Pitch Analysis

Voice-pitch analysis is a relatively new physiological measurement technique that gauges emotional reactions as reflected in physiological changes in a person's voice. Abnormal frequencies in the voice caused by changes in the autonomic nervous system are measured with sophisticated, audio-adapted computer equipment. Computerized analysis compares the respondent's voice pitch during warm-up conversations (normal range) with verbal responses to questions about his or her evaluative reaction to television commercials or other stimuli. This technique, unlike other physiological devices, does not require the researcher to surround subjects with mazes of wires or equipment.

voice-pitch analysis

A physiological measurement technique that records abnormal frequencies in the voice that are supposed to reflect emotional reactions to various stimuli.

Neurological Devices

The chapter's opening vignette described a technology that observed brain activity as a person went about everyday behaviors. More and more, we are able to observe what goes on in the consumer's mind. Neurological activity can reveal how much thought takes place and what types of feelings a person is probably experiencing. Similar processes involve things such as **magnetic resonance imaging (MRI)** or transcranial magnetic simulation.[20] If these things sound complicated, it's because they are. These tools allow actual direct observation of what is going on in the mind of a respondent by assessing and identifying where electromagnetic activity is taking place within the brain. Thus, these techniques may revolutionize research on information processing.

Marketing researchers employ the technology by having paid respondents view advertisements in an MRI machine.[21] The results help identify the patterns of cognitive and emotional reactions the ads may generate, at least when ads are viewed in an MRI machine. Thus, the tools remain obtrusive and expensive, both factors limiting their application in practice. However, advancing technology may enable smaller and portable devices more amenable to studying behavior

Magnetic Resonance Imagery (MRI) device

A machine that allows one to measure what portions of the brain are active at a given time.

Companies like Visiontrack specialize in research that tracks how the eye moves during an activity. Think about how useful this might be to companies considering product placements within video games or in designing more efficient instrument panels for airplanes.

©Barone Firenze/Shutterstock

in a more realistic setting. Researchers also will have to be concerned about the ethical implications of looking into someone's mind. Once these barriers are overcome, observations of brain activity may become a mainstay of observational marketing research.

Physiological measures have disadvantages and advantages. All of these devices assume that physiological reactions are associated with persuasiveness or predict a cognitive response. However, no strong theoretical evidence demonstrates exactly how physiological changes drive future sales. Another major problem with physiological research is the *calibration,* or sensitivity, of measuring devices. Identifying arousal is one thing, but precisely measuring *levels* of arousal is another. In addition, most of these devices are expensive and require an artificial setting for their use. However, as a prominent researcher points out, physiological measurement is coincidental: "Physiological measurement isn't an exit interview. It's not dependent on what was remembered later on. It's a live blood, sweat, and tears, moment-by-moment response, synchronous with the stimulus."[22]

TIPS OF THE TRADE

- Generally, observational data are most advantageous when researchers record the data without the conscious awareness of the person observed. Once someone knows that others are watching, the researcher cannot be sure how much that knowledge changes behavior.
- Marketing research often involves information processing. Researchers should strongly consider using measures of response latency when studying information processing. Computer-aided survey technology makes observing response latency easy and accurate.

- To avoid ethical issues, the anonymity of people whose behavior is captured using observational data collection should be protected at all times unless consent has been obtained to identify the person.
- Observational data, including Web traffic counts and conversational volume, become more reliable and meaningful when analyzed in conjunction with other types of data.

Source: © Cengage Learning 2013.

:: SUMMARY

1. Discuss the role of observation as a marketing research tool. Scientific observation is the systematic process of recording the behavioral patterns of people, objects, and occurrences as they are witnessed Ten kinds of observable phenomena are: 1) physical actions; 2) verbal behavior, such as sales conversations; 3) expressive behavior; 4) spatial relations and locations; 5) temporal patterns; 6) physical objects; 7) verbal and pictorial records; 8) neurological activity; 9) Internet activity; and 10) geographic information. Observational data is very advantageous in capturing what actually happened.

2. Know the difference between direct and contrived observation. The most advantageous observational data techniques are unobtrusive, meaning the observation takes place without the knowledge of the observed person. Direct observation involves watching and recording what naturally occurs, without creating an artificial situation. For some data, observation is the most direct or the only method of collection. For example, researchers can measure response latency, the time it takes individuals to choose between alternatives. Observation can also be contrived by creating the situations to be observed such as the case with mystery shoppers. This can reduce the time and expense of obtaining reactions to certain circumstances.

3. Identify ethical issues particular to research using observation. Contrived observation, hidden observation, and other observation research tools, including the use of Web tracking and smartphone data, have the potential to involve deception or violate one's privacy. For this reason, these methods often raise ethical concerns about subjects' right to privacy and right to be informed. The chapter includes a short checklist that can be useful in determining the morality of an observational data gathering approach. An over-riding concern when consent cannot or is not obtained is whether the person freely performs the observed behavior in public.

4. Explain the observation of physical objects and message content. Physical-trace evidence serves as a visible record of past events. Researchers may examine whatever evidence provides such a record, including inventory levels, the contents of garbage cans, or the items in a consumer's pantry. Researchers can take advantage of artifacts that are left behind to try and explain the behavior associated with that particular object. Content analysis obtains data by observing and analyzing the contents of the messages in written or spoken communications.

5. Describe major types of mechanical observation. Mechanical observation uses a variety of devices to record behavior directly. It may be an efficient and accurate choice when the situation or behavior to be recorded is routine, repetitive, or programmatic. National television audience ratings are based on mechanical observation (for example, PeopleMeters) and computerized data collection. Website traffic and content are monitored easily through traces left on computers. Barcode scanners automatically record purchase data and RFID tags can also track the movement of goods. Smartphones record various aspects of behavior including geographic location.

6. Summarize techniques for measuring physiological reactions. Physiological reactions, such as arousal or eye movement patterns, may be observed using a number of mechanical devices. Eye-tracking monitors identify the direction of a person's gaze, and a pupilometer observes and records changes in the diameter of the pupils of subjects' eyes, based on the assumption that a larger pupil signifies a positive attitude. A psychogalvanometer measures galvanic skin response as a signal of a person's emotional reactions. Voice-pitch analysis measures changes in a person's voice and associates the changes with emotional response. MRIs and similar devices allow recording of neurological (i.e., brain) activity.

:: KEY TERMS AND CONCEPTS

artifacts, *199*
click-through rate (CTR), *202*
content analysis, *200*
contrived observation, *196*
conversation volume, *203*
direct observation, *194*
eye-tracking monitor, *206*

hidden observation, *192*
observation, *190*
observer bias, *195*
magnetic resonance imagery (MRI) *207*
psychogalvanometer, *207*
pupilometer, *207*
response latency, *194*

scanner-based consumer panel, *204*
television monitoring, *201*
unobtrusive observation, *192*
visible observation, *192*
voice-pitch analysis, *207*

EXHIBIT 8.2-2 Observation Study Recording Form

Company Name _____

_____

Address: _____

Tulsa, Oklahoma

Activities: ___ 1 Vacant ___ 2 Retail ___ 3 Wholesale ___ 4 Manufacturing

___ 5 Service ___ 6 Other (Specify) _____

Retail SIC: ___ 52 ___ 53 ___ 54 ___ 55 ___ 56 ___ 57 ___ 58 ___ 59 ___ 60

Other Activities (describe): _____

_____

Is the Building: ___ 1 For Sale? ___ 2 For Rent?

Leasable Space: _____

Realtor's Name: _____

Realtor's Phone: _____

Rent (per sq. foot)

Is the Building Being: ___ 1 Restored? ___ 2 Remodeled?

Estimated Frontage (Feet): _____

Estimated Number of Stories: _____

Comments: _____

_____

_____

Conducting Marketing Experiments

CHAPTER

9

LEARNING OUTCOMES

After studying this chapter, you should be able to:

1. Know the basic characteristics of research experiments
2. Design an experiment using the basic issues of experimental design
3. Know ways of maximizing the validity of experiments, including the minimization of demand characteristics
4. Weigh the trade-off between internal and external validity
5. Recognize the appropriate uses of test-marketing
6. Avoid unethical experimental practices

Chapter Vignette:

Warning! This Product May Cause . . .

"What cigarette do you smoke, Doctor?" This was the question posed in a 1949 ad for Camel cigarettes. Not surprisingly, the result stated in the ad was that more doctors smoked Camels than any other cigarette. The intended inference here is obvious—if doctors choose Camels, then they must not cause as many harmful effects as those of other cigarettes! The whole question of smoking has advanced a great deal since that time. Inevitably, debates about smoking involve questions of cause.

- Does smoking cause cancer?
- Does smoking cause death?
- Does advertising cause people to smoke?

Warning labels say things like "Smoking causes lung cancer, heart disease, and emphysema." In U.S. courts, plaintiffs' attorneys and in some cases state governments have successfully argued that cigarette companies are responsible for the health problems and even deaths associated with long-term smoking.[1] As a result, tobacco companies have paid huge settlements. However, a U.K.-based tobacco company, Imperial Tobacco, faced with a £500,000 lawsuit filed on behalf of a cancer patient who had smoked Player Cigarettes for 40 years, is basing a legal defense on the notion that a lack of certainty remains over whether or not cigarettes cause cancer. They claim that the only evidence for this is statistical association and that many other factors are also statistically associated with the occurrence of cancer including a patient's socioeconomic status, childhood experiences (orientation toward healthy behaviors like exercise and diet), ethnicity, personality, and diet.

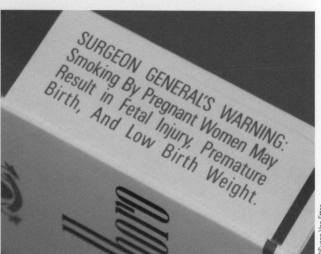

©Susan Van Etten

The defense is based on Imperial Tobacco's claim that no experimental evidence isolates the extent to which smoking truly causes cancer.[2] Further, they argued that advertising could not have caused the plaintiff to begin smoking. The Imperial defense was successful as the court ruled in their favor stating that the causal evidence was insufficient to hold the company responsible.

Nonetheless, many lawsuits in U.S. courts name the brand that a smoker first started smoking even if the person smoked many brands of cigarettes in the years and decades that followed. This tactic is based on the assumption that the branding and advertising efforts initially caused a person to smoke. The research evidence on this point is mixed, but researchers now are turning their attention toward experiments testing hypotheses related to the effectiveness of anti-smoking advertisements—particularly those aimed at adolescents. Typically, these experiments involve multiple groups of individuals, each subjected to a different set of conditions, and then each measured on variables related to their actual smoking behavior

or favorableness toward smoking.[3] For instance, a set of four groups are given magazines with different types of ads.

- Group 1 views a magazine with several actual ads for cigarettes.
- Group 2 views a magazine with several anti-smoking ads which emphasize negative effects on health.
- Group 3 views a magazine with several anti-smoking ads which emphasize negative effects on one's social life.
- Group 4 views a magazine with no cigarette or anti-smoking ads.

The researchers analyze the differences across groups to examine the effectiveness of the ads. In this case, groups 2 and 3 should be less favorably inclined toward smoking than either group 1 or group 4 if anti-smoking ads are effective. Then, the results from groups 2 and 3 can be compared to each other to see whether teens are more affected by fear of becoming ill or becoming less popular! The extent to which the researchers can truly establish causal evidence eventually will boil down to control.

Introduction

Most students are familiar with scientific experiments from studying physical sciences like physics and chemistry. The term *experiment* typically conjures up an image of a chemist surrounded by bubbling test tubes and Bunsen burners. Behavioral and physical scientists have used experimentation far longer than have marketing researchers. Nevertheless, both social scientists and physical scientists use experiments for much the same purpose.

Experiments are widely used in causal research designs. Experimental research allows a researcher to control the research situation so that *causal* relationships among variables may be evaluated. The marketing experimenter manipulates one or more independent variables and holds constant all other possible independent variables while observing effects on dependent variables. Variables may be controlled in an experiment to a degree not possible in a survey.

A simple example would be thinking about how changes in price might cause changes in sales. Price would be an independent variable and sales would be a dependent variable. The marketing research can experimentally control price by setting it at different levels and then study this problem by examining consumer reactions to each level.

A famous marketing experiment investigated the influence of brand name on consumers' taste perceptions. An experimenter manipulated whether consumers preferred the taste of beer in labeled or unlabeled bottles. One week respondents were given a six-pack containing bottles labeled only with letters (A, B, C). The following week, respondents received another six-pack with brand labels (like Budweiser, Coors, Miller, and so forth). The experimenter measured reactions to the beers after each tasting. In every case, the beer itself was the same. So, every person involved in the experiment drank the very same beer. Therefore, the differences observed in taste, the key dependent variable, could only be attributable to the difference in labeling. When the consumers participating in the experiment expressed a preference for the branded beer, the conclusion is that brand name does influence consumers' taste perceptions.

The Characteristics of Experiments

Examples are probably the best way to illustrate marketing experiments. Here, we illustrate the characteristics of experiments by describing a study aimed at testing hypotheses, inferring the potential causal effects of color. We will refer back to this example throughout this chapter and begin by describing the key characteristics of experiments in this section of the chapter.

By now, perhaps you've had an opportunity to explore the editing features of the Qualtrics survey platform. As the name implies, the tool edits a "survey." Typically, surveys are thought of in association with descriptive research designs. Consider the following points in trying to understand the role such tools may play in causal designs.

1. What types of variables can be measured using survey items created with Qualtrics?
2. Would it be possible to implement an experimental manipulation within or in conjunction with a Qualtrics survey application?
3. Is it possible to create a manipulation check with a Qualtrics survey item?
4. How might computer technology assist in randomly assigning subjects to experimental conditions?

Source: © Cengage Learning 2013.

Subjects

Let's take a look at an experiment investigating how color and lights might influence shoppers. This particular research is highly relevant for those involved in retail management and design. The key decisions facing managers is how to alter color and lighting to produce favorable consumer reactions. A corresponding research question is, "What is the effect of color and lighting on shopper patronage (patronage means how much someone would shop and buy in a store)?"[4]

Over two hundred female consumers participated in the experiment. Researchers refer to participants in experimental research as **subjects** rather than respondents—the term typically used for participants in survey research. This is because the researcher subjects research participants to some experimental treatment. In addressing the color and lighting research question, the experimental task involved asking subjects to provide responses to a "new fashion store" concept. The hypothetical new store would sell women's clothing and accessories to the fashion-minded professional woman.

subjects

The sampling units for an experiment, usually human participants in research who are subjected to some experimental manipulation.

Experimental Conditions

Perhaps the characteristic that most differentiates experimental research from survey research is the manner in which independent variables are created rather than simply measured. The illustration experiment involves two relevant independent variables. Fictitious store environments were created for the experiment. Four different hypothetical store environments were created corresponding to different combinations of the independent variable values. Thus, the only thing differing between the four is the particular combination of the predominant store color and the type of lighting.

The experimenter created the color independent variable by variously designing the new store as either predominantly blue or predominantly orange. Similarly, the experimenter created the lighting independent variable by designing the hypothetical store as either having bright or soft lights. Exhibit 9.1 illustrates the four different experimental conditions created by combining the two possible values for each independent variable. An **experimental condition** refers to one of the possible levels of an experimental variable manipulation.

The procedures assigned subjects randomly to one of these four conditions. As a result, each subject group experienced a store with one of the four color and lighting combinations, as shown

experimental condition

One of the possible levels of an experimental variable manipulation.

215

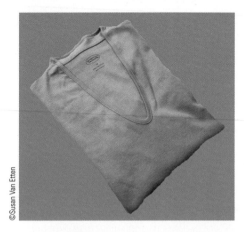 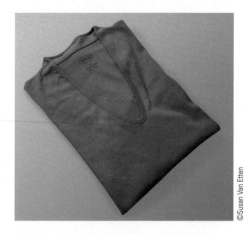

©Susan Van Etten

©Susan Van Etten

EXHIBIT **9.1**

Experimental Conditions in Color and Lighting Experiment

		Color	
		Blue	**Orange**
Lighting:	Soft	¼ of Participants	¼ of Participants
	Bright	¼ of Participants	¼ of Participants

in Exhibit 9.1. Thus, all participants within a group received the same description. Subjects in different groups received different descriptions. By analyzing differences between the groups, the researcher can see what effects occur due to the two experimentally controlled independent variables.

Independent variables that are not experimental conditions can also be included as a means of statistical control in the analysis of experiments. Researchers refer to these as either blocking variables or covariates. **Blocking variables** are categorical variables like a subject's gender or ethnicity. For example, researchers may group results based on whether respondents are male or female. On the other hand, a continuous variable that is expected to show a statistical relationship with the dependent variables is known as a **covariate**. Once statistical analysis begins, blocking variables are treated in much the same way as experimental variables and covariates are treated like a regression variable. We'll cover the statistical analysis of experiments later in the text.

blocking variables

Categorical variables included in the statistical analysis of experimental data as a way of statistically controlling or accounting for variance due to that variable.

covariate

A continuous variable included in the statistical analysis as a way of statistically controlling for variance due to that variable.

Effects

The key outcome, or dependent variable, in this example is a subject's perception of how much he or she would patronize the store. In this case, a rating scale asking how much each participant thought they would actually visit and buy things at the store was created. The possible scores ranged from 0 (would not shop) to 300 (definitely would shop). A higher score means higher patronage. Effects are the characteristics of experiments that allow testing of hypotheses. We can classify effects in several ways. Here, we will focus on the difference between main effects and interaction effects.

Main Effects

main effect

The experimental difference in dependent variable means between the different levels of any single experimental variable.

A **main effect** refers to the experimental difference in means between the different levels of any single experimental variable. In this case, there are two potential main effects, one for color and one for lighting.

Exhibit 9.2 shows the average patronage score for each experimental condition. The results show that among experimental subjects who rated a blue store, an average patronage score of

EXHIBIT **9.2**
Consumer Average Patronage
Scores in Each Condition

		Color		
		Blue	**Orange**	
Lighting:	**Soft**	148.5	140.1	144.7
	Bright	159.1	122.6	140.4
		153.8	131.8	

Source: © Cengage Learning 2013.

153.8 was reported, which is considerably higher than the average of 131.8 reported by subjects who rated an orange store. The lighting experimental variable, however, doesn't seem to make much difference. Subjects in the soft lighting condition reported an average of 144.7 and subjects in the bright lighting condition reported only a slightly lower average of 140.4.

Thus, the conclusion at this point seems that changing a store's color can change consumer patronage. A blue store is better than an orange store! On the other hand, lighting doesn't seem to make much difference. Or does it?

Interactions

An **interaction effect** is due to a specific combination of independent variables. In this case, it's possible that the combination of color and lighting creates effects that are not clearly represented in the two main effects.

Experimental results are often shown with a line graph, as shown in Exhibit 9.3. Main effects are illustrated when the lines are at different heights, as is the case here. Notice the blue line is higher than the orange line. The midpoints of the lines correspond to the means of 153.8 and 131.8 for the blue and orange condition, respectively. A lighting main effect is less obvious because the difference between the midpoint between the two soft points (144.7) is not too different than the corresponding height of the two bright points (140.4). When the lines have very different slopes, an interaction is likely present. In this case, the combination of lights and color is presenting an interaction leading to the following interpretation.

The best possible reaction occurs when the store has a blue color with bright lights and the worst combination occurs when the store is orange with bright lights. In contrast, the means are essentially the same for either color when the lights are soft. So, lights may indeed matter. When the lights are soft, there is little difference in patronage between a blue and orange store. But, when the lights are bright, there is quite a difference between blue and orange.

The pattern of results depicted in Exhibit 9.3 can be contrasted with those from another experiment, shown in Exhibit 9.4 on the next page. Here, researchers conducted an experiment to see how different promotions offered by a nightclub might affect the amount of drinks a college student

interaction effect

Differences in dependant variable means due to a specific combination of independent variables.

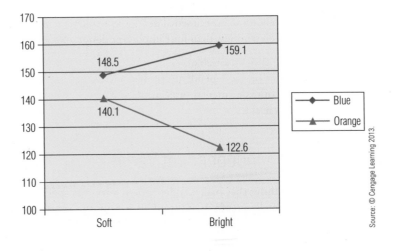

EXHIBIT **9.3**
Experimental Graph Showing
Results within Each Condition

Source: © Cengage Learning 2013.

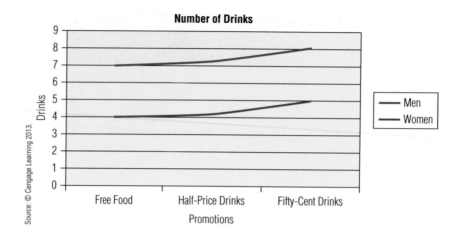

Source: © Cengage Learning 2013.

would have during the promotion.[5] The researchers were also interested in potential differences between men and women—a blocking variable. Notice that the line for men is higher than the line for women, suggesting a main effect of sex; men have more drinks than women. Also, the mean number of drinks is higher for the fifty-cent drink promotion than for either of the other two. But, in contrast to our illustration above, the lines are parallel to each other, suggesting that no interaction effect has occurred. In other words, men and women respond to the promotions in the same way.

Summary of Experimental Characteristics

Experiments differ from ordinary survey research. The differences can be understood by identifying characteristics of experiments. These characteristics include the following:

- Experiments use subjects instead of respondents.
- Experimental variables become the key independent variables. The researcher creates the experimental variables rather than simply measuring them. Measured independent variables are called blocking variables or covariates in experiments.
- Experimental effects are determined by differences between groups formed in the experiment. Main effects are differences in the means based on a single variable. Interaction effects are differences in means based on combinations of two or more variables.

Basic Issues in Experimental Design

Experimental design is a major research topic. In fact, there are courses and books devoted only to that topic.[6] Here, an introduction into experimental design is provided. The terminology introduced in describing experimental characteristics will be helpful in learning how to implement a simple experimental design. Fortunately, most experimental designs in marketing are relatively simple.

Experimental designs involve no less than four important design elements:

1. manipulation of the independent variable
2. selection and measurement of the dependent variable
3. selection and assignment of experimental subjects
4. control over extraneous variables

Manipulation of the Independent Variable

Recall from Chapter 3, the thing that makes independent variables special in experimentation is that the researcher can actually create its values. This is how the researcher manipulates, and therefore controls, independent variables. In our color experiment, the researcher manipulated the

• • • • • • •

Marketing research sometimes involves experiments that manipulate different elements of physical environments.

values of the color independent variable by assigning it a value of either blue or orange. Experimental independent variables are hypothesized to be causal influences. Therefore, experiments are very appropriate in causal designs.

An **experimental treatment** is the term referring to the way an experimental variable is manipulated. For example, the illustration manipulates the store environment experimental treatment by assigning consumers to evaluate either a blue or orange store. Thus, there were two levels (or values) of the color variable. A medical researcher may manipulate an experimental variable by treating some subjects with one drug and the other subjects with a separate drug. Experimental variables often involve treatments with more than two levels. For instance, prices of $229, $269, and $299 might represent treatments in a pricing experiment examining how price causes sales for a small under-counter LCD television.

experimental treatment

The term referring to the way an experimental variable is manipulated.

Experimental variables like these can not only be described as independent variables, but they also can be described as a *categorical variable* because they take on a value to represent some classifiable or qualitative aspect. Color, for example, is either orange or blue. Advertising copy style is another example of a categorical or classificatory variable that a researcher could manipulate in an experiment. In other situations, an independent variable may truly exist as a *continuous variable*. When this is the case, the researcher must select appropriate levels of that variable as experimental treatments. For example, lighting can vary from dark to any level of brightness. Price can take on any value but the researcher will only include levels representing relevant distinctions in price in an experiment. Before conducting the experiment, the researcher decides on levels that would be relevant to study. The levels should be noticeably different and realistic.

Experimental and Control Groups

In perhaps the simplest experiment, the researcher manipulates an independent variable over two treatment levels resulting in two groups: an experimental group and a control group. An **experimental group** is one in which an experimental treatment is administered. A **control group** is one in which no experimental treatment is administered. For example, consider an experiment studying how advertising affects sales. In the experimental group, the advertising budget may be set at $200,000. In the control condition, advertising may remain at zero or may not change from its current level. By holding conditions constant in the control group, the researcher controls potential sources of error in the experiment. Sales (the dependent variable) in the two treatment groups are compared at the end of the experiment to determine whether the level of advertising

experimental group

A group of subjects to whom an experimental treatment is administered.

control group

A group of subjects to whom no experimental treatment is administered.

Although this type of procedure is often followed, if our tastes and digestive systems react differently to different foods at different times of the day, systematic error is introduced into the experiment. Furthermore, because the night classes contain students who are older on average, the professors may reach the conclusion that students perform better when they eat cookies, when it may really be due to the fact that students who are older perform better no matter what they are fed.

Randomization

randomization

The random assignment of subject and treatments to groups; it is one device for equally distributing the effects of extraneous variables to all conditions.

Randomization—the random assignment of subject and treatments to groups—is one device for equally distributing the effects of extraneous variables to all conditions. Randomizing assignments does not eliminate nuisance variables but controls for them because they likely exist to the same degree in every experimental cell. All cells should yield similar average scores on the dependent variables if it were not for the experimental treatments administered in a particular cell. In other words, the researcher would like to set up a situation where everything in every cell is the same except for the experimental treatment. Random assignment of subjects allows the researcher to make this assumption, thereby reducing the chance of systematic error. With proper randomization, the characteristics of each experimental group tend to be the same as the population characteristics.

Matching

Matching subjects on the basis of pertinent background information is another technique for controlling systematic error. Matching involves assigning subjects in a way that a particular characteristic is the same in each group. If a subject's sex is expected to influence dependent variable responses, as in a taste test, then the researcher may make sure that there are equal numbers of men and women in each experimental cell. In general, if a researcher believes that certain extraneous variables may affect the dependent variable, he or she can make sure that the subjects in each group are the same on these characteristics.

For example, in a taste test experiment for a dog food, it might be important to match the dogs in various experimental groups on the basis of age or breed. That way, the same number of basset hounds and dobermans will test formula A, formula B, and formula C. Although matching can be a useful approach, the researcher can never be sure that sampling units are matched on all characteristics. Here, for example, even though breeds can be matched, it is difficult to know if all dogs live in the same type of environment (indoors, outdoors, spacious, cramped, with table scraps or without, and so on).

Repeated Measures

repeated measures

Experiments in which an individual subject is exposed to more than one level of an experimental treatment.

Experiments that expose an individual subject to more than one level of an experimental treatment involve a **repeated measures** design. Although this approach has advantages, including being more economical because the same subject provides data on multiple conditions, the design has drawbacks that limit its usefulness. We will discuss these in more detail later.

Extraneous Variables

The fourth decision about the basic elements of an experiment concerns control over variables that may systematically influence the dependent variable(s). Earlier we classified total survey error into two basic categories: random sampling error and systematic error. The same dichotomy applies to all research designs, but the terms *random (sampling) error* and *systematic error* are more frequently used when discussing experiments.

Experimental Confounds

We have already discussed how systematic error can occur when extraneous variables or the conditions of administering the experiment influence the dependent variables. When this occurs, the results will be confounded because all extraneous variables have not been controlled for or eliminated. A **confound** in an experiment means that an alternative explanation exists beyond the experimental variables for any observed differences in the dependent variable. Once a potential confound is identified, the validity of the experiment is severely questioned.

confound

An experimental confound means that there is an alternative explanation beyond the experimental variables for any observed differences in the dependent variable.

Recall from the Research Snapshot on page 221 that the experimental procedures involved a taste test. The Research Snapshot illustrates how a confound can ruin an experiment. Sea Snapper fish sticks were always presented on a blue plate and Captain John's fish sticks were always presented on a goldish-colored plate. The plate's color is confounding the explanation that the difference in brands is responsible for the difference in liking. Is the difference due to the color or the product quality?

In a simple experimental group–control group experiment aimed at employee task efficiency, if subjects in the experimental group are always administered a treatment (an energy drink) in the morning and then have their efficiency measured also in the morning, and the control group always has their efficiency measured in the afternoon, a constant error has been introduced. In other words, the results will show a difference not only due to the treatment, but also due to the added efficiency that naturally occurs in the morning. In such a situation, time of day represents a confound. On the other hand, other types of error are random and not constant; for example, the natural fluctuations in efficiency that occur from day to day. Random errors are less of a problem for experiments than are constant errors because they do not cause systematic changes in outcomes.

Identifying Extraneous Variables

Most students of marketing realize that the marketing mix variables—price, product, promotion, and distribution—interact with uncontrollable forces in the market, such as competitors' activities and consumer trends. Thus, marketing experiments are subject to the effect of extraneous variables. Because extraneous variables can produce confounded results, researchers must make every attempt to identify them before the experiment.

The chapter vignette illustrates how important isolating causes can be in developing theoretical explanations. Does cigarette advertising cause young people to smoke? One of the primary reasons for the inconclusiveness of this debate is the failure for most of the research to control for extraneous variables.[8] For instance, consider a study in which two groups of U.S. high school students are studied over the course of a year. One is exposed to a greater percentage of foreign television media in which American cigarettes are more often shown in a flattering and glamorous light. In fact, the programming includes cigarette commercials. The other group is a control group in which their exposure to media is not controlled. At the end of the year, the experimental group reports a greater frequency and incidence of cigarette smoking. Did the increased media exposure involving cigarettes cause smoking behavior?

Although the result seems plausible at first, the careful researcher may ask the following questions:

■ Was the demographic makeup of the two groups the same? Although it is clear that the ages of the two groups are likely the same, it is well known that different ethnic groups have different smoking rates. Approximately 28 percent of all high school students report smoking, but the rate is higher among Hispanic teens, for example.[9] Therefore, if one group contained more Hispanics or Asians, we might expect it to report different smoking rates than otherwise.

■ How did the control group fill the time consumed by the experimental group in being exposed to the experimental treatment? Could it be that it somehow dissuaded them from smoking? Perhaps they were exposed to media with more anti-smoking messages?

■ Were the two groups of the same general achievement profiles? Those who are high in the need for achievement may be less prone to smoke than are other students.

■ Although it is a difficult task to list all possible extraneous factors, some that even sound unusual can sometimes have an effect. For example, did the students have equally dispersed birthdays? Researchers have even shown that smoking rates correspond to one's birthday, meaning that different astrological groups have different smoking rates.[10]

Because an experimenter does not want extraneous variables to affect the results, he or she must control or eliminate such variables. It is always better to spend time thinking about how to control for possible extraneous variables before the experiment because often there is nothing that can be done to salvage results after a confounding effect is identified.

Demand Characteristics and Experimental Validity

demand characteristic

Experimental design element or procedure that unintentionally provides subjects with hints about the research hypothesis.

What Are Demand Characteristics? The term **demand characteristic** refers to an experimental design element that unintentionally provides subjects with hints about the research hypothesis. Researchers cannot reveal the research hypotheses to subjects before the experiment or else they can create a confounding effect. Think about the retail atmospherics experiment. If the subjects were told before they participated that they were going to be involved in an experiment to see if they liked stores that were predominantly orange or predominantly blue, the researcher would never be sure if their responses to the dependent variable were really due to the differences in the experimental stimuli or due to the fact that the subjects were trying to provide a "correct" response. In addition, once subjects know the hypotheses, there is little hope that they will respond naturally.

demand effect

Occurs when demand characteristics actually affect the dependent variable.

So, knowledge of the experimental hypothesis creates a confound. This particular type of confound is known as a **demand effect**. Demand characteristics make demand effects very likely.

Experimenter Bias and Demand Effects

Demand characteristics are aspects of an experiment that *demand* (encourage) that the subjects respond in a particular way. Hence, they are a source of systematic error. If participants recognize the experimenter's expectation or demand, they are likely to act in a manner consistent with the experimental treatment. Even slight nonverbal cues may influence their reactions.

The person administering experimental procedures often creates prominent demand characteristics. If an experimenter's presence, actions, or comments influence the subjects' behavior or sway the subjects to slant their answers to cooperate with the experimenter, the experiment has introduced *experimenter bias*. When subjects slant their answers to cooperate with the experimenter, they are exhibiting behaviors that might not represent their behavior in the marketplace. For example, if subjects in an advertising experiment understand that the experimenter is interested in whether they changed their attitudes in accord with a given advertisement, they may answer in the desired direction. Acting in this manner reflects a demand effect rather than a true experimental treatment effect.

Reducing Demand Characteristics

Although it is practically impossible to eliminate demand characteristics from experiments, researchers can take several steps aimed at reducing them. Many of these steps make it difficult for subjects to know what the researcher is trying to find out. Some or all of these may be appropriate in a given experiment:

The experimenter unintentionally can create a demand effect by smiling, nodding, or frowning at the wrong time.

1. Use an experimental disguise.
2. Isolate experimental subjects.
3. Use a "blind" experimental administrator.
4. Administer only one experimental treatment level to each subject.

Experimental Disguise

The experimental administrator can tell subjects that the purpose of the experiment is somewhat different from the actual purpose. Most often, administrators simply tell less than the complete "truth" about what is going to happen. For instance, in the retail atmosphere study, the instructions informed subjects that the study sought their reaction to a new retail store concept. This really is true, but the instructions included nothing about color, lighting, or any other potential experimental effect.

In other cases, more deceit may be needed. Psychologists studying how much pain one person may be willing to inflict on another might use a ruse, telling the subject that they are actually interested in the effect of pain on human performance. The researcher tells the actual subject to administer a series of questions to another person (who is actually a research assistant) and to provide the person with an increasingly strong electric shock each time an incorrect answer is given. In reality, the real dependent variable has something to do with how long the actual subject will continue to administer shocks before stopping.

A *placebo* is an experimental deception involving a false treatment. A **placebo effect** refers to the corresponding effect in a dependent variable that is due to the psychological impact that goes along with knowledge that a treatment has been administered. A placebo is particularly important when the experimental variable involves physical consumption of some product. The placebo should not be different in any manner that is actually noticeable by the research subject. If someone is told that a special food additive will suppress appetite, and they are supposed to sprinkle it on their dinner before eating as part of an experiment, another group should receive a placebo that looks exactly like the actual food additive but actually is some type of inert compound. Both groups are likely to show some difference in consumption compared to someone undergoing no effect. The difference in the actual experimental group and the placebo group would represent the true effect of the additive.

Placebo effects exist in marketing research. For example, when subjects are told that an energy drink is sold at a discount price, they believe it is significantly less effective than when it is sold at

placebo effect

The effect in a dependent variable associated with the psychological impact that goes along with knowledge of some treatment being administered.

the regular, non-discounted price.[11] Later, we will return to the ethical issues involved in experimental deception.

Isolate Experimental Subjects

Researchers should minimize the extent to which subjects are able to talk about the experimental procedures with each other. Although it may be unintentional, discussion among subjects may lead them to guess the experimental hypotheses. For instance, it could be that different subjects receive different treatments. The experimental integrity will be higher when each only knows enough to participate him/herself and the procedures prevent one subject from being concerned about other subjects.

Use a "Blind" Experimental Administrator

When possible, the research assistants actually administering the experiment do not know the experimental hypotheses. Ignorance can be bliss in this case as the big advantage is that if the administrator does not know what exactly is being studied, he/she will not likely give off clues that result in demand effects. Like the subjects, administrators often do their job best when they know only enough guide subjects through the task.

Administer Only One Experimental Condition Per Subject

When subjects observe more than one experimental treatment condition, they are much more likely to guess the experimental hypothesis. Despite the cost advantages, most researchers should avoid administering multiple treatments to an individual subject. In the retail atmospherics example, if subjects responded first to a blue retail store concept, and then saw the same store that was exactly the same except the walls had become orange, then they are very likely to know that the researcher is interested in color.

Establishing Control

The major difference between experimental research and descriptive research is an experimenter's ability to control variables by either holding conditions constant or manipulating the experimental variable. If the color of beer causes preference, a brewery experimenting with a new clear beer must determine the possible extraneous variables other than color that may affect an experiment's results and attempt to eliminate or control those variables. Marketing theory tells us that brand image and packaging design are important factors in beer drinkers' reactions. Therefore, the researcher may wish to control the influence of these variables. He or she may eliminate these two extraneous variables by packaging the test beers in plain brown packages without any brand identification.

When extraneous variables cannot be eliminated, experimenters may strive for **constancy of conditions**. This means that subjects in all experimental groups participate in identical conditions except for the differing experimental treatments. The principle of matching discussed earlier helps make sure that constancy is achieved.

constancy of conditions

Means that subjects in all experimental groups are exposed to identical conditions except for the differing experimental treatments.

A supermarket experiment involving four test products shows the care that must be taken to hold all factors constant. The experiment required that all factors other than shelf space remain constant throughout the testing period. In all stores the shelf level (i.e., height) that had existed before the tests was to stay the same throughout the test period. Only the *amount* of shelf space (the treatment) was supposed to change. One problem involved store personnel accidentally changing shelf level when stocking the test products, creating an alternative explanation for any change in sales. Thus, the researcher sought to minimize this problem by auditing each store four times a week. In this way, a change in shelf height could be detected in a minimum amount of time. The experimenter personally stocked as many of the products as possible, and the cooperation of stock clerks also helped reduce treatment deviations.

If an experimental method requires that the same subjects be exposed to two or more experimental treatments, an error may occur due to the *order of presentation*. For instance, if subjects are examining the effects of different levels of graphical interface on video game enjoyment, and they are asked to view each of four different levels, the order in which they are presented may influence enjoyment. Subjects might perform one level simply because it follows a very poor level. **Counterbalancing** attempts to eliminate the confounding effects of order of presentation by requiring that one-fourth of the subjects be exposed to treatment A first, one-fourth to treatment B first, one-fourth to treatment C first, and finally one-fourth to treatment D first. Likewise, the other levels are counterbalanced so that the order of presentation is rotated among subjects.

counterbalancing

Attempts to eliminate the confounding effects of order of presentation by requiring that one-fourth of the subjects be exposed to treatment A first, one-fourth to treatment B first, one-fourth to treatment C first, and finally one-fourth to treatment D first.

Basic versus Factorial Experimental Designs

In *basic experimental designs* a single independent variable is manipulated to observe its effect on a single dependent variable. However, we know that complex marketing dependent variables such as sales, product usage, and preference are influenced by several factors. The simultaneous change in independent variables such as price and advertising may have a greater influence on sales than if either variable is changed alone. *Factorial experimental designs* are more sophisticated than basic experimental designs and allow for an investigation of the interaction of two or more independent variables.

Laboratory Experiments

A marketing experiment can be conducted in a natural setting (a field experiment) or in an artificial or laboratory setting. In social sciences, the actual laboratory may be a behavioral lab, which is somewhat like a focus group facility. However, the experimental procedures may turn a classroom or a place in a shopping center into an experimental lab.

In a **laboratory experiment** the researcher maximizes control over the research setting and extraneous variables. For example, some advertising researchers recruit subjects and bring them to the agency's office or perhaps a mobile unit designed for research purposes. Researchers then expose subjects to a television commercial within the context of a program that includes competitors' ads among the commercials shown. While viewing the ads, a lie detector-type device measures the subjects' physiological arousal. The researcher measures trial purchase intentions for the focal product as well. In a short time span, the marketer is able to collect information on emotional responses and consumer decision making. Our retail atmospheric experiment also illustrates a laboratory experiment.

Other laboratory experiments may be more controlled or artificial. For example, a **tachistoscope** allows a researcher to experiment with the visual impact of advertising, packaging, and so on by controlling the amount of time a subject sees a visual image. Each stimulus (for example, package design) is projected from a slide to the tachistoscope at varying exposure lengths (one-tenth of a second, two-tenths, three-tenths, and so on). The tachistoscope simulates the split-second duration of a customer's attention to a package in a mass display.

laboratory experiment

The researcher has more complete control over the research setting and extraneous variables.

tachistoscope

Device that controls the amount of time a subject is exposed to a visual image.

field experiments

Research projects involving experimental manipulations that are implemented in a natural environment.

Field Experiments

Field experiments are research projects involving experimental manipulations implemented in a natural environment. They can be useful in fine-tuning marketing strategies and determining sales forecasts for different marketing mix designs.

McDonald's conducted a field experiment testing the Triple Ripple, a three-flavor ice cream product. Based on the results, McDonald's dropped the idea because the experiment revealed that

Facilities like this one can break down the food that companies sell and tell them exactly what it should taste like. Is this a good way to test the taste of new products?

Image courtesy of Susan Van Etten

History

history effect

Occurs when a change other than the experimental treatment occurs during the course of an experiment that affects the dependent variable.

A **history effect** occurs when a change other than the experimental treatment occurs during the course of an experiment that affects the dependent variable. A common history effect occurs when competitors change their marketing strategies during a test marketing experiment. History effects are particularly prevalent in repeated measures experiments that take place over an extended time. If we wanted to assess how much a change in recipe improves individual subjects' consumption of a food product, we would first measure their consumption and then compare it with consumption after the change. Because several weeks may pass between the first and second measurement, there are many things that could occur that would also influence subjects' diets.

Although it may sound extreme, examining the effect of a dietary supplement on various health-related outcomes may require that a subject be confined during the experiment's course. This may take several weeks. Without confining the subject in something like a hospital setting, there would be little way of controlling food and drink consumption, exercise activities, and other factors that may also affect the dependent variables.

cohort effect

Refers to a change in the dependent variable that occurs because members of one experimental group experienced different historical situations than members of other experimental groups.

A special case of the history effect is the **cohort effect**, which refers to a change in the dependent variable that occurs because members of one experimental group experienced different historical situations than members of other experimental groups. For example, two groups of managers used as subjects may be in different cohorts because one group encountered different experiences over the course of an experiment. If the experimental manipulation involves different levels of financial incentives and performance is the dependent variable, one group may be affected by an informative article appearing in a trade magazine during the experiment. Because the other group participated prior to this group, members of that group could not benefit from the article. Therefore, the possibility exists that the article rather than the change in incentive is truly causing differences in performance.

Maturation

maturation effect

A function of time and the naturally occurring events that coincide with growth and experience.

A **maturation effect** is a function of time and the naturally occurring events that coincide with growth and experience. Experiments taking place over longer timespans may see lower internal validity as subjects simply grow older or more experienced. Suppose an experiment were designed to test the impact of a new compensation program on sales productivity. If this program were tested over a year's time, some of the salespeople probably would mature as a result of more selling experience or perhaps gain increased knowledge. Their sales productivity might improve because of their knowledge and experience rather than the compensation program.

Testing

testing effects

A nuisance effect occurring when the initial measurement or test alerts or primes subjects in a way that affects their response to the experimental treatments.

Testing effects are also called *pretesting effects* because the initial measurement or test alerts or primes subjects in a way that affects their response to the experimental treatments. Testing effects only occur in a before-and-after study. A before-and-after study is one requiring an initial baseline measure be taken before an experimental treatment is administered. So, before-and-after experiments are a special case of a repeated measures design. For example, students taking standardized achievement and intelligence tests for the second time usually do better than those taking the tests for the first time. The effect of testing may increase awareness of socially approved answers, increase attention to experimental conditions (that is, the subject may watch more closely), or make the subject more conscious than usual of the dimensions of a problem.

Instrumentation

instrumentation effect

A nuisance that occurs when a change in the wording of questions, a change in interviewers, or a change in other procedures causes a change in the dependent variable.

A change in the wording of questions, a change in interviewers, or a change in other procedures used to measure the dependent variable causes an **instrumentation effect**, which may jeopardize internal validity. If the same interviewers ask questions for both before and after measurement, some problems may arise. With practice, interviewers may acquire increased skill in interviewing, or they may become bored and decide to reword the questionnaire in their own terms. To avoid this problem, new interviewers are hired, but different individuals are also a source of extraneous variation due to instrumentation variation. There are numerous other sources of instrument decay or variation. Again, instrumentation effects are problematic with any type of repeated measures design.

Selection

The selection effect is a sample bias that results from differential selection of respondents for the comparison groups, or sample selection error, discussed earlier.

Mortality

If an experiment takes place over a period of a few weeks or more, some sample bias may occur due to the **mortality effect (sample attrition)**. Sample attrition occurs when some subjects withdraw from the experiment before it is completed. Mortality effects may occur if subjects drop from one experimental treatment group disproportionately from other groups. Consider a sales training experiment investigating the effects of close supervision of salespeople (high pressure) versus low supervision (low pressure). The high-pressure condition may misleadingly appear superior if those subjects who completed the experiment did very well. If, however, the high-pressure condition caused more subjects to drop out than the other conditions, this apparent superiority may be due to the fact that only very determined and/or talented salespeople stuck with the program.

mortality effect (sample attrition)

Occurs when some subjects withdraw from the experiment before it is completed.

External Validity

External validity is the accuracy with which experimental results are generalizable beyond the experimental subjects. External validity increases as subjects comprising a sample truly represent a population and when the results extend to market segments or other groups of people. The higher the external validity, the more researchers and managers can count on the fact that any results observed in an experiment will also be seen in the "real world" (marketplace, workplace, sales floor, and so on).

external validity

Is the accuracy with which experimental results can be generalized beyond the experimental subjects.

SUV safety continues to improve, but car companies, including GM, Jeep, Toyota, and Suzuki, still face liability lawsuits based on claims that a design contributed to a high propensity of rollover.[12] The companies experiment with various types of suspensions and test the equipment in labs. Once the companies design minimizes rollover problems in the lab, they move outside to a test track and see how a real vehicle handles. However, even this test leaves room for lawyers to argue that the tests lack external validity. After all, a track is not a highway and the test drivers are not typical SUV owners. Lab experiments are associated with low external validity because experimental procedures exact demanding control but do not adequately represent real world intricacies. In other words, the experimental conditions may be too artificial. When a study lacks external validity, the researcher will have difficulty repeating the experiment with any change in subjects, settings, or time.

Student Surrogates

Basic researchers often use college students as experimental subjects.[13] Convenience, time, money, and a host of other practical considerations often lead to using students as research subjects. This practice is widespread in academic studies. Some evidence shows that students are quite similar to household consumers, but other evidence indicates that they do not provide sufficient external validity to represent most populations. This is particularly true when students substitute or play the role of business people.

The issue of external validity represents a key concern in predicting how representative an experiment's results may be. Students are easily accessible, but they often are not representative of the total population. This is not always the case, however, and sometimes researchers focus on behaviors for which students have some particular expertise. Research directed at understanding how young adults react to Facebook promotions or how different studying techniques affect test performance can have a great deal of internal and external validity using students. This is because students fit within the population of interest. However, researchers wishing to conduct an experiment addressing a research question aimed at understanding how renovating church facilities affects clergy

Mechanical Students

"Who needs extra credit?" Ever get asked that question in class? Well, then, you know the answer. The bulk of experimental psychological research relies on student subjects and counts on them performing their duty to execute faithfully and honestly the instructions provided. However, are students equally able and motivated to do that? It turns out that male students are more likely to participate late in a term compared to female students. Also, the more conscientious students are, the more likely they are to participate early in the term. As a consequence, students with better grades participate early and those who are desperate for extra credit late in the term jump on the opportunity. If these factors also influence response quality then researchers may find different results for an experiment conducted in week 2 as opposed to week 13!

Students may become mechanical and simply move through the procedures, motivated only by getting through and receiving credit. Enter Mechanical Turk. Amazon provides opportunities for browsers to become "workers" and participate in "human intelligence tasks (HIT)" for small amounts of pay. If a browser is bored, perhaps they'll take place in a short experiment on price policies for 10 cents. These "workers" opt into the experiment by clicking through an invitation link placed on the site. Early research suggests that Mechanical Turk workers tend to be female (three-quarters) and average about 30 years old. In addition, based on how they respond to a question like:

Have you ever had a fatal heart attack while watching television?

They appear to pay at least as much attention to the experiment as do students because students answer "yes" as often as HIT workers. Thus, mechanical subjects may replace mechanical students.

Sources: Paolacci, G., J. Chandler, and P.G. Ipeirotis (2010), "Running Experiments on Mechanical Turk," *Judgment and Decision-Making*, 5 (August), 411–19; Witt, E.A., M.B. Donnelon, and M. J. Orlando (2011), "Timing and Selection Effects within a Psychology Subjects Pool: Personality and Sex Matter," *Personality and Individual Differences*, 50 (February), 355–59.

members' job satisfaction would probably not benefit much from using typical undergraduate business students as subjects. Why would anyone expect these students to behave like clergy?

Other times, researchers are only interested in whether or not some effect might exist at all under any situation; then, students are as good as any other human subjects. This places the emphasis predominantly on internal validity with no consideration of generalizability. So, students or other convenience samples are sometimes very useful and provide an adequate way of testing whether an hypothesized effect can occur.

Not all student subjects are the same. For instance, the Research Snapshot suggests that the time of the semester can affect which students participate in university research. Thus, an effect that exists at the end of the term may look a little different than the effect that might exist at the beginning of a term. Technology provides some alternatives to student subjects and more researchers are taking advantage of these opportunities. People looking for something to do on the Internet provide ready access sometimes for a very minimal cost.[14] The extent to which these Internet workers are better than student–subjects is still unknown and worthy of more research.

Trade-Offs Between Internal and External Validity

Naturalistic field experiments tend to have greater external validity than artificial laboratory experiments. Marketing researchers often must trade internal validity for external validity. A researcher who wishes to test advertising effectiveness by manipulating treatments via a split–cable (some households get one ad and others another) experiment has the assurance that the advertisement will be viewed in an externally valid situation, the subjects' homes. However, the researcher has no assurance that an interruption (for example, a phone call from a market researcher) will not have an influence that will reduce the internal validity of the experiment. Laboratory experiments with many controlled factors usually are high in internal validity, whereas field experiments generally have less internal validity, but greater external validity. Ideally, results from lab experiments would be followed up with a type of field test.

Using Test-Marketing

The most common type of field marketing experiment is the test market. Test-marketing has three broad primary uses in marketing research. Each use can be broken down more specifically to look at some issue in close detail. The three broad uses are as follows:

1. Forecasting the success of a newly developed product.
2. Testing hypotheses about different options for marketing mix elements.
3. Identifying weaknesses in product designs or marketing strategies.

Forecasting New Product Success

Test markets frequently provide pilot tests for new products. The basic idea is simple. A product is marketed on a small scale under actual market conditions and the results allow a prediction of success or failure once the product is introduced on a large scale. Do people really want skinny beers? Heineken used a test-market to forecast the success of Heineken Premium Light (HPL) beer which led Miller to test its own skinny beer (MGD 64) version and now these beers have substantial market share.[15]

Companies using test markets should realize that a new product concept also involves issues like advertising, pricing, supply chains, and retail placement. These issues may also be manipulated within a test market. Estimates can then be made about the optimal advertising level, the need for product sampling, retail channel fit, or perhaps even advertising and retail channel selection interaction. Test-marketing permits evaluation of the entire new product concept, not just the physical good itself.

A researcher conducting a test market may evaluate not only new products' sales as a dependent variable, but also existing products' sales as relevant dependent variables. This was a major concern in the introduction of HPL and MGD 64. Test-marketing allows a firm to determine whether a new offering will cannibalize sales from existing products, meaning that consumers are choosing the new offering as a replacement for another product offered by the same company. If Miller's MGD 64 sales in a test market are impressive but sales of their other beers drop proportionately, then Miller would be less inclined to go through all the effort and expense of a full-scale new product launch.

Testing the Marketing Mix

Test markets are equally useful as a field experiment manipulating different marketing plans for existing products. A manager can study any element of the marketing mix with a test market.

As we all know, retailers rely heavily on weekly flyers distributed through newspapers or through direct mail. This is particularly true in France, where retail advertising historically faces greater restrictions, including limited television advertisements. In France, the average French household receives over 12 kg (26.4 lbs) of retail flyers annually![16] Yet, many have little idea about the effectiveness of different approaches. Should the flyers simply promote low price, or should they emphasize products related to a specific theme? In fact, different flyer styles can significantly affect not only sales, but retailer image, too.[17]

The most effective distribution channel may also be indicated in a test market. DVDs and Blue-ray disks are facing increased competition from other technologies that allow consumers to access movies disc-less. Paramount recently test-marketed a different channel for the distribution of a motion picture.[18] In December of 2007, Paramount released *Jackass 2.5,* actually the third in the *Jackass* series of films, for online distribution at the same time the movie was released to theaters. The online version was free, but contained embedded advertisements. Paramount was testing to see how consumers would warm up to this novel method of distribution.

• • • • • • •

Test-marketing can be used to determine the impact of different promotional approaches on sales and brand image.

©Susan Van Etten

Identifying Product Weaknesses

Test-market experimentation also allows identification of previously undetected product or marketing plan weaknesses. The company can deal with the weaknesses before the committing to the actual sales launch. Although often this use of test markets is accidental, in the sense that it isn't the reason for conducting the test markets, companies save huge sums of resources by spotting problems before the full-scale marketing effort begins. Often, this use of test marketing occurs when a product underperforms in at least one location. Researchers can then follow up with other research approaches to try and reveal the reason for the lack of performance. Once identified, product modifications address these faults specifically.

McDonald's test-marketed pizza periodically for years. The first test market provided lower-than-expected sales results. The reasons for the underperformance included a failure to consider competitors' reactions and problems associated with the small, single-portion pizza, which was the only way McPizza was sold. Additionally, McPizza didn't seem to bring any new customers to McDonald's. In the next round of test marketing, the marketing strategy repositioned the pizza, shifting to a 14-inch pizza that was only sold from about 4 P.M. until closing. With still underwhelming results, McDonald's test-marketed "Pizza Shoppes" within the test McDonald's where employees could be seen assembling ingredients on ready-made pizza dough. Although the concept is still alive, McDonald's has shied away from pizza for the U.S. adult market. A McPizza Happy Meal remains as a sole pizza concept with promise for American stores. Pizza-like products, however, exist and succeed at many McDonald's locations in other nations.

When a product fails its market test, the test market does not fail! In most cases, this represents an important *research success*. Encountering problems in a test-market either properly leads the company to introduce the new product or to make the planned change in marketing strategy. Thus, decision makers avoid a huge mistake. In addition, test-market results may lead management to make adjustments that will turn the poor test-market results into a market success. The managerial experience gained in test-marketing can be extremely valuable, even when the performance results are disappointing.

Projecting Test-Market Results

Test-marketing is all about generalizing results. In other words, researchers do a trial test on a small scale with the hope that the small scale results will match those achieved in a full-scale product introduction. Therefore, external validity is a key consideration in designing a test market. Test markets are not appropriate for research questions that require very rigorous control of internal validity. However, the fundamental reason that test markets are conducted is the hope that results can be accurately projected from the sample to the entire market or population of customers. Researchers take several steps to try to make these projections as accurate as they possibly can.

Most researchers support sales data with consumer survey data during test markets. These help monitor consumer awareness and attitudes toward the test-marketed product as well as the repeat-purchase likelihood. Frequently this information is acquired via consumer panels.

Estimating Sales Volume: Some Problems

Test-marketing is all about estimating how well the product involved will do in the marketplace. Researchers project sales based on how well the product performs in the test market. Numerous methodological factors cause problems in estimating national sales results based on regional tests. Often, these problems result from mistakes in the design or execution of the test market itself.

Overattention

If managers give too much attention to a new product launch within a test market, the product may be more successful than it would under more normal marketing conditions. In the test market, the firm's advertising agency may make sure that the test markets have excellent television coverage (which may or may not be representative of the national television coverage). If salespeople are aware of the test market, they may spend unusual amounts of time making sure the new product is available or displayed better. This also means that managers should avoid any added incentives that would encourage extra sales efforts to sell the test-marketed product.

Unrealistic Store Conditions

The test market should offer the product under the same conditions that would likely exist under real conditions. If greater effort leads to a relatively advantageous but unrealistic merchandising advantage, the results will not be valid. For example, extra shelf facings, eye-level stocking, and other conditions resulting from unrealistic distribution efforts would probably distort the test market.

This situation may result from research design problems or overattention, as previously described. For example, if retailers know that someone is paying more attention to their efforts with a given product, they may give it artificially high distribution and extra retail support.

Reading the Competitive Environment Incorrectly

Another common mistake is to assume that the competitive environment will be the same nationally as in the test market. If competitors are unaware of a test market, the results will not measure competitors' reactions to company strategy. Competitors' responses after a national introduction may differ substantially from the way they reacted in the test market. On the other hand, competitors may react to a test market by attempting to undermine it. If they know that a firm is testing, they may attempt to disrupt test-market results with increased promotions and lower prices for their own products, among other potential acts of **test-market sabotage**.

test-market sabotage

Intentional attempts to disrupt the results of a test market being conducted by another firm.

When Starbucks test-marketed its supermarket brand coffee in Chicago, Procter & Gamble broadcast television commercials touting Millstone coffee's victory over Starbucks in taste tests. The commercials lampooned Starbucks for being more interested in selling T-shirts and novelties than coffee. P&G also offered free samples of Millstone to disrupt the result of Starbucks' test market.[19]

Time Lapse

One relatively uncontrolled problem results from the time lapse between the test-market experiment and the national introduction of the product. Often, the time period between the test market and national introduction is a year or more. Given the time needed to build production capacity, develop channels of distribution, and gain initial sales acceptance, this may be unavoidable. However, the longer the time between the test market and the actual selling market, the less accurate one should expect the results to be.

Advantages of Test-Marketing

This discussion of test-marketing should make it clear that test markets are advantageous in ways that are very difficult to match with other research approaches. The key advantage of test-marketing is the real-world setting in which the experiment is performed. Although focus groups and surveys also can be useful in describing what people may like in a new product, the actual behavior of consumers in a real test-market location is far more likely to lead to accurate projections.

A second advantage of test-marketing is that researchers can easily communicate results to management. Although the experiment itself can be difficult to implement for a host of reasons, most related to small-scale or temporary marketing, the data analysis is usually very simple. Very often, the same procedures used in any simple experiment provide a way of producing test-market results. As we will see, this relies heavily on comparing means in some way. Researchers find marketing managers much more receptive to these types of results than they may be to results drawn from complicated mathematical models or qualitative approaches relying on deep subjective interpretation. Many consumer industries depend heavily on test-market results for help in decision making. The Research Snapshot illustrates how marketing managers in the fast-food industry can use test-marketing.

Disadvantages of Test-Marketing

Test markets also have disadvantages. Although the power of test markets in providing accurate predictions are apparently such that companies would use test markets for all major marketing changes, this is hardly the case. The disadvantages are such that test markets are used less frequently than one might think.

Cost

Test-marketing is very expensive. Consider that for most new products, companies have to actually create production facilities on a small scale, develop distribution within selected test-market cities, arrange media coverage specific to those locations, and then have systems and people in place to carefully monitor market results. All of this leads to high cost overall and very high unit costs. Heineken faced all these issues in test-marketing HPL. As a result, each six-pack could cost several times over the actual selling price. However, when HPL was introduced throughout the United States, the economies of scale that come with full-scale marketing left unit costs below the selling price.

Test-marketing a packaged-goods product typically costs millions. As with other forms of marketing research, decision makers must weigh the value of the information against the research costs. The expense of test-marketing certainly is a primary reason why marketing managers refuse to use the approach. Although they do reduce error in decision making, they are not perfect and certainly some risk remains in basing decisions on test-market results. If they were risk-free, managers would use them far more frequently. Because they are not risk-free and are so expensive, managers may decide to make go or no-go decisions based on less expensive techniques that are often less accurate.

Time

Test markets cost more than just money. Test markets cannot be put together overnight. Simply planning a test market usually takes months. Actually implementing one takes much longer. On top of the time for planning and implementation, researchers also must decide how long is long

© Susan Van Etten

The Hidden in Hidden Valley Ranch

A few years ago, Hidden Valley Ranch (HVR) conducted a field market experiment to examine how effective three new flavors of salad dressings would be in the marketplace. Thus, there were three levels of the experimental variable, each representing a different flavor. HVR had to produce small batches of each flavor, get them bottled, and ship them to their sales representatives, who then had to stock the dressings in the participating retail stores. All of this was very expensive and the costs to produce each bottle used in a test market were almost $20.

So, the first day of the test was consumed with sales reps placing the products in the salad dressing sections of retail stores. The second day, each rep went back to each store to record the number of sales for each flavor. By the third day, all of the bottles of all flavors had sold!! Amazing! Was every flavor a huge success? Actually, one of HVR's competitors had sent their sales reps around beginning on the second day of the test to buy every bottle of the new HVR dressings in every store it had been placed in. Thus, HVR was unable to produce any sales data (the dependent variable) and the competitor was able to break down the dressing in their labs and determine the recipe.

This illustrates one risk that comes along with field tests. Once a product is available for sale, there are no secrets. Also, you risk espionage of this type that can render the experiment invalid.

Source: © Cengage Learning 2013.

enough. In other words, when is the amount of data collected sufficient to have confidence in drawing valid conclusions?

The appropriate time period for a test market varies depending on the research objectives. Sometimes, as in Procter & Gamble's testing of its unique new products Febreze, Dryel, and Fit Fruit & Vegetable Wash, the research takes several years. In other situations, as in P&G's testing of Encaprin pain reliever (a product that ultimately failed in national distribution), the time period may be shorter. HPL's test markets lasted less than a year, relatively short by most standards.

Thus, even a quickly planned and implemented test market can cost the firm a year or more in time. During this time, competitors are also trying to gain competitive advantage. The fear that competitors may make a big move first puts added pressure on marketing managers to move quickly. For this reason, the time costs associated with test markets are a primary reason for forgoing them.

How long should a test market be? Test markets should be long enough for consumers to become aware of the product, have a chance to purchase it, consume it, and repurchase it at least one more time. Thus, it must be longer than the average purchase cycle for that particular product. A test market that is too short may overestimate sales, because typically the early adopters are heavy users of the product. Thus, projections are based on consumers who are far from average.

> Time must be allowed for sales to settle down from their initial honeymoon level. In addition, the share and sales levels must be allowed to stabilize. After the introduction of a product, peaks and troughs will inevitably stem from initial customer interest and curiosity as well as from competitive product retaliation.[20]

Loss of Secrecy

As pointed out in the Research Snapshot, one drawback to actual field experimentation is that the marketplace is a public forum. Therefore, secrets no longer exist. In the case of a new product, not only does the competition know about the new product, but a competitor can sometimes benefit from the test market by monitoring the same dependent variables as the sponsoring firms. This may cause them to launch a competing product. In some cases, the competitor can even beat the originating company to the national marketplace.

Selecting test markets is, for the most part, a sampling problem. The researcher seeks a sample of test-market cities that is representative of the population comprised of all consumers in the relevant marketing area. If a new product is being launched throughout Australia, for example, the researcher must choose cities that are typical of all Australians.

EXHIBIT 9.6
Popular Test-Markets and Selected Demographic Characteristics

City	2010 Population	Median Age	Percent of Households w/Children	Hispanic Proportion (Percent)
Cedar Rapids, IA	126,326	34.7	28.9%	3.3%
Eau Claire, WI	65,883	36.0	36.1%	1.9%
Grand Junction, CO	58,566	38.8	32.1%	13.9%
Pittsfield, MA	44,737	39.6	35.9%	5.0%
Wichita Falls, TX	140,553	31.9	35.5%	18.9%
Wichita, KS	382,368	33.4	36.9%	15.3%
Midland, TX	111,147	32.3	32.9%	37.6%
Entire U.S.A.	308,745,538	37.2	36.9%	15.3%

Thus, test-market cities should represent the entire competitive marketplace. For companies wishing to market a product through the United States, there is no single ideal test-market city. Nevertheless, the researcher must usually avoid cities that are not representative of the nation. Regional or urban differences, atypical climates, unusual ethnic compositions, or different lifestyles may dramatically affect a marketing program. Sometimes, although the researchers may wish to sell a product throughout the entire region of the United States, they may have a certain benefit segment in mind. Food companies may consider introducing a product for segments that enjoy spicy food, for example. In this case, they may choose cities known to favor spicier, more flavor-filled foods, such as New Orleans and San Antonio. In this case, those test-market city populations fit the benefit segment and in this way represent the relevant population better than more typical cities.

Certain cities are used repeatedly for test-market operations because researchers see them as typical of U.S. consumers overall. Whereas some larger cities like Tampa; Peoria, Illinois; and San Antonio are attractive test-markets, test-markets often take place in smaller cities. Exhibit 9.6 above lists several of the most popular U.S. test-markets.[21] Their popularity lies in how close they come to duplicating the average U.S. demographic profile.

Americans and Canadians are similar in many respects. However, one shouldn't assume that a product that is successful in the United States will be successful in Canada. Thus, even after a successful American launch, a company may wish to conduct a test market in Canada. In addition, even if Canadians like a new product, a unique marketing approach may be in order. Generally, Calgary, Alberta, represents a prime test-market location for the Canadian market. When Italy's Podere Castorani Winery wished to expand to Canada, Calgary provided the test-market location. Likewise, when Shell introduced a fast-pay charge system, Calgary again proved a suitable test market. Edmonton also is frequently used to test-market products. Imperial Tobacco selected Edmonton for a test market of SNUS, a smokeless, spitless tobacco product, positioned as a safe alternative relative to smoking cigarettes.[22]

Like the United States, Canada is comprised of many different ethnic segments. Companies should also be aware that French Canada is quite different from the rest of the country. Edmonton may represent Canadians well enough but not French Canadians. Thus, companies may consider a test-market in Quebec City, Quebec, to see how French Canadian consumers will react.

Test-marketing in Europe can be particularly difficult. Although companies can test their products country by country, the sheer costs involved with test-marketing motivate firms to look for cities more representative of large parts of Europe. Copenhagen, Denmark, is one such city. Although the population is somewhat homogenous demographically, it is also multilingual and receptive to new ideas.[23] Copenhagen is particularly representative of northern Europe. Other cities to be considered include Frankfurt, Germany; Birmingham, England; and Madrid, Spain.

Ethical Issues in Experimentation

Ethical issues with experimentation were discussed in Chapter 4 so we touch on them lightly here. The question of deception is a key ethical dilemma in experimentation. Although deception is necessary in most experiments, when debriefing procedures return subjects to their prior condition, then the experiment is probably consistent with good moral standards. When subjects have been injured significantly or truly psychologically harmed, debriefing will not return them to their formal condition and the experiment should not proceed. Therefore, we offer additional commentary on debriefing.

Researchers should debrief experimental subjects following an experimental procedure. In fact, many academic researchers, such as those conducting basic marketing research, are required to debrief subjects by their university IRB procedures. Debriefing experimental subjects by communicating the purpose of the experiment and the researcher's hypotheses about the nature of consumer behavior is expected to counteract negative effects of deception, relieve stress, and provide an educational experience for the subject.

Proper debriefing allows the subject to save face by uncovering the truth for himself. The experimenter should begin by asking the subject if he has any questions or if he found any part of the experiment odd, confusing, or disturbing. This question provides a check on the subject's suspiciousness and effectiveness of manipulations. The experimenter continues to provide the subject cues to the deception until the subject states that he believes there was more to the experiment than met the eye. At this time the purpose and procedure of the experiment [are] revealed.[24]

Debriefing therefore is critical because it allows us to return subjects to normal. If this cannot be done through a simple procedure like debriefing, the experiment is likely unethical. If an experimenter, for example, took 100 nonsmokers, divided them into 4 groups of 25, and had them smoke 20 or 50 cigarettes a day for 5 years (manipulation 1) that were either called Nicky's or BeFrees (manipulation 2), no debriefing could restore them to normal and therefore, this experiment should never be conducted.

Additionally, there is the issue of test markets and efforts extended toward interfering with a competitor's test market. When a company puts a product out for public consumption, they should be aware that competitors may also now freely consume the product. If a competitor buys a lot of the product, the test-market results will be misleading. Further, any design secret is probably no longer secret as competitors dissect the new product. When a company actively attempts to sabotage or invalidate another company's test market or they aim to infringe on some patent/copyright protection, those acts are ethically questionable.

● ● ● ● ● ● ●

Miami is not considered as representative of the U.S. population as is Peoria, IL.

TIPS OF THE TRADE

- Experiments test for causal evidence and thus represent the primary tool for causal research designs.
- Experimental manipulations in marketing research should possess the following characteristics:
    - Comprise distinct categories or magnitudes
    - Two, three or, at most, four treatment levels per experimental variable—particularly when multiple experimental variables are used in a single study
    - Administered randomly across subjects
- Experimental graphs are useful in displaying results, particularly when interactions are involved.
- Laboratory experiments provide greater internal validity at the cost of lower external validity.

- That's how student subjects or subjects from an online HIT pool are justified as legitimate.
- Field experiments, including test markets, increase external validity at the cost of internal validity.
- Traditional test markets remain expensive and technology offers some virtual alternatives. Test markets also take a lot of time and involve a loss of secrecy.
- When a product can easily be duplicated by competitors who obtain an actual product, then a test market may not be wise.

Source: © Cengage Learning 2013.

∷ SUMMARY

1. Know the basic characteristics of research experiments. Independent variables are created through manipulation in experiments rather than through measurement. The researcher creates unique experimental conditions that each representing a unique level of an independent variable. Researchers refer to human sampling units as subjects in an experiment rather than respondents. This is because researchers subject them to experimental manipulations. Experimental manipulations are examined for the extent to which they affect outcomes. Main effects are due to differences in observed outcomes based on any single experimental variable. Interaction effects are due to combinations of independent variables.

2. Design an experiment using the basic issues of experimental design. Systematic experimental error occurs because sampling units (research subjects) in one experimental cell are different from those in another cell in a way that affects the dependent variable. In an experiment involving how people respond to color, the researcher would not want to have all males in one color group and all females in another. Randomization is an important way of minimizing systematic experimental error. If research subjects are randomly assigned to different treatment combinations, then the differences among people that exist naturally within a population should also exist within each experimental cell. Additionally, the researcher must try to control for all possible extraneous variables. Extraneous variables can render any causal inference as spurious. Control is necessary to reduce the possibility of confounding explanations.

3. Know ways of maximizing the validity of experiments, including the minimization of demand characteristics. Demand characteristics are experimental procedures that somehow inform the subject about the actual research purpose. Demand effects can result from demand characteristics. When this happens, the results are confounded. Demand characteristics can be minimized by following these simple rules: using an experimental disguise, isolating experimental subjects, using a "blind" experimental administrator, and administering only one experimental treatment combination to each subject. A between-subjects design means that every subject receives only one experimental treatment combination. The main advantages of between-subjects designs are the reduced likelihood of demand effects and simpler analysis and presentation, all of which can improve validity.

4. Weigh the trade-off between internal and external validity. Lab experiments offer higher internal validity because they maximize control of extraneous variables. High internal validity is a good thing because we can be more certain that the experimental variable is truly the cause of any variance in the dependent variable. Field experiments maximize external validity because they take place in a more natural setting meaning that the results are more likely to generalize to the actual business situation. The increased external validity comes at the expense of internal validity.

5. Recognize the appropriate uses of test-marketing. Major uses of test-marketing include forecasting the success of a newly developed product, testing hypotheses about different options for marketing mix elements, and identifying weaknesses in product designs or marketing strategies. The two major advantages of test markets discussed in the chapter are the real-world setting and the ease in interpretation and communication of results. These advantages have to be weighed against several key disadvantages. These include the great amount of money that it costs to conduct a test market; the length of time it takes to design, implement, and analyze a test market; and the loss of secrecy that comes when the product is marketed publicly.

6. Avoid unethical experimental practices. Experiments involve deception. Additionally, research procedures sometimes expose subjects to stressful or possibly dangerous manipulations. Every precaution should be made to ensure that subjects are not harmed. Debriefing subjects about the true purpose of the experiment following its conclusion is important for the ethical treatment of subjects. If debriefing can restore subjects to their preexperimental condition, the experimental procedures are likely consistent with ethical practice. If the procedures changes subjects in some way that makes it difficult to return them to their prior condition, then the experimental procedures probably go beyond what ethical researchers consider appropriate.

:: KEY TERMS AND CONCEPTS

between-subjects design, *229*
blocking variables, *216*
cell, *220*
cohort effect, *230*
confound, *223*
constancy of conditions, *226*
control group, *219*
counterbalancing, *227*
covariate, *216*
demand characteristic, *224*
demand effect, *224*
experimental condition, *215*

experimental group, *219*
experimental treatment, *219*
external validity, *231*
field experiments, *227*
history effect, *230*
instrumentation effect, *230*
interaction effect, *217*
internal validity, *229*
laboratory experiment, *227*
main effect, *216*
manipulation check, *229*
maturation effect, *230*

mortality effect (sample attrition), *231*
placebo effect, *225*
randomization, *222*
repeated measures, *222*
subjects, *215*
systematic or nonsampling error, *221*
tachistoscope, *227*
test-market sabotage, *235*
test units, *221*
testing effects, *230*
within-subjects design, *229*

:: QUESTIONS FOR REVIEW AND CRITICAL THINKING

1. Define experimental condition, experimental treatment, and experimental group. How are these related to the implementation of a valid manipulation?

2. A tissue manufacturer that has the fourth-largest market share plans to experiment with a fifty-cent-off coupon during November and a buy-one, get-one-free coupon during December. The experiment will take place at Target stores in St. Louis and Kansas City. In addition, coupons will be issued either through Groupon.com or in the local newspaper. Sales will be recorded by scanners from which mean tissue sales for each store for each month can be computed and interpreted.

   a. What are the experimental variable and the dependent variable?

   b. Prepare a mock experimental graph that shows hypothetical results (simply guess at what the mean values for each experimental condition would be).

   c. What types of people would make good subjects for this experiment?

3. What is the difference between a *main effect* and an *interaction* in an experiment? In question 2, what will create a main effect? Is an interaction possible?

4. In what ways might the design in question 2 yield systematic or nonsampling error?
5. How can experimental graphs be used to show main effects and interactions?
6. What purpose does the random assignment of subjects serve?
7. Why is an experimental confound so damaging to the conclusions drawn from an experiment?
8. What are demand characteristics? How can they be minimized?
9. **ETHICS** Suppose researchers were experimenting with how much more satisfied consumers are with a "new and improved" version of some existing product. How might the researchers design a placebo within an experiment testing this research question? Is using such a placebo ethical or not?
10. If a company wanted to know whether to implement a new management training program based on how much it would improve ROI in its southwest division, would you recommend a field or lab experiment?
11. **'NET** Suppose you wanted to test the effect of three different e-mail requests inviting people to participate in a survey posted on the Internet. One simply contained a hyperlink with no explanation, the other said if someone participated $10 would be donated to charity, and the other said if someone participated he or she would have a chance to win $1,000. How would this experiment be conducted differently based on whether it was a between-subjects or within-subjects design? What are the advantages of a between-subjects design?
12. What is a manipulation check? How does it relate to internal validity?
13. Define internal validity and external validity. It's been said that external validity decreases when internal validity is high. Do you believe that is so? Explain your answer.
14. The idea of nonspurious association was introduced in Chapter 3. How does a confounding variable affect whether an association is spurious or nonspurious?
15. Why is a test market usually considered an experiment?
16. When is test-marketing likely to be conducted? When is it not as appropriate? Which type of validity is most relevant to test-marketing?
17. What are the advantages and disadvantages of test-marketing?
18. **ETHICS** What role does debriefing play in ensuring that experimental procedures are consistent with good ethical practice?
19. **ETHICS** A university researcher asks students to participate in an experiment that takes four hours to complete in the last week of a semester. Another researcher conducts the same experiment using online respondents paid $1 to participate. Contrast these two approaches, including a discussion of any ethical issues that might be involved.

∵ RESEARCH ACTIVITIES

1. Consider the situation of a researcher approached by Captain John's in the Research Snapshot on page 221.
   a. Provide a critique of the procedures used to support the claim that Sea Snapper's product is superior. Prepare it in a way that it could be presented as evidence in court.
   b. Design an experiment that would provide a more valid test of the research question, "Do consumers prefer Sea Snapper fish sticks compared to Captain John's fish sticks?"

2. Conduct a taste test involving soft drinks with a group of friends. Pour them several ounces of three popular soft drinks and simply label the cups A, B, and C. Make sure they are blind to the actual brands. Then, let them drink as much as they want and record how much of each they drink. You may also ask them some questions about the drinks. Then, allow other subjects to participate in the same test, but this time, let them know what the three brands are. Record the same data and draw conclusions. Does brand knowledge affect behavior and attitudes about soft drinks?

Examining Product Failure at No-Charge Electronics

Case 9.1

No-Charge Electronics owner Buzz Auphf needs to know how much product failure affects customer loyalty. Buzz contacts David Handy, a local market researcher, and they ultimately decide on examining a research question asking, "How do current customers react to different levels of product failure?" David designs the following experiment to examine the causal effect of product failure on customer purchase intentions, satisfaction, and loyalty.

The experiment is implemented via e-mail using a sample of current and prospective customers. Three free MP3 movies are provided as an incentive to participate. Subjects are asked to click through to an Internet site to download a product that will enhance their computer's graphics capability. In the low-failure condition, after the subjects click to the site, there is no change in the graphics of their computers. In the high-failure condition, once they click through to the site, the subjects' computers go into an infinite loop of obscene graphical images until a message arrives, indicating that a severe virus has infected their computer and some files may be permanently damaged. This goes on for 45 minutes with no remedy. At that time, a debriefing message pops up telling subjects that it was all part of an experiment and that their computer should now function properly. Prepare a position statement either agreeing or disagreeing that the experiment is consistent with good ethical practice.

Source: © Cengage Learning 2013.

Tooheys

Case 9.2

Sixty-six willing Australian drinkers helped a federal court judge decide that Tooheys didn't engage in misleading or deceptive advertising for its 2.2 beer. The beer contains 2.2 percent alcohol, compared to 6 percent for other beers leading to a claim that could be interpreted as implying it was non-alcoholic.

Volunteers were invited to a marathon drinking session after the Aboriginal Legal Service claimed Tooheys' advertising implied beer drinkers could imbibe as much 2.2 as desired without becoming legally intoxicated. Drunken driving laws prohibit anyone with a blood-alcohol level above 0.05 from getting behind the wheel in Australia.

So, an experiment was conducted to see what happens when a lot of 2.2 is consumed. But the task wasn't easy or that much fun. Some subjects couldn't manage to drink the required 10 "middies," an Aussie term for a beer glass of 10 fluid ounces, over the course of an hour.

Thirty-six participants could manage only nine glasses. Four threw up and were excluded. Two more couldn't manage the "minimum" nine glasses and had to be replaced.

Justice J. Beaumont observed that consuming enough 2.2 in an hour to reach the 0.05 level was "uncomfortable and therefore an unlikely process." Because none of the ads mentioned such extreme quantities, he ruled they couldn't be found misleading or deceptive.[25]

Questions

1. Would a lab experiment or a field experiment be more "valid" in determining whether Tooheys could cause a normal beer consumer to become intoxicated? Explain.

2. Describe an alternate research design that would have higher validity.

3. Is the experiment described in this story consistent with good ethical practice? Likewise, comment on how the design described in part 2 would be made consistent with good ethical practices.

4. Is validity or ethics more important?

Source: © Cengage Learning 2013.

correlation between the NPS and things like profitability could be misleading. Alternatively, some firms have broken their organizations down into functions (service, sales, etc.) and developed an NPS for each area, claiming the information obtained is richer and more useful. However, despite the shortcomings, it is doubtful that competitive firms would trade even a single promoter for dozens of detractors or even a handful of passively satisfied customers. So, this single item certainly helps managers know the score![1]

Introduction

Anyone who has ever followed a recipe knows the importance of good measurement. Following a recipe may seem easy, but understanding the quantities represented and the units of measure can be critical. Confuse salt with sugar or tablespoons for teaspoons and the dish is ruined. Just as in the culinary arts, researchers can measure business and marketing in more than one way. Also, researchers often may have to use imperfect measurement devices. Measure a concept poorly and the "recipe" is a likely disaster. Only in this case, the poorly implemented "recipe" makes for bad business decisions not just a bad dinner.

What to Measure

Managers can't know if their business is performing well without good measurement. However, researchers may not always know exactly what defines good business performance. Measures cannot be any better than the concepts' definitions.

measurement

The process of describing some property of a phenomenon of interest, usually by assigning numbers in a reliable and valid way.

The decision statement, corresponding research questions, and research hypotheses determine what concepts researchers need to measure. **Measurement** is the process of describing some property of a phenomenon, usually by assigning numbers, in a reliable and valid way. The numbers convey information about the phenomenon. When numbers are used, the researcher must have a rule for assigning a number to an observation in a way that provides an accurate description.

We can illustrate measurement by thinking about the way instructors assign students' grades. A grade represents a student's performance in a class. Students with higher performance should receive a different grade than do students with lower performance. Even the apparently simple concept of student performance is measured in many different ways. Consider the following options:

1. A student can be assigned a letter corresponding to his/her performance, as is typical of U.S.-based grading systems.
   a. A — Represents excellent performance
   b. B — Represents good performance
   c. C — Represents average performance
   d. D — Represents poor performance
   e. F — Represents failing performance
2. A student can be assigned a number from 1 to 20, which is the system more typically used in France.
   a. 20 — Represents outstanding performance
   b. 11–20 — Represent differing degrees of passing performance
   c. Below 11 — Represent failing performance
3. A student can be assigned a number corresponding to a percentage performance scale.
   a. 100 percent — Represents a perfect score, indicating the best performance.
   b. 60–99 percent — Represents differing degrees of passing performance, each number representing the proportion of correct work.
   c. 0–59 percent — Represents failing performance but still captures proportion of correct work.
4. A student can be assigned one of two letters corresponding to performance.
   a. P — Represents a passing mark
   b. F — Represents a failing mark

Take a look at the section of the student survey shown in the screenshot. Suppose someone thought the items made a composite scale and you are asked to analyze its quality. Answer the following questions:

1. Is the level of measurement nominal, ordinal, interval, or ratio?
2. Assuming the scale items represent studying concentration, do you think any of the items need to be reverse-coded before a summated scale could be formed? If so, which ones?
3. Using the data for these items, compute the coefficient α and draw a conclusion about the scale's reliability.

4. At this point, how much can be said about the scale's validity? Are there any items that do not belong on the scale?

Source: © Cengage Learning 2013.

Each measurement scale has the potential of producing error or a lack of validity. Exhibit 10.1 illustrates a common student performance measurement application.

Often, instructors may use a percentage scale all semester long and then at the end, have to assign a letter grade for a student's overall performance. Does this produce any potential measurement problems? Consider two students who have percentage scores of 79.4 and 70.0, respectively. The most likely outcome using a conventional ten–point spread when these scores are translated into "letter grades" is that each receives a C (70–79 percent range for a C). Consider a third student who finishes with a 69.0 percent average and a fourth student who finishes with a 79.9 percent average.

Which students are happiest with this arrangement? The first two students receive the same grade, even though their scores are 9.4 percent apart. The third student gets a grade lower (D) performance than the second student, even though their percentage scores are only 1.0 percentage point different. The fourth student, who has a score only 0.5 percent higher than the first student,

Student	Percentage Grade	Difference from Next Highest Grade	Letter Grade
1	79.4%	0.5%	C
2	70.0%	9.4%	C
3	69.0%	1.0%	D
4	79.9%	NA	B

EXHIBIT **10.1**
Are There Any Validity Issues with This Measurement?

Source: © Cengage Learning 2013.

would receive a B. Thus, the measuring system (final grade) suggests that the fourth student outperformed the first (presuming that 79.9 is rounded up to 80) student (B versus C), but the first student did not outperform the second (each gets a C), even though the first and second students have the greatest difference in percentage scores.

One can make a case that error exists in this measurement system. All measurement, particularly in the social sciences, contains error. Researchers, if we are to represent concepts truthfully, must make sure that the measures used are accurate enough to yield correct conclusions. Making use of measures requires that the flaws in measures are at least somewhat understood. When this is the case, researchers can sometimes account for the error statistically. Ultimately, research would be impossible without measurement.

Concepts

concept

A generalized idea that represents something of identifiable and distinct meaning.

A researcher has to know what to measure before knowing how to measure something. Hopefully, the research questions make the relevant concepts clear. A **concept** can be thought of as a generalized idea that represents something of identifiable and distinct meaning. Demographic concepts such as *age*, *sex*, and *number of children* are relatively concrete having relatively unambiguous meanings. They present few problems in either definition or measurement. Other concepts are more abstract. Concepts such as *loyalty, personality, performance, channel power, trust, corporate culture, customer satisfaction, value,* and so on are more difficult to both define and measure. Involvement seems like a simple idea until the researcher tries to unambiguously define it and measure it. Recently, marketing managers use the term *engagement* to represent how much a consumer is interested in and interacting with a brand. If engagement and involvement are different concepts, marketing researchers are challenged to develop distinct measurement scales for each concept.[2]

Operational Definitions

operationalization

The process of identifying scale devices that correspond to properties of a concept involved in a research process.

scale

A device providing a range of values that correspond to different characteristics or amounts of a characteristic exhibited in observing a concept.

correspondence rules

Indicate the way that a certain value on a scale corresponds to a true value of a concept.

Researchers measure concepts through a process known as **operationalization**. This process involves identifying scales that correspond to properties of the concept. **Scales**, just as a scale you may use to check your weight, provide a range of values that correspond to different characteristics in the concept being measured. In other words, scales provide **correspondence rules** that indicate that a certain value on a scale corresponds to a value of a concept. Hopefully, they do this in a truthful way.

Here is an example of a correspondence rule: "Assign numerals 1 through 7 according to how much individual customers trust a sales representative. If a customer judges a sales representative as completely trustworthy, assign a 7. If the sales rep is perceived as completely untrustworthy, assign the numeral 1. Numbers in between represent varying degrees of trust." The opening vignette describes the concept of NPS and its correspondence rules and every professor uses correspondence rules to transfer marks for a term into a grade.

Variables

Researchers use the variance in concepts to make meaningful diagnoses. Therefore, when we defined *variables*, we really were suggesting that variables capture different values of a concept. Scales capture a concept's variance and, as such, the scales provide the researcher's variables. Consider the following hypothesis:

> *H1: Experience is related positively to job performance.*

The hypothesis implies a relationship between two variables, experience and job performance. The variables capture variance in the experience and performance concepts. One employee may have 15 years of experience and be a top performer. A second may have 10 years' experience and be a good performer. The scale used to measure experience is quite simple in this case and would involve simply providing the number of years an employee has been with the company. Job performance is captured by a scale providing a correspondence rule with which a supervisor places an employee into a performance category.

> *"Not everything that can be counted counts, and not everything that counts can be counted."*
>
> —ALBERT EINSTEIN

Constructs

Sometimes a single variable cannot capture a concept alone. Using multiple variables to measure one concept often provides a more complete account of some concept than could any single variable. Even in the physical sciences, scientists apply multiple measurements to obtain more accurate representations.

A **construct** is a term used for concepts that are measured with multiple variables. For instance, when a marketing researcher wishes to measure a sales person's customer orientation, several variables like these may be used, each captured on a 1-to-5 scale of some type:

1. I offer the product that is best suited to a customer's problem.
2. A good employee has to have the customer's best interests in mind.
3. I try to find out what kind of products will be most helpful to a customer.[3]

Operational definitions translate conceptual definitions into measurement scales. An operational definition is like a manual of instructions or a recipe: even the truth of a statement like "Gaston likes seafood gumbo" depends on the recipe and the ingredients. Different instructions lead to different results.[4]

construct

A term used to refer to concepts measured with multiple variables.

Levels of Scale Measurement

Marketing researchers use many scales. Not all scales capture the same richness in a measure and not all concepts require a rich measure. But, a researcher can classify all measures based on the way they represent distinctions between observations of a variable. The four levels or types of scale measurement are *nominal, ordinal, interval,* and *ratio level scales*. Traditionally, the level of scale measurement is important because it determines the mathematical comparisons that are allowable. Each of the four scale levels offers the researcher progressively more power in analyzing and testing the validity of a scale.

Nominal Scale

Nominal scales represent the most elementary level of measurement. A nominal scale assigns a value to an object for identification or classification purposes. The value can be a number, but does not have to be a number, because nominal scales do not represent quantities. In this sense, a

nominal scales

Represent the most elementary level of measurement in which values are assigned to an object for identification or classification purposes only.

● ● ● ● ● ● ●

Athletes wear nominal numbers on their jerseys.

©karnizz/Shutterstock

nominal scale is truly a qualitative scale. Nominal scales are extremely useful even though some may consider them elementary.

Marketing researchers use nominal scales quite often. For instance, suppose Barq's Root Beer experimented with three different types of sweeteners (cane sugar, corn syrup, or fruit extract) in an effort to decide which created the best tasting soft drink. Basically, Barq's researchers designed a taste-test experiment. Experimental subjects taste one of the three recipes and then rate how much they like it and how likely they would be to buy that particular drink. The researchers would like the subjects to remain blind to the recipe so that the knowledge does not bias their perceptions. Thus, when subjects are actually asked to taste one of the three root beers, the drinks are labeled X, Y, or Z, not cane sugar, corn syrup, or fruit extract. The X, Y, and Z become the measuring system that represents the variance in sweeteners.

Nominal scaling is arbitrary in the sense that each label can be assigned to any of the categories without introducing error; for instance, in the root beer example, the researcher can assign the letter Z to any of the three options without damaging scale validity. Cane sugar could just as properly be labeled Z as X, or Y or even A, or B. The researcher might use numbers instead of letters without any change in the validity of the measuring system. If so, cane sugar, corn syrup, and fruit extract might be identified with the numbers 1, 2, and 3, respectively, or even 543, −26, and 8080, respectively. Either set of numbers is equally valid because the numbers are not representing different quantities. They are simply identifying the type of sweetener.

We encounter nominal numbering systems all the time. Uniform numbers are nominal numbers. Tom Brady is identified on the football field by his jersey number. What is his number? Airport terminals are identified with a nominal numbering system. In the Atlanta airport, a departing traveler has to go through terminals T, A, B, C, D, and E before reaching a departure gate atter minal F. School bus numbers are nominal in that they simply identify a bus. Elementary school buses sometimes use both a number and an animal designation to help small children get on the right bus. So, bus number "8" may also be the "tiger" bus.

The first drawing in Exhibit 10.2 depicts the number 7 on a horse's colors. This is merely a label to allow bettors and racing enthusiasts to identify the horse. The assignment of a 7 to this horse does not mean that it is the seventh-fastest horse or that it is the seventh biggest, or anything else meaningful. But, the 7 does let you know when you have won or lost your bet!

EXHIBIT **10.2**

Nominal, Ordinal, Interval, and Ratio Scales Provide Different Information

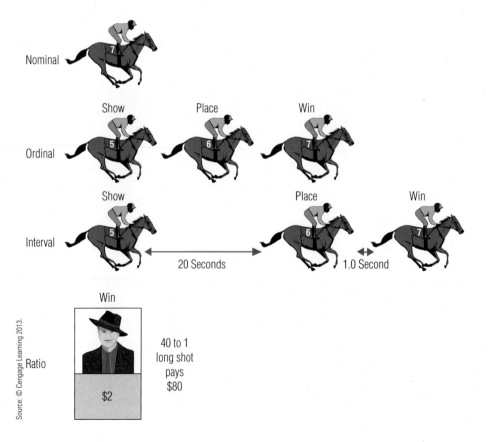

Source: © Cengage Learning 2013.

EXHIBIT **10.3**
Facts About the Four Levels of Scales

Level	Examples	Numerical Operations	
Nominal	Yes – No Female – Male Buy – Did Not Buy Postal Code: ____	Counting	• Frequencies • Mode
Ordinal	Rankings Choose from the Following: • Dissatisfied • Satisfied • Very Satisfied • Delighted Indicate Your Level of Education: • HS Diploma • Some College • Bachelor's Degree • Graduate Degree	Counting and Ordering	• Frequencies • Mode • Median • Range
Interval	100-Point Job Performance Ratings Assigned by Supervisors: 0% = Worst Performers 100% = Best Performers Temperature-Type Attitude Scales: Low Temperature = Bad Attitude High Temperature = Good Attitude	Common Arithmetic Operations	• Mean • Median • Variance • Standard Deviation
Ratio	Amount Purchased Salesperson Sales Volume Likelihood of performing some act: • 0% = No Likelihood to • 100% = Certainty Number of stores visited Time spent viewing a particular web page Number of web pages viewed	All Arithmetic Operations	• Mean • Median • Variance • Standard Deviation

Source: © Cengage Learning 2013.

Exhibit 10.3 lists some nominal scales commonly used by marketing researchers. Nominal scale properties mean the numbering system simply identifies things.

Ordinal Scale

Ordinal scales have nominal properties, but they also allow things to be categorized based on how much of some concept they possess. In other words, an ordinal scale is a ranking scale. When a professor assigns an A, B, C, D, or F to a student at the end of the semester, he or she is using an ordinal scale. An A represents greater performance than B, which is greater performance than B, and so forth.

ordinal scales

Ranking scales allowing things to be arranged based on how much of some concept they possess.

Questionnaires often ask research participants to *rank-order* things based on preference. So, preference is the concept, and the ordinal scale lists the options from most to least preferred, or vice versa. In this sense, ordinal scales are somewhat arbitrary, but not nearly as arbitrary as a nominal scale. Five objects can be ranked from 1 to 5 (least preferred to most preferred) or 1 to 5 (most preferred to least preferred) with no loss of meaning.

When business professors take some time off and go to the race track, even they know that a horse finishing in the "show" position has finished after the "win" and "place" horses (see the second drawing in Exhibit 10.2). The order of finish can be accurately represented by an ordinal scale using an ordered number rule:

- Assign 1 to the "win" position
- Assign 2 to the "place" position
- Assign 3 to the "show" position

the result is a discrete value that can be coded 1, 2, or 3, respectively. This is also an ordinal scale to the extent that it represents an ordered arrangement of agreement. Nominal and ordinal scales are discrete measures.

Certain statistics are most appropriate for discrete measures. Exhibit 10.3 shows statistics for each scale level. The largest distinction is between statistics used for discrete versus continuous measures. For instance, the central tendency of discrete measures is best captured by the mode. When a student wants to know what the most likely grade is for MKTG4311, the mode will be very useful. Observe the results below from the previous semester:

A	5 Students	D	6 Students
B	20 Students	F	6 Students
C	12 Students		

The mode is a "B" because more students obtained that value than any other value. Therefore, the "average" student would expect a B in MKTG4311.

Continuous Measures

continuous measures

Measures that reflect the intensity of a concept by assigning values that can take on any value along a scale range.

Continuous measures are those assigning values anywhere along a scale range in a place that corresponds to the intensity of some concept. Ratio measures are continuous measures. Thus, when we measure sales for each salesperson using the dollar amount sold, we are assigning continuous measures. A number line could be constructed ranging from the least amount sold to the most and a spot on the line would correspond exactly to a sales person's performance.

Strictly speaking, interval scales are not necessarily continuous. Consider the following common type of survey question:

	Strongly Disagree	Disagree	Neutral	Agree	Strongly Agree
I enjoy participating in online auctions	1	2	3	4	5

This is a discrete scale because only the values 1, 2, 3, 4, or 5 can be assigned. Furthermore, it is an ordinal scale because it only orders based on agreement. We really have no way of knowing that the difference in agreement somebody marking a 5 and somebody marking a 4 is the same as the difference in agreement between somebody marking a 2 and somebody marking 1. The scale difference is 1 in either case but is the difference in true agreement the same? There is no way to know. Therefore, the mean is not an appropriate way of stating central tendency, and we really shouldn't use many common statistics on these responses.

However, as a scaled response of this type takes on more values, the error introduced by assuming that the differences between the discrete points are equal becomes smaller. This may be seen by imagining a *Likert scale* with a thousand levels of agreement rather than three or four. The differences between the different levels become so small with a thousand levels that only tiny errors could be introduced by assuming each interval is the same. Therefore, marketing researchers generally treat interval scales containing five or more categories of response as interval. When fewer than five categories are used, this assumption is inappropriate. So, interval scales are treated as continuous when five or more categories are used.

The researcher should keep in mind, however, the distinction between ratio and interval measures. Errors in judgment can be made when interval measures are treated as ratio. For example, attitude is usually measured with an interval scale. An attitude of zero means nothing. In fact, attitude would only have meaning in a relative sense. Therefore, attitude takes on meaning when one person's response is compared to another or through another comparison.

The mean and standard deviation may be calculated from continuous data. Using the actual quantities for arithmetic operations is permissible with ratio scales. Thus, the ratios of scale values are meaningful. A ratio scale has all the properties of nominal, ordinal, and interval scales. However, the same cannot be said in reverse. An ordinal scale, for example, has nominal properties, but it does not have interval or ratio properties.

Reliable and Valid Index Measures

Earlier, we distinguished constructs as concepts that require multiple variables to measure them adequately. Looking back to the chapter vignette, could it be that multiple items will be required to adequately represent customer promotion? Likewise, a consumer's commitment toward a brand or store is usually represented by multiple items. An **attribute** is a single characteristic or fundamental feature of an object, person, situation, or issue.

attribute

A single characteristic or fundamental feature of an object, person, situation, or issue.

Indexes and Composites

Multi-item instruments for measuring a construct are either called *index measures* or *composite measures*. An **index measure** assigns a value based on how characteristic an observation is of the thing being measured. Indexes often are formed by putting several variables together. For example, researchers often form a social class index using three weighted variables: income, occupation, and education. Sociologists see occupation as the single best indicator and it gets the highest weight. A person with a highly prestigious occupation and a graduate degree but lacking a very high income would be more characteristic of high social class than one with a very high income but lacking formal education and a prestigious occupation.

index measure

An index assigns a value based on how much of the concept being measured is associated with an observation. Indexes are formed by putting several variables together systematically.

With an index, the different attributes may not be strongly correlated with each other. A person's income does not always relate strongly to their education. The American Consumer Satisfaction Index (ACSI) provides a level of American consumers' general satisfaction with businesses based on scores across diverse and unrelated industries and competitors within those industries. Readers are likely not surprised to know that Americans appear more satisfied with soft drinks than they are with cable TV companies based on this index.[6]

Composite measures also assign a value based on a mathematical derivation of multiple variables. For example, restaurant satisfaction may be measured by combining questions such as "How satisfied are you with your restaurant experience today? How pleased are you with your visit to our restaurant? How satisfied are you with the overall service quality provided today?" For most practical applications, composite measures and indexes are computed in the same way.[7] However, composite measures are distinguished from index measures in that the composite's indicators should be both theoretically and statistically related to each other. In the customer satisfaction items listed above, one can hardly imagine that respondents would say they were highly satisfied and then provide a low score for how pleased they felt. That simply wouldn't make a lot of sense. Likewise, they should show correlation.

composite measures

Assign a value to an observation based on a mathematical derivation of multiple variables.

Computing Scale Values

Exhibit 10.4 demonstrates how a researcher creates a composite measure from individual rating scales. This particular scale assesses how much a consumer trusts a website.[8] This particular composite represents a **summated scale**. A summated scale is created by simply summing the response to each item making up the composite measure. In this case, the consumer would have a trust score of 13 based on responses to five items. A researcher may sometimes choose to average the scores rather than summing them. The advantage to this is that the composite measure is expressed on the same scale as are the items that make it up. So, instead of a 13, the consumer would have a score of 2.6. The information content is the same.

summated scale

A scale created by simply summing (adding together) the response to each item making up the composite measure. The scores can be but do not have to be averaged by the number of items making up the composite scale.

Recoding Made Easy

Most survey-related software makes scale recoding easy. The screenshot shown here is from SPSS, perhaps the most widely used statistical software in survey-related marketing research. All that needs to be done to reverse-code a scale is to go through this click-through sequence:

1. Click on transform.
2. Click on recode.
3. Choose to recode into the same variable.
4. Select the variable(s) to be recoded.
5. Click on old and new values.
6. Use the menu that appears to enter the old values and the matching new values. Click add after entering each pair.
7. Click continue.

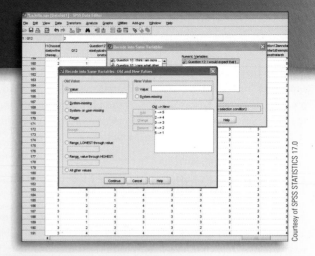

Courtesy of SPSS STATISTICS 17.0

This would successfully recode variable X13 in this case. Other software, including Qualtrics, provide easy procedures like these for recoding variables. A recoding routine can be employed in Excel as well by employing the appropriate formula in a new column.

Source: © Cengage Learning 2013.

EXHIBIT 10.4

Computing a Composite Scale

Item	Strongly Disagree (SD) → Strongly Agree (SA)				
This site appears to be more trustworthy than other sites I have visited.	SD	(D)	N	A	SA
My overall trust in this site is very high.	SD	D	(N)	A	SA
My overall impression of the believability of the information on this site is very high.	SD	(D)	N	A	SA
My overall confidence in the recommendations on this site is very high.	SD	(D)	N	A	SA
The company represented in this site delivers on its promises.	SD	D	N	(A)	SA

Computation:
Scale Values: SD = 1, D = 2, N = 3, A = 4, SA = 5

Thus, the Trust score for this consumer is
2 + 3 + 2 + 2 + 4 = 13

Source: © Cengage Learning 2013.

reverse coding

Means that the value assigned for a response is treated oppositely from the other items.

Sometimes a response may need to be reverse-coded before computing a summated or averaged scale value. **Reverse coding** means that the value assigned for a response is treated oppositely from the other items. If a sixth item was included on the trust scale that said, "I do not trust this website," reverse coding would be necessary to make sure a composite made sense. The content of this item is the reverse of trust (distrust), so the item score is reversed for consistency. Thus, on a 5-point scale, the values are:

- 5 becomes 1
- 4 becomes 2
- 3 stays 3
- 2 becomes 4
- 1 becomes 5

The Research Snapshot shows how a recode can be carried out using SPSS.

Reliability

Reliability is an indicator of a measure's internal consistency. Consistency is the key to understanding reliability. A measure is reliable when different attempts at measuring something converge on the same result. If a professor's marketing research tests are reliable, a student should tend toward consistent scores on all tests. In other words, a student that makes an 80 on the first test should make scores close to 80 on all subsequent tests. If it is difficult to predict what students would make on a test by examining their previous test scores;the tests probably lack reliability.

reliability

An indicator of a measure's internal consistency.

Internal Consistency

Internal consistency is a term used by researchers to represent a measure's homogeneity. An attempt to measure trust may require asking several similar but not identical questions. The set of items that make up a measure comprise a *battery* of scale items. *Internal consistency* of a multiple-item measure can be measured by correlating scores on subsets of items making up a scale.

The **split-half method** of checking reliability takes half the items from a scale (for example, odd-numbered items) and checks them against the results from the other half (even-numbered items). The two scale *halves* should correlate highly. They should also produce similar scores. However, multiple techniques exist for estimating scale reliability.

Coefficient alpha(α) is the most commonly applied estimate of a composite scale's reliability.[9] Coefficient α estimates internal consistency by computing the average of all possible split-half reliabilities for a multiple-item scale. The coefficient demonstrates whether or not the different items converge. Many researchers use α as the sole indicator of a scale's quality largely because statistical programs like SPSS and SAS's JMP readily provide the result. A full accounting of measurement quality though should also include other indicators of validity as shown below. Coefficient α can only take on values ranging from 0, meaning no consistency among items (they are all statistically independent), to 1, meaning complete consistency (all items correlate perfectly with each other).

Generally speaking, researchers consider scales exhibiting a coefficient α between 0.80 and 0.96 as possessing very good reliability. Scales with a coefficient α between 0.70 and 0.80 are considered to have good reliability, and an α value between 0.60 and 0.70 indicates fair reliability. When the coefficient α is below 0.60, the scale has poor reliability.[10] Researchers generally report coefficient α for each composite measure involved in a study.

internal consistency

Represents a measure's homogeneity or the extent to which each indicator of a concept converges on a common meaning.

split-half method

A method for assessing internal consistency by checking the results of one-half of a set of scaled items against the results from the other half.

coefficient alpha (α)

The most commonly applied estimate of a multiple item scale's reliability. It represents the average of all possible split-half reliabilities for a construct.

Test-Retest Reliability

The **test-retest method** of determining reliability involves administering the same scale or measure to the same respondents at two separate times to test for stability. If the measure is stable over time, the test, administered under the same conditions each time, should obtain similar results. Test-retest reliability represents a measure's repeatability.

Suppose a researcher at one time attempts to measure buying intentions and finds that 12 percent of a population is willing to purchase a product. A few weeks later under similar conditions, the researcher assesses intentions in the population again and finds the result to be 12 percent. The measure thus, appears reliable. High-stability correlation or consistency between two measures at time 1 and time 2 indicates high reliability.

Assume that a person does not change his or her mind about dark beer with time. A scale item like the one shown below:

I prefer dark beer to all other types of beer.

Should produce the same score in November 2012 as it would in April 2013 or November 2013. When a measuring instrument produces unpredictable results from one testing to the next, the results lack consistency and suggest an unreliable measure. Research based on unreliable measures is itself unreliable because of measurement error.

Reliability is a necessary but not sufficient condition for validity. A reliable scale may not be valid. For example, a purchase intention measurement technique may consistently indicate that

test-retest method

Administering the same scale or measure to the same respondents at two separate points in time to test for stability.

Reliability

Scale: Positive Feelings

Case Processing Summary

		N	%
Cases	Valid	457	100.0
	Excluded[a]	0	.0
	Total	457	100.0

a. Listwise deletion based on all variables in the procedure.

Reliability Statistics

Cronbach's Alpha	N of Items
.960	5

Item-Total Statistics

	Scale Mean if Item Deleted	Scale Variance if Item Deleted	Corrected Item-Total Correlation	Cronbach's Alpha if Item Deleted
Excited...	14.58	51.459	.859	.955
Happy	14.16	51.611	.886	.950
Interested	14.04	50.138	.891	.949
Pleased	14.29	51.352	.910	.946
Satisfied	14.30	51.603	.886	.950

Here are some results from using a software package to estimate coefficient α for a five-item scale measuring the positive feelings shoppers had during a shopping trip. The results show a value of 0.96 for the scale. Also, the item-total statistics indicate that all the items correlate highly with the scale. Overall, these are positive results.

validity

The accuracy of a measure or the extent to which a score truthfully represents a concept.

face (content) validity

Extent to which individual measures' content match the intended concept's definition.

20 percent of those sampled are willing to purchase a new product. Whether the measure is valid depends on whether 20 percent of the population indeed purchases the product. A reliable but invalid instrument will yield consistently inaccurate results. Perhaps you've come across results from polls or other research in the media that appear reliable but inaccurate in this manner?

Validity

Good measures should be both precise and accurate. Reliability represents how precise a measure is in that the different attempts at measuring the same thing converge on the same point. Accuracy deals more with how a measure assesses the intended concept. **Validity** is the accuracy of a measure or the extent to which a score truthfully represents a concept.

Achieving validity is not a simple matter. Researchers who study job performance often result to asking employees to self-rate their own performance. A multiple-item, self-rated performance scale is usually reliable, but does one's opinion reflect his/her actual job performance? Perhaps some bias creeps in, causing the scale to represent something besides true job performance.

Researchers need to know if their measures are valid. The question of validity expresses the researcher's concern with accurate measurement. Validity addresses the problem of whether a measure indeed measures what it is supposed to measure. When a measure lacks validity, any conclusions based on that measure are also likely faulty.

Students should be able to empathize with the following validity problem. Consider the controversy about highway patrol officers using radar guns to clock speeders. An officer clocks a driver at 75 mph in a 55 mph zone. However, the same radar gun registered 28 mph when aimed at a house. The error occurred because the radar gun had picked up impulses from the electrical system of the squad car's idling engine. The house was probably not speeding—and the radar gun was probably not completely valid.

Establishing Validity

Researchers attempt to assess validity in many ways. The following questions represent some of these approaches:

■ Is there a consensus among my colleagues that my attitude scale measures represent the definition of an attitude?
■ Does my measure correlate with other measures of the same concept?
■ Does the behavior expected from my measure predict actual observed behavior?

The three basic aspects of validity are *face* or *content validity, criterion validity,* and *construct validity.*

Face (content) validity refers to the extent to which individual measures' content match the intended concept's definition. One way to check this involves using a few expert judges to judge how well each item in a scale represents the concept definition. This test provides evidence of face validity when the judges tend to agree that the items' content matches the concept. If expert judges cannot be used, the researcher him/herself must carefully inspect each item's content.

A golfer may hit reliable but not valid putts and thus tend to miss them in some repeated fashion. This golfer's putts tend to converge to the left of—rather than in—the hole!

Criterion validity addresses the question, "Does my measure correlate with measures of the similar concepts or known quantities?" Criterion validity may be classified as either *concurrent validity* or *predictive validity,* depending on the time sequence in which the new measurement scale and the criterion measure are correlated. If the researcher applies the new measure at the same time as the criterion measure, then concurrent validity is relevant. Predictive validity is established when a new measure predicts a future event. The two measures differ only on the basis of a time dimension.

A practical example of predictive validity is illustrated by a commercial research firm's test of the relationship between a rough commercial's effectiveness (as determined, for example, by recall scores) and a finished commercial's effectiveness (also by recall scores). Ad agencies test animatic, photomatic, or live-action rough commercials before developing actual finished commercials. One marketing research consulting firm suggests that this testing has high predictive validity. Rough commercial recall scores provide correct estimates of the final finished commercial recall scores more than 80 percent of the time.[11]

Construct validity exists when a measure reliably measures and truthfully represents a unique concept. Construct validity consists of several components, including:

- Face or content validity
- Convergent validity
- Criterion or validity
- Discriminant validity

Construct Validity

Exists when a measure reliably measures and truthfully represents a unique concept; consists of several components including face validity, convergent validity, criterion validity, and discriminant validity.

criterion validity

The ability of a measure to correlate with other standard measures of similar constructs or established criteria.

construct validity

Exists when a measure reliably measures and truthfully represents a unique concept; consists of several components including face validity, convergent validity, criterion validity, and discriminant validity.

convergent validity

Depends on internal consistency so that multiple measures converge on a consistent meaning.

discriminant validity

Represents how unique or distinct is a measure; a scale should not correlate too highly with a measure of a different construct.

Convergent validity depends on internal consistency meaning that multiple measures converge on a consistent meaning. Highly reliable scales contain convergent validity. Criterion validity and face validity were discussed in the preceding paragraphs. **Discriminant validity** represents how unique or distinct is a measure. A scale should not correlate too highly with a measure of a different construct. For example, a customer satisfaction measure should not correlate too highly with a cognitive dissonance scale if the two concepts are truly different. As a rough rule of thumb, when two scales are correlated above 0.75, discriminant validity may be an issue. Multivariate procedures like factor analysis can be useful in establishing construct validity. The reader is referred to other sources for a more detailed discussion.[12]

Reliability vs. Validity

The differences between reliability and validity can be illustrated by picturing target shooting, as illustrated in Exhibit 10.5. Suppose someone fires a competitive shooter fires an equal number of rounds with a century-old rifle and a modern rifle.[13] The shots from the older gun end up considerably scattered, but those from the newer gun cluster closely together. The inconsistency of the old rifle compared with that of the new one indicates lower reliability.

The target on the right of the exhibit shows results from a new, low-priced air gun. All the shots cluster tightly but on the edge of the target. The shots fired with the new gun indicate a reliable tool because they are consistent with each other. The shots are reliable, but not valid because they miss the target by a substantial margin. If you've tried to target shoot at a carnival, you may have used a gun like this.

What Is an Attitude?

What does one mean when they accuse someone of having a "bad attitude"? The idea is that one's disposition about the relevant matter is not positive and the result is less than productive behavior. Formally, an **attitude** is a social-psychological concept defined as a relatively enduring predisposition to respond consistently to various things including people, activities, events, and objects. Attitudes are predispositions toward behavior and as such represent rules that inform a person of the appropriate reaction in a given situation. If someone has a negative attitude toward broccoli, then that person is likely to avoid eating, smelling, or even approaching any dish with the obvious presence of broccoli. If a fan "loves the Bulldogs," he or she is more likely to buy tickets to their games and to attend them. Additionally, attitudes are latent constructs and because of this, they are not directly observable.

Attitudes are thought to have three components:

attitude

An enduring disposition to consistently respond in a given manner to various aspects of the world; composed of affective, cognitive, and behavioral components.

■ An affective component that expresses how much affinity someone has toward the relevant matter. More simply, this is the feeling of liking or not liking something. For example, a consumer might say "I love Chick-fil-A." This expresses strong affinity.

EXHIBIT 10.5
Reliability and Validity on Target

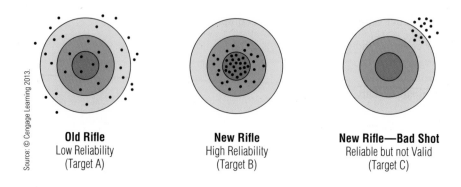

Source: © Cengage Learning 2013.

Old Rifle
Low Reliability
(Target A)

New Rifle
High Reliability
(Target B)

New Rifle—Bad Shot
Reliable but not Valid
(Target C)

- A cognitive component that represents a person's awareness and knowledge of the relevant matter; in other words, what a person believes about the subject matter. When someone says, "Chick-fil-A has a wide selection," they are expressing a belief about this particular consumer alternative. Together with other relevant beliefs about Chick-fil-A, the beliefs comprise knowledge, which need not be correct to shape attitude.

- A behavioral component representing the action undertaken as a result of the affective and cognitive components. If the attitude is positive, the person will display approach responses. If the attitude is negative, the person will display avoidance reactions. "I'll never eat at Chick-fil-A again" expresses a behavioral component of a negative attitude. Researchers often capture the behavioral component using intentions toward future behavior.

Sometimes researchers need to study overall attitude. Other times, they may focus on one of these components more than others. Whenever overall attitude or any of these components are measured through survey research, the researcher is conducting attitudinal research.

Research results generally show that attitudes do predict behavior with at least some accuracy and for this reason; marketing managers place a great deal of importance on attitudes. If a marketing approach changes consumers' aggregate attitude about a product, sales volume will increase accordingly. If employees' aggregate attitude about their job improves, their work output is likely to increase in proportion. Further, if knowledge about a product can be changed, the product can be repositioned to capture anew market. For example, Lucozade was transformed from a liquid nutritional supplement for pediatric digestive illness patients into a sports and fitness drink for adults.[14]

This brand transformation required careful coordination of communications with consumers that involved advertising and merchandising. Additionally, a great deal of survey research tracked consumers' attitudes along the way.

Attitudinal Rating Scales

Researchers face a wide variety of choices in measuring attitudinal concepts. One reason for the variety is that no complete consensus exists over just what constitutes an attitude or an attitudinal variable. Researchers generally agree, however, that the affective, cognitive, and behavioral components of an attitude can each be measured effectively. However, attitudes may also be interpreted using qualitative techniques like those discussed in Chapter 5. Even if no agreement exists

Image courtesy of Susan Van Etten

Lucozade was transformed from a product for children with stomach problems into a sports, fitness, and energy product for adults. Attitudinal research helped track this brand transformation.

over the precise boundaries delineating attitudinal variables from others, researchers widely apply approaches used to measure attitude components in measuring many attitude-like variables.

Physiological Measures

Research may assess the affective (emotional) components of attitudes through physiological measures like galvanic skin response (GSR), blood pressure, magnetic resonance imaging (MRI),and pupil dilation. These measures provide a means of assessing affect without verbally questioning the respondent. In general, they can provide a gross measure of likes or dislikes, but they are not extremely sensitive to the different gradients of an attitude. Researchers studying attitudes toward music used a physiological approach in studying what types of music tend to become popular.[15] MRI recordings, for instance, showing brain activity consistent with increased liking, correlate positively with purchases of music.

Rating Scales

In contrast to physiological measures, an entire class of psychological measures involve gaining a respondent's structured response to a specific query or stimulus. Often, the research asks the respondent to ranking, rate, sort, or choose one of multiple responses as a way of indicating a response. A **ranking task** requires the respondent to rank-order a small number of stores, brands, feelings, or objects on the basis of overall preference or some characteristic of the stimulus. **Rating** requires the respondent to estimate the magnitude or the extent to which some characteristic exists. Ratings produce quantitative scores.

The rating task involves marking a response indicating one's position using one or more attitudinal or cognitive scales. A **sorting** task might present the respondent with several product concepts on cards and require the respondent to classify the concepts by placing the cards into stacks each representing a different meaning. Another type of attitude measurement is a **choice** between two or more alternatives. If a respondent chooses one object over another, the researcher assumes that the respondent prefers the chosen object, at least in this setting.

Marketing researchers commonly use rating scales to measure attitudes. This section discusses many rating scales designed to enable respondents to report the intensity of their attitudes. In its most basic form, attitude scaling requires that an individual agree or disagree with a statement or indicate how much a term describes his or her feeling. For example, respondents in a political poll may be asked whether they either agree or disagree with a statement like, "Politicians are likable." Or, an individual might indicate whether he or she likes or dislikes jalapeño bean dip. This type of self-rating scale merely classifies respondents into one of two categories, thus having only the properties of a nominal scale, and the types of mathematical analysis that may be used with this basic scale are limited.

Simple attitude scaling can be a practical way of implementing a survey when questionnaires are extremely long, when respondents have little education, or for other specific reasons. In fact, a number of simplified scales are merely checklists where a respondent indicates past experience, preference, or likes and dislikes simply by checking an item. A recent checklist survey showed that 77 percent of small business owners believe small and medium-size businesses "have less bureaucracy," 76 percent said smaller companies "have more flexibility" than large ones, and 73 percent were optimistic heading into 2008 as opposed to 75 percent indicating optimism at the end of 2006. Looking back, these results may have signaled economic problems. Researchers can get simple but useful answers like these very quickly through simple questioning techniques.

Most attitude theorists believe that attitudes vary along a continuum. Thus, the purpose of an attitude scale is to find an individual's position on the continuum. However, simple nominal scales do not allow for fine distinctions between attitudes. Several other scale approaches make foe more precise measurements. The following sections describe popular techniques for measuring attitudes.

---

ranking

A measurement task that requires respondents to rank-order a small number of stores, brands, or objects on the basis of overall preference or some characteristic of the stimulus.

rating

A measurement task that requires respondents to estimate the magnitude of a characteristic or quality that a brand, store, or object possesses.

sorting

A measurement task that presents a respondent with several objects or product concepts and requires the respondent to arrange the objects into piles or classify the product concepts.

choice

A measurement task that identifies preferences by requiring respondents to choose between two or more alternatives.

Measuring the Affect Component

Not all rating approaches are the same. Exhibit 10.6 displays an interesting approach to get respondents to rate their affect toward some object. Respondents are asked to choose a "manikin" from each row to show not only their general affective state (like or dislike), but the degree to which they get emotionally aroused (the middle row), and how much the thing being rated makes them feel small (unimportant) or important. This approach is useful in all manner of measures involving emotion.

Source: © Cengage Learning 2013.

EXHIBIT 10.6
Novel Approach to Rating Affect
Source: Morris, J.D. (1995), "Observations:SAM: The Self-Assessment Manikin: An Efficient Cross-Cultural Measurement of Emotional Response," *Journal of Advertising Research*, 35, 63–68.

©Tyler Olson/Shutterstock

● ● ● ● ● ● ●

Generally, consumers act in a way consistent with their attitudes. Therefore, attitudes are a popular marketing research topic.

Category Scales

The simplest rating scale contains only two response categories: agree/disagree. For instance, a researcher might include a simple question like this:

I like the idea of attending Cool State University.

   ☐ *Yes*   ☐ *No*

Expanding the response categories provides the respondent with more flexibility in the rating task. Even more information is provided if the categories are ordered according to a particular descriptive or evaluative dimension. Consider the following question:

How often do you think favorably about attending Cool State University?

☐ *Never*   ☐ *Rarely*   ☐ *Sometimes*   ☐ *Often*   ☐ *Very often*

category scale

A rating scale that consists of several response categories, often providing respondents with alternatives to indicate positions on a continuum.

This **category scale** measures attitude with greater sensitivity than a two-point response scale. By having more choices, the potential exists to provide more information. However, a researcher will create measurement error if he/she uses a category scale for something that is truly bipolar (yes/no, female/male, member/non-member, and so on).

Response category wording is an extremely important factor. Exhibit 10.7 shows some common wordings used in category scales measuring common marketing research variables. As you

EXHIBIT 10.7 Selected Category Scales

Quality				
Excellent	Good	Fair	Poor	
Very good	Fairly good	Neither good nor bad	Not very good	Not good at all
Well above average	Above average	Average	Below average	Well below average
Importance				
Very important	Fairly important	Neutral	Not so important	Not at all important
Interest				
Very interested	Somewhat interested			Not very interested
Satisfaction				
Completely satisfied	Somewhat satisfied	Neither satisfied nor dissatisfied	Somewhat dissatisfied	Completely dissatisfied
Very satisfied	Quite satisfied	Somewhat satisfied	Not at all satisfied	
Frequency				
All of the time	Very often	Often	Sometimes	Hardly ever
Very often	Often	Sometimes	Rarely	Never
All of the time	Most of the time	Some of the time	Just now and then	
Truth				
Very true	Somewhat true	Not very true	Not at all true	
Definitely yes	Probably yes	Probably no	Definitely no	
Uniqueness				
Very different	Somewhat different	Slightly different	Not at all different	
Extremely unique	Very unique	Somewhat unique	Slightly unique	Not at all unique

can see, the more categories, the more difficulty a researcher has in coming up with precise and readily understandable category labels.

The Likert Scale

The Likert scale may well be the most commonly applied scale format in marketing research. Likert scales are simple to administer and understand. Likert scales were developed by and named after RensisLikert, a twentieth-century social scientist. With a **Likert scale**, respondents indicate their attitudes by checking how strongly they disagree or agree with carefully constructed statements. The scale results reveal the respondent's attitude ranging from very positive to very negative. Individuals generally choose from multiple response alternatives such as strongly agree, agree, neutral, disagree, and strongly disagree. Researchers commonly employ five choices, although they also often use six, seven, or even more response points. In the following example, from a study of food-shopping behavior, there are five alternatives:

Likert scale

A measure of attitudes designed to allow respondents to rate how strongly they disagree or agree with carefully constructed statements, ranging from very positive to very negative attitudes toward an object.

I like to go to Walmart when buying food for my family.				
Strongly Disagree	Disagree	Neutral	Agree	Strongly Agree
☐	☐	☐	☐	☐
(1)	(2)	(3)	(4)	(5)

Researchers assign scores to each possible response. In this example, numerical scores of 1, 2, 3, 4, and 5 are assigned to each level of agreement, respectively. Here, strong agreement indicates the most favorable attitude on the statement, and a numerical score of 5 is assigned to this response.

Realize that if the statement were worded in a way that indicated dislike for shopping for food at Walmart, a 5 would mean a less favorable attitude about this activity. For example, responses to the item above could even be combined with those from an item like this:

Walmart is a bad place to shop for fresh foods.				
Strongly Disagree	Disagree	Neutral	Agree	Strongly Agree
☐	☐	☐	☐	☐
(1)	(2)	(3)	(4)	(5)

However, before a composite scale could be created, the responses to this item would have to be reverse coded, as shown previously. An attitude score is arbitrary and has little cardinal meaning—in other words, attitude scores are at best interval and not ratio. They could also just as easily be scored so that a higher score indicated less favorable attitudes. However, the convention is to score attitude scales so that a higher score means a more favorable attitude.

Selecting Items for a Likert Scale

Typically, a researcher will use multiple items to represent a single attitudinal concept. The researcher may generate a large number of statements before putting together the final questionnaire. A pretest may be conducted using these items, allowing for an *item analysis* to be performed. The item analysis helps select items that evoke a wide response (meaning all respondents are not selecting the same response point such as all strongly agree) allowing the item to discriminate among those with positive and negative attitudes. Items are also analyzed for clarity or unusual response patterns. Thus, the final Likert items should be clearly understood and elicit an accurate range of responses corresponding to respondents' true attitudes.

Assessing Item and Scale Quality

Another big advantage of using multiple items is that one can assess reliability and validity using a wide range of statistical approaches. For instance, coefficient α for reliability can only be assessed with multiple items. Later chapters will discuss multivariate procedures for assessing validity in more detail. These are also facilitated by using multiple items. In the end, only a set of items that show acceptable reliability and validity should be summed or averaged for scores representing hypothetical constructs. Unfortunately, not all researchers are willing or able to thoroughly assess reliability and validity. Without this assessment, the researcher has no way of knowing exactly what the items represent or how well they represent anything of interest.

Semantic Differential

semantic differential

A measure of attitudes that consists of a series of bipolar rating scales with opposite terms on either end.

A **semantic differential** is a scale type on which respondents describe their attitude using a series of bipolar rating scales. Bipolar rating scales involve respondents choosing between opposing adjectives—such as "good" and "bad," "modern" and "old-fashioned," or "clean" and "dirty." One adjective anchors the beginning and the other the end (or poles) of the scale. The subject makes repeated judgments about the concept under investigation on each of the scales. Exhibit 10.8 shows an example semantic differential approach for assessing consumer attitudes toward hypermarts.

EXHIBIT 10.8

An Example of a Semantic Differential Scale

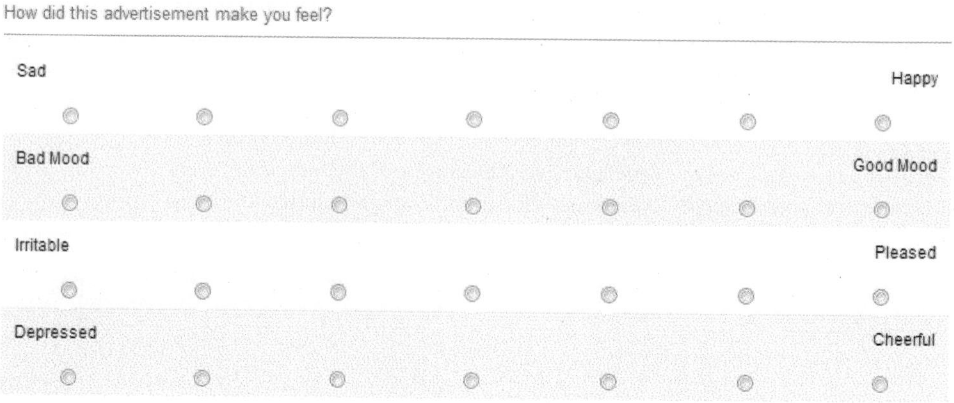

Source: © Cengage Learning 2013.

The scoring of the semantic differential can be illustrated using the scale bounded by the anchors "complex" and "simple." Respondents are instructed to check the place that indicates the nearest appropriate adjective. From left to right, the scale intervals represent the belief that the stimulus is somewhere between extremely simple and extremely complex. One advantage provided by using scale labels over each category is the ability to influence the distribution of responses. If, for instance, respondents are expected to respond toward the extremely complex end of the scale, the research may try an unbalanced labeling with the neutral answer appearing closer to the left end of the scale rather than right in the middle.

Extremely Simple	Very Simple	Slightly Simple	Neither Simple nor Complex	Slightly Complex	Very Complex	Extremely Complex
☐	☐	☐	☐	☐	☐	☐
(−3)	(−2)	(−1)	(0)	(1)	(2)	(3)

Semantic Differentials and Meaning

The semantic differential technique originally was developed as a method for measuring the meanings of objects or the "semantic space" of interpersonal experience.[16] Researchers see the semantic differential as versatile and useful in a wide variety of business situations.

When opposites are available, the semantic differential is a good scale choice. In typical attitude or image studies, simple anchors such as very unfavorable and very favorable work well. However, the validity of the semantic differential depends on finding scale anchors that are semantic opposites and this can sometimes prove difficult. For example, consider the following scale in which the respondent is asked to place a check on the space closest to the way they feel about the phrase:

Shopping at Bebe makes me:

Happy __ __ __ __ __ __ Sad

Few would question that sad is the opposite of happy. However, what if this were combined with an item capturing how angry shopping at Bebe makes a respondent feel? Then, what would the opposite of angry be? Clearly, using happy as the opposite of angry would present a problem because the items above suggests happy is the opposite of sad. Thus, a semantic differential may not be best for capturing anger unless a distinctive and unambiguous opposite exists.

Scoring Semantic Differentials

Like Likert scales, a numerical score can be assigned to each position on a semantic differential scale. For a seven-point semantic differential the scores could be 1, 2, 3, 4, 5, 6, 7 or −3, −2, −1, 0, +1, +2, +3. Marketing researchers generally assume that the semantic differential provides interval data. This assumption does have critics who argue that the data have only ordinal properties because the numerical scores are arbitrary and there is no way of knowing that the differences between choices are equal. Practically, the vast majority of social science researchers treat semantic differential scales as metric (at least interval). This is justified because the amount of error introduced by assuming the intervals between choices are equal (even though this is uncertain at best) is fairly small.

Constant-Sum Scale

A **constant-sum scale** demands that respondents divide points among several attributes to indicate their relative importance. Suppose Samsung wishes to determine the importance of smartphone attributes such as Internet capability, text messaging, app availability, voice clarity, and economical service plan. Respondents might divide a constant sum of 100 points to indicate the relative importance of those attributes:

constant-sum scale

A measure of attitudes in which respondents are asked to divide a constant sum to indicate the relative importance of attributes; respondents often sort cards, but the task may also be a rating task.

Divide 100 points among the following characteristics of a smart phone indicating how important each characteristic is when selecting a new phone.

Internet Capability	0
Ease of Text Messaging	0
App Availability	0
Voice Clarity	0
Economical Service Plan	0
Total	0

Source: © Cengage Learning 2013.

The constant-sum scale requires respondents to understand that their responses should total to the total number of points. In the case above, that number is 100. As the number of stimuli increases, this technique becomes increasingly complex. Fortunately, electronic questionnaires eliminate math errors by having the software trigger an error notice whenever responses do not match the total. The respondent could adjust the responses until the sums do indeed match the total. If respondents follow the instructions correctly, the results will approximate interval measures.

This technique may be used for measuring brand preference. The approach, which is similar to the paired-comparison method, is as follows:

Divide 100 points among the following brands based on your degree of preference for each:

Coca-Cola	30
Pepsi-Cola	25
Dr. Pepper	45
Total	100

Although the constant sum scale is widely used, strictly speaking, the scale is flawed because the last response is completely determined by the way the respondent has scored the other choices. Although this is probably somewhat complex to understand, the fact is that practical reasons often outweigh this concern.

Graphic Rating Scales

graphic rating scale

A measure of attitude that allows respondents to rate an object by choosing any point along a graphic continuum. Electronic slider scales work much the same way.

A **graphic rating scale** presents respondents with a graphic continuum. The respondents are allowed to choose any point on the continuum to indicate their attitude. Exhibit 10.9 shows a traditional graphic scale, ranging from one extreme position to the opposite position. Typically a respondent's score is determined by measuring the length (in millimeters) from one end of the graphic continuum to the point marked by the respondent. Many researchers believe that scoring in this manner strengthens the assumption that graphic rating scales of this type are interval scales. Alternatively, the researcher may divide the line into predetermined scoring categories (lengths) and record respondents' marks accordingly. In other words, the graphic rating scale has the advantage of allowing the researcher to choose any interval desired for scoring purposes. Electronic questionnaires allow the use of a slider scale. The sliders function much the same as a graphics rating scale.

EXHIBIT 10.9
Graphic Rating Scale

Source: © Cengage Learning 2013.

Please evaluate each attribute in terms of how important it is to you by placing an X at the position on the horizontal line that most reflects your feelings.

Seating comfort	Not important _____	Very important
In-flight meals	Not important _____	Very important
Airfare	Not important _____	Very important

Graphic rating scales are not limited to straight lines as sources of visual communication. Picture response options or another type of graphic continuum may be used to enhance communication with respondents.

Research to investigate children's attitudes has used happy-sad face scales. Exhibit 10.9 illustrates one such approach. Here, the respondent chooses an attitude by sliding the scale up and down using the tab to the right of the face. As the respondent moves the tab up or down, the face smiles or frowns, correspondingly. The first respondent is fairly pleased with the idea of hot breakfast items at Starbucks. However, the second respondent has a very negative attitude toward the idea. Notice the position of the tab corresponding to each face.

Among the attitude rating approaches discussed in this chapter, Likert scales and semantic differentials account for the majority of applications. The Research Snapshot suggests that attitudes can help make a story complete.

Click, Click, Click

Marketing metrics, as discussed earlier, are clearly increasingly being applied. The quantitative results can be extremely useful in helping determine how much some marketing tactic is really worth. For example, when marketers use a banner ad on a Web site, the ad agency can monitor the way click-through rates change with varying ad placements and characteristics. For example, do click-throughs become more likely when the ad is placed in a content consistent site such as an ad for an airline in on island resort's website? Using metrics like this, the ad agency might be able to inform clients how much an ad placement is worth.

However, recent research suggests these numbers do not tell the whole story because they ignore consumer attitudes. A banner ad, for instance, may affect consumer awareness and attitudes even if a consumer does not click through to view the contents of the actual Web page. For example, when British Airways introduced its Club World perks for good customers, the click-through rate on banner ads may have been low, but a test showed that respondents who were exposed to the ads were approximately 20 percent more likely to be aware of Club

World than respondents who were not exposed to these ads. Thus, the click metrics did not tell the whole story. Similarly, leading financial institutions supplement their marketing metrics with attitudinal research to better understand which consumers are likely to become loyal. The attitudinal research helps firms better understand the customer-based brand equity. In the end, behavioral metrics have not replaced attitudinal research. The two approaches complement each other quite well.

Sources: Howell, N., "Looking Deeper," *New Media Age* (December 1, 2005), 24–25; Taylor, S.A. and G.L. Hunter, "Understanding Brand Equity in Financial Services," *Journal of Services Marketing*, 21, no. 4 (2007), 241–52.

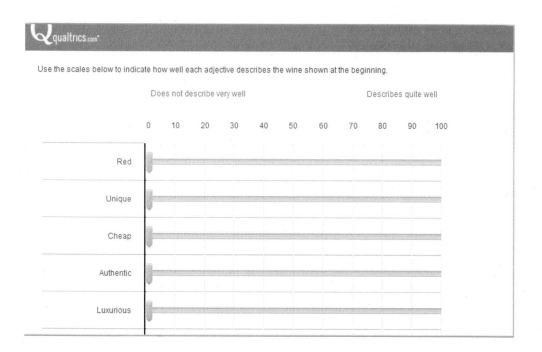

Ranking

A ranking is different than a rating scale in that respondents simply order alternatives on a characteristic. Consumers often rank-order their preferences so, in this sense, ranking scales have considerable validity. An ordinal scale may be developed by asking respondents to rank-order (from most preferred to least preferred) a set of objects or attributes. Respondents easily understand the task of rank-ordering product attributes or arranging a set of brand names according to preference. Like the constant-sum scale however, the ranking scale suffers from inflexibility in that if we know how someone ranked five out of six alternatives, we know the answer to the sixth. Thus, a respondent does not rate each category independently as in a typical ratings scale. Additionally, ordinal scaling only allows us to know that one option is preferred over another—not how much one option is preferred over another.

> *"My tastes are very simple. I only want the best."*
>
> —OSCAR WILDE

paired comparison

A measurement technique that involves presenting the respondent with two objects and asking the respondent to pick the preferred object; more than two objects may be presented, but comparisons are made in pairs.

Paired Comparisons

Consider a situation in which a chain saw manufacturer learned that a competitor had introduced a new lightweight (6-pound) chainsaw. The manufacturer's lightest chainsaw weighed 9 pounds. Executives wondered if they needed to introduce a 6-pound chainsaw into the product line. The research design employed a **paired comparison** approach. The company built a prototype of a 6-pound chainsaw. Then, they painted both the 9- and 6-pound saws from their competitor the same color as their own 9- and 6-pound chainsaws. Then, color differences would not be responsible for any preferences. Respondents then saw two chainsaws at a time and picked the one they preferred. Three pairs of comparisons allowed the researchers to determine the saw each respondent liked best.

The following question illustrates the typical format for asking about paired comparisons.

I would like to know your overall opinion of two brands of adhesive bandages. They are Curad and Band-Aid. Overall, which of these two brands—Curad or Band-Aid—do you think is the better one? Or are both the same?

Curad is better. ____
Band-Aid is better. ____
They are the same. ____

If researchers wish to compare four brands of pens on the basis of attractiveness or writing quality, six comparisons $[(n)(n-1)/2]$ will be necessary. Paired comparisons sometimes require respondents to assess similarity instead of preference by asking which of the two choices is more similar to a third choice. With either similarity or preference, if the number of comparisons is too large, respondents become fatigued and do not carefully discriminate the choices.

Direct Assessment of Consumer Attitudes

Attitudes, as hypothetical constructs, cannot be observed directly. We can, however, infer one's attitude by the way he or she responds to multiple attitude indicators. The researcher can then sum the scores on the multiple indicators of attitude. Consider the following three semantic differential items that may capture a consumer's attitude toward Microsoft Word:

very bad ___ ___ ___ ___ ___ ___ ___very good

very unfavorable ___ ___ ___ ___ ___ ___ ___very favorable

very negative ___ ___ ___ ___ ___ ___ ___ very positive

A summed score over these three items would represent a latent (unobservable) attitude construct. How do you feel about Microsoft Word? Use the scale to find your score.

The decision whether to use ranking, sorting, rating, or a choice technique is determined largely by the problem definition and especially by the type of statistical analysis desired. For example, ranking provides only ordinal data, limiting the statistical techniques that may be used.

How Many Scale Categories or Response Positions?

Should a category scale have four, five, or seven response positions or categories? Or should the researcher use a graphic scale with an infinite number of positions? The original developmental research on the semantic differential indicated that five to eight points is optimal. However, the researcher must determine the number of meaningful positions that is best for the specific project. This issue of identifying how many meaningful distinctions respondents can practically make is basically a matter of sensitivity. For example, how sensitively can students discriminate the difficulty of college courses? The answer to the question may help determine the number of response categories.

The number of response categories can influence research conclusions. Think about a service employee asked to respond to an item asking about job satisfaction using a two-point response scale of either "no" or "yes." Can the two-point scale adequately capture the range of responses that employees might actually feel? Would we really expect that all people who respond "yes" have the same amount of satisfaction? Typically, a yes or no satisfaction question will yield about 80 percent "yes" responses. In other words, the data are typically skewed with a small number of scale points. If the scale is expanded to the typical five-point Likert format, the "yes" responses are likely to be spread across multiple categories. Similarly, a scale with too few points may suppress variance that truly exists. Thus, a scale should be adequately sensitive to capture a respondent's opinion or feelings.

What happens if the same question is asked with scales of varying numbers of response categories? Some research suggests that skewness is reduced by including more scale points, particularly for attitudinal- and satisfaction-type items. Additionally, including more scale points produces less extreme patterns of results with typical responses closer to the midpoint of the scale. Thus, as long as adding category responses does not become taxing to respondents, more categories are better than fewer. However, scales with five-to-ten scale points typically display results suggesting they are appropriate for use in statistical procedures like regression.[17]

Recent research suggests a caveat to this finding. The research finds that less capable respondents sometimes provide more valid responses with fewer rather than more scale points.[18] In addition, the inclusion of labels over all scale points tends to produce slightly more acquiescence bias than a scale with labels only on the end point. As a result, the use of labels over all choices is preferable when scores will be compared directly across respondents but scores with only the ends labeled work are preferable for use with statistics like regression analysis.

Balanced or Unbalanced Rating Scale?

The fixed-alternative format may be balanced or unbalanced. For example, the following question, which asks about parent-child decisions relating to television program watching, is a **balanced rating scale**:

> *Who decides which movies your family will see?*

Child decides all of the time.	*Child decides most of the time.*	*Child and parent decide together.*	*Parent decides most of the time.*	*Parent decides all of the time.*
____	____	____	____	____

balanced rating scale
A fixed-alternative rating scale with an equal number of positive and negative categories; a neutral point or point of indifference is at the center of the scale.

This scale is balanced because a neutral point, or point of indifference, is at the center of the scale.

Unbalanced rating scales may be used when responses are expected to be distributed at one end of the scale, producing a skewed distribution. The skewed distribution may indicate error and can also interfere with the ability to draw meaningful statistical inferences. Marketing researchers often face situations where "end-piling" will occur. One reason for this is that researchers often ask questions for which respondents are fully expected to give more positive than negative responses. For instance, satisfaction scales (job or customer) generally show this pattern. After all, if an employee has stayed in one job for some years or a customer has already selected a place to do business, we should expect that they would provide a positive response. Unbalanced scales, such as the following one, may mitigate this type of "end piling":

unbalanced rating scale
A fixed-alternative rating scale that has more response categories at one end than the other, resulting in an unequal number of positive and negative categories.

Completely Dissatisfied	Dissatisfied	Somewhat Satisfied	Satisfied	Completely Satisfied
☐	☐	☐	☐	☐

The scale contains three "satisfied" responses and only two "dissatisfied" responses above. Researchers choose between a balanced or unbalanced scale, depending on the nature of the concept or knowledge about attitudes toward what is measured. When researchers expect respondents are predisposed toward one end of a concept or the other, unbalanced scales are appropriate.

Satisfaction and importance scores usually skew toward positive responses so unbalanced scales may better capture any true variance that exists.

Forced-Choice Scales?

forced-choice rating scale

A fixed-alternative rating scale that requires respondents to choose one of the fixed alternatives.

In many situations, a respondent does not have a strong attitude or opinion toward an issue. A **forced-choice rating scale** compels the respondent to answer using a design or technical aspect. Design-wise, the scale can eliminate a neutral response. A balanced scale with an even number of scale choices accomplishes this task. Consider the Likert item shown below:

	Strongly Disagree	Disagree	Slightly Disagree	Slightly Agree	Agree	Strongly Agree
The U.S. Federal Tax Code is fair to all American taxpayers	1	2	3	4	5	6

Source: © Cengage Learning 2013.

Technically, software can require a respondent to fill in an answer before finishing the survey. Unanswered items are flagged with an indicator.

non-forced-choice scale

A fixed-alternative rating scale that provides a "don't know" or "no opinion" category or allowing respondents to indicate that they cannot say which alternative is their choice.

Some IRBs suggest that forcing a response by using survey technology borders on unethical. One way around this problem is to use a **non-forced-choice scale**, including a "no opinion" category, as in the following example:

How does your attitude toward Community Bank compare with your attitude toward First National Bank?

☐ *Community Bank is much better than First National Bank.*
☐ *Community Bank is better than First National Bank.*
☐ *Community Bank is worse than First National Bank.*
☐ *Community Bank is much worse than First National Bank.*
☐ *Don't know.*

Asking this type of question allows the investigator to separate respondents who cannot make an honest comparison. The argument for forced choice is that people really do have attitudes, even if they are only somewhat knowledgeable about alternatives and should be able to answer the question. Respondents are not provided with an easy out by simply selecting "neutral." The use of forced-choice questions is associated with higher incidences of "no answer." Perhaps when respondents really can't make up their mind, they will leave an item blank if they are given that choice.

Opponents of the forced-choice approach argue that error results when respondents are required to answer questions for which they lack a firm position and they argue that response rates will be lower because respondents will quit when forced to answer questions. However, research indicates that forced-choice items do not tend to produce greater error supporting the argument that people do have some opinion on practically all issues.[19] Further, the total survey response rate and item response rate (leaving items blank or choosing "don't know") is not affected by force-choice approaches. Thus, researchers can apply forced choice responses without significant risk of harming the survey process.

"Refusing to have an opinion is a way of having one, isn't it?"

—LUIGI PIRANDELLO

Single or Multiple Items?

Whether to use a single item or a measure made up from responses to several items depends on several characteristics of the phenomenon.

- The complexity of the phenomenon measured
- The number of dimensions of the phenomenon
- The level of abstraction of the phenomenon

Hopefully, the definition of the concept studied makes answers to these questions simple. A single item can assess some very simple or concrete concepts.

"Did you watch *American Idol* last night?"

_____ yes _____ no

"Do you like pistachio ice cream?"

Don't Like at All _____ _____ _____ _____ _____ Like a Lot

Other indices such as social class require multiple items to form an index. Latent constructs like the personality trait of extraversion generally require multiple item scales.

Attitudes and Intentions

Behavioral researchers often model behavior as a function of intention, which in turn, is considered a function of attitudes. Attitudes are considered a function of a person's beliefs about anactivity weighted by their evaluations of those characteristics. This type of research is sometimes referred to as a **multi-attribute model** or reasoned action approach. For example, a consumer's attitude to opt in to SMS advertising can be modeled by their intention to do so, which in turn, is a function of their attitude.[20] Likewise, a researcher may first measure attitude as a way of knowing how likely a consumer would be to respond to a survey request posted on Facebook.

multi-attribute model

A model that constructs an attitude score based on the multiplicative sum of beliefs about an option times the evaluation of those belief characteristics.

Multi-Attribute Attitude Score

Attitudes are modeled with a multi-attribute approach by taking belief scores assessed with a type of rating scale like those described and multiplying each belief score by an evaluation also supplied using a type of rating scale, and then summing each resulting product. For instance, a series of Likert statements might assess a respondent's beliefs about the reliability, price, service, and styling of a Honda Fit.

	Strongly Disagree	Disagree	Neutral	Agree	Strongly Agree
The Honda Fit is the most reliable car in its class.	SD	D	N	A	SA
The Honda Fit has a low price for a car of its type.	SD	D	N	A	SA
I know that my Honda dealer will provide great service if I buy a Honda Fit.	SD	D	N	A	SA
The Honda Fit is one of the most stylish cars you can buy.	SD	D	N	A	SA

Then, respondents may use a simple rating scale to assess how good or bad each characteristic is. For example, the scale may appear something like this with instructions for the respondent to indicate the relative evaluation of each characteristic.

All things considered ...							
Buying a car that is reliable is							
Very bad	☐	☐	☐	☐	☐	☐	Very good
Buying a car with a low price is							
Very bad	☐	☐	☐	☐	☐	☐	Very good
Buying a car from a dealer with excellent service is							
Very bad	☐	☐	☐	☐	☐	☐	Very good
Buying a car with the latest styling is							
Very bad	☐	☐	☐	☐	☐	☐	Very good

The respondent's attitude toward buying a Honda Fit would be found by multiplying beliefs by evaluations. If a respondent provided the following belief scores using Likert scales for each belief item

Honda Fit reliability	*5*
Honda Fit pricing	*3*
Honda Fit dealer service	*2*
Honda Fit styling	*1*

and the following evaluation scores using the rating scale shown in the preceding

Reliability	*6*
Low pricing	*3*
Dealer service	*4*
Styling	*2*

then her attitude score could be computed as

Beliefs	×	Evaluations	=	(B)(E)
5		6		30
3		3		9
2		4		8
1		2		2
	Total			49

The multi-attribute attitude score for this consumer would be 49. A researcher may also ask respondents to rate a competitor's product. In this case, the product might be a Chevy Aveo. Using the same four characteristics, a score for the competitor can be obtained. The scores can then be compared to see which brand has a competitive advantage in terms of consumer attitudes.

Marketing researchers employ this approach frequently. The key advantages lie in how diagnostic the results can be. Not only can a researcher provide management with feedback on the relative attitude scores, but he or she can also identify characteristics that are most in need of being improved. In particular, poor belief scores on characteristics that respondents rate very favorably (or as highly important) indicate the characteristics that managers should change to improve competitive positioning. In this case, the Fit does well on reliability, and the strong belief score on this characteristic is largely responsible for shaping this consumer's attitude. If the Chevy Aveo scored only a 2 on reliability, the result would diagnose a problem that managers should address. The Aveo has a relatively low score on a very meaningful characteristic.

Behavioral Intention

According to reasoned action theory, people form intentions consistent with the multi-attribute attitude score. Intentions represent the behavioral expectations of an individual toward an attitudinal object. Typically, the component of interest to marketers is a buying intention, a tendency to seek additional information, or plans to visit a showroom. Category scales for measuring the behavioral component of an attitude ask about a respondent's likelihood of purchase or intention to perform a future action, using questions such as the following:

> *How likely is it that you will purchase a Honda Fit?*
>
> ____*I definitely will buy.*
> ____*I probably will buy.*
> ____*I might buy.*
> ____*I probably will not buy.*
> ____*I definitely will not buy.*

The attitude scores obtained above should correlate positively with the behavioral intent scores.

TIPS OF THE TRADE

- Hypotheses reveal the concepts to measure during the research.
- Coefficient α provides an estimate of scale reliability. It is only applicable to multiple item scales—particularly those with three or more items to be formed into a composite. The following guide can be used in judging the results from estimating coefficient α.
  - Above 0.8, very good reliability
    - Scale can be used as is from a reliability standpoint.
  - From 0.7 to 0.79, good reliability
    - Scale can be used as is from a reliability standpoint.
  - From 0.6 to 0.69, fair reliability
    - Scale can be used as is with caution.
    - Below 0.6, further refinement or modifications to the scale must be made before using.
  - Whenever there is a question about the number of scale points to use, it is better to use more rather than fewer scale points.
- Forced-choice questions have their place in marketing research
  - When using an even number of scale points, researchers should consider providing an option outside of the scale for respondents who simply cannot reach a decision.
- Attitude scores have no absolute meaning so results for more than one company are needed to provide reference.

Source: © Cengage Learning 2013.

:: SUMMARY

1. Determine what needs to be measured based on a research question or hypothesis. Researchers can determine what concepts must be measured by examining research questions and hypotheses. A hypothesis often states that one concept is related to another or that differences in an outcome concept will be observed across different groups. Therefore, the concepts listed in the hypotheses must have operational measures if the research testing them is performed.

2. Distinguish levels of scale measurement. Four levels of scale measurement can be identified. Each level is associated with increasingly more complex properties. Nominal scales assign numbers

recognize what a researcher means by common wine terms such as *Champagne* and *Burgundy*. They understand the terminology and see items using such terms as *accurately worded*. However, respondents with less expertise may interpret the same questions differently. These respondents may inaccurately associate all sparkling wine with "champagne" and may think of a California "burgundy" when answering the question (Champagne and Burgundy are both names that refer specifically to wines from regions in France).[3] Thus, even relatively simple questions can produce inaccurate answers.

Question Phrasing: Open- or Close-Ended Statements?

Questions can be phrased in any one of many ways. The research may choose from many standard question formats developed over time in previous research studies. This section presents a classification of question types and provides some helpful guidelines for writing questions.

Open-Ended Response versus Fixed-Alternative Questions

Two basic types of questions can be identified based on the amount of freedom respondents have in answering. The following sections define open-ended or closed question formats.

open-ended response questions

Questions that pose a problem and ask respondents to answer in their own words.

Open-ended response questions pose a problem or topic and ask respondents to answer in their own words. If the question is asked in a personal interview, the interviewer may probe for more information, as in the following examples:

■ What search engines can you think of other than Google.com?
■ How do you feel about the political and economic situation today?
■ What things do you like most about your iPad?
■ Why do you avoid buying clothes at Walmart?
■ How much extra are you willing to pay for an electric car?

fixed-alternative questions

Questions in which respondents are given specific, limited-alternative responses and asked to choose the one closest to their own viewpoint.

Open-ended response questions are free-answer questions. **Fixed-alternative questions**—sometimes called *closed-ended questions*—give respondents a limited number of specific alternative responses from which to choose. For example:

Do you blog/have your own Myspace/Facebook-type (or other social networking) page?	
Yes	No
☐	☐

How much time daily do you spend working on your blog/Myspace/Facebook-type page?			
I don't blog	less than 30 minutes a day	30 minutes to 1 hour a day	more than one hour/day
☐	☐	☐	☐

How much time do you spend studying Marketing Research weekly?			
Less than an hour	Between 1 and 2 hours	Between 2 and 3 hours	Greater than 3 hours
☐	☐	☐	☐

Studying for me is:						
Important						Not Important
○	○	○	○	○	○	○
Not Essential						Essential
○	○	○	○	○	○	○
Boring						Exciting
○	○	○	○	○	○	○

Courtesy of Qualtrics.com

How much more are you willing to pay for an electric car as opposed to a diesel car with the same horesepower?

- ○ $0
- ○ $1 - $249
- ○ $250 - $749
- ○ $750 - $1,499
- ○ $1,500 - $2,999
- ○ More than $3,000

Using Open-Ended Response Questions

Open-ended response questions offer several advantages. They are particularly beneficial when the researcher implements an exploratory research design. At this point, the relevant range of responses is not even known. Consider the open-ended question above concerning willingness to pay for an electric car. Are consumers willing to pay anything extra? What is the most that people might be willing to pay? Early on, the researcher may have no good idea of what to expect. The initial responses may be helpful in assessing ranges of responses that might be useful in developing structured responses used in a descriptive design. However, researchers can employ numeric open-ended responses with some confidence based on evidence suggesting that open-ended willingness to pay measures accurately forecast demand.[4]

Open-ended questions also identify which words and phrases people spontaneously give to the free-response question. Respondents are free to answer with whatever is at the top of their minds. By obtaining free and uninhibited responses, the researcher may find some unanticipated reaction toward the product. Such responses will reflect the flavor of the language that people use in talking about goods or services and thus may provide a source of new ideas for advertising copywriting or ways to word structured scale items.

Open-ended response questions also are valuable at the beginning of an interview. They are good first questions because they allow respondents to warm up to the questioning process and can stimulate memory for past events. The following question illustrates an open-ended question as an opener:

In the space below, tell us about an incident in which you felt a strong sense of nostalgia:

This may be followed up with structured questions about how the sense of nostalgia influences feelings about brands or retailers. Further, the open-ended response provides the potential for interpretive research approaches that potentially provide deep insights into the experience.

Open-ended responses also offer some disadvantages. The cost of administering open-ended response questions is on average higher than that of administering fixed-alternative questions. As each respondent's written answer offers a somewhat unique perspective, someone must manually summarize, categorize, or interpret the responses. Once a classification scheme is developed, a data editor can code responses within each data record.

Another potential disadvantage of open-ended responses is an increased possibility of interviewer bias. In an oral interview, interviewer instructions state that answers are to be recorded verbatim. Rarely does even the best interviewer record every word spoken by the respondent. Interviewers have a tendency to take shortcuts. When this occurs, the interviewer may well introduce error because the final answer may reflect a combination of the respondent's and interviewer's ideas.

Also, articulate individuals tend to give longer answers to open-ended response questions. Such respondents often are better educated and from higher-income groups and therefore may not be representative of the entire population, and yet they may give a large share of the responses.

Fixed-Alternative Questions

In contrast, fixed-alternative questions require less interviewer skill, take less time, and are easier for the respondent to answer. This is because answers to closed questions are classified into standardized groupings prior to data collection. Standardizing alternative responses to a question provides comparability of answers, which facilitates coding, tabulating, and ultimately interpreting the data.

However, when a researcher is unaware of the potential responses to a question, fixed-alternative questions obviously cannot be used. If the researcher assumes what the responses will be but is in fact wrong, he or she will have no way of knowing the extent to which the assumption was incorrect. Sometimes this type of error comes to light after the questionnaire has been used. Consider for instance the fixed-alternative question above about willingness to pay for an electric car. What if those particular categories were chosen without careful consideration of the potential range of responses and the more than half of respondents select "more than $3,000." Then, the question format has likely suppressed variation and should probably have included categories above $3,000.

Unanticipated alternatives emerge when respondents believe that closed answers do not adequately reflect their feelings. They may make comments to the interviewer or write additional answers on the questionnaire indicating that the exploratory research did not yield a complete array of responses. After the fact, researchers can't do very much to correct a closed question that does not provide a valid set of alternatives. Therefore, a researcher may find exploratory research with open-ended responses valuable before writing a descriptive questionnaire. The researcher should strive to ensure that there are sufficient response choices to include the relevant range of responses as well as an "other" choice for respondents who do not see their answer among the choice set.

How much more are you willing to pay for an electric car as opposed to a diesel car with the same horesepower?

- ○ $0
- ○ $1 - $249
- ○ $250 - $749
- ○ $750 - $1,499
- ○ $1,500 - $2,999
- ○ More than $3,000
- ○ Other _____

Also, a fixed-alternative question may tempt respondents to check an answer that is more prestigious or socially acceptable than the true answer. Rather than stating that they do not know why they chose a given product, they may select an alternative among those presented, or as a matter of convenience, they may select a given alternative rather than think of the most correct response.

Most questionnaires mix open-ended and closed questions. As we have discussed, each form has unique benefits. In addition, a change of pace can eliminate respondent boredom and fatigue.

Types of Fixed-Alternative Questions

This section identifies and classifies different types of fixed-alternative questions.

The **simple-dichotomy (dichotomous-alternative) question** requires the respondent to choose one of two alternatives. The answer can be a simple "yes" or "no" or a choice between "this" and "that." For example:

Did you make any calls with your home (landline) phone during the 7 days?

☐ *Yes*   ☐ *No*

Several types of questions provide the respondent with *multiple-choice alternatives*. The **multiple-choice question** requires the respondent to choose one—and only one—response from among several possible alternatives. For example:

Courtesy of Qualtrics.com

The **frequency-determination question** is a multiple-choice question that asks for an answer about the general frequency of occurrence. For example:

Courtesy of Qualtrics.com

Attitude rating scales, such as the Likert scale, semantic differential, Stapel scale, and so on, are fixed-alternative questions too. These scales were discussed in Chapter 10.

The **checklist question** allows the respondent to provide multiple answers to a single question. The respondent indicates past experience, preference, and the like merely by checking off items.

simple-dichotomy (dichotomous-alternative) question

A fixed-alternative question that requires the respondent to choose one of two alternatives.

multiple-choice question

A fixed-alternative question that requires the respondent to choose one response from among multiple alternatives.

frequency-determination question

A fixed-alternative question that asks for an answer about general frequency of occurrence.

checklist question

A fixed-alternative question that allows the respondent to provide multiple answers to a single question by checking off items.

In many cases the choices are adjectives that describe a particular object. A typical checklist question might ask the following:

Please check which of the following sources you use to get financial news?

- Personal stock broker
- Wall Street Journal
- Bloomberg
- The Financial Times
- Television News Programs
- Local Newspapers
- USA Today
- Facebook Friends

A major problem in developing dichotomous or multiple-choice alternatives is the framing of response alternatives. There should be no overlap among categories. Alternatives should be *mutually exclusive,* meaning only one dimension of an issue should be related to each alternative. The following listing of income groups illustrates a common error:

- Under $15,000
- $15,000–$35,000
- $35,000–$55,000
- $55,000–$75,000
- $75,000 or more

How many people with incomes of $35,000 will be in the second group, and how many will be in the third group? A respondent who actually had a $35,000 income could equally as likely choose either. Researchers have no way of knowing how a true $35,000-per-year respondent responded. Grouping alternatives without forethought about analysis is likely to diminish accuracy.

Also, few people relish being in the lowest category. To negate the potential bias caused by respondents' tendency to avoid an extreme category, researchers often include a category lower than the lowest expected answers.

Phrasing Questions for Self-Administered, Telephone, and Personal Interview Surveys

The means of data collection—telephone interview, personal interview, self-administered questionnaire—will influence what is the best question format and phrasing. In general, questions for mail, Internet, and telephone surveys must be less complex than those used in personal interviews. Questionnaires for telephone and personal interviews should be written in a conversational style. Exhibit 11.1 illustrates how a question may be revised for a different medium.

In a telephone survey about attitudes toward police services, the questionnaire not only asked about general attitudes such as how much respondents trust their local police officers and whether the police are "approachable," "dedicated," and so on, but also provided basic scenarios to help respondents put their expectations into words. For example, the interviewer asked respondents to imagine that someone had broken into their home and stolen items, and that the respondent called the police to report the crime. The interviewer asked how quickly or slowly the respondent expected the police to arrive.[5]

EXHIBIT **11.1**
Best Question Formats Vary
by the Interview Medium

Format for Internet or snail-mail self-administered survey:

How satisfied are you with your mobile phone service provider?

○ Very Dissatisfied

○ Quite dissatisfied

○ Somewhat dissatisfied

○ Slightly dissatisfied

○ Neither satisfied or dissatisfied

○ Slightly satisfied

○ Somewhat satisfied

○ Quite satisfied

○ Very satisfied

Format for telephone or personal interview:

How satisfied are you with your mobile phone service provider? Would you say that you are very dissatisfied, dissatisfied, neither dissatisfied or satisfied, satisfied, or very satisfied?

_____very dissatisfied
_____dissatisfied
_____neither
_____satisfied
_____very satisfied

Source: © Cengage Learning 2013.

When a question is read aloud, remembering the alternative choices can be difficult. Consider the following question from a personal interview:

> *There has been a lot of discussion about the potential health risks to nonsmokers from secondhand tobacco smoke. How serious a health threat to you personally is the inhaling of this secondhand smoke, often called* passive smoking: *Is it a very serious health threat, somewhat serious, not too serious, or not serious at all?*

1. Very serious
2. Somewhat serious
3. Not too serious
4. Not serious at all
5. (Don't know)

The last portion of the question was a listing of the four alternatives that serve as answers. The interviewer uses the listing at the end to remind respondents of the alternatives. The fifth alternative, "Don't know," is in parentheses because, although the interviewer knows it is an acceptable answer, it is not read. The researcher only uses this response when the respondent truly cannot provide an answer.

Avoiding Mistakes

No hard-and-fast rules determine how to develop a questionnaire. Fortunately, research experience has yielded some guidelines that help prevent the most common mistakes.

Simpler Is Better

Words used in questionnaires should be readily understandable to all respondents. The researcher usually has the difficult task of adopting the conversational language of people at the lower education levels without talking down to better-educated respondents. Remember, not all people have the vocabulary of a college graduate. Many consumers, for instance, have never gone beyond a high school education.

❝I don't know the rules of grammar. . . . If you're trying to persuade people to do something, or buy something, it seems to me you should use their language, the language they use every day, the language in which they think. We try to write in the vernacular.❞

—DAVID OGILVY

Respondents can probably tell an interviewer whether they are married, single, divorced, separated, or widowed, but providing their *marital status* may present a problem. The technical jargon of top corporate executives should be avoided when surveying retailers or industrial users. "Brand image," "positioning," "marginal analysis," and other corporate language may not have the same meaning for or even be understood by a store owner-operator in a retail survey. The vocabulary used in the following question from an attitude survey on social problems probably would confuse many respondents:

> *When effluents from a paper mill can be drunk and exhaust from factory smokestacks can be breathed, then humankind will have done a good job in saving the environment. . . . Don't you agree that what we want is zero toxicity, meaning no effluents?*

Besides being too long, complex, and confusing, this question is leading.

Avoid Leading and Loaded Questions

leading question

A question that suggests or implies certain answers.

Leading and loaded questions are a major source of bias. A **leading question** suggests or implies certain answers. A media study of environmental consciousness asked consumers this question:

Many concerned individuals are washing their clothes less often because of concerns for the environment. How has concern for the environment affected your washing behavior?

- ○ Wash rarely
- ○ Wash less often
- ○ Wash about the same
- ○ Wash more often
- ○ Was much more

Close

The potential "bandwagon effect" implied in this question threatens the study's validity. *Partial mention of alternatives* is a variation of this phenomenon:

What do you usually drink first thing in the morning?

- ○ Coke
- ○ Coffee
- ○ Milk

This item may produce an artificially high percentage of Coke, coffee, and milk drinkers because other categories, such as water or juice, do not appear.

loaded question

A question that suggests a socially desirable answer or is emotionally charged.

A **loaded question** suggests a socially desirable answer or is emotionally charged. Consider the following question:

What most influences your opinion on controversial political issues?

- ○ Analysis based on knowledge
- ○ Media officials
- ○ Late night comedians
- ○ Coworker opinion

Most respondents will choose the first response. Why? Even though the question is not that emotionally charged, the first response builds self-esteem more so than the other choices by making the choice seem logical and well thought out.

Certain answers to questions are more socially desirable than others. For example, a truthful answer to the following classification question might be painful:

Where did your rank academically in your high school graduation class?

○ 1st (top) quarter

○ 2nd quarter

○ 3rd quarter

○ 4th (bottom) quarter

When taking personality or psychographic tests, respondents frequently can interpret which answers are most socially acceptable even if those answers do not portray their true feelings. For example, what are the socially desirable answers to the following questions on a self-confidence scale?

	Strongly Disagree	Disagree	Neither Agree nor Disagree	Agree	Strongly Agree
I am capable of handling myself in most social situations	○	○	○	○	○
I seldom fear that my actions will cause others to have low opinions of me	○	○	○	○	○

Courtesy of Qualtrics.com

An experiment conducted in the early days of polling illustrates the unpopularity of change.[6] Comparable samples of respondents were simultaneously asked two questions about the presidential succession. One sample was asked,

> *"Would you favor or oppose adding a law to the Constitution preventing a president from succeeding him/herself more than once?"*

The other sample was asked,

> *"Would you favor or oppose changing the Constitution in order to prevent a president from succeeding him/herself more than once?"*

Fifty percent of respondents answered negatively to the first question. For the second question, 65 percent of respondents answered negatively. Thus, the public would rather add to than change the Constitution.

Asking respondents "how often" they use a product or visit a store leads them to generalize about their habits, because there usually is some variance in their behavior. In generalizing, a person is likely to portray an *ideal* behavior rather than an *average* behavior. For instance, brushing your teeth after each meal may be ideal, but busy people may skip brushing occasionally. An introductory **counterbiasing statement** or preamble to a question that reassures respondents that their "embarrassing" behavior is not abnormal may yield truthful responses:

> *Some people have the time to brush three times daily but others do not. How often did you brush your teeth yesterday?*

If a question embarrasses the respondent, it may elicit no answer or a biased response. This is particularly true with respect to personal or classification data such as income or education. The problem may be mitigated by introducing the section of the questionnaire with a statement such as this:

> *To help classify your answers, we'd like to ask you a few questions. Again, your answers will be kept in strict confidence.*

counterbiasing statement

An introductory statement or preamble to a potentially embarrassing question that reduces a respondent's reluctance to answer by suggesting that certain behavior is not unusual.

split-ballot technique

Using two alternative phrasings of the same question for respective halves of a sample to elicit a more accurate total response than would a single phrasing.

A question statement may be leading because it is phrased to reflect either the negative or the positive aspects of an issue. To control for this bias, the wording of attitudinal questions may be reversed for 50 percent of the sample. This **split-ballot technique** is used with the expectation that two alternative phrasings of the same question will yield a more accurate total response than will a single phrasing. For example, in a study on economy car buying behavior, one-half of a sample of imported-car purchasers received a questionnaire in which they were asked to agree or disagree with the statement:

"Small domestic cars are cheaper to operate than small imported cars."

The other half of the import-car owners received a questionnaire in which the statement read:

"Small imported cars are cheaper to operate than small domestic cars."

The results to the two questions were averaged to get an opinion score for perceived economy of imports versus domestics.

Avoid Ambiguity: Be as Specific as Possible

Items on questionnaires often are ambiguous because they are too general. Consider such indefinite words as *often, occasionally, regularly, frequently, many, good,* and *poor.* Each of these words has many different meanings. For one consumer *frequent* reading of *Fortune* magazine may be reading six or seven issues a year. Another consumer may think reading two issues a year is frequent.

Questions such as the following one, used in a study measuring the reactions of consumers to a television boycott, should be interpreted with care:

Qualtrics.com

Please indicate the statement that best describes your family's television viewing during the boycott of the Exploration Network.

○ We did not watch the Exploration Network

○ We watched hardly any programs on the Exploration Network

○ We occasionally watched programs on the Exploration Netowrk

○ We watched a lot of programs on the Exploration Network

Close

Some marketing scholars suggest that the rate of diffusion of an innovation is related to the perception of product attributes such as *divisibility,* which refers to the extent to which the innovation may be tried or tested on a limited scale.[7] An empirical attempt to test this theory using semantic differentials was a disaster. Pretesting found that the bipolar adjectives *divisible–not divisible* were impossible for consumers to understand because they did not have the theory in mind as a frame of reference. A revision of the scale used these bipolar adjectives:

Testable ___ ___ ___ ___ ___ ___ ___ *Not testable*
(sample use possible)   *(sample use not possible)*

However, the question remained ambiguous because the meaning was still unclear sending the researchers back for more pretesting using more concrete wording such as "can you try before you buy?"

A brewing industry study on point-of-purchase advertising (store displays) asked:

What degree of durability do you prefer in your point-of-purchase advertising?

○ Permanent (lasting more than 6 months)

○ Semipermanent (lasting 1 to 6 months)

○ Temporary (lasting less than 1 month)

Here the researchers clarified the terms *permanent, semipermanent,* and *temporary* by defining them for the respondent. However, the question remained somewhat ambiguous. Beer marketers often use a variety of point-of-purchase devices to serve different purposes—in this case, what is the purpose? In addition, analysis was difficult because respondents were merely asked to indicate a preference rather than a *degree* of preference. Thus, the meaning of a question may not be clear because the frame of reference is inadequate for interpreting the context of the question.

A student research group asked this question:

> *What media do you rely on most?*

> ☐ *Television*

> ☐ *Radio*

> ☐ *Internet*

> ☐ *Newspapers*

This question is ambiguous because it does not ask about the content of the media. "Rely on most" for what—news, sports, finance, entertainment?

Avoid Double-Barreled Items

A question covering several issues at once is referred to as a **double-barreled question** and should always be avoided. Making the mistake of asking two questions rather than one is easy—for example,

> **Please indicate how much you agree with the following statement:**
> **Labor unions and management are most responsible for the current economic crisis.**

When a respondent agrees, so they mean both unions and management, unions or management are responsible? One cannot tell.

When multiple questions are asked in one question, the results may be exceedingly difficult to interpret. Consider the following question from a magazine's survey entitled "How Do You Feel about Being a Woman?":

double-barreled question

A question that may induce bias because it covers two or more issues at once.

Between you and your husband, who does the housework (cleaning, cooking, dishwashing, laundry) over and above that done by any hired help?

⊙ I do all of it

⊙ I do almost all of it

⊙ I do over half

⊙ We split the work fifty-fity

⊙ My hustand does over half

Courtesy of Qualtrics.com

The answers to this question do not tell us if the wife cooks and the husband washes the dishes. The Research Snapshot provides additional insight into this question.

A survey by a consumer-oriented librarian asked a sample of visitors,

> *Are you satisfied with the present system of handling "closed-reserve" and "open-reserve" readings?*

> ☐ *Yes*   ☐ *No*

A respondent may feel torn between a "yes" to one part of the question and "no" to the other part. The answer to this question does not tell the researcher which problem or combination of problems concerns the library patron. Further, a Likert statement from a study dealing with student perceptions of managerial ethics:

Top international sales managers sometimes buy liquor and prostitutes for important customers.

Strongly Disagree	Disagree	Neither Agree or Disagree	Agree	Strongly Agree
◎	◎	◎	◎	◎

The item intends to discover students' attitudes about selling as a career.[8] However, perhaps this would be better as two separate questions rather than one to learn respondents' specific beliefs. Then no ambiguity would exist about what sales managers might buy for customers. A sales manager who takes a customer out for dinner may buy drinks but might never think of buying prostitutes. So, as is, what would a strongly agree or strongly disagree response really mean?

Avoid Making Assumptions

Consider the following question:

Should Macy's continue its excellent gift wrapping program?

◎ yes

◎ No

This question has a built-in assumption: that people believe the gift-wrapping program is excellent. By answering "yes," the respondent implies that the program is, in fact, excellent and that things are fine just as they are. When a respondent answers "no," the opinion is to discontinue the program implying that it isn't excellent. But, perhaps the respondent thinks Macy's should wrap gifts but doesn't buy the built-in excellence assumption. What answer would that respondent mark?

Another frequent mistake is assuming that the respondent had previously thought about an issue. For example, the following question appeared in a survey concerning Jack-in-the-Box:

> **"Do you think Jack-in-the-Box restaurants should consider changing their name?"**

Respondents have not likely thought about this question beforehand. Most respondents answered the question even though they had no prior opinion concerning the name change. Researchers that desire an informed opinion will end up with responses based on too low a level of involvement in a case like this.

Avoid Taxing Respondents Memory

A simple fact is that sometimes, we can't remember everything. Researchers writing questions about past behavior or events should recognize that certain questions may make serious demands on the respondent's memory. Writing questions about prior events requires a conscientious attempt to minimize the problems associated with forgetting.

In many situations, respondents cannot recall details without some type of assistance. For example, a telephone survey conducted during the 24-hour period following the airing of the Super Bowl might establish whether the respondent watched the Super Bowl and then asked:

> **Do you recall any commercials on that program?**

Who Really Does Housework?

Who does housework? What seems like a simple question becomes not so simple when one needs a precise answer. One recent survey suggests that on average, women spent approximately 42 hours a week doing housework compared to approximately 23 hours a week for men. According to these results, women do almost twice as much housework as men. On closer inspection however, these results suggests that the average married couple spends 65 hours a week doing housework. Really? Do couples really put in nearly 10 hours a day on housework?

That result doesn't seem plausible on first glance but a number of factors related to survey design may influence the result. First, what is housework? Does housework include driving the kids to school, driving to the grocery store or driving to work? Does it include time going out to get the newspaper or time spent perusing food catalogs for recipe ideas? A broader definition of housework will yield higher numbers. Second, respondents who do very little housework are not that likely to report to such a survey. Thus, response bias may occur based on the type of person who does respond. Third, the question is prone to socially desirable responding. The socially desirable response for both men and women is to admit to doing a significant amount of housework.

Perhaps an interesting side note is that the more couples report doing housework, the higher the frequency of intimacy

they report. On top of this, men report an average of 34 hours a week of work outside the home and women about 20. This doesn't seem to leave a lot of time for other activities. Perhaps one factor behind the apparent relationship is that respondents who report a lot of housework exhibit a response pattern using the upper ends of scales more than the lower parts. The end result, if researchers want accurate answers to such questions, they should insure anonymity, have a very good definition of the phenomena being studied, and be able to convey that definition in a survey instrument. Sometimes, behavioral evidence can validate (or invalidate) survey results. People who do more housework do not have more children than other couples. Does this behavioral result say anything about potential bias in the survey results?

Sources: Craig, L. and P. Simminski (2011), "If Men Do More Housework, Do Their Wives Have More Babies?" Social Indicators Research, 101 (2), 255–58. Shellenbarger, S. (2009), "Housework Pays Off Between the Sheets," Wall Street Journal, (October 21), D1–D3.

If the answer is positive, the interviewer might ask, "What brands were advertised?" These two questions measure **unaided recall**, because they give the respondent no clue as to the brand of interest.

If the researcher suspects that the respondent may have forgotten the answer to a question, he or she may rewrite the question in an **aided-recall** format—that is, in a format that provides a clue to help jog the respondent's memory. For instance, the question about an advertised beer in an aided-recall format might be "Do you recall whether there was a brand of beer advertised on that program?" or "I am going to read you a list of beer brand names. Can you pick out the name of the beer that was advertised on the program?" Aided recall is less taxing to the respondent's memory.

Telescoping and squishing are two additional consequences of respondents' forgetting the exact details of their behavior. *Telescoping* occurs when respondents believe that past events happened more recently than they actually did. The opposite effect, *squishing,* occurs when respondents think that recent events took place longer ago than they really did. A potential solution to this problem may be to refer to a specific event that is memorable—for example, "How often have you gone to a sporting event since the World Series?" Because forgetting tends to increase over time, the question may concern a recent period: "How often did you watch any HBO program last week?"

In situations in which "I don't know" or "I can't recall" is a meaningful answer, simply including a "don't know" response category may solve the question writer's problem. Exhibit 11.2 summarizes some key wording mistakes and tips on minimizing them.

unaided recall

Asking respondents to remember something without providing any clue.

aided-recall

Asking the respondent to remember something and giving them a clue to help.

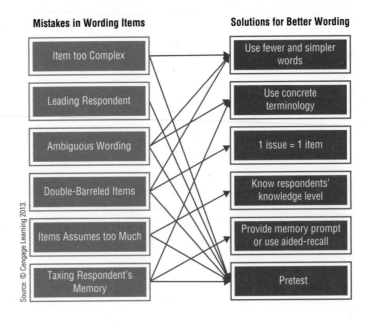

Order Bias

Question Sequence

The order of questions, or the question sequence, may serve several functions for the researcher. If the opening questions are interesting, simple to comprehend, and easy to answer, respondents' cooperation and involvement can be maintained throughout the questionnaire. Asking easy-to-answer questions teaches respondents their role and builds their confidence.

A mail survey among department store buyers drew an extremely poor return rate. A substantial improvement in response rate occurred, however, when researchers added some introductory questions seeking opinions on pending legislation of great importance to these buyers. Respondents completed all the questions, not only those in the opening section.

In their attempt to "warm up" respondents toward the questionnaire, student researchers frequently ask demographic or classificatory questions at the beginning. This generally is not advisable, because asking for personal information such as income level or education may embarrass or threaten respondents. Asking potentially embarrassing questions or personal questions at the end of the questionnaire usually is better. At that point, the respondent may be comfortable with the questioning in general but also, if the respondent breaks off at that point, the researcher still has a nearly complete questionnaire to work with.

order bias

Results when a particular sequencing of questions affects the way a person responds or when the choices provided as answers favors one response over another.

Order bias results when a particular sequencing of questions affects the way a person responds or when the choices provided as answers favors one response over another. In political elections involving candidates lacking high visibility, such as elections for county commissioners and judges, the first name listed on a ballot often receives the most votes. For this reason, election boards should consider ballots that list candidate's names in different positions across voters as a way of equaling out any votes that just go to the first person on the list.

Asking specific questions before asking about broader issues is a common cause of order bias. For example, bias may arise if questions about happiness with life in general are asked before asking about happiness with specific aspects of one's life. Consider the following three questions (each rated out of 100 points):

1. Tell us how happy you are with your life in general? _____
2. Tell us how happy you are with your marriage? _____
3. Tell us how happy you are with your career achievements? _____

Responses to question 1 are on average higher when asked in this order. Asking questions 2 and/or 3 first significantly lowers average reported happiness with life. Respondents may overlook specific aspects when answering the general question but then overweight these aspects relative to other nonmentioned aspects.[9] Specific questions may thus influence the more general ones more than general questions will influence specific ones.

As a result of this bias, ask general questions before specific questions to obtain the best idea of the true overall impression. This procedure, known as the **funnel technique**, allows the researcher to understand the respondent's overall frame of reference before asking more specific questions. The funnel technique reduces bias from one or two specific items.

funnel technique

Asking general questions before specific questions in order to obtain unbiased responses.

Randomized Presentations

Consider how later answers might be biased by previous questions in this questionnaire on environmental pollution:

Mark the response that best matches your feelings about the severity of each environmental issue.

	Not Severe	Somewhat Severe	Severe	Very Severe	Extremely Severe
Air pollution from automobiles	○	○	○	○	○
Air pollution from open fires	○	○	○	○	○
Air pollution from industrial smoke	○	○	○	○	○
Air pollution from foul odors	○	○	○	○	○
Noise pollution from airplanes	○	○	○	○	○
Noise pollution from cars, trucks, scooters, motorcycles	○	○	○	○	○
Noise pollution from industry	○	○	○	○	○
Noise pollution from loud music	○	○	○	○	○

Courtesy of Qualtrics.com

Not surprisingly, researchers found that the responses to the air pollution questions were highly correlated—in fact, almost identical. With attitude scales, *anchoring effect also may exist*. The first concept measured tends to become a comparison point from which one makes subsequent evaluations. One way to avoid order bias is to randomize question order. Each respondent receives the questions in a different order depending upon the randomization routine. For instance, a set of twenty questions can be assigned positions using random numbers to assign the order. Internet surveys make randomizing question order convenient and easy. Randomization of items on a questionnaire susceptible to the anchoring effect reduces bias.[10]

A related problem is bias caused by the order of alternatives on closed questions. To avoid this problem, researchers can employ electronic questionnaires making randomization of the choices easy. This makes sense for multiple-choice responses that do not have a logical order. For instance, a question asking respondents to choose their favorite brand of potato chip could randomize the alternatives to avoid the one on top getting more responses just out of convenience. Alternatively, the standard Likert scale format is logically ordered from 1 representing the strongest disagreement (lowest agreement) to 5, in the case of a 5-point scale, representing the highest agreement. Randomizing the response order in such a case could be confusing to the respondent. With complete randomization, question order is random and respondents see response alternatives in different random positions.

Not surprisingly, marketing researchers rarely print alternative questionnaires with either randomized questions or responses. If printed questionnaires are used, randomization would make data coding very difficult and create a high opportunity for coding error. Thus, printed survey instruments are disadvantageous when randomization is needed.

Randomized Response Techniques

Researchers who need to ask embarrassing or incriminating questions sometimes employ randomized response approaches that try to demonstrate to the respondent that even the researcher would not be able to know how the responded answered the question. **Randomized response techniques** involve randomly assigning respondents to answer either the question of interest (embarrassing) or a mundane and unembarrassing question. Researchers use an approach like this when studying sensitive issues including sexually transmitted diseases, sexual behaviors, pornography consumption, cigarette consumption, abortion, and voting behaviors, among other things.[11] The following illustration gives an idea of how this works.

Suppose a marketing researcher was studying relationships between manufacturing firms' sales personnel and a retail firms' buying agents. The researcher wants the answer to this question:

H) Have you every lied about a product's shipping date in order to close a deal?

Rather than asking this question alone. The survey offers respondents an alternate question:

T) Choose a card from the deck provided. Is the card red?

Alternate questions H and T are followed by a single "yes" or "no" response scale. The instructions then tell respondents to flip a coin. If the flip turns out heads, respondents should answer question H. If the flip turns out tails, respondents should answer question T. In this way, respondents get the idea (which is true) that the researcher can't tell what question the respondent answered.

However, in any group of respondents, the percentage of people who lied can be obtained based on the observed numbers of yes responses and the known statistical probability of a coin flip. In other words, any difference from 50 percent yes is attributed to the presumably honest answers of respondents.[12] Thus, researchers can address hypotheses involving whether or not automobile industry personnel lie about delivery dates more often than computer industry personnel or whether one culture or sex differs from another. The use of randomized response techniques remains controversial based in part on the willingness and ability of respondents to follow procedures. For now, researchers should consider using the approach when studying relatively capable respondents.

Survey Flow

Survey flow refers to the ordering of questions through a survey. Just above, we discussed order bias as one aspect of survey flow. Other aspects of survey flow can affect response quality. This section discusses issues that facilitate good flow and thereby valid responses.

Oftentimes certain sections of a questionnaire are irrelevant to a particular respondent. Asking a question that does not apply to the respondent or that the respondent is not qualified to answer may be irritating or cause a biased response or even a survey breakoff. A **breakoff** means the respondent stops answering questions resulting in an incomplete survey. We'll have more breakoffs later in the chapter.

A **filter question** can serve as a **branching** mechanism directing respondents to an appropriate part of the questionnaire using skip logic. Asking:

"Where do you generally have check-cashing problems in Springfield?"

may elicit a response even though the respondent has had no check-cashing problems. He or she may wish to please the interviewer with an answer. The respondent could first encounter a filter question such as:

"Do you ever have a problem cashing a check in Springfield? _____Yes _____No"

The responses provided would branch respondents who say yes to questions about the places where checks cannot be cashed while respondents who say no skip to the next block of questions.

Exhibit 11.3 gives an example of a flowchart plan for a survey addressing a rental car company's sponsorship of a top racer in the Tour de France bicycle race. In this case, the company (Eurocar) is evaluating the sponsorship's effectiveness across different markets and potential markets.

EXHIBIT **11.3**
Survey Flow for Tour de France Sponsorship

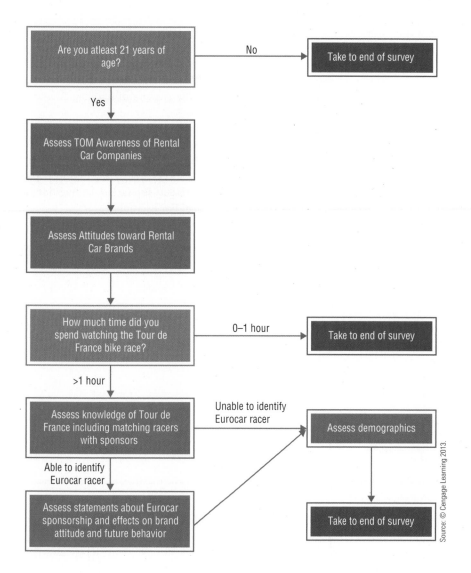

The first question serves as a filter and qualifies respondents based on whether or not they are old enough to rent a car. Next, respondents provide unaided top of mind awareness and then rate attitudes toward rental car companies including Eurocar. Respondents then reveal whether they spent any significant time viewing the Tour de France. If the respondent viewed for more than one hour, questions assessing the respondent's awareness of sponsorships are provided and so forth. The survey allows research questions involving how much the awareness of Eurocar is affected by the sponsorship and how attitudes toward the company might be changed relative to the sponsorship.

Good survey flow, sometimes called layout, and physical attractiveness are crucial in mail, Internet, and other self-administered questionnaires. For different reasons, a good layout in questionnaires designed for face-to-face and telephone interviewers is also important.

Traditional Questionnaires

A good layout is neat and attractive, and the instructions for the interviewer should be easy to follow. The responses "It Depends," "Refused," and "Don't Know" enclosed in a box to the side indicate that these answers are acceptable but responses from the 5-point scale are preferred.

Survey researchers can increase response rates by investing in an attractive and well-designed questionnaire. Self-response printed questionnaires should never be overcrowded. Margins should be of decent size, white space should be used to separate blocks of print, and the unavoidable columns of multiple boxes should be kept to a minimum. A question should not begin on one page and end on another page. Splitting questions may cause a respondent to read only part of a question, to pay less attention to answers on one of the pages, or to become confused. For web-based surveys, again do not crowd a page and try to minimize the amount of scrolling a respondent has to do to see all the items.

Questionnaires should be designed to appear as short as possible. A booklet form of questionnaire is preferable to stapling a large number of pages together. Also, do not try to put too many questions on a page—paper or electronic. In situations in which it is necessary to conserve space on the questionnaire or to facilitate data entry or tabulation of the data, a multiple-grid layout may be used. The **multiple-grid (matrix table) question** presents several similar questions and corresponding response alternatives arranged in a grid format. For example:

multiple-grid (matrix table) question

Several similar questions of the same format all arranged in a grid format.

On your recent flight to San Francisco, ...

	No	Yes	Not sure
Did you depart on time?	○	○	○
Did you use the departure lounge?	○	○	○
Did the gate agent address you by name?	○	○	○
Was the airplane clean?	○	○	○
Did the pilot inform you of any turbulence in route?	○	○	○
Were you satisfied with the airline's service?	○	○	○

Courtesy of Qualtrics.com

By using several forms, special instructions, and other tricks of the trade, the researcher can design the questionnaire to facilitate the interviewer's job of following interconnected questions. Exhibit 11.4 illustrates portions of an interview form used by a telephone interviewer. Note how the layout and easy-to-follow instructions for interviewers in Questions 1, 2, and 3 help the interviewer follow the question sequence.

Instructions are often capitalized or printed in bold to alert the interviewer that it may be necessary to proceed in a certain way. For example, if a particular answer is given, the interviewer or respondent may be instructed to skip certain questions or go to a special sequence of questions. To facilitate coding, fixed alternative responses can be precoded when possible, as in Exhibit 11.4.

Layout is extremely important when questionnaires are long or require the respondent to fill in a large amount of information. In many circumstances, using headings or subtitles to indicate groups of questions will help the respondent grasp the scope or nature of the questions to be asked. Thus, at a glance, the respondent can follow the logic of the questionnaire.

Survey Technology

Many guidelines for laying out paper questionnaires apply to Internet questionnaires too. Given the increasing reliance on Internet or Web-based surveys, we discuss many survey flow issues in this important context. Survey software programs like Qualtrics allow several special features that facilitate design and allow important data to be collected that may be difficult otherwise. Smartphones and tablet computers also provide another medium for administering surveys. These same software programs often provide formats amenable to these media as well. Earlier, we learned how

EXHIBIT **11.4**
Telephone Questionnaire
with Skip Questions

1. Did you take the car you had checked to the Standard Auto Repair Center for repairs?

    −1 Yes   **(SKIP TO Q. 3)**   −2 No

2. **(IF NO, ASK:)** Did you have the repair work done?

    −1 Yes   −2 No

    ↓   ↓

1. Where was the repair work done?_____   1. Why didn't you have the car repaired?

    _____   _____

                                                     _____

                                                     _____

2. Why didn't you have the repair work done
   at the Standard Auto Repair Center?_____

    _____

    _____

    _____

3. **(IF YES TO Q. 1, ASK:)** How satisfied were you with the repair work? Were you . . .

    −1 Very satisfied

    −2 Somewhat satisfied

    −3 Somewhat dissatisfied

    −4 Very dissatisfied

    (IF SOMEWHAT OR VERY DISSATISFIED:) In what way were you dissatisfied?

    _____

    _____

    _____

4. **(ASK EVERYONE:)** Do you ever buy gas at the 95th Street Standard Center?

    −1 Yes   −2 No   **(SKIP TO Q. 6)**

5. **(IF YES, ASK:)** How often do you buy gas there?

    −1 Always

    −2 Almost always

    −3 Most of the time

    −4 Part of the time

    −5 Hardly ever

6. Have you ever had your car washed there?

    −1 Yes   −2 No

7. Have you ever had an oil change or lubrication done there?

    −1 Yes   −2 No

electronic questionnaire designs facilitate randomization. Here, we learn about a few other features of self-administered Internet surveys.

Response Quality

Once a respondent agrees to participate, he or she has an ethical obligation to complete the task in a responsible fashion. However, this is not always the case. For instance, the researcher can build in questions that test whether or not the respondent is paying attention. Consider the following item:

Choose "disagree" to this item for administrative purposes.

- ⊙ Strongly Disagree
- ⊙ Disagree
- ⊙ Neutral
- ⊙ Agree
- ⊙ Strongly Agree

Suppose a respondent chooses "strongly agree." Obviously, he or she is not responding responsibly. At this point, the researcher can build in branching or skip logic that breaks the survey off if a respondent selects anything other than "disagree". An alternative is to build in a popup that reminds the respondent to pay attention. With a paper-and-pencil survey, a data entry coder would have to spot the lack of quality responses manually once the surveys are complete adding to the administrative expense.

Timing

Respondents can be timed as they move through electronic surveys. The total time that someone spends responding to a survey is routinely recorded. However, timers can also be set for individual pages or individual questions. Timing data can be used to provide behavioral data and to help identify types of respondent error.

Typically, "timing questions" record the amount of time a respondent took before clicking somewhere on a page, the amount of time until they made the last click on a page, and the total amount of time they spent on a page. The time a respondent spent on a page can be an important outcome in studies involving attitude change or information processing. For example, ad features may be built in precisely to encourage consumers to spend more time viewing the ad. Timing also can provide another check on response quality. For instance, if respondents spend less time on a page than it takes to read a question, then they are not likely paying very close attention and, as a result, the response quality is called into question.

Similarly, if the total time spent responding is too fast, then the respondent may be marking responses randomly or without paying attention.[13] Respondents who take one and one-half standard deviations less time than average appear particularly likely to be offering "satisficing" responses leading to substantially high response error.

Physical Features

Tracking Interest

heat map question

A graphical question that tracks the parts of an image or advertisement that most capture a respondent's attention.

Electronic questionnaires sometimes allow us to come close to tracking behavior beyond timing using special question types such as a heat map. Exhibit 11.5 displays a **heat map question** tracking the way a respondent views an advertisement for a watch. The dashed lines that form a grid would not be visible to the respondent. However, any cursor activity in each grid would be recorded, allowing the respondent to know what parts of the ad captured the respondent's attention the most. This type of question mimics behavioral pupil tracking and provides an indication of what parts of an advertisement or image capture the most attention.

Status Bar

status bar

In an Internet questionnaire, a visual indicator that tells the respondent what portion of the survey he or she has completed.

With a paper questionnaire, a respondent can flip through a questionnaire and know about how many questions are in a survey. Multiple page Web-based surveys do not provide this opportunity. However, the researcher may provide a **status bar** as a visual indicator of questionnaire length. The

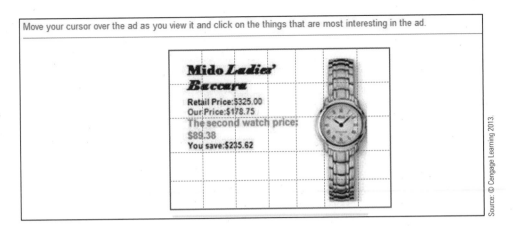

Move your cursor over the ad as you view it and click on the things that are most interesting in the ad.

Source: © Cengage Learning 2013.

EXHIBIT 11.5
Tracking Points of Interest
Using a Heat Map

status bar usually resembles a thermometer and the more the bar is filled the closer the respondent is to the finish. Exhibit 11.6 shows an online survey page including a status bar at the bottom of the page. In this case, the respondent appears to be nearly finished.

Status bars are a matter of courtesy to the respondent. However, when a survey involves multiple branches, the status bar can sometimes be misleading. The survey in the exhibit initially asked a filter question, "Do you drive an automobile?" Respondents who indicated no were taken immediately to the end of the survey. Thus, the more branching a survey involves, the less useful the status bar becomes.

Prompting

Web-based surveys allow limited interactivity. One useful piece of feedback comes in the form of a prompt message. **Prompting**, in this form, informs the respondent that he/she has skipped an item or provided implausible information. In Exhibit 11.6, the message tells the respondent that

EXHIBIT 11.6
Illustration of Status Bar
and Prompts

Sorry, you cannot continue until you correct the following:

• Issue 1
  • *Please answer this question.*

Please answer this question.

Please select the car your drive most often from the alternatives shown below.

Make

Model

Year

When do you believe you would be in the market to purchase a new car or truck?

○ 0-6 months

○ 7 months to 12 months

◉ 1 - 2 years

○ 3 - 5 years

○ Not in forseeable future

Survey Completion
0%   100%

>>

Source: © Cengage Learning 2013.

the question describing the car must be answered before moving forward with the survey. In this case, the researcher has set this question to be a forced response. In other instances, a prompt may indicate that implausible answers have been provided such as when a constant scale sum does not add up to the proper total.

Prompting of this type reduces item nonresponse (fewer items are skipped) at the expense of increasing break-offs.[14] Respondents may get frustrated with the demands to provide answers and simply quit answering all questions. This particularly true if the prompt asks a respondent to fill in open-ended items or items a respondent views as sensitive or personal. Overall, prompts should be used for critical questions because blank answers to these are practically equivalent to a survey nonresponse anyway.

Piping

piping software

Software that allows question answers to be inserted into later questions.

Survey software can systematically or randomly manipulate the questions a respondent sees. **Piping software** allows responses to a previous question to be inserted into later questions. For instance, a researcher studying vacation destinations conducts an online survey about consumer perceptions of their most recent vacation spot. After initial screening to make sure the person has taken a vacation in the past year, the respondent encounters this question:

In what place (resort area, city, or geographic region) did you spend the largest part of your most recent vacation?

Whatever the respondent writes in this box will be inserted into future questions about the destination. If the respondent put Disney World, the future question would appear as:

How many nights did you stay at Disneyworld?

Piping makes question wording much simpler because the respondent's answer replaces repetitive use of phrases such as "your most recent vacation destination."

Pretesting and Revising Questionnaires

Many novelists write, rewrite, revise, and rewrite again certain chapters, paragraphs, or even sentences. The researcher works in a similar world. Rarely does he or she write only a first draft of a questionnaire. Usually the questionnaire is tried out on a group, selected on a convenience basis, that is similar in makeup to the one that ultimately will be sampled. Although the researcher should not select a group too divergent from the target market—for example, selecting business students as surrogates for businesspeople—pretesting does not require a statistical sample. The pretesting process allows the researcher to determine whether respondents have any difficulty understanding the questionnaire and whether there are any ambiguous or biased questions. This process is exceedingly beneficial and may also involve not just the content of the questions but the method of asking as shown in the Research Snapshot on the next page. Making a mistake with twenty-five or fifty subjects can avoid the potential disaster of administering an invalid questionnaire to several hundred individuals.

For a questionnaire investigating teaching students' experience with Web-based instruction, the researcher had the questionnaire reviewed first by university faculty members to ensure the

©Nicholas Moore/Shutterstock

I Give Up!

The questionnaire design not only aims to get valid data—but design features also assist in getting data at all. No matter what the interview mode, a large portion of respondents give up before finishing and abandon the survey. With snail-mail questionnaires, the number is impossible to determine. However, phone interviews and online surveys allow an assessment of not only how many break-offs occur but also when they occur. When designing online surveys, keep the following guidelines in mind when attempting to minimize nonresponse problems due to break-offs:

■ Make sure the questionnaire is visually appealing and easy to read. Clutter causes respondents to give up.
■ Don't put too many questions on a single page or the task looks burdensome and leads respondents to give up.
■ Sensitive questions leads respondents to give up.
■ Respondents give up in the face of long questions.
■ Open-ended questions in a majority closed-ended survey leads resondents to give up.
■ The more sophisticated the sample, the more items capturing greater variance (like sliders and high response rates)

and those not containing labels on all response categories can be used effectively.

■ One important element in a pretest is estimating how many people give up without finishing.

Follow these rules and you won't have to give up on Web-based surveys.

Sources: Peychev, A. (2009), "Survey Breakoff," *Public Opinion Quarterly*, 71 (Spring), 74–97. Weijters, B., E. Cabooter, and N. Schillewaert (2010), "The Effect of Rating Scale Format on Response Styles: The Number of Response Categories and Response Category Labels," *International Journal of Research in Marketing*, 27, 236–47.

questions were valid, then asked twenty teaching students to try answering the questions and indicate any ambiguities they noticed. Their feedback prompted changes in the format and wording. Pretesting was especially helpful because the English-language questionnaire was used in a school in the United Arab Emirates, where English is spoken but is not the primary language.

Tabulating the results of a pretest helps determine whether the questionnaire will meet the objectives of the research. A **preliminary tabulation** often illustrates that, although respondents can easily comprehend and answer a given question, that question is inappropriate because it does not provide relevant information to help solve the marketing problem. Consider the following example from a survey among distributors of high-tech medical equipment such as MRI machines:

preliminary tabulation

A tabulation of the results of a pretest to help determine whether the questionnaire will meet the objectives of the research.

Please indicate the percentage of new client contacts that you have made in the last two years that originated from the following sources:

Email	0
Phone Call	0
Linked-In Message	0
Facebook Message	0
In-person Cold Call	0
Professional Meeting Attendance	0
Other _____	0
Other _____	0
Total	0

Courtesy of Qualtrics.com

Although this may seem like a simple question, pretesting may uncover potential problems. For instance, can respondents add up scores to total 100? If using an online format, the survey software can use a routine to prompt respondents should the scores not total to 100. But, if the task is too difficult, the researcher should revise the question. Also, is some other category frequent enough in occurrence to be listed as one of the options? If the open-ended boxes reveal some category showing up a lot, the item should include it as an explicit choice. If on the other hand, very few pretest respondents choose any response for "other," only one "other" response should be used to avoid confusion that may come from including two.

What administrative procedures should be implemented to maximize the value of a pretest? Administering a questionnaire exactly as planned in the actual study often is not possible. For example, mailing out a questionnaire might require several weeks that simply cannot be spared. Pretesting a questionnaire in this manner would provide important information on response rate but may not point out why questions were skipped or what questions are ambiguous or confusing. Personal interviewers can record requests for additional explanation or comments that indicate respondents' difficulty with question sequence or other factors. This is the primary reason why researchers employ interviewers often in pretest work. Self-administered questionnaires are not reworded as personal interviews, but interviewers are instructed to observe respondents and ask for their comments after they complete the questionnaire. When pretesting personal or telephone interviews, interviewers may test alternative wordings and question sequences to determine which format best suits the intended respondents.

No matter how the pretest is conducted, the researcher should remember that its purpose is to uncover any problems that the questionnaire may cause. Thus, pretests typically are conducted to answer questions about the questionnaire such as the following:

- Can the questionnaire format be followed by the interviewer [respondent for self-response]?
- Does the questionnaire flow naturally and conversationally?
- Are the questions clear and easy to understand?
- Can respondents answer the questions easily?
- Which alternative forms of questions work best?
- What overall and item response rates can be expected?

Pretests also provide means for testing the sampling procedure—to determine, for example, whether interviewers are following the sampling instructions properly and whether the procedure is efficient. Pretests also provide estimates of the response rates for mail surveys and the completion rates for telephone surveys.

Usually a questionnaire goes through several revisions. The exact number of revisions depends on the researcher's and client's judgment. The revision process usually ends when both agree that the desired information is being collected in an unbiased manner.

Designing Questionnaires for Global Markets

Marketing research is now a global enterprise. Researchers must take cultural factors into account when designing questionnaires. The most common problem involves translating a questionnaire into other languages. A questionnaire developed in one country may be difficult to translate because equivalent language concepts do not exist or because of differences in phrasing and vernacular. Although Spanish is spoken in both Mexico and Venezuela, one researcher found out that the Spanish translation of the English term *retail outlet* works in Mexico but not in Venezuela. Venezuelans interpreted the translation to refer to an electrical outlet.

Counting on an international audience to speak a common language such as English does not necessarily bridge these gaps, even when the respondents actually do speak more than one language. Cultural differences incorporate many shades of meaning that may not be captured by a survey delivered in a language used primarily for, say, business transactions. In a test of this idea, undergraduate students in twenty-four countries completed questionnaires about attitudes toward school and career. Half received the questionnaire in English, and half in their native language. The results varied, with country-to-country differences smaller when students completed the questionnaire in English.[15]

Some survey software tools like Qualtrics provide a free translation service that will allow one to write a survey in one language and have it administered in another. This may be useful for very exploratory surveys and as a first effort in translation. Marketing researchers usually apply more rigor in making sure the meanings match across languages.

International marketing researchers often have questionnaires back translated. **Back translation** is the process of taking a questionnaire that has previously been translated from one language to another and having it translated back again by a second, independent translator. The back translator is often a person whose native tongue is the language that will be used for the questionnaire. This process can reveal inconsistencies between the English version and the translation. For example, when a soft-drink company translated its slogan "Baby, it's cold inside" into Cantonese for research in Hong Kong, the result read "Small Mosquito, on the inside, it is very cold." In Hong Kong, *small mosquito* is a colloquial expression for a small child. Obviously the intended meaning of the advertising message had been lost in the translated questionnaire.[16]

back translation

Taking a questionnaire that has previously been translated into another language and having a second, independent translator translate it back to the original language.

TIPS OF THE TRADE

- Keep questionnaire wording simple
  - Use shorter words that have concrete meaning
  - Use shorter statements—one line is best—never more than two lines
  - When questioning about frequency, try to use numbers instead of vague terms like *rarely*.
- Design questionnaire for least capable respondent in the sampling frame
- In general, funnel respondents from general to specific questions
- Randomize question order when possible to avoid order bias

- Once a questionnaire exceeds a dozen questions, build in response quality checks that terminate the survey if a respondent gives an incorrect response
- Keep appearance of questionnaire neat and clean to avoid break-offs
- Pretests are invaluable in spotting things such as mistake-prone questions, projected overall response rates, item response rates based on break-offs.
  - A revised questionnaire is better than an initial questionnaire.

Source: © Cengage Learning 2013.

:: SUMMARY

1. Know the key decisions in questionnaire design. The data gathered via a questionnaire must be both relevant and accurate to be of value. A researcher systematically planning a survey faces several decisions that will shape the value of the questionnaire. What should be asked? How should questions be phrased? In what sequence should the questions be arranged? What questionnaire layout will best serve the research objectives? How can the questionnaire encourage complete responses? How should the questionnaire be pretested and revised if needed?

2. Choose between open-ended and fixed-alternative questions. Open-ended response questions pose some question and ask a respondent to answer in his or her own words. They provide the respondent with flexibility and may allow for meaningful, interpretive conclusions. Open-ended

Instead, Cadbury recruited a sample from a sensory panel. Panel members passed tests rating their sense of smell and even the rate at which they salivate. Cadbury trained the panelists for the gum-chewing job, teaching them to chew steadily along with the beats of a metronome.

Testers chewed samples of the gum for precisely three minutes, timing themselves with electronic clocks. At the end of each chewing period, a panel leader asked for comments. Panelists cleared their palates with crackers and water before trying the next sample. Eventually, the panelists provided enough feedback for the company to pinpoint winning flavor combinations and move on to engineering the production process.

Just as Cadbury needed a sample of gum chewers to make judgments about its products, sampling is a familiar part of daily life. A customer in a bookstore picks up a book, looks at the cover, and skims a few pages to get a sense of the writing style and content before deciding whether to buy. A high school student visits a college website to listen to a classroom lecture and view the notes. Selecting a university on the basis of one website visit may not be scientific sampling, but in a personal situation, it may be a meaningful and practical sampling experience. When measuring every item in a population is impossible, inconvenient, or too expensive, we intuitively take a sample.

Although sampling is commonplace in daily activities, these familiar samples are seldom scientific. For researchers, the process of sampling can be quite complex. Sampling is a central aspect of marketing research, requiring in-depth examination. Sampling does much to determine how realistic marketing results will be. This chapter explains the nature of sampling and ways to determine the appropriate sample design.

Introduction

sample

A subset, or some part, of a larger population.

population (universe)

Any complete group of entities that share some common set of characteristics.

population element

An individual member of a population.

census

An investigation of all the individual elements that make up a population.

The sampling process involves drawing conclusions about an entire population by taking measurements from only a portion of all population elements. Sampling makes research possible in cases where taking measurements from everyone or on everything is impossible. A **sample** is as a subset, or some part, of a larger population, from which researchers estimate population characteristics.

Sampling is defined in terms of the population being studied. A **population (universe)** is any complete group—for example, of people, sales territories, stores, products, or college students—whose members share some common set of characteristics. Each individual member is referred to as a **population element**.

Researchers could study every element of a population to draw some conclusion. A **census** is an investigation of all the individual elements that make up the population—a total enumeration rather than a sample. Thus, if we wished to know whether more adult Texans drive pickup trucks than sedans, we could contact every adult Texan and find out whether or not they drive a pickup truck or a sedan. We would then know the answer to this question definitively.

Why Sample?

At a wine-tasting, guests sample wine by having a small taste from multiple bottles of wine. From this, the consumer decides if he or she likes a particular wine. If each guest consumed the entire bottle before making a decision, he or she would be far too inebriated to have any idea about the other bottles. In addition, if the goal is to decide whether or not the wines taste good, giving each person a bottle of wine would soon get very expensive. Similarly, and for some of the same reasons, scientific studies try to draw conclusions about populations by measuring a small portion (sample) rather than taking a census.

Pragmatic Reasons

Applied marketing research projects usually have budget and time constraints. If Ford Motor Corporation wished to take a census of past purchasers' reactions to the company's recalls of defective models, the researchers would have to contact millions of automobile buyers. Some of them would be inaccessible (for example, out of the country), and it would be impossible to contact all these people within a short time period.

This survey asks a variety of questions of college students. Suppose you were an online university interested in studying the habits of college students in general. Consider the following questions:

1. How well do the results collected from this survey represent the market for undergraduate college students?
2. How well do the results represent American undergraduate college students? [Hint: Compare the profile on the questions shown below with data showing typical characteristics of American undergraduate students.]
3. How well do the results represent American business students?
4. Can the data be stratified in a way that would allow it to represent more specific populations? Explain your answer.

Source: © Cengage Learning 2013.

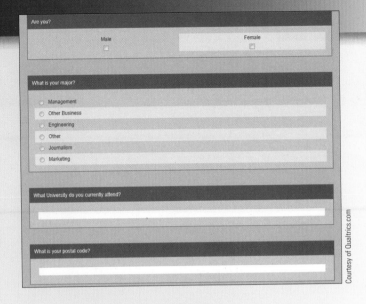

Courtesy of Qualtrics.com

A researcher who wants to investigate a population with an extremely small number of population elements may elect to conduct a census rather than a sample because the cost, labor, and time drawbacks would be relatively insignificant. For a company that wants to assess salespersons' satisfaction with its computer networking system, circulating a questionnaire to all twenty-five of its employees is practical. In most situations, however, many practical reasons favor sampling. Sampling cuts costs, reduces labor requirements, and gathers vital information quickly. These advantages may be sufficient in themselves for using a sample rather than a census, but there are other reasons. The Research Snapshot on page 317 describing the origins of the Gallup poll describe its very practical origins. Ultimately, sampling is a practical matter.

Accurate and Reliable Results

Another major reason for sampling is that most properly selected samples give results that are reasonably accurate. If the elements of a population are quite similar, only a small sample is necessary to accurately portray the characteristic of interest. Thus, a population consisting of 10,000 eleventh-grade students in all-boys Catholic high schools will require a smaller sample than a broader population consisting of 10,000 high school students from coeducational, public, secondary schools.

A visual example of how different-sized samples allow one to draw conclusions is provided in Exhibit 12.1. A sample is similar to a jigsaw puzzle that isn't solved yet. Even without looking at the box cover, the puzzler probably doesn't have to wait until every piece is in place to draw a conclusion of what the picture will be. However, as more pieces are put in place, which is analogous to more units being sampled, conclusions can be made with greater confidence. Thus, larger samples allow conclusions to be drawn with more confidence that they truly represent the population.

A sample may even on occasion be more accurate than a census. Interviewer mistakes, tabulation errors, and other nonsampling errors may increase during a census as workers suffer from burnout, fatigue, incompetence, or dishonesty. In a sample, increased accuracy may sometimes be possible because the fieldwork and tabulation of data can be more closely supervised. In a field survey, a small, well-trained, closely supervised group may do a more careful and accurate job of collecting information than a large group of nonprofessional interviewers who try to contact everyone. The U.S. Census Bureau conducts surveys on samples of populations as a way of checking the accuracy of the actual census of those populations. If the conclusions drawn from the sample disagree with the census results, the census is deemed inaccurate and becomes a candidate to be redone because an accurate census is required by law every ten years.

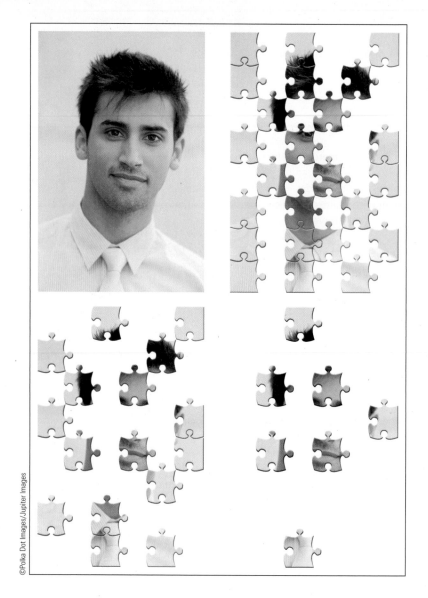

©Polka Dot Images/Jupiter Images

Destruction of Test Units

Many research projects, especially those in quality-control testing, require the destruction of the items being tested. If a manufacturer of firecrackers wished to find out whether each unit met a specific production standard, no product would be left after the testing. This is the exact situation in many marketing strategy experiments. For example, if an experimental sales presentation were presented to every potential customer, no prospects would remain to be contacted after the experiment. In other words, if there is a finite population and everyone in the population participates in the research and cannot be replaced, no population elements remain to be selected as sampling units. The test units have been destroyed or ruined for the purpose of the research project. Obviously, taking a census in these cases would not be too wise!

Identifying a Relevant Population and Sampling Frame

Before taking a sample, researchers must make several decisions. Exhibit 12.2 presents these decisions as a series of sequential stages, but the order of the decisions does not always follow this sequence. These decisions are highly interrelated. The steps listed in this exhibit are discussed here and in the next two chapters.

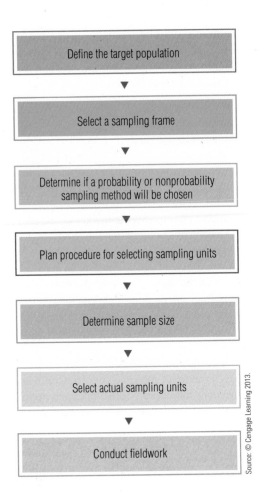

Source: © Cengage Learning 2013.

EXHIBIT **12.2**
Stages in the Selection of a Sample

Defining the Target Population

The first question in sampling is "what population are we trying to project?" In other words, what larger group is intended to be represented by using a sample? This question is rarely as easy as it may seem and often the matter isn't given much thought.

Polling agencies conduct research to predict election results. What is the relevant sample? *Registered voters* seems to be a reasonable choice and fortunately, a list of registered voters is generally available in public records. However, the actual election results will be determined by who actually votes, not who is registered to vote. If a study is supposed to represent those who actually will vote, registered voters no longer form the most relevant population. Identifying a sample that represents likely voters is much more difficult because no such list exists.

The population must be defined accurately for the research to produce good results. One survey concerning organizational buyer behavior had purchasing agents whom sales representatives regularly contacted rate preferred product characteristics. After the research proved less than helpful, investigators discovered that industrial engineers were actually making the purchasing decisions. For consumer research, the appropriate population element frequently is the household rather than an individual member of the household. This presents some problems if household lists are not available or if input cannot be obtained from the entire household.

Consider how difficult identifying a relevant population is for a company like Anthropologie or Bebe. What is the population of "fashion consumers"? However, the entire population of fashion consumers is likely not relevant for either of these companies. Clearly, no precise list of population members exists in this case. Even if they are directing a study at "loyal customers," questions such as defining a loyal or a disloyal consumer remain. Companies that use loyalty cards can maintain a list, but the presumption is that only these consumers are truly loyal. In other words, no consumers that do not have a card are loyal. This assumption may be reasonable but is clearly not perfect. Thus, a sample drawn from this list is more precisely described as representing the population of customers who have a loyalty card than as representing truly loyal customers.

One approach for defining the target population is to ask and answer questions about crucial population characteristics. This list illustrates the process:

- Is a list available that matches our population? If so, can we use it? Is valid contact information available and can they be reached with an appropriate communication method?
  - A mobile phone service provider like Verizon or AT&T would have a list of all of its customers.
- Who are we not interested in?
  - Researchers studying the behavior of retail buyers (who make decisions for retailers about what will be sold in the store) are not interested in undergraduate college students.
- What are the relevant market segment characteristics?
  - Companies generally appeal only to specific market segments. For example, consider Abercrombie and Fitch's (A&F) brand Image. Certainly, A&F shoppers belong to a specific market segment with specific characteristics.
- Are we only interested in a regional population? If so, how do we determine the borders?
  - For example, does the "U.K. market" include England, Scotland, and Wales (Great Britain)? Or does it include only England, or does it also include Northern Ireland, or maybe even the Republic of Ireland, which is not actually part of the United Kingdom?
  - What states comprise the southern United States or the western United States? Does either include Hawaii?
- Should the study include multiple populations?
  - When launching a new product in multiple countries, each country may constitute a distinct population rather than the entire population. Each population may need to be contacted through a different medium with a different approach.

Answers to these questions help researchers and decision makers focus on the right populations of potential respondents. The sample is implemented using the tangible, identifiable characteristics that also define the population. A baby food manufacturer might define the population as women of childbearing age. However, a more specific *operational definition* would be women between the ages of 18 and 50. Although this definition by age may exclude a few women who are capable of childbearing and include some who are not, it is still more explicit and provides a manageable basis for the sample design. Perhaps there are other reasons why this isn't a perfect population description. One important thing to remember is that if the population members cannot be reached by an appropriate communication method, they cannot be part of a sample.

Obviously, A&F caters to a specific market segment with specific demographic and lifestyle characteristics. A researcher studying A&F customers would err by studying the "clothing market."

George Gallup's Nation of Numbers

Civil engineers conduct surveys using a transit that takes measures at specific points and from that information, he/she generates a description of a piece of land. In somewhat the same way, George Gallup pioneered sampling theories that allow a sample survey to determine public opinion. You didn't have to talk to everybody, he said, as long as you randomly selected interviews according to a sampling plan.

Most of Gallup's work was based on the idea of random sampling. Today, truly random sampling has become increasingly difficult based on changes in the methods of communication. Door-to-door sampling is almost unheard of and even random-digit dialing will likely lead to systematic variation from the characteristics of most populations. Although most polling agencies stick to telephone interviews to predict things like election outcomes, with varying success, major companies have turned to the Web to generate samples. The results are not perfect, but companies like Proctor & Gamble, General Mills, and McDonald's are discovering ways that the shortcomings of online samples can be corrected using many of the same techniques that phone interviewers have used for years. The ease and convenience of online surveying offers a tremendous advantage just as Gallup found that sampling offered an advantage over canvassing an entire population. Thus, online surveys, just like sampling, are here to stay.

Sources: Excerpted from "George Gallup's Nation of Numbers," *Esquire* (December 1983), pp. 91–92; Helm, B., "Online Polls: How Good Are They?" *BusinessWeek* 4088 (June 16, 2008), 86.

The Sampling Frame

In practice, the sample will be drawn from a list of population elements that often differ somewhat from the defined target population. A list of elements from which the sample may be drawn is called a **sampling frame**. The sampling frame is also called the *working population* because these units will eventually provide units involved in analysis. A simple example of a sampling frame would be a list of all members of the American Medical Association.

A **sampling frame error** occurs when certain sample elements are excluded or when the entire population is not accurately represented in the sampling frame. An election poll relying on a telephone directory as a sampling frame uses households with listed phone numbers, not households who are likely to vote. Phone directories also underrepresent people with disabilities. Some disabilities, such as hearing and speech impairments, might make telephone use impossible. However, when researchers in Washington State tested for this possible sampling frame error by comparing Census Bureau data on the prevalence of disability with the responses to a telephone survey, they found the opposite effect. The reported prevalence of a disability was actually higher in the phone survey.[2] How could this be? Perhaps it has something to do with the likelihood that a member of the sample would be available to take a call. The Research Snapshot describes this issue in more detail.

In practice, almost every list excludes some members of the population. For example, would a university e-mail directory provide an accurate sampling frame for a given university's student population? Perhaps the sampling frame excludes students who registered late and includes students who have resigned from the university. The e-mail directory also will likely list only the student's official university e-mail address. However, many students may not ever use this address, opting to use a private e-mail account instead. Thus, the university e-mail directory could not be expected to perfectly represent the student population. However, a perfect representation isn't always possible or needed.

Sampling Services

Some firms, called *sampling services* or *list brokers*, specialize in providing lists or databases that include the names, addresses, phone numbers, and e-mail addresses of specific populations. Lists offered by companies such as this are compiled from subscriptions to professional journals, credit

sampling frame

A list of elements from which a sample may be drawn; also called working population.

sampling frame error

An error that occurs when certain sample elements are not listed or are not accurately represented in a sampling frame.

card applications, warranty card registrations, and a variety of other sources. One sampling service obtained its listing of households with children from an ice cream retailer who gave away free ice cream cones on children's birthdays. The children filled out cards with their names, addresses, and birthdays, which the retailer then sold to the mailing list company.

A valuable source of names is Equifax's series of city directories. Equifax City Directory provides complete, comprehensive, and accurate business and residential information. The city directory records the name of each resident over eighteen years of age and lists pertinent information about each household. The reverse directory pages offer a unique benefit. A **reverse directory** provides, in a different format, the same information contained in a telephone directory. Listings may be by city and street address or by phone number, rather than alphabetical by last name. Such a directory is particularly useful when a retailer wishes to survey only a certain geographical area of a city or when census tracts are to be selected on the basis of income or another demographic criterion.

reverse directory

A directory similar to a telephone directory except that listings are by city and street address or by phone number rather than alphabetical by last name.

Online Panels

online panels

Lists of respondents who have agreed to participate in marketing research along with the e-mail contact information for these individuals.

Online survey services routinely provide access to **online panels** for a modest fee. The panel consists of a list of e-mail addresses with each address identifying an individual who has agreed to participate in research surveys. Qualtrics, the company that hosts the survey involved in the Survey This! Features, provides access to such services. Typical online panels contain millions of potential respondents. The more specific the profile requested, the more expensive the panel. Online panels are increasingly used to provide sampling frames in marketing research. Later, we discuss the advantages and disadvantages of using an online panel as a sampling frame.

Sampling Frames for International Marketing Research

The availability of sampling frames varies dramatically around the world. Not every country's government conducts a census of population. In some countries telephone directories are incomplete, no voter registration lists exist, and accurate maps of urban areas are unobtainable. However, in Taiwan, Japan, and other Asian countries, a researcher can build a sampling frame relatively easily because those governments release some census information. If a family changes households, updated census information must be reported to a centralized government agency before communal services (water, gas, electricity, education, and so on) are made available.[3] This information is then easily accessible in the local *Inhabitants' Register*. Fortunately, many of the online panels include members in nations around the world. The panels can be stratified by country or by region within a country just as they can in the United States. For example, if a company wishes to survey part-time fast-food employees in Canada and Japan, a panel can probably provide potential respondents.

sampling unit

A single element or group of elements subject to selection in the sample.

Sampling Units

The elements of a population must be selected according to a specified procedure when sampling. The **sampling unit** is a single element or group of elements that is eligible for selection via the sampling process. For example, an airline may sample passengers by taking every twenty-fifth name on a complete list of passengers flying on a specified day. In this case the sampling unit would be the same as the element. Alternatively, the airline could first select certain flights as the sampling unit and then select certain passengers on each flight. In this case the sampling unit would contain many elements.

primary sampling unit (PSU)

A term used to designate a unit selected in the first stage of sampling.

secondary sampling unit

A term used to designate a unit selected in the second stage of sampling.

tertiary sampling unit

A term used to designate a unit selected in the third stage of sampling.

If the target population has first been divided into units, such as airline flights, additional terminology must be used. A unit selected in the first stage of sampling is called a **primary sampling unit (PSU)**. A unit selected in a successive stage of sampling is called a **secondary sampling unit** or (if three stages are necessary) **tertiary sampling unit**. When there is no list of population elements, the sampling unit generally is something other than the population element. In a random-digit dialing study, the sampling unit will be telephone numbers.

Random Sampling and Nonsampling Errors

An advertising agency sampled a small number of shoppers in grocery stores that used Shopper's Video, an in-store advertising network. The agency hoped to measure brand awareness and purchase intentions. Investigators expected this sample to be representative of the grocery-shopping population. However, if a difference exists between the value of a sample statistic of interest (for example, the sample group's average willingness to buy the advertised brand) and the value of the corresponding population parameter (the population's average willingness to buy), a *statistical error* has occurred. Earlier, we introduced two basic causes of differences between statistics and parameters:

1. random sampling errors
2. systematic (nonsampling) error

An estimation made from a sample is not the same as a census count. **Random sampling error** is the difference between the sample result and the result of an accurate census. Of course, the result of a census is unknown unless someone actually takes one. Random sampling error occurs because of chance variation in the selection of sampling units. The sampling units, even if properly selected according to sampling theory, may not perfectly represent the population because of chance variation.

> **random sampling error**
> The difference between the sample result and the result of a census conducted using identical procedures.

Picture fifty students in a typical undergraduate research class. If the class is the population and the instructor uses a random sample of ten students to estimate the average height of a student in the class, a random selection process should make sure that the ten tallest students are not selected for the sample. Although this is theoretically possible, the odds that this would occur are astronomical. The difference between the average of the ten students and the actual average of the population (fifty students) represent random sampling error.

Random Sampling Error

Random sampling error will come back into play later when the issue of hypothesis testing surfaces. At this point, recognize that *random sampling error* is a technical term that refers *only* to statistical fluctuations that occur because of chance variations in the elements selected for the sample. Random sampling error is a function of sample size. As sample size increases, random sampling error decreases.

Let's return to the classroom of fifty students. If the researcher is very lazy, a sample of 1 can be used to estimate student height. The chance of randomly selecting the tallest student is 1 in 50, the same as the odds of selecting the student that matched the median. Either way, the confidence that the sample is matching the true population value should not be very high. A strong likelihood exists that by doubling the sample size to two observations, the estimated value could change a great deal. Conversely, if the researcher is very cautious, a sample of forty-nine might be taken. Now, even if the tallest person in the class is in the sample, there are forty-eight other observations that are also considered. The estimate of the average height now is much more confident. Also, the value should not change very much when one more observation is added to the calculation. When someone releases poll results and describes them with a margin of error of 3, 5, or 10 percent, that margin of error is determined by the sample size.

Systematic Sampling Error

Systematic (nonsampling) errors result from nonsampling factors, primarily the nature of a study's design and the correctness of execution. These errors are systematic in some way and *not* due to chance fluctuations. For example, in our classroom example, if a researcher chose a sampling frame consisting of all students sitting in the first two rows, a strong likelihood exists that systematic error would be introduced because shorter students tend to sit up front in an effort to see what is going on instead of the back of another student's head. Sample biases such as these account for a large portion of errors in marketing research. Errors due to sample selection problems are nonsampling errors and should not be classified as random sampling errors.

Systematic but not Obvious Sampling Error

We touched on some of these topics in earlier chapters. For example, telephone samples cannot represent the entire U.S. population because people without a landline phone usually share something in common with each other. For instance, they tend to be younger than average. Likewise, a random sample of U.S. homeowners would not represent all U.S. consumers because homeowners tend to be relatively older and more likely to have children than apartment dwellers. If a researcher cannot obtain a random, representative sample, he or she should aim to gather a sample that matches the population demographically.

Internet surveys allow researchers to reach a large sample rapidly—both an advantage and a disadvantage. Sample size requirements can be met overnight or in some cases almost instantaneously. A researcher can, for instance, release a survey during the morning in the Eastern Standard Time zone and have all sample size requirements met before anyone on the West Coast wakes up. If rapid response rates are expected, and a national sample is desired, steps must be taken to distribute the questionnaire evenly across all time zones. In addition, a survey released during the middle of the day, just like a phone sample conducted in the middle of the day, is likely to exclude people with full-time jobs in a systematic way because they are at work. Thus, the survey should probably remain active for a minimum of 12 hours or so.

The ease and low cost of an Internet survey also contributes to the flood of online questionnaires. As a result, frequent Internet users may be more selective about which surveys they bother answering. Researchers investigating college students' attitudes toward environmental issues found that those who responded to an e-mail request sent to all students at a school scored higher on environmental concern than students contacted individually through systematic sampling.[4] The researchers concluded that students who cared about the issues were more likely to respond to the online survey.

Website Visitors

Many Internet surveys use volunteer respondents who happen to visit an organization's website intentionally or by happenstance. These *unrestricted samples* are clearly not random samples. They may not even represent people with an interest in that particular website because of the haphazard manner by which many respondents arrived at a particular site.

A better technique for sampling website visitors is to select sampling units randomly. Survey software can be used to trigger a pop-up survey to each one-hundredth (or whatever number) visitor. Or, the software can even adjust the triggering of the survey based on information gathered on the respondent's Web behavior. For example, the opportunity to become a respondent might be timed so that at least 30 seconds have to be spent on the home page before the respondent becomes part of the sampling frame. This may prevent random page visitors from becoming a large part of the sample. Respondents who are selected to participate are first prompted to see if they would like to participate. If the person clicks "Yes," the site presents the questionnaire as a pop-up or as a new browser window.

Randomly selecting website visitors can cause a problem by overrepresenting frequent visitors. Several programming techniques and technologies (using cookies, registration data, or prescreening) are available to help accomplish more representative sampling based on site traffic. Cookies contain information that reveals the frequency of visits.

Panel Samples

Consumer panels provide a practical sampling frame in many situations. The panel company knows basic characteristics of each member. Panels become particularly useful in screening out sampling units who do not fit the characteristics of a relevant population. If the relevant population is men, the e-mail addresses belonging to female respondents are omitted from the frame. However, panels are not perfect.

Often panel members are compensated for their time with a sweepstakes, a small cash incentive, points that can be traded for products or donations to charities. The panel members may also contain a high proportion of respondents who simply like to fill out questionnaires or give their opinion. Either case presents the opportunity for sample bias. Fortunately, research suggests that personality variables do not relate strongly to panel membership.[5] However, attempts to validate survey results using different panels or different communication methods often show variance.[6] Thus, as the concern for representativeness increases, the more steps the researcher must take to ensure that the sampling units do indeed represent the population.

Consider Harris Interactive Inc., an Internet survey research organization, which maintains a panel of more than 6 million individuals internationally. A database this large allows the company to draw simple random samples, stratified samples, and quota samples from its panel members.[7] Harris Interactive oversamples, meaning sends disproportionately more invitations, to demographic groups known to under-respond such as males 18 to 24 years old. Practically all groups can be reached through panel surveys with the possible exception of the elderly (over 75 years of age) and the impoverished.

To ensure that survey results are representative, Harris Interactive uses a *propensity-weighting* scheme. The research company does parallel studies—by phone as well as over the Internet—to test the accuracy of its Internet data-gathering capabilities. Researchers look at the results of the telephone surveys and match those against the Internet-only survey results. Next, they use propensity weighting to adjust the results, taking into account the motivational and behavioral differences between the online and offline populations. (How propensity weighting adjusts for the difference between the Internet population and the general population is beyond the scope of this discussion.)

In addition to these steps, panel members may be asked screening questions to make sure that the screening characteristics are accurately working. For example, a researcher interested in coffee shop drinkers in the Midwest may want respondents to compare other shops to Starbucks. Thus, the population may be limited to consumers who frequent Starbucks. Although the online panel may be screened to include only communities where Starbucks has coffee shops, the researcher would be well advised to include screening questions that check on the familiarity of respondents with Starbucks.

Opting In

Survey Sampling International specializes in providing sampling frames and scientifically drawn samples.[8] The company offers more than 3,500 lists of high-quality, targeted e-mail addresses of individuals who have given permission to receive e-mail messages related to a particular topic of interest. Survey Sampling International's database contains millions of Internet users who **opt in**, **meaning they agree to be solicited for participation in surveys**. An important feature of Survey Sampling International's database is that the company has each individual confirm and reconfirm interest in communicating about a topic before the person's e-mail address is added to the company's database.

By whatever technique the sampling frame is compiled, it is important *not* to send unauthorized e-mail to respondents. If individuals do not *opt in* to receive e-mail from a particular organization, they may consider unsolicited survey requests to be spam. A researcher cannot expect high response rates from individuals who have not agreed to be surveyed. Spamming is not tolerated by experienced Internet users and can easily backfire, creating a host of problems—the most extreme being complaints to the Internet service provider (ISP), which may shut down the survey site.

Sites like Amazon's Mechanical Turk provide another opportunity for respondents to opt in to surveys. However, these respondents do not participate as members of any panel but rather as an unscreened, paid respondent. Therefore, respondents who participate after coincidentally or intentionally finding a survey on a website of this type are not random and cannot be considered representative of the general population.

opt in
To give permission to be solicited to participate in surveys.

● ● ● ● ● ● ●

Survey Sampling International concentrates its efforts on providing valid sampling frames. Notice how they place emphasis on profiling questions to help maintain the match between the sample and the population.

Image courtesy of Barry J. Babin

Less Than Perfectly Representative Samples

Random sampling errors and systematic errors associated with the sampling process may combine to yield a sample that is less than perfectly representative of the population. Exhibit 12.3 illustrates two nonsampling errors (sampling frame error and nonresponse error) related to sample design. The total population is represented by the area of the largest square. Sampling frame errors eliminate some potential respondents. Random sampling error (due exclusively to random, chance fluctuation) may cause an imbalance in the representativeness of the group. Additional errors will occur if individuals refuse to be interviewed or cannot be contacted. Such nonresponse error may also cause the sample to be less than perfectly representative. Notice that if the top half of the total population comes from one part of town, and the bottom half comes from another part of town; by the time the planned sample is reached, the portion from the lower part of the exhibit is overrepresented and this continues to the actual sample where 25 percent more of the sample (represented by four people as opposed to three) comes from the lower portion of town. The actual sample overrepresents this portion of town.

Probability versus Nonprobability Sampling

Several alternative ways to take a sample are available. The main alternative sampling plans may be grouped into two categories: probability techniques and nonprobability techniques.

In **probability sampling**, every element in the population has a *known, nonzero probability* of selection. The simple random sample, in which each member of the population has an equal probability of being selected, is the best-known probability sample.

In **nonprobability sampling**, the probability of any particular member of the population being chosen is unknown. The selection of sampling units in nonprobability sampling is quite arbitrary, as researchers rely heavily on personal judgment. Technically, no appropriate statistical techniques exist for measuring random sampling error from a nonprobability sample. Therefore, projecting the data beyond the sample is, technically speaking, statistically inappropriate. Nevertheless, researchers sometimes find nonprobability samples best suited for a specific researcher purpose. As a result, nonprobability samples are pragmatic and are used in market research.

Although probability sampling is preferred, this section on nonprobability sampling illustrates some potential sources of error and other weaknesses in sampling.

probability sampling

A sampling technique in which every member of the population has a known, nonzero probability of selection.

nonprobability sampling

A sampling technique in which units of the sample are selected on the basis of personal judgment or convenience; the probability of any particular member of the population being chosen is unknown.

EXHIBIT 12.3 Errors Associated with Sampling

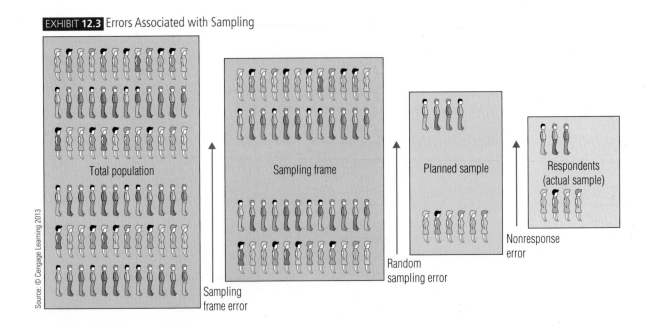

Source: © Cengage Learning 2013

Total population

Sampling frame

Planned sample

Respondents (actual sample)

Sampling frame error

Random sampling error

Nonresponse error

Convenience Sampling

As the name suggests, **convenience sampling** refers to sampling by obtaining people or units that are conveniently available. A research team may determine that the most convenient and economical method is to set up an interviewing booth from which to intercept consumers at a shopping center. Television stations often present person-on-the-street interviews that are presumed to reflect public opinion. Thus, whoever happens to walk by the reporter is surveyed on matters of the day. (Of course, the television station generally warns that the survey was "unscientific and random" [sic].) Comedians do these interviews and commonly demonstrate that the typical "person-on-the-street" can't answer basic questions like who is the vice president is or give the names of two U.S. Supreme Court justices.

Researchers generally use convenience samples to obtain a large number of completed questionnaires quickly and economically, or when obtaining a sample through other means is impractical. For example, many Internet surveys are conducted with volunteer respondents who, either intentionally or by happenstance come across a survey invitation on Facebook, Twitter, or some other website. Although this method produces a large number of responses quickly and at low cost, visitors to a website comprise a convenience sample. Respondents, thus, may not be representative because of the haphazard manner by which many of them arrived at the website or because of self-selection bias.

Similarly, research looking for cross-cultural differences in organizational or consumer behavior typically uses convenience samples. Rather than selecting cultures with characteristics relevant to the hypothesis being tested, the researchers conducting these studies often choose cultures to which they have access (for example, because they speak the language or have contacts in that culture's organizations). Further adding to the convenience, cross-cultural research often defines "culture" in terms of nations, which are easier to identify and obtain statistics about. But, complications exist with this approach, including the fact that many nations include several cultures and some people in a given nation may be more involved with the international business or academic community than with a particular ethnic culture.[9] Here again, the use of convenience sampling limits how well the research represents the intended population.

The user of research based on a convenience sample should remember that projecting the results beyond the specific sample is inappropriate. Convenience samples are best used for exploratory research when additional research will subsequently be conducted with a probability sample. University professors conducting marketing research will frequently use a student sample out of convenience. This can be appropriate if the emphasis in the research design is largely on internal validity. In other words, to see if the effect put forth in a hypothesis holds under circumstances allowing maximum control of outside effects. The use of student sample is inappropriate when the researcher intends the results to generalize to a larger population.

convenience sampling

The sampling procedure of obtaining those people or units that are most conveniently available.

"A straw vote only shows which way the hot air blows."

—O. HENRY

Judgment Sampling

Judgment (purposive) sampling is a nonprobability sampling technique in which an experienced individual selects the sample based on his or her judgment about some appropriate characteristics required of the sample member. Researchers select samples that satisfy their specific purposes, even if they are not fully representative. The consumer price index (CPI) is based on a judgment sample of market-basket items, housing costs, and other selected goods and services expected to reflect a representative sample of items consumed by most Americans. Test-market cities often are selected because they are viewed as typical cities whose demographic profiles closely match the national profile. A fashion manufacturer regularly selects a sample of key accounts that it believes are capable of providing information needed to predict what may sell in the fall. Thus, the sample is selected to achieve this specific objective.

judgment (purposive) sampling

A nonprobability sampling technique in which an experienced individual selects the sample based on personal judgment about some appropriate characteristics of the sample member.

Quota Sampling

Suppose your university administration wants to investigate the experiences of the undergraduate student body. Although 95 percent of the students are full-time, the administration may wish to ensure that both full-time and part-time students are included in the sample. In this case, the researcher may decide to have the sample of 200 students consist of 150 full-time and 50 part-time students. This quota would ensure that the part-time students are well represented, whereas strict probability sampling procedures might not include a sufficient number of those students (10).

quota sampling

A nonprobability sampling procedure that ensures that various subgroups of a population will be represented on pertinent characteristics to the exact extent that the investigator desires.

The purpose of **quota sampling** is to ensure that the various subgroups in a population are represented on pertinent sample characteristics to the exact extent that the investigators desire. Stratified sampling, a probability sampling procedure described in the next section, also has this objective, but it should not be confused with quota sampling. In quota sampling, the interviewer has a quota to achieve. For example, the interviewer may be assigned 100 interviews, 75 with full-time students, and 25 with part-time students. The interviewer is responsible for finding enough people to meet the quota. Aggregating the various interview quotas yields a sample that represents the desired proportion of each subgroup.

Possible Sources of Bias

The logic of classifying the population by pertinent subgroups is essentially sound. However, because respondents are selected according to a convenience sampling procedure rather than on a probability basis (as in stratified sampling), the haphazard selection of subjects may introduce bias. For example, a college professor hired some of his students to conduct a quota sample based on age. When analyzing the data, the professor discovered that almost all the people in the "under 25 years" category were college-educated. Interviewers, being human, tend to prefer to interview people who are similar to themselves.

Quota samples tend to include people who are easily found, willing to be interviewed, and middle class. Fieldworkers exercise considerable leeway in the selection of actual respondents. Interviewers often concentrate their interviewing in areas with heavy pedestrian traffic such as downtowns, shopping malls, and college campuses. Those who interview door-to-door learn quickly that quota requirements are difficult to meet by interviewing whoever happens to appear at the door. People who are more likely to stay at home generally share a less active lifestyle and are less likely to be meaningfully employed. One interviewer related a story of working in an upper-middle-class neighborhood. After a few blocks, he arrived in a neighborhood of mansions. Feeling that most of the would-be respondents were above his station, the interviewer skipped these houses because he felt uncomfortable knocking on doors that would be answered by these people or their hired help.

Advantages of Quota Sampling

The major advantages of quota sampling over probability sampling are speed of data collection, lower costs, and convenience. Although quota sampling has many problems, carefully supervised data collection may provide a representative sample of the various subgroups within a population. Quota sampling may be appropriate when the researcher knows that a certain demographic group is more likely to refuse to cooperate with a survey. For instance, if older men are more likely to refuse, a higher quota can be set for this group so that the proportion of each demographic category will be similar to the proportions in the population. A number of laboratory experiments also rely on quota sampling because it is difficult to find a sample of the general population willing to visit a laboratory to participate in an experiment.

Snowball Sampling

snowball sampling

A sampling procedure in which initial respondents are selected by probability methods and additional respondents are obtained from information provided by those initial respondents.

Snowball sampling involves using probability methods for selecting initial respondents and then obtaining additional respondents through information provided by those initial respondents. Researchers use this referral type approach when locating members of rare populations. Suppose a manufacturer of sports equipment is considering marketing a mahogany croquet set for serious adult players. This market is certainly small. An extremely large sample would be necessary to find 100 serious adult croquet players. It would be much more economical to survey, say, 300 people, find 15 serious croquet players, and ask them for the names of other croquet players.

Reduced sample sizes and costs are clear-cut advantages of snowball sampling. However, bias is likely to enter into the study because a person suggested by someone also in the sample has a higher probability of being similar to the first person. If there are major differences between those who are widely known by others and those who are not, this technique may present some serious problems. However, snowball sampling can locate and recruit heavy users, such as consumers who buy more than twenty-five houseplants each year. The approach may identify potential focus group participants and because generalizability is not a concern, the focus group organizer can use snowball sampling.

Probability Sampling

All probability sampling techniques employ chance selection procedures. The random probability process eliminates bias inherent in nonprobability sampling procedures. Note that the term *random* refers to the procedure for selecting the sample and not the data in the sample. *Randomness* characterizes a procedure whose outcome cannot be predicted because it depends on chance. Randomness should not be thought of as unplanned or unscientific—it is the basis of all probability sampling techniques. This section will examine the various probability sampling methods.

Simple Random Sampling

Simple random sampling is a sampling procedure ensuring that each element in a population has an equal chance of being included in a sample. Examples include drawing names from a hat and selecting the winning raffle ticket from a large drum. If the names or raffle tickets are thoroughly stirred, each person or ticket should have an equal chance of being selected. In contrast to other, more complex types of probability sampling, this process is simple in that only one stage of sample selection is required.

Although drawing names or numbers out of a fishbowl, rolling dice, or turning a roulette wheel may be an appropriate way to draw a sample from a small population, when populations consist of large numbers of elements, sample selection can be based on tabled random numbers or computer-generated random numbers (see **http://www.samurajdata.se/~cj/rnd.html** or **http://random.org** for simple random number generators).

Suppose a researcher is interested in selecting a simple random sample of all the Honda auto dealers in California, New Mexico, Arizona, and Nevada. Each dealer's name is assigned a number from 1 to 105. The numbers can be written on paper slips, and all the slips can be placed in a bowl. If a researcher desires a sample of 25, he or she can use a random number generator to randomly select a number between 1 and 105. For example, if 60 is the random number generated, then the dealer assigned that number is selected for the sample. This procedure can then be repeated until the sample of 25 is obtained. Alternatively, the researcher can use an online number generator to find 25 random numbers between 1 and 105 and produce the same result.

simple random sampling

A sampling procedure that assures each element in the population of an equal chance of being included in the sample.

"Make everything as simple as possible, but not simpler."

—ALBERT EINSTEIN

● ● ● ● ● ● ●

Random number tables can be found on the Internet. This is just one example.

RANDOM.ORG – Integer Generator

http://www.random.org/integers/?num=100&min=1&max=100&col=5&base=10&format=html&rnd=new

RANDOM.ORG – Integer Generator

Home Games Numbers Lists & More Drawings Web Tools Statistics Testimonials Learn More Login

RANDOM.ORG

Search RANDOM.ORG

True Random Number Service

Random Integer Generator

Here are your random numbers:

53	8	48	16	89
95	4	18	80	3
73	77	70	9	21
40	4	52	67	82
35	26	94	53	6
14	99	73	83	7
45	72	86	61	77
79	59	51	89	25
75	97	8	42	27
79	83	66	13	97
16	8	58	13	24
88	57	28	70	96
91	2	31	87	7
48	75	37	83	43
2	30	89	20	96
34	63	100	88	54
26	26	53	7	3
37	74	33	73	43
5	55	54	21	98
19	97	94	70	58

Timestamp: 2011-12-09 15:15:28 UTC

(Again!) (Go Back)

Note: The numbers are generated left to right, i.e., across columns.

+1 1.3k

Like 42k

Traditionally, random number tables have facilitated random sample selection. A number is first assigned to each element of the population (i.e., alphabetical, chronological, digits from a student number, etc.). Assuming the population is 99,999 or fewer, five-digit numbers may be selected from the table of random numbers merely by reading the numbers in any column or row, moving up, down, left, or right. A random starting point should be selected at the outset. For convenience, we will assume that we have randomly selected as our starting point the first five digits in columns 1 through 5, row 1, of the table generated by random.org, shown above. The first number in our sample would be 73265; moving down, the next numbers would be 34663, 62549, and so on.

The random-digit dialing technique of sample selection requires that a telephone interviewer identify the exchange or exchanges of interest (the first three numbers in a phone number after the area code) and then use a table of numbers to select the next four numbers. In practice, however, the exchanges are not always selected randomly. Researchers who wanted to find out whether black Americans with African ancestry prefer being called "black" or "African-American" narrowed their sampling frame by selecting exchanges associated with geographic areas where the proportion of this population was at least 30 percent. The reasoning was that this made the survey procedure far more efficient, considering that the researchers were trying to contact a group representing less than 15 percent of U.S. households. This initial judgment sampling raises the same issues we discussed regarding nonprobability sampling. In this study, the researchers found that respondents were most likely to prefer the term *black* if they had attended schools that were about half black and half white.[10] If such experiences influence the answers to the question of interest to the researchers, the fact that blacks who live in predominantly white communities are underrepresented may introduce bias into the results. The result reduces the generalizability of the results.

systematic sampling

A sampling procedure in which a starting point is selected by a random process and then every *n*th number on the list is selected.

Systematic Sampling Suppose a researcher wants to take a sample of 1,000 from a population of 200,000 names. With **systematic sampling**, he/she would draw every 200th name from a list of population members. This simple process illustrates how to find the interval between selected observations:

$$\text{Interval} = \frac{\text{Population Size}}{\text{Sample Size}} = \frac{200,000}{1,000} = 200$$

A starting point is selected randomly; then every *n*th number on the list is selected. In this case, the researcher selects every 200th name. Because the starting point may well not be at the beginning, this may actually yield only 199 names. A random number can be used to select one more if the sample needs to be exactly 1,000.

Exhibit 12.4 illustrates this process. Here, suppose someone wished to take a sample of the average monthly temperature in Colombia over a 100-month period. Thus, the exhibit shows the first in what will be a total of 104 total observations. If a sample of 20 is to be obtained, every fifth observation is taken. A die is rolled to find what the first observation will be. Thus, the sequence of selected observations is shown in the rows highlighted in green.

Although systematic sampling is not actually a random selection procedure, it does yield random results if the arrangement of the items is not in some sequence corresponding to the interval in some way. The problem of *periodicity* can occur otherwise. Returning to Exhibit 12.4, what would happen if the average temperature in this time period were compared with a historical average of 17 degrees and a sample was formed with a sampling interval of 12 and a random starting point of August? Obviously, the comparison would be biased because all of the readings would be summertime readings. This could hardly be considered random.

Stratified Sampling

stratified sampling

A probability sampling procedure in which simple random subsamples that are more or less equal on some characteristic are drawn from within each stratum of the population.

The usefulness of dividing the population into subgroups, or *strata,* whose members are more or less equal with respect to a characteristic, was illustrated in our discussion of quota sampling. The first step is the same for both stratified and quota sampling: choosing strata on the basis of existing information—for example, classifying retail outlets based on annual sales volume. However, the process of selecting sampling units within the strata differs substantially. In **stratified sampling**, a subsample is drawn using simple random sampling within each stratum. This is not true of quota sampling.

The reason for taking a stratified sample is to obtain a more efficient sample than would be possible with simple random sampling. Suppose, for example, that urban and rural groups have

EXHIBIT **12.4**
Systematically Sampling
from a List

	Observation	Month	Year	Average Temperature (C°)
Random Starting Point	1	January	2010	4
	2	February	2010	6
	3	March	2010	10
	4	April	2010	15
	5	May	2010	16
	6	June	2010	22
Select	7	July	2010	26
	8	August	2010	22
	9	September	2010	27
	10	October	2010	19
	11	November	2010	10
Select	12	December	2010	6
	13	January	2011	−2
	14	February	2011	9
	15	March	2011	9
	16	April	2011	12
Select	17	May	2011	18
	18	June	2011	26
	19	July	2011	30
	20	August	2011	31
	21	September	2011	24
Select	22	October	2011	14
	23	November	2011	12
	24	December	2011	7
	25	January	2012	5
	26	February	2012	4
Select	27	March	2012	9
	28	April	2012	14
	29	May	2012	18
	30	June	2012	24
	31	July	2012	24
Select	32	August	2012	25

Source: © Cengage Learning 2013.

widely different attitudes toward energy conservation, but members within each group hold very similar attitudes. Random sampling error will be reduced with the use of stratified sampling, because each group is internally homogeneous but there are comparative differences between groups. More technically, a smaller standard error may result from this stratified sampling because the groups will be adequately represented when strata are combined.

Another reason for selecting a stratified sample is to ensure that the sample will accurately reflect the population on the basis of the criterion or criteria used for stratification. This is a concern because occasionally simple random sampling yields a disproportionate number of one group or another and the sample ends up being less representative than it could be.

A researcher can select a stratified sample as follows. First, a variable (sometimes several variables) is identified as an efficient basis for stratification. A stratification variable must be a characteristic of the population elements known to be related to the dependent variable or other variables of interest. The variable chosen should increase homogeneity within each stratum and increase heterogeneity between strata. The stratification variable usually is a categorical variable or one easily converted into categories (that is, subgroups). For example, a pharmaceutical company interested in measuring how often physicians prescribe a certain drug might choose physicians' training area as a basis for stratification. In this example the mutually exclusive strata are MDs (medical doctors) and ODs (osteopathic doctors).

Next, for each separate subgroup or stratum, a list of population elements must be obtained. (If such lists are not available, they can be costly to prepare, and if a complete listing is not available, a true stratified probability sample cannot be selected.) Using a table of random numbers or some other device, a *separate* simple random sample is then taken within each stratum. Of course, the researcher must determine how large a sample to draw for each stratum. This issue is discussed in the following section.

Proportional versus Disproportional Sampling

proportional stratified sample

A stratified sample in which the number of sampling units drawn from each stratum is in proportion to the population size of that stratum.

If the number of sampling units drawn from each stratum is in proportion to the relative population size of the stratum, the sample is a **proportional stratified sample**. Sometimes, however, a researcher selects a disproportional stratified sample to try to obtain an adequate number of sampling units in each stratum. Sampling more heavily in a given stratum than its relative population size warrants is not a problem if the primary purpose of the research is to estimate some characteristic separately for each stratum and if researchers are concerned about assessing the differences among strata.

Suppose a research question concerned what was the average total bill of retail customers in Missouri based on the average total reported by retail stores. The percentage breakdown of Missouri retail outlets is presented in Exhibit 12.5. A proportional sample of retail stores would use the same percentages as in the population. However, the small percentage of warehouse club stores underrepresents the relative amount of money consumers spend in these large stores. To avoid underrepresenting the large warehouse clubs in the sample, the researcher can take a disproportional sample.

disproportional stratified sample

A stratified sample in which the sample size for each stratum is allocated according to analytical considerations.

In a **disproportional stratified sample** the sample size for each stratum is not allocated in proportion to the population size but is dictated by analytical considerations, such as variability in store sales volume. The logic behind this procedure relates to the general argument for sample size: as variability increases, sample size must increase to provide accurate estimates. Thus, the strata

EXHIBIT 12.5

Disproportional Sampling: Hypothetical Example

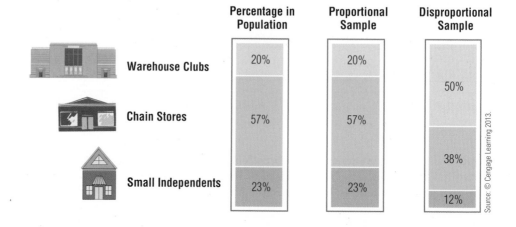

Source: © Cengage Learning 2013.

that exhibit the greatest variability are sampled more heavily to increase sample efficiency—that is, produce smaller random sampling error. Complex formulas (beyond the scope of an introductory course in marketing research) have been developed to determine sample size for each stratum. A simplified rule of thumb for understanding the concept of optimal allocation is that the stratum sample size increases for strata of larger sizes with the greatest relative variability. Other complexities arise in determining population estimates. For example, when disproportional stratified sampling is used, the estimated mean for each stratum has to be weighed according to the number of elements in each stratum in order to calculate the total population mean.

Cluster Sampling

Cluster sampling is an economical sampling approach that retains the characteristics of a probability sample. Consider a researcher who must conduct 500 personal interviews with physicians scattered throughout the United States. Travel costs are likely to be enormous because the amount of time spent traveling will be substantially greater than the time spent in the interviewing process. If a pharmaceutical marketer can assume the product will be equally successful in Phoenix and Baltimore, cluster sampling provides an alternative. The assumption is that respondents in a cluster that is sampled are the same as respondents in an unsampled cluster.

In **cluster sampling**, the primary sampling unit is no longer the individual element in the population (for example, grocery stores) but a larger cluster of elements located in proximity to one another (for example, cities). The *area sample* is the most popular type of cluster sample. A grocery store researcher, for example, may randomly choose several geographic areas as primary sampling units and then interview at a sample of grocery stores within the geographic clusters. Interviews are confined to these clusters only. No interviews occur in other clusters. Cluster sampling is classified as a probability sampling technique because of either the random selection of clusters or the random selection of elements within each cluster. Some examples of clusters appear in Exhibit 12.6.

Cluster samples become attractive when lists of a sample population are not available. For example, when researchers investigating employees and self-employed workers for a downtown revitalization project found that a comprehensive list of these people was not available, they decided to take a cluster sample, selecting organizations (business and government) involved in the project as the clusters. A sample of firms within the central business district was developed, using stratified probability sampling to identify clusters. Next, individual workers within the firms (clusters) were randomly selected and interviewed concerning the revitalization project.

cluster sampling

An economically efficient sampling technique in which the primary sampling unit is not the individual element in the population but a large cluster of elements; clusters are selected randomly.

Population Element	Possible Clusters in the United States
U.S. adult population	States Counties Metropolitan Statistical Areas Census Tracts Blocks Households
College seniors	Colleges
Manufacturing firms	Counties Metropolitan Statistical Areas Localities Plants
Airline travelers	Airports Planes
Sports fans	Football Stadiums Basketball Arenas Baseball Parks

EXHIBIT **12.6**
Examples of Clusters

Source: © Cengage Learning 2013.

Had Too Much?

When has a customer had too much to drink? Health and government agencies are interested in marketing research on consumers' reported consumption of alcoholic beverages. However, marketing research on the topic is complicated by multiple issues. Some respondents may view the topic as personally sensitive and be hesitant to respond or respond truthfully. Not only will this lead to respondent error but systematic sampling error may increase as these respondents opt out.

Moreover, if the intent is to represent the U.S. adult population, and the questions involve self-reported numbers of drinks and intoxication, what should the sampling frame be? Should the sampling frame take into account factors beyond demographics such as the height and weight of consumers? Should it account for situational factors and the types of service environments in which consumers drink? Research suggests large variations in the amount of drinks necessary for someone to become intoxicated based on these factors and other things

such as the amount and types of foods consumed while drinking. As in a lot of marketing research, what seems at first like a simple matter of asking a few questions, quickly becomes complex. In this case, trying to get a sampling frame and sampling scheme that adequately represents the relevant population is itself a question requiring a great deal of study.

Sources: Beck, M. (2011), "Testing the Limits of Tipsy," *Wall Street Journal*, (August 2), D. Reynolds, K. and L. Harris (2009), "Dysfunctional Customer Behavior Severity: An Empirical Examination," *Journal of Retailing*, 85 (3), 321–35.

Ideally a cluster should be as heterogeneous as the population itself—a mirror image of the population. A problem may arise with cluster sampling if the characteristics and attitudes of the elements within the cluster are too similar. For example, geographic neighborhoods tend to have residents of the same socioeconomic status. Students at a university tend to share similar beliefs. This problem may be mitigated by constructing clusters composed of diverse elements and by selecting a large number of sampled clusters.

Multistage Area Sampling

multistage area sampling

Sampling that involves using a combination of two or more probability sampling techniques.

Multistage area sampling is a cluster sampling approach involving multiple steps that combine some of the probability techniques already described. Typically, geographic areas are randomly selected in progressively smaller (lower-population) units. For example, a political pollster investigating an election in Texas might first choose counties within the state to ensure that different areas are represented in the sample. In the second step, precincts within the selected counties may be chosen. As a final step, the pollster may select blocks (or households) within the precincts, then interview all the blocks (or households) within the geographic area. Researchers may take as many steps as necessary to achieve a representative sample.

The Bureau of the Census provides maps, population information, demographic characteristics for population statistics, and so on, by several small geographical areas; these may be useful in sampling. Census classifications of small geographic areas vary, depending on the extent of urbanization within Metropolitan Statistical Areas (MSAs) or counties.

What Is the Appropriate Sample Design?

A researcher who must decide on the most appropriate sample design for a specific project will identify a number of sampling criteria and evaluate the relative importance of each criterion before selecting a sampling design. This section outlines and briefly discusses the most common criteria. The Research Snapshot illustrates how important the sampling design would be to any survey about U.S. drinking habits.

Degree of Accuracy

Selecting a representative sample can be crucial for a researcher desiring to make accurate predictions or forecasts. However, the degree of accuracy required or the researcher's tolerance for sampling and nonsampling error may vary from project to project, especially when cost savings or another benefit may be a trade-off for a reduction in accuracy.

For example, when the sample is part of an exploratory research project, accuracy may not be the highest priority. For other, more conclusive projects, the sample result must precisely represent a population's characteristics, and the researcher must be willing to spend the time and money needed to achieve that accuracy. When researchers use a convenience sample, they may sometimes even think backwards and only describe what population the results extend to based on the sample that can be obtained. Typically, a market research report will qualify results based on sampling characteristics.

Resources

The cost associated with the different sampling techniques varies tremendously. If the researcher's financial and human resources are restricted, certain options will have to be eliminated. For a typical graduate student working on a thesis or dissertation, conducting a representative, national survey is often out of the question because of limited resources. Managers concerned with the cost of the research versus the value of the information often will opt to save money by using a nonprobability sampling design rather than make the decision to conduct no research at all.

Time

A researcher who needs to meet a deadline or complete a project quickly will be more likely to select a simple, less time-consuming sample design. A researcher may have questions about an online panel and how well it represents the relevant population of consumers in the United States. However, he or she can obtain the online panel very quickly and may be willing to trade off speed for any increased accuracy that would come from drawing his or her own sampling frame.

Advance Knowledge of the Population

Advance knowledge of population characteristics, such as the availability of lists of population members, is an important criterion. In many cases, however, no list of population elements exists. This is especially true when the population element is defined by ownership of a particular product or brand, by experience in performing a specific job task, or on a qualitative dimension. A lack of adequate lists may automatically rule out systematic sampling, stratified sampling, or other sampling designs, or it may dictate that a preliminary study, such as a short telephone survey using random digit dialing, be conducted to generate information to build a sampling frame for the primary study. In many developing countries, things like reverse directories are rare. Thus, researchers planning sample designs have to work around this limitation.

National versus Local Project

Geographic proximity of population elements will influence sample design. When population elements are unequally distributed geographically, a cluster sample may become much more attractive. A sample that represents all households in the United States and Canada becomes the goal for the few household products that show no regional, demographic, or lifestyle bias. Few products exhibit this characteristic. For instance, market research investigating opinions of North Americans about the Smart Car would be served better by sampling from large urban areas rather than giving rural residents an equal chance of being included in the research.

TIPS OF THE TRADE

- Marketing research rarely requires a census.
- Online panels are a practical reality in marketing research. A sample can be obtained quickly and generally comes close to matching general population parameters.
- As with all panels, the researcher faces a risk that systematic error is introduced in some way. For example, this sample may be higher in willingness to give opinions or may be responding only for an incentive.
- Convenience samples do have appropriate uses in marketing research. Convenience samples (including student samples) are particularly appropriate when:
  - – Exploratory research is conducted.
  - – The researcher is primarily interested in internal validity (testing a hypothesis under any condition) rather than external validity (understanding how much the sample results project to a target population).
  - When cost and time constraints only allow a convenience sample:
    - – Researchers can think backwards and project on the population for whom the results apply to based on the nature of the convenience sample.
- The research report should address the adequacy of the sample. The report should qualify the generalizability of the results based on sample limitations.

Source: © Cengage Learning 2013.

∷ SUMMARY

1. Explain reasons for taking a sample rather than a complete census. Sampling involves drawing conclusions about an entire population by taking measurements from only a portion of that population. The practical nature of research is clearly illustrated in sampling. Sampling is used because of the practical impossibility of measuring every population member. Seldom would a researcher have the time or budget to do so. Also, a researcher would rarely need to measure every unit, as a well-designed and executed sampling plan can yield results that may even be more accurate than an actual census. Samples also are needed in cases where measurement involves destruction of the measured unit.

2. Describe the process of identifying a target population and selecting a sampling frame. The first problem in sampling is to define the target population. Incorrect or vague definition of this population is likely to produce misleading results. The chapter contains an example list of questions that illustrate considerations needed in making a decision about the relevant population. A sampling frame is a list of elements, or individual members, of the overall population from which the sample is drawn. A sampling unit is a single element or group of elements subject to selection in the sample. Sometimes, a list of actual population members exists and can serve as a sampling frame. More often, the researcher will need the assistance of a directory, panel, or mailing list in forming the sampling frame.

3. Compare random sampling and systematic (nonsampling) errors with an emphasis on how the Internet is intertwined with this issue. Two sources of discrepancy between the sample results and the population parameters exist. One, random sampling error, arises from chance variations of the sample from the population. Random sampling error is a function of sample size and may be estimated using the central-limit theorem (discussed in a later chapter). Systematic, or nonsampling, error comes from sources such as sampling frame error, mistakes in recording responses, or nonresponses from persons who are not contacted or who refuse to participate. When researchers do not have an accurate list of population members, some type of systematic error becomes very likely. Internet surveys and consumer panels are very convenient but make truly random selection difficult. Thus, when these methods are chosen, extra care needs to be taken to make sure that the sample has characteristics that indeed allows it to represent the target population.

4. Identify the types of nonprobability sampling, including their advantages and disadvantages. The two major classes of sampling methods are probability and nonprobability techniques. Nonprobability techniques include convenience sampling, judgment sampling, quota sampling, and snowball sampling. They are convenient to use, but more subject to systematic sampling error. Sorting out the systematic sampling error from the random sampling error also proves problematic.

5. Summarize various types of probability samples. Probability samples are based on chance selection procedures. These include simple random sampling, systematic sampling, stratified sampling, and cluster sampling. With these techniques, random sampling error can be accurately predicted. The process for selecting sample units from a population is described in the chapter. A true probability sample can be costly both in terms of money and time.

6. Discuss how to choose an appropriate sample design. A researcher who must determine the most appropriate sampling design for a specific project will identify a number of sampling criteria and evaluate the relative importance of each criterion before selecting a design. The most common criteria concern accuracy requirements, available resources, time constraints, knowledge availability, and analytical requirements. Internet sampling presents some unique issues. Researchers must be aware that samples may be unrepresentative because not everyone has a computer or access to the Internet. Convenience samples drawn from website visitors can create problems. Drawing a probability sample from an established consumer panel whose members opt in can be effective.

:: KEY TERMS AND CONCEPTS

census, *312*
cluster sampling, *329*
convenience sampling, *323*
disproportional stratified sample, *328*
judgment (purposive) sampling, *323*
multistage area sampling, *330*
nonprobability sampling, *322*
online panels, *318*
opt in, *321*

population (universe), *312*
population element, *312*
primary sampling unit (PSU), *318*
probability sampling, *322*
proportional stratified sample, *328*
quota sampling, *324*
random sampling error, *319*
reverse directory, *318*
sample, *312*

sampling frame, *317*
sampling frame error, *317*
sampling unit, *318*
secondary sampling unit, *318*
simple random sampling, *325*
snowball sampling, *324*
stratified sampling, *326*
systematic sampling, *326*
tertiary sampling unit, *318*

:: QUESTIONS FOR REVIEW AND CRITICAL THINKING

1. If you decide whether you want to see a new movie or television program on the basis of the "coming attractions" or television commercial previews, are you using a sampling technique? Could this be described as a scientific sampling technique?

2. What is the difference between a population and a sample? What are the reasons why a sampling process is so often used in place of a census? Why is it that a population can sometimes be as accurate as, or more accurate than, a census?

3. How can a market researcher try to be confident that the target population involved in some research situation is defined properly?

4. How might the target population differ for a researcher doing separate projects for two retailing companies—one for A&F and one for Nordstrom?

5. Name some possible sampling frames for research questions involving the following:
   a. An online travel agency like Orbitz.com
   b. Online social network members

   c. Golf course greenskeepers (responsible for the condition of the golf course)
   d. Dog owners
   e. Harley-Davidson owners
   f. Tattoo wearers
   g. Minority-owned businesses
   h. Women over six feet tall
   i. Children who may consider engineering as a career
   j. Fast-food consumers in California

6. Describe the difference between a random and systematic sampling error.

7. What is a nonprobability sample? What are some examples?

8. Is a convenience sample ever appropriate? Explain.

9. When would a researcher use a judgment, or purposive, sample?

10. A telephone interviewer asks, "I would like to ask you about race. Are you Native American, Hispanic, African-American, Asian, or white?" After the respondent replies, the interviewer says, "We have conducted a large number of surveys with people of your background, and we do not need to question you

How good are the descriptive statistics discussed previously in helping make decisions like these? Before jumping to conclusions, consider some details seldom reported in media accounts of opinion results. The 60 and 55 percent figures come from a national consumer panel of 1,100 consumers. The 75 percent figure from parents is taken from a focus group of 12 consumers. The 40 percent top-box result is based on input from 150 GameCube owners in Texas aged 12 to 17 years old.

Knowing the size of the sample certainly helps us know how valuable the information is. In the first case, a sample of 1,100 means that sample result is likely within 2 to 3 percent of the actual population values. Thus, a majority of consumers and even gamers appear concerned. In the second case, a sample of 12 means that the true population value could actually be 100 percent, meaning all parents are not concerned about the effect of violence on their own children, or it could be practically 0 percent! Finally, in the third case, the sample of 150 consumers means the actual population value can be confidently projected to be between 32 and 48 percent.

Is there enough confidence to act? Not all decisions are the same. Enacting federal legislation is no small matter and steps that restrict market freedom should be considered only with very solid data. Thus, the sample of 1,100 provides a relatively high degree of confidence, but perhaps this alone isn't quite enough. The political and financial risks associated with a bad regulatory decision require very great precision. On the other hand, introducing a new video game, particularly if it is a variant of one that already exists, is not so risky and less precision is needed. If 40 percent is the benchmark upon which to make the go–no go decision for the firm, the 32 to 48 percent range may provide enough confidence to move forward. Although the firm might like more specific evidence, a larger sample will be costly in both money and time. Further, the longer the introduction is put off, the greater the risk that a competitor will be able to upstage the new introduction. So, at least in this case, bigger may not be better![1]

Introduction

The first portion of the chapter summarizes key statistical concepts necessary for understanding the theory that underlies the derivation of sample size. Students who need to review the basic aspects of statistics theory should pay particular attention to this material. Even those students who received good grades in elementary statistics classes probably will benefit from a quick review of these basic statistical concepts. The chapter then turns to issues related to sample size and the degree with which this affects the confidence with which population estimates can be made.

Raw data alone are seldom useful. They have to be organized and summarized to become useful and have the possibility of becoming actual market intelligence. The most basic ways for doing this include frequency distributions, proportions, and measures of central tendency and dispersion. Beyond these results, information about the sample helps decision makers know how much confidence can be placed in a given number.

Basic Descriptive and Inferential Statistics

Databases like those available through census.gov and the CIA *Factbook* present table after table of figures associated with numbers of births, number of workers by industry, populations, and other data that represent *statistics*. Specifically, these tables provide descriptive statistics. Another type of statistics, *inferential statistics*, allows inferences about a whole population from a sample. For example, when a firm test-markets a new product in Sacramento and Birmingham, it wishes to make an inference from these sample markets to predict what will happen throughout the United States. So, two applications of statistics exist: (1) to describe characteristics of the population or sample and (2) to generalize from a sample to a population.

What Are Sample Statistics and Population Parameters?

The primary purpose of inferential statistics is to make a judgment about a population, or the total collection of all elements about which a researcher seeks information. A sample is a subset or

Using data from the Survey This! feature, try to come up with answers to these questions:

1. Suppose a marketing manager was trying to determine how many students had only one e-mail account that they used regularly. Their intention is to market additional Internet services to students who have only one or no e-mail account.

   a. What is the proportion of students in the sample that have more than one e-mail account?
   b. If the student population is 5 million students, what sample size is needed to estimate the actual proportion of students with more than one active e-mail account within +/–1 percent?
   c. What sample size is needed to estimate the actual proportion of students with more than one active e-mail account within +/–5 percent?
   d. If the decision to launch this marketing activity involves an investment of approximately $75,000 for this

company (with median annual revenues of $3M), what level of precision would you recommend?

Source: © Cengage Learning 2013.

---

relatively small portion of the total number of elements in a given population. Data from a sample are always uncertain but when data come from all elements of a population, certainty is possible.

Sample statistics are measures computed from sample data. Population parameters are measured characteristics of a specific population. Sample statistics are used to make inferences (guesses) about population parameters.[2] In our notation, we will generally represent population parameters with Greek lowercase letters—for example, μ or α—and sample statistics with English letters, such as X or S.

sample statistics
Variables in a sample or measures computed from sample data.

Frequency Distributions

One of the most common ways to summarize a set of data is to construct a *frequency table*, or **frequency distribution**. The process begins with recording the number of times a particular value of a variable occurs. This is the frequency of that value. Exhibit 13.1 represents a frequency distribution of respondents' answers to a question that asked how much money they currently had in the local university credit union bank account (all were customers of the credit union).

frequency distribution
A set of data organized by summarizing the number of times a particular value of a variable occurs.

Amount	Frequency (Number of People Who Hold Deposits in Each Range)
Under $3,000	499
$3,000 – $4,999	530
$5,000 – $9,999	562
$10,000 – $14,999	718
$15,000 or more	811
	3,120

EXHIBIT 13.1
Frequency Distribution of Deposits

Source: © Cengage Learning 2013.

Source: © Cengage Learning 2013.

EXHIBIT 13.2
Percentage Distribution
of Deposits

Amount	Percent (Percentage of People Who Hold Deposits in Each Range)
Under $3,000	16
$3,000 – $4,999	17
$5,000 – $9,999	18
$10,000 – $14,999	23
$15,000 or more	26
	100

percentage distribution

A frequency distribution organized into a table (or graph) that summarizes percentage values associated with particular values of a variable.

probability

The long-run relative frequency with which an event will occur.

A similar method is a distribution of relative frequency, or a **percentage distribution**. To develop a frequency distribution of percentages, divide the frequency of each value by the total number of observations, and multiply the result by 100. Based on the data in Exhibit 13.1, Exhibit 13.2 shows the percentage distribution of deposits; that is, the percentage of people holding deposits within each range of values.

Probability is the long-run relative frequency with which an event will occur. Inferential statistics uses the concept of a probability distribution, which is conceptually the same as a percentage distribution except that the data are converted into probabilities. Exhibit 13.3 shows the probability distribution of the credit union deposits.

Proportions

proportion

The percentage of elements that meet some criterion.

Frequencies can also be expressed in terms of percentages. When a frequency distribution portrays only a single characteristic in terms of a percentage of the total, it defines the **proportion** of occurrence. A proportion, such as the proportion of tenured professors at a university, indicates the percentage of population elements that successfully meet a standard concerning the particular characteristic. A proportion may be expressed as a percentage, a fraction, or a decimal value. In the example used here and illustrated in Exhibit 13.3, the probabilities are equal to the proportion of consumers in each deposit category. For example, 23 percent have a bank balance between $10,000 and $14,999.

Top-Box Scores

top-box score

Proportion of respondents who chose the most positive choice in a multiple-choice question.

Managers are often very interested in the proportion of consumers choosing extreme responses. A **top-box score** generally refers to the portion of respondents who choose the most favorable response toward an option usually related to buying behavior. Typically, the top-box results show the portion of consumers who would most likely recommend a business to a friend or most likely to make a purchase. The logic is that respondents who choose the most extreme response are really quite unique compared to the others. Managers are often asking what the top-box score or number is.[3]

EXHIBIT 13.3
Probability Distribution
of Deposits

Source: © Cengage Learning 2013.

Amount	Probability
Under $3,000	.16
$3,000 – $4,999	.17
$5,000 – $9,999	.18
$10,000 – $14,999	.23
$15,000 or more	.26
	1.00

Measures of Central Tendency

On a typical day, a sales manager counts the number of sales calls each sales representative makes. He or she wishes to inspect the data to find the center, or middle area, of the frequency distribution. Put another way, what is the most typical number of sales calls? Central tendency can be measured with the mean, median, or mode. Each is determined in a slightly different way.

The Mean

We all have been exposed to the average known as the **mean**. The mean is simply the arithmetic average, and it is a common measure of central tendency. To express this mathematically, we use the summation symbol, the capital Greek letter **sigma** (Σ). A typical use might look like this:

$$\sum_{i=1}^{n} X_i$$

mean

A measure of central tendency; the arithmetic average.

which is a shorthand way to write the sum:

$$X_1 + X_2 + X_3 + X_4 + X_5 + \cdots + X_n$$

Below the Σ is the initial value of an index, i in this case, and above it is the final value of i, which also equals n, the total number of observations.

Suppose a sales manager supervises the eight salespeople listed in Exhibit 13.4. To express the sum of the salespeople's calls in Σ notation, we just number the salespeople (this number becomes the index number) and associate subscripted variables with their numbers of calls:

We then write an appropriate Σ formula and evaluate it:

$$\sum_{i=1}^{8} X_i = X_1 + X_2 + X_3 + X_4 + X_5 + X_6 + X_7 + X_8$$
$$= 4 + 3 + 2 + 5 + 3 + 3 + 1 + 5$$
$$= 26$$

This notation is the numerator in the formula for the arithmetic mean:

$$\text{Mean} = \frac{\sum_{i=1}^{n} X_i}{n} = \frac{26}{8} = 3.25$$

The notation $\sum_{i=1}^{n} X_i$ means add together all the Xs whose subscripts are between 1 and n inclusive, where n equals 8 in this case. The formula shows that the mean number of sales calls in this example is 3.25.

Index		Salesperson	Variable		Number of Calls
1	=	Mike	X_1	=	4
2	=	Patty	X_2	=	3
3	=	Billie	X_3	=	2
4	=	Bob	X_4	=	5
5	=	John	X_5	=	3
6	=	Frank	X_6	=	3
7	=	Chuck	X_7	=	1
8	=	Samantha	X_8	=	5
		Total		=	26

EXHIBIT 13.4

Number of Sales Calls per Day by Salesperson

Researchers generally wish to know the population mean, μ (lowercase Greek letter *mu*), which is calculated as follows:

$$\mu = \frac{\sum_{i=1}^{N} X_i}{N}$$

where

N = number of members in the population

Often we will not have enough data to calculate the population mean, μ, so we will calculate a sample mean, $\overline{X}$(read "X bar"), with the following formula:

$$\overline{X} = \frac{\sum_{i=1}^{n} X_i}{n}$$

where

n = number of observations made in the sample

More likely than not, you already know how to calculate a mean. However, knowing how to distinguish among the symbols Σ, μ, and X is helpful to understand statistics.

In this introductory discussion of the summation sign (Σ), we have used detailed notation that includes the subscript for the initial index value (i) and the final index value (n). However, from this point on in the chapter, we'll omit the details for simplicity and the symbol Σ will mean summed overall observations in the sample.

The mean is the most widely applied measure of central tendency. However, the mean can sometimes be misleading, particularly when extreme values or outliers are present. Thus, researchers sometimes rely on other central tendency indicators.

The Median

median

A measure of central tendency that is the midpoint; the value below which half the values in a distribution fall.

The next measure of central tendency, the **median**, is the midpoint of the distribution, or the 50th percentile. In other words, the median is the value below which half the values in the sample fall. In the sales manager example, 3 is the median because half the observations are greater than 3 and half are less than 3. In cases like this, with an even number of observations, the median equals the average of the two middle observations, in this case both are 3.

The median is a better indicator of central tendency in the presence of extreme values or outliers. For instance, a professor gives a marketing research test and one student makes a 99, another makes a 98, the next highest grade is 51, and the remaining 17 grades range from 30 to 50. If the professor curves the grades so that everyone who scores "above average" will pass, the result could be only 5 or 6 students passing as the mean would be on the order of 46. Perhaps the students would prefer a curve based around the median which would mean that half of the students would pass by definition.

The Mode

mode

A measure of central tendency; the value that occurs most often.

In fashion merchandizing, *mode* refers to the most popular fashion. In statistics the **mode** is the measure of central tendency that identifies the value that occurs most often. In our example of sales calls, Patty, John, and Frank each made three sales calls. The value 3 occurs most often, so 3 is the mode. The mode is determined by listing each possible value and noting the number of times each value occurs. The mode is the best measure of central tendency for data that is less than interval and for data approaching a unimodal distribution with one large peak (many observations have the same response with relatively few other responses).

Measures of Dispersion

The mean, median, and mode summarize the central tendency of frequency distributions. Accurate analysis of data also requires knowing the tendency of observations to depart from the central tendency. Thus, another way to summarize the data is to calculate the dispersion of the data, or

	Units Product A	Units Product B
January	196	150
February	198	160
March	199	176
April	200	181
May	200	192
June	200	200
July	200	201
August	201	202
September	201	213
October	201	224
November	202	240
December	202	261
Average	**200**	**200**

EXHIBIT 13.5
Sales Levels for Two Products with Identical Average Sales

Source: © Cengage Learning 2013.

how the observations vary from the mean. Consider, for instance, the twelve-month sales patterns of the two products shown in Exhibit 13.5. Both have a mean monthly sales volume of 200 units, but the dispersion of observations for product B is much greater than that for product A. There are several measures of dispersion.

The Range

The simplest measure of dispersion is the range. It is the distance between the smallest and the largest values of a frequency distribution. In Exhibit 13.5, the range for product A is between 196 units and 202 units (6 units), whereas for product B the range is between 150 units and 261 units (111 units). The range does not take into account all the observations; it merely tells us about the extreme values of the distribution.

Just as people may be fat or skinny, distributions may be fat or skinny. Although we do not expect all observations to be exactly like the mean, in a skinny distribution they will lie a short distance from the mean. Product A is an example; the observations are close together and reasonably close to the mean. In a fat distribution, such as the one for product B, they will be spread out. Exhibit 13.6 illustrates this concept graphically with two frequency distributions that have identical modes, medians, and means but different degrees of dispersion.

The interquartile range is the range that encompasses the middle 50 percent of the observations—in other words, the range between the bottom quartile (lowest 25 percent) and the top quartile (highest 25 percent).

Deviation Scores

A method of calculating how far any observation is from the mean is to calculate individual deviation scores. To calculate a deviation from the mean, use the following formula:

$$d_{i_i} = X_i - \overline{X}$$

For the value of 150 units for product B for the month of January, the deviation score is -50; that is, $150 - 200 = -50$. If the deviation scores are large, we will have a fat distribution because the distribution exhibits a broad spread.

EXHIBIT **13.6**
Low Dispersion versus High
Dispersion

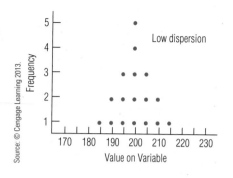

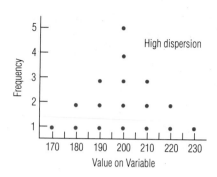

Why Use the Standard Deviation?

Statisticians have derived several quantitative indexes to reflect a distribution's spread, or variability. The *standard deviation* is perhaps the most valuable index of spread, or dispersion. Students often have difficulty understanding it. Learning about the standard deviation will be easier if we first look at several other measures of dispersion that may be used. Each of these has certain limitations that the standard deviation does not.

First is the average deviation. We compute the average deviation by calculating the deviation score of each observation value (that is, its difference from the mean), summing these scores, and then dividing by the sample size (n):

$$\text{Average deviation} = \frac{\Sigma(X_i - \overline{X})}{n}$$

Although this measure of spread seems interesting, it is never used. Positive deviation scores are canceled out by negative scores with this formula, leaving an average deviation value of zero no matter how wide the spread may be. Hence, the average deviation is a useless spread measure.

One might correct for the disadvantage of the average deviation by computing the absolute values of the deviations. In other words, we ignore all the positive and negative signs and use only the absolute value of each deviation. The formula for the mean absolute deviation is:

$$\text{Mean absolute deviation} = \frac{\Sigma|X_i - \overline{X}|}{n}$$

Although this procedure eliminates the problem of always having a zero score for the deviation measure, it becomes even more useful to express deviations in terms of variance.

VARIANCE

Another means of eliminating the sign problem caused by the negative deviations canceling out the positive deviations is to square the deviation scores. The following formula gives the mean squared deviation:

$$\text{Mean squared deviation} = \frac{\Sigma(X_i - \overline{X})^2}{n}$$

This measure is useful for describing the sample variability. However, we typically wish to make an inference about a population from a sample, and so the divisor $n - 1$ is used rather than n in most pragmatic marketing research problems.[4] The divisor changes from n to $n - 1$ to provide an unbiased estimator. This new measure of spread, called **variance**, has the following formula:

variance

A measure of variability or dispersion. Its square root is the standard deviation.

$$\text{Variance} = S^2 = \frac{\Sigma(X_i - \overline{X})^2}{n - 1}$$

Variance is a very good index of dispersion. The variance, S^2, will equal zero if and only if each and every observation in the distribution is the same as the mean. The variance will grow larger as the observations tend to differ increasingly from one another and from the mean.

STANDARD DEVIATION

Although the variance is frequently used in statistics, it has one major drawback. The variance reflects a unit of measurement that has been squared. For instance, if measures of sales in a territory are made in dollars, the mean number will be reflected in dollars, but the variance will be in

X	$(X - \bar{X})^1$	$(X - \bar{X})^2$
4	$(4 - 3.25) = \quad .75$	.5625
3	$(3 - 3.25) = \quad -.25$	.0625
2	$(2 - 3.25) = -1.25$	1.5625
5	$(5 - 3.25) = \quad 1.75$	3.0625
3	$(3 - 3.25) = \quad -.25$	.0625
3	$(3 - 3.25) = \quad -.25$	.0625
1	$(1 - 3.25) = -2.25$	5.0625
5	$(5 - 3.25) = \quad 1.75$	3.0625
Σ^a	^{0}	13.5000

$$n = 8 \qquad \bar{X} = 3.25$$

$$S = \sqrt{\frac{\Sigma(X - \bar{X})^2}{n - 1}} = \sqrt{\frac{13.5}{8 - 1}} = \sqrt{\frac{13.5}{7}} = \sqrt{1.9286} = 1.3887$$

[a] The summation of this column is not used in the calculation of the standard deviation.

EXHIBIT 13.7
Calculating a Standard Deviation: Number of Sales Calls per Day for Eight Salespeople

Source: © Cengage Learning 2013.

squared dollars. Because of this, statisticians often take the square root of the variance. Using the square root of the variance for a distribution, called the **standard deviation**, eliminates the drawback of having the measure of dispersion in squared units rather than in the original measurement units. The formula for the standard deviation is

$$S = \sqrt{S^2} = \sqrt{\frac{\Sigma(X_i - \bar{X})^2}{n - 1}}$$

standard deviation

A quantitative index of a distribution's spread, or variability; the square root of the variance for a distribution.

Exhibit 13.7 illustrates that the calculation of a standard deviation requires the researcher to first calculate the sample mean. In the example with eight salespeople's sales calls (Exhibit 13.4), we calculated the sample mean as 3.25. Exhibit 13.7 illustrates how to calculate the standard deviation for these data.

At this point we can return to thinking about the original purpose for measures of dispersion. We want to summarize the data from survey research and other forms of marketing research. Indexes of central tendency, such as the mean, help us interpret the data. In addition, we wish to calculate a measure of variability that will give us a quantitative index of the dispersion of the distribution. We have looked at several measures of dispersion to arrive at two very adequate means of measuring dispersion: the variance and the standard deviation. The term given is for the sample standard deviation, S.

The term for the population standard deviation, σ, which is conceptually very similar, has not been given. Nevertheless, you should understand that σ measures the dispersion in the population and S measures the dispersion in the sample. These concepts are crucial to understanding statistics. Remember, the student must learn the language of statistics to use it in a research project. If you do not understand the language at this point, review this material now.

Distinguish Between Sample and Sample Distribution

Roulette is a common casino game and a casino may contain many roulette wheels. If someone wanted to know whether the roulette wheels were fair, they may make many observations of which number the ball lands on as the result of a spin. The results would follow some pattern. It might not be possible to record the results of all spins of the roulette wheel, but someone could

By recording the results of spins of the roulette wheel, one could find the distribution of the results. If the wheel is fair, what should the distribution look like?

probably record results over a several-hour period on one or more wheels. This basic image provides the idea behind statistical distributions.

The Normal Distribution

normal distribution

A symmetrical, bell-shaped distribution that describes the expected probability distribution of many chance occurrences.

One of the most common probability distributions in statistics is the **normal distribution**, commonly represented by the *normal curve*. This mathematical and theoretical distribution describes the expected distribution of sample means and many other chance occurrences. The normal curve is bell shaped, and almost all (99.7 percent) of its values are within ±3 standard deviations from its mean. An example of a normal curve, the distribution of IQ scores, appears in Exhibit 13.8. The IQ score is normed to 100 meaning that 100 is an average IQ score. In this example, 1 standard deviation for IQ equals 15. Someone with an IQ score of 70 is 2 standard deviations below average and scores better than 2.14 percent of others. A person scoring 145 is 3 standard deviations above average and better than 99.8 percent of others.

standardized normal distribution

A purely theoretical probability distribution that reflects a specific normal curve for the standardized value, *z*.

The **standardized normal distribution** is a specific normal curve that has several characteristics:

1. It is symmetrical about its mean.
2. The mean identifies the normal curve's highest point (the mode) and the vertical line about which this normal curve is symmetrical.

EXHIBIT 13.8

Normal Distribution:
Distribution of Intelligence
Quotient (IQ) Scores

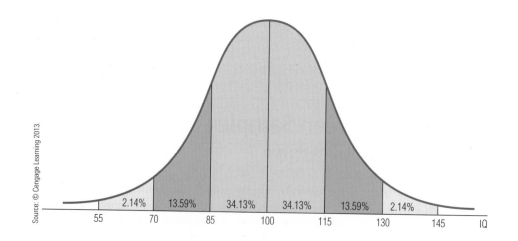

Source: © Cengage Learning 2013.

	2.14%	13.59%	34.13%	34.13%	13.59%	2.14%	
55	70	85	100	115	130	145	IQ

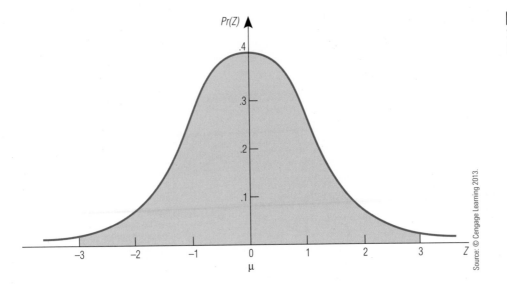

Source: © Cengage Learning 2013.

EXHIBIT 13.9
Standardized Normal Distribution

3. The normal curve has an infinite number of cases (it is a continuous distribution), and the area under the curve has a probability density equal to 1.0.
4. The standardized normal distribution has a mean of 0 and a standard deviation of 1.

Exhibit 13.9 illustrates these properties. Exhibit 13.10 is a summary version of the typical standardized normal table found at the end of most statistics textbooks. A more complex table of areas under the standardized normal distribution can be found on the Internet at **http://www.mathsisfun.com/data/standard-normal-distribution-table.html** or in the statistical appendix on the **www.cengage.com/marketing/zikmund**.

The standardized normal distribution is a purely theoretical probability distribution, but it is a most useful distribution in inferential statistics. Statisticians have spent a great deal of time and effort making it convenient for researchers to find the probability of any portion of the area under the standardized normal distribution. All we have to do is transform, or convert, the data from other observed normal distributions to the standardized normal curve. In other words, the standardized normal distribution is extremely valuable because we can translate, or transform, any normal variable, X, into the standardized value, Z. Exhibit 13.11 illustrates how either a skinny distribution or a fat distribution can be converted into the standardized normal distribution. This ability to transform normal variables has many pragmatic implications for the marketing researcher.

Computing the standardized value, Z, of any measurement expressed in original units is simple: Subtract the mean from the value to be transformed, and divide by the standard deviation (all

> *"To study the abnormal is the best way of understanding the normal."*
>
> —WILLIAM JAMES

EXHIBIT 13.10 Standardized Normal Table: Area Under Half of the Normal Curve[a]

Z Standard Deviations from the Mean (Units)	Z Standard Deviations from the Mean (Tenths of Units)[a]									
	.0	.1	.2	.3	.4	.5	.6	.7	.8	.9
0.0	.000	.040	.080	.118	.155	.192	.226	.258	.288	.315
1.0	.341	.364	.385	.403	.419	.433	.445	.455	.464	.471
2.0	.477	.482	.486	.489	.492	.494	.495	.496	.497	.498
3.0	.499	.499	.499	.499	.499	.499	.499	.499	.499	.499

[a]Area under the segment of the normal curve extending (in one direction) from the mean to the point indicated by each row-column combination. For example, about 68 percent of normally distributed events can be expected to fall within 1.0 standard deviation on either side of the mean (0.341 × 2). An interval of almost 2.0 standard deviations around the mean will include 95 percent of all cases (.477 + .477).

Source: © Cengage Learning 2013.

EXHIBIT **13.11**

Standardized Values can be Computed from Flat or Peaked Distributions Resulting in a Standardized Normal Curve

Source: © Cengage Learning 2013.

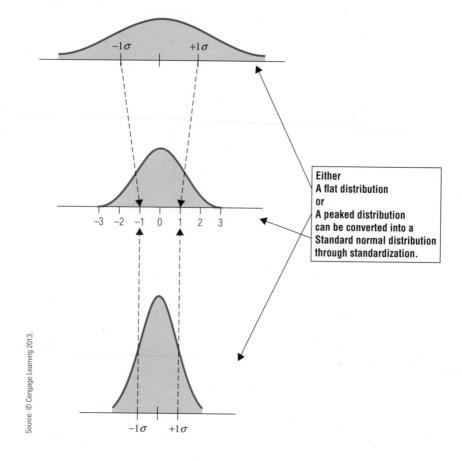

Either
A flat distribution
or
A peaked distribution
can be converted into a
Standard normal distribution
through standardization.

expressed in original units). The formula for this procedure and its verbal statement follow. In the formula, note that σ, the population standard deviation, is used for calculation.[5]

$$\text{Standardized value} = \frac{\text{Value to be transformed} - \text{Mean}}{\text{Standard deviation}}$$

$$Z = \frac{X - \mu}{\sigma}$$

where

μ = hypothesized or expected value of the mean

Suppose that in the past a toy manufacturer has experienced mean sales, μ, of 9,000 units and a standard deviation, σ, of 500 units during September. The production manager wishes to know whether wholesalers will demand between 7,500 and 9,625 units during September of the upcoming year. Because no tables are available showing the distribution for a mean of 9,000 and a standard deviation of 500, we must transform our distribution of toy sales, X, into the standardized form using our simple formula. The following computation shows that the probability (Pr) of obtaining sales in this range is equal to 0.893:

$$Z = \frac{X - \mu}{\sigma} = \frac{7,500 - 9,000}{500} = -3.00$$

$$Z = \frac{X - \mu}{\sigma} = \frac{9,625 - 9,000}{500} = 1.25$$

Using Exhibit 13.10, we find that

When $Z = -3.00$, the area under the curve (probability) equals 0.499.
When $Z = 1.25$, the area under the curve (probability) equals 0.394.

Thus, the total area under the curve is $0.499 + 0.394 = 0.893$. (The area under the curve corresponding to this computation is the shaded areas in Exhibit 13.12.) The sales manager, therefore, knows there is a 0.893 probability that sales will be between 7,500 and 9,625.

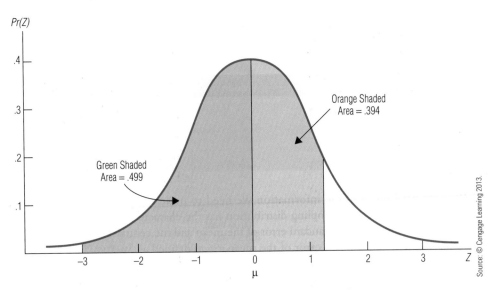

Source: © Cengage Learning 2013.

EXHIBIT 13.12
Standardized Distribution
Curve

Population Distribution and Sample Distribution

Before we outline the technique of statistical inference, three additional types of distributions must be defined: population distribution, sample distribution, and sampling distribution. When conducting a research project or survey, the researcher's purpose is not to describe the sample of respondents, but to make an inference about the population. As defined previously, a population, or universe, is the total set, or collection, of potential units for observation. The sample is a smaller subset of this population.

A frequency distribution of the population elements is called a **population distribution**. The mean and standard deviation of the population distribution are represented by the Greek letters μ and σ. A frequency distribution of a sample is called a **sample distribution**. The sample mean is designated $\overline{X}$, and the sample standard deviation is designated S.

population distribution
A frequency distribution of the elements of a population.

sample distribution
A frequency distribution of a sample.

Sampling Distribution

The concepts of population distribution and sample distribution are relatively simple. However, we must now introduce another distribution, which is the crux of understanding statistics: the *sampling distribution of the sample mean*. The sampling distribution is a theoretical probability distribution that in actual practice would never be calculated. Hence, practical, business-oriented students have difficulty understanding why the notion of the sampling distribution is important. Statisticians, with their mathematical curiosity, have asked themselves, "What would happen if we were to draw a large number of samples (say, 50,000), each having n elements, from a specified population?" Assuming that the samples were randomly selected, the sample means, $\overline{X}$s, could be arranged in a frequency distribution. Because different people or sample units would be selected in the different samples, the sample means would not be exactly equal. The shape of the sampling distribution is of considerable importance to statisticians. If the sample size is sufficiently large and if the samples are randomly drawn, we know from the central-limit theorem that the sampling distribution of the mean will be approximately normally distributed.

A formal definition of the sampling distribution is as follows:

> A **sampling distribution** *is a theoretical probability distribution that shows the functional relation between the possible values of some summary characteristic of n cases drawn at random and the probability (density) associated with each value over all possible samples of size n from a particular population.*[6]

The sampling distribution's mean is called the *expected value* of the statistic. The expected value of the mean of the sampling distribution is equal to μ. The standard deviation of a sampling distribution of $\overline{X}$ is called **standard error of the mean** ($S_{\overline{X}}$) and is approximately equal to:

$$S_{\overline{X}} = \frac{\sigma}{\sqrt{n}}$$

sampling distribution
A theoretical probability distribution of sample means for all possible samples of a certain size drawn from a particular population.

standard error of the mean
The standard deviation of the sampling distribution.

Source: © Cengage Learning 2013.

EXHIBIT 13.15
Calculation of Population
Mean

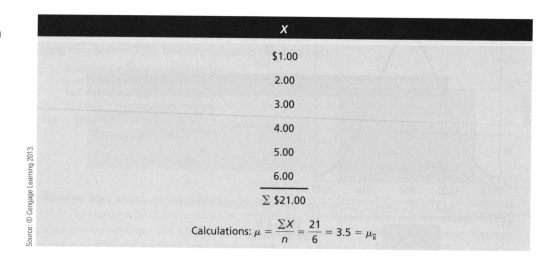

X
$1.00
2.00
3.00
4.00
5.00
6.00
Σ $21.00

Calculations: $\mu = \dfrac{\Sigma X}{n} = \dfrac{21}{6} = 3.5 = \mu_{\bar{x}}$

Estimation of Parameters and Confidence Intervals

A retailer such as Land's End may rely on sampling and statistical estimation to prepare for Christmas orders. The company can expect that 28 days after mailing its Christmas catalog, it will see a peak in Internet and phone orders amounting to X percent of total Christmas orders. With this information, the company can tell within 5 percent how many ties it will sell by Christmas. Making a proper inference about population parameters is highly practical for a marketer that must have the inventory appropriate for a short selling season.

Suppose you are a product manager for Con-Agra Foods and you recently invited Facebook Friends of Swiss Miss to test a reformulated Swiss Miss Healthy Cocoa Mix. The results of the research indicate that when the product was placed in 800 homes, 80 percent of respondents said they would buy it when available in a store: 76 percent among those not previously trying a low-calorie cocoa and 84 percent among those who had. How can you be sure there were no statistical errors in this estimate? How confident can you be of these figures?

Students often wonder whether statistics are really used in the business world. The two situations just described provide examples of the need for statistical estimation of parameters and the value of statistical techniques as managerial tools.

Point Estimates

Our goal in using statistics is to make an estimate about population parameters. A population mean, μ, and standard deviation, σ, are constants, but in most instances of marketing research, they are unknown. To estimate population values, we are required to sample. As we have discussed, $\bar{X}$ and S are random variables that will vary from sample to sample with a certain probability (sampling) distribution. The Research Snapshot above discusses estimates of Olympic game viewership.

Consider a practical example of a prospective racquetball entrepreneur who wishes to estimate the average number of days players participate in this sport each week. When statistical inference is needed, the population mean, μ, is a constant but unknown parameter. To estimate the average number of playing days, we could take a sample of 300 racquetball players throughout the area where our entrepreneur is thinking of building club facilities. If the sample mean, $\bar{X}$, equals 2.6 days per week, we might use this figure as a **point estimate**. This single value, 2.6, would be the best estimate of the population mean. However, we would be extremely lucky if the sample estimate were exactly the same as the population value. A less risky alternative would be to calculate a confidence interval.

point estimate

An estimate of the population mean in the form of a single value, usually the sample mean.

©chalabala/Shutterstock

Are You Facebook Normal?

Are you normal? Well, now one can get help in answering this question just by going to the Internet. Put the question in a search engine and you'll come to quite a few websites willing to answer the question for you. A quiz at **www.blogthings.com** consists of twenty questions covering things like whether or not you change towels every day, whether you have closer to $40 or $100 on hand, whether you are comfortable using the bathroom with another person in the room, and so forth. Once the user finishes the quiz, the site provides him/her with a normal score by comparing the responses to the overall distribution of responses. Similarly, Facebook users can test

how "normal" they are and compare their normalness to their Facebook friends. This Facebook app asks questions about how much you like your body, how you really feel about the people you know, and whether you think you are mentally ill. Over 2,000,000 people have respondent to these questions and one's normalness is determined against that distribution. The author of this book scored 55 percent normal on blogthings but only 19 percent normal according to Facebook. I suppose that brings us back to test reliability!

Source: © Cengage Learning 2013.

Confidence Intervals

If we specify a range of numbers, or interval, within which the population mean should lie, we can be more confident that our inference is correct. A **confidence interval estimate** is based on the knowledge that $\mu = \overline{X} \pm$ a small sampling error. After calculating an interval estimate, we can determine how probable it is that the population mean will fall within this range of statistical values. In the racquetball project, the researcher, after setting up a confidence interval, would be able to make a statement such as "With 95 percent confidence, I think that the average number of days played per week is between 2.3 and 2.9." This information can be used to estimate market demand because the researcher has a certain confidence that the interval contains the value of the true population mean.

The crux of the problem for a researcher is to determine how much random sampling error to tolerate. In other words, what should the confidence interval be? How much of a gamble should be taken that μ will be included in the range? Do we need to be 80 percent, 90 percent, or 99 percent sure? The **confidence level** is a percentage or decimal that indicates the long-run probability that the results will be correct. Traditionally, researchers have used the 95 percent confidence level. Although there is nothing magical about the 95 percent confidence level, it is conventional to select this confidence level in our examples.

As mentioned, the point estimate gives no information about the possible magnitude of random sampling error. The confidence interval gives the estimated value of the population parameter, plus or minus an estimate of the error. We can express the idea of the confidence interval as follows:

$$\mu = \overline{X} \pm \text{a small sampling error}$$

More formally, assuming that the researchers select a large sample (more than thirty observations), the small sampling error is given by

$$\text{Small sampling error} = Z_{c.l.} \, S_{\overline{X}}.$$

where

$Z_{c.l.}$ = value of Z, or standardized normal variable, at a specified confidence level (*c.l.*)

$S_{\overline{X}}$ = standard error of the mean

The precision of our estimate is indicated by the value of $Z_{c.l.} \, S_{\overline{X}}$. It is useful to define the range of possible error, E, as follows:

$$E = Z_{c.l.} \, S_{\overline{X}}$$

confidence interval estimate

A specified range of numbers within which a population mean is expected to lie; an estimate of the population mean based on the knowledge that it will be equal to the sample mean plus or minus a small sampling error.

confidence level

A percentage or decimal value that tells how confident a researcher can be about being correct; it states the long-run percentage of confidence intervals that will include the true population mean.

Thus,

$$\mu = \overline{X} \pm E$$

where

$\overline{X}$ = sample mean (commonly pronounced X-bar)

E = range of sampling error

or

$$\mu = \overline{X} \pm Z_{c.l.}\, S_{\overline{X}}.$$

The expression of "confidence" using $\pm E$ is stated as one-half of the total confidence interval. One-half of the interval is less than the mean and the other half is greater than the mean.

The following step-by-step procedure can be used to calculate confidence intervals:

1. Calculate $\overline{X}$ from the sample.
2. Assuming σ is unknown, estimate the population standard deviation by finding S, the sample standard deviation.
3. Estimate the standard error of the mean, using the following formula:

$$S_{\overline{X}} = \frac{S}{\sqrt{n}}$$

4. Determine the Z-value associated with the desired confidence level. The confidence level should be divided by 2 to determine what percentage of the area under the curve to include on each side of the mean.
5. Calculate the confidence interval.

The following example shows how calculation of a confidence interval can be used in preparing a demographic profile, a useful tool for market segmentation. Suppose you plan to open a sporting goods store to cater to working women who play golf. In a survey of 100 women in your market area, you find that the mean age $(\overline{X})$ is 37.5 years, with a standard deviation (S) of 12.0 years. Even though 37.5 years is the "expected value" and the best guess for the true mean age in the population (μ), the likelihood is that the mean is not exactly 37.5. Thus, a confidence interval around the sample mean computed using the steps just given will be useful:

1. $\overline{X}$ = 37.5 years
2. S = 12.0 years
3. $S_{\overline{X}} = \dfrac{12.0}{\sqrt{100}} = 1.2$
4. Suppose you wish to be 95 percent confident—that is, assured that 95 times out of 100, the estimates from your sample will include the population parameter. Including 95 percent of the area requires that 47.5 percent (one-half of 95 percent) of the distribution on each side be included. From a Z-table (see Exhibit 13.10 or the full table available on the companion website), you find that 0.475 corresponds to the Z-value 1.96.
5. Substitute the values for $Z_{c.l.}$ and $S_{\overline{X}}$ into the confidence interval formula:

$$\mu = 37.5 \pm (1.96)(1.2)$$

$$= 37.5 \pm 2.352$$

You can thus expect that μ is contained in the range from 35.15 to 39.85 years. Intervals constructed in this manner will contain the true value of μ 95 percent of the time.

Step 3 can be eliminated by entering S and n directly in the confidence interval formula:

$$\mu = \overline{X} \pm Z_{c.l.}\frac{S}{\sqrt{n}}$$

Remember that $S/\sqrt{n}$ represents the standard error of the mean, $S_{\overline{X}}$. Its use is based on the central-limit theorem.

If you wanted to increase the probability that the population mean will lie within the confidence interval, you could use the 99 percent confidence level, with a Z-value of 2.57. You may want to calculate the 99 percent confidence interval for the preceding example; you can expect that μ will be in the range between 34.416 and 40.584 years.

We have now examined the basic concepts of inferential statistics. You should understand that sample statistics such as the sample means, $\overline{X}$s, can provide good estimates of population parameters such as μ. You should also realize that there is a certain probability of being in error when you estimate a population parameter from sample statistics. In other words, there will be a random sampling error, which is the difference between the survey results and the results of surveying the entire population. If you have a firm understanding of these basic terms and ideas, which are the essence of statistics, the remaining statistics concepts will be relatively simple for you. The Research Snapshot shows how simple descriptive statistics can be used to contrast Walmart and Target shoppers.

Sample Size

Random Error and Sample Size

When asked to evaluate a marketing research project, most people, even those with little marketing research training, begin by asking, "How big was the sample?" Intuitively we know that the larger the sample, the more accurate the research. This is in fact a statistical truth; random sampling error varies with samples of different sizes. In statistical terms, increasing the sample size decreases the width of the confidence interval at a given confidence level. When the standard deviation of the population is unknown, a confidence interval is calculated using the following formula:

$$\text{Confidence interval} = \overline{X} \pm Z\frac{S}{\sqrt{n}}$$

Observe that the equation for the plus or minus error factor in the confidence interval includes n, the sample size:

$$E = Z\frac{S}{\sqrt{n}}$$

If n increases, E is reduced.

We already noted that it is not necessary to take a census of all elements of the population to conduct an accurate study. The laws of probability give investigators sufficient confidence regarding the accuracy of data collected from a sample. Knowledge of the characteristics of the sampling distribution helps researchers make reasonably precise estimates.

Students familiar with the law of diminishing returns in economics will easily grasp the concept that increases in sample size reduce sampling error at a *decreasing rate*. For example, doubling a sample of 1,000 will reduce random sampling error by 1 percentage point, but doubling the sample from 2,000 to 4,000 will reduce random sampling error by only another half percentage point. More technically, random sampling error is inversely proportional to the square root of n. Thus, the main issue becomes one of determining the optimal sample size.

Factors in Determining Sample Size for Questions Involving Means

Three factors are required to specify sample size: (1) the variance, or heterogeneity, of the population; (2) the magnitude of acceptable error; and (3) the confidence level. Suppose a researcher wishes to find out whether nine-year-old boys are taller than four-year-old boys. Intuitively we know that even with a very small sample size, the correct information probably will be obtained. This is based on the fact that the determination of sample size depends on the research question and the variability within the sample.

Target and Walmart Shoppers Really Are Different

Scarborough Research conducts ongoing consumer research about American consumer habits. The result is a sample including over 220,000 adults in eighty-one designated market areas used to estimate characteristics of the U.S. population. In 2011, Walmart renewed an effort to win back customers who defected for other mass merchandisers, namely Target. But, how different are those segments?

When survey respondents identified the stores in which they shop, 40 percent named both Target and Walmart. However, 31 percent shopped at Walmart but not Target and 12 percent shopped at Target but not Walmart. Target shoppers who shunned Walmart were more likely to shop at more upscale stores, including Macy's and Nordstrom. To a Target-only shopper, value is defined by style, selection, quality, and a pleasant experience. Walmart shoppers who stay away from Target were more likely to shop at discounters such as Dollar General and

Kmart. Walmart shoppers define value in a utilitarian way by emphasizing price and one-stop shopping convenience. Digging a little deeper, research suggests that not all Walmart shoppers are alike. Walmart recently tried adding more upscale brands hoping consumers would morph the image into something closer to Target. However, they soon cut back on this new strategy based on reduced sales from the core segment.

How accurately do you think the Scarborough sample captures these two stores segments?

Sources: Merrilees, B., and D. Miller (2010), "Brand Morphing across Segments," *Journal of Business Research*, 63 (November), 1129–34; *Stores Magazine* (2005), "Walmart versus Target," 87 (November), 14; Troy, M. (2011), "Loyalty on the Line as Walmart Ads Tempt Target Shoppers," Retailtoday. com (April), accessed August 14, 2011.

The *variance*, or *heterogeneity*, of the population is the first necessary bit of information. In statistical terms, this refers to the *standard deviation* of the population. Only a small sample is required if the population is homogeneous. For example, predicting the average age of graduate students requires a smaller sample than predicting the average age of people who visit the zoo. As *heterogeneity* increases, so must sample size. A pharmaceutical company testing the effectiveness of an acne medicine, for instance, should require a sample large enough to account for the varying range of skin types.

The *magnitude of error*, or the confidence interval, is the second necessary bit of information. Defined in statistical terms as E, the magnitude of error indicates how precise the estimate must be. It indicates a certain precision level. From a managerial perspective, the importance of the decision in terms of profitability will influence the researcher's specifications of the range of error. If, for example, favorable results from a test-market sample will result in the construction of a new plant and unfavorable results will dictate not marketing the product, the acceptable range of error probably will be small; the cost of an error would be too great to allow much room for random sampling errors. In other cases, the estimate need not be extremely precise. Allowing an error of $\pm\$1,000$ in total family income instead of $E = \pm50$ may be acceptable in most market segmentation studies.

The third factor of concern is the *confidence level*. In our examples, we will typically use the 95 percent confidence level. This, however, is an arbitrary decision based on convention; there is nothing sacred about the 0.05 chance level (that is, the probability of 0.05 of the true population parameter being incorrectly estimated). Exhibit 13.16 summarizes the information required to determine sample size.

Estimating Sample Size for Questions Involving Means

Once the preceding concepts are understood, determining the actual size for a simple random sample is quite easy. The researcher must follow three steps:

1. Estimate the standard deviation of the population.
2. Make a judgment about the allowable magnitude of error.
3. Determine a confidence level.

Variable	Symbol	Typical Source of Information
Standard deviation	S	Pilot study or rule of thumb
Magnitude of error	E	Managerial judgment or calculation ($ZS_{\bar{x}}$)
Confidence level	$Z_{c.l.}$	Managerial judgment

EXHIBIT **13.16**
Statistical Information Needed to Determine Sample Size for Questions Involving Means

Source: © Cengage Learning 2013.

The only problem is estimating the standard deviation of the population. Ideally, similar studies conducted in the past will give a basis for judging the standard deviation. In practice, researchers who lack prior information conduct a pilot study to estimate the population parameters so that another, larger sample of the appropriate sample size may be drawn. This procedure is called *sequential sampling* because researchers take an initial look at the pilot study results before deciding on a larger sample to provide more precise information.

A rule of thumb for estimating the value of the standard deviation is to expect it to be one-sixth of the range. If researchers conducting a study on television purchases expected the price paid to range from $100 to $700, a rule-of-thumb estimate for the standard deviation would be $100.

For the moment, assume that the standard deviation has been estimated in some preliminary work. If our concern is to estimate the mean of a particular population, the formula for sample size is

$$n = \left(\frac{ZS}{E}\right)^2$$

where

Z = standardized value that corresponds to the confidence level

S = sample standard deviation or estimate of the population standard deviation

E = acceptable error amount, plus or minus error factor (recall the range is one-half of the total confidence interval)[8]

Suppose a survey researcher studying annual expenditures on lipstick wishes to have a 95 percent confidence level ($Z = 1.96$) and a range of error (E) of less than $2. If the estimate of the standard deviation is $29, the sample size can be calculated as follows:

$$n = \left(\frac{ZS}{E}\right)^2 = \left(\frac{(1.96)(29)^2}{2}\right) = \left(\frac{56.84}{2}\right)^2 = 28.42^2 = 808$$

If a range of error (E) of $4 is acceptable, sample size can be reduced:

$$n = \left(\frac{ZS}{E}\right)^2 = \left(\frac{(1.96)(29)}{4}\right)^2 = \left(\frac{56.84}{4}\right)^2 = 14.21^2 = 202$$

Thus, doubling the range of acceptable error reduces sample size requirements dramatically. Stated conversely in a general sense, doubling sample size will reduce error by only approximately one-quarter. Thus, the added precision may often not be worth the added costs.

Population Size and Sample Size

The ACNielsen Company estimates television ratings. Throughout the years, it has been plagued with questions about how it is possible to rate 100 million plus television homes with a sample of approximately 5,000 households. The answer to that question is that in most cases the size of the population does not have a major effect on the sample size. As we have indicated, the variance of the population has the largest effect on sample size. However, a finite correction factor may be needed to adjust a sample size that is more than 5 percent of a finite population. If the sample is large relative to the population, the foregoing procedures may overestimate sample size, and the researcher may need to adjust sample size. The finite correction factor is:

$$\sqrt{\frac{(N - n)}{(N - 1)}}$$

where

N = population size
n = sample size

Determining Sample Size for Proportions

Researchers frequently are concerned with determining sample size for problems that involve estimating population proportions or percentages. When the question involves the estimation of a proportion, the researcher requires some knowledge of the logic for determining a confidence interval around a sample proportion estimation (p) of the population proportion (π). For a confidence interval to be constructed around the sample proportion (p), an estimate of the standard error of the proportion (S_p) must be calculated and a confidence level specified.

The precision of the estimate is indicated by the value $Z_{c.l.}S_p$. Thus, the plus-or-minus estimate of the population proportion is

$$\text{Confidence interval} = p \pm Z_{c.l.}S_p$$

If the researcher selects a 95 percent probability for the confidence interval, $Z_{c.l.}$ will equal 1.96 (from Z-table). The formula for S_p is

$$S_p = \sqrt{\frac{pq}{n}} \text{ or } S_p = \sqrt{\frac{p(1 - p)}{n}}$$

where

S_p = estimate of the standard error of the proportion

p = proportion of successes

$q = 1 - p$, or proportion of failures

Suppose that 20 percent of a sample of 1,200 television viewers recall seeing an advertisement. The proportion of successes (p) equals 0.2, and the proportion of failures (q) equals 0.8. We estimate the 95 percent confidence interval as follows:

$$\text{Confidence Interval} = p \pm Z_{c.l.}S_p$$

$$= 0.2 \pm 1.96S_p$$

$$= 0.2 \pm 1.96\sqrt{\frac{p(1 - p)}{n}}$$

$$= 0.2 \pm 1.96\sqrt{\frac{0.2(1 - 0.2)}{1,200}}$$

$$= 0.2 \pm 1.96\sqrt{\frac{0.16}{1,200}}$$

$$= 0.2 \pm 1.96(0.0115)$$

$$= 0.2 \pm 0.023$$

Thus, the population proportion who see an advertisement is estimated to be included in the interval between 0.177 (0.2 − 0.023) and 0.223 (0.2 + 0.023), or roughly between 18 and 22 percent, with 95 percent confidence (95 out of 100 times).

Sample size for a proportion requires the researcher to make a judgment about confidence level and the maximum allowance for random sampling error. Furthermore, the size of the proportion influences random sampling error, so an estimate of the expected proportion of successes must be made, based on intuition or prior information. The formula is

$$n = \frac{Z_{c.l.}^2 \, pq}{E^2}$$

where

n = number of items in sample

$Z_{c.l.}^2$ = square of the confidence level in standard error units

p = estimated proportion of successes

$q = 1 - p$, or estimated proportion of failures

E^2 = square of the maximum allowance for error between the true proportion and the sample proportion, or $Z_{c.l.} S_p$ squared

Suppose a researcher believes that a simple random sample will show that 60 percent of the population (p) recognizes the name of an automobile dealership. The researcher wishes to estimate with 95 percent confidence ($Z_{c.l.} = 1.96$) that the allowance for sampling error is not greater than 3.5 percentage points (E). Substituting these values into the formula gives

$$n = \frac{(1.96)^2(0.6)(0.4)}{0.035^2}$$

$$= \frac{(3.8416)(0.24)}{0.001225}$$

$$= \frac{0.922}{0.001225}$$

$$= 753$$

Determining Sample Size on the Basis of Judgment

Just as sample units may be selected to suit the convenience or judgment of the researcher, sample size may also be determined on the basis of managerial judgments. Using a sample size similar to those used in previous studies provides the inexperienced researcher with a comparison with other researchers' judgments.

Another judgmental factor that affects the determination of sample size is the selection of the appropriate item, question, or characteristic to be used for the sample size calculations. Several different characteristics affect most studies, and the desired degree of precision may vary for these items. The researcher must exercise some judgment to determine which item will be used. Often the item that will produce the largest sample size will be used to determine the ultimate sample size. However, the cost of data collection becomes a major consideration, and judgment must be exercised regarding the importance of such information.

Another consideration stems from most researchers' need to analyze various subgroups within the sample. For example, suppose an analyst wishes to look at differences in retailers' attitudes by geographic region. The analyst will want to make sure to sample an adequate number of retailers in the New England, Mid-Atlantic, and South Atlantic regions to ensure that subgroup comparisons are reliable. There is a judgmental rule of thumb for selecting minimum subgroup sample size: Each subgroup to be separately analyzed should have a minimum of 100 units in each category of the major breakdowns. The total sample size is computed by totaling the sample sizes necessary for these subgroups.

TIPS OF THE TRADE

- Measures of central tendency are often used.
  - The mean is the most commonly used measure of central tendency.
  - The median is more appropriate than the mean as a measure of central tendency when the data display extreme values or outliers.
  - The mode is most appropriate as a measure of central tendency when the data are less than interval.
- Sample size estimates often require some estimate of the standard deviation that will exist in the sample.
- Larger samples allow predictions with greater precision that can be expressed over a smaller range.
  - Increases in precision usually require disproportionately large increases in sample size.
- The amount of risk involved in a decision should be strongly considered in making decisions about the sample.
  - Only the riskiest of decisions require very large samples (i.e., thousands of respondents).
  - Samples of 300 to 500 respondents can provide adequate results for many marketing decisions that do not involve extremely high risk.

Source: © Cengage Learning 2013.

:: SUMMARY

1. Use descriptive statistics indicating central tendency and dispersion to make inferences about a population. Calculating a mean and a standard deviation to "describe" or profile a sample is a commonly applied descriptive statistical approach. Inferential statistics investigate samples to draw conclusions about entire populations. If a mean is computed and then compared to a preconceived standard, then inferential statistics are being implemented. A frequency distribution shows how frequently each response or classification occurs. A simple tally count illustrates a frequency distribution. A proportion indicates the percentage of group members that have a particular characteristic. Three measures of central tendency are commonly used: the mean, the median, and the mode. These three values may differ, and care must be taken to understand distortions that may arise from using the wrong measure of central tendency. Measures of dispersion further describe a distribution. The range is the difference between the largest and smallest values observed. The most useful measures of dispersion are the variance and standard deviation.

2. Distinguish among population, sample, and sampling distributions. The techniques of statistical inference are based on the relationship among the population distribution, the sample distribution, and the sampling distribution. The population distribution is a frequency distribution of the elements of a population. The sample distribution is a frequency distribution of a sample. A sampling distribution is a theoretical probability distribution of sample means for all possible samples of a certain size drawn from a particular population. The sampling distribution's mean is the expected value of the mean, which equals the population's mean. The standard deviation of the sampling distribution is the standard error of the mean, approximately equal to the standard deviation of the population, divided by the square root of the sample size.

3. Explain the central-limit theorem. The central-limit theorem states that as sample size increases, the distribution of sample means of size n, randomly selected, approaches a normal distribution. This means that even if a distribution has a non-normal distribution, the distribution of averages taken from samples of these numbers is normally distributed. This allows inferential statistics to be used. This theoretical knowledge can be used to estimate parameters and determine sample size.

4. Use confidence intervals to express population estimates. Estimating a population mean with a single value gives a point estimate. The confidence interval estimate is a range of numbers within which the researcher is confident that the population mean will lie. The confidence level is a percentage that indicates the long-run probability that the confidence interval estimate will be correct. Many research problems involve the estimation of proportions. Statistical techniques may be used to determine a confidence interval around a sample proportion.

5. Understand the major issues in specifying sample size. The statistical determination of sample size requires knowledge of (1) the variance of the population, (2) the magnitude of acceptable error, and (3) the confidence level. Several computational formulas are available for determining sample size. Furthermore, a number of easy-to-use tables have been compiled to help researchers calculate sample size. The main reason a large sample size is desirable is that sample size is related to random sampling error. A smaller sample makes a larger error in estimates more likely.

:: KEY TERMS AND CONCEPTS

central-limit theorem, *348*
confidence interval estimate, *351*
confidence level, *351*
frequency distribution, *337*
mean, *339*
median, *340*
mode, *340*

normal distribution, *344*
percentage distribution, *338*
point estimate, *350*
population distribution, *347*
probability, *338*
proportion, *338*
sample distribution, *347*

sample statistics, *337*
sampling distribution, *347*
standard deviation, *343*
standard error of the mean, *347*
standardized normal distribution, *344*
top-box score, *338*
variance, *342*

:: QUESTIONS FOR REVIEW AND CRITICAL THINKING

1. What is the difference between descriptive and inferential statistics?

2. Suppose the speed limits in thirteen countries in miles per hour are as follows:

Country	Highway Miles per Hour
Italy	87
France	82
Hungary	75
Belgium	75
Portugal	75
Great Britain	70
Spain	62
Denmark	62
Netherlands	62
Greece	62
Japan	62
Norway	56
Turkey	56

What is the mean, median, and mode for these data? Feel free to use your computer (statistical software or spreadsheet) to get the answer. Which is the best measure of central tendency for this data?

3. Prepare a frequency distribution for the data in question 2.

4. Why is the standard deviation rather than the average deviation typically used?

5. Calculate the standard deviation for the data in question 2.

6. Draw three distributions that have the same mean value but different standard deviation values. Draw three distributions that have the same standard deviation value but different mean values.

7. A manufacturer of MP3 players surveyed 100 retail stores in each of the firm's sales regions. An analyst noticed that in the South Atlantic region the average retail price was $165 (mean) and the

standard deviation was $30. However, in the Mid-Atlantic region the mean price was $170, with a standard deviation of $15. What do these statistics tell us about these two sales regions?

8. What is the sampling distribution? How does it differ from the sample distribution?

9. What would happen to the sampling distribution of the mean if we increased sample size from 5 to 25?

10. Suppose a fast-food restaurant wishes to estimate average sales volume for a new menu item. The restaurant has analyzed the sales of the item at a similar outlet and observed the following results:

   $\overline{X} = 500$ (mean daily sales)
   $S = 100$ (standard deviation of sample)
   $n = 25$ (sample size)

   The restaurant manager wants to know into what range the mean daily sales should fall 95 percent of the time. Perform this calculation.

11. In the example on page 355 of research on lipstick, where $E = \$2$ and $S = \$29$, what sample size would we require if we desired a 99 percent confidence level?

12. Suppose you are planning to sample cat owners to determine the average number of cans of cat food they purchase monthly. The following standards have been set: a confidence level of 99 percent and an error of less than 5 units. Past research has indicated that the standard deviation should be 6 units. What is the required sample size?

13. What is a standardized normal curve?

14. **ETHICS** Using the formula in this chapter, a researcher determines that at the 95 percent confidence level, a sample of 2,500 is required to satisfy a client's requirements. The researcher actually uses a sample of 1,200, however, because the client has specified a budget cap for the survey. What are the ethical considerations in this situation?

15. Draw the distribution that should result from an honest roulette wheel. Draw the distribution from a dishonest roulette wheel. Assuming samples of 500 spins were taken from each wheel, what would the distribution of sample means of 10 look like for each wheel?

16. Go to http://www.researchinfo.com. Click on "Market Research Calculators." Which of the calculators can be used to help find the sample size required? How big of a sample is needed to make an inference about the U.S. population +/−5 percent? How large a sample is needed to make an inference about the population of Norway +/−5 percent? Remember, population statistics can be found in the *CIA World Factbook* online. Comment.

17. A random number generator and other statistical information can be found at http://www.random.org. Flip some virtual coins. Perform twenty flips with an Aurelian coin. Perform twenty flips with a Constatius coin. Perform frequency tables for each result. What conclusion might you draw? Would the result change if you flipped the coins 200 times or 2,000 times?

:: RESEARCH ACTIVITIES

1. Look up at least five academic articles in an area of interest to you that involve survey research. Do they all discuss the sample and sample size? From any description about the sample provided, can the reader make a judgment about what population the statistics generalize too (presuming inferential statistics are involved)?

2. Use an online library service to find basic business research studies that report a "response rate" or number of respondents compared to number of contacts. You may wish to consult journals such as the *Journal of Business Research*, the *Journal of Marketing*, the *Journal of the Academy of Marketing Science*, or the *Journal of Personal Selling and Sales Management*. Find at least ten such studies. What is the average response rate across all of these studies? Do the resulting sample sizes seem adequate? Write a brief report on your findings.

Coastal Star Sales Corporation

Case 13.1

Download the data sets for this case from www.cengage.com/marketing/zikmund *or request them from your instructor.*

Coastal Star Sales Corporation is a West Coast wholesaler that markets leisure products from several manufacturers. Coastal Star has an 80-person sales force that sells to wholesalers in a six-state area, which is divided into two sales regions. Case Exhibit 13.1−1 shows the names of a sample of eleven salespeople, some descriptive information about each person, and sales performance for each of the last two years.

Questions

1. Calculate a mean and a standard deviation for each variable.
2. Set a 95 percent confidence interval around the mean for each variable.
3. Calculate the median, mode, and range for each variable.
4. Organize the data for current sales into a frequency distribution with three classes: (a) under $500,000, (b) $500,000 to $999,999, and (c) $1,000,000 and over.
5. Organize the data for years of selling experience into a frequency distribution with two classes: (a) less than five years and (b) five or more years.
6. Convert the frequency distributions from question 5 to percentage distributions.

Source: © Cengage Learning 2013.

CASE EXHIBIT 13.1–1 Salesperson Data: Coastal Star Sales Corporation

				Sales	
Region	**Salesperson**	**Age**	**Years of Experience**	**Previous Year**	**Current Year**
Northern	Jackson	40	7	$ 412,744	$ 411,007
Northern	Gentry	60	12	1,491,024	1,726,630
Northern	La Forge	26	2	301,421	700,112
Northern	Miller	39	1	401,241	471,001
Northern	Mowen	64	5	448,160	449,261
Southern	Young	51	2	518,897	519,412
Southern	Fisk	34	1	846,222	713,333
Southern	Kincaid	62	10	1,527,124	2,009,041
Southern	Krieger	42	3	921,174	1,030,000
Southern	Manzer	64	5	463,399	422,798
Southern	Weiner	27	2	548,011	422,001

Analysis and Reporting

CHAPTER 14
Basic Data Analysis

CHAPTER 15
Testing for Differences Between Groups and for Relationships Among Variables

CHAPTER 16
Communicating Research Results

CHAPTER 14

:::::: Basic Data Analysis

LEARNING OUTCOMES

After studying this chapter, you should be able to

1. Prepare qualitative data for interpretation or data analysis
2. Know what descriptive statistics are and why they are used
3. Create and interpret tabulation and cross-tabulation tables
4. Perform basic data transformations
5. Understand the basics of testing hypotheses using inferential statistics
6. Be able to use a p-value to make statistical inferences
7. Conduct a univariate *t*-test

Chapter Vignette:

"Don't Tell Me!"

Most people think that the last thing businesses like to hear is a consumer complaint. However, a bigger problem may occur when consumers don't complain. Complaints can provide key data that allows businesses to improve the way they deal with customers. By improving service, the businesses keep more customers and become more profitable. Thus, when consumers truly have a problem, management should welcome complaints. From another perspective, a relatively large number of complaints indicates a potential problem with management. Thus, many businesses set specific targets for minimizing complaints. Realizing that some consumers are chronic complainers, most of these targets don't strive for perfection but settle on a reasonable number. For instance, a business may set a target of fewer than twenty-five complaints per week. Research is needed to help set the target and then assess firm performance against that standard.

Who complains the most? A recent study examined the demographics of the "complainer." Among 162 complainers in the sample (out of 237 consumers in total with 75 reporting no bad experiences in the last twelve months), the results reveal how many people in each group make up the "complainer":

Age:	< 25	26–39	40–53	54 or more
Percentage	43.6	35.3	66.7	65.9

Does this mean that older people are more likely to complain? Does this mean that older consumers are better sources of marketing information or just chronic complainers that the firm may be better off without? Perhaps part of the answer lies in drawing meaning from basic statistics like these.[1]

Introduction

We now turn to research tools that allow researchers to make inferences. As researchers, we infer whether or not a condition exists in a population based on what we observe in a sample. Alternatively, the research could be more exploratory and the researcher could be using statistics simply to search for some pattern within the data. On rare occasions, the data may represent a census of a population, in which case no statistical inferences are necessary because parameters are known. Descriptive statistical tools like these provide a straightforward way of succinctly describing the information content within a data set.

Coding Qualitative Responses

Researchers often summarize and bring meaning to qualitative data by developing a type of logical coding scheme. The interpretation of these responses may be aided by some type of computer analysis. A researcher will even combine an interpretive approach with basic quantitative analyses to address a research question. Either way, some coding is necessary. Any mistakes in coding can dramatically change the conclusions. **Coding** represents the way a specific meaning is assigned to a response within previously edited data. Codes represent the meaning in data by assigning some measurement symbol to different categories of responses. This may be a number, letter, or word. The proper form of coding can be tied back to the level of measurement present. Nominal measurement can be represented by a word, letter, or any identifying mark. On the other hand, numbers typically are most appropriate for ordinal, interval, or ratio measures.

Thus, **codes** often, but not always, are numerical symbols. However, they are more broadly defined as rules for interpreting, classifying, and recording data. In interpretive research, numbers are seldom used for codes. In qualitative research, the codes are usually words or phrases that represent themes. For example, a qualitative researcher may apply a code to a hermeneutic unit describing in detail a respondent's reactions to several different glasses of wine. After reading through the text several times, and applying a word-counting routine, the researcher realizes that appearance, the nose (aroma), and guessing (trying to guess what the wine will be like or what type of wine is in the glass) are important themes. A code is assigned to these categories. After considerable thought and questioning of the experience, the researcher builds a network, or grounded theory, that suggests how a wine may be associated with feelings of romance.

coding

The process of assigning a numerical score or other character symbol to previously edited data.

codes

Rules for interpreting, classifying, and recording data in the coding process; also, the actual numerical or other character symbols assigned to raw data.

Structured Qualitative Responses and Dummy Variables

Qualitative responses to structured questions such as "yes" or "no" can be stored in a data file with letters such as "Y" or "N." Alternatively, they can be represented with numbers, one each to represent the respective category. Because this represents a nominal numbering system, the actual numbers used are arbitrary.

Even though the codes are numeric, the variable is classificatory. Any numbers assigned serve only to separate affirmative from negative responses. For statistical purposes the research may consider adopting **dummy coding** for dichotomous responses like yes or no. Dummy coding assigns a 0 to one category and a 1 to the other. So, for yes/no responses, a 0 could be "no" and a 1 would be "yes." Similarly, a "1" could represent a female respondent and a "0" would be a male respondent. Dummy coding provides the researcher with more flexibility in how structured, qualitative responses are analyzed statistically. Dummy coding can be used when more than two categories exist, but because a dummy variable can only represent two categories, multiple dummy variables are needed to represent a single qualitative response that can take on more than two categories. In fact, the rule is that if k is the number of categories for a qualitative variable, $k - 1$ dummy variables are needed to represent the variable.

An alternative to dummy coding is **effects coding**. Effects coding is performed by assigning a $+1$ to one value of a dichotomous variable and a -1 to the other. Dummy coding is more widely used in general, although effects coding has some advantages in the way experimental results are

dummy coding

Numeric "1" or "0" coding where each number represents an alternate response such as "female" or "male."

effects coding

An alternative to dummy coding using the values of −1 and 1 to represent two categories of responses.

SURVEY THIS!

Take a look at the section of the student survey shown.

Compute the appropriate descriptive statistic for each question using the data from the results for your class or school (across all sections of marketing research classes taking the survey). What conclusions would you draw from these results?

Source: © Cengage Learning 2013.

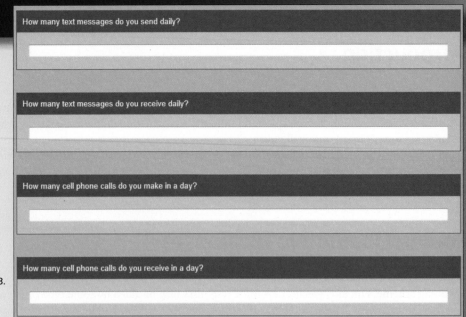

How many text messages do you send daily?

How many text messages do you receive daily?

How many cell phone calls do you make in a day?

How many cell phone calls do you receive in a day?

Courtesy of Qualtrics.com

presented. Either way is an acceptable technique for coding structured qualitative data. Either way, the qualitative data is now represented in a way that facilitates basic data analysis.

Class coding is another approach that can be used if the data are not going to be directly used to perform computations. **Class coding** assigns numbers to categories in an arbitrary way merely as a means of identifying some characteristic. If packages come in three colors, the class codes may be 1 for blue, 2 for red, and 3 for green. This coding works for representing treatment conditions in experimental variables.

class coding

Coding that assigns numbers to categories in an arbitrary way merely as a means of identifying some characteristic.

The Nature of Descriptive Analysis

descriptive analysis

The elementary transformation of raw data in a way that describes the basic characteristics such as central tendency, distribution, and variability.

Perhaps the most basic statistical analysis is descriptive analysis. **Descriptive analysis** is the elementary transformation of data in a way that describes the basic characteristics such as central tendency, distribution, and variability. A researcher takes responses from 1,000 American consumers and tabulates their favorite soft drink brand and the price they expect to pay for a six-pack of that product. The mode for favorite soft drink and the average price across all 1,000 consumers would be descriptive statistics that describe central tendency in two different ways. Averages, medians, modes, variance, range, and standard deviation typify widely applied descriptive statistics.

Descriptive statistics can summarize responses from large numbers of respondents in a few simple statistics. When a sample is used, the sample descriptive statistics are used to make inferences about characteristics of the entire population of interest. The researcher examining descriptive statistics for any particular variable is using univariate statistics. Descriptive statistics are simple but powerful. Because they are so simple, descriptive statistics are used very widely.

In an earlier chapter, we learned that the level of scale measurement can help the researcher choose the most appropriate statistical tool. Exhibit 14.1 shows the specific descriptive statistic appropriate for each level of measurement. Also, remember that all statistics appropriate for lower-order scales (nominal is the lowest) are suitable for higher-order scales (ratio is the highest). So, a frequency table could also be used for interval or ratio data. Frequencies can be represented graphically as shown and are a good way of visually depicting typical survey results.

Consider the following data. Sample consumers were asked where they most often purchased beer. The result is a nominal variable which can be described with a frequency distribution (see the bar chart in Exhibit 14.1). Ten percent indicated they most often purchased beer in a drug store, 45 percent indicated a convenience store, 35 percent indicated a grocery store, and 7 percent indicated a specialty store. Three percent listed "other" (not shown in the bar chart). The mode is

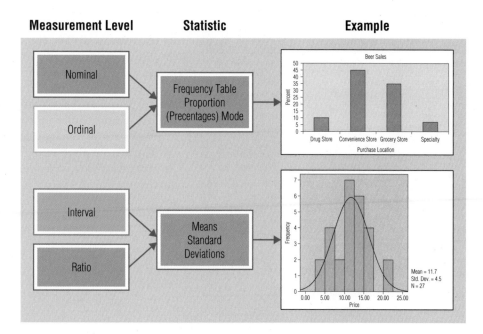

Measurement Level   Statistic   Example

Source: © Cengage Learning 2013.

EXHIBIT 14.1
Levels of Scale Measurement and Suggested Descriptive Statistics

convenience store because more respondents chose this than any other category. A similar distribution may have been obtained if the chart plotted the number of respondents ranking each store as their favorite type of place to purchase beer.

The bottom part of Exhibit 14.1 displays example descriptive statistics for interval and ratio variables. In this case, the chart displays results of a question asking respondents how much they typically spend on a bottle of wine purchased in a store. The mean and standard deviation are displayed beside the chart as 11.7 and 4.5, respectively. Additionally, the frequency distribution is shown with a histogram. A **histogram** is a graphical way of showing the frequency distribution in which the height of a bar corresponds to the frequency of a category. Histograms are useful for any type of data, but with continuous variables (interval or ratio) the histogram is useful for providing a quick assessment of the distribution of the data. A normal distribution line is superimposed over the histogram providing an easy comparison to see if the data are skewed or multi-modal.

histogram

A graphical way of showing a frequency distribution in which the height of a bar corresponds to the observed frequency of the category.

Creating and Interpreting Tabulation

Tabulation refers to the orderly arrangement of data in a table or other summary format. When this tabulation process is done by hand the term *tallying* is used. Counting the different ways respondents answered a question and arranging them in a simple tabular form yields a **frequency table**. The actual number of responses to each category is a variable's frequency distribution. A simple tabulation of this type is sometimes called a *marginal tabulation*.

Simple tabulation tells the researcher how frequently each response occurs. This starting point for analysis requires the researcher to count responses or observations for each category or code assigned to a variable. A frequency table showing where consumers generally purchase beer can be computed easily. The tabular results that correspond to the chart would appear as follows:

tabulation

The orderly arrangement of data in a table or other summary format showing the number of responses to each response category; tallying.

frequency table

A table showing the different ways respondents answered a question.

Response	Frequency	Percent	Cumulative Percentage
Drug store	50	10	10
Convenience store	225	45	55
Grocery store	175	35	90
Specialty	35	7	97
Other	15	3	100

Source: © Cengage Learning 2013.

Image courtesy of Susan Van Etten

Websites like this one provide a secondary data source in the form of descriptive statistics or details that can easily be used to compute tabulations, means, cross-tabulations, and so on.

The frequency column shows the tally result or the number of respondents listing each store, respectively. The percent column shows the total percentage in each category. The cumulative percentage shows the percentage indicating either a particular category or any preceding category as their preferred place to purchase beer. From this chart, the mode indicates that the typical consumer buys beer at the convenience store because more people indicated this as their top response.

Similarly, a recent tabulation of Americans' responses to the simple question of "Who is your favorite movie star?" Overall, Johnny Depp, Denzel Washington, John Wayne, Harrison Ford, and Angeline Jolie are the top five based on frequency of being mentioned as the favorite among 2,000 respondents.[2] However, the response varied by generation. For respondents aged 18 to 33 (Echo Boomers), Johnny Depp is the favorite. For respondents aged 34 to 45 (Gen X), Denzel Washington is the preferred movie star as is the case for Boomers (46–64), and John Wayne leads the pack among the Matures (62+). The idea that generation may influence choice of favorite movie star brings us to cross-tabulation.

Cross-Tabulation

A frequency distribution or tabulation can address many research questions. As long as a question deals with only one categorical variable, tabulation is probably the best approach. Although frequency counts, percentage distributions, and averages summarize considerable information, simple tabulation may not yield the full value of the research. **Cross-tabulation** is the appropriate technique for addressing research questions involving relationships among multiple less than interval variables. A cross-tabulation is a combined frequency table. Cross-tabulation allows the inspection and comparison of differences among groups based on nominal or ordinal categories. One key to interpreting a cross-tabulation table is comparing the observed table values with hypothetical values that would result from pure chance.

Exhibit 14.2 summarizes a cross-tabulations from consumers' responses to different ways of obtaining music in the United States.[3] The study contrasts a questionable method of obtaining music online (downloading from illegal file sharing site) by a basic demographic variable—generation. A sample of 214 consumers of varying ages provide the data. When given a choice between obtaining a music file via the Internet, a total of 165 of the 214 would choose to purchase it legally from a site like iTunes, whereas 49 would obtain it for free even if the download were illegal. The cross-tabulation comes by looking at how generation membership (a less than interval

cross-tabulation

The appropriate technique for addressing research questions involving relationships among multiple less than interval variables; results in a combined frequency table displaying one variable in rows and another in columns.

EXHIBIT 14.2

Cross-Tabulation from Consumer Ethics Survey

Generation	Purchase	Download	Total
Echo Boomer	18	35	53
Gen X	41	12	53
Boomer	54	1	55
Mature	53	0	53
	165	49	214

Source: © Cengage Learning 2013.

variable) influences choice of methods to obtain the music. Results in Exhibit 14.2 breaks down the results and suggest that the echo boomer generation displays a preference toward obtaining the music illegally (35 of 53), whereas older generations tend toward purchasing the music rather than downloading illicitly.

Contingency Tables

Exhibit 14.3 shows example cross-tabulation results using contingency tables. A **contingency table** is a data matrix that displays the frequency of some combination of possible responses to multiple variables. Two-way contingency tables, meaning they involve two less than interval variables, are used most often. A three-way contingency table involves three less than interval variables. Beyond three variables, contingency tables become difficult to analyze and explain easily.

Two variables are depicted in the contingency table shown in panel A:

■ Row Variable: Biological Sex _____M _____F
■ Column Variable: "Do you shop at Target? YES or NO".

Several conclusions can be drawn initially by examining the row and column totals:

1. Two hundred and twenty-five men and 225 women responded, as seen in the row totals column. This means that altogether 450 consumers responded.
2. Out of this 450 total consumers, 330 consumers indicated that "yes" they do shop at Target and 120 indicated "no," they do not shop at Target. This can be observed in the column totals at the bottom of the table. These row and column totals often are called **marginals** because they appear in the table's margins.

Researchers usually are more interested in the inner cells of a contingency table. The inner cells display conditional frequencies (combinations). Using these values, we can draw some more specific conclusions:

3. Out of 330 consumers who shop at Target, 150 are male and 180 are female.
4. Alternatively, out of the 120 respondents not shopping at Target, 75 are male and 45 are female.

contingency table

A data matrix that displays the frequency of some combination of possible responses to multiple variables; cross-tabulation results.

marginals

Row and column totals in a contingency table, which are shown in its margins.

EXHIBIT **14.3**
Different Ways of Depicting the Cross-Tabulation of Biological Sex and Target Patronage

(A) Cross-Tabulation of Question "Do you shop at Target?" by Sex of Respondent			
	Yes	No	Total
Men	150	75	225
Women	180	45	225
Total	330	120	450

(B) Percentage Cross-Tabulation of Question "Do you shop at Target?" by Sex of Respondent, Row Percentage			
	Yes	No	Total (Base)
Men	66.7%	33.3%	100% (225)
Women	80.0%	20.0%	100% (225)

(C) Percentage Cross-Tabulation of Question "Do you shop at Target?" by Sex of Respondent, Column Percentage		
	Yes	No
Men	45.5%	62.5%
Women	54.5%	37.5%
Total	100%	100%
(Base)	(330)	(120)

Source: © Cengage Learning 2013.

This finding helps us know whether the two variables are related. If men and women equally patronize Target, we would expect that hypothetically 165 of the 330 shoppers would be male and 165 would be female. Clearly, these hypothetical expectations (165m/165f) are not observed. What is the implication? A relationship exists between respondent sex and shopping choice. Specifically, Target shoppers are more likely to be female than male. Notice that the same meaning could be drawn by analyzing non-Target shoppers.

A two-way contingency table like the one shown in part A is referred to as a *2 × 2 table* because it has two rows (Men and Women) and two columns (Yes and No). Each variable has two levels. A two-way contingency table displaying two variables one (the row variable) with three levels and the other with four levels would be referred to as a *3 × 4 table*. Any cross-tabulation table may be classified according to the number of rows by the number of columns (*R by C*).

Percentage Cross-Tabulations

statistical base

The number of respondents or observations (in a row or column) used as a basis for computing percentages.

When data from a survey are cross-tabulated, percentages help the researcher understand the nature of the relationship by making relative comparisons simpler. The total number of respondents or observations may be used as a **statistical base** for computing the percentage in each cell. When the objective of the research is to identify a relationship between answers to two questions (or two variables), one of the questions is commonly chosen to be the source of the base for determining percentages. For example, look at the data in parts A, B, and C of Exhibit 14.3. Compare part B with part C. Selecting either the row percentages or the column percentages will emphasize a particular comparison or distribution. The nature of the problem the researcher wishes to answer will determine which marginal total will serve as a base for computing percentages.

Elaboration and Refinement

"The more we study, the more we discover our ignorance."

—PERCY BYSSHE SHELLEY

elaboration analysis

An analysis of the basic cross-tabulation for each level of a variable not previously considered, such as subgroups of the sample.

The *Oxford Universal Dictionary* defines *analysis* as "the resolution of anything complex into its simplest elements." Once a researcher has examined the basic relationship between two variables, he or she may wish to investigate this relationship under a variety of different conditions. Typically, a third variable is introduced into the analysis to elaborate and refine the researcher's understanding by specifying the conditions under which the relationship between the first two variables is strongest and weakest. In other words, a more elaborate analysis asks, "Will interpretation of the relationship be modified if other variables are simultaneously considered?"

Elaboration analysis involves the basic cross-tabulation within various subgroups of the sample. The researcher breaks down the analysis for each level of another variable. If the researcher has cross-tabulated shopping preference by sex (see Exhibit 14.3) and wishes to investigate another variable (say, marital status), a more elaborate analysis may be conducted. Exhibit 14.4 breaks down the responses to the question "Do you shop at Target?" by sex and marital status. The data show women display the same preference whether married or single. However, married men are much more likely to shop at Target than are single men. The analysis suggests that the original conclusion about the relationship between sex and shopping behavior for women be retained. However, a relationship that was not discernible in the two-variable case is evident. Married men more frequently shop at Target than do single men.

The finding is consistent with an interaction effect. The combination of the two variables, sex and marital status, is associated with differences in the dependent variable. Interactions between

EXHIBIT 14.4

Cross-Tabulation of Marital Status, Sex, and Responses to the Question "Do You Shop at Target?"

	Single		Married	
	Men	**Women**	**Men**	**Women**
"Do you shop at Target?"				
Yes	55%	80%	86%	80%
No	45%	20%	14%	20%

variables examine moderating variables. A **moderator variable** is a third variable that changes the nature of a relationship between the original independent and dependent variables. Marital status is a moderator variable in this case. The interaction effect suggests that marriage changes the relationship between sex and shopping preference.

In other situations the addition of a third variable to the analysis may lead us to reject the original conclusion about the relationship. When this occurs, the elaboration analysis suggests the relationship between the original variables is spurious.

moderator variable

A third variable that changes the nature of a relationship between the original independent and dependent variables.

How Many Cross-Tabulations?

Surveys may ask dozens of questions and hundreds of categorical variables can be stored in a data warehouse. Computer-assisted marketing researchers can "fish" for relationships by cross-tabulating every categorical variable with every other categorical variable. Thus, every possible response becomes a possible explanatory variable. A researcher addressing an exploratory research question may find some benefit in such a fishing expedition. Software exists that can automatically search through volumes of cross-tabulations. These may even provide some insight into the market segment structure for some product. Alternatively, the program may flag the cross-tabulations suggesting the strongest relationship. CHAID (chi-square automatic interaction detection) software exemplifies software that makes searches through large numbers of variables possible. Data-mining can be conducted with CHAID or similar techniques and may suggest useful relationships. A recent application paired promotion types against the type of product and suggests that coupons work best in getting consumers to come to your restaurant but television advertising works best in selling automobiles.[4]

Outside of exploratory research, researchers should conduct cross-tabulations that address specific research questions or hypotheses. When hypotheses involve relationships among two categorical variables, cross-tabulations are the right tool for the job.

Data Transformation

Simple Transformations

Data transformation (also called *data conversion*) is the process of changing the data from their original form to a format suitable for performing a data analysis that will achieve research objectives. Researchers often modify the values of scalar data or create new variables. For example, many researchers believe that less response bias will result if interviewers ask respondents for their year of birth rather than their age. This presents no problem for the research analyst, because a simple data transformation is possible. The raw data coded as birth year can easily be transformed to age by subtracting the birth year from the current year.

In earlier chapters, we discussed recoding and creating summated scales. These also are common data transformations.

Collapsing or combining adjacent categories of a variable is a common form of data transformation used to reduce the number of categories. A Likert scale may sometimes be collapsed into a smaller number of categories. For instance, consider the following Likert item administered to a sample of state university seniors:

data transformation

Process of changing the data from their original form to a format suitable for performing a data analysis addressing research objectives.

"All that we do is done with an eye to something else."

—ARISTOTLE

	Strongly Disagree	Disagree	Neutral	Agree	Strongly Agree
I am satisfied with my college experience at this university.	☐	☐	☐	☐	☐

The following frequency table describes results for this survey item:

Strongly Disagree	Disagree	Neutral	Agree	Strongly Agree
110	30	15	35	210

EXHIBIT **14.5**
Bimodal Distributions Are Consistent with Transformations into Categorical Values

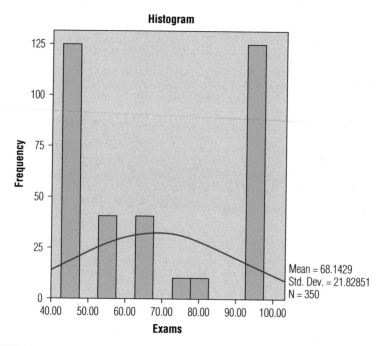

Histogram

Mean = 68.1429
Std. Dev. = 21.82851
N = 350

Source: Adapted from 1987 Nielsen Television Report.

The distribution is bimodal because two peaks exist in the distribution, one at either end of the scale. Because the vast majority of respondents (80 percent = (110 + 210)/400) indicated either strongly disagree or strongly agree, the variable closely resembles a categorical variable. Customers either strongly disagreed or strongly agreed with the statement. So, the research may wish to collapse the responses into two categories. Although multiple ways exist to accomplish this, the researcher may assign the value zero to all respondents who either strongly disagreed or disagreed and the value one to all respondents who either agreed or strongly agreed. Respondents marking neutral would be excluded from analysis.

Perhaps the 110 dissatisfied students differ in an important way from the 210. Perhaps their exam scores are also bimodal. Exhibit 14.5 shows an example of a bimodal distribution.

Problems with Data Transformations

median split

Dividing a data set into two categories by placing respondents below the median in one category and respondents above the median in another.

Researchers often perform a median split to collapse a scale with multiple response points into two categories. The **median split** means respondents below the observed median go into one category and respondents above the median go into another. Although this is common, the approach is best applied only when the data do indeed exhibit bimodal characteristics. When the data are unimodal, such as would be the case with normally distributed data, a median split will lead to error.

Exhibit 14.6 illustrates this problem. Clearly, most respondents either slightly agree or slightly disagree with this statement. The central tendency could be represented by the median of 3.5, a mean of 3.5, or the mode of 3.5 (3 and 4 each have the same number of responses so the mode is set between the two). The "outliers," if any, appear to be those not indicating something other than slight agreement or slight disagreement. In all likelihood, the respondents indicating slight disagreement are more similar to those indicating slight agreement than they are to those respondents indicating strong disagreement. Yet, the recode places values 1 and 3 in the same new category, but places values 3 and 4 in a different category (see the recoding scheme in Exhibit 14.6). The distribution does not support a median split into two categories and so a transformation collapsing these values into agreement and disagreement is inappropriate.

When a sufficient number of responses exist and a variable is ratio, the researcher may choose to delete one-fourth to one-third of the responses around the median to effectively ensure a

Wine Index Can Help Retailers

Indexes can be very useful, and researchers are sometimes asked to create index values from secondary data.

Using 1968 U.S. wine consumption as a base (just over 4 liters/person), the current wine consumption index for the United Kingdom is 5.1, South Africa's index value is 1.7, Israel's index is 0.2, Luxembourg's wine index is 13.4 (54.3 liters/person/year), but the top of the list is Vatican City where the just under 1,000 residents have a wine index of 17.3! U.S. consumption is over 9 liters per person for an index of 2.3 today.

This information would be helpful in making decisions about the amount of space and attention given to wine in different countries. Similarly, U.S. retailers could compute wine or beer indices by state. Policy agencies could also chart indices on alcohol consumption that may be helpful in regulating underage consumption.

Sources: Per capita consumption figures derived from The Wine Institute, http://www.wineinstitute.org/as accessed August 17, 2011.

bimodal distribution. This helps to mitigate the logical inconsistency illustrated in Exhibit 14.6. Median splits should always be performed only with great care and with adequate justification, though, as the inappropriate collapsing of continuous variables into categorical variables ignores the information contained within the untransformed values. Justification for a median slit commonly is found in the ability to apply a more parsimonious statistical approach than would be possible using the raw data values.

EXHIBIT **14.6**
The Problem with Median Splits with Unimodal Data

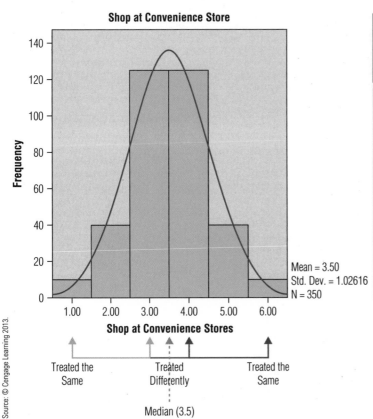

Shop at Convenience Store

Mean = 3.50
Std. Dev. = 1.02616
N = 350

Source: © Cengage Learning 2013.

Frequency Distribution: X1 = I Do most of my Shopping at Convenience stores.		
Response Category (Code)	**Counts**	**Cumulative Percentage**
Strongly Disagree (1)	10	2.86%
Disagree (2)	40	14.29%
Slightly Disagree (3)	125	50.00%
Slightly Agree (4)	125	85.71%
Agree (5)	40	97.14%
Strongly Agree (6)	10	100.00%
Median = 3.5		
Recode to Complete Data Transformation:		
Old Values	1 2 3 4 5 6	
New Values	1 1 1 2 2 2	

Index Numbers

index numbers

Scores or observations recalibrated to indicate how they relate to a base number.

The consumer price index and wholesale price index are secondary data sources that are frequently used by marketing researchers. Price indexes, like other **index numbers**, represent simple data transformations that allow researchers to track a variable's value over time and compare a variable(s) with other variables. Recalibration allows scores or observations to be related to a certain base period or base number.

For instance, if the data are time-related, a base year is chosen. The index numbers are then computed by dividing each year's activity by the base-year activity and multiplying by 100. Index numbers require ratio measurement scales. Marketing managers may often chart consumption in some category over time. Grocers may wish to chart the U.S. wine consumption index. Using 1968 as a base year (4.05 liters per year), the 2011 U.S. wine consumption index is about 2.3, meaning that the typical American consumer drinks 9.3 liters of wine per year (see the Research Snapshot above).[4]

Tabular and Graphic Methods of Displaying Data

Tables, graphs, and charts may simplify and clarify data. Graphical representations of data may take a number of forms, ranging from a computer printout to an elaborate pictograph. Tables, graphs, and charts, however, all facilitate summarization and communication. For example, see how the simple frequency table and histogram shown in Exhibit 14.6 provide a summary that quickly and easily communicates meaning that would be more difficult to see if all 350 responses were viewed separately.

Today's researcher has many convenient tools to quickly produce charts, graphs, or tables. Even basic word processing programs include chart functions that can construct the chart within the text document. Bar charts (histograms), pie charts, curve/line diagrams, and scatter plots are among the most widely used tools. Some choices match well with certain types of data and analyses.

> *"The thing to do is to supply light."*
> —WOODROW WILSON

Hypothesis Testing Using Basic Statistics

Descriptive research and causal research designs often climax with hypotheses tests. Generally, hypotheses should be stated in concrete fashion so that the method of empirical testing seems almost obvious.

Empirical testing typically involves inferential statistics. This means that an inference can be made about some population based on observations of a sample representing that population. Statistical analysis can be divided into several groups based on how many variables are involved:

univariate statistical analysis

Tests of hypotheses involving only one variable.

bivariate statistical analysis

Tests of hypotheses involving two variables.

multivariate statistical analysis

Statistical analysis involving three or more variables or sets of variables.

- **Univariate statistical analysis** tests hypotheses involving only one variable.
- **Bivariate statistical analysis** tests hypotheses involving two variables.
- **Multivariate statistical analysis** tests hypotheses and models involving multiple (three or more) variables or sets of variables.

For now, the focus is on univariate statistics. Thus, we examine statistical tests appropriate for drawing inferences about a single variable.

Hypothesis Testing Procedure

Hypotheses are tested by comparing an educated guess with empirical reality. The process can be described as follows:

- First, the hypothesis is derived from the research objectives. The hypothesis should be stated as specifically as possible and should be theoretically sound.

■ Next, a sample is obtained and the relevant variables are measured. In univariate tests, only one variable is of interest.

■ The measured value obtained in the sample is compared to the value either stated explicitly or implied in the hypothesis. If the value is consistent with the hypothesis, the hypothesis is supported. If the value is not consistent with the hypothesis, the hypothesis is not supported.

A univariate hypothesis consistent with the chapter vignette would be:

H1: The average number of children per family in ZIP code 70360 is greater than 1.5.

If a sample is drawn from this ZIP code and the average number of children per family is 0.075, the hypothesis is not supported. If the average number of children is 3.3, the hypothesis is supported. As the mean becomes smaller and approaches the theoretical expected value of 1.5, the chance becomes smaller that the hypothesis can indeed be supported. The exact point where the hypothesis changes from not being supported to being supported depends on how much risk the researcher is willing to accept and on the variability of the measure.

Univariate hypotheses are typified by tests comparing some observed sample mean against a benchmark value. The test addresses the question, is the sample mean truly different from the benchmark? But, how different is really different? If the observed sample mean is 1.55 and the benchmark is 1.50, would the hypothesis still be supported? Probably not! When the observed mean is so close to the benchmark, we do not have sufficient confidence that a second set of data using a new sample taken from the same population might not produce a finding conflicting with the benchmark. In contrast, when the mean turns out well above 1.50, perhaps 3.3, then we could more easily trust that another sample would not produce a mean equal to or less than 1.50.

Although the terminology of *null* and *alternative hypotheses* is common in statistical theory, it is also commonly confusing. Therefore, we'll avoid using the term *null hypothesis* when at all possible. Students usually understand hypothesis testing more easily by focusing on what the findings should look like if the proposed hypothesis is true. If the hypothesis above is true, an observed sample's mean should be noticeably greater than 1.50. We test to see if this idea can be supported by the empirical evidence. A statistical test's significance level or p-value becomes a key indicator of whether or not a hypothesis can be supported.

Significance Levels and p-values

A **significance level** is a critical probability associated with a statistical hypothesis test that indicates how likely it is that an inference supporting a difference between an observed value and some statistical expectation is true. The term **p-value** stands for probability-value and is essentially another name for an *observed* or *computed* significance level. Exhibit 14.7 discusses interpretations of p-values for different kinds of statistical tests. The probability in a p-value is that the statistical expectation (null) for a given test is true. So, low p-values mean there is little likelihood that the statistical expectation is true. This means the researcher's hypothesis positing (suggesting) a difference between an observed mean and a population mean, or between an observed frequency and a population frequency, or for a relationship between two variables, is likely supported.

Traditionally, researchers have specified an acceptable significance level for a test prior to the analysis. Later, we will discuss this as an acceptable amount of Type I error. For most applications, the acceptable amount of error, and therefore the acceptable significance level, is 0.1, 0.05, or 0.01. If the p-value resulting from a statistical test is less than the pre-specified significance level, then a hypothesis implying differences is supported.

significance level

A critical probability associated with a statistical hypothesis test that indicates how likely an inference supporting a difference between an observed value and some statistical expectation is true. The acceptable level of Type I error.

p-value

Probability value, or the observed or computed significance level; p-values are compared to significance levels to test hypotheses.

Type I and Type II Errors

Hypothesis testing using sample observations is based on probability theory. We make an observation of a sample and use it to infer the probability that an observation is true within the population the sample represents. Because we cannot make any statement about a sample with complete

Source: © Cengage Learning 2013.

EXHIBIT 14.7
p-Values and Statistical Tests

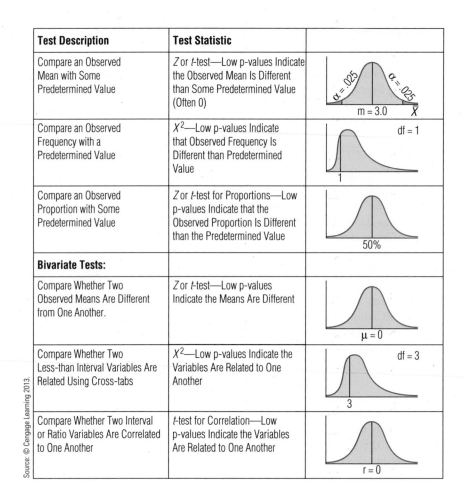

Test Description	Test Statistic	
Compare an Observed Mean with Some Predetermined Value	Z or t-test—Low p-values Indicate the Observed Mean Is Different than Some Predetermined Value (Often 0)	$\alpha = .025$ $\alpha = .025$ $m = 3.0$ $\bar{X}$
Compare an Observed Frequency with a Predetermined Value	X^2—Low p-values Indicate that Observed Frequency Is Different than Predetermined Value	df = 1 1
Compare an Observed Proportion with Some Predetermined Value	Z or t-test for Proportions—Low p-values Indicate that the Observed Proportion Is Different than the Predetermined Value	50%
Bivariate Tests:		
Compare Whether Two Observed Means Are Different from One Another.	Z or t-test—Low p-values Indicate the Means Are Different	$\mu = 0$
Compare Whether Two Less-than Interval Variables Are Related Using Cross-tabs	X^2—Low p-values Indicate the Variables Are Related to One Another	df = 3 3
Compare Whether Two Interval or Ratio Variables Are Correlated to One Another	t-test for Correlation—Low p-values Indicate the Variables Are Related to One Another	r = 0

certainty, there is always the chance that an error will be made. When a researcher makes the observation using a census, meaning that every unit (person or object) in a population is measured, then conclusions are certain. Researchers very rarely use a census though and thus, they are susceptible to two types of inferential errors (see Research Snapshot).

Type I Error

Type I error

occurs when a condition that is true in the population is rejected based on statistical observations

Suppose the observed sample mean described above leads to the conclusion that the mean is greater than 1.5 when in fact the true population mean is equal to 1.5. A **Type I error** has occurred. A **Type I error** occurs when a condition that is true in the population is rejected based on statistical observations. When a researcher sets an acceptable significance level a priori (α), he or she is determining how much tolerance he or she has for a Type I error. Simply put, a Type I error occurs when the researcher concludes that there is a statistical difference based on a sample result when in reality one does not exist in the population. When testing for relationships, a Type I error occurs when the researcher concludes a relationship exists when in fact one does not exist.

Type II error

Conversely, if our null hypothesis is indeed false, but we conclude that we should not reject the null hypothesis, we make what is called a Type II error. In this example, our null hypothesis that the mean is equal to 1.5 is not true in the population. However, our sample data indicates the mean does not differ from 1.5. So, a Type II error is the probability of failing to reject a false hypothesis.

The Law and Type I and Type II Errors

Although most attorneys and judges do not concern themselves with the statistical terminology of Type I and Type II errors, they do follow this logic. For example, our legal system is based on the concept that a person is innocent until proven guilty. Assume that the null hypothesis is that the individual is innocent. If we make a Type I error, we will send an innocent person to prison. Our legal system takes many precautions to avoid Type I errors. A Type II error would occur if a guilty party were set free (the null hypothesis would have been accepted). Our society places such a high value on avoiding Type I errors that Type II errors are more likely to occur.

Source: © Cengage Learning 2013.

©Michael Newman/PhotoEdit

This incorrect decision is called beta (β). In practical terms, a Type II error means that our sample does not show a difference between an observed mean and a benchmark when in fact the difference does exist in the population. Alternatively, for correlation-type relationships, a **Type II error** is created when the sample data suggests that a relationship does not exist when in fact a relationship does exist. Such an occurrence is related to statistical power. A sample size is sometimes too small to provide the power needed to find a relationship.

Unfortunately, without increasing sample size the researcher cannot simultaneously reduce Type I and Type II errors. They are inversely related. Thus, reducing the probability of a Type II error increases the probability of a Type I error. In marketing problems, Type I errors generally are considered more serious than Type II errors. Thus more emphasis is placed on determining the significance level, α, than in determining β.[5]

Type II error

created when the sample data suggests that a relationship does not exist when in fact a relationship does exist

Univariate Tests of Means

At times, a researcher may wish to compare some observation against a preset standard. A univariate t-test is appropriate for testing hypotheses involving an observed mean against a specified value such as a sales target. The t-distribution, like the standardized normal curve, is a symmetrical, bell-shaped distribution with a mean of 0 and a standard deviation of 1.0. When sample size (n) is larger than 30, the t-distribution and Z-distribution are almost identical. Therefore, although the t-test is strictly appropriate for tests involving small sample sizes with unknown standard deviations, researchers commonly apply the t-test for comparisons involving the mean of an interval or ratio measure. The precise height and shape of the t-distribution vary with sample size.

More specifically, the shape of the t-distribution is influenced by its degrees of freedom (df). The degrees of freedom are determined by the number of distinct calculations that are possible given a set of information. In the case of a univariate t-test, the degrees of freedom are equal to the sample size (n) minus one. If a sample size is 46 (n = 46) then the degrees of freedom for a univariate t-test is 45 (df = 46 − 1 = 45).

Exhibit 14.8 illustrates t-distributions for 1, 2, 5, and an infinite number of degrees of freedom. Notice that the t-distribution approaches a normal distribution rapidly with increasing sample size. This is why, in practice, marketing researchers usually apply a t-test even with large samples. The practical effect is that the conclusion will be the same because the distributions are so similar with large samples and the correspondingly larger numbers of degrees of freedom.

EXHIBIT 14.8

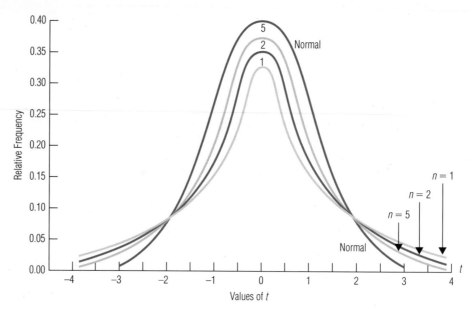

Source: From ZIKMUND/BABIN/CARR/GRIFFIN, Business Research Methods (with Qualtrics Card), 8E. © 2010 Cengage Learning.

Another way to look at degrees of freedom is to think of adding four numbers together when you know their sum—for example,

4

2

1

+X

12

The value of the fourth number has to be 5. The values of the first three digits could change to any value (freely vary), but the fourth value would have to be determined for the sum to still equal to 12. In this example there are three degrees of freedom. Degrees of freedom can be a difficult concept to understand fully. For most basic statistical analyses, the user only needs to remember the rule for determining the number of degrees of freedom for a given test. Today, with computerized software packages, the number of degrees of freedom is provided automatically for most tests.

Ultra-luxury car makers may set a sales goals that involves selling 1,000 cars per year or fewer worldwide as a means of deciding whether to put that car into production. The research question of "will sales exceed 1,000 cars?" involves a univariate analysis? More specifically, a univariate t-test may result from survey data of prospective customers.

To calculate a t statistic, one uses this formula:

$$t = \frac{\overline{X} - \mu}{S_{\overline{X}}}$$

with $n - 1$ degrees of freedom. Suppose a researcher for a luxury car manager believes that the average number of cars sold would be 20 per week. The manager records the number of sales for the first 25 weeks of a new prototype production run. Are the sales different from 20 per week? The substantive hypothesis is

H1: μ # 20

1. The researcher calculates a sample mean and standard deviation. In this case, suppose $\overline{X} = 22$ and S (sample standard deviation) = 5.

©KENCKO photography/Shutterstock

2. The standard error is computed ($S_{\overline{X}}$):

$$S_{\overline{X}} = \frac{S}{\sqrt{n}}$$
$$= \frac{5}{\sqrt{25}}$$
$$= 1$$

3. The researcher then finds the *t*-value associated with the desired level of confidence level or statistical significance. If a 95 percent confidence level is desired, the significance level is 0.05.
4. The critical values for the *t*-test are found by locating the upper and lower limits of the confidence interval. The result defines the regions of rejection. This requires determining the critical value of *t*. For 24 degrees of freedom ($n = 25$, $d.f. = n - 1$), the critical *t*-value is 2.064.
5. The formula provides this result:

$$t_{abs} = \frac{\overline{X} - \mu}{S_{\overline{X}}}$$

$$t_{abs} = \frac{22 - 20}{1} = \frac{2}{1} = 2$$

The observed mean of 22 is inserted for the sample mean ($\overline{X}$) and the hypothesized value of 20 is inserted for the population mean (μ). We can see that the observed *t*-value of 2.00 is less than the critical *t*-value of 2.064 at the 0.05 level when there are $25 - 1 = 24$ degrees of freedom. As a result, the p-value is greater than 0.05 and the hypothesis is not supported. We cannot conclude with 95 percent confidence that the mean is not 20.

The Z-distribution and the t-distribution are very similar, and thus the Z-test and *t*-test will provide much the same result in most situations. However, when the population standard deviation (σ) is known, the Z-test is most appropriate. When σ is unknown (the situation in most business research studies), and the sample size greater than 30, the Z-test also can be used. When σ is unknown and the sample size is small, the *t*-test is most appropriate.

TIPS OF THE TRADE

- A frequency table can be a very useful way to depict basic tabulations.
- Cross-tabulation and contingency tables are a simple and effective way to examine relationships among less than interval variables.
  - When a distinction can be made between independent and dependent variables (that are nominal or ordinal), the convention is that rows are independent variables and columns are dependent variables.

- A continuous variable that displays a bimodal distribution is appropriate for a median split.
  - Median splits should be performed on variables that display a normal distribution only with caution.
  - Importantly, median splits on continuous variables should be performed only after deleting one-fourth to one-third of the responses around the median to help prevent logically inconsistent classifications.

Source: © Cengage Learning 2013.

:: SUMMARY

1. Prepare qualitative data for interpretation or data analysis. Qualitative data interpretation benefits from coding. Coding can help identify key themes. Coding involves assigning some representative value to units of data having similar meaning. One of the most basic forms of coding is dummy coding. Dummy coding involves representing dichotomies with values of 0 and 1.

2. Know what descriptive statistics are and why they are used. Descriptive analyses provide descriptive statistics. These include measures of central tendency and variation. Statistics such as the mean, mode, median, range, variance, and standard deviation are all descriptive statistics. These statistics provide a basic summary describing the basic properties of a variable.

3. Create and interpret tabulation and cross-tabulation tables. Statistical tabulation is another way of saying that we count the number of observations in each possible response category. In other words, tabulation is the same as tallying. Tabulation is an appropriate descriptive analysis for less-than interval variables. Frequency tables and histograms are used to display tabulation results. Cross-tabulation is the appropriate technique for assessing relationships among multiple less than interval variables. The key to interpreting a cross-tabulation result is to compare actual observed values with hypothetical values that would result from pure chance. When observed results vary from these values, a relationship is indicated.

4. Perform basic data transformations. Data transformations are often needed to assist in data analysis and involve changing the mathematical form of data in a systematic way. Basic data transformations include reverse coding, summating scales, creating index numbers, and collapsing a variable based on a median split.

5. Understand the basics of testing hypotheses using inferential statistics. Hypothesis testing can involve univariate, bivariate, or multivariate statistics. Hypotheses are derived from research questions and should be stated in specific and testable terms. A sample is drawn. The sample represents a relevant population and then an inference about the population is made based on the descriptive statistics developed from the sample.

6. Using p-values to make statistical inferences. A p-value is the probability value associated with a statistical test. The probability in a *p*-value is the probability that the expected value for some test distribution is true. In other words, for a *t*-test, the expected value of the *t*-distribution is 0. If a researcher is testing whether or not a variable is significantly different from 0, then the p-value that results from the corresponding computed *t*-value represents the probability that the true population mean is actually 0. For most marketing research hypotheses, a low p-value supports the hypothesis. If a p-value is lower than the researcher's acceptable significance level (i.e., 0.05), then the hypothesis is usually supported.

7. Conduct a univariate *t*-test. A univariate *t*-test allows a researcher to test inferences comparing a sample observation against a predetermined standard. Often, the predetermined standard represents some benchmark such as a sales target or scrap rate. The *t*-test results allow an inference about a relevant population based on the mean derived from a sample.

:: KEY TERMS AND CONCEPTS

bivariate statistical analysis, *372*
class coding, *364*
coding, *363*
codes, *363*
contingency table, *367*
cross-tabulation, *366*
data transformation, *369*
descriptive analysis, *364*
dummy coding, *363*

effects coding, *363*
elaboration analysis, *368*
frequency table, *365*
histogram, *365*
index numbers, *372*
marginals, *367*
median split, *370*
moderator variable, *369*
multivariate statistical analysis, *372*

p-value, *373*
significance level, *373*
statistical base, *368*
tabulation, *365*
Type I error, *374*
Type II error, *375*
univariate statistical analysis, *372*

:: QUESTIONS FOR REVIEW AND CRITICAL THINKING

1. How does coding allow qualitative data to become useful to a researcher?
2. What are five descriptive statistics used to describe the basic properties of variables?
3. What is a histogram? What is the advantage of overlaying a normal distribution over a histogram?
4. A survey asks respondents to respond to the statement "My work is interesting." Interpret the frequency distribution shown here (taken from an SPSS output):

Category Label	Code	Abs. Freq.	Rel. Freq. (Pct.)	Adj. Freq. (Pct.)	Cum. Freq. (Pct.)
Very true	1	650	23.9	62.4	62.4
Somewhat true	2	303	11.2	29.1	91.5
Not very true	3	61	2.2	5.9	97.3
Not at all true	4	28	1.0	2.7	100.0
	•	1,673	61.6	Missing	
	Total	2,715	100.0	100.0	
Valid cases	1,042		Missing cases	1,673	

5. Use the data in the following table to
   a. prepare a frequency distribution of the respondents' ages
   b. cross-tabulate the respondents' genders with cola preference
   c. identify any outliers

Individual	Gender	Age	Cola Preference	Weekly Unit Purchases
John	M	19	Coke	2
Al	M	17	Pepsi	5
Bill	M	20	Pepsi	7
Mary	F	20	Coke	2
Jim	M	18	Coke	4
Karen	F	16	Coke	4
Tom	M	17	Pepsi	12
Sassi	F	22	Pepsi	6
Amie	F	20	Pepsi	2
Dawn	F	19	Pepsi	3

6. Data on the average size of a soda (in ounces) at all thirty major league baseball parks are as follows: 14, 18, 20, 16, 16, 12, 14, 16, 14, 16, 16, 16, 14, 32, 16, 20, 12, 16, 20, 12, 16, 16, 24, 16, 16, 14, 14, 12, 14, 20. Compute descriptive statistics for this variable. Comment on the results.

7. The following computer output shows a cross-tabulation of frequencies and provides frequency number (N) and row (R) percentages.
   a. Interpret this output including an impression about whether or not the row and column variables are related.
   b. Critique the way the analysis is presented.

Have You Read a Book in Past 3 Months?	Have High School Diploma?		
	Yes	No	Total
Yes	489	174	663
	73.8	26.2	
No	473	378	851
	55.6	44.4	
	......	......	......
TOTAL	962	552	1514

8. List and describe at least three basic data transformations.
9. What conditions suggest that a ratio variable should be transformed into a dichotomous (two group) variable represented with dummy coding?

10. **ETHICS** A data processing analyst for a research supplier finds that preliminary computer runs of survey results show that consumers love a client's new product. The employee buys a large block of the client's stock. Is this ethical?

11. Use a website such as **http://www.styledrops.com** to find some prices for 4 Prada handbags, 4 Gucci handbags, 4 Yves Saint Laurent handbags, 4 Burberry handbags, and 4 Ferragamo handbags. Enter these into a spreadsheet. Using the lowest-priced Prada handbag as a base, compute an index displaying the price of all other handbags. Which brand offers the best value in your opinion? Compute the appropriate statistic for central tendency using the spreadsheet or some other software. Use the chart feature to depict the prices as a frequency distribution.

12. Describe the basic hypothesis testing procedure.
13. What is a p-value and how is it used?
14. A researcher is asked to determine whether or not a productivity objective (in dollars) of better than $75,000 per employee is possible. A productivity test is done involving twenty employees. What conclusion would you reach? The sales results are as follows:

28,000	105,000	58,000	93,000	96,000
67,000	82,500	75,000	81,000	59,000
101,000	60,500	77,000	72,500	48,000
99,000	78,000	71,000	80,500	78,000

:: RESEARCH ACTIVITIES

1. Go thewebsite for the Chicago Cubs baseball team (**http://chicago.cubs.mlb.com**). Use either the schedule listing or the stats information to find their record in the most recent season. Create a data file with a variable indicating whether each game was won or lost and a variable indicating whether the game was played at home in Wrigley Field or away from home. Using a computer and software such as Excel, SPSS, or SAS product:

   a. Compute a frequency table and histogram for each variable.

   b. Use cross-tabulations to examine whether a relationship exists between where the game is played (home or away) and winning.

   c. Extra Analysis: Repeat the analyses for the Houston Astros baseball team (**http://www.astros.com**). What does this suggest for the relationship between playing at home and winning?

Body on Tap

Case 14.1

A few years ago Vidal Sassoon, Inc., took legal action against Bristol-Myers over a series of TV commercials and print ads for a shampoo that had been named Body on Tap because of its beer content.[10] The prototype commercial featured a well-known high fashion model saying, "In shampoo tests with over 900 women like me, Body on Tap got higher ratings than Prell for body. Higher than Flex for conditioning. Higher than Sassoon for strong, healthy-looking hair."

The evidence showed that several groups of approximately 200 women each tested just one shampoo. They rated it on a six-step qualitative scale, from "outstanding" to "poor," for 27 separate attributes, such as body and conditioning. It became clear that 900 women did not, after trying both shampoos, make product-to-product comparisons between Body on Tap and Sassoon or between Body on Tap and any of the other brands mentioned. In fact, no woman in the tests tried more than one shampoo.

The claim that the women preferred Body on Tap to Sassoon for "strong, healthy-looking hair" was based on combining the data for the "outstanding" and "excellent" ratings and discarding the lower four ratings on the scale. The figures then were 36 percent for Body on Tap and 24 percent (of a separate group of women) for Sassoon.

When the "very good" and "good" ratings were combined with the "outstanding" and "excellent" ratings, however, there was only a difference of 1 percent between the two products in the category of "strong, healthy-looking hair."

The research was conducted for Bristol-Myers by Marketing Information Systems, Inc. (MISI), using a technique known as *blind monadic testing*. The president of MISI testified that this method typically is employed when what is wanted is an absolute response to a product "without reference to another specific product." Although he testified that blind monadic testing was used in connection with comparative advertising, that was not the purpose for which Bristol-Myers retained MISI. Rather, Bristol-Myers wished to determine consumer reaction to the introduction of Body on Tap. And Sassoon's in-house research expert stated flatly that blind monadic testing cannot support comparative advertising claims.

Question

Comment on the professionalism of the procedures used to make the advertising claim. Why do you believe the researchers performed the data transformations described?

Source: © Cengage Learning 2013.

Premier Motorcars

Case 14.2

Premier Motorcars is the new Fiat dealer in Delavan, Illinois. Premier Motorcars has been regularly advertising in its local market area that the new Fiat 500 averages 30 miles to a gallon of gas and mentions that this figure may vary with driving conditions. A local consumer group wishes to verify the advertising claim. To do so, it selects a sample of recent purchasers of the Fiat 500. It asks them to drive their cars until at least two tanks of gasoline have been used up and then calculate the mileage in miles per gallon. The researcher can then calculate descriptive statistics indicating what the actual mileage of the Fiat 500 is based on the observations from the sample. The data in Case Exhibit 14.2–1 portray the results of the tests.

Questions

1. Formulate a statistical hypothesis appropriate for the consumer group's purpose.
2. Calculate the mean average miles per gallon. Compute the sample variance and sample standard deviation.
3. Construct the appropriate statistical test for your hypothesis, using a 0.05 significance level.

Source: Case prepared by Mitch Griffin, Bradley University.

CASE EXHIBIT 14.2–1 Miles per Gallon Information

Purchaser	Miles per Gallon	Purchaser	Miles per Gallon
1	30.9	13	27.0
2	24.5	14	26.7
3	31.2	15	31.0
4	28.7	16	23.5
5	35.1	17	29.4
6	29.0	18	26.3
7	28.8	19	27.5
8	23.1	20	28.2
9	31.0	21	28.4
10	30.2	22	29.1
11	28.4	23	21.9
12	29.3	24	30.9

Source: Case prepared by Mitch Griffin, Bradley University.

©Zoran Karapanceev/Shutterstock

Testing for Differences Between Groups and for Relationships Among Variables

LEARNING OUTCOMES

After studying this chapter, you should be able to

1. Choose the appropriate statistic
2. Construct a cross-tabulation table and the corresponding χ^2 statistic
3. Use a *t*-test to compare a difference between two means
4. Conduct a one-way analysis of variance test (ANOVA)
5. Appreciate the practicality of modern statistical software packages
6. Use the GLM to represent a generalized statistical model

CHAPTER

15

Chapter Vignette:

Doubling Down

How many times have you heard somebody try to blame something on "big business"? Well, people make up businesses. Interestingly though, many people have double standards when laying moral blame for the same actions.

John is about to trade in his car and knows that some repair is needed that is not obvious but needs to be fixed to avoid permanent damage to the car. John takes the car to Carmax, where an agent named Patrice greets him. Should John tell Patrice about the problem? Is that the morally correct thing to do?

By now, you've probably made some judgment of John's action should he not disclose the problem. Put the shoe on the other foot now. What if Patrice, the Carmax sales agent, were selling a car with the same problem to John? Should she disclose the problem to John? Does your moral judgment of this act differ from the one above? If you would judge John's act as less

morally incorrect than Patrice's, then you, like a large number of people, are displaying a double standard. A dubious act performed by a consumer is judged as more ethical than the very same act performed by someone associated with a business.

Researchers build hypotheses around this double standard and test them using simple tests of differences between ethical judgments. The research puts various dubious scenarios before experimental subjects and asks them to rate how ethical the person's behavior was using a scale ranging from 1 = totally unethical to 7 = total ethical. These scenarios were split across 127 subjects so that half read a scenario involving a consumer engaging in the act while the other half read the same scenario with the exception that a businessperson performs the same act. Across the four scenarios, the results show:

The differences between the means support the double standard hypothesis. When a consumer performs the act,

| | Scenario: | | | |
Act Performed by:	Deceive in Negotiation	Hide Product Defect	Overstate 3rd Party Offer	Apply Time Pressure
Consumer	5.4	3.7	5.3	6.0
Business	3.6	1.7	3.4	5.0

subjects judge the act more ethically. However, given that the results come from a sample and not a census, a statistical test is needed to judge how confident one can be about a conclusion that the means are different between the two conditions. In this case, an independent samples *t*-test confirms that the means are significantly different with 95 percent confidence.

One reason for the difference may be neutralization, or more simply, the extent to which excuses are available for an otherwise unethical act. For instance, if subjects excuse the consumer based on the thought that his/her action "won't really hurt anybody," then the act is judge as more ethical. Correlational studies shed light on this issue. This chapter sheds light on statistical tools researchers use to reach such conclusions.[1]

©Bloomberg via Getty Images

Sources: De Bock, T. and P. V. Kenhove (2011), "Double Standards: The Role of Techniques of Neutralization," *Journal of Business Ethics,* 99, 283–296. Vermeir, I. and P. V. Kenhove (2008), "Gender Differences in Double Standards," *Journal of Business Ethics,"* 81, 281–298.

Introduction

The vignette describes ethical judgment comparisons across two experimental groups. If we look at the customer (business) condition as a categorical variable and ethical judgments as an interval variable, these comparisons really involve drawing inferences about how one experimental variable influences another, ethical judgments. A surprising number of inferences involve two variables. In fact, sometimes researchers reduce a more complex analysis to a two-variable comparison because presenting the results becomes very simple. This chapter illustrates some common ways that such statistical tests can be performed.

What is the Appropriate Test Statistic?

In marketing research, differences in behavior, characteristics, beliefs, opinions, emotions, or attitudes are commonly examined. For example, in the most basic experimental design, the researcher tests differences between subjects assigned to an experimental group and subjects assigned to the control group. A survey researcher may be interested in whether male and female consumers purchase a product in the same amount. Business researchers may also test whether or not business units in Europe are as profitable as business units in the United States. Such tests are bivariate **tests of differences** when they involve only two variables: a variable that acts like a dependent variable and a variable that acts as a classification variable.

test of differences

An investigation of a hypothesis stating that two (or more) groups differ with respect to measures on a variable.

Exhibit 15.1 on the next page illustrates that the type of measurement, the nature of the comparison, and the number of groups to be compared influence the statistical choice. Often researchers are interested in testing differences in mean scores between groups or in comparing how two groups' scores are distributed across possible response categories. We will focus our attention on these issues.[2] The rest of the chapter focuses on how to choose the right statistic for two-group comparisons and perform the corresponding test. Exhibit 15.1 on the next page provides a frame of reference for the rest of the chapter by illustrating various possible comparisons involving a few golfers.

More generally, choosing the right statistic boils down to what type and how many variables are involved in the research question being examined. In this text, practically all the hypotheses can be expressed either as tests of differences between groups or as relationships among variables.

EXHIBIT 15.1 Some Bivariate Hypotheses

Information	Golfer Dolly	Lori	Mel	Hypothesis or Research Question	Level of Measurement Involved	Statistic Used	Comment	Result
Average Driver Distance (meters)	135	150	185	Lori hits her drives further than Dolly	Golfer = Nominal; Drive Distance = Ratio	Independent Samples t-test to compare mean distance	The data for Lori and Dolly are used.	Supported ($t = 2.07$, df = 56, $p < .05$)
σ	30	25	30					
Average 7-Wood Distance (meters)	140	145	150	Mel hits her driver further than her 7-wood	Club = Nominal (7-wood or driver); 7-Wood Distance = Ratio	Paired-Samples t-test to compare mean distances for Mel	Only the data for Mel are used (std of diff = 30)	Supported ($t = 6.39$, df = 29, $p < .05$)
σ	30	30	30					
Sample size (number of balls hit)	28 drives 28 7-woods	30 drives 28 7-woods	29 drives 28 7-woods	A relationship exists between golfers and 7-wood distance	Golfer = Nominal; Distance = Ratio	One-Way ANOVA to compare means for the three groups	All data for 7-wood distance are used (MSE = 30)	Not supported ($F = 0.83$, ns)
Number of Drives in Fairway	4	22	11	Mel drives the ball more accurately than Dolly	Golfer = Nominal; Accuracy = Nominal (Right, Fairway, Left)	Cross-Tabulation with χ^2 Statistic	Resulting cross tabulation table is 2 rows × 3 columns (rows = golfer and columns = accuracy (fairway, right left)	Supported ($\chi^2 = 10.3$, df = 3, $p < .05$)
Drives missing right of fairway	16	7	9	A relationship exist between golfers and accuracy	Golfer = Nominal; Accuracy = Nominal (Right, Fairway, Left)	Cross-Tabulation with χ^2 Statistic	Cross-tabulation is now 3 rows × 3 columns	Supported ($\chi^2 = 23.7$, df = 4, $p < .05$)
Drives missing left of fairway	8	1	9					

Generally, we can group variables based on whether they are dependent or independent. Dependent variables respond to independent variables.

By answering the question of how many independent variables (IV) and the scale level of the variables, finding an appropriate statistic is easy. Exhibit 15.2 provides a useful guide in choosing a test statistic under these circumstances. Notice that in several cases the appropriate statistic would be beyond the scope of this text. Fortunately, the tests that are described here are very commonly used in marketing research and account for a large bulk of inferential tests. Users may find it useful to refer back to this particular exhibit when trying to decide which statistical tool fits a given research question or hypothesis.

Market research reports very often involve cross-tabulation tables. For instance, if a researcher is interested in testing whether male golfers will select a domestic or imported name brand, the research question involves a categorical (nominal) independent variable, a consumer's sex, and a categorical (nominal) dependent variable, brand type. Thus, the test would involve a single less than interval dependent variable and a single less than interval independent variable. The appropriate tool therefore is a χ^2 test computed from the corresponding 2 (Male/Female) × 2 (Domestic/Imported) cross-tabulation table.

EXHIBIT 15.2
Choosing the Right Statistic

Independent Variables:	Dependent Variables		
	1 Nominal / Ordinal DV	1 at Least Interval DV	More than 1 DV
1 Nominal/Ordinal IV	Cross-Tabulation with χ^2 Test	t-test or One-Way ANOVA	Multivariate Analysis
2 or More Nominal/Ordinal IVs	Cross-Tabulation with χ^2 Test	n-Way ANOVA	Multivariate ANOVA
At Least 1 Nominal/Ordinal IV and at Least 1 Interval or Ratio IV	Multivariate Analyses—(Logistic Regression)	Full-Factorial ANCOVA	Multivariate MANCOVA
1 Interval/Ratio IV	t-test	Simple Regression	Multivariate Regression
1 or More Interval/Ratio IVs	Multivariate Analyses—(Logistic Regression)	Multiple Regression	Multivariate Analyses such as Path Model

Color Code:

    Beyond the Scope of this Text   Dependent Variable Condition

    Variations of the GLM illustrated in Chapter   Bivariate test illustrated in Chapter

    Independent Variable Condition

Source: © Cengage Learning 2013.

SURVEY THIS!

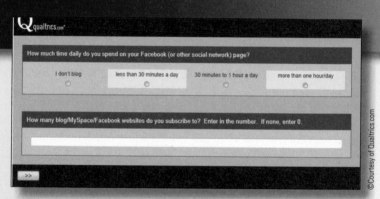

Are men or women more preoccupied with their smartphones and social networking sites? You may be able to answer this question by looking at the data from the student survey. Test the following hypotheses using data obtained from the survey:

H₁: Women are more likely than men to have a Facebook site.

H₂: Men are more likely to have more than one e-mail address.

H₃: Women check their e-mail more often than do men.

H₄: Men spend more time online daily than do women.

H₅: The better a student feels about their living arrangements, the more time they spend studying.

Source: © Cengage Learning 2013.

Cross-Tabulation Tables: The χ^2 Test for Goodness-of-Fit

Cross-tabulation was introduced in the previous chapter as a way of representing relationships between variables. Cross-tabulations are intuitive and easily understood. They also lend themselves well to graphical analysis using tools like bar charts.

Researchers use two-variable cross-tabulations the most because the results are very easily communicated. Cross-tabulations are much like tallying. When two variables exist, each with two categories, four cells result. Each cell contains the count of observations matching a particular combination of characteristics. The χ^2 distribution provides a means for testing the statistical significance of a contingency table. In other words, the bivariate χ^2 test examines the statistical significance of relationships among two less than interval variables.

The χ^2 test for a contingency table involves comparing the observed frequencies (O_i) with the expected frequencies (E_i) in each cell of the table. The goodness- (or closeness-) of-fit of the observed distribution with the expected distribution is captured by this statistic. Remember that the convention is that the row variable is considered the independent variable and the column variable is considered the dependent variable. Cross-tabulation is appropriate when both variables are nominal or ordinal; however, interval variables are sometimes used in a cross-tabulation if the range is very small—meaning the variable only takes on values of 1, 2, or 3, for example. Once a variable has more than four categories, a cross-tabulation table can be difficult to interpret.

We could use a χ^2 test to examine a research question asking whether or not Papa John's restaurants were more likely to be located in a stand-alone location or in a shopping center. The univariate (one-dimensional) analysis suggests that the majority of the locations (60 percent) are stand-alone units:

Location	One-Way Frequency Table
Stand-alone	60 stores
Shopping Center	40 stores
Total	100 stores

Is there any effect of location on Papa John's restaurants? Suppose the researcher analyzes the situation further by examining the following bivariate hypothesis:

Stand-alone locations are more likely to be profitable than are shopping center locations.

Although the researcher is unable to obtain the dollar figures for profitability of each unit, a press release indicates which Papa John's units were profitable and which were not. Cross-tabulation using a χ^2 test is appropriate because:

- The independent variable (location) is less than interval.
- The dependent variable (profitable/not profitable) is less than interval.

The data can be recorded in the following 2 × 2 contingency table:

Location	Profitable	Not Profitable	Total
Stand-alone	50	10	60
Shopping Center	15	25	40
Totals	65	35	100

> *"You got to be careful if you don't know where you're going, because you might not get there."*
>
> —YOGI BERRA

Several conclusions appear evident. One, it seems that more stores are profitable than not profitable (65 versus 35, respectively). Secondly, more of the profitable restaurants seem to be in stand-alone locations (50 out of 65). However, is the difference strong enough to be statistically significant?

Is the observed difference between stand-alone and shopping center locations the result of chance variation due to random sampling? Is the discrepancy more than sampling variation? The χ^2 test allows us to conduct tests for significance in the analysis of the $R \times C$ contingency table (where R = row and C = column). The formula for the χ^2 statistic is the same as that for one-way frequency tables:

$$\chi^2 = \sum \frac{(O_i - E_i)^2}{E_i}$$

where

χ^2 = chi-square statistic
O_i = observed frequency in the ith cell
E_i = expected frequency in the ith cell

Again, as in a univariate χ^2 test, a frequency count of data that nominally identify or categorically rank groups is acceptable.

If the researcher's hypothesis is true, the frequencies shown in the contingency table should not resemble a random distribution. In other words, if location has no effect on profitability, the profitable and unprofitable stores would be spread evenly across the two location categories. This is really the logic of the test in that it compares the observed frequencies with the theoretical expected values for each cell.

After obtaining the observations for each cell, the expected values for each cell must be obtained. The expected values for each cell can be computed easily using this formula:

$$E_{ij} = \frac{R_i C_j}{n}$$

where

R_i = total observed frequency count in the ith row
C_j = total observed frequency count in the jth column
n = sample size

Only the total column and total row values are needed for this calculation. Thus, the calculation could be performed before the data are even tabulated. The following values represent the expected values for each cell:

Location	Profitable	Not Profitable	Total
Stand-alone	(60 × 65)/100 = 39	(60 × 35)/100 = 21	60
Shopping Center	(40 × 65)/100 = 26	(40 × 35)/100 = 14	40
Totals	65	35	100

Notice that the row and column totals are the same for both the observed and expected contingency matrices. These values also become useful in providing the substantive interpretation of the relationship. Variance from the expected value indicates a relationship.

The actual bivariate χ^2 test value can be calculated in the same manner as for a univariate test. The one difference is that the degrees of freedom are obtained by multiplying the number of rows minus one $(R - 1)$ times the number of columns minus one $(C - 1)$ rather than simply the number of cells minus one:

$$\chi^2 = \sum \frac{(O_i - E_i)^2}{E_i}$$

with $(R - 1)(C - 1)$ degrees of freedom. The observed and expected values can be plugged into the formula as follows:

$$\chi^2 = \frac{(50 - 39)^2}{39} + \frac{(10 - 21)^2}{21} + \frac{(15 - 26)^2}{26} + \frac{(25 - 14)^2}{4}$$

$$= 3.102 + 5.762 + 4.654 + 8.643$$

$$= 22.16$$

The number of degrees of freedom equals 1:

$$(R - 1)(C - 1) = (2 - 1)(2 - 1) = 1$$

From an Internet chi-square calculator (such as **www.danielsoper.com/statcalc/calc11.aspx**) or the chi-square distribution table on the companion website (**www.cengage.com/marketing/zikmund**), we see that the critical value at the 0.05 probability level with 1 d.f. is 3.84. Thus, we are 95 percent confident that the observed values do not equal the expected values. Before the hypothesis can be supported, however, the researcher must check and see that the deviations from the expected values are in the hypothesized direction. Because the difference between the stand-alone locations' observed profitability and the expected values for that cell are positive, the hypothesis is supported. Location is associated with profitability. Thus, testing the hypothesis involves two key steps:

1. Examine the statistical significance of the observed contingency table.
2. Examine whether the differences between the observed and expected values are consistent with the hypothesized prediction.

Proper use of the χ^2 test requires that each expected cell frequency (E) have a value of at least 5. If this sample size requirement is not met, the researcher should take a larger sample as a way of increasing the frequency.

JMP is a new user-friendly statistics software package from SAS. The JMP screenshot shows a cross-tabulation result depicting whether or not the type of coupon that guests as a water park used for admission influenced whether that customer would upgrade their ticket to a season pass. The mosaic frame at the top of the output depicts in colors the proportion of each cou-pon type that either said "yes," "no," or "maybe" to an upgrade. The contingency table shows the cross-tabulation results. Two numbers are depicted in each cell with the top number showing the observed cell frequency count and the bottom number showing the expected cell frequency count. A large difference between the observed and expected counts provides a clue to interpretation. The final results show the chi-square statistic result.

In this case, the χ^2 of just over 19 is significant, as indicated by the p value of less than 0.001, suggesting a relationship. In this case, the $5 off coupon produced 46 upgrades out of 80 respondents

The cross-tab window in SAS. In this case, a cross-tab between the variables salespeople and store would be conducted.

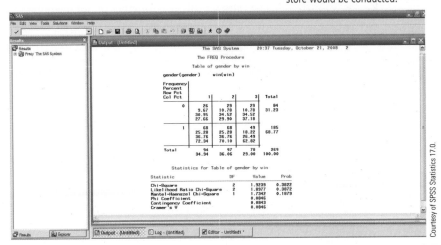

Courtesy of SPSS Statistics 17.0.

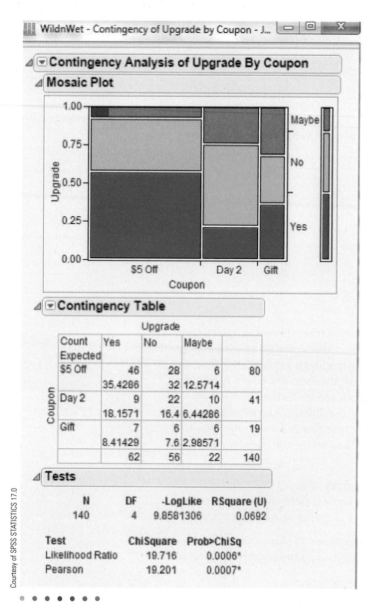

A cross-tabulation result from SAS JMP showing a significant relationship between Coupon type and a dependent variable upgrade.

redeeming that coupon—more than ten more than the statistical expected value. The Day 2 coupon converted only 9 of 41 respondents while producing 22 no's. The free gift coupon does not reveal a distinct pattern. As a result, the $5 off coupon is recommended as the most effective of these coupons in getting customers to upgrade to a season pass.

The *t*-Test for Comparing Two Means

Independent Samples *t*-Test

When a researcher needs to compare means for a variable grouped into two categories based on some less-than interval variable, a *t*-test is appropriate. One way to think about this is as testing the way a dichotomous (two-level) independent variable is associated with changes in a continuous dependent variable. Several variations of the *t*-test exist.

Most typically, the researcher will apply the **independent samples *t*-test**, which tests the differences between means taken from two independent samples or groups. So, for example, if we measure the price for some designer jeans at 30 different retail stores, of which 15 are Internet-only stores (pure clicks) and 15 are traditional stores, we can test whether or not the prices are different based on store type with an independent samples *t*-test. The *t*-test for difference of means assumes the two samples (one Internet and one traditional store) are drawn from normal distributions and that the variances of the two populations are approximately equal (homoscedasticity).

Independent Samples *t*-test Calculation

The *t*-test actually tests whether or not the differences between two group means is zero. Not surprisingly, this idea can be expressed as the difference between two population means:

$$\mu_1 = \mu_2, \text{which is equivalent to,} \, \mu_1 - \mu_2 = 0$$

However, because this is inferential statistics, we test the idea by comparing two sample means:

$$(\overline{X}_1 - \overline{X}_{2=0}).$$

A verbal expression of the formula for *t* is

independent samples *t*-test

A test for hypotheses stating that the mean scores for some interval- or ratio-scaled variable grouped based on some less-than interval classificatory variable are not the same.

$$t = \frac{\text{Sample Mean 1} - \text{Sample Mean 2}}{\text{Variability of random means}}$$

Thus, the *t*-value is a ratio with information about the difference between means (provided by the sample) in the numerator and the standard error in the denominator. The question is whether the observed differences have occurred by chance alone. To calculate *t*, we use the following formula:

$$t = \frac{\overline{X}_1 - \overline{X}_2}{S_{X_1 - \overline{X}_1}}$$

where

$\overline{X}_1$ = mean for group 1

$\overline{X}_2$ = mean for group 2

$S_{\overline{X}_1 - \overline{X}_2}$ = pooled, or combined, standard error of difference between means

A **pooled estimate of the standard error** is a better estimate of the standard error than one based on the variance from either sample. The pooled standard error of the difference between means of independent samples can be calculated using the following formula:

pooled estimate of the standard error

An estimate of the standard error for a t-test of independent means that assumes the variances of both groups are equal.

$$S_{\overline{X}_1 - \overline{X}_2} = \sqrt{\left(\frac{(n_1 - 1)S_1^2 + (n_2 - 1)S_2^2}{n_1 + n_2 - 2}\right)\left(\frac{1}{n_1} + \frac{1}{n_2}\right)}$$

where

S_1^2 = variance of group 1

S_2^2 = variance of group 2

n_1 = sample size of group 1

n_2 = sample size of group 2

Are business majors or sociology majors more positive about a career in business? A t-test can be used to test the difference between sociology majors and business majors on scores on a scale measuring attitudes toward business. We will assume that the attitude scale is an interval scale. The result of the simple random sample of these two groups of college students is shown below:

Business Students	Sociology Students
$\overline{X}_1$ = 16.5	$\overline{X}_2$ = 12.2
S_1 = 2.1	S_2 = 2.6
n_1 = 21	n_2 = 14

A high score indicates a favorable attitude toward business. This particular t-test tests whether the difference in attitudes between sociology and business students is significant. A higher t-value is associated with a lower p-value. As the t gets higher and the p-value gets lower, the researcher has more confidence that the means are truly different. The relevant data computation is

$$S_{\overline{X}_1 - \overline{X}_2} = \sqrt{\left(\frac{(n_1 - 1)S_1^2 + (n_2 - 1)S_2^2}{n_1 + n_2 - 2}\right)\left(\frac{1}{n_1} + \frac{1}{n_2}\right)}$$

$$= \sqrt{\left(\frac{(20)(2.1)^2 + (13)(2.6)^2}{33}\right)\left(\frac{1}{21} + \frac{1}{14}\right)}$$

$$= 0.797$$

The calculation of the t-statistic is:

$$t = \frac{\overline{X}_1 - \overline{X}_2}{S_{\overline{X}_1 - \overline{X}_2}}$$

$$t = \frac{16.5 - 12.2}{0.797}$$

$$= \frac{4.3}{0.797}$$

$$= 5.395$$

In a test of means between groups, degrees of freedom are calculated as follows:

$$d.f. = n - k$$

where

$n = n_1 + n_2$
$k =$ number of groups

In our example *d.f.* equals 33 (21 + 14 − 2). If the 0.01 level of significance is selected, reference to the tabled values of the *t*-distribution (see **www.cengage.com/marketing/zikmund** or a Web based p-value calculator) yields the critical *t*-value. The critical *t*-value of 2.75 must be surpassed by the observed *t*-value if the hypothesis test is to be statistically significant at the 0.01 level. The calculated value of *t*, 5.39, exceeds the critical value of *t* for statistical significance, so it is significant at $\alpha = 0.01$. The p-value is less than 0.01. In other words, this research shows that business students have significantly more positive attitudes toward business than do sociology students. The Research Snapshot provides an overview of situations calling for an independent samples *t*-test.

Practically Speaking

In practice, computer software is used to compute the *t*-test results. Exhibit 15.3 displays a typical *t*-test printout. These particular results examine the following research question:

RQ: Does religion relate to price sensitivity in restaurants?

This question was addressed by asking a sample of 100 consumers to report how much they would be willing to pay per person for a nice dinner at one of the better restaurants in town. A research assistant showed each respondent a menu from the restaurant and then asked the respondent what amount per person he or she would pay (including tip) if dining there. The sample included 57 Catholics and 43 Protestants. Because no direction of the relationship is stated (no hypothesis is offered), a two-tailed test is appropriate. Although instructors still find some value in having students learn to perform the *t*-test calculations, practitioners almost always generate and interpret computer generated results today.

EXHIBIT 15.3 Independent Samples *t*-Test Results

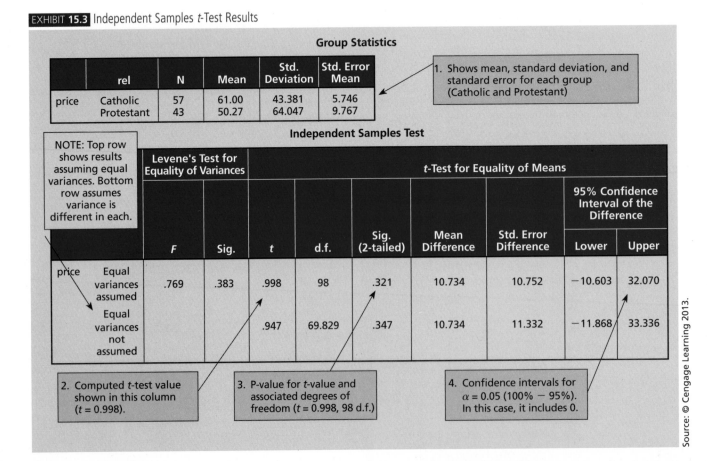

Group Statistics

	rel	N	Mean	Std. Deviation	Std. Error Mean
price	Catholic	57	61.00	43.381	5.746
	Protestant	43	50.27	64.047	9.767

1. Shows mean, standard deviation, and standard error for each group (Catholic and Protestant)

Independent Samples Test

NOTE: Top row shows results assuming equal variances. Bottom row assumes variance is different in each.

		Levene's Test for Equality of Variances		*t*-Test for Equality of Means					95% Confidence Interval of the Difference	
		F	Sig.	t	d.f.	Sig. (2-tailed)	Mean Difference	Std. Error Difference	Lower	Upper
price	Equal variances assumed	.769	.383	.998	98	.321	10.734	10.752	−10.603	32.070
	Equal variances not assumed			.947	69.829	.347	10.734	11.332	−11.868	33.336

2. Computed *t*-test value shown in this column (*t* = 0.998).

3. P-value for *t*-value and associated degrees of freedom (*t* = 0.998, 98 d.f.)

4. Confidence intervals for $\alpha = 0.05$ (100% − 95%). In this case, it includes 0.

Source: © Cengage Learning 2013.

Marketing Expert "T-eeze"

When is an independent samples *t*-test appropriate? Once again, we can find out by answering some simple questions:

- Is the dependent variable interval or ratio?
- Can the dependent variable scores be grouped based upon some meaningful categorical variable?
- Does the grouping result in scores drawn from independent samples (hint: means that one respondent's score on the dv does not influence another respondent's score on the dv)?
- Are two groups involved in the research question?

When the answer to all questions is "yes," an independent samples *t*-test is appropriate. Often, business researchers may wish to examine how some process varies between novices and experts. Consider the following example.

Researchers looked at the difference in decision speed for expert and novice salespeople faced with the same situation. Decision speed is a ratio dependent variable and the scores are grouped based on whether or not the salesperson is an expert or a novice. Thus, this categorical variable produces two groups.

The results across 40 respondents, 20 experts and 20 novices, are shown at the bottom left.

The average difference in decision time is 38 seconds. Is this significantly different from 0? The calculated *t*-test is 2.76 with 38 d.f. The one-tailed p-value is 0.0045; thus the conclusion is reached that experts do take less time to make a decision than do novices.

Marketers often want to know differences in key variables like price perception and satisfaction across different groups. A recent study examined differences in the perceptions of prices at hypermarkets. The results indicate that married men believe that prices are higher (+0.186) than do married women. Perhaps a further study could compare price perceptions of married consumers against single consumers or examine which group shows the most expertise by assessing accuracy in price perceptions between groups. Are men or women price experts?

Sources: Shepherd, D. G., S. F. Gardial, M. G. Johnson, and J. O. Rentz, "Cognitive Insights into the Highly Skilled or Expert Salesperson," *Psychology and Marketing,* 23 (February 2006), 115–138; Green, R. D.. and H.C. Chen (2011), "Spousal Purchasing Behavior as an Influence on Brand Equity," *International Journal of Management and Marketing Research,* 3, 1–17.

The interpretation of the *t*-test is made simple by focusing on either the p-value or the confidence interval and the group means. Here are the basic steps:

1. Examine the difference in means to find the "direction" of any difference. In this case, Catholics are willing to pay over $10 more than Protestants.
2. Compute or locate the computed *t*-test value. In this case, $t = 0.998$.
3. Find the p-value associated with this *t* and the corresponding degrees of freedom. Here, the p-value (two-tailed significance level) is 0.321. This suggests a 32 percent chance that the means are actually equal given the observed sample means. Assuming a 0.05 acceptable type I error rate (α), the appropriate conclusion is that the means are not significantly different.
4. The difference can also be examined using the 95 percent confidence interval ($-10.603 < \overline{X}_1 - \overline{X}_2 < 32.070$). Because the confidence interval includes 0, we lack sufficient confidence that the true difference between the population means is not really 0. The result suggests that it may well be 0.

A few points are worth noting about this particular result. First, strictly speaking, the *t*-test assumes that the two population variances are equal. A slightly more complicated formula exists which will compute the *t*-statistic assuming the variances are not equal.[3] The software provides both results when reporting independent samples *t*-test results. The sample variances appear considerably different in this case as evidenced by the standard deviations for each group (43.4, 64.0). Nonetheless, the conclusions are the same using either assumption. In marketing research, we often deal with values that have variances close enough to assume equal variance. This isn't always the case in the physical sciences, where variables may take on values of drastically different magnitude. Thus, the rule of thumb in marketing research is to use the equal variance assumption. In the vast majority of cases, the same conclusion will be drawn using either assumption.

Second, notice that even though the means appear to be not so close to each other, the statistical conclusion is that they are the same. The substantive conclusion is that Catholics and Protestants would not be expected to pay different prices. Why is it that means do not appear to be similar, yet that is the conclusion? The answer lies in the variance. Respondents tended to provide very wide ranges of acceptable prices. Notice how large the standard deviations are compared to the mean for each group. Because the *t*-statistic is a function of the standard error, which is a function of the standard deviation, a lot of variance means a smaller *t*-value for any given observed difference. When this occurs, the researcher may wish to double-check for outliers. A small number of wild price estimates could be inflating the variance for one or both groups. An additional consideration would be to increase the sample size and test again.

Third, a *t*-test is used even though the sample size is greater than thirty. Strictly speaking, a *Z*-test can test this difference. Researchers often employ a *t*-test even with large samples. As samples get larger, the *t*-test and *Z*-test tend to yield the same results. Although a *t*-test can be used with large samples, a *Z*-test should not be used with small samples. Also, a *Z*-test can be used in instances where the population variance is known ahead of time.

Paired-Samples *t*-Test

What happens when a researcher needs to compare two means that are not from independent samples? Such might be the case when the same respondent provides two comparable scores; for instance, when a respondent rates both how much he or she likes shopping on retail websites and how much he or she likes shopping in real retail stores. Because the liking scores are both provided by the same person, the assumption that they are independent is not realistic. Additionally, if one compares the prices the same retailers charge in their stores with the prices they charge on their websites, the samples cannot be considered independent because each pair of observations is from the same sampling unit.

paired-samples *t*-test

An appropriate test for comparing the scores of two interval variables drawn from related populations.

A **paired-samples *t*-test** is appropriate in this situation. The idea behind the paired-samples *t*-test can be seen in the following computation:

$$t = \frac{\overline{d}}{s_s / \sqrt{n}}$$

where $\overline{d}$ is the average difference between means, *sd* is the standard deviation of the observed differences between means, and *n* is the number of observed differences between means. The test has degrees of freedom equal to one minus the total number of paired differences. Researchers also can compute the paired-samples *t*-test using statistical software. For example, using SPSS, the click-through sequence would be:

Analyze → Compare Means → Paired-Samples t-test

A dialog box then appears in which the "paired variables" should be entered. When a paired-samples *t*-test is appropriate, the two numbers being compared are usually scored as separate variables.

Exhibit 15.4 displays a paired samples *t*-test result. A sample of 208 amusement park consumers was asked to rate how satisfied they felt both before and after visiting a new water rapids ride. The research question is, "How does the new water attraction affect customer satisfaction?" Each respondent provided two satisfaction scores much as in a within-subjects experimental design. The bar chart depicts the means for each variable (satisfied1 is the score before and satisfied2 is the score after riding the new attraction). The *t*-test results suggest that average difference of −0.40 (rounded to two decimals) is associated with a *t*-value of −4.8. As can be seen using either the p-value ($p < 0.0001$) or the confidence interval ($-0.24 < \overline{d} < -0.56$), which does not include 0, the difference is significantly different from 0. Therefore, the results suggest that the new attraction may not have been such a good idea!

Management researchers have used paired-samples *t*-tests to examine the effect of downsizing on employee morale. For instance, job satisfaction for a sample of employees can be measured immediately after the downsizing. Some months later, employee satisfaction can be measured again. The difference between the satisfaction scores can be compared using a paired-samples *t*-test. Results suggest that the employee satisfaction scores increase within a few months of the downsizing as evidenced by statistically significant paired-samples *t*-values.[4]

Satisfaction Before and After Ride

EXHIBIT **15.4**
Illustration of Paired-Samples
t-Test Results

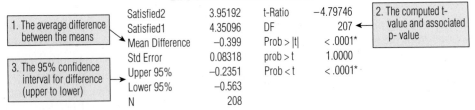

Difference: Satisfied2-Satisfied1

1. The average difference between the means	Satisfied2	3.95192	t-Ratio −4.79746
	Satisfied1	4.35096	DF 207
	Mean Difference	−0.399	Prob > |t| < .0001*
3. The 95% confidence interval for difference (upper to lower)	Std Error	0.08318	prob > t 1.0000
	Upper 95%	−0.2351	Prob < t < .0001*
	Lower 95%	−0.563	
	N	208	

2. The computed t-value and associated p-value

Source: © Cengage Learning 2013.

The *Z*-Test for Comparing Two Proportions

What type of statistical comparison can be made when the observed statistics are proportions? Suppose a researcher wishes to test the hypothesis that wholesalers in the northern and southern United States differ in the proportion of sales they make to discount retailers. Testing whether the population proportion for group 1 (p_1) equals the population proportion for group 2 (p_2) is conceptually the same as the *t*-test of two means. This section briefly describes **Z-test for differences of proportions**, which requires a sample size greater than thirty.

The test is appropriate for a hypothesis of this form:

$$H_0: \pi_1 = \pi_2$$

which may be restated as

$$H_0: \pi_1 - \pi_2 = 0$$

Comparison of the observed sample proportions p_1 and p_2 allows the researcher to ask whether the difference between two *large* random samples occurred due to chance alone. The Z-test statistic can be computed using the following formula:

$$Z = \frac{(p_1 - p_2)(\pi_1 - \pi_2)}{S_{p_1 - p_2}}$$

where

p_1 = sample proportion of successes in group 1

p_2 = sample proportion of successes in group 2

$\pi_1 - \pi_2$ = hypothesized population proportion 1 minus hypothesized population proportion 2

$S_{p_1 - p_2}$ = pooled estimate of the standard error of differences in proportions

To calculate the standard error of the differences in proportions, use the formula

$$S_{p_1 - p_2} = \sqrt{\bar{p}\,\bar{q}\left(\frac{1}{n_1} + \frac{1}{n_2}\right)}$$

Z-test for difference of proportions

A technique used to test the hypothesis that proportions are significantly different for two independent samples or groups.

where

$\bar{p}$ = pooled estimate of proportion of successes in a sample

$q = 1 - \bar{p}$, or pooled estimate of proportion of failures in a sample

n_1 = sample size for group 1

n_2 = sample size for group 2

To calculate the pooled estimator, $\bar{p}$, use the formula

$$\bar{p} = \frac{n_1 p_1 + n_2 p_2}{n_1 + p_2}$$

One-Way Analysis of Variance (ANOVA)

analysis of variance (ANOVA)

Analysis involving the investigation of the effects of one treatment variable on an interval-scaled dependent variable—a hypothesis-testing technique to determine whether statistically significant differences in means occur between two or more groups.

When the means of more than two groups or populations are compared, one-way **analysis of variance (ANOVA)** is the appropriate statistical tool. ANOVA involving only one grouping variable is often referred to as *one-way* ANOVA because only one independent variable is involved. Another way to define ANOVA is as the appropriate statistical technique to examine the effect of a less than interval independent variable on an at least interval dependent variable. Thus, a categorical independent variable and a continuous dependent variable are involved. An independent samples *t*-test can be thought of as a special case of ANOVA in which the independent variable has only two levels. When more levels exist, the *t*-test alone cannot handle the problem.

The statistical null hypothesis for ANOVA is stated as follows:

$$\mu_1 = \mu_2 = \mu_3 = \cdots = \mu_k$$

The symbol k is the number of groups or categories for an independent variable. In other words, all group means are equal. The substantive hypothesis tested in ANOVA is[6]:

At least one group mean is not equal to another group mean.

As the term *analysis of variance* suggests, the problem requires comparing variances to make inferences about the means.

The chapter vignette discussed how a sample of prices taken from the Internet could be explained by the source of the price. Specifically, the independent variable could be thought of as "source," meaning either Internet or multi-channel retailer. The dependent variable is price. Because only two groups exist for the independent variable, either an independent samples *t*-test or one-way ANOVA could be used. The results would be identical.

However, assume that source involved three group levels. Prices would now be compared based on whether the retailer was a bricks-and-clicks retailer (multi-channel, meaning real and virtual stores), a bricks-only store (only physical stores), or a clicks-only retailer (virtual or Internet stores only). One-way ANOVA would be the choice for this analysis.

Simple Illustration of ANOVA

ANOVA's logic is fairly simple. Look at the data table, which describes how much coffee respondents report drinking each day based on which shift they work (GY stands for graveyard shift, which is typically from about 5:00 P.M. until about 1:00 A.M.).

Day	1
Day	3
Day	4
Day	0
Day	2
GY	7
GY	2
GY	1

GY	6
Night	6
Night	8
Night	3
Night	7
Night	6

The following table displays the means for each group and the overall mean:

Shift	Mean	Std. Deviation	N
Day	2.00	1.58	5
GY	4.00	2.94	4
Night	6.00	1.87	5
Total	4.00	2.63	14

Exhibit 15.5 plots each observation with a bar. The long blue vertical line illustrates the total range of observations. The lowest is 0 cups and the highest is 8 cups of coffee for a range of 8. The overall mean is 4 cups. Each group mean is shown with a different-colored line that matches the bars corresponding to the group. The day shift averages 2 cups of coffee a day, the graveyard shift 4 cups, and the night shift 6 cups of coffee per day.

Here is the basic idea of ANOVA. Look at the dark double-headed arrow in Exhibit 15.5. This line represents the range of the differences between group means. In this case, the lowest mean is 2 cups and the highest mean is 6 cups. Thus, the blue vertical line corresponds to the total variation (range) in the data and the thick double-headed black vertical line corresponds to the variance accounted for by the group differences. As the thick black line accounts for more of the total variance, then the ANOVA model suggests that the group means are not all the same, and in particular, not all the same as the overall mean. This also means that the independent variable, in this case work shift, explains the dependent variable. Here, the results suggest that knowing when someone works explains how much coffee they drink. Night-shift workers drink the most coffee.

Partitioning Variance in ANOVA

The responses to any continuous variable contain a certain amount of variance. We have been discussing variable comparisons created by separating observations into groups. ANOVA works by breaking the total variance in a response down into components that are either due to a grouping variable or due to variance within groups.

EXHIBIT 15.5 Illustration of ANOVA Logic

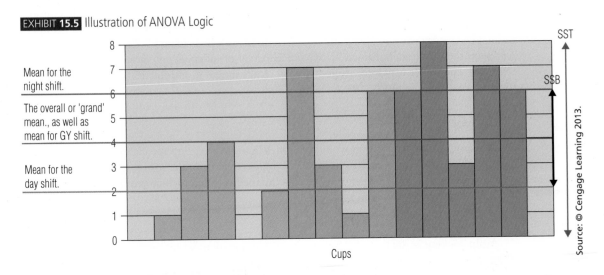

Source: © Cengage Learning 2013.

Total Variability

An implicit question with the use of ANOVA is, "How can the dependent variable best be predicted?" Absent any additional information, the error in predicting an observation is minimized by choosing the central tendency, or mean for an interval variable. For the coffee example, if no information was available about the work shift of each respondent, the best guess for coffee drinking consumption would be 4 cups. The total error (or variability) that would result from using the **grand mean**, meaning the mean over all observations, can be thought of as:

grand mean

The mean of a variable over all observations.

$$SST = Total \ of \ (observed \ value - grand \ mean)^2$$

Although the term *error* is used, this really represents how much total variation exists among the measures.

Using the first observation, the error of observation would be:

$$(1 \ cup - 4 \ cups)^2 = 9$$

The same squared error could be computed for each observation and these squared errors totaled to give SST.

Between-Groups Variance

ANOVA tests whether "grouping" observations explains variance in the dependent variable. In Exhibit 15.5, the three colors reflect three levels of the independent variable, work shift. Given this additional information about which shift a respondent works, the prediction changes. Now, instead of guessing the grand mean, the group mean would be used. So, once we know that someone works the day shift, the prediction would be that he or she consumes 2 cups of coffee per day. Similarly, the graveyard and night-shift predictions would be 4 and 6 cups, respectively. Thus, the **between-groups variance** can be found by taking the total sum of the weighted difference between group means and the overall mean as shown:

between-groups variance

The sum of differences between the group mean and the grand mean summed over all groups for a given set of observations.

$$SSB = Total \ of \ n_{group}(Group \ Mean - Grand \ Mean)^2$$

The weighting factor (n_{group}) is the specific group sample size. Let's consider the first observation once again. Because this observation is in the day shift, we predict 2 cups of coffee will be consumed. Looking at the day shift group observations in Exhibit 15.5, the new error in prediction would be:

$$(2 \ cups - 4 \ cups)^2 = (2)^2 = 4$$

The error in prediction has been reduced from 3 using the grand mean to 2 using the group mean. This squared difference would be weighted by the group sample size of 5, to yield a contribution to SSB of 20.

Next, the same process could be followed for the other groups yielding two more contributions to SSB. Because the graveyard shift group mean is the same as the grand mean, that group's contribution to SSB is 0. Notice that the night-shift group mean is also 2 different than the grand mean, like the day shift, so this group's contribution to SSB is likewise 20. The total SSB then represents the variation explained by the experimental or independent variable. In this case, total SSB is 40. The reader may look at the statistical results shown in Exhibit 15.6 to find this value in the sums of squares column.

Within-Group Error

Finally, error within each group would remain. Whereas the group means explain the variation between the total mean and the group mean, the distance from the group mean and each individual observation remains unexplained. This distance is called **within-group error or variance**. The values for each observation can be found by:

within-group error or variance

The sum of the differences between observed values and the group mean for a given set of observations; also known as total error variance.

$$SSE = Total \ of \ (Observed \ Mean - Group \ Mean)^2$$

Again, looking at the first observation, the SSE component would be:

$$SSE = (1 \ cup - 2 \ cups)^2 = 1 \ cup$$

EXHIBIT 15.6 Interpreting ANOVA

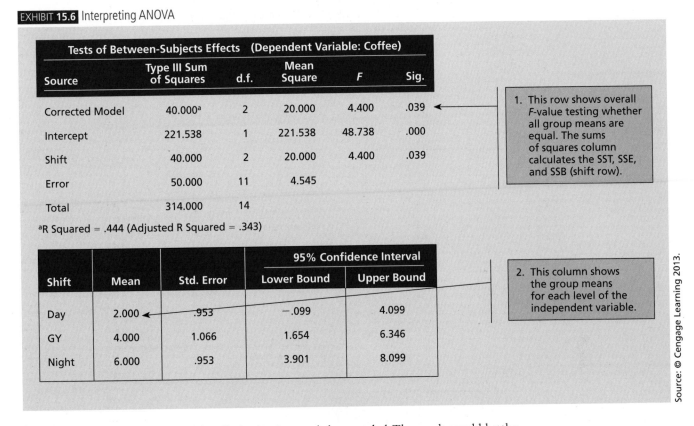

Tests of Between-Subjects Effects (Dependent Variable: Coffee)					
Source	Type III Sum of Squares	d.f.	Mean Square	F	Sig.
Corrected Model	40.000[a]	2	20.000	4.400	.039
Intercept	221.538	1	221.538	48.738	.000
Shift	40.000	2	20.000	4.400	.039
Error	50.000	11	4.545		
Total	314.000	14			

[a]R Squared = .444 (Adjusted R Squared = .343)

1. This row shows overall F-value testing whether all group means are equal. The sums of squares column calculates the SST, SSE, and SSB (shift row).

			95% Confidence Interval	
Shift	Mean	Std. Error	Lower Bound	Upper Bound
Day	2.000	.953	−.099	4.099
GY	4.000	1.066	1.654	6.346
Night	6.000	.953	3.901	8.099

2. This column shows the group means for each level of the independent variable.

This process could be computed for all observations and then totaled. The result would be the total error variance—a name sometimes used to refer to SSE since it is variability not accounted for by the group means. These three components are used in determining how well an ANOVA model explains a dependent variable.

The *F*-Test

The **F-test** is the key statistical test for an ANOVA model. The *F*-test determines whether there is more variability in the scores of one sample than in the scores of another sample. The key question is whether the two sample variances are different from each other or whether they are from the same population. Thus, the test breaks down the variance in a total sample and illustrates why ANOVA is *analysis of variance*.

The *F*-statistic (or *F*-ratio) can be obtained by taking the larger sample variance and dividing by the smaller sample variance. Using tabled values of the *F*-distribution (see **www.cengage.com/marketing/zikmund**) is much like using the tables of the *Z*- and *t*-distributions that we have examined previously. These tables portray the *F*-distribution, which is a probability distribution of the ratios of sample variances. These tables indicate that the distribution of *F* is actually a family of distributions that change quite drastically with changes in sample sizes. Thus, degrees of freedom must be specified. Inspection of an *F*-table allows the researcher to determine the probability of finding an *F* as large as a calculated *F*.

F-test

A procedure used to determine whether there is more variability in the scores of one sample than in the scores of another sample.

Using Variance Components to Compute *F*-Ratios

In ANOVA, the basic consideration for the *F*-test is identifying the relative size of variance components. The three forms of variation described briefly above are:

1. SSE—variation of scores due to random error or within-group variance due to individual differences from the group mean. This is the error of prediction.
2. SSB—systematic variation of scores between groups due to manipulation of an experimental variable or group classifications of a measured independent variable or between-group variance.
3. SST—the total observed variation across all groups and individual observations.

The Research Snapshot provides additional insight into the mechanics of ANOVA. In addition, the Web resources provided with the text provide some illustrations of how to perform an analysis like this using SPSS, SAS, or EXCEL.

SAS:

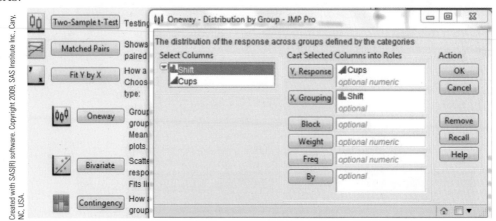

SPSS:

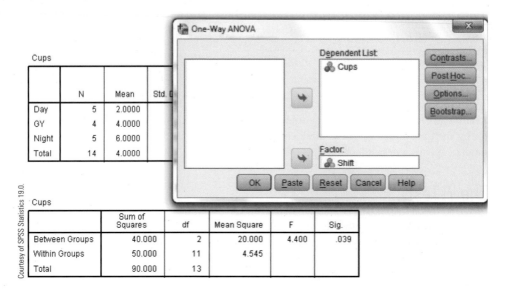

EXCEL:

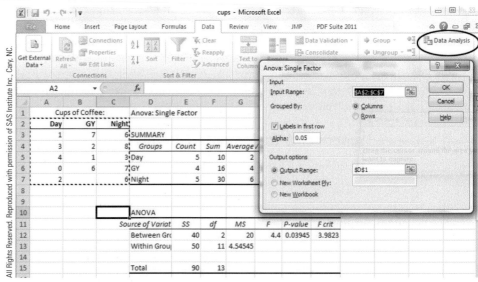

Is the Price Right?

©Diego Cervo/Shutterstock

Marketing researchers often find themselves in situations where they would like to test relationships between a combination of nominal and continuous variables with some continuous dependent variable.

Some marketing researchers recently sought to explore combinations of wine label characteristics and the way they influence how much a consumer is willing to pay. The research questions involved whether or not customers are willing to pay (WTP) a higher price when a) the label describes the wine with a technical versus casual description (EXP1), b) the wine is from France or Oregon (EXP2), and c) when the consumers wine knowledge varies (Q5_2). Consumers tasted a wine (actually in all cases they tasted the same wine) and were shown the bottle. The label contained the two experimental variables: the description of the wine (either technical or casual) and the origin of the wine (France/Oregon). Wine knowledge was assessed based on the results of a 100-point test assessing how knowledgeable each respondent was about wine. The model can be expressed as:

The researchers examine the research question using a GLM approach within SPSS. They agree that a 0.1 Type I error rate is acceptable in this analysis. After opening the data file, the researcher chose analyze, general linear model, then univariate. After entering the correct variables the program produces the results:

$$WTP = Y_{WTP} + \Delta EXP1 + \Delta EXP2 + \Delta EXP1 \star EXP2 + BQ5_2$$

Means by Condition

		Description		
		Casual	Technical	Overall
Place of Origin	Oregon	22.04	24.69	23.37
	France	33.59	26.89	30.24
Overall:		27.82	25.8	26.8

The ANOVA table suggests that the model explains a significant amount of variance in WTP. The wine's origin significantly affects WTP. Subjects are willing to pay an average of $30.50 when the wine is French but only $23.53 when they believe it is from Oregon. In addition, the interaction between origin and the presentation of information is significant as seen by the F of 4.86 for EXP1XEXP2. The means by condition suggests that presenting a technical description results in a higher price when the wine is from Oregon ($25.74 versus $21.32) but a lower price when the wine is from France ($33.94 versus $27.06). Finally, the parameter estimate (not shown here) for wine knowledge is −0.09, suggesting that for every point higher in wine knowledge, the subjects are willing to pay 9 cents less for the wine. As a decision maker for a wine company, how could you use this information?

Source: © Cengage Learning 2013.

Univariate Analysis of Variance

Tests of Between-Subjects Effects

Dependent Variable:WTP

Source	Type III Sum of Squares	df	Mean Square	F	Sig.
Corrected Model	2714.807[a]	4	678.702	4.239	.003
Intercept	27818.172	1	27818.172	173.762	.000
Q5_2	558.065	1	558.065	3.486	.065
Exp1	39.563	1	39.563	.247	.620
Exp2	1233.614	1	1233.614	7.706	.007
Exp1 * Exp2	766.289	1	766.289	4.786	.031
Error	16009.383	100	160.094		
Total	96353.000	105			
Corrected Total	18724.190	104			

a. R Squared =.145 (Adjusted R Squared = .111)

Thus, we can partition total variability into *within-group variance* and *between-group variance*. The F-distribution is a function of the ratio of these two sources of variances:

$$F = f\left(\frac{SSB}{SSE}\right)$$

A larger ratio of variance between groups to variance within groups implies a greater value of F. If the F-value is large, the results are likely to be statistically significant.

A Different but Equivalent Representation

F also can be thought of as a function of the between-group variance and total variance.

$$F = f\left(\frac{SSB}{SST - SSB}\right)$$

In this sense, the ratio of the thick black line to the blue line representing the total range of data presents the basic idea of the F-value.

Practically Speaking

Exhibit 15.6 displays the ANOVA result for the coffee-drinking example. Again, one advantage of living in modern times is that even a simple problem like this one need not be hand computed. Even though this example presents a small problem, one-way ANOVA models with more observations or levels would be interpreted similarly.

The first thing to check is whether or not the overall model F is significant. In this case, the computed $F = 4.40$ with 2 and 11 degrees of freedom. The p-value associated with this value is 0.039. Thus, we have high confidence in concluding that the group means are not all the same. Second, the researcher must remember to examine the actual means for each group to properly interpret the result. Doing so, the conclusion reached is that the night-shift people drink the most coffee, followed by the graveyard-shift workers, and then lastly, the day-shift workers.

Statistical Software

Manual calculations play little role in analyzing marketing research data today. Businesses increasingly rely on analytics that come from market data. Learning calculations can sometimes be useful in understanding how various statistics work, but the researcher usually has access to statistical software that facilitates statistical analysis by quickly and easily providing results for t-tests, cross-tabulations, ANOVA, GLM and more. Some of the most common statistical software packages are SPSS, now owned by IBM, SAS, and a new user-friendly product from SAS called JMP. Excel also includes a data analysis package that provides basic univariate and bivariate statistical results. The Excel Data Analysis component is an "add-in" that can be easily added in the Excel options. The one-way ANOVA is called Simple Anova in the Data Analysis package. Basic JMP components also become available on the Excel toolbar if both packages are installed on a computer. Most universities provide students with access to one or more of these software packages.

General Linear Model

general linear model (GLM)

A way of explaining and predicting dependent variable based on fluctuations (variation) from its mean. The fluctuations are due to changes in independent variables.

Multivariate dependence techniques are variants of the **general linear model (GLM)**. Simply, the GLM is a way of modeling a process based on how different variables cause fluctuations from the average dependent variable. Fluctuations can come in the form of group means that differ from the overall mean as in ANOVA or in the form of a significant slope coefficient as in regression.

GLM Equation

The basic idea can be thought of as follows:

$$\hat{Y}_i = \overline{Y} + \Delta X + \Delta F + \Delta XF$$

Here, $\overline{Y}\ \overline{Y}$ represents a constant, which can be thought of as the overall mean of the dependent variable, ΔX and ΔF represent changes due to main effect independent variables (such as experimental variables) and blocking independent variables (such as covariates or grouping variables), respectively, and ΔXF represents the change due to the combination (interaction effect) of those variables. Realize that Y_i in this case could represent multiple dependent variables, just as X and F could represent multiple independent variables. This form is an ANOVA representation. An ANCOVA representation would add a continuous covariate (X_c):

$$\hat{Y}_i = \overline{Y} + \Delta X + \Delta F + \Delta XF + BXc$$

B is a regression coefficient, as described below.

Regression analysis and n-way ANOVA represent common forms that the GLM can take. SAS and SPSS both contained programs specifically referred to by GLM. They are particularly useful in analyzing data from experiments but GLM can also be used to produce regression results.

Regression Analysis

Simple regression investigates a *straight-line relationship* of the type:

$$Y = \alpha + \beta X,$$

where Y is a continuous dependent variable and X is an independent variable that is usually continuous, although a dichotomous nominal or ordinal variables can be included in the form of a dummy variable. Alpha (α) and beta (β) are two parameters that must be estimated so that the equation best represents a given set of data. These two parameters determine the height of the regression line and the angle of the line relative to horizontal. When these parameters change, the line changes. Together, they represent the changes from the overall mean of the dependent variable for a regression form of the GLM. Regression techniques have the job of estimating values for these parameters that make the line *fit* the observations the best.

The result is simply a linear equation, or the equation for a line, just as in basic algebra! Parameter α represents the Y intercept (where the line crosses the y-axis) and β is the slope coefficient. The slope is the change in Y associated with a change of one unit in X. Slope may also be thought of as rise over run. That is, how much Y rises (or falls if negative) for every one unit change in the X-axis. A mathematical estimation of the line completes the regression progress by providing estimates for the intercept (b_0) and slope coefficient (b_1).

$$Y_i = b_0 + b_1 X_1 + e_i$$

Interpreting Multiple Regression Analysis

Multiple regression analysis is an extension of simple regression analysis, allowing a metric dependent variable to be predicted by multiple independent variables. Thus, one dependent variable is explained by more than one independent variable. When trying to explain sales, plausible independent variables include prices, economic factors, advertising intensity, and consumers' incomes in the area. A simple regression equation can be expanded to represent multiple regression analysis:

$$Y_i = b_0 + b_1 X_1 + b_2 X_2 + b_3 X_3 + \cdots + b_n X_n + e_i$$

multiple regression analysis

An analysis of association in which the effects of two or more independent variables on a single, interval-scaled dependent variable are investigated simultaneously.

Parameter Estimate Choices

The estimates for α and β are the key to regression analysis. In most business research, the estimate of β is most important. The explanatory power of regression rests with β because this is where the direction and strength of the relationship between the independent and dependent variable is explained. A Y-intercept term is sometimes referred to as a constant because α represents a fixed point. An estimated slope coefficient is sometimes referred to as a regression weight, regression coefficient, parameter estimate, or sometimes even as a *path* estimate. The term *path estimate* is a descriptive term adapted because of the way hypothesized causal relationships are often represented in diagrams:

$$\boxed{X} \xrightarrow{\beta_1} \boxed{Y}$$

For all practical purposes, these terms are used interchangeably. Parameter estimates can be presented in either raw or standardized form. One potential problem with raw parameter estimates is due to the fact that, like covariance values, they reflect the measurement scale range. So, if a simple regression involves distance measured with miles, very small parameter estimates may indicate a strong relationship. In contrast, if the very same distance is measured with centimeters, a very large parameter estimate would be needed to indicate a strong relationship. Generally, the raw slope coefficient is abbreviated with a small letter **b**.

Researchers often explain regression results by referring to a **standardized regression coefficient (β)**. A standardized regression coefficient, like a correlation coefficient, provides a common metric allowing regression results to be compared to one another no matter what the original scale range may have been. Due to the mathematics involved in standardization, the standardized Y-intercept term is always 0.

Researchers use shorthand to label regression coefficients as either "raw" or "standardized." The most common shorthand is as follows:

- **B**$_0$ or b_0—raw (unstandardized) Y-intercept term; an estimate of what was referred to as α above.
- **B**$_1$ or $\boldsymbol{\beta}_1$—raw regression coefficient or estimate.
- $\boldsymbol{\beta}_1$—standardized regression coefficients.

The bottom line is that when the actual units of measurement are the focus of analysis, such as might be the case in trying to forecast sales during some period, raw (unstandardized) coefficients are most appropriate. When the goal is explanation of some outcome by examining a series of relationships, standardized regression coefficients are more appropriate because they allow for the size of the relationship for each independent variable can be compared directly. A β of 0.6 is a stronger relationship than a β of 0.2. With unstandardized coefficients, this comparison cannot be directly made.

Steps in Interpreting a Multiple Regression Model

Multiple regression models often are used to test a proposed theoretical model. For instance, a researcher may be asked to develop and test a model explaining business unit performance. Why do some business units outperform others? Multiple regression models can be interpreted using these steps:

1. Examine the model F-test. If the test result is not significant, the model should be dismissed and there is no need to proceed to further steps.
2. Examine the individual statistical tests for each parameter estimate. Independent variables with significant results can be considered a significant explanatory variable.
3. Examine the model R^2. No cutoff values exist that can distinguish an acceptable amount of explained variation across all regression models. However, the absolute value of R^2 is more important when the researcher is more interested in prediction than explanation. In other words, the regression is run for pure forecasting purposes. When the model is more oriented toward explaining which variables are most important in explaining the dependent variable, cutoff values for the model R^2 are inappropriate.
4. A next step would be to diagnose multicollinearity. Simply put, this is the extent to which the independent variables are redundant. A detailed discussion of this topic is beyond the scope of this particular text. However, a simple check for problems can be obtained by taking a look at the Variance Inflation Factors (VIF). Most statistical packages allow these to be computed. VIFs of between 1 and 2 are generally not indicative of problems with multicollinearity. As they become larger, the results become more susceptible to interpretation problems because of overlap in the independent variables.

Exhibit 15.7 illustrates this step-by-step process, using regression results from a SAS output. The regression model explains marketing employees' bonuses for a *Fortune* 500 company. The independent variables are Tools (a dummy variable representing whether the employee uses a new social network mining tool coded 1 if the employee installed the software and 0 if not), Hours (number of hours working in field per week), and Exp (experience in the industry in years). In

standardized regression coefficient (β)

The estimated coefficient indicating the strength of relationship between an independent variable and dependent variable expressed on a standardized scale where higher absolute values indicate stronger relationships (range is from –1 to 1).

Source: © Cengage Learning 2013.

EXHIBIT 15.7
Interpreting Multiple
Regression Results

ANOVA[b]

Model		Sum of Squares	df	Mean Square	F	Sig.
1	Regression	638686.188	3	212895.396	50.446	.000[a]
	Residual	700568.540	166	4220.292		
	Total	1339254.728	169			

a. Predictors: (Constant), Exp, Hours, Tools
b. Dependent Variable: Bonus

3. The model explains 47.7% of the total variation in the dependent variable (Bonus).

Model	R	R Square	Adjusted R Square	Std. Error of the Estimate
1	.691[a]	.477	.467	64.96378

1. The regression model explains a significant portion of the variance in Bonus

Coefficients[a]

Model		Unstandardized Coefficients		Standardized Coefficients	t	sig.	Collinearity Statistics	
		B	Std. Error	Beta			Tolerance	VIF
1	(Constant)	166.552	25.965		6.414	.000		
	Tools	−3.425	10.517	−.018	−.326	.745	.991	1.009
	Hours	4.519	.367	.691	12.299	.000	.999	1.001
	Exp	−.102	.318	−.018	−.320	.750	.992	1.008

a. Dependent Variable: Bonus

2. The individual parameter estimates suggest that HOURS significantly and positively influences Bonus.

4. The VIFS are all close to 1.0 suggesting no problems with multicollinearity.

this case, the researcher is using a maximum acceptable Type I error rate of 0.05. The conclusion reached from this analysis is that hours spent in the field pays off in increased bonus amounts ($\beta = 0.69, p < 0.05$).

TIPS OF THE TRADE

- Cross-tabulations are widely applied in market research reports and presentations.
  - Take advantage of graphical tools like bar charts to present cross-tabulation results in presentations and reports.
  - Cross-tabulations are appropriate for research questions involving predictions of categorical dependent variables using categorical independent variables. These are usually nominal or ordinal.
    - When more than four categories exist, cross-tabulation tables can become difficult to present clearly.
    - Independent variables are placed in rows and dependent variables are placed in columns.
- A *t*-test can be used to compare means.
  - An independent samples *t*-test predicts a continuous (interval or ratio) dependent variable with a categorical (nominal or ordinal) independent (grouping) variable.

- A paired samples *t*-test compares means from two different responses from the same sampling unit. Therefore, the sampling is dependent.
- A one-way ANOVA extends the concept of an independent samples *t*-test to more than two groups.
  - Don't be fooled by the fact that it involves an *F*-test instead of a *t*-test. They are mathematically related and, in fact, an *F*-value is the square of a *t*-value that would result from the same analysis.
  - Stat packages usually have an ANOVA package or a one-way ANOVA package. However, general linear model (GLM) procedures can also conduct these tests and offer more flexibility when multiple independent variables are involved.
- Simple hand calculations can be useful in learning what statistical procedures actually do. However, in conducting actual tests, take advantage of computer software whenever permissible.

Source: © Cengage Learning 2013.

:: SUMMARY

1. Choose the appropriate statistic. A skilled researcher can quickly determine the appropriate statistic for a given research question. In this chapter, we learned that if the researcher can distinguish independent from dependent variables, know how many of each is involved in the analysis, and know the level of scale measurement for each, choosing the right statistic is easy.

2. Construct a cross-tabulation table and the corresponding χ^2 statistic. Bivariate statistical techniques analyze scores on two variables at a time. A cross-tabulation is a useful way of depicting and analyzing the way two categorical variables are related to one another. For instance, a nominal independent variable may be used to predict a nominal dependent variable. Cross-tabulations are very useful and lend themselves well to depicting results in charts. The χ^2 statistic is the test statistic appropriate for testing relationships among variables used in a cross-tabulation table. Higher χ^2 values are generally associated with lower p-values and therefore greater probability of a relationship between the row and column variable. The process of testing a hypothesis using a χ^2 statistic is similar in concept to practically all the hypotheses testing procedures that follow.

3. Use a t-test to compare a difference between two means. When a researcher needs to compare means for a variable grouped into two categories based on a less than interval variable, a t-test is appropriate. An independent samples t-test examines whether a dependent variable like price differs based on a grouping variable like biological sex. Statistically, the test examines whether the difference between the mean for men and women is different from 0. Larger t-values are associated with smaller p-values and statistical significance. A paired-samples t-test examines whether or not the means from two variables that are not independent are different. A common situation calling for this test is when the two observations are from the same respondent or sampling unit. A simple before-and-after test calls for a paired-sample t-test so long as the dependent variable is continuous.

4. Conduct a one-way analysis of variance test (ANOVA). ANOVA is the appropriate statistical technique to examine the effect of a less than interval independent variable on an at least interval dependent variable. Conceptually, ANOVA partitions the total variability into three types: total variation, between-group variation, and within-group variation. As the explained variance represented by SSB becomes larger relative to SSE or SST, the ANOVA model is more likely significant, indicating that at least one group mean is different from another group mean.

5. Appreciate the practicality of modern statistical software packages. Hand calculations using a simple calculator can sometimes be a good way for getting the feel of exactly what a statistic is doing; however, even small applications are usually better performed with the help of statistical software whether it is Excel, SPSS, SAS, JMP, or another package. This saves time and helps reduce mathematical errors.

6. Use the GLM to represent a generalized statistical model. The general linear model is a widely used way of representing statistical effects as systematic deviations from the population mean. ANOVA and linear regression are among the most common forms of the GLM. The results should be analyzed based on how well they account for variation in the dependent variable and based on what specific independent variables relate significantly to the dependent variable.

:: KEY TERMS AND CONCEPTS

analysis of variance (ANOVA), *396*
between-groups variance, *398*
F-test, *399*
general linear model (GLM), *402*
grand mean, *398*

independent samples t-test, *390*
multiple regression analysis, *403*
paired-samples t-test, *304*
pooled estimate of the standard error, *391*
standardized regression coefficient (β), *404*

test of differences, *384*
within-group error or variance, *398*
Z-test for differences of proportions, *395*

:: QUESTIONS FOR REVIEW AND CRITICAL THINKING

1. What statistical test of differences is appropriate in the following situations?
   a. Average campaign contributions (in $) of Democrats, Republicans, and Independents for comparison.
   b. Advertising managers and brand managers have responded "yes," "no," or "not sure" to an attitude question. The advertising and brand managers' responses will be compared.
   c. One-half of a sample received an incentive in a mail survey while the other half did not. A comparison of response rates is desired.
   d. A researcher believes that married men will push the grocery cart when grocery shopping with their wives. How would the hypothesis be tested?
   e. A manager wishes to compare the job performance of a salesperson before ethics training with the performance of that same salesperson after ethics training.

2. Perform a χ^2 test on the following data (hint: set up a spreadsheet to perform the calculations):
   a. Increased regulation is the best way to ensure safe products.

	Agree	Disagree	No Opinion
Managers	58	66	8
Line Employees	34	24	10
Totals	92	90	18

   b. Ownership of residence.

	Yes	No
Male	25	20
Female	16	14

3. Interpret the following computer cross-tab output including a χ^2 test. Variable EDUCATION is a response to "What is your highest level of educational achievement?" HS means a high school diploma, SC means some college, BS means a bachelor's degree, and MBA means a master of business administration. Variable WIN is how well the respondent did on a set of casino games of chance. A 1 means they would have lost more than $100, a 2 means they approximately broke even, and a 3 means they won more than $100. What is the result of exploring a research question that education influences performance on casino gambling? Comment on your conclusion and any issues in interpreting the result.

The SAS System
The FREQ Procedure
Table of Education by Win

EDUCATION Frequency Percent Row Pct Col Pct	Win			Total
	1	2	3	
MBA	3	10	4	17
	1.12	3.72	1.49	6.32
	17.65	58.82	23.53	
	3.19	10.31	5.13	
BS	11	19	12	42
	4.09	7.06	4.46	15.61
	26.19	45.24	28.57	
	11.70	19.59	15.38	
SC	33	30	27	90
	12.27	11.15	10.04	33.45
	35.67	33.33	30.00	
	35.11	30.93	34.62	
HS	47	38	35	120
	17.47	14.13	13.01	44.61
	29.17	31.67	29.17	
	50.00	39.18	44.57	
Total	94	97	78	269
	34.94	36.06	29.00	100.00

Statistics for Table of education by win

Statistic	DF	Value	Prob
Chi-Square	6	7.5275	0.2748
Sample Size = 269			

4. A store manager's computer-generated list of all retail sales employees indicates that 70 percent are full-time employees, 20 percent are part-time employees, and 10 percent are furloughed or laid-off employees. A sample of 50 employees from the list indicates that there are 40 full-time employees, 6 part-time employees, and 4 furloughed/laid-off employees. Conduct a statistical test to determine whether the sample is representative of the population.

5. Test the following hypothesis using the data summarized in the table below. Interpret your result:

   H1: Internet retailers offer lower prices for DVD players than do traditional in-store retailers.

Retail Type	DVD Player Average Price	Standard Deviation	n
E-tailers	$371.95	$50.00	25
Multichannel retailers	$360.30	$45.00	25

6. Selected territories in a company's eastern and western regions were rated for sales potential based on the company's evaluation system. A sales manager wishes to conduct a *t*-test of means to determine whether there is a difference between the two regions. Conduct this test, preferably using a statistical software package, and draw the appropriate conclusion:

Region	Territory	Rating	Region	Territory	Rating
West	1	74	East	8	81
West	2	88	East	9	63
West	3	78	East	10	56
West	4	85	East	11	68
West	5	100	East	12	80
West	6	114	East	13	79
West	7	98	East	14	69

How would this result change if the company only had seven territories in the West and seven in the East?

7. How does an independent samples *t*-test differ from the following?

   a. one-way ANOVA
   b. paired-samples *t*-test
   c. a χ^2 test

8. Are *t*-tests or *Z*-tests used more often in marketing research? Why?

9. A sales force received some management-by-objectives training. Are the before/after mean scores for salespeople's job performance statistically significant at the 0.05 level? The results from a sample of employees are as follows (use your computer and statistical software to solve this problem):

Skill	Before	After	Skill	Before	After
Carlos	4.84	5.43	Tommy	4.00	5.00
Sammy	5.24	5.51	Laurie	4.67	4.50
Melanie	5.37	5.42	Ronald	4.95	4.40
Philippe	3.69	4.50	Amanda	4.00	5.95
Cargill	5.95	5.90	Brittany	3.75	3.50
Dwight	4.75	5.25	Mathew	3.85	4.00
Amy	3.90	4.50	Alice	5.00	4.10
Kallua	3.20	3.75	Jake	4.00	5.15

10. Using the "CAR" data that accompanies the text (see website), consider the following problem. The data describe attitudes of car owners from Germany and the United States toward their automobiles. The variable "ATT" is how much respondents like their current car (attitude), "ATTNEW" is their attitude toward a new car called the Cycle. The "COUNTRY" variable is self-explanatory. The "SPEND" variable is how much the respondents spend on average on products to keep their cars clean (in euros). Using SPSS or other statistical software, test the following hypotheses:

    H1: The owners' attitudes toward the Cycle are more favorable than attitudes toward their current cars.

    H2: Germans like their cars more than Americans.

11. Interpret the following output examining group differences for purchase intentions. The three groups refer to consumers from three states: Florida, Minnesota, and Hawaii.

Tests of Between-Subjects Effects
Dependent Variable: int2

Source	Type III Sum of Squares	d.f.	Mean Square	F	Sig.
Corrected Model	681.746[a]	2	3340.873	3.227	0.043
Intercept	308897.012	1	308897.012	298.323	0.000
State	6681.746	2	3340.873	3.227	0.043
Error	148068.543	143	1035.444		
Total	459697.250	146			
Corrected Total	154750.289	145			

[a]R Squared = 0.043 (Adjusted R Squared = 0.030)

Source: © Cengage Learning 2013.

Law
Dependent Variable: int2

State	Mean	Std. Error	95% Confidence Interval	
			Lower Bound	Upper Bound
F	37.018	4.339	28.441	45.595
M	50.357	4.965	40.542	60.172
H	51.459	4.597	42.373	60.546

Source: © Cengage Learning 2013.

12. The following table gives a football team's season-ticket sales, percentage of games won, and number of active alumni for the years from 1998 to 2007.

Year	Season-Ticket Sales	Percentage of Games Won	Number of Active Alumni
1998	4,995	40	NA
1999	8,599	54	3,450
2000	8,479	55	3,801
2001	8,419	58	4,000
2002	10,253	63	4,098
2003	12,457	75	6,315
2004	13,285	36	6,860
2005	14,177	27	8,423
2006	15,730	63	9,000
2007	15,805	70	9,500
2008	15,575	72	9,530
2009	15,900	75	9,550
2010	14,010	80	9,560
2011	12,500	82	9,575

Source: © Cengage Learning 2013.

a. Estimate a regression model for sales = Percentage of games won.
b. Estimate a regression model for sales = Number of active alumni.
c. Estimate a multiple regression model predicting sales using variables of your choice.
d. If *sales* is the dependent variable, which of the two independent variables do you think explains sales better? Explain.

13. Interpret the following GLM results. Following from an example in the chapter, *performance* is the performance rating for a business unit manager. *Sales* is a measure of the average sales for that unit. *Experience* is the number of years the manager has been in the industry. The variable *dummy* has been added. This variable is a 0 if the manager has no advanced college degree and a 1 if the manager has an MBA. Do you have any recommendations?

14. Interpret the following regression results. All of the variables are the same as in number 2. These results are produced with a regression program instead of the GLM-univariate ANOVA program.
a. What do you notice when the results are compared to those in number 2? Comment.
b. List the independent variables in order from greatest to least in terms of how strong the relationship is with performance.
c. When might one prefer to use an ANOVA program instead of a multiple regression program?

```
                     The SAS System
                    The GLM Procedure
              Dependent Variable: Performance

                              Sum of
Source              DF       Squares     Mean Square   F Value    Pr > F

Model                3   173.6381430    57.8793810     13.87    <0.0001
Error               36   150.2341040     4.1731696
Corrected Total     39   323.8722470


          R-Square    Coeff Var     Root MSE    Performance Mean
          0.536132    2.514731      2.042834         81.23468


Source              DF    Type III SS    Mean Square   F Value    Pr > F
Dummy                1   136.9511200    136.9511200     32.82    <0.0001
Sales                1    22.4950649     22.4950649      5.39    0.0260
Experience           1     2.2356995      2.2356995      0.54    0.4689

Level of      -------Performance-------  ----------Sales----------  ----Experience--------
Dummy   N      Mean        Std Dev       Mean         Std Dev       Mean          Std Dev
0      22   79.4848842   1.78987031   15979.7723   2008.32604   23.8984087     8.27327485
1      18   83.3733171   2.50773844   16432.0080   2015.18863   20.6788050     8.96324112
```

```
                           The SAS System
                           The REG Procedure
                            Model: MODEL1
                     Dependent Variable: performance

                    Number of Observations Read 40
                    Number of Observations Used 40
```

Analysis of Variance

Source	DF	Sum of Squares	Mean Square	F Value	Pr > F
Model	3	173.63814	57.87938	13.87	<0.0001
Error	36	150.23410	4.17317		
Corrected Total	39	323.87225			

Root MSE	2.04283	R-Square	0.5361	
Dependent Mean	81.23468	Adj R-Sq	0.4975	
Coeff Var	2.51473			

Parameter Estimates

Variable	Label	DF	Parameter Estimate	Standard Error	t Value	Pr > |t|	Standardized Estimate
Intercept	Intercept	1	72.68459	2.88092	25.23	<0.0001	0
Dummy	Dummy	1	3.80621	0.66442	5.73	<0.0001	0.66546
Sales	Sales	1	0.00038324	0.00016507	2.32	0.0260	0.26578
Experience	Experience	1	0.02829	0.03866	0.73	0.4689	0.08475

:: RESEARCH ACTIVITIES

1. **ETHICS/'NET** How ethical is it to do business in different countries around the world? An international organization, Transparency International, keeps track of the perception of ethical practices in different countries. Visit the website and search for the latest corruption indices (**http://www.transparency.org/policy_and_research/surveys_indices/cpi/**). Using the data found here for 2010, test the following research questions.

   a. Are nations from Europe and North America perceived as more ethical than nations from Asia, Africa, and South America? Include Australia and New Zealand with Europe.

   b. Are there differences among the corruption indices between 2005 and 2010?

2. **'NET** The Federal Reserve Bank of St. Louis maintains a database called FRED (Federal Reserve Economic Data). Navigate to the FRED database at **http://research.stlouisfed.org/fred2**. You'll notice a link to the civilian unemployment rate. Randomly select two, 10-year periods between 1970 and today and then compare average figures. What statistical tests are appropriate? Was there a difference in unemployment across the periods?

Case 15.1

Old School versus New School Sports Fans

Download the data sets for this case from **www.cengage.com/marketing/zikmund** or request them from your instructor.

Three academic researchers investigated the idea that, in American sports, there are two segments with opposing views about the goal of competition (i.e., winning versus self-actualization) and the acceptable/desirable way of achieving this goal.[7] Persons who believe in "winning at any cost" are proponents of sports success as a product and can be labeled new school (NS) individuals. The new school is founded on notions of the player before the team, loyalty to the highest bidder, and high-tech production and consumption of professional sports. On the other hand, persons who value the process of sports and believe that "how you play the game matters" can be labeled old school (OS) individuals. The old school emerges from old-fashioned American notions of the team before the player, sportsmanship, and loyalty above all else, and competition simply for "love of the game."

New School/Old School was measured by asking agreement with ten attitude statements. The scores on these statements were combined. Higher scores represent an orientation toward old school values. For purposes of this case study, individuals who did not answer every question were eliminated from the analysis. Based on their summated scores, respondents were grouped into low-score, middle-score, and high-score groups. Case Exhibit 15.1–1 shows the SPSS computer output of a cross-tabulation to relate the gender of the respondent (GENDER) with the New School/Old School (OLDSKOOL) grouping.

Questions

Is this form of analysis appropriate?
Interpret the computer output and critique the analysis.
Explore the GLM (general linear model) procedure in SAS or SPSS by testing a model using show_off as the dependent variable and gender as the independent variable (a fixed effect in the SPSS GLM window and a class variable in SAS Proc GLM).

CASE EXHIBIT 15.1–1 SPSS Output

OLDSKOOL * GENDER Crosstabulation

			GENDER		Total
			women	men	
OLDSKOOL	high	Count	9	17	26
		% within OLDSKOOL	34.6%	65.4%	100.0%
		% within GENDER	10.6%	9.2%	9.6%
		% of Total	3.3%	6.3%	9.6%
	low	Count	45	70	115
		% within OLDSKOOL	39.1%	60.9%	100.0%
		% within GENDER	52.9%	37.8%	42.6%
		% of Total	16.7%	25.9%	42.6%
	middle	Count	31	98	129
		% within OLDSKOOL	24.0%	76.0%	100.0%
		% within GENDER	36.5%	53.0%	47.8%
		% of Total	11.5%	36.3%	47.8%
Total		Count	85	185	270
		% within OLDSKOOL	31.5%	68.5%	100.0%
		% within GENDER	100.0%	100.0%	100.0%
		% of Total	31.5%	68.5%	100.0%

Chi-Square Tests

	Value	df	Asymp. Sig. (2-sided)
Pearson Chi-Square	6.557[a]	2	.038
Likelihood Ratio	6.608	2	.037
N of Valid Cases	270		

[a]0 cells (.0%) have expected count less than 5. The minimum expected count is 8.19.

Source: © Cengage Learning 2013.

Case 15.2

International Operations at CarCare Inc.

CarCare is considering expanding its operations beyond the United States. The company wants to know whether it should target countries with consumers who tend to have a positive attitude toward their current cars. It has gathered data on U.S. and German car owners. The data are included in the "car" data set that can be viewed on the website at **www.cengage.com/marketing/zikmund** (car.sav or car.xls) or available from your instructor. Using the data, conduct a correlation and simple

regression analysis using spending as the dependent variable and attitude toward the current car as the independent variable.

1.   Test the hypothesis: Attitude toward one's car is related positively to spending for car-care products.
2.   Would you recommend they do more research to identify nations with relatively favorable attitudes toward the cars they own?

Source: © Cengage Learning 2013.

⣿⣿ Communicating Research Results

LEARNING OUTCOMES

After studying this chapter, you should be able to

1. Define the parts of a research report following a standard format
2. Explain how to use tables for presenting numerical information
3. Summarize how to select and use the types of research charts
4. Know how to give an effective oral presentation
5. Discuss the importance of Internet reporting and research follow-up

Chapter Vignette:

Effective Research Is a Stone's Throw Away

© Susan Van Etten

The Rosetta Stone represents one of the greatest findings in the history of communication. The stone dates back to several centuries before Christ but was discovered near the ancient city of Rosetta, Egypt, at the end of the eighteenth century. What made this discovery so special? The etchings on the stone represented a decree to the peoples of that time that was not only written in hieroglyphics but also in ancient Greek. French and British researchers worked for decades and eventually produced a translation between the ancient Greek and the hieroglyphic script. They learned that hieroglyphics were not just pictures but that over time, hieroglyphics had developed into a language with symbols that took on phonetic characteristics including sound. This breakthrough meant that scores of ancient etchings could now communicate effectively because of the translation code made possible by the Rosetta Stone.[1]

Fortunately, marketing researchers don't have to write research reports on stones, but effective communication can still be pretty hard! The research report is the tool that translates what most people could not possibly understand into a useful report that communicates important information for business managers, marketing executives, policy makers, or other marketing researchers. Marketing practitioners lack working knowledge of multivariate data analysis, ethnography, phenomenology, or most other technical aspects of marketing research. So, even if researchers conduct the marketing research properly, the research can still be a complete failure if the researcher is unable to produce a user-friendly, concise, and actionable research report. In fact, science itself is of little use unless one can effectively communicate its meaning.[2]

In fact, employers often view excellent writing skills as a necessary requisite when evaluating marketing research candidates. Unfortunately, these same employers are often disappointed with technical employees' communication skills. These employees are expected not only to write formal research reports, but also to make effective oral presentations and increasingly, to deliver effective and accurate communication via Internet media including online meetings, blogs, and even tweets. Imagine the chore of translating results of a months-long research project into a 140-character tweet![3] Sounds like a job for another Rosetta Stone!

Introduction

Researchers can easily be tempted into rushing through the research report. By the time the report is written, the researchers may well feel exhausted or burned out and ready to move on to something new. All the "real" work has been done; it just has to be put on paper. This feeling can be disastrous, however. If people who need to use the research results have to wade through a disorganized presentation, are confused by technical jargon, or find sloppiness of language or thought, they will probably discount the report and make decisions without it, just as if the project had never been done. So, the research report is a crucial means for communicating the whole project. This chapter explains the communication of research results using written reports, presentations, and follow-up conversations.[4] The Research Snapshot on page 416 shows how difficult accurate communication can be.

What Is a Marketing Research Report?

A **research report** is a formal presentation and/or written statement that communicates research results and draws appropriate conclusions following from the research. A market research report is directed to the client or management team who initiated the research. If the proposal's deliverables include specific managerial recommendations, they are included and highlighted in the report. In fact, they should be a logical conclusion of the report contents. A basic marketing researcher writes a very similar report but it often takes the form of a white paper or scholarly research paper targeted for publication in a research journal such as the *Journal of Marketing* or the *Journal of the Academy of Marketing Science*. More often than not, a written research report will also be supported by a formal presentation delivered in person or via the Internet.

More and more research companies are finding a ready research market for marketing research reports sold online for a fee. Several websites serve as brokers or warehouses for reports on virtually any business topic. For example, Research and Markets (**http://www.researchandmarkets.com**) offers hundreds of thousands of research reports through its website. These reports are compiled from some of the top consulting firms and leading publishers around the world. Potential customers can preview these reports by examining a summary of each. At an average price of about $4,000 per piece, they had best be very well done and communicate clearly or the customer is not likely to use this service again.

research report

An oral presentation or written statement of research results, strategic recommendations, and/or other conclusions to a specific audience.

"It is a luxury to be understood."

—RALPH WALDO EMERSON

Report Format

Every significant research project produces at least one report. Report contents are specific to each report. However, researchers tend to follow some conventions with respect to the **report format**. This research report format results from a consensus about the ordered parts and contents that comprise a professional research report or paper. The goal of the format is making sure

report format

A standard outline that marketing research reports use as a guide to make sure that the key elements are presented in a logical and usable order.

Now, the end is near. The Survey This! feature has covered quite a bit of ground about marketing research students' preferences and behaviors. The topics include how students interact with technology, preferences for communicating, studying, and how they spend their time, among other things. Additionally, you may be interested in comparing how different groups of respondents are similar or alike. Perhaps you are curious about some of these issues. Develop at least three research questions. Examine these questions using the data from the survey. Prepare a written report and slide show presentation that could be used to brief an interested audience of businesspeople who wish to better serve this particular market. Try to pick issues that you are truly curious about and you'll find yourself anxious to get to the answer!

When I think of my school, I feel: (semantic differential scale with rows)
- Inferior / Superior
- Critical / Sympathetic
- Remote / Close
- Happy / Sad
- Involved / Ambivalent
- Proud / Embarrassed
- Dissatisfied / Satisfied
- Malcontent / Content
- In Control / Out of Control

Courtesy of Qualtrics.com

Source: © Cengage Learning 2013.

the document is user-friendly. Large research companies use standard templates that allow the researcher to fill in the custom information derived from the specific research project. These large companies also may employ a technical writing staff to assist in the production of reports. Not every report fits the exact template and occasionally the some reports may omit a section or include other sections that are not part of the basic template. But, most research projects will follow an outline that includes the major elements shown below:

1. Title page
2. Letter of transmittal
3. Letter of authorization
4. Table of contents (and lists of figures and tables)
5. Executive summary
   a. Objectives
   b. Results
   c. Conclusions
   d. Recommendations
6. Body
   a. Introduction
      1. Background
      2. Objectives
   b. Methodology
   c. Results
   d. Limitations
   e. Conclusions and recommendations
7. Appendix
   a. Data collection forms
   b. Detailed calculations
   c. General tables
   d. Bibliography
   e. Other support material

This format is illustrated graphically in Exhibit 16.1.

EXHIBIT 16.1 Report Format

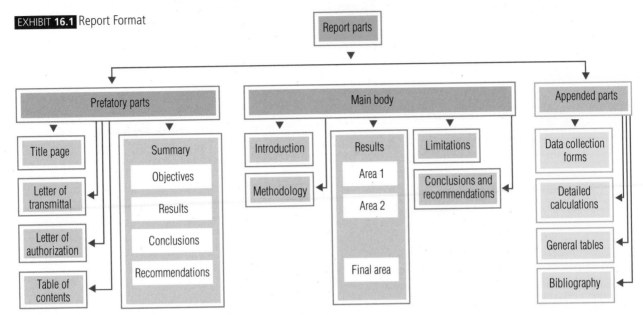

Source: © Cengage Learning 2013.

Tailoring the Format to the Project

The format of a research report may need to be adjusted for two reasons: (1) to obtain the proper level of formality and (2) to decrease the complexity of the report. The format given here is for the most formal type of report, such as one for a large project done within an organization or one done by a research agency for a client company. This type of report is usually bound in a permanent cover and may be hundreds of pages long.

In less formal reports, each part is shorter, and some parts are omitted. The situation may be compared to the way people's clothing varies according to the formality of the occasion. The most formal report is dressed, so to speak, in a tuxedo or long evening gown. It includes the full assortment of prefatory parts—title fly page, title page, letters of transmittal and authorization, and table of contents. Like changing into an everyday business suit, dropping down to the next level of formality involves eliminating parts of the prefatory material that are not needed in this situation and reducing the complexity of the report body. In general, as the report moves down through the sport coat and slacks and then blue jeans stages, more prefatory parts are dropped, and the complexity and length of the report body are reduced.

How does the researcher decide on the appropriate level of formality? The general rule is to include all the parts needed for effective communication in the particular circumstances—and no more. This depends on how far up in management the report is expected to go and how routine the matter is. A researcher's immediate supervisor does not need a 100-page, "black-tie" report on a routine project. However, the board of directors does not want a one-page "blue jeans" report on a big project that backs a major expansion program. The formal report to top management may later be stripped of some of the prefatory parts (and thus reduced in formality) for wider circulation within the company.

The Parts of the Report

Typically, research reports follow the same general outline. Research reports are a form of technical writing and as such, readers may well expect the paper to follow this format. Here, the old adage, "If it ain't broke, don't fix it," truly applies.

Title Page

The *title page* provides a name for report, tells for whom the report was prepared (when prepared for a specific entity and not for public consumption), tells who performed the research and wrote the report, and gives the date of release or presentation. The report's title should give a concise

> *"The covers of this book are too far apart."*
>
> —AMBROSE BIERCE

Statistics Show 20 Percent of Report Statistics Are Misleading. Oh Yeah??!!

People may not like math, but when it comes to making judgments, people like numbers. Just consider how many news stories in the paper or news report poll results, trends, or other statistics. Similarly, many ads make claims backed up by statistics. Consider these "facts" taken from newspaper reports:

"Visa announced that its new credit card will carry an adjustable rate set monthly at four percent above the prime rate, in line with other variable-rate cards."

This is a common mistake: confusing *percentage* and *percentage points*. A rate set so slightly above the prime rate would be an unusually good bargain. For example, at the time of this writing, the U.S. federal prime rate is 3.25 percent; prime plus 4 percent would be just 3.38 percent, far below the rates charged by most credit cards. The writer probably meant Visa would charge prime rate plus four percentage points, which in this example would be 7.25 percent.

©Nisimo/Shutterstock

"Battling Hunger, a food pantry, said it delivered 110,000 tons of food to Detroit last Thanksgiving. The food was delivered to help residents there overcome the effects of a severe economic slump, particularly in the automobile industry."

Can you spot any problems with such statements? Looking carefully, each of these examples is potentially misleading. Misleading reports may not have to do with the numbers themselves, but with other details such as the units of measure or standards of comparison. In this case, 110,000 tons equals 220 million pounds of food. Can that be reasonable? Even if the food pantry served a million people—all of Detroit plus some suburbanites—it would have distributed 220 pounds of food to each individual. Not likely. When numbers are this unrealistic, the writer should check the calculations, including the decimal point's location, and the units. Perhaps this writer meant 110,000 pounds or 110 tons.

"More Americans tell pollsters they are currently more often happy than worried."

This seems simple enough. However, what the story does not point out is that the poll results contain only results taken on the weekend. People who are polled on weekdays give the opposite picture—they are more worried than happy. So, pay attention to the details before jumping to conclusions.

Sources: Based on Bialik, C. (2009), "In Ads, 1 Out of 5 Stats is Bogus," *Wall Street Journal* (March 11), 12; Carl Bialik, "Monitoring the Numbers in the News," *Wall Street Journal*, January 20, 2006, http://online.wsj.com/article/SB113764595134250640.html, accessed August 17, 2011; Bialik, C. (2011), "U.S. News—The Numbers Guy: Happy? Statisticians Aren't Buying It," *Wall Street Journal* (March 26), 2.

indication of the purpose of the research project. Researchers are often challenged to come up with a title that is both descriptive and brief. Generally, a shorter title is better and a good rule of thumb is not to extend the title far beyond twelve words. The title page also provides contact information for both the preparer and recipient. On confidential reports, the title page lists the names of individuals to whom the report should be circulated. Formal reports are often bound and covered with a title fly page which lists only the name of the report.

Letter of Transmittal

Relatively formal and very formal reports include a *letter of transmittal*. Its purpose is to release or deliver the report to the recipient. It also serves to establish some rapport between the reader and the writer. This is the one part of the formal report in which a personal or even slightly informal tone should be used. The transmittal should not dive into the report findings except in the broadest terms.

A transmittal letter's opening paragraph releases the report and briefly identifies the factors of authorization. The letter comments generally on findings and matters of interest regarding the research. The closing section expresses the writer's personal interest in the project just completed and in doing additional, related work. Overall, the letter explains how the report represents a key deliverable and invites further discussion on the matter.

Letter of Authorization

The *letter of authorization* is a letter to the researcher that approves the project, details who has responsibility for it, and describes the resources available to support it. Because the researcher would not write this letter personally, writing guidelines will not be discussed here. In many situations, simply referring to the authorization in the letter of transmittal is sufficient. If so, the letter of authorization need not be included in the report. In some cases, though, the reader may be unfamiliar with the authorization or may need detailed information about it. In such cases, the report should include this letter, preferably an exact copy of the original.

The Table of Contents

A *table of contents* is essential to any report more than a few pages long. It should list the divisions and subdivisions of the report with page references. The table of contents is based on the final outline of the report, but it should include only the first-level subdivisions. For short reports it is sufficient to include only the main divisions. If the report includes many figures or tables, a list of these should immediately follow the table of contents.

The Executive Summary

The *summary*, or *executive summary* as it is called more often, briefly explains why the research project was conducted, what aspects of the problem were considered, what the outcome was, and what should be done. It is a vital part of the report. Studies have indicated that nearly all managers read a report's summary, whereas only a minority read the rest of the report. Thus, the writer's only chance to produce an impact may be in the summary.

The summary should be written only after the rest of the report has been completed. It represents the essence of the report. Executive summaries should be one page long (or, at most, two pages), so the writer must carefully sort out what is important enough to be included in it. Several pages of the full report may have to be condensed into one summarizing sentence. Some parts of the report may be condensed more than others; the number of words in the summary need not be in proportion to the length of the section being discussed. The summary should be written to be self-sufficient. In fact, the summary is often detached from the report and circulated by itself.

The summary contains four elements. First, it states the objectives of the report, including the most important background information and the specific purposes of the project. Second, it presents the methodology and the major results and then the conclusions. These are opinions based on the results and constitute an interpretation of the results. Finally come recommendations, or suggestions for action, based on the conclusions. In many cases, managers prefer not to have recommendations included in the report or summary. Whether or not recommendations are included should be clear from the particular context of the report.

The Body

The *body* constitutes the bulk of the report. It begins with an **introduction section** setting out the background factors that made the project necessary as well as the objectives of the report. It continues with discussions of the methodology, results, and limitations of the study and finishes with conclusions and recommendations based on the results.

The introduction explains why the researchers conducted the project and what questions the research addresses. It should include the basic authorization and submittal data. The relevant background comes next. Enough background should be included to explain why the project was worth doing, but unessential historical factors should be omitted. The research should address

introduction section

The part of the body of a research report that discusses background information and the specific objectives of the research.

the question of how much background is enough by referring to the needs of the audience. A government report that will be widely circulated requires more background than a company's internal report on customer satisfaction. The last part of the introduction explains exactly what question or decision statement motivated the project. This includes the statement of the problem and research questions as originally stated in the research proposal. Each research question presented here should have a corresponding subheading in the results section of the report.

research methodology section

The part of the body of a report that presents the findings of the project. It includes tables, charts, and an organized narrative.

The second part of the body is the **research methodology section**. This part is a challenge to write because it must explain technical procedures in a manner appropriate for the audience. Complex technical details can be included in a technical appendix. Sometimes, the report includes a glossary of technical terms. Four points should be included in the research methodology section:

1. *Research design.* Was the study exploratory, descriptive, or causal? Did the data come from primary or secondary sources? Were results collected by survey, observation, or experiment? A copy of the survey questionnaire or observation form should be included in the appendix. Why was this particular design suited to the study?
2. *Sample design.* What was the target population? What sampling frame was used? What sample units were used? How were they selected? How large was the sample? What was the response rate? Detailed computations to support these explanations should be saved for the appendix.
3. *Data collection and fieldwork.* How many and what types of fieldworkers were used? What training and supervision did they receive? Was the work verified? This section is important for establishing the degree of accuracy of the results.
4. *Analysis.* This section should outline the general statistical methods used in the study, but the information presented here should not overlap with what is presented in the results section.

results section

The part of the body of a report that presents the findings of the project. It includes tables, charts, and an organized narrative.

The **results section** presents the crucial evidence that allows conclusions to be drawn. This section should present in some logical order, those findings of the project that bear on the decision statement(s). The results should be organized as a continuous narrative, designed to be convincing but not to oversell the project. Summary tables and charts should be used to aid the discussion. These may serve as points of reference to the data being discussed and free the prose from excessive facts and figures. Research should save comprehensive or detailed charts, however, for an appendix.

Because no research is perfect, its limitations should be indicated. If problems arose with nonresponse error or sampling procedures, these should be discussed. However, the discussion of limitations should avoid overemphasizing the weaknesses; its aim should be to provide a realistic basis for assessing the results.

conclusions and recommendations section

The part of the body of a report that provides opinions based on the results and suggestions for action.

The last part of the body is the **conclusions and recommendations section**. As mentioned earlier, conclusions are opinions based on the results, and recommendations are suggestions for action. The conclusions and recommendations should be presented in this section in more detail than in the summary, and the text should include justification as needed.

Appendix

An *appendix* presents the "too . . . " material. Any material that is too technical or too detailed to go in the body should appear in an appendix. This includes materials of interest only to some readers or subsidiary materials not directly related to the objectives. Some examples of appendix materials are data collection forms, detailed calculations, discussions of highly technical questions, detailed or comprehensive tables of results, and a bibliography (if appropriate). Appendices increasingly appear only in electronic form residing on secure web pages accessible by following links in the main report.

Basic Marketing Research Report

The outline described applies especially to applied market research projects. When basic research reports are written, such as might be submitted and potentially published in an academic business journal, the outline changes slightly because some components become irrelevant. A common outline used in basic marketing research proceeds as follows:

1. Abstract
2. Introduction
3. Background
   a. Literature Review
   b. Hypotheses
4. Research Methods
5. Results
6. Discussion
   a. Implications
   b. Limitations
   c. Future Research
7. Conclusions
8. References
9. Appendixes

Using Tables Effectively

Used properly, **graphic aids** can clarify complex points or emphasize a message. Used improperly or sloppily, they can distract or even mislead a reader. Graphical aids work best when they are an integral part of the text. The graphics should always be interpreted in the text. This does not mean that the writer should exhaustively explain an obvious chart or table, but it *does* mean that the text should point out the key elements of any graphic aid and relate them to the discussion in progress.

Several types of graphic aids may be useful in research reports including tables, charts, maps, and diagrams. The following discussion briefly covers the most common ones, tables and charts. The reader interested in other types of graphic material should consult more specialized sources.

graphic aids

Pictures or diagrams used to clarify complex points or emphasize a message.

Creating Tables

Tables are most useful for presenting numerical information, especially when the results involve several pieces of information all addressing a single point. For example, consider how hard following the information in Exhibit 16.2 might be with only narrative text and no graphical aids. Using tables allows a writer to point out significant features without getting bogged down in detail. The body of the report should include only relatively short summary tables, with comprehensive tables reserved for an appendix.

EXHIBIT **16.2** Basic Data Table Illustration

Number of Graphic → **Table 162E. Bottled Water Sales Volume—2001 to 2011** ← Title | Column Headings
(In millions of $US)

Country	2001	2002	2003	2004	2005	2006	2007	2008	2009	2010	2011
World-wide	55,618	59,543	63,950	66,916	71,092	75,851	81,112	84,866	88,862	93,239	98,058
United States	10,247	11,413	12,253	13,214	14,343	15,610	16,966	17,010	17,107	17,217	17,343
Germany	9,427	9,979	10,577	10,728	11,281	11,958	12,648	13,293	13,931	14,573	15,212
China	1,497	1,752	2,214	2,589	3,246	4,028	4,971	6,108	7,474	9,122	11,104
Italy	5,824	6,135	6,500	6,675	6,972	7,276	7,590	7,910	8,231	8,547	8,862
France	4,191	4,251	4,287	4,323	4,364	4,409	4,520	4,620	4,706	4,782	4,851
Japan	2,445	2,682	2,973	3,236	3,374	3,531	3,702	3,887	4,091	4,319	4,573
Brazil	2,620	2,651	2,713	2,884	3,059	3,224	3,390	3,578	3,780	4,009	4,268

Note: Sales volume based on average retail price per liter by total liters sold by country.
Source: Data Monitor Interactive Consumer Database.

Row Headings

Notes including sources

Each table should include the following elements:

- *Number.* The number is indexed to the List of Exhibits/Tables/Figures/Charts provided along with the TOC. For an electronic report, this list may be hyperlinked to the graphics list for easy navigation. Some authors prefer to use the term *exhibit* to refer to all tables, charts, figures—all graphics in general. Others prefer to number tables, charts, and figures separately.
- *Title.* The title should indicate the contents of the table and be complete enough to be intelligible without referring to the text.
- *Stubheads and bannerheads.* The stubheads contain the captions for the rows of the table, and the bannerheads (or boxheads) contain those for the columns.
- *Notes.* Any explanations or qualifications for particular table entries or sections should be given in notes placed at the bottom of the table or footnotes appearing at the bottom of the page.
- *Source notes.* If a table is based on material from one or more secondary sources rather than on new data generated by the project, the sources should be acknowledged, usually below the table.

Using Charts Effectively

Charts translate numerical information into visual form so that relationships may be easily grasped. The accuracy of the numbers is reduced to gain this advantage. Each chart should include the following elements:

- *Figure number.* Charts (and other illustrative material) should be numbered in a separate series from tables. The numbers allow for easy reference from the text. If there are many charts, a list of them should be included after the table of contents.
- *Title.* The title should describe the contents of the chart and be independent of the text explanation. The number and title may be placed at the top or bottom of the chart.
- *Explanatory legends.* Enough explanation should be put on the chart to spare the reader a need to look at the accompanying text. Such explanations should include labels for axes, scale numbers, and a key to the various quantities being graphed.
- *Source and footnotes.* Any secondary sources for the data should be acknowledged. Footnotes may be used to explain items, although they are less common for charts than for tables.

Charts are subject to distortion, whether unintentional or deliberate. Researchers must use special care to faithfully represent true scale values in all graphical aids. In fact, scale values can be intentionally altered in an effort to skew the interpretation of the data. Intentionally altering scales for this purpose is clearly unethical and unintentionally doing so is sloppy.

A particularly severe kind of distortion comes from treating unequal intervals as if they were equal; this generally results from a deliberate attempt to distort data. Exhibit 16.3 shows this type of distortion. Here, both charts show average quarterly gas prices for regular gas in the Gulf region of the United States over a five-year period. The top frame makes the case that gas prices have really been quite stable during this period. However, the bottom frame shows a fairly sharp spike in prices during 2008. The two charts supposedly showing the same data tell quite a different story. On close inspection, however, the two charts are not using the same intervals. The data from the top chart omit observations for three-quarters of 2008, allowing the reader to draw the conclusion that gas prices have been stable. When those observations are added to the chart so that equal quarterly intervals are used between observations, the picture becomes much clearer.

Researchers sometimes are tempted to choose the scale values for axes on charts in a way that may make a small finding seem much larger than it really is. This also can occur by accident as statistical tools that generate such graphs may automatically insert inappropriate minimum and maximum values. Consider Exhibit 16.4. Here the results of an experiment testing the difference between two alternative advertising designs on purchase intention are displayed in both frames. Subjects recorded their purchase intentions after viewing one of the ads using a 10-point scale scored from 1 (Extremely Unlikely to Buy) to 10 (Very Likely to Buy). Both frames display exactly the same data. However, would the conclusion be the same? Frame A

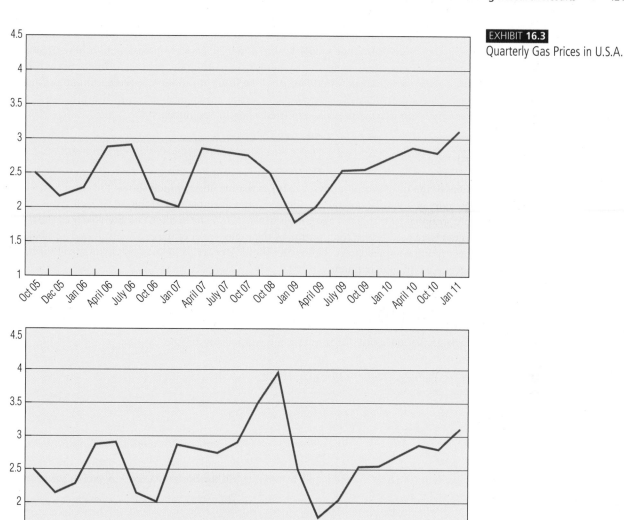

EXHIBIT 16.3
Quarterly Gas Prices in U.S.A.

Source: © Cengage Learning 2013.

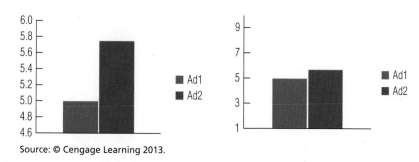

EXHIBIT 16.4
Axes Values Can Influence
Interpretation

Source: © Cengage Learning 2013.

makes ad 2 seem much more advantageous relative to ad 1. In contrast, frame B leads to the conclusion that there is very little difference between the two. In this case, frame A is misleading because notice that the y-axis uses a minimum value of 4.6 and a maximum value of 6.0, whereas frame B uses the actual scale minimum and maximum values of 1 and 10. Similar distortions can occur when using charts to interaction effects. Again, great caution should be taken in making sure that the chart can be used to help support the old adage, "Statistics don't lie, but liars use statistics."

Marketing researchers should always try to present results as faithfully as possible. In this case, using the entire scale range would lead to a more accurate conclusion. In other instances where a larger range of values may be in play, perhaps in plotting the price someone actually paid for their last car, the minimum axes value need not be 0, but it should reflect the minimum plausible price that someone would pay. For example, one may set the scale range in this instance by the actual minimum and maximum prices reported across all respondents.

Pie Charts

One of the most useful kinds of charts is the pie chart, which shows the composition of a total quantity at a particular time. As shown in the example in Exhibit 16.5, each angle, or "slice," is proportional to its percentage of the whole. Companies often use pie charts to show how revenues were used or the composition of their sales. Each of the segments should be labeled with its description and percentage. The writer should not try to include too many small slices; about six slices is a typical maximum.

Line Graphs

Line graphs are useful for showing the relationship of one variable to another. The dependent variable generally is shown on the vertical axis, and the independent variable on the horizontal axis. The most common independent variable for such charts is time, but it is by no means the only one. Exhibit 16.6 depicts a *simple line graph*.

Bar Charts

A bar chart shows changes in the value of a dependent variable (plotted on the vertical axis) at discrete intervals of the independent variable (on the horizontal axis). A simple bar chart is shown in Exhibit 16.7.

EXHIBIT 16.5

A Simple Pie Chart with Slices Representing the Frequency of Sales at Each Price Level

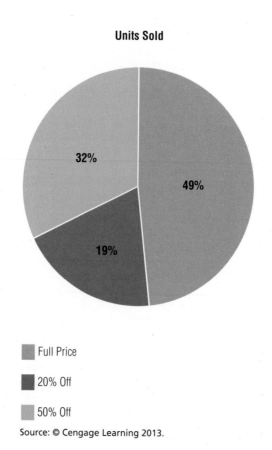

Source: © Cengage Learning 2013.

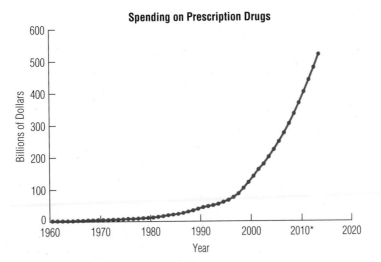

EXHIBIT **16.6**
Simple Line Graph

*Projected data for 2004–2014.

Source: Data from U.S. Census Bureau, *Statistical Abstract of the United States,* 2006, table 118, p. 98.

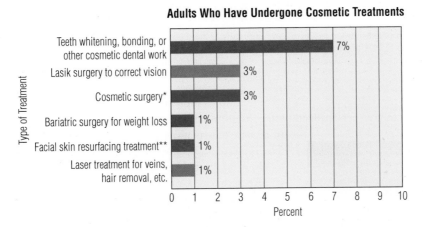

EXHIBIT **16.7**
Simple Bar Chart

*Includes face lift, chin implant, tummy tuck, etc.
**Includes chemical peels, laser abrasion, etc.

Source: Data from Harris Interactive, "Despite Risks, Adults Not Shying Away from Cosmetic Surgery and Other Treatments," news release, February 13, 2006, http://www.harrisinteractive.com. Accessed April 4, 2006.

The *multiple-bar chart* (see Exhibit 16.8) shows how multiple variables are related to the primary variable. In each of these cases, each bar or segment of the bar needs to be clearly identified with a different color or pattern. The writer should not use too many divisions or dependent variables. Too much detail obscures the essential advantage of charts, which is to make relationships easy to grasp. In this chart, the user can see both the general downward trend in overall sales post-2007 as well as the fluctuations in sales by brands. The Ford F-150 appears to have fared well relative to other best-sellers, as evidenced by its relatively high increase in sales in 2010.

The Oral Presentation

The conclusions and recommendations of most research reports are presented orally as well as in writing. The purpose of an **oral presentation** is to highlight the most important findings of a research project and provide clients or line managers with an opportunity to ask questions. The oral presentation may be as simple as a short video conference with a manager at the client organization's location or as formal as a report to the company board of directors. One rule stands above all when preparing a presentation—be as straightforward as possible.

oral presentation

A spoken summary of the major findings, conclusions, and recommendations, given to clients or line managers to provide them with the opportunity to clarify any ambiguous issues by asking questions.

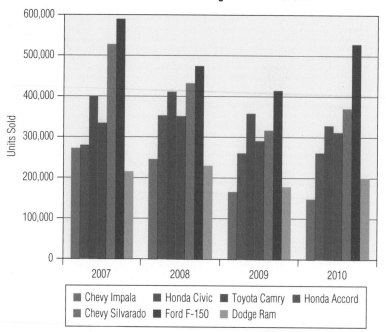

Recent Best Selling Cars in the U.S.A.

Source: "Forbes.com - 10 Best Selling Vehicles of 2007," http://www.autospies.com/news/Forbes-com-10-Best-Selling-Vehicles-of-2007-23985/, accessed December 22, 2008; Jacqueline Mitchell, "The Year's Best- And Worst-Selling Cars," http://www.forbes.com/2008/12/03/2008-car-sales-forbeslife-cx_jm_1203cars.html, accessed December 22, 2008.

Realize this rule applies also in nontraditional presentation formats. Today's researcher has to be prepared to give personalized presentations to busy executives and to use Internet-based tools to prepare presentations that can be viewed at the user's leisure. The Research Snapshot discusses these trends briefly.

In a traditional oral presentation, preparation is the key to effectiveness. Communication specialists often suggest that a person preparing an oral presentation begin at the end. In other words, while preparing a presentation, a researcher should think about what he or she wants the client to know when it has been completed. The researcher should select the three or four most important findings for emphasis and rely on the written report for a full summary. The researcher also needs to be ready to defend the results of the research. This is not the same as being defensive; instead, the researcher should be prepared to deal in a confident, competent manner with the questions that arise. Remember that even the most reliable and valid research project is worthless if the managers who must act on its results are not convinced of its importance.

As with written reports, researchers need to adapt the presentation to the audience. Delivering an hour-long formal speech when a 10-minute discussion is what management asked for (or vice versa) will reflect poorly on both the presenter and the report. The terminology also needs to be appropriate for the audience. A group of marketing researchers can tolerate more jargon than a group of managers.

Lecturing or reading to the audience is sure to impede communication at any level of formality. The presenter should refrain from reading prepared text word for word. By relying on brief notes, familiarity with the subject, and as much rehearsal as the occasion calls for, the presenter will foster better

RESEARCH SNAPSHOT

Presentation Today?

©Stuart Jenner/Shutterstock

In the 1960s, a marketing research presentation probably meant going through key results using a flip chart and magic marker. In the 70s and 80s, the presenter turned to overhead projectors. The LCD projector and the common types of presentation software that we use today became the tool of choice in the late 1990s. The projectors have become increasingly small and portable, enabling presentations to be given just about anywhere where a power source is available.

However, the modern marketing researcher doesn't even need a projector. Increasingly, tablet computers are used to give presentations to small groups. In fact, the researcher doesn't even need to be present for the presentation as Skype-type software programs and communication enable delivery of the presentation over the Internet. In either case, the researcher needs to be keenly aware how the presentation format will affect communication. A tablet computer offers a small screen so even fewer words per slide are the rule. For remote presentations, the researcher may wish to take advantage of on-screen annotations that allow the user to easily know where in the screen the key information can be found and to include any additional explanations. Similarly, if the presentation is to be completely canned and viewed by the users without the presence of the researcher, these types of visual and voice-over annotations can be extremely useful. These technological tools are real trends in presentations today.

Sources: Brodkin, J. (2011), "The Complicated New Face of Personal Computing," *Network World*, 28 (1/10), 12–16; Pharmaceutical Executive (2011), "iDeal Tool of Sales Trade," 31 (May), 84–86.

communication. He or she should avoid research jargon and use short, familiar words. The presenter should maintain eye contact with the audience and repeat the main points. Because the audience cannot go back and replay what the speaker has said, an oral presentation often is organized around a standard format: "Tell them what you are going to tell them, tell them, and tell them what you just told them."

Graphic and other visual aids can be as useful in an oral presentation as in a written one. Presenters can choose from a variety of media. Slides, overhead-projector acetates, and on-screen computer-generated graphics are useful for larger audiences. For smaller audiences, the researcher may put the visual aids on posters or flip charts. Another possibility is to make copies of the charts for each participant, possibly as a supplement to one of the other forms of presentation. Still another is to use a small personal computer or a tablet computer to flip through a presentation. This latter option is best if the audience is only one person.

Whatever medium is chosen, each visual aid should be designed to convey a simple, attention-getting message that supports a point on which the audience should focus its thinking. As they do in written presentations, presenters should interpret graphics for the audience. The best slides are easy to read and interpret. Large typeface, multiple colors, bullets that highlight, and other artistic devices can enhance the readability of charts.

Using gestures during presentations also can help convey the message and make presentations more interesting. Also, invite participation from the audience. Here are some tips on actually making the presentation:[6]

- Generally, introduce yourself while displaying the title of the presentation. Acknowledge any others who materially assisted in the project.
- Open up your arms to embrace your audience. Keep your arms between your waist and shoulders.
- Drop your arms to your sides when not using them.

Some gestures are used to draw attention to points illustrated by visual aids. For these, gesturing with an open hand can seem more friendly and can even release tension related to nervousness. In contrast, a nervous speaker who uses a laser pointer may distract the audience as the pointer jumps around in the speaker's shaky hand.[7]

Reports on the Internet

Many clients want numerous employees to have access to research findings. One easy way to share data is to make executive summaries and reports available on a company intranet. In addition, a company can use information technology on the Internet to design questionnaires, administer surveys, analyze data, and share the results in a presentation-ready format. Real-time data capture allows for beginning-to-end reporting. A number of companies offer fully Web-based research management systems—for example, many companies also provide online research reports on key topics of interest.

The Research Follow-Up

research follow-up

Recontacting decision makers and/or clients after they have had a chance to read over a research report in order to determine whether additional information or clarification is necessary.

Research reports and oral presentations should communicate research findings so that managers can make business decisions. In many cases, the manager who receives the research report is unable to interpret the information and draw conclusions relevant to managerial decisions. For this reason, effective researchers do not treat the report as the end of the research process. They conduct a **research follow-up**, in which they recontact decision makers and/or clients after the latter have had a chance to read over the report. The purpose is to determine whether the researchers need to provide additional information or clarify issues of concern to management. Just as marketing research may help an organization learn about its customers' satisfaction, the research follow-up can help marketing research staffers ensure the satisfaction of their customers, marketing managers.

TIPS OF THE TRADE

- Research reports, like all communications, are interpreted by the receiver. Try to be clear and unambiguous in preparing the research report.
  - Research reports should generally follow the principles of good technical writing.
  - Whenever possible, have someone else proof the report and slides before submitting them to the client or editor.
  - Whenever possible, stick to the standard outline for the paper.
- The executive summary is critically important because on occasion it is the only part read in detail by the client.
  - Keep it short—about 400 words maximum, except for the longest reports.
  - Highlight the key findings with bullet points.
  - Write it last—after finishing the rest of the report and presentation.
- Consider the audience in preparing the report and presentation.
  - Make the communication understandable.
  - Avoid jargon and put any complex statistical output in a technical appendix.
- Use charts and tables to illustrate findings.
- Presentation slides should be clear and legible.
  - Err toward larger font, not smaller.
  - Err toward fewer words, not more.
- When slides are posted for viewing via the Internet, annotate complex issues with pop-ups or balloon inserts.

Source: © Cengage Learning 2013.

∷ SUMMARY

1. Define the parts of a research report following a standard format. A research report is an oral or written presentation of research findings directed to a specific audience to accomplish a particular purpose. Report preparation is the final stage of the research project. The consensus is that the format for a research report should include certain prefatory parts, the body of the report, and appended parts. The report format should be varied to suit the level of formality of the particular situation. The prefatory parts of a formal report include a title page, letters of transmittal and authorization, a table of contents, and a summary.

2. Explain how to use tables for presenting numerical information. Tables present large amounts of numerical information in a concise manner. They are especially useful for presenting several pieces of information about each item discussed. Short tables are helpful in the body of the report; long tables are better suited for an appendix. Each table should include a number, title, stubheads and bannerheads, footnotes for any explanations or qualifications of entries, and source notes for data from secondary sources.

3. Summarize how to select and use the types of research charts. Charts present numerical data in a way that highlights their relationships. Each chart should include a figure number, title, explanatory legends, and a source note for secondary sources. Pie charts show the composition of a total (the parts that make up a whole). Line graphs show the relationship of a dependent variable (on the vertical axis) to an independent variable (horizontal axis). Most commonly, the independent variable is time. Bar charts show changes in a dependent variable at discrete intervals of the independent variable—for example, comparing one year with another or one subset of the population with another. Researchers need to pay careful attention to avoid distorted interpretations of graphics based on manipulations of the scale values used on axes or any other intentional or careless inaccuracy.

4. Know how to give an effective oral presentation. Most research projects are reported on orally as well as in writing, so the researcher needs to prepare an oral presentation. The presentation should defend the results without being defensive. The presentation must be tailored to the situation and the audience. The presenter should practice delivering the presentation in a natural way, without reading to the audience. Graphic aids are useful supplements when they are simple and easy to read. Gestures also add interest and emphasis.

5. Discuss the importance of Internet reporting and research follow-up. Posting a summary of results online gives clients ready access to that information. Some online survey software processes the data and displays results in a presentation-ready format. In the follow-up stage of a research project, the researchers recontact decision makers after submitting the report. This helps the researchers determine whether they need to provide further information or clarify any issues of concern to management.

∷ KEY TERMS AND CONCEPTS

conclusions and recommendations
    section, *418*
graphic aids, *419*
introduction section, *417*

oral presentation, *423*
report format, *413*
research follow-up, *426*
research methodology section, *418*

research report, *413*
results section, *418*

∷ QUESTIONS FOR REVIEW AND CRITICAL THINKING

1. What are the parts of a market research report?
2. How does an applied market research report differ from a basic or marketing research report?
3. What types of tables might be used to describe some of the various statistical tests discussed in previous chapters?
4. What is the difference between a *basic marketing research paper* and *an applied market research report?*
5. What is a *pie chart?* What is a *bar chart?* When might one be preferable over the other?

6. How might a marketing research unintentionally distort results of an independent *t*-test examining brand A's customer satisfaction against brand B's customer satisfaction where customer satisfaction is measured on a 0- to 100-point satisfaction scale (0 = no satisfaction to 100 = complete satisfaction)? How might the researcher intentionally distort the interpretation of these results?

7. What are some basic business research journals? Find some published research reports in these journals. How do they meet the standards set forth in this chapter?

8. What rules should be followed when preparing slides for computer-generated presentations?

9. **ETHICS** What ethical concerns arise when you prepare (or read) a report?

10. **ETHICS** A researcher working for Hi Time prepares a bar chart comparing the number of customers visiting two competing booths at a fashion trade show. One booth is the Hi Time booth; the other is for a competing company, So Cool. First, the chart is prepared as shown here:

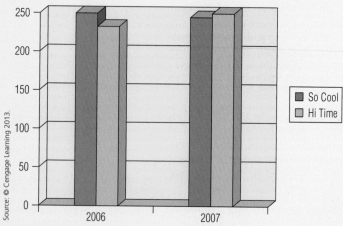

In preparing for a presentation to the Hi Time Board, the client tells the researcher that the chart doesn't seem to reflect the improvements made since 2008. Therefore, the researcher prepares the chart as shown here:

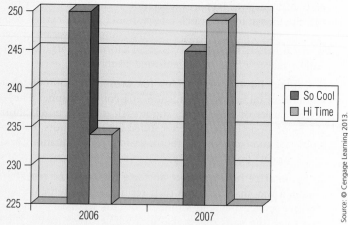

a. What has reformatting the bar chart accomplished?

b. Was it ethical for the client to ask for the bar chart to be redrawn?

c. Would it be ethical for the researcher to use the new chart in the presentation?

11. Prepare an exhibit like 16.2 that shows the per-capita bottled water consumption for the countries listed. Population stats for each country can be found in the CIA *Factbook* discussed in an earlier chapter. Sort the countries from most to least consumption per capita. Which exhibit would be more valuable for someone looking for opportunities in the bottled water industry?

Source: © Cengage Learning 2013.

:: RESEARCH ACTIVITIES

1. Input "Starbucks" or "McDonald's" in an Internet search engine available through your library's reference service or even a general search engine such as Google News. Look at the articles for that company. Limit the search by using the word "report." Find one of the articles that actually presents research reports, such as consumer reactions to a new product. Prepare PowerPoint slides that contain appropriate charts to present the results.

2. Consider question 11 and prepare a short presentation that summarizes the results from both the overall bottled water market and the per-capita market. Annotate the presentation so that it can serve as a stand-alone presentation.

Consumer Price Knowledge

Case 16.1

A recent study investigated one major area of marketing decisions: pricing practices. Specifically, the study addressed consumer knowledge and attitudes about the practice of online retailers adjusting their prices according to customer characteristics, such as how frequently they buy from the retailer. Price discrimination has long been commonplace in many industries but the Internet provides a way of implementing large scale price discrimination. Realize that price discrimination isn't always a bad thing for individual consumers as sometimes he or she is the beneficiary of a low price.

For example, a rental car company may offer a consumer a low rate on a rental car if the person's recent Web history has shown a search for hotels. Someone who goes straight to the rental car site may not get such a discount. Another website selling cameras charged different prices for the same model depending on whether the visitor to the site had previously visited sites that supply price comparisons. In general, price discrimination is legal unless it discriminates by race or sex or involves antitrust or price-fixing laws (such as two competitors agreeing to charge certain prices).

The study consisted of telephone interviews conducted with a sample of 1,500 adults, screened to find persons who had used the Internet in the preceding thirty days. The questionnaire gathered demographic data and data about Internet usage. In addition, the interviewer read seventeen statements about basic laws and practices related to price discrimination and the targeting of consumers according to their shopping behaviors. Respondents were asked whether each of these statements was true or false. Case Exhibits 16.1–1 through 16.1–4 summarize some of the results from this study.

CASE EXHIBIT 16.1–1
Selected Information about the Sample

Sex	
Male	48%
Female	52%
Online Connection at Home	
Dial-up connection only	31%
Cable modem (with/without dial-up)	18%
DSL (with/without dial-up)	25%
Cable or DSL with another method	13%
Don't know	4%
No connection at home	9%
Self-Ranked Expertise Navigating the Internet	
Beginner	14%
Intermediate	40%
Advanced	34%
Expert	12%

Source: Joseph Turow, Lauren Feldman, and Kimberly Meltzer, "Open to Exploitation: American Shoppers Online and Offline," APPC report, June 2005, p. 15, downloaded at http://www.annenbergpublicpolicycenter.org. Reprinted by permission.

Source: © Cengage Learning 2013.

CASE EXHIBIT 16.1–2
Responses to Selected Knowledge Questions

Statement	Response*		
	True	**False**	**Don't Know**
Companies today have the ability to follow my activity across many sites on the web.	**80%**	8%	12%
It is legal for an *online* store to charge different people different prices at the same time of day.	**38%**	29%	33%
By law, a site such as Expedia or Orbitz that compares prices on different airlines must include the lowest airline prices.	37%	**32%**	31%
It is legal for an *offline* store to charge different people different prices at the same time of day.	29%	**42%**	29%
When a website has a privacy policy, it means the site will not share my information with other websitesor companies.	59%	**25%**	16%

*When the numbers do not add up to 100%, it is because of a rounding error. **Boldface** type indicates the correct answer.

Source: Joseph Turow, Lauren Feldman, and Kimberly Meltzer, "Open to Exploitation: American Shoppers Online and Offline," APPC report, June 2005, p. 20, downloaded at http://www.annenbergpublicpolicycenter.org. Accessed April 5, 2006. Reprinted by permission.

Questions

1. The information provided here is not detailed enough for a formal report, but assume that you are making an informal report in a preliminary stage of the reporting process. Which of these findings do you want to emphasize as your main points? Why?
2. Prepare a written summary of the findings, using at least two tables or charts.
3. Prepare two tables or charts that would be suitable to accompany an oral presentation of these results. Are they different from the visual aids you prepared for question 2? Why or why not?

A Final Note on Marketing Research

Hopefully, after reading and studying the material in this book, you can now understand and apply basic processes that help identify key information needs and turn raw data into intelligence. Thus, after sifting through a vast sea of information, this intelligence helps someone make a better decision, which, in turn, helps make someone's life better. The consumer who gets something of greater value is better off and the people who produced and marketed the product also are better off. Marketing research is a very important and useful area of knowledge that can lead to meaningful skills. The set of cases that follows provides the reader with one last chance to gain experience through real-world applications of marketing research. If you are still hungry for more about marketing research, there are many more advanced topics that can increase your skills in one of the specialized areas of research!

Source: © Cengage Learning 2013.

CASE EXHIBIT **16.1–3**

Responses to Selected Attitude Questions

Statement	Response*			
	Agree	Disagree	Neutral	Don't Know
It's okay if a store charges me a price based on what it knows about me.	8%	91%	—	1%
It's okay if an *online* store I use charges different people different prices for the same products during the same hour.	11%	87%	1%	1%
It would bother me to learn that other people pay less than I do for the same products.	76%	22%	1%	1%
It would bother me if websites I shop at keep detailed records of my buying behavior.	57%	41%	2%	1%
It's okay if a store I shop at frequently uses information it has about me to create a picture of me that improves the services it provides for me.	50%	41%	2%	1%

*When the numbers do not add up to 100%, it is because of a rounding error.

Source: Joseph Turow, Lauren Feldman, and Kimberly Meltzer, "Open to Exploitation: American Shoppers Online and Offline," APPC report, June 2005, p. 22, downloaded at http://www.annenbergpublicpolicycenter.org. Accessed April 7, 2006. Reprinted by permission.

CASE EXHIBIT **16.1–4**

Predicting Knowledge Score from Selected Demographics

	Unstandardized Regression Coefficient (B)	Standardized Regression Coefficient (β)
Education	0.630*	0.200
Income	0.383*	0.150
Self-perceived ability to navigate Internet	0.616*	0.149
Constant	2.687	
R^2	0.148	

*Significance <0.001 level.

Source: Joseph Turow, Lauren Feldman, and Kimberly Meltzer, "Open to Exploitation: American Shoppers Online and Offline," APPC report, June 2005, p. 29, downloaded at http://www.annenbergpublicpolicycenter.org. Accessed April 6, 2006. Reprinted by permission.

PART SIX

Comprehensive Cases with Computerized Databases

CASE 1
Say It Ain't So! Is This the Real Thing?

CASE 2
TABH, INC., Automotive Consulting

CASE 3
Knowing the Way

Case 1 Say It Ain't So! Is This the Real Thing?

INTRODUCTION

David Ortega is the lead researcher for an upscale restaurant group hoping to add another chain that would compete directly with the upscale Smith and Wollensky restaurants (**http://www.smith-andwollensky.com**). The Smith and Wollensky Restaurant Group operates a handful of iconic restaurants around the country. The average check for a customer at Smith and Wollensky is approximately $80 to $90.[1] Whenever a new venture of this type is planned, one has to wonder whether there are enough customers willing to pay premium prices given the large number of lesser priced alternatives. In fact, David learns that Smith and Wollensky is giving some thought to opening a lesser priced "Grill" that would be positioned so that the average customer check would be about half that of the original. Maybe the best way to position the new restaurant group would be as a premium value offering high quality steaks and service but at a more modest price. What is it that people are willing to pay for and what sacrifices can be made to deliver a high value experience if not a luxurious experience? How can he create a unique experience at a lower price without falling into a mere dinner house category? These are the questions facing David Ortega.

RESEARCH APPROACH

After considering how to study the issue, David decides a qualitative research approach will be useful. He hopes to develop a deep understanding of how the fine dining experience offers value—and perhaps some insights into what intangibles create value for consumers in general. After considering the different options, he decides on a phenomenological approach. The primary tool of investigation is conversational interviewing. David plans to enter into casual conversations with businesspeople in the lounge of the downtown Ritz Carlton. He begins the conversation by commenting on the wine he is sipping—something like, "It isn't bad, but it's hard to believe they get $15 for just one glass of this stuff."

RESULTS

Two weeks later, David has completed "conversations" with five consumers. He found them very willing and free to talk about the things they indulge in. He develops a field log of notes from the consumers' comments. The notes are recorded verbatim.[2] The following field notes are highlighted:

Respondent	Date/Time	Text
Joe, wm, 55, attorney	12/5/08 – 10:15 PM	Well, wine doesn't have to be expensive to be good. Beyond some basic price point . . . maybe $14 a bottle . . . I find a lot of good wines. But, the wine has to fit the situation. It has to add something. A fake Rolex will tell time; but a real Rolex tells you about you. I don't mind paying for something that's unique—even though it might not be my cup of tea. Chateau Masur is like that. It's from Lebanon! It isn't always elegant or delicious, but it is always real. You always know it comes from some place very unique and is made under the most trying circumstances.
Sally, hf, 45, medical sales	12/7/08 – 5:45 PM	We pay too much for a lot of stuff though. I like things to be genuine. When you ask for crab you get crab—not Krab with a "K." It's made of fish you know! . . . I love old neighborhood Italian restaurants. They aren't always expensive. But, they have character. I think that it is very easy to spoil. I might not want a checkered red and white table cloth at home, but the Italian restaurant has to have one. I have to smell the garlic from the parking lot. And, that cheap Chianti, the kind with the basket cradle—it had better be from Italy—it tastes sooo good there. You know, you could pay more, but a nice dinner there with a couple of friends is worth a lot.

		You know, the people who make great wine or who have great restaurants kind of luck into it. I don't think they really ever sent out a survey asking what the restaurant or the wine should be like. I think they said "I am going to make this the way that I want it to be . . ." and it just happens to be right! They are so committed to the product that it works—no matter the price. But commitment like that costs a little more usually—although they aren't in it for the money.
Hebert, wm, 40, oil executive	12/8/08 – 11:00 PM	How old is it? The older it is, the more it is worth—yeah! I like this French wine that has "depuis 1574," maybe its name is Hugel (trying to recall). Imagine the same family running that company for hundreds of years. I like to think about the family in the vineyards—the old man on a tractor with his sons running around the sides. Their kids are hanging around the barn. . . .
		You know, you can buy cheap things and get cheated too. We are free to be cheated at any price point! (laughter) I remember bringing home a bottle of "Louisiana Hot Sauce." Man, that stuff didn't have any heat to it at all. When I looked at the bottle, do you know where it was from? . . . Man, it was from Tennessee . . . can you believe that, Louisiana Hot Sauce from Tennessee!! What a scam. . . . .
		When I buy something nice, I want it to be real. Burgundy should be from Burgundy. Bordeaux should be from Bordeaux. Champagne should be from Champagne—not Texas or California! (laughter) Because I know in Champagne, they know how to make Champagne—sparkling wine. They have perfected the methods over hundreds of years. A good glass of Champagne is worth what you pay!
Angela, bf, 60, insurance executive	12/9/08 – 6:45 PM	Look at this hotel . . . when you just look at the price you think "this is crazy!" But, look at the attention to detail. Cleaning the floor is a production. Have you noticed the way they turn down your bed? Taking care of the plants is serious business to these people. I've stayed at a place like this in Florida—I loved it. At first, I couldn't put my finger on it. Then, it hit me. The place smelled like Florida. They have a way of giving everything the smell of sweet grass and citrus. It's terrific. Another one in California smelled of sandalwood and cypress. You have to be willing to pay more for people that care so much about what they do. Maybe that's your wine? Those smells make me think of those special places. When I drink a wine, I think about where it comes from too.
Burt, wm, 35, sales	12/9/08 – 9:30 PM	It's okay for something to be cheap . . . even fake! As long as I know it's fake. I've got three fake Rolexes. This one looks pretty good . . . looks genuine . . . but look at the way the second hand moves . . . it's jumping. A real one wouldn't do that!!
		I ate with this guy the other night who sent back a bottle of wine after ordering it. When the waiter pulled the cork, it didn't have Domaine Mas Blanc written on it—that's the name of the wine. He said, "How do I know it is real?" At first I thought he was crazy but after I looked at my fake Rolex . . . you know, I think he was right. When you spend $100 for a bottle, you want real stuff. But, if you spend $10 for a bottle of wine in a restaurant, who the hell cares? You didn't pay for it to be real . . . one day, when I pony up ten grand for a real Rolex, I'll send back the fakes!

Note: w = white; h = hispanic, f = female, m = male, etc.

RESULTS

David decides to use a word count to try to identify the main themes. Hopefully, these themes can help clarify the business problem. Perhaps if the information can't answer the questions above, it will point him in the right direction. Whatever the case, David feels the project has helped him better understand the total value proposition offered by restaurants, wines, hotels, and other products.

Questions

1. Comment on the research approach. Do you feel it was an appropriate choice?
2. **ETHICS** David did not inform these respondents that he was doing marketing research during these conversations. Why do you think he withheld this information and was it appropriate to do so?
3. **'NET** Using the Internet, try to identify at least three restaurants that Smith and Wollensky competes with and three with whom the new S&W Grill may compete.
4. Try to interpret the discussions above. You may use one of the approaches discussed in the text. What themes should be coded? What themes occur most frequently? Can the different themes be linked together to form a unit of meaning?
5. What is the result of this research? What should David report back to the restaurant group?

[1]MacNealy, Jeremy (2006), "Smith and Wollensky on the Grill," The Motley Fool, http://www.fool.com/News/mft/2006/mft06040425.htm, accessed October 2, 2011.
[2]For more comments along this same line, see Beverland, M., "The Real Thing: Branding Authenticity in the Luxury Wine Trade," Journal of Business Research 59 (February 2006), 251–258; Beverland, M., "Crafting Brand Authenticity: The Case of Luxury Wines," Journal of Management Studies, 42 (July 2005), 103–29; and Wolff, C., "Blending High Style and Authenticity," Lodging Hospitality, 61 (November 1, 2005), 72–76.

Case 2 TABH, INC., Automotive Consulting

(Download the data sets for this case from www.cengage. com/marketing/zikmund or request them from your instructor.) TABH consulting specializes in research for automobile dealers in the United States, Canada, Mexico, and Europe. Although much of their work is done on a pay-for fee basis with customers such as dealerships and dealership networks selling all major makes of automobiles, they also produce a monthly "white paper" that is sold via their website. This off-the-shelf research is purchased by other research firms and by companies within the auto industry itself. This month, they would like to produce a white paper analyzing the viability of college students attending schools located in small college towns as a potentially underserved market segment.

TABH management assigns a junior analyst named Michel Gonzalez to the project. Lacking time for a more comprehensive study, Michel decides to contact the traffic department at Cal Poly University in Pomona, California, and at Central Missouri State University in Warrensburg, Missouri. Michel wishes to obtain data from the students' automobile parking registration records. Although both schools are willing to provide anonymous data records for a limited number of students, Cal Poly offers Michel a chance to visit during the registration period, which just happens to be next week. As a result, not only can Michel get data from students' registration forms, but a small amount of primary data can be obtained by intercepting students near the registration window. In return, Michel is asked to purchase a booth at the Cal Poly career fair.

As a result, Michel obtains some basic information from students. The information results in a small data set consisting of the follow observations for 100 undergraduate college students in Pomona, California.

Variable	Description
Sex	Student's sex dummy coded with 1 = female and 0 = male
Color	Color of a student's car as listed on his or her registration form
Major	Student's major field of study (Business, Liberal Arts (LA), or Engineering (ENG))
Grade	Student's grade record reported as the mode (A, B, or C)
Finance	Whether the student financed the car he or she is driving or paid for it with cash, coded 0 = cash payment and 1 = financed
Residence	Whether the student lives on campus or commutes to school, coded 0 = commute and 1 = on campus
Animal	Michel asks each student to quickly draw a cartoon about the type of car they would like to purchase. Students are told to depict the car as an animal in the cartoon. Although Michel expects to interpret these cartoons more deeply when time allows, the initial coding specifies what type of animal was drawn by each respondent. When Michel was unsure of what animal was drawn, a second researcher was conferred with to determine what animal was depicted. Some students depicted the car as a dog, some as a cat, and some as a mule.

The purpose of the white paper is to offer car dealers considering new locations a comparison of the profile of a small-town university with the primary market segments for their particular automobile. For instance, a company specializing in small pickup trucks appeals to a different market segment than does a company specializing in two-door economy sedans. Many small towns currently do not have dealerships, particularly beyond the "Big 3." Although TABH cannot predict with certainty who may purchase the white paper, it particularly wants to appeal to companies with high sales growth in the United States, such as Kia (http://www.kia.com), Hyundai (http://www.hyundai-motor.com), and potentially European auto dealerships currently without significant U.S. distribution, such as Smart (http://www.smart.com), among others. TABH also hopes the white paper may eventually lead to a customized project for one of these companies. Thus, the general research question is:

What are the automobile market segment characteristics of students attending U.S. universities in small towns?

This question can be broken down into a series of more specific questions:

* *What segments can be identified based on identifiable characteristics of students?*
* *How do different segments view a car?*
* *What types of automobiles would be most in demand?*

Questions

1. What types of tests can be performed using the data that may at least indirectly address the primary research question?
2. What do you think the primary conclusions of the white paper will be based on the data provided?
3. Assuming a small college town lacked an auto dealership (beyond Ford, GM, and Chrysler), what two companies should be most interested in this type of location? Use the Internet if necessary to perform some cursory research on different car companies.
4. What are the weaknesses in basing decisions on this type of research?
5. Are there key issues that may diminish the usefulness of this research?
6. What kinds of themes might emerge from the cartoon drawings?
7. Are there any ethical dilemmas presented in this case?

Case 3 **Knowing the Way**

The Swamp Palace museum is an interactive museum that teaches visitors the ways of life on the swamps of the southern United States. Visitors can visit over 100 exhibits demonstrating the ecology of the swamp and the habits of the animals and insects that call the swamp home. Additionally, the museum includes several fast-food and full-service restaurants and opportunity for swimming and several thrill rides. The park covers over forty acres and includes miles and miles of pathways.

The park was originally supported with one time government funding but now it has to become self-supporting. After five years of operation, the park has not lacked for visitors but has struggled just to break even. The Swamp Palace has sought help from the Marketivity Group to help them address the long-term viability of the park. Initially, the Swamp Palace conducts exploratory research employing a participant-observer technique in which trained interviewers pretend to be park guests and engage in dialog with museum patrons. After employing interpretive techniques to the data gathered in these interviews, the Marketivity Group reports the exploratory results to management. A report emphasizes these key findings:

1. Patrons who complain tend to base their complaints over deficiencies in quality. Happy patrons voice nothing indicating a low quality theme.
2. Patrons also express a theme around value. Unhappy patrons believe the value offered by the park is low based in part on what is perceived as a high admission price.
3. Patrons express the difficulty in getting around in the park as a key theme. Even happy patrons joke about how difficult it is to find their way around.
4. As groups get larger, at least one member of the group was unhappy about having to accompany the others to the park.

After further subsequent discussions, Marketivity is hired to undertake a further study aimed at helping in addressing these decision statements:

- In what ways can Swamp Palace use technology to improve a customer's ability to effectively navigate around the museum?
- In what ways can Swamp Palace increase return visits by customers?
- Is participation in online coupon programs an effective way of increasing patronage and value?

Several technologies are considered as ways of enhancing value. One is a mobile phone app that will provide oral and visual navigation aids around the park. For instance, if someone says "take me to the Blind Bayou Bar," the phone will give directions using prominent museum landmarks. Second, Swamp Palace is considering subscribing to an Internet coupon program that would provide patrons with discounts. Marketivity translates these statements into several research questions including the following:

1. Do patrons who use a mobile phone navigation app report higher service quality and have an improved experience relative to those who do not?
2. Do patrons who use the mobile phone app have a greater likelihood of upgrading to a season pass?
3. Do patrons who use a coupon report more positive price perceptions?
4. Do patrons who use the mobile phone app have a greater likelihood of upgrading to a season pass?
5. What factors contribute to improved value perceptions?

Marketivity implements a quasi-experimental design over a one-week period in August. A sample of 200 visitors are randomly intercepted before entering the park. Approximately half are given the opportunity to download a free navigation app for their cell phone. Similarly, about half are invited to go to a kiosk and download a coupon from the internet. The park provides Marketivity with employees to intercept the patrons and explain the research procedures. Upon exiting the park, the patrons are taken to a desk where they fill out a short questionnaire. The employee then keys the data into the computer. The variables in the data set are described in the table below.

Name	Description*	Values
Wayf	A variable indicating whether the patron was provided the mobile phone app on entering the park	Yes or No
Groupn	A variable indicating whether the patron used a Groupon discount to enter the park	1 = Yes / 2 = No
SQ1	Employees at SPM offer high-quality service	5-point Likert (SD to SA)
SQ2	The attractions at SPM are high in quality	5-point Likert (SD to SA)
SQ3	The food quality at SPM is very good	5-point Likert (SD to SA)
SQ4	The service at SPM is excellent overall	5-point Likert (SD to SA)
SQ5	The quality of SPM is very good	5-point Likert (SD to SA)
VAL1	The time I spent at SPM was truly a joy	5-point Likert (SD to SA)
VAL2	I enjoyed being engaged in exciting activities during my visit to SPM	5-point Likert (SD to SA)
VAL3	While at SPM, I was able to forget my problems	5-point Likert (SD to SA)
VAL4	I think SPM offers guests a lot of value	5-point Likert (SD to SA)
PriceP	The admission price is very fair	5-point Likert (SD to SA)
	Use the terms below to describe your feelings about your overall experience at the museum:	
FEEL1	Favorable ------- Unfavorable	7-point Semantic Differential
FEEL2	Exciting ------- Boring	7-point Semantic Differential

FEEL3	Happy ------- Sad	7-point Semantic Differential
FEEL4	Delighted ------- Terrible	7-point Semantic Differential
UPGRADE	Whether respondent agreed to upgrade their ticket to a season pass	1=No / 2=Yes / 3= Undecided
Gender	Sex of respondent	1=Female / 2=Male
Age	Age group	1=less than 18 / 2= 19-24 / 3=25-35 / 4 = 36 - 45 / 5 = 46 or more
Others	How many others were with the patron	0=None / 1=1 / 2=2 / 3=3 / 4= more than 3

*Notes: Missing values in the data set are indicated by either an empty cell (sometimes with a . in the cell) or by the numeral 9. SPM stands for Swamp Place Museum, SD = Strongly Disagree (1) and SA = Strongly Agree (5).

Questions

1. Do frequencies on Gender, Others, and Age. Are any problems evident with coding? Take any necessary corrective actions.
2. Compute a composite scale for the five SQ items and the four VAL items. Compute a coefficient alpha for each of the resulting service quality and value scales.
3. Perform an appropriate test of each research question RQ1, RQ2, RQ3, RQ4, and RQ5.
4. List an additional research question that can be addressed with a one-way ANOVA. Conduct the test.
5. List an additional research question that can be addressed with a GLM model. Conduct the test.
6. Summarize the implications for the decision statements that arise from the tests above. Make sure you cover whether the park should invest in the navigation system and coupon technologies.

ENDNOTES

Chapter 1

1 Felten, E. (2010), "It's Better for Whose Environment?" *Wall Street Journal* (October 4), D12.Vranica, S. (2010), "Sun Chips Bag to Lose Its Crunch," *Wall Street Journal* (October 6), B8. Beer, J. (2010), "Breaking Down the Sun Chips Bag Story," *Marketing Magazine*, 115 (10/25), 6.

2 Zmuda, N. (2009), "Facebook Turns Focus Group with Splenda Product-Sampling App," *Advertising Age*, 80 (7/13), 18.

3 "U.S. Coffee Makers Perky as Consumption Increases," *Nations Restaurant Business*, 36 (April 22, 2002), 34; "U.S. Specialty Coffee Market in 30 Year Renaissance," http://www.cnn.com, December 15, 2000.

4 "Coffee: Demographics," in *The 2008 Beverage Market Research Handbook* (Loganville, GA: Richard K. Miller & Associates, 2008), 98–100.

5 http://www.starbucks.com/about-us/our-heritage, accessed January 23, 2011.

6 Wallace, B. (2010), "The World's Most Caffeinated Country," *Bloomberg Businessweek*, 4177 (May 3), 74.

7 Garvin, Andrew P., "Evolve Approach to Serve Complex Market," *Marketing News* (September 15, 2005), 22.

8 Gibson, Lawrence D., "Quo Vadis Marketing Research?" *Marketing Research*, 12 (Spring 2000), 36–41.

9 Matthew, A., "FDA Delays DTC Draft Guidance to Study How Consumers Use Brief Summaries," *Medical Marketing and Media*, 39 (November 2004), 10.

10 See, for example, Babin, Barry J., J. C. Chebat, and Richard Michon, "Perceived Appropriateness and its Effect on Quality, Affect and Behavior," *Journal of Retailing and Consumer Services*, 11 (September 2004), 287–98.

11 Ferrell, O. C., T. L. Gonzalez-Padron, T. Hult, and I. Maignan (2010), "From Market Orientation to Stakeholder Orientation," *Journal of Public Policy and Marketing*, 29 (Spring), 93–96; Sin, Leo Y. M., Alan C. B. Tse, Oliver H. M. Yau, Raymond P. M. Chow, Jenny S.Y. Lee, and Lorett B. Y. Lau, "Relationship Marketing Orientation: Scale Development and Cross-Cultural Validation," *Journal of Business Research*, 58 (February 2005), 185–94; Nakata, C., and K. Sivakumar, "Instituting the Marketing Concept in a Multinational Setting: The Role of National Culture," *Journal of the Academy of Marketing Science*, 29 (Summer 2001), 255–75; Day, G., "The Capabilities of Market-Driven Organizations," *Journal of Marketing*, 58 (October 1994), 37–52.

12 Gaudoin, T. (2011), "Luggage: An Open and Shut Case," *Wall Street Journal*, (January 28), C12.

13 Stoll, J. D., "GM Weighs More Layoffs, Sale of Brands," *Wall Street Journal* (July 7, 2008), A1. Mitchell, J. (2010), "U.S. Investigates Saturn Steering Reports," *Wall Street Journal*, (December 16), A10.

14 Lee, Ruby P., Gillian Naylor ,and Qimei Chen (2011), "Linking Customer Resrouces to Firm Success: The Role of Marketing Program Implementation," *Journal of Business Research*, 64 (April), 394–400; Sin, Leo Y. M., Alan C. B. Tse, Oliver H. M.Yau, Raymond P. M. Chow, Jenny S.Y. Lee, and Lorett B.Y. Lau, "Relationship Marketing Orientation: Scale Development and Cross-Cultural Validation," *Journal of Business Research*, 58 (February 2005), 185–94; Nakata, C., and K. Sivakumar, "Instituting the Marketing Concept in a Multinational Setting: The Role of National Culture," *Journal of the Academy of Marketing Science*, 29 (Summer 2001), 255–75; Ward, James C., M. D. Hutt, and Peter H. Reingen, "Evolving Patterns of Organizational Beliefs in the Formation of Strategy," *Journal of Marketing*, 58 (April 1994), 96–110.

15 *Professional Builder*, "David Weekley Homes Reign in Fort Worth Market," 69 (December, 2004), 31–34.

16 *USA Today* (2010), "Not Even in NFL yet, Tim Tebow: Already a Marketing Trendsetter," (April 19), C11.

17 Bojanic, D. C. (2011), "The Impact of Age and Family Life Experiences on Mexican Visitor Shopping Expenditures," *Tourism Management*, 32 (April), 405–14.

18 Wyner, Gordon A., "Biz Problems Can Get Solved With Research," *Marketing News* (September 15, 2005), 33–34.

19 Kesmodel, D., and D.Yadron (2010), "E-Cigarettes Spark New Smoking War," *Wall Street Journal* (August 25), A1–A12.

20 See Allenby, Greg M., Thomas S. Shively,Yang Sha, and Mark J. Garratt, "A Choice Model for Packaged Goods: Dealing with Discrete Quantities and Quantity Discounts," *Marketing Science*, 23 (Winter 2004), 14–21.

21 Ofir, Chezy, "Reexamining Latitude of Price Acceptability and Price Thresholds: Predicting Basic Consumer Reaction to Price," *Journal of Consumer Research*, 30 (March 2004), 612–21.

22 Bonamici, Kate, "Big-Foot Dips Toe in Coffee," *Fortune*, 149 (January 26, 2004), 70.

23 Syam, S., and A. Bhatnagar (2010), "A Decision Model for E-commerce-enabled Partial Market Exit," *Journal of Retailing*, 86 (December), 401–13.

24 Ulin, J. (2010), "Internet Distribution, Downloads and On-demand Streaming—A New Paradigm," *The Business of Media Distribution*, 292–341.

25 Gardyn, Rebecca, "Same Name, New Number: AT&T's Brand Image Gets a Needed Boost from a Well-Rounded Hero," *American Demographics* (March 2001), 56.

26 Schneider, Lars-Peter, and Bettina T. Cornwell, "Cashing in on Crashes via Brand Placement in Computer Games," *International Journal of Advertising*, 24, no. 3 (2005), 321–42.

27 Low, George S., "Correlates of Integrated Marketing Communications," *Journal of Advertising Research* (May 2000).

28 Hein, Kenneth, "Best Buy Calls the 'Odd' Squad: Group of Tech 'Geeks' Gets Spotlight in National Branding Spot," *Brandweek*, 45 (October 18, 2004), 11; *DSN Retailing Today*, "Best Buy Turns On the Geek Appeal. (CE & Entertainment)," 42 (February 24, 2004), 22.

29 Garretson, Judith, and Scot Burton, "The Role of Spokescharacters as Advertisement and Package Cues in Integrated Marketing Communications," *Journal of Marketing*, 69 (October, 2005), 118–32.

30 Li, L.Y. (2011), "Marketing Metrics' Usage: Its Predictors and Implications of Customer Relationship Management," *Industrial Marketing Management*, 40 (January), 139–48.

31 Roberts, W. A. (2009), "Making a Mint," *Prepared Foods*, 178 (October), 37–40.

32 *Express Magazine*, "You Say Tomato, I say Tomahto," (Spring 2006), 19.

Chapter 2

1 Granados, N., A. Gupta, and R. J. Kauffman (2008), "Designing Online Selling Mechanisms: Transparency Levels and Prices," *Decision Support Systems* (November), 729–45; Beirne, M., "Southwest Airlines Delivers Fare Offers with DING!" *Brandweek* (2006), www.brandweek.com/bw/news/recent_cisplay-jsp?vnu_content_id=1002765480, accessed June 16, 2008; McCarthy, S. (2010), "Better Odds of Getting Your Bags," *Wall Street Journal* (December 2), D1–D7.

2 Koening, M., and J. Meisnner (2010), "List Pricing versus Dynamic Pricing: Impact on Revenue Risk," *European Journal of Operations Research*, 204 (August), 505–12.

3 McCartney, S. (2011), "Whatever You Do, Don't Buy an Airline Ticket On …." *Wall Street Journal* (July 27), D1–D5.

4 Steel, E., and G. A. Fowler (2010), "Facebook Touts Selling Power of Friendship," *Wall Street Journal* (July 7), B1.

5 "SAS helps ImpactRX Provide Real Time Marketing Intelligence to Pharma Companies," *Business Wire* (March 17, 2008), retrieved July 14, 2008, from ABI/INFORM Dateline database (document ID: 1447327611).

6 Modern Materials Handling (2009), "Bringing Plants and Purchases Closer Together," 64 (October), 40.

7 Baraniuk, R. B. (2011), "More is Less: Signal Processing and the Data Deluge," *Science*, 331 (February), 717–18.

8 Smith, D. G., and D. Strutton (2010), "Has e-Marketing come of Age? "Modeling Historical Influences on Post-Adoption Era Consumer Internet Behaviors," *Journal of Business Research*, 63 (October), 950–56.

9 Cited in Bernoff, J. (2009), "Be Smart about Customer Intelligence," *Marketing News*, 43 (November 30), 12.

10 Evan, A., G. Shankaranarayanan, and P.B. Berger (2010), "Managing the Quality of Marketing Data: Cost/Benefit Tradeoffs and Optimal Configuration," *Journal of Interactive Marketing*, 24 (August), 209–21.

11 Zhou, K. Z., and C. B. Li (2010), "How Strategic Orientations Influence the Building of Dynamic Capability in Emerging Markets," *Journal of Business Research*, 63 (March), 224–31.

12 Fergueson, R. B. (2004), "Marines Deploy RFID," *e-Week*, 21 (November), 37; "Benefits of RFID Becoming More Visible," *DSN Retailing Today* (August 8, 2005), 22.

13 Fielding, M. (2010), "C'est Délicieux," *Marketing News*, 44 (September 5), 6.

14 Ante, S. E. (2011), "Billboards Join Wired Age," *Wall Street Journal*, (February 4), B10.

15 Steel, E. (2010), "Some Data-Miners Ready to Reveal What They Know," *Wall Street Journal*, (December 3), B1–B2.

16 Rigby, D., and C. Zook (2002), "Open-Market Innovation," *Harvard Business Review* (October), 80–89.

17 http://internetworldstats.com, accessed February 9, 2011.

18 "A Better Web Through Higher Math," http://www.businessweek.com, accessed November 12, 2005.

19 Efrati, A. (2011), "Google Says Being Cheated," *Wall Street Journal* (February 2), A1.

20 Gallagher, D. (2010), "Is Your Videogame Machine Watching You?" *Wall Street Journal*, (November 11), 8.

21 Gabriel, A. R. (2010), "Building Relationships," *Wall Street & Technology*, 28 (December), 16–17; Lamont, J. (2010), "Real-time Fraud Measures," *KMWorld*, 19 (Jul/Aug), 12–21.

22 Troung, A. (2011), "Social Media Week Checks Into Hong Kong," *Wall Street Journal* (February 9),

23 Hill, K. (2011), "Whac-A-Mole," *Forbes*, 187 (1/17), 36; Vascellaro, J. E. (2010), "Suit to Snuff Out 'History Sniffing' Takes Aim at Tracking Web Users," *Wall Street Journal*, (December 6), B1–B2.

24 Schurer, L. A. E. (2011), "Secret Texting…Pass It On," *Wall Street Journal* (February 4), B11.

25 Steel (2010).

Chapter 3

1 Haytko, D., "Message from the Guest Editor," *Marketing Education Review*, 18 (Spring 2008), 1; Anwar, A., M. Al-Shami, and S. A. Ahmed, "Developing a Market-Oriented MBA Program: Practitioners' Views from GCC Countries," *Journal of International Marketing & Marketing Research*, 31 (October 2006), 129–39.

2 Krakovsky, M. (2010), "Degrees, Distance, and Dollars," *Communications of the ACM*, 53 (September), 18–19.

3 Cited in Conant, J. (2008), *The Irregulars*, Simon & Schuster: New York.

4 Zahay, Debra, Abbie Griffin, and Elisa Fredericks (2004), "Sources, Uses, and Forms of Data in the New Product Development Process," *Industrial Marketing Management*, 33 (October), 658–66.

5 Hara, Yoshika (2002), "New Industry Awaits Human-Friendly Bipeds—'Personal Robots' Get Ready to Walk on the Human Side," *Electronic Engineering Times* (September 16), 157–59.

6 Bocchi, Joe, Jacqueline K. Eastman, and Cathy Owens Swift (2004), "Retaining the Online Learner: Profile of Students in an Online MBA Program and Implications for Teaching Them," *Journal of Education for Business* (March/April 2004), 245–253.

7 Data Monitor (2010), "Global-Organic Food Industry Profile (Chapter 7)," *Datamonitor*, RC 199–853, 8–25.

8 *RFF Retailer* (2008), "What's the Deal with Whole Foods?" (August 12), 12.

9 Bocchi, Eastman, and Swift (2004); Carr, S., "As Distance Education Comes of Age, the Challenge is Keeping the Students," *Chronicle of Higher Education* (2000) 23, A1.; Moskal and Dziuban, "Present and Future Directions for Assessing Cybereducation: The Changing Research Paradigm," in L. R. Vandervert, L.V. Chavinina, and R. A. Cornell, Eds., *Cybereducation: The Future of Long-Distance Learning* (2001), New York: P. D. Moskal and C. G. Dziuban, Liebert, 157–184.

10 Hamilton, R., and A. Chernov (2010), "The Impact of Product Line Extensions and Consumer Goals on the Formation of Price Image," *Journal of Marketing Research*, 47 (February), 51–62.

11 Thomas, Jerry W. (2005), "Skipping MR a Major Error," *Marketing News*, (March 4), 50.

12 Kolb, B. (2008), "The Marketing Research Process," Marketing Research for Nonprofit, Community and Creative Organizations, 21–41.

13 A. Einstein and L. Infeld, *The Evolution of Physics* (New York: Simon and Schuster, 1942), p. 95.

14 See Bhardwaj, S., I. Palaparthy, and A. Agrawal, "Exploration of Environmental Dimensions of Servicescapes: A Literature Review," *The Icfai Journal of Marketing Management*, 7, no. 1 (2008), 37–48 for a relevant literature review.

15 Perdue, B. C., and J. O. Summers, "Checking the Success of Manipulations in Marketing Experiments," *Journal of Marketing Research*, 23 (November 1986), 317–26.

16 See, for example, Kwok, S., and M. Uncles, "Sales Promotion Effectiveness: The Impact of Consumer Differences at an Ethnic-Group Level," *Journal of Product and Brand Management*, 14, no. 3 (2005), 170–86.

17 Babin, B. J., D. M. Hardesty, and T. A. Suter (2003), "Color and Shopping Intentions: The Effect of Price Fairness and Perceived Affect," *Journal of Business Research*, 56 (July), 541–51.

18 See Hauser, J., O. Toubie, T. Evgeniou, R. Befurt, and D. Dzyabura (2010), "Disjunctions of Conjunctions: Cognitive Simplicity and Consideration Sets," *Journal of Marketing Research*, 47 (June), 485–496 for a study demonstrating how consumers use simplifying approaches in making important decisions.

Chapter 4

1 Sources: Aldhous, P. and P. McKenna (2010), "Hey Green Spender, Spend a Buck on Me," *New Scientist*, 205 (February 20), 6–9. Veal, G. J. and S. Mouzas (2011), "Changes the Rules of the Game: Business Responses to New Regulation," *Industrial Marketing Management*, 40 (February), 290–300. Pandol, C. A., "The Issue with Green Marketing: Is Green a Good Idea," http://www.usc.edu/org/InsightBusiness/ib/articles/articlescontent/08_4_Cristina%20 Pandol.html, accessed March 6, 2011.

2 Vasishhtha, P. (2010), "Y Worry?" *Advisor Today*, 105 (March), 26–27. Lanzoni, G., and N. Marcus (2004), "Seeking Market Research/Competitive Intelligence," *LIMRA's Market Facts Quarterly*, 23(1), 20–23.

3 http://nielsen.com/content/corporate/global/en.html, accessed March 9, 2011.

4 Jdpower.com, accessed March 9, 2011.

5 Data taken from Honomichl, J. (2010), "Global Top 25: 2010 Honomichl Report," *Marketing News*, (August 30), 16.

6 Russell-Bennett, R., J. R. McColl-Kennedy, and L.V. Coote (2007), "Involvement, Satisfaction, and Brand Loyalty in a Small Business Services Setting," *Journal of Business Research*, 60 (December), 1253–62.

7 Kinnear, Thomas C., and Ann Root, eds., *Survey of Marketing Research* (Chicago: American Marketing Association, 1994).

8 See Izzo, G. Martin, and Scott J. Vitell, "Exploring the Effects of Professional Education on Salespeople: The Case of Autonomous Agents," *Journal of Marketing Theory & Practice*, 11 (Fall 2003), 26–38; Loe, Terry, and William A. Weeks, "An Empirical Investigation of Efforts to Improve Sales Students' Moral Reasoning," Journal *of Personal Selling and Sales Management*, 20 (Fall 2000), 243–52; Michaelides, P., and P. Gibbs (2006), "Technological Skills and the Ethics of Marketing Research," *Business Ethics: A European Review*, 15 (January), 44–52.

9 Barnett, Tim, and Sean Valentino, "Issue Contingencies and Marketers' Recognition of Ethical Issues, Ethical Judgments and Behavioral Intentions," *Journal of Business Research*, 57 (April 2004), 338–46.

10 Robin, D. P., R. E. Reidenbach, and B. J. Babin, "The Nature,

Measurement and Stability of Ethical Judgements in the Workplace," *Psychological Reports*, 80 (1997), 563–80.

11 Michaelides and Gibbs (2006).

12 A firm that conducts surveys and is not involved in selling or telemarketing is generally considered exempt from federal do not call legislation. For more on the do-not-call legislation, see www.donotcall.gov.

13 Gillin, Donna L., "The Evolution of Privacy Legislation: How Privacy Issues Are Changing Research," *Marketing Research*, 13 (Winter 2001), 6–7.

14 Jarvis, Steve, "CMOR Finds Survey Refusal Rate Still Rising," *Marketing News*, 36 (February 4, 2002), 4.

15 Gillin, Donna (2001).

16 Kozinets, R.V. (2002), "The Field Behind the Screen: Using Netnography for Marketing Research in Online Communities," *Journal of Marketing Research*, 39 (February), 61–72.

17 Ahuja, R. D., M. Walker, and R. Tadepalli, "Paternalism, Limited Paternalism and the Pontius Pilate Plight When Researching Children," *Journal of Business Ethics*, 32 (July 2001), 81–92; Clegg, A., "Out of the Mouths of Babes," *Marketing Week* (June 23, 2005), 43.

18 Spangenberg, E., B. Grohmann, and D. E. Sprott, "It's Beginning to Smell (and Sound) a Lot Like Christmas: The Interactive Effects of Ambient Scent and Music in a Retail Setting," *The Journal of Business Research*, 58 (November 2005), 582–89; Michon, Richard, Jean-Charles Chebat, and L. W. Turley, "Mall Atmospherics: The Interaction Effects of the Mall Environment on Shopping Behavior," *Journal of Business Research*, 58 (May 2005), 576–83.

19 Hein, K. (2008), "Marketers Use Hypnosis to Mine Deep Thoughts," Adweek, 49 (March 24), 4.

20 Akaah, I.P., and E.A. Riordan (1990), "The Incidence of Unethical Practice in Marketing Research: An Empirical Investigation," *Journal of the Academy of Marketing Sciences*, 90 (Spring), 143–52.

21 Carrigan, M., and M. Kirkup, "The Ethical Responsibilities of Marketers in Retail Observational Research: Protecting Stakeholders through the 'Ethical Research' Covenant," *International Journal of Retail, Distribution and Consumer Research*, 11 (October 2001), 411–35.

22 Robinson, K. (2009), "Wal-Mart Push Polls Chicago, Claims 74% Support for New Store," *Chicago Sun Times*, (July 29), http://chicagoist.com/2009/07/29/is_wal-mart_push_polling_chicago.php, accessed March 13, 2011.

23 Brennan, M., S. Benson, and Z. Kearns (2005), "The Effect of Introductions on Telephone Survey Participation Rates," *International Journal of Market Research*, 47(1), 65–74.

24 *Marketing News* (1995), "Marketers Value Honesty in Marketing Researchers," 29 (June 5), 27.

Chapter 5

1 Sayre, Shay (2001), *Qualitative Methods for Marketplace Research* (Sage: Thousand Oaks, CA).

2 Entertainment Newsweekly, "Electronic Arts Inc.; EA Brings Entries' Fifth Annual Goofy versus Regular Skateboarding Competition to Skate," (September 26, 2008), 181; Montgomery, T., "Vans' Second Life," *OC Metro*, (October 11, 2007), 24.

3 Schawbel, D. (2010), "Three Steps to Establishing an Entreprenur Brand," *Businessweek.com*, (December 13), 5.

4 Carofano, J. (2007), "Skate High," *Footwear News*, 63 (January 29), 116–17.

5 Sayre, Shay (2001); Morse, Janice M., and Lyn Richards (2002), *Readme First for a User's Guide to Qualitative Methods* (Sage: Thousand Oaks, CA).

6 See, for example, May, Carl (2005), "Methodological Pluralism: British Sociology and the Evidence-Based State: A Reply to Payne et al.," *Sociology*, 39 (July), 519–28; Achenbaum, A. A. (2001), "When Good Research Goes Bad," *Marketing Research*, 13 (Winter), 13–15; Wade, K. R. (2002), "We Have Come Upon the Enemy: And They are Us," *Marketing Research*, 14 (Summer), 39.

7 Babin, Barry J., William R. Darden, and Mitch Griffin, "Work and/or Fun: Measuring Hedonic and Utilitarian Shopping Value," *Journal of Consumer Research*, 20 (March 1994), 644–56.

8 Semon, Thomas T. (2002), "You Get What You Pay For: It May be Bad MR," *Marketing News*, 36 (April 15), 7.

9 Hamel, G., and C. K. Prahalad, "Corporate Imagination and Expeditionary Marketing," *Harvard Business Review* (July–August 1991), 85.

10 Martens, Claire (2004), "Sometimes a Great Notion Isn't Yet a Great Product," *Harvard Management Update* (March), 3–4.

11 Thompson, Craig J. (1997), "Interpreting Consumers: A Hermeneutical Framework for Deriving Marketing Insights from the Tests of Consumers' Consumption Stories," *Journal of Marketing Research*, 34 (November), 438–55 (see pp. 443–44 for quotation).

12 Thompson (1997)

13 Although we refer to a hermeneutic unit as being text-based here for simplicity, they can actually also be developed using pictures, videotapes, or artifacts as well. Software such as ATLAS.ti will allow files containing pictures, videos, and text to be combined into a hermeneutic unit.

14 Rubinson, J. (2010), "Marketers, Researchers, Lend Me Your Ears," *Brandweek*, 51 (February 15), 34.

15 Morse, Janice M., and Lyn Richards (2002).

16 Winsome, S. J., and P. Johnson (2000), "The Pros and Cons of Data Analysis Software for Qualitative Research," *Journal of Nursing Scholarship*, 32(4), 393–97.

17 See Feldman, Stephen P., "Playing with the Pieces: Deconstruction and the Loss of Moral Culture," *Journal of Management Studies*, 35 (January 1998), 59–79.

18 Louella, Miles (2003), "Living their Lives," *Marketing* (UK) (December 11), 27–28.

19 Reid, D. M., "Changes in Japan's Post-Bubble Business Environment: Implications for Foreign-Affiliated Companies," *Journal of International Marketing*, 7, no. 3 (1999), 38–63.

20 Silber, I., A. Israeli, A. Bustin, and O.B. Zyi (2009), "Recover Strategies for Service Failures: The Case of Restaurants," *Journal of Hospitality Marketing & Management*, 18 (July), 730–41.

21 Strauss, A. L., and J. Corbin, *Basics of Qualitative Research* (Sage Publications: Newbury Park, CA, 1990).

22 Geiger, S., and D. Turley, "Personal Selling as a Knowledge-Based Activity: Communities of Practice in the Sales Force," *Irish Journal of Management*, 26 (2005), 61–70.

23 Beverland, M., "The Components of Prestige Brands," *Journal of Business Research*, 59 (February 2006), 251–58; Beverland, M., and F.J. Farrelly (2010), "The Quest for Authenticity in Consumption: Consumers' Purposive Choices of Authentic Cues to Shape Experienced Outcomes," *Journal of Consumer Research*, 36 (February), 838–56.

24 Harwood, Jonathan (2005), "Philip Morris Develops Smokeless Cigarette," *Marketing Week*, 28 (March 31), 5.

25 Woodyard, C. (2010), "Buick Wants to Know How They Really Feel," *USA Today*, (July 20), 3B.

26 See Palan, K. M., and R. E. Wilkes, "Adolescent-Parent Interaction in Family Decision Making," *Journal of Consumer Research*, 24 (September 1997), 159–70; Haytko, Diana L., and Julie Baker, "It's All at the Mall: Exploring Adolescent Girls' Experiences," *Journal of Retailing*, 80 (Spring 2004), 67–83.

27 Godes, David, and Dina Mayzlin (2004), "Using On-Line Conversations to Study Word-of-Mouth Communications," *Marketing Science*, 23, 545–60.

28 Babin, Barry J., William R. Darden, and James S. Boles (1995), "Salesperson Stereotypes, Consumer Emotions, and Their Impact on Information Processing," *Journal of the Academy of Marketing Science*, 23 (Spring), 94–105.

29 Murphy, Ian (1996), "Aided by Research, Harley Goes Whole Hog," *Marketing News*, 30 (December 2), 16–17.

30 Boddy, C. (2005), "A Look at the Evidence for the Usefulness, Reliability and Validity of Projective Techniques in Marketing Research," *International Journal of Marketing Research*, 47(3), 239–54.

31 Boddy (2005).

32 Heather, R. P. (1994), "Future Focus Groups," *American Demographics* (January 1), 6.

33 Arnold, M. (2010), "Sermo Offers On-Demand Physician Focus Groups," *Medical Marketing & Media*, 44 (November), 28.

34 Creamer, Mathew (2005), "Slowly, Marketers Learn How to Let Go and Let Blog," *Advertising Age*, 76 (October 31), 1–35.

35 Fass, Allison (2005), "Collective Opinion," *Forbes*, 176 (November 28), 76–79.

36 Godes, David, and Dina Mayzlin (2004), "Using On-Line Conversations to Study Word-of-Mouth Communications," *Marketing Science*, 23, 545–60.

37 Mayo-Smith, D. (2010), "Could You Retweet that Please?" *NZ Business*, 24 (March), 54.

38 Casteleyn et al. (2008).

39 Kozinets, R. (2002), "The Field Behind the Screen: Using Netnography for Marketing Research in Online Communities," *Journal of Marketing Research*, 39 (February), 61–72.

40 Smith, A., R. Bolton, and J. Wagner, "A Model of Customer Satisfaction with Service Encounters Involving Failure and Recovery," *Journal of Marketing Research*, 36 (August 1999), 356–72; Bolton, R., and T. M. Bronkhorst, "Quantitative Analysis of Depth Interviews," *Psychology & Marketing*, 8 (Winter 1991), 275–97.

41 Wooliscroft, B., R. D. Tamilia, and S. J. Shapiro (2006), *A Twenty-First Century Guide to Aldersonian Marketing Thought* (Springer, New York, NY).

42 Klahr, S. (2000), "Getting' Buggy With It," *Advertising Age's Creativity*, 8 (May), 9.

Chapter 6

1 "Licensed to Snoop," *Human Resources* (June 2008), 57–58; Marks, P., "Pentagon Sets Its Sights on Social Networking Websites," *New Scientist* (June 9, 2006), http://www.newscientist.com/article/mg19025556.200, accessed August 6, 2008; Lowry, Tom, "Obama's Secret Weapon," *BusinessWeek* (July 7, 2008), 56–57.

2 Aggarwal, S.C. (2008), "Child Labour in India: Magnitude, Trends and Distribution," *International Journal of Employment Studies*, 16 (October), 1–30.

3 Bachman, K. (2007), "Arbitron, Nielsen Face Off in Out of Home TV Ratings," *Mediaweek*, 17 (August 6), 6.

4 http://www.npd.com/corpServlet?nextpage=food-beverage-national-eating-trends_s.html, accessed April 2, 2011.

5 Grow, Brian, "Yes, Ma'am, That Part Is in Stock," *BusinessWeek*, (August 1, 2005), p. 32; "Servigistics Pricing: Maximizing the Profitability of Your Service Network," Servigistics, http://www.servigistics.com, accessed February 7, 2006.

6 Prasso, Sheridan, "Battle for the Face of China," *Fortune*, 152 (December 12, 2005), p. 156–61.

7 Charles, Susan K., "Custom Content Delivery," Online, (March–April 2004), p. 24–29; Fleming, Lee, "Digital Delivery: Pushing Content to the Desktop," *Digital Information Group* (January 31, 1997), p. 7.

8 Weltz, S. (2010), "Back to the Future: Why Push Technologies and Search are about to Explode," *Venture Beat*, http://venturebeat.com/2010/07/26/back-to-the-future-why-push-technologies-and-search-are-about-to-explode/, accessed April 2, 2011.

9 https://www.cia.gov/library/publications/the-world-factbook/geos/ez.html, accessed April 2, 2011.

10 "Seeking New Beer Drinkers in the High Andes," Global Agenda, (September 6, 2005), p. 1; and "China Ranked Largest Beer Consumer in 2004," *Kyodo News International* (December 15, 2005); Knight Ridder Tribune Business News, p. 1; Switzer, T. (2011), "No Beer, Please – We're Ozzis," *Maclean's*, 124 (2/7), 40. Additional Exhibit Sources: https://www.cia.gov/library/publications/the-world-factbook/index.html, accessed April 4, 2010. www.just-drinks.com, accessed April 4, 2011.

11 This section is based on Levy, Michael and Barton Weitz, *Retail Management* (Homewood, IL: Richard D. Irwin, 1992), pp. 357–58.

12 For illustrations, see Mesak, H., A. Bari, B. J. Babin, L. Birou, and A. Jurkus (2011), ""Optimum Advertising Policy Over Time for Subscriber Service Innovations in the Presence of Service Cost Learning and Customers' Disadoption," *European Journal of Operations Research*, 211 (June), 642–49.: Puneet, M., J.P. Dube', K.Y. Goh, and P.K. Chintagunta (2006), "The Effect of Banner Advertising on Internet Purchasing, Journal of Marketing Research, 43 (February), 98–108.

13 See Hanna, R., A. Rohm, and V. Crittenden (2011), "We're All Connected: The Power of Social Media Ecosystem," *Journal of Interactive Marketing*, 1–9.

14 Rao, Srikumar S. (1996), "The Hot Zone," *Forbes* (November 18), 8.

15 Mehta, N. (2007), "Investigating Consumers' Purchase Incidence and Brand Choice Decisions Across Multiple Product Categories: A Theoretical and Empirical Analysis," *Marketing Science*, 26 (Mar/Apr), 457–79.

16 *Wall Street Journal* (2011), "Macy's Catalogs Shoppers' Habits," (March 23), B5.

17 Totty, Michael (2005), "Making Searches Work at Work," *Wall Street Journal* (December 19), http://online.wsj.com, accessed February 10, 2006.

18 Weiss, A. M., N. H. Lurie, and D. J. MacInnis (2008), "Listening to Strangers: Whose Responses Are Valuable, How Valuable Are They, and Why?" *Journal of Marketing Research*, 45 (August), 425–36.

19 Based on 2008 data—the latest available as of this writing.

20 "Hispanic-Owned Businesses: Growth Projections, 2004–2010," *HispanicBusiness.com Store*, http://www.hbinc.com, accessed April 7, 2011.

21 http://money.cnn.com/magazines/fortune/fortune500/2010/full_list/, accessed April 6, 2011.

22 Neff, Jack (2001), "Wal-Mart Takes Stock in RetailLink System," *Advertising Age*, (May 21), p. 6.

23 Harris Interactive (2011), "Recent Crisis in Japan has had Little Impact on Americans' Views of Nuclear Power: Poll," http://www.harrisinteractive.com/NewsRoom/PressReleases/tabid/446/mid/1506/articleId/744/ctl/ReadCustom%20Default/Default.aspx, accessed April 6, 2011.

24 See Federal Grants Wire, "National Trade Data Bank (NTDB)," http://www.federalgrantswire.com, accessed April 6, 2011.

Chapter 7

1 Swientek, B (2003), "Using Consumer Insights to Guide Package Design: Traditional Research Can Give You Answers. But…" *Brand Packaging* (March 1), accessed at www.interbrand.com, June 30, 2008.

2 Vascellaro, Jessica E. (2005), "Who'll Give Me $50 for This Purse from Nana?" *Wall Street Journal* (December 28), D1–D2.

3 Brown, M.R., R.K. Bhadury, and N.K. Pope (2010), "The Impact of Comedic Violence on Viral Advertising Effectiveness," *Journal of Advertising*, 39 (Spring), 49–65.

4 Exhibit revised with assistance of Christo Boshoff, Stellenbosh University.

5 Cull, William L., Karen G. O'Connor, Sanford Sharp, and Suk-fong S. Tang (2005), "Response Rates and Response Bias for 50 Surveys of Pediatricians," *Health Services Research*, 40 (February), 213.

6 Lee, Eunkyu, Michael Y. Hu, and Rex S. Toh (2004), "Respondent

Noncooperation in Surveys and Diaries: An Analysis of Item Non-response and Panel Attrition," *International Journal of Market Research*, 46 (Autumn 2004), 311.

7 Douglas Aircraft (undated), Consumer Research, p. 13.

8 For an interesting study of extremity bias, see Baumgartner, Hans and Jan-Benedict E. M. Steenkamp (2001), "Response Styles in Marketing Research: A Cross-National Investigation," *Journal of Marketing Research* (May), 143–56.

9 Raven, G. (2008), "Major Holocaust Polls Show Built-In Bias," *Journal of Historical Review*, 15, no. 1, accessed at http://www.ihr.org/jhr/v15/v15n1p25_Raven.html, April 18, 2011.

10 Network World (2009), "Goodbadugly," [NOTE – WRITTEN AS ONE WORD] 26 (December 21), 5.

11 Wasserman, Todd, Gerry Khermouch and Jeff Green (2000), "Mining Everyone's Business," *BrandWeek* (February 28), 34.

12 Hof, Robert D. (2005), "The Power of Us," *BusinessWeek* (June 20), 74–82.

13 Hernandes, Sigfredo A. and Carol J. Kaufman (1990), "Marketing Research in Hispanic Barrios: A Guide to Survey Research," *Marketing Research* (March), 11–27.

14 Vicente, P. and E. Reis (2010), "Who is Missing from Mobile Phone Surveys? An Analysis of European Countries," *International Journal of Marketing Management*, 5 (Summer), 15(2000), 26; www.marketingcharts.com, accessed April 22, 2011.

15 Asia Pulse (2011), "China's Mobile Phone Penetration Reaches 64.4% in 2010," (February 14), 1, ProQuest DOI 852745352, indicates 859 million Chinese with mobile phones at the end of 2010.

16 Business Middle East (2010), Database:telecommunications (September), 12.

17 Brick, J. M., P. D. Brick, S. Dipko, S. Presser, C. Tucker, and Y. Yuan (2007), "Cell Phone Survey Feasibility in the U.S.: Sampling and Calling Cell Numbers Versus Landline Numbers," *Public Opinion Quarterly*, 71 (Spring), 23–39.

18 Vicente and Reis (2010); Vicente, P.E. Reis and M. Santos (2009), "Using Mobile Phones for Survey Research," *International Journal of Marketing Research*, 51 (5), 613–33.

19 Curtin, Richard, Stanley Presser, and Eleanor Singer (2005), "Changes in Telephone Survey Nonresponse over the Past Quarter Century," *Public Opinion Quarterly* (Spring), 69 (1), 87–95.

20 Cuneo, Alice Z. (2004), "Researchers Flail as Public Cuts the Cord," *Advertising Age* (November 15), 3–52.

21 Callegaro, M., H.L. McCutheon, and J. Ludwig (2010), "Who's

Calling? The Impact of Caller ID on Telephone Survey Response," *Field Methods*, 22 (May 12), 175–91.

22 Hembroff, Larry A. Debra Rusz, Ann Rafferty, Harry McGee, and Nathaniel Ehrlich (2005), "The Cost-Effectiveness of Alternative Advance Mailings in a Telephone Survey," *Public Opinion Quarterly*, 69 (Summer), 232–45.

23 Brennan, Mike, Susan Benson, and Zane Kearns (2005), "The Effect of Introductions on Telephone Survey Participation Rates," *International Journal of Market Research*, 47, (1), 65–74.

24 Roster, C.A., R.D. Rogers, and G. Albaum (2007), "A Comparison of Response Characteristics from Web and Telephone Surveys," *International Journal of Marketing Research*, 46 (Fall), 359–73; Albaum, G., C.A. Roster, J. Wiley, J. Rossiter, and S.M. Smith (2010), "Designing Web Surveys in Marketing Research: Does Use of Forced Answering Affect Completion Rates?" *Journal of Marketing Theory and Practice*, 18 (Summer), 285–93; Ocal, Yasmine (2011), "Reponse Rates in Major Marketing Journals: Analysis and Commentary," presentation at AMS World Marketing Congress, July 20, Reims, France.

25 Göritz, Anja S. (2004), "Recruitment for On-Line Access Panels," *International Journal of Market Research*, 46 (4), 411–25.

26 Shih, T.H. and S. Fan (2009), "Comparing Response Rates in E-mail and Paper Surveys: A Meta-Analysis," *Educational Research Review*, 4, 26–40.

27 Fricker, Scott, Mirta Galesic, Roger Tourangeau, and Ting Yan (2005), "An Experimental Comparison of Web and Telephone Surveys," *Public Opinion Quarterly*, 69 (Fall), 370–92.

28 Albaum et al. (2010).

29 Porter, P. R. and M. E. Whitcomb (2007), "Mixed-Mode Contacts in Internet Surveys: Paper Is Not Necessarily Better," *Public Opinion Quarterly*, 71 (Winter), 635–48.

30 Gruen, T., T. Osmonbekov, and A. J. Czaplewski (2006), "eWOM: The Impact of Customer-to-Customer Online Know-How Exchange on Customer Value and Loyalty," *Journal of Business Research*, 59 (April), 449–56.

31 Shih and Fan (2009).

32 Ocal and Babin (2011).

33 Braunsberger, K., H. Wybenga, and R. Gates (2007), "A Comparison of Reliability between Telephone and Web-Based Surveys," *Journal of Business Research*, 60 (July), 758–64.

Chapter 8

1 Based on Thomas Mucha (2005), "This Is Your Brain on Advertising," *Business 2.0* (August 2005), 8 (August), 47–49; Peter Laybourne

and David Lewis, "Neuromarketing: The Future of Consumer Research?" *Admap* (May), pp. 28–30.

2 Dumas, A. (2007), "The Limits of Market Research Methods," Advertising Age, 78 (October 18), 27.

3 Abrams, Bill, *The Observational Research Handbook* (Chicago: NTC Business Books, 2000), pp. 2, 105.

4 Redmond, E. C. and C. J. Griffith (2003), "A Comparison and Evaluation of Research Methods Used in Consumer Food Safety Studies," *International Journal of Consumer Studies*, 27 (January), 17–33.

5 Phillips, A. (2011), "Researchers, Snoppers and Spies—The Legal and Ethical Challenges Facing Observational Research," *International Journal of Marketing Research*, 52 (2), 275–78.

6 Phillips (2011).

7 Judah, G., R. Aunger, W.P. Schmidt, S. Michie, S. Granger, and V. Curtis (2011), "Experimental Pretesting of Hand-Washing," *American Journal of Public Health*, 99 (September 2), S405–411.

8 "About Nielsen Media Research," Nielsen Media Research, http://www.nielsenmedia.com, accessed February 24, 2006.

9 "The Portable People Meter System," Arbitron, http://www.arbitron.com, accessed December 17, 2008.

10 "About the PreTesting Company" and "Television," PreTesting Company, http://www.pretesting.com, accessed February 24, 2006.

11 Conley, Lucas (2005), "At 1600 Pennsylvania Avenue, Of Course, It's 'Rush Limbaugh,' " *Fast Company* (February), 91, 29; Dina ElBoghdady (2004), "Advertisers Tune In to New Radio Gauge," *Washington Post* (October 25, 2004), http://www.washingtonpost.com; "iBiquity and Mobiltrak: Bringing Radio into the Digital Age," Bear Stearns Equity Research, February 8, 2005, http://www.bearstearns.com.

12 Hampp, A. (2010), "Can Paramount Stir Up Some Buzz for Paranormal Sequel?" *Advertising Age*, 81 (Oct. 18), 6.

13 Walmsley, A. (2010), "A Lot of Buzz About Nothing," *Marketing* (November 24), 12.

14 Kiley, David (2006), "Google: Searching for an Edge in Ads," *BusinessWeek* (January 30), 80–82. infotrac.galegroup.com. See also Pieter Sanders and Bram Lebo, "Click Tracking: A Fool's Paradise?" *Brandweek* 46 (June 6, 2005), 46; Klaassen, A., M. Creamer, A. Hampp, and E. Tan (2007), "10 Lessons from the Ad Age Digital Marketing Conference," *Advertising Age* (March 12), 42.

15 Neff, Jack (2005), "Aging Population Brushes Off Coloring," *Advertising Age*, 76 (July 25), 3–49.

16 Horovitz, B. (2007), "Marketers Take a Close Look at Your Daily Routines,"

USA Today, www.usatoday.com/money/advertising/2007-04-29-watching-marketing_N.htm, accessed August 10, 2008.

17 Starr, R. G. and K.V. Fernandez (2007), "The Mindcam Methodology: Perceiving through the Native's Eye," *Qualitative Market Research: An International Journal*, 10, no. 2, 168–82.

18 Hotz, R.L. (2011), "The Really Smart Phone," *Wall Street Journal*, C1.

19 Stringer, Kortney (2005) "Eye-Tracking Technology for Marketers," *Detroit Free Press* (August 1), downloaded from http://www.highbeam.com/doc/1G1-134701284.html, accessed December 18, 2008; Hill, D. (2007), "Face Value," *Marketing Research*, 19 (Fall), 9–14.

20 Lee, N. and A.J. Broderick (2007), "The Past, Present and Future of Observational Research in Marketing," *Qualitative Market Research: An International Journal*, 10, no. 2, 121–29.

21 Yoon, C., R. Gonzalez, and J.R. Bettman (2009), "Using fMRI to Inform Marketing Research: Challenges and Opportunities," *Journal of Marketing Research*, 46, 17–19; Reimann, M., O. Schilke, B. Weber, C. Neuhaus, and J. Zaichkowski (2011), "Functional Magnetic Resonance Imaging in Consumer Research: A Review and Application," *Psychology & Marketing*, 28 (June), 608–37.

22 Krugman's, Herbert B. (1981), statement is quoted in "Live, Simultaneous Study of Stimulus, Response Is Physiological Measurement's Great Virtue," *Marketing News* (May 15), pp. 1, 20.

Chapter 9

1 See http://www.law.com and search key terms such as *cigarettes*, *tobacco*, *Brown and Williamson*, and so on for some examples.

2 Doward, J. (2003), "Cigarette Giant to Deny Cancer Link," *The Observer* (October 5), http://www.guardian.co.uk/society/2003/oct/05/smoking.cancercare, accessed May 16, 2011; Seenan, Gerard (2005), "Smoker's Widow Loses Legal Fight," *The Observer* (June 1). http://www.guardian.co.uk/society/2005/jun/01/smoking.publichealth1, accessed May 16, 2008.

3 See for example, Bolton, L.E., J.B. Cohen, and P.N. Bloom, "Does Marketing Products as Remedies Create "Get Out of Jail Free Cards'?" *Journal of Consumer Research* 33 (June 2006), 71–84; Smith, K. H. and M. A. Stutts, "The Influence of Individual Factors on the Effectiveness of Message Content in Antismoking Advertisements Aimed at Adolescents," *The Journal of Consumer Affairs* 40 (2006), 261–93; Zhao, G. and C. Pechmann, "The Impact of

Regulatory Focus on Adolescents' Response to Antismoking Advertising Campaigns," *Journal of Marketing Research* 44 (November 2007), 671–87.

4 Babin, Barry J., David M. Hardesty, and Tracy A. Suter (2003), "Color and Shopping Intentions: The Intervening Effect of Price Fairness and Perceived Affect," *Journal of Business Research* 56 (July), 541–51.

5 Christie, J., D. Fisher, J. Kozup, S. Smith, S. Burton, and E. Creyer, "The Effects of Bar-Sponsored Alcohol Beverage Promotions Across Binge and Nonbinge Drinkers," *Journal of Public Policy and Marketing*, 20 (Fall 2001), 240–53.

6 Shadish, William R., Thomas D. Cook, and Donald T. Campbell (2002), *Experimental and Quasi Experimental Designs for Generalized Causal Inference* (Geneva, IL: Houghton Mifflin).

7 Like Dragnet, the story is true but the brand names are fictitious.

8 Reitter, Robert N. (2003), "Comment: American Media and the Smoking-Related Behaviors of Asian Adolescents," *Journal of Advertising Research* 43 (March), 12–13.

9 Lach, Jennifer, "Up in Smoke," *American Demographics*, 22 (March 2000), 26.

10 Mitchell, Vincent-Wayne and Sarah Haggett (1997), "Sun-Sign Astrology in Market Segmentation: An Empirical Investigation," *Journal of Consumer Marketing* 14, no. 2, 113–31.

11 Shiv, Baba, Ziv Carmon, and Dan Aneley (2005), "Placebo Effects of Marketing Actions: Consumers May Get What They Pay for," *Journal of Marketing Research* 42 (November), 383–93.

12 White, J.B. (2010), "Why Toyota Rolled Over for its SUVs," *Wall Street Journal* (April 21), D1–D2.

13 Peterson, Robert A. (2001), "On the Use of Students in Social Science Research: Evidence from a Second Order Meta Analysis," *Journal of Consumer Research* 28 (December), 450–61.

14 Bonabeau, E. (2009), "Decisions 2.0: The Power of Collective Intelligence," *Sloan Management Review*, 50 (February), 45–50.

15 Riell, H. (2008), "Getting Back to Beer," *Convenience Store Decisions* 19 (February), 14.

16 Riste, Christine (2002), "La suprématie contée des prospectus," *Libre Service Actualité-LSA* (January 17), 1751.

17 Babin, B.J. and Adilson Borges, "Product Category and Promotional Theme Congruency: Its Effect on Preference and Retail Store Image," in *Development in Marketing Science*, H. Spotts, Ed. (Academy of Marketing Science, Coral Gables, FL, 2005).

18 "*Jackass 2.5* to Test Market for Online Film Release," CBC News,

http://www.cbc.ca/arts/film/story/2007/12/13/jackass-online.html?ref=rss, accessed August 24, 2008.

19 Neff, Jack (1998), "Millstone," *Advertising Age* (June 29), S16.

20 Cadbury, N.D., "When, Where, and How to Test Market," *Harvard Business Review* (May–June 1975), 96–105.

21 Neff, Jack (2001), "Average City, USA," *Advertising Age* 72 (July 9), 12.

22 Ramage, Norma, "Testing, Testing 1, 2, 3," *Marketing Magazine* 110 (July 2005), 1196; CNW_Telbec, "Imperial Tobacco Canada Lives Up to Its Corporate Social Responsibility Promise," *Groupe CNW* (2007), http://www.newswire.ca/fr/releases/archive/September2007/12/c7976.html, accessed November 12, 2008.

23 "How to Open the Northern European Market," U.S. Commercial Service Denmark (2006), http://www.buyusa.gov/denmark, accessed January 22, 2006.

24 Tybout, Alice M. and Gerald Zaltman (1974), "Ethics in Marketing Research: Their Practical Relevance," *Journal of Marketing Research* 21 (November), 357–68.

25 Reprinted with permission from Lee Martin, Geoffrey "Drinkers Get Court Call," *Advertising Age* (May 20, 1991). Copyright © 1991 Crain Communications, Inc.

Chapter 10

1 Reichheld, F.F., "The One Number You Need to Grow," *Harvard Business Review* 81 (2003), 46–54; Keiningham, T. L., B. Cooil, T.W. Andreassen, and L. Aksoy, "A Longitudinal Examination of the Net Promoter and Firm Revenue Growth," *Journal of Marketing* 71 (2007), 39–51; Grisaffe, D.B., "Questions About the Ultimate Question: Conceptual Considerations in Evaluating Reichheld's Net Promoter Score (NPS)," *Journal of Consumer Satisfaction, Dissatisfaction and Complaining Behavior* 20 (2007), 36–53; Mitchell, A., "The Only Number You Need to Know Does Not Add Up to Much," *Marketing Week* (March 6, 2008), 22–23.

2 See Mollen, A. and Wilson, H. (2010). "Engagement, telepresence and interactivity in online consumer experience: Reconciling scholastic and managerial perspectives," *Journal of Business Research*, 63, 919–25.

3 Periatt, J.A., S.A. LeMay, and S. Chakrabarty, "The Selling Orientation-Customer Orientation (SOCO) Scale: Cross-Validation of the Revised Version," *Journal of Personal Selling and Sales Management*, 24 (Winter 2004), 49–54.

4 Anderson, Barry F., *The Psychology Experiment* (Monterey, CA: Brooks/Cole, 1971), p. 26.

5 Cohen, Jacob, "Things I Have Learned (So Far)," *American*

Psychologist, 45 (December 1990), 1304–312.

6 Arnold, Catherine, "Satisfaction's the Name of the Game," *Marketing News*, 38 (October 15, 2004), 39–45. Also, see http://www.theacsi.org.

7 In more advanced applications such as those involving structural equations analysis, a distinction can be made between reflective composites and formative indexes. See Hair, J.F., W.C. Black, B.J. Babin, R. Anderson, and R. Tatham, *Multivariate Data Analysis*, 6th ed. (Upper Saddle River, NJ: Prentice Hall, 2006).

8 Bart, Yakov, Venkatesh Shankar, Fareena Sultan, and Glen L. Urban, "Are the Drivers and Role of Online Trust the Same for All Web Sites and Consumers? A Large-Scale Exploratory Study," *Journal of Marketing*, 69 (October 2005), 133–52.

9 Cronbach, Lee J., "My Current Thoughts on Coefficient Alpha and Successor Procedures," *Center for the Study of Evaluation Report*, 64, no. 3 (2004), http://epm.sagepub.com/cgi/content/short/64/3/391, accessed October 25, 2008.

10 Hair et al. (2009)

11 Burke Marketing Research, "Rough Commercial Recall Testing," Cincinnati, OH (undated).

12 Hair et al. (2009)

13 Cox, Keith K. and Ben M. Enis, *The Marketing Research Process* (Pacific Palisades, CA: Goodyear, 1972); Kerlinger, Fred N., *Foundations of Behavioral Research*, 3rd ed. (Ft. Worth: Holt, Rinehart and Winston, 1986).

14 Howell, N., "Looking Deeper," *New Media Age* (December 1, 2005), 24–25.

15 Hotz, R.L. (2011), "Songs Stick in Teens' Heads," *Wall Street Journal* (June 13), AA1.

16 Osgood, Charles, George Suci, and Percy Tannenbaum, *The Measurement of Meaning* (Urbana: University of Illinois Press, 1957). Seven-point scales were used in the original work; however, subsequent researchers have modified the scale to have five points, nine points, and so on.

17 Peterson, R.A. and W. Wilson, "Measuring Customer Satisfaction: Fact and Artifact," *Journal of the Academy of Marketing Science* 20 (Spring 1992), 61–71; Dawes, J., "Do Data Characteristics Change According to the Number of Scale Points Used? An Experiment Using 5-Point, 7-Point and 10-Point Scales," *International Journal of Market Research* 50, no. 1 (2008), 61–77.

18 Weigters, B., E. Cabooter, and N. Schillewaert (2010), "The Effect of Rating Scale Format on Response Styles: The Number of Response Categories and Response Category Labels," *International Journal of Research in Marketing*, 27 (September), 236–47.

19 Roster, C.A., R.D. Rogers, and G. Albaum (2007), "A Comparison of Response Characteristics from Web and Telephone Surveys," *International Journal of Marketing Research*, 46 (Fall), 359–73. Albaum, G., C.A. Roster, J. Wiley, J. Rossiter, and S.M. Smith (2010), "Designing Web Surveys in MarketingResearch: Does Use of Forced Answering Affect Completion Rates?" *Journal of Marketing Theory and Practice*, 18 (Summer), 285–93.

20 See Muk, A., "Consumers' Intentions to Opt in to SMS Advertising," *International Journal of Advertising*, 26, no. 2 (2007), 177–98; Summers, T.A., "Predicting Purchase Intention of a Controversial Luxury Apparel Product," *Journal of Fashion Marketing & Management*, 10, no. 4 (2006), 405–19, for examples.

Chapter 11

1 Sources: de Jong, M. G., R. Pieters and J.P. Fox (2010), "Reducing Social Desirability Bias Through Item Randomized Response : An Application to Measure Underreported Desires," *Journal of Marketing Research*, 47 (February), 14–27. Cnn.com (2011), "Why Some Dissatisfied Users are Shunning Facebook," (6/20), http://articles.cnn.com/2011-06-20/tech/people.shunning.facebook_1_facebook-user-active-users-popular-social-networking-site?_s=PM:TECH, accessed July 13, 2011.

2 Smith, Robert, David Olah, Bruce Hansen and Dan Cumbo, "The Effect of Questionnaire Length on Participant Response Rate: A Case Study in the U.S. Cabinet Industry," *Forest Products Journal* 53 (November–December 2003), 31.

3 Giraud, G., C. Tebby, and C. Amblard (2011), "Measurement of Consumers' Wine-Related Knowledge," INRA UMR CESAER Working Paper, Dijon, France.

4 Miller, K.M., R. Hofstetter, H. Krohmer, and Z.J. Zhang (2011), "How Should Consumers' Willingness to Pay Be Measured? An Empirical Comparison of State-of-the-Art Approaches?" *Journal of Marketing Research*, 48 (February), 172–84.

5 Donahue, Amy K. and Joanne M. Miller, "Citizen Preferences and Paying for Police," *Journal of Urban Affairs* 27, no.4 (2005), 419–35.

6 Roll, Charles W., Jr. and Albert H. Cantril, *Polls: Their Use and Misuse in Politics* (New York: Basic Books, 1972), pp. 106–7.

7 Other product attributes are relative advantage, compatibility, complexity, and communicability.

8 Dawson, L., "Will Feminization Change the Image of the Sales Profession?" *Journal of Personal Selling*

and Sales Management 12 (Winter 1992), 21–32.

9 Lietz, P. (2010), "Research into Questionnaire Design: A Summary of the Literature," *International Journal of Market Research*, 52 (2), 249–72.

10 Malhotra, Neil (2008), "Completion Time and Response Order Effects in Web Surveys," *Public Opinion Quarterly*, 22 (5), 914–34.

11 Holbrook, A.L. and J.A. Krosnick (2010), "Measuring Voter Turnout by Using Randomized Response Technique: Evidence Calling into Question the Method's Validity," *Public Opinion Quarterly*, 74, 328–43. De Jong, M. G., R. Pieters and J. P. Fox (2010), "Reducing Social Desirability Bias Through Item Randomized Response: An Application to Measure Underreported Desires," *Journal of Marketing Research*, 47 (February), 14–27.

12 See Holbrook and Krosniek (2010) for more details on computation.

13 Malhotra (2008).

14 Peychev, A. (2009), "Survey Breakoff," *Public Opinion Quarterly*, 71 (Spring), 74–97.

15 Harzing, Anne-Wil, "Does the Use of English-Language Questionnaires in Cross-National Research Obscure National Differences?" *International Journal of Cross Cultural Management* 5, no. 2 (2005): 213–24.

16 Cateora, Philip R., *International Marketing* (Homewood, IL: Richard D. Irwin, 1990), pp. 387–89.

Chapter 12

1 Based on Deborah Ball, "As Chocolate Sags, Cadbury Gambles on a Piece of Gum," *Wall Street Journal* (January 12, 2006), A1; Clews, M.L. (2009), "Burtons Adds Healthier Products to Cadbury Brunch Range," *Marketing Week*, 32 (2/12), 64.

2 Kinne, Susan and Tari D. Topolski, "Inclusion of People with Disabilities in Telephone Health Surveillance Surveys," *American Journal of Public Health* 95, no. 3 (March 2005): 512–17.

3 Brock, Sabra E. "Marketing Research in Asia: Problems, Opportunities, and Lessons," *Marketing Research* (September 1989), p. 47.

4 Rideout, Bruce E., Katherine Hushen, Dawn McGinty, Stephanie Perkins, and Jennifer Tate, "Endorsement of the New Ecological Paradigm in Systematic and E-Mail Samples of College Students," *Journal of Environmental Education* 37 (winter 2005), 3–11.

5 Krosnick, J., "The Distinguishing Characteristics of Frequent Survey Participants," *Proceedings of Midwestern Political Science Association* 1 (2006).

6 Krosnick, J., D. Rivers, and N. Norman, "Web Survey Methodologies: A Comparison of

Survey Accuracy," *Proceedings of the American Association for Public Opinion Research* 1 (2005).

7 Harris Interactive (2011), "Sampling Support and Design," http://www.harrisinteractive.com/vault/HI_SP_Sheet_SamplingSupportandDesign.pdf, accessed August 3, 2011.

8 See http://ssisamples.com, accessed August 3, 2011.

9 Craig, C.S. and S.P. Douglas (2011), "Assessing Cross-Cultural Theory and Research: A Commentary Issue," *Journal of Business Research*, 64 (June), 625–27.

10 Sigenman, Lee, Steven A. Tuch. and Jack K. Martin, "What's in a Name? Preference for 'Black' versus 'African-American' among Americans of African Descent," *Public Opinion Quarterly* 69 (fall 2005), 429–38.

11 Based on Gene Mueller, "It's Hard to Figure Number of Anglers," *Washington Times* (March 20, 2005), downloaded from InfoTrac at http://web3.infotrac.galegroup.com; Atlantic Coastal Cooperative Statistics Program, "About Us: Committees," http://www.accsp.org, accessed March 16, 2006; Atlantic States Marine Fisheries Commission, "About Us," http://www.asmfc.org, accessed March 16, 2006.

Chapter 13

1 "Gaming News," *Marketing News*, 42 (February 1, 2008), 39; Hellebusch, S. J., "Know Sample Quantity for Clearer Results," *Marketing News*, 40 (September 15, 2006), 23–26; Sheth-Voss, P., "How Big Should Your Sample Be?" *Marketing Research*, 20 (Summer 2008), 25–29.

2 Most of the statistical material in this book assumes that the population parameters are unknown, which is the typical situation in most applied research projects.

3 See Jurik, R., M. Moody, and J. Seal, "The Mean vs. the Top Box(es) Scores," *Marketing Research*, 20 (Summer 2008), 41–42.

4 The reasons for this are related to the concept of degrees of freedom, which will be explained later. At this point, disregard the intuitive notion of division by n, because it produces a biased estimate of the population variance.

5 In practice, most survey researchers will not use this exact formula. A modification of the formula, $Z = (X - \mu)/S$, using the sample standard deviation in an adjusted form, is frequently used.

6 Hayes, William L. *Statistics* (New York: Holt, Rinehart and Winston, 1963), p. 193.

7 Wonnacott, Thomas H., and Ronald J. Wonnacott. *Introductory Statistics*, 2nd ed. (New York: Wiley, 1972), p. 125.

8 Note that the derivation of this formula is (1) $E = ZS_x$; (2) $E = ZS/\sqrt{n}$ $\sqrt{n}\_$ (3) $\sqrt{n}$— $\sqrt{n}$— ZS/E; (4) $n = (ZS/E)^2$.

Chapter 14

1 Sources: Phau, I., and M. Baird (2008), "Complainers versus non-Complainers Retaliatory Responses Towards Service Dissatisfactions," *Marketing Intelligence & Planning*, 26, 567–604. Ramsey, R. D. (2010), "How to Handle Customer Complaints," *The American Salesman*, 55 (June), 25–30.

2 Corso, R. A. (2011), "Johnny Depp is America's Favorite Actor, While Denzel Washinton is Number 2: Last Year's Number One, Clint Eastwood, Drops to Number 9 on the List," Harris Interactive press release (January 12).

3 Dilmperi, A., T. Kin g, and C. Dennis (2011), "Pirates of the Web: The Curse of Illegal Downloading," *Journal of Retailing and Consumer Services*, 18 (March), 132–40.

4 See Schultz, D. E., and M.P. Block (2011), "How U.S. Consumers View In-Store Promotions," *Journal of Business Research*, 54 (January), 51–54.

5 http://www.wineinstitute.org/resources/statistics, accessed August 17, 2011.

6 See a comprehensive statistics text such as Hair et al. (2010; Multivariate Data Analysis) for a more detailed explanation.

Chapter 15

1 Sources: De Bock, T., and P.V. Kenhove (2011), "Double Standards: The Role of Techniques of Neutralization," *Journal of Business Ethics*, 99, 283–96; Vermeir, I., and P.V. Kenhove (2008), "Gender Differences in Double Standards," *Journal of Business Ethics*, 81, 281–98.

2 Three nonparametric tests—the Wilcoxon matched-pairs signed ranks test, the Kruskal-Wallis test, and the Mann–Whitney U test can also be used but are not described here.

3 The formula is not shown here but it can be found in most basic statistics books.

4 See, for example, Armstrong-Stassen, M. (2002), "Designated Redundant but Escaping Lay-Off: A Special Group of Lay-Off Survivors," *Journal of Occupational and Organizational Psychology*, 75 (March), 1–13.

Chapter 16

1 Dowling, Mike, "Mr. Dowling's Rosetta Stone Page," http://www.mrdowling.com/604-rosettastone.html, accessed August 21, 2011; Singh (2011), "The Decipherment of Hieroglyphs," BBC History, http://bbc.co.uk/history/ancient/egyptians/decipherment_01.shtml, www.bbc.co.uk/history/ancient/egyptians/decipherment_01.shtml, accessed October1, 2011.

2 Yore, L. D., M. K. Florence, T. W. Pearso,n and A. J. Weaver (2006), "Written Discourse in Scientific Communities: A Conversation with Two Scientists about Their Views of Science, Use of Language, Role of Writing in Doing Science, and Compatibility between Their Epistemic Views and Language," *International Journal of Science Education* 28 (February), 109–41.

3 Sullivan, E. A., "Twitterpated: Marketers Enamored of Online Communication System," *Marketing News* (October 15, 2008), 8.

4 The original version of this chapter was written by John Bush, Oklahoma State University, and appeared in William G. Zikmund, *Business Research Methods* (Hinsdale, IL: Dryden Press, 1984).

5 "A Speech Tip," *Communication Briefings* 14, no. 2 (1995), p. 3.

6 These guidelines, adapted with permission from Marjorie Brody (President, Brody Communications, 1200 Melrose Ave., Melrose Park, PA 19126), appeared in "How to Gesture When Speaking," *Communication Briefings* 14, no. 11 (1995), p. 4.

7 "Tips of the Month," *Communication Briefings* 24, no. 7 (May 2005), p. 1.

8 Based on Bridis, Ted, "Study: Shoppers Naïve about Online Pricing," *Information Week* (June 1, 2005), downloaded from InfoTrac at http://web2.infotrac.galegroup.com; Annenberg Public Policy Center (APPC), "Annenberg Study Shows Americans Vulnerable to Exploitation in the Online and Offline Marketplace," news release (June 1, 2005), http://www.annenbergpublicpolicycenter.org; Turow, Joseph, Lauren Feldman, and Kimberly Meltzer, "Open to Exploitation: American Shoppers Online and Offline," APPC report (June 2005), downloaded at http://www.annenbergpublicpolicycenter.org.

INDEX

A

ACNielsen Company, 36, 62–63, 130, 145–146, 175–176, 203
Acquiescence bias, 157
Active research, 80–81
Administrative error, 158
Advocacy research, 85
Affect component, 263
Aided recall, 293
American Consumer Satisfaction Index (ACSI), 133, 142, 255, 278
Analysis
    of data, 13–14, 64
    diagnostic, 51
    forecast, 76
    market-basket, 137
    site analysis techniques, 146
Analysis of variance (ANOVA), 369
ANOVA. *See* One-way analysis of variance (ANOVA)
Appendix (research report), 418
Applied marketing research, 7–8
Applied Research, 7–8
Arbitron, 75, 130, 145, 201
Artifacts, 199
Attitudes, 260–261
Attitudinal rating scales
    balanced vs. unbalanced, 271–272
    behavioral intention, 275
    category scales, 264–265
    constant-sum scale, 267–268
    definition of, 261–262
    direct assessment, 270
    forced-choice scales, 272
    graphic rating scale, 268–269
    Likert scale, 265
    measuring affect component, 263
    measuring scale quality, 266
    multi-attribute score, 273–274
    number of scale categories, 270–271
    operational definitions, 248–249
    paired comparisons, 270
    physiological measures, 262
    ranking, 269–270
    semantic differential, 266–267
Attributes, 255

B

Back translation, 305
Balanced rating scale, 271–272
Bar charts, 422–423
Basic experimental designs, 227
Basic marketing research, 8
Behavioral intention, 275
Behavioral tracking, 35
Benefits vs. costs, 20–21
Best Buy and integrated marketing, 18–19
Between-groups variance, 398
Between-subjects design, 228–229
Bias, 6, 8–9, 156–157, 195
Bivariate statistical analysis, 372
"Blind" experimental administrator, 226
Blocking variables, 216
Branching, 296
Breakoff, 296
Business research. *See* Research

C

Callbacks, 164, 169, 179
Case studies, 106
Categorical variables, 218–219
Category scale, 264
Causal inference, 52
Causal research, 51–54
Causality, 52–53
Cause-and-effect relationships, 52–53
Cell, 220
Census, 312
Central location interviewing, 170
Central tendency, 339–340
Central-limit theorem, 348–350
Charts (research reports)
    bar charts, 422–423
    line graphs, 422
    pie charts, 422
    use of, 420–422
Checklist question, 285
Children, interviewing, 82–83
Children's Online Privacy Protection Act (COPPA), 82
Choice, 262
Class coding, 364
Click rate, 178
Click-through rate (CTR), 202
Cloud computing, 198
Cluster sampling, 329–330
Coding, 363
Coding qualitative responses, 363–364
Coefficient alpha (α), 257
Cohort effect, 230
Collages, 115

Communication
  computerized voice-activated
    telephone interviews, 164
  smartphones, 151, 205–206
  technology for, 21
  telephone interviews, 165–170
Complemetary evidence, 194
Composite measures, 255–256
Compustat, 37, 133
Computer-assisted telephone
    interviewing (CATI), 164
Concept testing, 102
Concepts, 248
Conclusions and recommendations
    selection, 418
Concomitant variation, 52
Confidence interval estimate, 351
Confidence intervals, 350–353
Confidence levels, 351
Confidentiality, 82, 90
Confirmatory research, 100
Conflict of interest, 90–91
Constancy of conditions, 226
Constant-sum scale, 267–268
Construct, 249
Construct validity, 259–260
Consumer attitude research, 145
Consumption behavior data, 145
Content analysis, 200–201
Content providers, 38
Contingency table, 367–368
Continuous measures, 254–255
Contrived observation, 196–197
Control group, 219
Convenience sampling, 323
Convergent validity, 248
Conversation volume, 203
Conversations, 113–114
Cookies, 40, 203
COPPA (Children's Online Privacy
    Protection Act), 82
Correlation, 52–53
Correspondence rules, 248
Counterbalancing, 227
Counterbiasing statement, 289
Covariate, 216
Cover letter, 174
Criterion validity, 260
Cross-checks, 131
Cross-functional teams, 77–78
Cross-tabulation, 366
  contingency tables, 367–368
  elaboration and refinement of,
    368–369
  number of, 369
  percentage cross-tabulations, 368
  use of, 366–367

Cultural cross-validation, 22–23
Culture, 104–105
Custom research, 74, 75
Customer discovery, 138
Customer orientation, 9–10
Customer relationship management
    (CRM), 32, 75, 138

D

Data
  conversion, 130
  definition of, 28
  external, 140
  internal, 139
  internal and proprietary data, 139–140
  proprietary, 139
  qualitative, 100–101
  quantative, 101
  reliability and validity of, 130–131
  scanner, 35
  secondary. see Secondary data
  secondary data sources, 140–145
  single-source, 137
Data analysis, 13–14, 64
Data archives
  data wholesalers, 36
  financial databases, 37
  statistical databases, 36–37
  video databases, 37
Data conversion, 130. see also Data
    transformation
Data interchange, electronic, 37–38
Data mining, 137
Data Monitor, 134
Data processing error, 158
Data quality, 29
Data specialists, 36
Data technology, ethics of, 41–42
Data transformation, 130, 369
  definition of, 130
  index numbers, 372
  problems with, 370–371
  simple transformations, 369–370
  tabular and graphic data display, 372
Data warehouse, 33
Data wholesalers, 36
Database, 33
Database marketing, 138
Data-collection, 64
David-Brown Index, 14
Debriefing, 83, 239
Deception, in research, 83
Decision support system (DSS)
  characteristics of, 31–33
  databases and data warehousing, 33
  input management, 33–37

Deep-packet inspection, 197–198
Degrees of freedom (df), 375
Deliverables, 56
Delivery information acquisition
    devices (DIADs), 30
Demand characteristics, 224–226
Demand effect, 224
Dependent variable, 220
Depth interview, 112–113
Descriptive analysis, 364–365
Descriptive research, 49–51
Deviation scores, 342–343
  standard deviation, 342–343
Diagnostic analysis, 51
DIALOG catalog, 36
Dichotomous-alternative (simple-
    dichotomy) question, 285
Differences, testing for. See Test of
    differences
Direct observation, 194–196
Director of marketing research, 75,
    76–77
Discrete measures, 253–254
Discriminant validity, 260
Discussion guide, 116
Dispersion, measures for
  deviations, 341
  range, 341
  standard deviation, 342–343
Disproportional stratified sample, 328
Distribution
  normal distribution, 343–348
  population and sample, 347
  sampling, 347–348
Distribution research, sample, 17–18,
    343–348
Do-not-call legislation, 80
Door-to-door interviews, 164
Double-barreled question, 291
Drop-off method, 176
Dummy coding, 363
Dynamic pricing, 27

E

E-cigarettes, 16
Effects coding, 363–364
Elaboration analysis, 368
Electronic data interchange (EDI),
    37–38
E-mail surveys, 177–178
Emotion, and research, 123
Empirical testing, 61
Enterprise search, 139–140
Entrap, 198
Environmental scanning, 36, 39, 133–134
Estimates of parameters, 350

Ethical dilemma, 78
Ethical issues. *see also* Rights and
   obligations
   and client sponsor, 84–86
   conflicts of interest, 91–92
   data technology, 41–42
   in experimentation, 239
   and human observation, 197–198
   idealism, 79–81
   and online research, 121
   and participant, 80–84
   privacy, 80–82, 86
   relativism, 78
   and the researcher, 86–90
   of society at large, 90
   and surveys, 183–184
Ethics, data technology, 41–42, 81
Ethnography, 104–105
Experimental condition, 215
Experimental design
   and basic vs. factorial designs, 227
   and extraneous variables, 223–224
   and laboratory experiments, 227
   manipulation of independent variable,
      218–220
   matching for, 222
   randomization of, 222
   repeated measures for, 222
   and sample selection and errors,
      221–222
   selection of dependant variable, 220
Experimental disguise, 225
Experimental group, 219
Experimental treament, 219
Experimental validity
   between-subjects designs, 228–229
   and demand characteristics, 224–226
   and experimental control, 226–227
   external, 231–232
   and field experiments, 227–228
   internal, 229–231
   internal vs. external, 232–233
   and market testing, 233–238
Experimental variable, 53
Experimenter bias, 224
Experiments
   and consent, 84
   definition of, 53–54
   effects of, 216–218
   experimental conditions, 215–216
   and small sample research, 100
   sujects of, 214–215
Exploratory research, 48–49, 100–102,
   121–123
External data, 140
External data sources, 140–145
External validity, 231

Extremity bias, 157
Eye-tracking monitor, 206

F

Face (content) validity, 258
Face-to-face interview, 80, 119
Fact-finding, research data, 132–134
Factorial designs, 227
Federal Trade Commission (FTC), 87
Field experiments, 227–228
Field notes, 115
Filter question, 296–297
Financial databases, 37
Fixed alternative questions, 282
Focus blog, 119
Focus group interview
   advantages of, 108–109
   as diagnostic tools, 111–112
   disadvantages of, 117–118
   environmental concerns, 111
   illustration of, 109
   moderator for, 111
   outline for, 116–117
   respondents to, 110–111
Focus groups, 59
Forced-choice rating scales, 272
Forecast analysis, 76
Forrester Research, 203
Free-association techniques, 114–116
Frequency distribution, 337–338
Frequency table, 365–366
F-test, 399–402
Funnel technique, 295

G

Gallup, 61, 75, 161, 188, 196, 317
General linear model (GLM)
   GLM equation, 402–403
   regression analysis, 403–405
Geo-demographics, 15
Geolocation technologies, 41
Global marketing research,
   21–23, 30
Goodness-of-fit, 387–390
Grand mean, 398
Graph theory, 38
Graphic aids, 419
Graphic rating scale, 268–269
Grounded theory, 105–106

H

Harley-Davidson, 13, 115
Harm, protection from, 83–84
Harris/Interactive, 61, 145, 196, 321
Heat map question, 300

Hermeneutic unit, 103
Hermeneutics, 103–104
"human intelligence tasks" (HIT), 232
Hidden observation, 192
Hidden Valley Ranch, 237
Histogram, 365
History effect, 230
History sniffing, 41
Honesty, 88–90
Human subjects review committee, 84

I

Idea generation, 101
Idealism, 79
Implicit consent, 81
Incentives, use of, 174
Independent samples *t*-test, 390
Independent variables, manipulation of
   categorical variables, 218–219
   experimental and control groups,
      219–220
   more than one variable, 220
   treatment levels, 220
Index measure, 255–256
Index numbers, 372
Index of retail saturation, 136
Information, characteristics of, 28–31
Information completeness, 29
Information technology, 40
Informed consent, 80
INFOSCAN, 144–145
In-house research, 70–73
Input management
   behavioral tracking, 35
   internal records, 33–34
   outside vendors, 36
   proprietary marketing research, 34
   salesperson input, 34–35
   web tracking, 35–36, 38–39
Institutional Review Board (IRB), 84,
   197
Instrumentation effect, 230
Integrated marketing communication, 18
Integrated marketing mix, 18–19
Interaction effect, 217
Interactive survey approaches, 160
Interest, conflicts in, 91–92
Internal consistency, 257
Internal data, 139–140
Internal validity, 229–231
Internet, 38–40, 140
Internet presentations, 426
"Internet privacy", 80
Internet surveys, 178–181
Interpretation, 163, 196, 363
Interpretative software, 121

Interval scales, 252
Interview techniques. *see also* Personal
    interviews
    and children, 82–83
    conversations, 113–114
    conversational tools, 103, 113–114
    depth procedure, 113
    face-to-face, 80
    focus group. *see* Focus groups
    free-association and sentence
        completion, 114–116
    probing, 101
    projective techniques, 115–116
    push pull, 87–88
    semi-structured, 114
    semi-structured interviews, 114–115
    technology for, 118–121
Interviewer bias, 157
Interviewer cheating, 159
Interviewer error, 159
Intranet, 40
Introduction section, 417
Inventories, 199–200
Item nonresponse, 162

J

J.D. Power, 73
Joint Advertising, Market Research &
    Studies (JAMRS), 140
Judgement (purposive) sampling, 323
Junior analyst, 75

K

Keying mail with codes, 176
Keyword search, 38–39

L

Laboratory experiment, 227
Laddering, 112
Leading questions, 288–290
Letter of authorization, 417
Letter of transmittal, 416–417
Likert scale, 265
Limited research service companies, 74
Line graphs, 422
Literature review, 58
Loaded question, 288–290

M

Magnetic resonance imagery (MRI), 189,
    207
Magnitude of error, 354
    estimating, 354
Mail survey, 171–173
    characteristics of, 171–173

increasing response rates, 174–176
    response rates, 173–174
Main effect, 216
Mall-intercept interviews, 164
Manager of decision support systems, 76
Manipulation, 53–54
Manipulation check, 229
Marginal tabulation, 365
Marginals, 367–368
Market dynamism, 30
Market intelligence, 28
Market tracking, 133
Market-basket analysis, 137
Marketing channel, 17
Marketing concept, 9, 13–14
Marketing ethics, 78
Marketing metrics, 19, 269
Marketing mix, 16–19
Marketing performance, 19
Marketing research. *See* Research
Marketing Research Corporation of
    America (MRCA), 145
Market-share data, 144–145
Matrix table (multiple-grid) question,
    296
Maturation effect, 230
McCann-Erickson, 122
Mean, 339–340, 375–377
Measurement
    concept of, 248
    definition of, 246–248
    index measures and composites,
        255–256
    operational definitions, 248–249
    reliability, 257–258
    scale measurements. *see* Scale
        measurement
    validity, 258–260
Mechanical observation
    camera surveillance, 205
    monitoring website traffic, 202–204
    scanner-based research, 204–205
    smartphones, 205–206
    television and radio monitoring,
        201–202
Mechanical Turk, 232
Media sources, marketing, 143–144
Median, 340
Median split, 370–371
Mistakes, avoiding (questionnaires)
    ambiguity, 290–291
    assumptions, 292
    double-barreled items, 291–292
    leading and loaded questions, 288–290
    and memory taxing, 292–293
    simpler is better, 287–288
Mobiltrak, 202
Mode, 340

Model building, 340
    advertising response, 137
    analysis of trade sites, 135–137
    and estimating market potential,
        134–135
    and sales forecasting, 135
Moderator, 111
Moderator variable, 369
Mortality effect (sample attrition), 231
Multi-attribute model, 275
Multi-choice question, 285
Multiple regression analysis, 403
Multiple-grid (matrix table) question,
    298
Multistage area sampling, 330
Multivariate statistical analysis, 372
Mystery shoppers, 83, 196

N

National Eating Trends (NET), 132–133,
    145
National Family Opinion (NFO), 145
National Trade Data Bank (NTDB),
    146–147
Net promotion score (NPS), 245, 248
Netnography, 120–121
Neural network, 137
Neuroco, 189
Neurological devices, 207–208
Neuromarketing, 189
NFC (near-field-communication), 30–31
No contracts, 155
Nominal scales, 249
Non-forced-choice scale, 272
Noninteractive survey approaches, 160
Nonprobability sampling
    convenience, 323
    judgement (purposive), 323
    quota, 323–325
Nonrespondents, 155
Nonresponse errors, 155
Nonsampling or systematic error,
    221–222
Nonspurious association, 52–53
Normal distribution, 344

O

Objectives, for research
    data mining, 137–138
    database and CRM management, 138
Objectives, secondary data
    fact-finding, 132–134
    model building, 134–137
Observation
    complementary evidence, 194
    content analysis, 200–201

contrived, 196–197
definition of, 190
direct, 194–196
ethical issues of, 197–198
of human behavior, 193–194
mechanical, 201–206
nature of, 191–192
observable phenomena, 190–191
of physical objects, 198–201
physiological reactions, 206–208
Observer bias, 195
One-way analysis of variance (ANOVA)
example of, 396–397
F-test, 399–402
partitioning variance in, 397–399
practical uses for, 402
Online focus group, 119
Online panels, 318
Open data partnership, 42
Open source innovation, 38
Open-ended response questions, 282–284
Operational definitions, 248–249
Operationalization, 248–249
Opt in, 321
Oral presentation, 423–425
Order bias, 294–296
Ordinal scale, 251
Outside agency, 70–73

P

Paired comparisons, 270
Paired-samples t-test, 304
Participant-observations, 104
Passive research, 81
Percentage distribution, 338
Performance-monitoring research, 19
Periodicals, marketing, 141–142
Personal interviews
advantages of, 160–162
callbacks, 164, 169, 179
central location interviewing, 170
characteristics of phone interviews, 167–170
computerized voice-activated telephone interviews, 170
disadvantages of, 162–163
door-to-door, 164
mobile phones, 166–167
phrasing for, 286–287
telephone interviews, 165–166
Phenomenology, 103–104
Philosophical issues, in research. See Ethical issues
Physiological reactions, observation of
eye-tracking, 206–207
neurological devices, 207–208

psychogalvanometer, 207
pupilometer, 207
voice-pitch analysis, 207
Picture frustration, 115
Pie charts, 422
Piggyback, 108
Pilot study, 59
Piping software, 302
Placebo, 82
Placebo effect, 225–226
Point estimates, 350
Polk Company, 144
Pooled estimate of the standard error, 391
Population (universe), 312
Population distribution, 347
Population element, 312
Population parameter, 154
Population parameters
frequency distributions, 337–338
proportions, 338
sample statistics, 336–337
top-box scores, 338
POS (point of sale), 28
Predictive analytics, 41
Preliminary tabulation, 303
Pretest, 59
Pretesting, 183
Pricing, 27
dynamic, 27
Pricing research, 17
Primary sampling unit (PSU), 318
Privacy, 80–82, 86
PRIZM data, 140, 145–146
Probability, 338
Probability sampling, 322
simple random sampling, 325–326
stratified sampling, 326–328
Probing, 101
Product oriented, 9
Product research, 16
Production oriented, 9
Profitability, 10–11
Projective technique, 115–116
Promotion research, 18
Prompting, 301–302
Proportion, 338
Proportional stratified sample, 328
Proprietary data, 139
Proprietary marketing research, 34
Pseudo-research, 87
Psychogalvanometer, 207
Public opinion research, 145
Pull technology, 40
Pupilometer, 207
Purposive (judgement) sampling, 323
Push poll, 87
Push technology, 40
P-value, 373

Q

Qualitative data, 100–101
Qualitative marketing research
definition of, 97
exploratory research, 121–123
and exploratory research designs, 100–103
free-association and sentence completion, 114–116
and idea generation, 101
and probing, 101
vs. quantitative marketing research, 98–100
technology for, 118–121
uses of, 97–98
Qualitative research orientations
case studies, 106
ethnography, 104–105
grounded theory, 105–106
phenomenology, 103–104
Qualitative research techniques
common tools, 107
conservations, 113–114
depth interviews, 112–113
focus group. see Focus groups
Qualitative responses, coding. See Coding qualitative responses
Quantified electroencephalography (QEEG), 189
Quantitative data, 101
Quantitative marketing research, 98–100
Question sequence, 294–295
Questionnaire design
accuracy of, 281–282
basic considerations, 280–281
for global markets, 304–305
relevancy of questions, 281
Questionnaire formats
fixed-alternative questions, 284–286
open-ended questions, 282–284
phrasing for, 286–287
Questionnaires
avoiding mistakes. see Mistakes, avoiding (questionnaires)
mail questionnaires. see Mail survey
order bias, 294–296
pretesting of, 302–304
self-administered, 171
survey flow, 296–298
survey technology, 298–302
Quota sampling, 323–325

R

Random digit dialing, 167
Randomization, 222
Randomized presentations, 295

Randomized response techniques, 296
Range, 341
Ranking, 269–270
Rating scales, 262
Ratio scales, 253
Recall, 293
Refusals, 156
Regression analysis, 403–405
Relationship marketing, 12
Relativism, 78
Relevance, 40
Reliability, 257–258
Repeated measures, 222
Replicable, 122
Report format, 413
Research
    analyzing marketing performance, 19
    applied, 7–8
    basic, 8
    and children, 82–83
    definition of, 5–7
    ethical issues in. *see* Ethical issues
    examples of, 3–4
    in-house vs. outside agency, 70–72
    and marketing concept, 13–14
    mispresentation of, 88–90
    need for, 19–21
    purpose of, 87–88
    and strategic management orientation,
        9–12
    and strategic marketing management,
        14–16
    in twenty-first century, 21–23
    types of, 16–19, 47–54
    working in, 72–78
Research, types of
    causal research, 51–53
    descriptive research, 49–51
    distribution research, 17–18
    experiments, 53–54
    exploratory research, 48–49
    pricing research, 17
    product research, 16
    promotion research, 18
    uncertainty, influences of, 54–55
Research analyst, 75
Research assistants, 76
Research design, 61–63
Research firms, size
    large firms, 76
    midsized firms, 75–76
    small firms, 74–75
Research follow-up, 413, 426
Research methodology section, 418
Research objectives
    and exploratory research, 58
    and hypothesis, 60–61

and preliminary research, 56–57
and previous research, 58–60
and the research proposal, 58
stating, 60
and theory, 60
Research process
    alternatives in, 55–56
    analyzing data, 64
    analyzing data for, 64
    collecting data, 64
    defining objectives of, 56–61
    and drawing conclusions, 64–65
    planning a design, 61–63
    sampling, 63–64
Research program, 65
Research project, 65
Research proposal, 58
Research reports, 413
    basic reports, 418–419
    follow-up of, 426
    and the internet, 426
    oral presentation of, 423–425
    parts of the report, 415–418
    and report format, 413–415
    use of charts, 420–423
    use of tables, 419–420
Research suppliers
    limited research service companies,
        74, 75
    standardized research service, 74
    syndicated service, 73
Researcher, 87–88
    and purpose of research, 87–88
Researcher-depende4nt, 97
Respondent error
    nonresponse error, 155–156
    response bias, 156–158
Respondents, 152
Response bias, 156–158
Response latency, 194
Response rate, mail surveys, 173–176
Results section, 418
Retail Forward, 74
Reverse coding, 256
Reverse directory, 318
RFID (radio frequency identification),
    30–31
RFID tag, 204–205
Right to Privacy
    active research, 80–81
    passive research, 81
Rights and obligations
    of participant, 80–84
    and privacy, 80–82, 86
    of researcher, 86–90
    of society at large, 90
    of user (client sponsor), 84–86

Roper Starch Worldwide, 145
Rosetta stone and communication,
    412–413

S

Sample bias, 156
Sample design, 331–332
Sample selection error, 158
Sample size
    estimates and means, 354–355
    factors in determining, 353–354
    and judgement, 357
    and population size, 355
    for proportions, 356–357
Sample statistics, 337
Sample survey, 152
Sampling
    accurate results from, 313–314
    cluster sampling, 329–330
    defintion of target population,
        315–316
    destruction of test units, 314
    and imperfect samples, 322
    non-probability, 322–325
    planning a sample, 63–64
    planning for, 63–64
    probability, 325–328
    probability vs. non-probability, 322
    proportional vs. disproportional,
        328–329
    random sampling error, 319
    reasons for, 312–313
    and sampling frame, 317–318
    and sampling units, 318
    systematic sampling error, 319–321
Sampling, statistics for
    central-limit theorem, 348–350
    confidence intervals, 350–353
    distribution vs. sample, 343–348
    measures of central tendency, 339–340
    measures of dispersion, 340–343
    point estimates, 350
    population parameters, 336–338
    problems with, 335–336
    random error, 353
    sample size, 353–358
Sampling distribution, 347–348
Sampling error, 154, 221–222
Sampling frame, 317
Sampling frame error, 317
Sampling unit, 318
Scale, 246
Scale measurement
    continuous measures, 254–255
    discreet measures, 253–254
    interval scale, 252–253

nominal scale, 249–251
   ordinal scale, 251–252
   ratio scale, 253
Scale values, computing, 255–256
Scanner data, 35
Scanner-based consumer panel, 204
Scientific decision process, 122–123
Scientific method, 8–9
Search engine, 35
Secondary data
   advantages of, 128–129, 129
   data mining, 137–138
   disadvantages of, 129–132
   fact-finding, 132–134
   model building, 134–137
Secondary data sources
   external, 140–145
   government agencies, 146–147
   internal and proprietary data,
      139–140
   single-source, 145–146
Secondary sampling unit, 318
Secrecy, loss of, 237–238
Self-administered questionnaires, 171,
   286–287
Self-selection bias, 156
Semantic differential, 266–267
Semi-structured interviews, 115
Sensing systems, 28
Sensory panel, 312
Sequential sampling, 355
Service monitoring, 88
Significance level, 373
Simple random sampling, 325
Simple-dichotomy (dichotomous-
   alternative) question, 285
Single-source data, 145–146
Site analysis techniques, 146
Smart agent software, 40
Smart poster, 31
Snowball sampling, 324
Social desirability bias, 158
Social networking, 120
Sorting, 262
Split-ballot technique, 290
Split-half method, 257
SPSS, 256
Spyware, 81
Stakeholder orientation, 9
Standard deviation, 342–343
Standard error of the mean, 347–348
Standardized normal distribution,
   344–347
Standardized regression coefficient (β),
   404
Standardized research service, 74
Statistical Abstract of the United States, 36

Statistical base, 368
Statistical databases, 36–37
Statistics. *see also* Sampling, statistics for
   central-limit theorem, 348–350
   confidence intervals, 350–353
   JMP software, 389
   measures of central tendency,
      339–340
   measures of dispersion, 340–343
   population parameters, 336–338
   problems with, 335–336, 416
   random error, 353
   sample size, 353–358
   software for, 402
   test of differences, 384–387
   testing for differences. *see* Test of
      differences
   t-test, 390–395
   χ^2 test (goodness-of-fit), 386–390
Status bar, 300–301
Strategetic management orientation,
   9–12
Stratified sampling, 326–328
Streaming media, 118–119
Student surrogates, 231–232
Subjective results, 99
Subjects, 215
Summated scale, 255–256
Supply chain, 17
Survey flow, 296–297
Survey technology
   physical features of, 300–302
   and response quality, 299–300
   and timing, 300
Surveys
   and administrative error, 158–159
   advantages and disadvantages of,
      153–154
   choosing best approach, 181–182
   definition of, 61–62
   ethics of, 183–184
   interactive survey approaches, 160
   internet surveys, 178–181
   mail questionnaires. *see* Mail survey
   non-interactive media, 160
   personal interviews. *see* Personal
      interviews
   respondent error and, 155–158
   sampling errors in, 154–155
   text message, 181
   types of information gathered, 152–153
Symptoms, 48
Syndicated service, 73
Systematic or nonsampling error,
   221–222
Systematic sampling, 326
Systemic error, 154

T

Table of contents (research report),
   417
Tables (research reports), 419–420
Tabulation, 365
   cross-tabulation, 366–369
   definition of, 365–366
Tachistoscope, 227
Tallying, 365
Target markets, 15–16
Technology. *see also* Mechanical
   observation
   and communication, 21
   DIADs, 30
   e-mail surveys, 177–178
   ethics of data technology, 41–42, 81
   information technology, 40
   internet, 38–40
   internet presentations of report, 426
   internet surveys, 178–181
   JMP, 389
   NFC, 31, 32
   for qualitative marketing research,
      118–121
   RFID tag, 30–31
   smartphones, 151, 205–206
   spyware, 81
   survey technology, 298–302
   telephone interviews, 165–170
   text message surveys, 181
   UPC, 35
Telephone interviews, 165–170,
   286–287
Television monitoring, 201
Temporal sequence, 52
Tertiary sampling unit, 318
Test of differences, 60
   choosing appropriate, 384–386
   cross-tabulation tables, 387–390
   general linear model, 402–405
   one-way analysis of variance
      (ANOVA), 396–402
   procedure for, 372–373
   significance levels, 373–375
   t-test, 390–395
   univariate tests of means, 375–377
   Z-test, 395–396
Test units, 221
Testing effects, 230
Test-market sabotage, 235
Test-marketing
   advantages of, 236
   disadvantages of, 236–238
   and estimating sales volumes,
      235–236
   and forecasting success, 233

Test-marketing (*continued*)
  and identifying product weaknesses, 234
    projecting results of, 235
    and texting marketing mix, 233
    using, 233
Test-retest method, 257
Text message surveys, 181
Text mining, 121
Thematic apperception test (TAT), 115, 122–123
Themes, 106
Theory, 60
Timeliness, 30
Title page (research report), 415–416
Top-box score, 338
Total value management, 19
Trade associations, marketing, 144
T-test for differences of proportions
  definition of, 390–392
  paired-samples, 394–395
  practical uses, 392–394
  using, 375–377
Type I error, 374
Type II error, 374–375

Unaided recall, 293
Unbalanced rating scale, 271–272
Uncertainty and research, 54–55
Uniform resource locator (URL), 38
Univariate statistical analysis, 372
Universal product code (UPC), 35, 144–145, 204–205
Unobtrusive methods, 64
Unobtrusive observation, 192
U.S. Census of Population, 142–143

Validity, 258
Validity, external, 231–232
Validity, internal, 229–231
Vans, 96
Variance, 342
Video conferencing, 118–119
Video databases, 37
Visible observation, 192
Voice-pitch analysis, 207

Way-finding, 192
Web tracking, 35–36, 38–39, 202–204
Within-group error or variance, 398
Within-subjects design, 228–229
World Factbook, 146
W.R. Simmons and Associates, 145

χ^2 test for goodness-of-fit, 387–390

Yankelovich MONITOR, 145
Yield management systems, 26–27

Z-test for differences of proportions, 375–377, 395–396